JOHN WILLIS'

THEATRE WORLD

1975–1976 SEASON

VOLUME 32

CROWN PUBLISHERS, INC.
ONE PARK AVENUE
NEW YORK, N.Y. 10016

"Not So Long Ago"
(1920)

with Philip Merivale and Basil
Rathbone in "The Swan" (1923)

as Juliet
(1929)

"Three Sisters"
(1926)

"L'Aiglon"
(1934)

"The Cradle Song"
(1934)

with Joseph Schildkraut
in "The Cherry Orchard" (194

"Mary Stuart"
(1957)

with Una O'Connor in
"The Starcross Story"
(1954)

"The Seagull"
(1964)

2

1927   1945   1946   1975

TO
EVA LeGALLIENNE

who for six decades has been an actress of consummate skill, a dauntless supporter of the classics, a creative and innovative producer-director, an heroic crusader for repertory, and who, justifiably, has earned immortal fame in the historical records of the American theatre.

"A CHORUS LINE"

Martha Swope Photos

Winner of 1976 Pulitzer Prize, New York Drama Critics Circle
Award, 9 Antoinette Perry ("Tony") Awards, Drama Desk Award, and Special Theatre World Award

CONTENTS

EDITOR: JOHN WILLIS

Assistant Editor: Don Nute

Staff: Alberto Cabrera, Fred Ortiz, Stanley Reeves, William Schelble, Paul Woodson

Staff Photographers: Joe Abeles, Bert Andrews, Ron Reagan, Van Williams

THE SEASON IN REVIEW
June 1, 1975–May 31, 1976

In addition to the exciting preparations for our American Bicentennial Celebration, the theatre season opened with the brightest prospects in over two decades. More backers were gambling on new productions, more actors were anxiously anticipating employment, and more productions were available than theatres to book them. However, almost immediately, dark clouds of union demands dimmed the optimistic horizon. On August 4, 1975, a new code went into effect for Off Off Broadway theatres and showcases. It would have annihilated a majority of houses where most experimental productions are staged, and where many performers have the opportunity to display and develop their talents. Instantaneously, there were loud protests of resentment from Actors Equity Association, and on Aug. 26 its members revoked the code. On September 18, Broadway's longest strike began. The musicians union forced all 9 Broadway musicals to close for 25 long days and nights. Plays without music and Off Broadway productions were not affected, but several new productions were postponed or cancelled. Although a settlement did not seem imminent, compromises were made, and on October 12 an agreement was reached that enabled theatres to re-open. The hits continued their sell-out business, but the shows doing marginal business had to struggle for survival. Theatrical advertising on television became an important factor in firing adrenalin back into Broadway's veins. At the season's conclusion, from the financial viewpoint, Broadway's box office receipts hit a record high (almost $71 million, according to *Variety's* statistical report), and the road had its second highest recorded grosses. In November, because of the unsavory atmosphere surrounding the Times Square area, producers, theatre owners and performers began a concerted effort to eradicate the mid-town peep shows, massage parlors, topless bars, loitering and soliciting. The League of New York Theatre Owners and Producers voted a levy on all New York and touring companies to promote this worthwhile project. They also accepted the general trend for an 8 o'clock curtain rather than last season's experimental 7:30 curtain.

From the creative and critical viewpoint, the season's quality was somewhat inconsistent. A surprising feature was the overwhelming number of revivals—due in part to the paucity of new playwrights who defected to the more lucrative tv "factories." Five of the revivals were produced at JFK Center in Washington especially for the bicentennial, and subsequently transferred to New York. They were "The Skin of Our Teeth" with Martha Scott, Alfred Drake, and a memorable characterization by Elizabeth Ashley; "Sweet Bird of Youth" with Christopher Walken and Irene Worth who received a "Tony" for best actress of the year; "The Royal Family" with Eva LeGallienne, George Grizzard, Sam Levene, and the scintillating Rosemary Harris; "Long Day's Journey into Night" with Zoe Caldwell, Jason Robards and Michael Moriarty; "The Heiress" with Jane Alexander and Richard Kiley. Other noteworthy revivals were "Death of a Salesman" with excellent performances by George C. Scott, Teresa Wright and James Farentino; "The Glass Menagerie" with Maureen Stapleton and Rip Torn; "The Lady from the Sea" with Vanessa Redgrave's Broadway debut; "Ah, Wilderness!" with Geraldine Fitzgerald, Richard Backus and Paul Rudd; and "Who's Afraid of Virginia Woolf?" with Colleen Dewhurst, Ben Gazzara, Maureen Anderman and Richard Kelton—superior in almost every respect to the original production. Musical revivals include "Very Good Eddie," "Hello, Dolly!," and "My Fair Lady" with commendable performances by Ian Richardson, Christine Andreas, Jerry Lanning and George Rose. The ever-popular Katharine Hepburn had a successful limited engagement in a less than mediocre English import, "A Matter of Gravity." Julie Harris again proved her great talent in the solo play about Emily Dickinson, "The Belle of Amherst." Richard Burton demonstrated his box office power by playing to SRO audiences for 12 weeks in last season's holdover, "Equus," and Liza Minnelli did likewise for 5 weeks in "Chicago" during Gwen Verdon's absence.

The outstandingly successful musicals were "Chicago" with gratifying performances by Gwen Verdon, Chita Rivera and

Jerry Orbach, "Bubbling Brown Sugar" with show-stoppers Vivian Reed, Avon Long and Chip Garnett, "The Robber Bridegroom," and the incomparable "A Chorus Line." Another musical feature of the Broadway season was sold-out concerts by Paul Anka, Shirley MacLaine, and Frank Sinatra with Ella Fitzgerald and Count Basie. Several much-heralded and eagerly anticipated musicals were sadly disappointing failures: "Rockabye Hamlet," "Home Sweet Homer," "Treemonisha," "Rex," and "1600 Pennsylvania Avenue."

The Antoinette Perry (Tony) Award for best play went to "Travesties," a British import that also received the New York Drama Critics Circle citation. Its star, visiting artist John Wood, was voted a "Tony" as best actor for his bravura performance. Best actress and actor in a musical were Donna McKechnie of "A Chorus Line" and George Rose of "My Fair Lady." For best supporting performances, "Tonys" were awarded Shirley Knight of "Kennedy's Children," Edward Hermann of "Mrs. Warren's Profession," Kelly Bishop and Sammy Williams of "A Chorus Line." Special "Tonys" were presented George Abbott, Richard Burton, Circle in the Square's producers, and Washington, D.C.'s Arena Stage—the first "Tony" to a regional company. Alexander H. Cohen's televised production of the "Tony" presentations was again an exemplary format. New York Drama Critics Circle cited the dramatically powerful "Streamers" as best American play, and the visually opulent "Pacific Overtures" as best musical. The Pulitzer Prize, 9 "Tonys," 6 Drama Desk Awards, and a Special Theatre World Award went to the indisputably deserving "A Chorus Line." Since its Off Broadway premier last season, it has continuously played to capacity audiences.

Off Broadway again declined both quantitatively and qualitatively. Severe financial crises confronted most non-profit institutional companies, and necessitated appeals for support. The Brooklyn Academy of Music, the oldest performing arts center in the country, renovated and restored its Music Hall with a new name, Playhouse. It re-opened Dec. 2, 1975 with "Sweet Bird of Youth." To everyone's gratification, the Academy again imported the Royal Shakespeare Company who performed in its innovative and critically-praised "Henry V." Other notable Off Broadway productions include the superior revivals by The Acting Company and the Phoenix Company, Lincoln Center's "Trelawny of the 'Wells,'" "Hamlet," "Mrs. Warren's Profession" with Lynn Redgrave a perfect Vivie, "The Threepenny Opera" and "Streamers" with a memorable cast headed by Dorian Harewood and Paul Rudd, the Public Theater's "Jesse and the Bandit Queen" with Dixie Carter making an impressive debut, "Rich and Famous" with praiseworthy performers Anita Gillette, Ron Leibman and William Atherton, Equity Library Theatre's hit revival of "Follies," the delightful revue "Tuscaloosa's Calling. . . .," "Vanities," and Circle Repertory Theatre's "Knock Knock" that was transferred to Broadway. As always, Guy Lombardo beautifully produced another musical under the stars at Jones Beach, providing the usual enjoyable summer experience. This year it was "Oklahoma!"

In addition to the outstanding performers already mentioned, recognition should be given Danny Aiello, Lewis Arlt, Pamela Blair, Northern J. Callaway, John Cullum, Moses Gunn, Linda Hopkins, Ken Howard, Cleavon Little, Priscilla Lopez, Mako, Keith McDermott, Estelle Parsons, Anthony Perkins, Gilbert Price, Madeleine Renaud, Charles Repole, Rachel Roberts, Isao Sato, Virginia Seidel, Daniel Seltzer, John Shea, Carole Shelley, Donald Sinden, Nancy Snyder, Meryl Streep, Kristoffer Tabori, Donna Theodore, and Dick Anthony Williams.

As is endemic to every season, productions were born that deserved longer life, but failed to attract enough patrons to survive. Among this season's victims were the trilogy under the title "The Norman Conquests," "Lamppost Reunion," "The Poison Tree," and "Yentl" with a stellar performance by Tovah Feldshuh. In retrospect, it was a richly rewarding year for the "main stem of the Big Apple," as well as for the mainstream of theatre throughout the United States.

Donna McKechnie,
Robert LuPone
in "A Chorus Line"

John Wood
in "Travesties"

BROADWAY CALENDAR
June 1, 1975 through May 31, 1976

Eva LeGallienne, Rosemary Harris
in "The Royal Family"

ony
ins
quus"

Christopher Walken,
Irene Worth
in "Sweet Bird of Youth"

Chita Rivera, Gwen Verdon
in "Chicago"

FORTY-SIXTH STREET THEATRE
Opened Tuesday, June 1, 1975.*
Robert Fryer and James Cresson present:

CHICAGO

Book, Fred Ebb, Bob Fosse; Music, John Kander; Lyrics, Fred Ebb; Based on the play "Chicago" by Maurine Dallas Watkins; Directed and Choreographed by Bob Fosse; Settings, Tony Walton; Costumes, Patricia Zipprodt; Lighting, Jules Fisher; Musical Director, Stanley Lebowsky; Orchestrations, Ralph Burns; Dance Music Arrangements, Peter Howard; Sound, Abe Jacob; Hairstylist, Romaine Green; Produced in association with Martin Richards; Managerial Associate, Frank Scardino; Wardrobe Supervisor, Louise Van Dine; Assistant Conductor, Art Wagner; Production Assistant, Vicki Stein; Assistant-Choreographer, Tony Stevens; Assistant to Director, Kathryn Doby; Original Cast Album, Arista Records.

CAST

Velma Kelly	Chita Rivera†9
Roxie Hart	Gwen Verdon†1
Fred Casely	Christopher Chadman†2
Sergeant Fogarty	Richard Korthaze
Amos Hart	Barney Martin†3
Liz	Cheryl Clark
Annie	Michon Peacock†4
June	Candy Brown†5
Hunyak	Graciela Daniele†6
Mona	Pamela Sousa
Martin Harrison	Michael Vita
Matron	Mary McCarty
Billy Flynn	Jerry Orbach
Mary Sunshine	M. O'Haughey
Go-to-Hell Kitty	Charlene Ryan†7
Harry	Paul Solen
Aaron	Gene Foote†10
The Judge	Ron Schwinn
Court Clerk	Gary Gendell†8

STANDBYS AND UNDERSTUDIES: Roxie, Lenora Nemetz; Matron, Mary Sunshine, Marsha Bagwell; Velma, Michon Peacock; Amos, Richard Korthaze; Dance Alternates, Hank Brunjes, Monica Tiller

MUSICAL NUMBERS: "All That Jazz," "Funny Honey," "Cell Block Tango," "When You're Good to Mama," "Tap Dance," "All I Care About,"."A Little Bit of Good," "We Both Reached for the Gun," "Roxie," "I Can't Do It Alone," "Chicago after Midnight," "My Own Best Friend," "I Know a Girl," "Me and My Baby," "Mister Cellophane," "When Velma Takes the Stand," "Razzle Dazzle," "Class," "Nowadays," "R.S.V.P." "Keep It Hot"

A musical vaudeville in two acts. The action takes place in the late 1920's in Chicago, Illinois.

General Managers: Joseph Harris, Ira Bernstein
Press: The Merlin Group, Cheryl Sue Dolby, Harriett Trachtenberg, Harold Lubin, Ron Harris
Stage Managers: Phil Friedman, Robert Corpora, Paul Phillips, Nick Malekos, Craig Jacobs

* Still playing May 31, 1976.
† Succeeded by: 1. Lenora Nemetz, Liza Minnelli during Miss Verdon's illness, 2. Gary Gendell, 3. Rex Everhart, 4. Joan Bell, 5. Karen G. Burke, Sally Neal, 6. Sandra Brewer, Candace Tovar, 7. Fern Fitzgerald, 8. Ross Miles, 9. Lenora Nemetz, 10. Laurent Giroux

Martha Swope Photos

Top Left: Gwen Verdon, Jerry Orbach

Gwen Verdon, Chita Rivera

Lenora Nemetz

Chita Rivera, Gwen Verdon
Above: Rex Everhart

9

PALACE THEATRE
Opened Tuesday, June 10, 1975.*
The Negro Ensemble Company in cooperation with Woodie King, Jr., presents:

THE FIRST BREEZE OF SUMMER

By Leslie Lee; Director, Douglas Turner Ward; Scenery, Edward Burbridge; Costumes, Mary Mease Warren; Lighting, Thomas Skelton; Production Administrator, Gerald S. Krone; Management Associates, Phyllis Restaino, Donald Tirabassi, Thelma Cooper; Production Assistant, Sandra L. Ross; Wardrobe Supervisor, Margaret Faison; Technical Director, Dik Krider

CAST

Gremmar	Frances Foster
Nate Edwards	Charles Brown
Lou Edwards	Reyno
Aunt Edna	Barbara Montgomery
Milton Edwards	Moses Gunn
Hattie	Ethel Ayler
Lucretia	Janet League
Sam Greene	Carl Crudup
Briton Woodward	Anthony McKay
Reverend Mosely	Lou Leabengula Myers
Hope	Petronia
Joe Drake	Peter DeMaio
Gloria Townes	Bebe Drake Hooks
Harper Edwards	Douglas Turner Ward†

UNDERSTUDIES: Jerry Cleveland, Bill Cobbs, Bebe Drake Hooks, Lou Leabengula Myers, Petronia, Roland Sanchez, Martha Short-Goldsen, Samm-Art Williams

A drama in two acts. The action takes place at the present time in a small city in the Northeast on a Thursday afternoon through Sunday night.

General Management: Dorothy Olim Associates
Press: Howard Atlee, Clarence Allsopp, Meg Gordean, Owen Levy
Stage Managers: Horacena J. Taylor, Jerry Cleveland

* Closed July 20, 1975 after 48 performances and 5 previews.
† Succeeded by Samm-Art Williams

Bert Andrews Photos

Left: Ethel Ayler, Charles Brown, Moses Gunn, Reyno Top: Ethel Ayler, Reyno

Moses Gunn, Peter DeMaio

Frances Foster, Ethel Ayler, Barbara Montgomery

CIRCLE IN THE SQUARE THEATRE
Opened Thursday, June 26, 1975.*
Circle in the Square Theatre (Theodore Mann, Artistic Director; Paul Libin, Managing Director) presents:

DEATH OF A SALESMAN

By Arthur Miller; Director, George C. Scott; Scenery, Marjorie Kellogg; Costumes, Arthur Boccia; Lighting, Thomas Skelton; Incidental Music, Craig Wesson; Production Associate, E. J. Oshins; Hairstylist, Roberto Fernandez; Wardrobe Supervisor, Sydney Brooks; Production Assistants, Nancy Cook, Johnny Clontz, Gordon Bendall, Bernard Ferstenberg, Anne Oberbroeckling, Guy Martin, Jacqueline Jacobus, Rose Avallone

CAST

Linda Loman	Teresa Wright
Willy Loman	George C. Scott†1
Happy	Harvey Keitel†2
Biff	James Farentino
Bernard	Chuck Patterson
First Woman	Patricia Quinn
Charley	Dotts Johnson
Uncle Ben	Ramon Bieri
Howard Wagner	Pirie MacDonald
Jenny	Helen Harrelson
Stanley	Mordecai Lawner
Miss Forsythe	Bara-Cristin Hansen
Letta	Joanne Jonas
Second Woman	Julie Garfield
Second Waiter	Craig Wasson

STANDBYS AND UNDERSTUDIES: Willy, Roy Poole; Linda, Helen Harrelson; Happy, Biff, Bruce Weitz; Howard, Stanley, Michael Durrell; Charley, Bernard, Arthur French; Miss Forsythe, Letta, Katherine De Hetre.

A drama in two acts. The action takes place in Willy Loman's house, and in various offices he visits in New York City and Boston.

Company Manager: William Conn
Press: Merle Debuskey, Susan L. Schulman
Stage Managers: Randall Brooks, James Bernardi

* Closed Aug. 24, 1975 after limited engagement of 71 performances and 23 previews. For original production, see THEATRE WORLD, Vol. 5. Original cast included Lee J. Cobb, Mildred Dunnock, Cameron Mitchell, Arthur Kennedy.
† Succeeded by: 1. Roy Poole during Mr. Scott's illness, 2. Martin Sheen

Inge Morath Photos

Top: Harvey Keitel, Teresa Wright, James Farentino, George C. Scott

George C. Scott

11

MARK HELLINGER THEATRE
Opened Tuesday, September 9, 1975.*
Ken Marsolais with The Kennedy Center-Xerox American
Bicentennial Theatre presents:

THE SKIN OF OUR TEETH

By Thornton Wilder; Director, Jose Quintero; Sets, Eugene Lee;
Costumes, Franne Lee; Lighting, Ken Billington; Produced by
Roger L. Stevens and Richmond Crinkley for Kennedy Center;
Wardrobe Supervisor, Kathleen Foster; Associate Producer, Scott/-
Bloom Productions Ltd.

CAST

Announcer/Professor/Mr. Tremayne	Alexander Reed
Sabina	Elizabeth Ashley
Mr. Fitzpatrick	F. J. O'Neil
Mrs. Antrobus	Martha Scott
Dinosaur	Roi Petersen
Mammoth/Monkey Man	Denny Dillon
Telegraph Boy/Assistant Announcer	Barry Livingston
Gladys	Janet Grey
Henry	Steve Railsback
Mr. Antrobus	Alfred Drake
Doctor/Fred Bailey	Lee Sherman
Judge	Joseph C. Davies
Homer/Announcer	Norman Michael Chase
Miss E. Muse/Conveener's Wife	Eda Seasongood
Miss T. Muse	Josephine Nichols
Miss M. Muse	Betty Lynd
Fortune Teller	Charlotte Jones
Defeated Candidate	Douglas Fisher
Hester	Yuye Fernandes
Ivy	Gertrude Jeannette
Chair Pushers	Philip Lindsay, Roi Petersen
Drum Majorettes	Betty Lynd, Kristina Callahan, Kate Kellery, Yuye Fernandes
Conveeners	Richard DeFabees, Joseph C. Davies, Douglas Fisher, J. F. Hall, Steven Kelly, Lee Sherman, Alexander Reed, Barry Livingston

UNDERSTUDIES: Sabina, Misses Muse, Kristina Callahan; Antrobus, Alexander Reed; Mrs. Antrobus, Ivy, Eda Seasongood; Fortune Teller, Hester, Josephine Nichols; Henry, Richard DeFabees;
Tremayn, Philip Lindsay; Gladys, Kate Kellery; Fitzpatrick, Bailey,
J. F. Hall; Mammoth, Betty Lynd; Announcer, Douglas Fisher

A comedy in three acts. The action takes place at the present time
in a home in Excelsior, NJ., and on Atlantic City's boardwalk.

General Manager: Leonard Soloway
Company Manager: James Mennen
Press: Betty Lee Hunt, Maria Cristina Pucci, Bill Evans
Stage Managers: Martin Herzer, David Taylor, Steven Kelly,
Betty Lynd

* Closed Sept. 13, 1975 after 7 performances and 7 previews. Original production opened Nov. 18, 1942 with Tallulah Bankhead,
Florence Eldridge, Fredric March, Montgomery Clift and played
359 performances. See THEATRE WORLD, VOL. 12 for 1955
revival with Mary Martin, Helen Hayes, George Abbott that
played 22 performances.

Richard Braaten Photos

Elizabeth Ashley, Charlotte Jones

**Martha Scott Top: Elizabeth
Ashley, Alfred Drake**

CIRCLE IN THE SQUARE
Opened Thursday, September 18, 1975.*
Circle in the Square (Theodore Mann, Artistic Director; Paul Libin, Managing Director) in association with the Long Wharf Theatre presents:

AH, WILDERNESS!

By Eugene O'Neill; Director, Arvin Brown; Scenery, Steven Rubin; Costumes, Bill Walker; Lighting, Ronald Wallace; Production Associate, Johnny Clontz; Hairstylist, Roberto Fernandez; Wardrobe Supervisor, Sydney Brooks; Production Assistants, Gordon Bendall, Tom Smith, Jolly Nelson, Frank Storch, Nancy Shutter

CAST

Tommy Miller	Glenn Zachar
Mildred Miller	Christina Whitmore
Arthur Miller	Paul Rudd
Essie Miller	Geraldine Fitzgerald
Lily Miller	Teresa Wright
Sid Davis	John Braden
Nat Miller	William Swetland
Richard Miller	Richard Backus
David McComber	Ralph Drischell
Norah	Linda Hunt
Wint Selby	Sean G. Griffin
Belle	Suzanne Lederer
Bartender	Stephen Mendillo
Salesman	Don Gantry
Muriel	Swoosie Kurtz

STANDBYS: Essie, Shirley Bryan; Arthur, Richard, Wint, Thomas Leopold; Belle, Mildred, Muriel, Norah, Alexandra Stoddart

A comedy in 3 acts and 7 scenes. The action takes place in the Miller home in a small Connecticut town on July 4, 1906.

Company Manager: William Conn
Press: Merle Debuskey, Susan L. Schulman
Stage Managers: Nina Seely, James Bernardi

* Closed Nov. 23, 1975 after limited engagement of 85 performances and 19 previews. Original production opened Oct. 2, 1933 at the Guild Theatre with George M. Cohan, Marjorie Marquis, Elisha Cook, Jr., and ran for 289 performances.

Inge Morath, Sy Friedman Photos

Top: entire cast

**Teresa Wright, John Braden
Above: Richard Backus, Swoosie Kurtz**

Ronald Dennis, Don Percassi, Priscilla Lopez,
Renee Baughman

SHUBERT THEATRE
Opened Sunday, October 19, 1975.*
Joseph Papp presents a New York Shakespeare Festival Production in association with Plum Productions:

A CHORUS LINE

Conceived, Choreographed and Directed by Michael Bennett; Book, James Kirkwood, Nicholas Dante; Music, Marvin Hamlisch; Lyrics, Edward Kleban; Co-Choreographer, Bob Avian; Musical Direction and Vocal Arrangements, Don Pippin; Associate Producer, Bernard Gersten; Setting, Robin Wagner; Costumes, Theoni V. Aldredge; Lighting, Tharon Musser; Sound, Abe Jacob; Music Coordinator, Robert Thomas; Orchestrations, Bill Byers, Hershy Kay, Jonathan Tunick; Assistant to choreographers and dance captain, Baayork Lee; Wardrobe Mistress, Alyce Gilbert; Hairstylist, Harvey's Bazaar; Original Cast Album by Columbia Records

CAST

Roy .... Scott Allen†16
Kristine .... Renee Baughman†1
Sheila .... Carole (Kelly) Bishop†17
Val .... Pamela Blair†2
Mike .... Wayne Cilento
Butch .... Chuck Cissel
Larry .... Clive Clerk
Maggie .... Kay Cole†3
Richie .... Ronald Dennis†4
Tricia .... Donna Drake
Tom .... Brandt Edwards
Judy .... Patricia Garland†5
Lois .... Carolyn Kirsch†6
Don .... Ron Kuhlman†7
Bebe .... Nancy Lane†8
Connie .... Baayork Lee†9
Diana .... Priscilla Lopez†10
Zach .... Robert LuPone†11
Mark .... Cameron Mason
Cassie .... Donna McKechnie†12
Al .... Don Percassi†13
Frank .... Michael Serrecchia
Greg .... Michel Stuart†14
Bobby .... Thomas J. Walsh
Paul .... Sammy Williams†15
Vicki .... Crissy Wilzak

UNDERSTUDIES: Al, Mike, John Mineo; Paul, Richie, Chuck Cissel; Kristine, Connie, Maggie, Donna Drake; Don, Mark, Brandt Edwards; Cassie, Sheila, Carolyn Kirsch; Diana, Bebe, Carole Schweid; Larry, Greg, Bobby, Michael Serrecchia; Val, Judy, Crissy Wilzak; Zach, Clive Clerk

MUSICAL NUMBERS: "I Hope I Get It," "I Can Do That," "And. ...," "At the Ballet," "Sing!," "Hello Twelve, Hello Thirteen, Hello Love," "Nothing," "Dance: Ten; Looks: Three," "The Music and the Mirror," "One," "The Tap Combination," "What I Did for Love"

A musical performed without intermission. The action takes place at an audition at the present time in this theatre.

Company Managers: Patricia Carney, Sally Campbell
Press: Merle Debruskey, Bob Ullman, Bruce Cohen
Stage Managers: Jeff Hamlin, Frank Hartenstein, Scott Allen

* Still playing May 31, 1976. Cited as Best Musical by New York Drama Critics Circle; winner of Pulitzer Prize; received "Tony" for Best Musical, Best Book of a Musical, Best Score, Best Director of a Musical, Best Lighting, Best Choreographer, Best Actress in a Musical (Donna McKechnie), Best Featured Actress in a Musical (Carole (Kelly) Bishop), Best Featured Actor in a Musical (Sammy Williams); presented a Special Theatre World Award to every member of the creative staff and original cast.
†*Succeeded by: 1. Cookie Vazquez, 2. Barbara Monte-Britton, 3. Lauree Berger, 4. Winston DeWitt Hemsley, 5. Sandahl Bergman, 6. Vickie Frederick, 7. David Thome, 8. Gillian Scalici, 9. Lauren Kayahara, 10. Carole Schweid, Rebecca York, 11. Joe Bennett, 12. Ann Reinking, 13. Bill Nabel, 14. Justin Ross, 15. George Pesaturo, 16. Danny Ruvolo, 17. Kathrynann Wright

Martha Swope Photos

Top Left: Donna McKechnie, Carole (Kelly) Bishop, Baayork Lee, Nancy Lane, Patricia Garland, Renee Baughman, Kay Cole, Priscilla Lopez, Pamela Blair, Robert LuPone

Pamela Blair, Sammy Williams,
Cameron Mason Top: Chuck Cissel,
Thomas J. Walsh, Kelly Bishop, Clive Clerk,
Joe Bennett, Wayne Cilento

Ann Reinking, Joe Bennett

THE LITTLE THEATRE
Opened Thursday, October 16, 1975.*
Joe Garofalo presents:

LAMPPOST REUNION

By Louis LaRusso II; Director, Tom Signorelli; Scenery, Robert
U. Taylor; Lighting, Spencer Mosse; Costumes, Judy Dearing; Production Assistant, Tony Golden; Wardrobe Mistress, Marilyn Amaral; Associate Producer, Barry Singer

CAST

Biggie . . . . Danny Aiello
Mac . . . . Frank Quinn†
Tommy . . . . Frank Bongiorno
Jobby . . . . George Pollock
Fred . . . . Gabriel Dell

STANDBYS: Biggie, Fred, Nick LaPadula; Tommy, Jobby, George
Poulos; Mac, Ron Ryan

General Manager: Ashton Springer
Company Manager: Bob McDonald
Press: Max Eisen, Carl Samrock
Stage Managers: Paul Austin, Richard Lalli, Gary Stein

* Closed Dec. 21, 1975 after 76 performances.
† Succeeded by Tom Signorelli

**Right Top: Frank Bongiorno,
George Pollock, Gabriel Dell**

Gabriel Dell, Frank Quinn

Gabriel Dell, Danny Aiello, Frank Quinn

BOOTH THEATRE

Opened Monday, October 20, 1975.*

Joseph Papp presents a New York Shakespeare Festival Production of:

THE LEAF PEOPLE

By Dennis J. Reardon; Director, Tom O'Horgan; Settings, John Conklin; Costumes and Makeup, Randy Barcelo; Lighting, John McLain; Sound, Roger Jay; Original Music, Xantheus Roh Leempoor; Associate Producer, Bernard Gersten; Assistant to director, Susan Elkind; Wardrobe Supervisor, Alfred Calamoneri

CAST

The Fishbellies:
First Interpreter	Grayson Hall
Second Interpreter	Anthony Holland
Shaughnessy (Shaw)	Tom Aldredge
Meatball	Ernesto Gonzalez
P. Sigmund Furth	Lane Smith
Steven	Ted LePlat
Michelle	Denise Delapenha
Anna Ames	Margaret Hall

The Leaf People:
Sutreeshay	Geanine-Michele Capozzoli
Gitaucho (Meesho)	Raymond J. Barry
The Sound (Keet)	Leon Morenzie
Leeboh	William Parry
Mayteemo	James Sbano
Monkey Man (Mututahsh)	Ernesto Gonzalez
Keerah	Denise Delapenha
Yawahlapeetee (Rubber Ball)	Joanna Featherstone
Kreetahshay (Chicken Mother)	Susan Batson
Green Father (Shay Tahndor)	Roy Brocksmith
Jeeshoom	Francisco Blackfeather
Kahleemshoht	Ron Capozzoli
Choolkahnoor	Jeffrey David-Owen
Lahbayneezh	Jelom Vieira
Treekah	Josevaldo Machado
Zhahbahroosh	Ric Lavin
Lohzhoodish	Soni Moreno
Lohmoheetet	Jeannette Ertelt

UNDERSTUDIES: Ron Capozzoli, Jeffrey David-Owen, Jeannette Ertelt, Ric Lavin, Soni Moreno, William Parry, James Sbano

A drama in 2 acts and 16 scenes. The action takes place in early October of 1973 in the Amazon Rain Forest.

Company Manager: Maurice Schaded
Press: Merle Debuskey, Leo Stern
Stage Managers: Galen McKinley, William Schill, Ron Capozzoli

* Closed Oct. 26, 1975 after 8 performances and 42 previews.

Barry Kramer-Joseph Abeles Photos

**Top: Joanna Featherstone, Tom Aldredge,
Raymond Barry (R) Ted LePlat, Lane Smith,
Margaret Hall**

**Susan Batson, Leon Morenzie
Above: Grayson Hall, Anthony Holland**

URIS THEATRE
Opened Tuesday, October 21, 1975.*
(Moved to Palace Theatre, Nov. 3, 1975)
Adela Holzer, James Nederlander and Victor Lurie present the
Houston Grand Opera Association Production of:

TREEMONISHA

By Scott Joplin; Conceived and Directed by Frank Corsaro; Choreography, Louis Johnson; Orchestration and Music Supervision, Gunther Schuller; Conductor, Gunther Schuller; Sets and Costumes, Franco Colavecchia; Lighting, Nananne Porcher; Artistic Consultant, Vera Brodsky Lawrence; Presented by arrangement with the Dramatic Publishing Company; Assistant Director, David Drisin; Production Associate, Marion Kinsella; Wardrobe Mistress, Billie White; Assistant Choreographer and Dance Captain, James Thurston

CAST

Zodzetrick .... Ben Harney
Ned...................................... Willard White
Monisha................................... Betty Allen
                           Matinees: Lorna Myers
Treemonisha .... Carmen Balthrop
                           Matinees: Kathleen Battle
Remus .... Curtis Rayam
Andy .... Kenneth Hicks
Lucy.................................... Cora Johnson
Parson Alltalk.......................... Edward Pierson
Simon .... Raymond Bazemore
Cephus.............................. Dwight Ransom
Luddud................................ Dorceal Duckens

CHORUS: Earl L. Baker, Kenneth Bates, Barbara Christopher, Steven Cole, Ella Eure, Gregory Gardner, Melvin Jordan, Patricia McDermott, Janette Moody, Marion Moore, Vera Moore, Lorna Myers, Glover Parham, Patricia Pates, William Penn, Dwight Ransom, Cornel Richie, Patricia Rogers, Christine Spencer, Walter Turnbull, Gloria Turner, Peter Whitehead, Arthur Williams, Barbara Young

DANCERS: Clyde-Jacques Barrett, Thea Barnes, Dwight Baxter, Renee Brailsford, Karen Burke, Veda Jackson, Reggie Jackson, Julia Lema, Anita Littleman, Rick Odums, Dwayne Phelps, Ivson Polk, Mabel Robinson, Martial Roumain, Katherine Singleton, James Thurston, Bobby Walker, Pamela Wilson

An opera in two acts and three scenes. The action takes place on a plantation in Arkansas, northeast of Texarkana and three or four miles from the Red River.

MUSICAL NUMBERS: "The Bag of Luck," "The Corn-Huskers," "We're Goin' Around," "The Wreath," "The Sacred Tree," "Surprise," "Treemonisha's Bringing Up," "Good Advice," "Confusion," "Superstition," "Treemonisha in Peril," "Frolic of the Bears," "Wasp Nest," "The Rescue," "We Will Rest Awhile," "Going Home," "Aunt Dinah Has Blowed de Horn," "I Want to See My Child," "Treemonisha's Return," "Wrong Is Never Right," "Abuse," "When Villains Ramble Far and Near," "Conjuror's Forgiven," "We Will Trust You as Our Leader," "A Real Slow Drag"

General Manager: Nelle Nugent
Company Manager: John Scott
Press: Michael Alpert, Marilyn LeVine, Joshua Ellis, Warren Knowlton
Stage Managers: Ben Janney, Elizabeth Caldwell, Clinton Davis

* Closed Dec. 14, 1975 after 64 performances and 6 previews.

Top: Carmen Balthrop, Curtis Rayam, also Right with Willard White, Betty Allen

18

Ben Harney, Dorceal Duckens, Kenneth Hicks, Carmen Balthrop Above: Willard White, Carmen Balthrop, Betty Allen

AMBASSADOR THEATRE

Opened Wednesday, October 22, 1975.*
(Moved to Edison Theatre December 3, 1975)
Lee Apostoleris presents the Center Theatre Group/Mark Taper Forum & Lee Apostoleris production of:

ME AND BESSIE

Conceived and Written by Will Holt and Linda Hopkins; Director, Robert Greenwald; Special Dance Sequences, Lester Wilson; Musical Director, Howlett Smith; Setting, Donald Harris; Costumes, Pete Menefee; Lighting, Tharon Musser; Assistant to producer, Monica Boscia; Music Coordinator, Earl Shendell; Sound, James Travers; Original Cast Album by Columbia Records.

CAST

Bessie Smith............................. Linda Hopkins
Man .... Lester Wilson
Woman..................................... Gerri Dean
Understudies: Thomas M. Pollard, Alfre Woodard

MUSICAL NUMBERS: "I Feel Good," "God Shall Wipe All Tears Away," "Moan You Moaners," "New Orleans Hop Scop Blues," "Romance in the Dark," "Preach Them Blues," "A Good Man Is Hard to Find," "T'Ain't Nobody's Bizness If I Do," "Gimme a Pigfoot," "Put It Right Here," "You've Been a Good Ole Wagon," "Trombone Cholly," "Jazzbo Brown," "After You've Gone," "There'll Be a Hot Time in the Old Town Tonight," "Empty Bed Blues," "Kitchen Man," "Mama Don't 'Low," "Do Your Duty," "Fare Thee Well," "Nobody Knows You When You're Down and Out," "Trouble," "The Man's All Right"

A "musical evening" in two acts.

General Manager: Emanuel Azenberg
Press: Merlin Group, Sandy Manley, Elizabeth Rodman
Stage Managers: Martin Herzer, Bethe Ward

* Still playing May 31, 1975.

Right: Linda Hopkins

Gerri Dean, Linda Hopkins, Lester Wilson

EUGENE O'NEILL THEATRE
Opened Thursday, October 23, 1975.*
Cheryl Crawford, Moe Septee, The Chelsea Theater with Mrs.
Victor H. Potamkin present the Chelsea Theater Center of
Brooklyn Production of:

YENTL

By Leah Napolin and Isaac Bashevis Singer; Conceived and Di-
rected by Robert Kalfin; Scenery, Karl Eigsti; Costumes, Carrie F.
Robbins; Lighting, William Mintzer; Music, Mel Marvin; Associate
Producer, Paul B. Berkowsky; Hairstylist, Kenneth Davis; Assistant
Director, Philip Littell

CAST

Yentl	Tovah Feldshuh
Reb Todrus/Fulcha/Laibish/Cantor/ Messenger/Musician	Bernie Passeltiner
Rivka/Necheleh/Chambermaid	Mary Ellen Ashley
Lemmel/Yussel/Wedding Jester/Dr. Solomon/ Mohel/Musician	Leland Moss
Reb Nata/The Shamus/Zelig	Reuben Schafer
Nehemiah/Rabbi/Sheftel	Albert M. Ottenheimer
Mordecai/Feitl	Hy Anzell
Shmuel, Zisheh/Musician	Stephen DePietri
Moishe/Gershon/Chaim/Musician	David Eric
Dovid/Yitzhok/Musician	Michael James Stratford
Treitl/Reb Alter	Herman O. Arbeit
Avigdor	John V. Shea
Raizeleh/Avram	Robin Bartlett
Finkl/Berel	Diane Tarleton
Zelda-Leah/Shimmel	Madeline Shaw
Hadass	Lynn Ann Leveridge
Frumka	Natalie Priest
Pesheh	Blanche Dee
Yachna	Rita Karin
Zlateh	Elaine Grollman

UNDERSTUDIES: Yentl, Robin Bartlett; Avigdor, Michael James
Stratford; Hadass, Necheleh, Zelda-Leah, Raizelen, Chambermaid,
Diane Tarleton; Yachna, Pesheh, Frumka, Mary Ellen Ashley; Reb
Todrus, Mordecai, Herman O. Arbeit; Lemmel, Stephen DePietri;
Messenger, Fulcha, David Eric; Reb Nata, Leland Moss; Zelig,
Rabbi, Reb Alter, Bernie Passeltiner; Cantor, Sheftel, Feitl, Reuben
Schafer; Zlateh, Rivka, Necheleh, Chambermaid, Madeline Shaw;
Dovid, Shmuel, Chaim, Richard Manheim

A drama in two acts. The action takes place in the villages of
Yanev, Zamosc, Bechev and Lublin, Poland in the year 1873.

General Manager: Paul B. Berkowsky
Company Manager: Gino Giglio
Press: Betty Lee Hunt, Maurice Turet, Maria Cristina Pucci, Bill
Evans
Stage Managers: Clint Jakeman, Richard Manheim

* Closed May 2, 1976 after 223 performances and 11 previews.

Laura W. Pettibone Photos

Leland Moss, Bernie Passeltiner, Tovah Feldshuh
Top Right: John V. Shea, Tovah Feldshuh

Tovah Feldshuh
Above: Lynn Ann Leveridge, John V. Shea

ANTA THEATRE
Opened Sunday, October 26, 1975.*
Barry M. Brown, Burry Fredrik, Fritz Holt, Sally Sears in association with Robert V. Straus present the American Bicentennial Theatre Production of:

SUMMER BRAVE

By William Inge; Director, Michael Montel; Scenery, Stuart Wurtzel; Costumes, Donald Brooks; Lighting, David Segal; Dance Staging, Michel Stuart; Produced for the Kennedy Center and Xerox Corp. by Roger L. Stevens and Richmond Crinkley; Wardrobe Supervisor, Sydney Smith; Production Assistants, Allan Sobek, Jay Levy

CAST

Millie Owens	Sheila K. Adams
Newsboy	Bill Barrett
Bomber	Mark Kologi
Beano	Miles Chapin
Madge Owens	Jill Eikenberry
Alan Seymour	Peter Weller
Flo Owens	Nan Martin
Hal Carter	Ernest Thompson
Rosemary Sydney	Alexis Smith
Mrs. Helen Potts	Martha Greenhouse
Irma Kronkite	Patricia O'Connell
Christine Schoenwalder	Alice Drummond
Howard Bevans	Joe Ponazecki

UNDERSTUDIES: Mrs. Potts, Flo, Irma, Alice Drummond; Howard, F. J. O'Neil; Madge, Millie, Christine, Stephanie Kurz; Alan, Hal, Richard DeFabees; Bomber, Beano, Bill Barrett; Newsboy, Jason La Padura

A drama in three acts. The action takes place in a small Kansas town in the early 1950's.

General Management: Marvin A. Krauss Associates
Company Manager: David Wyler
Press: Shirley Herz
Stage Managers: Dyanne Hochman, Jason LaPadura, Bill Barrett

* Closed Nov. 9, 1975 after 18 performances and 3 previews. This was William Inge's re-write of his Pulitzer-Prize play "Picnic."

Richard Braaten, Bill Barrett Photos

Top: Nan Martin, Alexis Smith, Alice Drummond, Jill Eikenberry, Patricia O'Connell, Joe Ponazecki

Alexis Smith, Ernest Thompson
Above: Jill Eikenberry, Peter Weller, Nan Martin, Martha Greenhouse

ETHEL BARRYMORE THEATRE
Opened Thursday, October 30, 1975.*
David Merrick, Doris Cole Abrahams, Burry Fredrik in association with S. Spencer Davids and Eddie Kulukundis present the Royal Shakespeare Company Production of:

TRAVESTIES

By Tom Stoppard; Director, Peter Wood; Scenery and Costumes, Carl Toms; Lighting, Robert Ornbo; Movement, William Chappell; Musical Supervision, Grant Hossack; Slide Drawings, Robert P. Vannutt; Wardrobe Mistress, Kathleen Foster; Production Assistant, Susan Cordon; Hairstylist, Tony Marrero

CAST

Tristan Tzara	Tim Curry
Cecily Carruthers	Beth Morris
James Joyce	James Booth
Gwendolen Carr	Meg Wynn Owen
Nadezhda Krupskaya	Frances Cuka
Vladimir Ilyich Ulyanov	Harry Towb
Henry Carr	John Wood
	Matinees: David Dukes
Bennett	John Bott

UNDERSTUDIES: Henry, David Dukes; Tzara, Bill Biskup; Gwendolen, Cecily, Kate McGregor-Stewart; Joyce, John Bott; Lenin, Bennett, John Clarkson; Nadya, Lila Martin

A comedy in two acts. The action takes place in Zurich in 1917 in a section of the public library, and in the drawing room of Henry Carr's apartment.

General Manager: Helen L. Nickerson
Company Manager: John Caruso
Press: Solters & Roskin, Bud Westman
Stage Managers: Alan Hall, Bill Biskup

* Closed March 13, 1976 after 156 performances and 3 previews. Winner of "Tony," and New York Drama Critics Circle Awards for Best Play of the 1975–76 season. John Wood also received a "Tony" for Best Actor.

Sophie Baker Photos

John Wood, John Bott
Top: John Wood

Frances Cuka, Harry Towb

Meg Wynn Owen, Tim Curry, John Bott, James Booth, Beth Morris, John Wood
Top: Tim Curry, John Bott, John Wood

JOHN GOLDEN THEATRE

Opened Monday, November 3, 1975.*
Michael Harvey in association with Robert Colby presents:

KENNEDY'S CHILDREN

By Robert Patrick; Director, Clive Donner; Designed by Santo
Loquasto; Lighting, Martin Aronstein; Associate Producer, Ramon
Getzov; Production Assistant, Christopher Cara; Wardrobe Supervisor, Arlene Konowitz

CAST

Wanda	Barbara Montgomery
Bartender	Douglas Travis
Sparger	Don Parker
Mark	Michael Sacks
Rona	Kaiulani Lee
Carla	Shirley Knight

UNDERSTUDIES: Wanda, Rona, Carla, Giulia Pagano; Mark,
Sparger, Douglas Travis; Bartender, Robert T. O'Rourke

A drama in two acts. The action takes place in a bar on the lower
East Side of New York City, on a rainy February afternoon in 1974.

General Manager: Jay Kingwill
Company Manager: Robert Frissell
Press: David Powers, William Schelble
Stage Managers: Mark Wright, Robert T. O'Rourke

* Closed Jan. 4, 1976 after 72 performances and 5 previews. Shirley
Knight received a 1976 "Tony" for Best Performance by a Featured Actress.

Martha Swope Photos

**Right: Kaiulani Lee, Shirley Knight,
Barbara Montgomery**

Barbara Montgomery, Don Parker, Douglas Travis, Shirley Knight, Kaiulani Lee, Michael Sacks

MINSKOFF THEATRE
Opened Thursday, November 6, 1975.*
Robert Cherin in association with Theatre Now, Inc. presents:

HELLO, DOLLY!

Book, Michael Stewart; Based on play "The Matchmaker" by
Thornton Wilder; Music and Lyrics, Jerry Herman; Director, Lucia
Victor; Dances Re-Created by Jack Craig from original choreography by Gower Champion; Settings, Oliver Smith; Lighting, John
Gleason; Costumes, Robert Pusilio; Musical Director, Al Cavaliere;
Production Supervisor, Mitch Miller; Wardrobe Mistress, Kathleen
Donnelly; Production Associate, Camille Ranson; Production Assistant, Steven Goldstein; Assistant Conductor, Ben Payne

CAST

Mrs. Dolly Gallagher Levi	Pearl Bailey
Ernestina	Bessye Ruth Scott
Ambrose Kemper	Howard Porter
Horse	Kathy Jennings, Karen Hubbard
Horace Vandergelder	Billy Daniels
Ermengarde	Karen Hubbard
Cornelius Hackl	Terrence Emanuel
Barnaby Tucker	Grenoldo Frazier
Irene Molloy	Mary Louise
Minnie Fay	Chip Fields
Mrs. Rose	Birdie M. Hale
Rudolph	Jonathan Wynne
Judge	Ted Goodridge
Court Clerk	Ray Gilbert

TOWNSPEOPLE: Sally Benoit, Terry Gene, Pat Gideon, Ann Givin, Birdie M. Hale, Karen Hubbard, Gwen Humble, Eulaula Jennings, Francie Mendenhall, Bessye Ruth Scott, Sachi Shimizu, Guy
Allen, Don Coleman, Richard Dodd, Ray Gilbert, Charles Goeddertz, Ted Goodridge, Clark James, James Kennon-Wilson, Richard
Maxon, Charles Neal, Howard Porter, Jimmy Rivers, Ken Rogers,
David Staller, Teddy Williams, Jonathan Wynne

UNDERSTUDIES: Dolly, Birdie M. Hale; Vandergelder, Ted Goodridge; Irene, Pat Gideon; Cornelius, Jonathan Wynne; Minnie Fay,
Gwen Humble; Barnaby, Teddy Williams; Ermengarde, Eulaula
Jennings; Ernestina, Mrs. Rose, Lisa Brown; Rudolph, Guy Allen;
Ambrose, Ken Rogers; Clerk, Don Coleman; Dance Alternates, Ron
Crofoot, Lisa Brown

MUSICAL NUMBERS: "I Put My Hand In," "It Takes a
Woman," "Put on Your Sunday Clothes," "Ribbons Down My
Back," "Motherhood," "Dancing," "Before the Parade Passes By,"
"Elegance," "Waiters Gallop," "Hello, Dolly!," "It Only Takes a
Moment," "So Long, Dearie," Finale

A musical comedy in 2 acts and 15 scenes. The action takes place
in Yonkers, and New York City.

General Managers: Theatre Now, Inc., William C. Cohen,
Edward H. Davis, Norman E. Rothstein
Press: Betty Lee Hunt Associates, Maria Cristina Pucci, Bill
Evans, Maurice Turet
Stage Managers: Kenneth Porter, Robert Vandergriff, Richard
Maxon

* Closed Dec. 21, 1975 after limited engagement of 42 performances
and 3 previews. For original production with Carol Channing, see
THEATRE WORLD, Vol. 20.

Top Right: Billy Daniels, Pearl Bailey
Below: Mary Louise, Grenoldo Frazier,
Chip Fields, Terrence Emanuel

Pearl Bailey (C)

Larry Kert, Cyril Ritchard, Patrice Munsel,
Dick Shawn, Tammy Grimes, John Rait, Lillian Gish

ST. JAMES THEATRE
Opened Thursday, November 13, 1975.*
The Theatre Guild and Jonathan Conrow present:

A MUSICAL JUBILEE

Written by Max Wilk; Director, Morton DaCosta; Musical Supervision, Lehman Engel; Musical Director, John Lesko; Devised by Marilyn Clark and Charles Burr; Associate Producer, Merle D. King; Dance Arrangements and Musical Continuity, Trude Rittman; Orchestrations, Philip J. Lang, Hershy Kay, Elman Anderson; Scenery, Herbert Senn; Costumes, Donald Brooks; Lighting, Thomas Skelton; Choreography, Robert Tucker; Assistant to producer, William Dempsey; Assistant Conductor, Woody Kessler; Executive Assistant, Larusa Kay; Production Assistants, Jerry MacLaughlin, William McCarthy, Mary Jane Gibbons, Jack Hogan; Wardrobe Supervisor, Sammy Alterman; Assistant to director, Janet O'Morrison

CAST

Patrice Munsel	John Raitt †1
Tammy Grimes	Dick Shawn †2
Cyril Ritchard	Larry Kert
Lillian Gish	

Steven Boockvor, Eric Brotherson, Marcia Brushingham, Igors Gavon, Nana, David King, Jeanne Lehman, Bettye Malone, Estella Munson, Julie Pars, Dennis Perren, Leland Schwantes, Craig Yates

UNDERSTUDIES: Raitt, Igors Gavon; Munsel, Estella Munson; Grimes, Jeanne Lehman; Shawn, David King; Ritchard, Eric Brotherson; Kert, Craig Yates; Gish, Marcia Brushingham

MUSICAL NUMBERS: "Happy Days," "Whoa-Haw," "Lorena," "Sweet Betsy from Pike," "Skip to My Lou," "Hold on Abraham," "Bonnie Blue Flag," "Tipperary," "I Didn't Raise My Boy to Be a Soldier," "Mademoiselle from Armentieres," "Over There," "Battle Hymn of the Republic," "Wien, Wien, You're Calling Me," "I'm in Love with Vienna," "Der Shimmy," "I've Got Something," "Oh, The Women," "Gypsy Love," "And Her Mother Came Too," "Song of the Vagabonds," "Totem Tom Tom," "Serenade," "Violetta," "Moonstruck," "You Are Love," "I've Told Every Little Star," "Why Was I Born?," "The Best Things in Life Are Free," "They Didn't Believe Me," "The Song Is You," "Something Seems Tingle Ingleing," "Yankee Doodle Tune," "We're Blasé," "Poor Little Rich Girl," "You Go to My Head," "Find Me a Primitive Man," "I Guess I'll Have to Change My Plans," "Sophisticated Lady," "Love Me or Leave Me," "Gilbert the Filbert," "At the Moving Picture Ball," "The Green Eye of the Little Yellow God," "I Wanna Be Loved by You," "Miss Annabelle Lee," "How Jazz Was Born," "Ain't Misbehavin'," "I'm Just Wild about Harry," "Me and My Shadow," "Sometime I'm Happy," "Great Day," "Lullaby of Broadway," "Lucky Day," "If You Knew Susie," " 'S Wonderful," "Fascinating Rhythm," "Liza," "Where or When," "Hallelujah"

A musical entertainment in two acts.

General Manager: Victor Samrock
Press: Joel Wolhandler Associates, Sol Jacobson
Stage Managers: William Dodds, Marnel Sumner, James Frasher

* Closed Jan. 1, 1976 after 92 performances and 2 previews.
† Succeeded by: 1. Igors Gavon, 2. David King

Richard Braaten Photos

**Top Left: Dick Shawn, Lillian Gish, Tammy
Grimes, Patrice Munsel, Larry Kert**

EDISON THEATRE
   Opened Monday, November 24, 1975.*
   Rita Fredricks, Theatre Now, Inc., Norman Kean present:

BOCCACCIO

Based on stories from "The Decameron" by Giovanni Boccaccio; Dramatization and Lyrics, Kenneth Cavander; Music, Richard Peaslee; Director, Warren Enters; Musical Staging, Julie Arenal; Setting, Robert U. Taylor; Costumes, Linda Fisher; Lighting, Patrika Brown; Musical Director, Ken Bichel; Orchestrations and Arrangements, Walt Levinsky, Richard Peaslee; Hairstylist Steve Atha; Wardrobe Mistress, Barbara Sibella

CAST

Beltramo/Egano	Michael Zaslow
Giletta/Abbess.	Virginia Vestoff
Masetto/Ferondo	Armand Assante
Beatrice/Sister Teresa/Ferondo's Wife.	Caroline McWilliams
Isabella/Sister Angelica	D'Jamin Bartlett
Alibech/Sister Makaria	Jill Choder
Rustico/Brother Perdurabo/Leonetto.	Munson Hicks
Anichino/Nuto/Abbot	Richard Bauer

Standbys: Sheilah Rae, Michael Forella

MUSICAL NUMBERS: Introduction, "Masetto's Song," "Nuns Song," "God Is Good," "Now My Season's Here," "Only in My Song," "Egano D'Galluzzi," "Men Who Have Loved Me," "In the Garden," "Lucky Anichino," "Pretend You're Living," "Devil in Hell," "She Doctor," "Lover Like a Blind Man," "If You Had Seen," "Love Was Just a Game," "Madonna Isabella," "My Holy Prayer," "Hold Me Gently"

A musical in two acts. The action takes place at a villa outside Florence in the year 1348.

   General Managers: Theatre Now, Inc., Norman Kean
   Press: Les Schecter Associates
   Stage Managers: Ron Abbott, John Beven, Claudia Burk

* Closed Nov. 30, 1975 after 7 performances and 48 previews.

Kenn Duncan Photos

**Top: Virginia Vestoff, Armand Assante,
ill Choder, D'Jamin Bartlett, Caroline McWilliams
R) Richard Bauer, Munson Hicks, D'Jamin Bartlett**

**(front) Richard Bauer, Caroline McWilliams,
(back) Munson Hicks, Michael Zaslow**

Barry Nelson, Ken Howard, Estelle Parsons, Richard Benjamin, Paula Prentiss, Carole Shelley

MOROSCO THEATRE
Opened Sunday, December 7, 1975.*
Robert Fryer, James Cresson, Michael Codron in association with Martin Richards and Victor D'Arc present:

THE NORMAN CONQUESTS

By Alan Ayckbourn; Director, Eric Thompson; Scenery and Lighting, Robert Randolph; Costumes, Noel Taylor; Production Associate, Robert Linden; Wardrobe Supervisor, Louise Van Dine; Assistant to director, Richard Seff; Assistant to producers, Ron Parker; Associate to General Managers, Nancy Simmons

CAST

Norman	Richard Benjamin
Annie	Paula Prentiss†1
Tom	Ken Howard†1
Sarah	Estelle Parsons
Reg	Barry Nelson
Ruth	Carole Shelley†2

STANDBYS: Norman, Donegan Smith; Annie, Donna Wandrey; Tom, Richard Altman; Sarah, Laura Stuart; Reg, Richard Seff; Ruth, Elaine Hyman

A trilogy of comedies ("Table Manners," "Living Together," "Round and Round the Garden"), each with two acts and four scenes. The action takes place on three separate nights over a weekend in an English country house at the present time. Each play has the same cast and is seen from a different viewpoint: from the dining room, the living room, and the garden. They may be seen in any order.

General Managers: Joseph Harris, Ira Bernstein
Press: Betty Lee Hunt, Maria Cristina Pucci, Bill Evans
Stage Managers: Milt Commons, Donegan Smith

* Closed June 19, 1976 after 225 performances and 3 previews.

† Succeeded by: 1. Don Murray, Richard Altman, 2. Elaine Hyman

Top: Ken Howard, Carole Shelly (L) Richard Benjamin Barry Nelson, Estelle Parsons

Carole Shelley, Barry Nelson, Richard Benjamin, Don Murray, Paula Prentiss, Estelle Parsons Top: (L) Estelle Parsons, Barry Nelson, (R) Richard Benjamin, Carole Shelley

MARTIN BECK THEATRE

Opened Tuesday, November 25, 1975.*
James M. Nederlander, Victor Lurie and Michael Codron present:

HABEAS CORPUS

By Alan Bennett; Director, Frank Dunlop; Scenery and Costumes, Carl Toms; Lighting, Jennifer Tipton; Musical Arrangements, Dorothea Freitag; Dances, Riggs O'Hara; Production Associates, Sandra Mandel, Kim Sellon, Cathy Blaser; Wardrobe Supervisor, Rosalie Lahm; Hairstylist, Tiv Davenport

CAST

Arthur Wicksteed	Donald Sinden†1
Mrs. Swabb	June Havoc
Mrs. Wicksteed	Rachel Roberts
Dennis Wicksteed	Kristoffer Tabori†2
Constance Wicksteed	Jean Marsh
Canon Throbbing	Paxton Whitehead†3
Sir Percy Shorter	Ian Trigger
Lady Rumpers	Celeste Holm
Felicity Rumpers	Constance Forslund
Mr. Shanks	Richard Gere
Mr. Purdue	Stephen D. Newman†4
Patient	Leo Leyden†5

and the Hove Palm Court Trio

UNDERSTUDIES: Arthur, Canon, Stephen D. Newman; Mrs. Wicksteed, Mrs. Swabb, Lady Rumpers, Joyce Worsley; Constance, Felicity, Holly Villaire; Dennis, Shanks, Purdue, Tom Everett; Shorter, Leo Leyden

A comedy in two acts. The action takes place at the present time in a refined English seaside resort, in the Wicksteed's home, and on the West Pier.

General Manager: Nelle Nugent
Company Manager: James Turner
Press: Michael Alpert, Marilynn LeVine, Joshua Ellis
Stage Managers: Frank Bayer, Louis Pulvino

* Closed Feb. 15, 1976 after 95 performances and 7 previews.
† Succeeded by: 1. Paxton Whitehead, 2. Mark Baker, 3. Stephen D. Newman, Kristoffer Tabori, 4. Tom Everett, 5. Joyce Worsley

Martha Swope Photos

Top: Donald Sinden, Rachel Roberts
(R) Jean Marsh, June Havoc

30

Paxton Whitehead, Celeste Holm, Mark Baker
Constance Forslund Above: Forslund, Sinden,
Kristoffer Tabori

CIRCLE IN THE SQUARE THEATRE
Opened Thursday, December 18, 1975.*
Circle in the Square (Theodore Mann, Artistic Director; Paul Libin, Managing Director) presents:

THE GLASS MENAGERIE

By Tennessee Williams; Director, Theodore Mann; Scenery, Ming Cho Lee; Costumes, Sydney Brooks; Lighting, Thomas Skelton; Incidental Music, Craig Wasson; Production Associate, Atsumi Kolba; Wardrobe Supervisor, Virginia Merkel; Production Assistants, Gordon Bendall, Sandy Caltabiano, Susan Elrod, Bernard Ferstenberg, Robin Groves, Sharon Kolberg, Jolly Nelson, Susan Santiago, Tom Smith

CAST

Amanda, the mother...................... Maureen Stapleton
Tom, her son................................. Rip Torn
Laura, her daughter .... Pamela Payton-Wright
Jim, the gentleman caller....................... Paul Rudd

STANDBYS AND UNDERSTUDIES: Amanda, Nancy Marchand; Tom, Jim, Marco St. John; Laura, Sharon Morrison

A drama in two acts. The action takes place in an alley in St. Louis at the present time and in the past.

Company Manager: William Conn
Press: Merle Debuskey, Susan L. Schulman
Stage Managers: Randall Brooks, James Bernardi

* Closed Feb. 22, 1976 after 77 performances and 23 previews. For original production with Laurette Taylor, Eddie Dowling, Julie Haydon and Anthony Ross, see THEATRE WORLD, Vol. 1. It opened Mar. 31, 1945 at The Playhouse and ran for 563 performances. Revived Nov. 21, 1956 at City Center with Helen Hayes, James Daly, Lois Smith and Lonny Chapman for 15 performances (See THEATRE WORLD, Vol. 13). On May 4, 1965 it was revived at the Brooks Atkinson Theatre for 176 performances with Maureen Stapleton, George Grizzard, Piper Laurie and Pat Hingle. (See THEATRE WORLD, Vol. 21)

Inge Morath Photos

Right: Rip Torn, Maureen Stapleton
Top: Maureen Stapleton

Paul Rudd, Pamela Payton-Wright

Maureen Stapleton, Pamela Payton-Wright

BOOTH THEATRE
Opened Sunday, December 21, 1975.*
David Merrick, Max Brown, Byron Goldman present the
Goodspeed Opera House Production of:

VERY GOOD EDDIE

Book, Guy Bolton; Based on a farce by Phillip Bartholomae; Music, Jerome Kern; Lyrics, Schuyler Greene; Director, Bill Gile; Dances and Musical Numbers Staged by Bill Gile; Musical Direction and Arrangements, Russell Warner; Scenery and Lighting, Fred Voelpel; Costumes, David Toser; Special Consultant, Alfred Simon; Wardrobe Supervisor, Kathleen Foster; Hairstylist, Karol Coeyman

CAST

Steward	James Harder
Mr. Dick Rivers	David Christmas
Mme. Matroppo	Travis Hudson
Miss Elsie Lilly	Cynthia Wells
M. de Rougemont	Joel Craig
Mrs. Georgina Kettle	Spring Fairbank
Mr. Eddie Kettle	Charles Repole
Mr. Percy Darling	Nicholas Wyman
Mrs. Elsie Darling	Virginia Seidel
Al Cleveland	James Harder
Miss Lily Pond	Wendy Young
Miss Chrystal Poole	Karen Crossley
Miss Carrie Closewell	Gillian Scalici†
Miss Alwys Innit	Robin Herbert
Mr. Tayleurs Dumme	Russ Beasley
Mr. Dayr Thurst	Jon Engstrom
Mr. Dustin Stacks	Larry McMillan
Mr. Rollo Munn	Hal Shane

UNDERSTUDIES: Eddie, Jon Engstrom; Elsie, Robin Herbert; Steward, Joel Craig; Matroppo, Helon Blount; Rivers, de Rougemont, Russ Beasley; Percy, David Christmas; Georgina, Jo-Ann Cifalo; Elsie, Wendy Young

MUSICAL NUMBERS: "We're on Our Way," "Some Sort of Somebody," "Thirteen Collar," "Bungalow in Quogue," "Isn't It Great to Be Married," "Good Night Boat," "Left All Alone Again Blues," "Hot Dog!," "If You're a Friend of Mine," "Wedding Bells Are Calling Me," "Honeymoon Inn," "I've Got to Dance," "Moon Love," "Old Boy Neutral," "Babes in the Wood," "Katy-did," "Nodding Roses," Finale.

A musical in two acts and three scenes. The action takes place in 1913 on a Hudson River Dayliner, and in the Honeymoon Inn in the Catskill Mountains.

General Manager: Helen L. Nickerson
Company Manager: G. Warren McClane
Press: Max Eisen, Judy Jacksina, Warren Pincus
Stage Managers: Don Judge, Mark Potter, Pat Trott

* Still playing May 31, 1976.
† Succeeded by Jo-Ann Cifala

Left: Joel Craig, Travis Hudson Top:
Charles Repole, Virginia Seidel

Nicholas Wyman, Virginia Seidel,
Charles Repole, Spring Fairbank

entire cast

Bette Henritze, Robert E. Thompson
Right: Christine Andreas, Michael Allinson

YCEUM THEATRE
Opened Friday, December 26, 1975.*
Shepard Traube presents:

ANGEL STREET

By Patrick Hamilton; Director, Shepard Traube; Setting, Douglas
Schmidt; Costumes, Patricia Adshead; Lighting, Leon DiLeone

CAST

. Manningham	Dina Merrill
Manningham	Michael Allinson
cy	Christine Andreas†
beth	Bette Henritze
gh	Robert E. Thompson

Understudies: Eleanor Tauber, Alfred Karl

drama in three acts. The action takes place in 1880 in a house
ngel Street in the Pimlico district of London.

Manager: Max Gendel
Press: Lenny Traube
Stage Manager: Rick Ralston

sed Feb. 8, 1976 after 52 performances and 4 previews. Origi-
production with Judith Evelyn, Vincent Price, Leo G. Carroll
ened Dec. 5, 1941 and played 1293 performances. Revived Jan.
1948 at City Center for 14 performances with Uta Hagen, Jose
rrer and Richard Whorf. (See THEATRE WORLD, Vol. 4)

cceeded by Christine Ebersole
Bill Mitchell Photos

Michael Allinson, Dina Merrill

BILTMORE THEATRE
Opened Sunday, December 28, 1975.*
R. Tyler Gatchell, Jr., Peter Neufeld in association with Barnard S. Straus present:

MURDER AMONG FRIENDS

By Bob Barry; Director, Val May; Setting, Santo Loquasto; Costumes, Joseph G. Aulisi; Lighting, Jennifer Tipton; Associate Producers, Erv Tullman, Barry Potashnick; Production Supervisor, Pat Tolson; Hairstylist, Mr. Vincent of Enrico Caruso; Wardrobe Supervisor, Joe Busheme

CAST

Angela Forrester . . . . Janet Leigh
Ted Cotton . . . . Lewis Arlt
Palmer Forrester . . . . Jack Cassidy
Gertrude Saidenberg . . . . Jane Hoffman
Marshall Saidenberg . . . . Richard Woods
Larry . . . . Michael Durrell

STANDBYS: Angela, Holland Taylor; Palmer, John Aniston; Larry, Andrew Bloch; Ted, Ted Shackelford.

A mystery in two acts and four scenes. The action takes place at the present time in the Forrester townhouse throughout New Year's Eve.

General Management: Gatchell & Neufeld
Company Manager: James Mennen
Press: Betty Lee Hunt, Maria Cristina Pucci, Bill Evans
Stage Manager: Andrew Bloch

* Closed Jan. 11, 1976 after 17 performances and 8 previews.

Top: Jack Cassidy, Lewis Arlt
34 Right: Cassidy, Janet Leigh Below: Leigh, Arlt

Lewis Arlt, Michael Durrell,
Jane Hoffman, Richard Woods

HARKNESS THEATRE

Opened Monday, December 29, 1975.*
Michael Harvey and Harvey Frand present the Kennedy Center-Xerox Corporation Production of:

SWEET BIRD OF YOUTH

By Tennessee Williams; Director, Edwin Sherin; Scenery, Karl Eigsti; Costumes, Laura Crow; Lighting, Ken Billington; Wardrobe Supervisor, Cindy Chock; Produced in association with Brooklyn Academy of Music

CAST

Chance Wayne	Christopher Walken
Princess Kosmonopolis	Irene Worth
Fly	Flloyd Ennis
Maid	Bunny Kacher
George Scudder	Christopher Bernau
Hatcher	Richard Kuss
Boss Finley	Pat Corley
Tom Junior	Matthew Cowles
Charles	Philip Lindsay
Aunt Nonnie	Eugenia Rawls†
Heavenly Finley	Lisa Richards
Miss Lucy	Cathryn Damon
Stuff	Tom Stechschulte
Heckler	David Gale
Violet	Linda Martin
Scotty	Lanny Flaherty
Edna	Susan Kay Logan
Bud	Eric Loeb
Men in bar	Richard Babcock, Frank Rohrbach
Trooper	George Bamford
Baton Twirler	Alicia Enterline

UNDERSTUDIES: Chance, Christopher Bernau; Boss, Richard Kuss; Miss Lucy, Aunt Nonnie, Violet, Edna, Bunny Kacher; Heavenly, Maid, Susan Kay Logan; Tom Junior, Tom Stechschulte; Hatcher, Charles, Fly, Richard Babcock; Heckler, Scotty, Scudder, Eric Loeb; Man in bar, Dan Hild; Stuff, Bud, George Bamford

A drama in three acts and five scenes. The action takes place at the present time in the Royal Palms Hotel, and Boss Finley's house somewhere on the Gulf coast.

General Manager: Jay Kingwill
Company Manager: Albert Poland
Press: David Powers, William Schelble
Stage Managers: Mark Wright, Dan Hild

* Closed Feb. 7, 1976 after 48 performances and 4 previews. For original production, see THEATRE WORLD, Vol. 15. Paul Newman and Geraldine Page were starred, and played 375 performances.
† Succeeded by Elena Karam

Richard Braaten, David Fishman Photos

Right: Lanny Flaherty, Christopher Walken, Pamela Costello, Susan Logan, Cathryn Damon

Christopher Walken, Irene Worth (also top right)

Irene Worth

HELEN HAYES THEATRE

Opened Tuesday, December 30, 1975.*
Barry M. Brown, Burry Fredrik, Fritz Holt, Sally Sears present the American Bicentennial Theatre Production of:

THE ROYAL FAMILY

By George S. Kaufman and Edna Ferber; Director, Ellis Rabb; Scenery, Oliver Smith; Costumes, Ann Roth; Lighting, John Gleason; Original Music, Claibe Richardson; Produced for the Kennedy Center and Xerox Corp. by Roger L. Stevens and Richmond Crinkley; Produced in association with the McCarter Theatre Company; Wardrobe Supervisor, Clifford Capone; Hairstylist, Diane Stokes

CAST

Della	Rosetta LeNoire
Jo	John Remme
Hallboy	James C. Burge
McDermott	Sherman Lloyd
Herbert Dean	Joseph Maher†1
Kitty Dean	Mary Louise Wilson†2
Gwen Cavendish	Mary Layne†3
Perry Stewart	Forrest Buckman
Fanny Cavendish	Eva LeGallienne
Oscar Wolfe	Sam Levene
Julie Cavendish	Rosemary Harris
Tony Cavendish	George Grizzard†4
Chauffeur	Miller Lide
Gilbert Marshall	Donald Barton
Hallboys	Miller Lide, Mark Fleischman†5
Gunga	James C. Burge
Miss Peake	Eleanor Phelps†6

UNDERSTUDIES: Julie, Della, Kitty, Peake, Maria Cellario; Fanny, Eleanor Phelps, Shirley Bryan; Tony, Perry, James C. Burge; Oscar, Gilbert, Herbert, Miller Lide; Gwen, Peake, Pat De Rousie, Sandra LaVallee; Jo, McDermott, Mark Fleischman, John C. Vennema

A comedy in three acts. The action takes place in the duplex apartment of the Cavendishes in the East Fifties in New York during 1927–28.

General/Company Manager: David Lawlor
Press: Shirley Herz
Stage Managers: Helaine Head, Andre Love

* Closed July 18, 1976 after 233 performances. Original production opened at the Selwyn Dec. 28, 1927 with Haidee Wright, Ann Andrews and Otto Kruger and played 345 performances. Revived at City Center Jan. 21, 1951 for 16 performances with Ethel Griffies, Ruth Hussey, John Emery and Peggy Ann Garner. (See THEATRE WORLD, Vol. 7). Ellis Rabb received a 1976 "Tony" for Best Director.
† Succeeded by: 1. Richard Woods, 2. Peg Murray, 3. Ellen Fiske, 4. Ellis Rabb, Richard Council, 5. John C. Vennema, Andre Love 6. Margot Stevenson, Maria Cellario

Richard Braaten, Cliff Moore Photos

Left: James C. Burge, George Grizzard
Top: Rosemary Harris, Eva LeGallienne, Mary Layne

Rosemary Harris, Donald Barton

Ellis Rabb, Rosetta LeNoire, James Maher, Sam Levene, Mary Louise Wilson, Rosemary Harris, Eva LeGallienne, Mary Layne

PALACE THEATRE
Opened Sunday, January 4, 1976.*
The John F. Kennedy Center for the Performing Arts presents:

HOME SWEET HOMER

Book, Roland Kibbee, Albert Marre; Music, Mitch Leigh; Lyrics, Charles Burr, Forman Brown; Book and Musical Staging, Albert Marre; Scenery and Lighting, Howard Bay; Costumes, Howard Bay, Ray Diffen; Musical Direction, Ross Reimueller; Orchestrations, Buryl Red; Choreographic Assistant, Michael Mann; Assistant to director, Dwight Frye; Music Coordinator, Earl Shendell; Associate Conductor, Terrill Jory; Production Assistant, Kay Vance; Sound, Lennie Will; Wardrobe Supervisor, Angelo Quillici; Hairstylists, Gloria Rivera, Wayne Herndon.

CAST

Odysseus	Yul Brynner
Penelope	Joan Diener
Telemachus	Russ Thacker
Penelope's Suitors:	
Antinous	Martin Vidnovic
Pilokrates	Ian Sullivan
Ktesippos	Bill Mackey
Eurymachus	Daniel Brown
Leokritos	Brian Destazio
Pimteus	John Aristides
Melios	Bill Nabel
Polybos	Les Freed
King Alkinoos	Shev Rodgers
Nausikaa	Diana Davila
Nausikaa's Handmaidens:	
Therapina	Suzanne Sponsler
Melantho	Cecile Santos
Hippodameia	Christine Uchida
Kerux	Darel Glaser
Dekati Evdomi VII	P. J. Mann

UNDERSTUDIES: Odysseus, Shev Rodgers; Penelope, Karen Shepard; Telemachus, Darel Glaser; Nausikaa, Suzanne Sponsler; Antinous, Daniel Brown; Alkinoos, Ian Sullivan; Swing, Linda Byrne.

MUSICAL NUMBERS: "The Tales," "The Future," "The Departure," "Home Sweet Homer," "The Ball," "How Could I Dare to Dream," "I Never Imagined Goodbye," "Love Is the Prize," "Penelope's Hand," "He Will Come Home Again," "Did He Really Think," "I Was Wrong," "The Rose," "Tomorrow," "The Contest," "He Sang Songs"

A musical performed without intermission.

General Managers: Wolsk & Azenberg, Douglas C. Baker
Press: Betty Lee Hunt, Maria Cristina Pucci, Rugh Cage
Stage Managers: Patrick Horrigan, Gregory A. Hirsch

* Closed Jan. 4, 1976 after one performance and 11 previews.

**Top: Shev Rodgers, Diana Davila,
Yul Brynner, Russ Thacker (also right)**

Yul Brynner, Diana Davila Above: Joan Diener

Opened Thursday, January 8, 1976.*
Emanuel Azenberg, William W. Bradley, Marvin A. Krauss
and Irving Siders present:

THE POISON TREE

By Ronald Ribman; Director, Charles Blackwell; Settings, Marjorie Kellogg; Costumes, Judy Dearing; Lighting, Martin Aronstein; Production Manager, Henry Velez: Wardrobe Supervisor, Josephine Zampredi; Production Assistant, Michael Connors

CAST

Albert Heisenman	Danny Meehan
Walter Turner	Daniel Barton
Officer Lowery	Gene O'Neill
Officer DiSantis	Peter Masterson
Sgt. Coyne	Robert Symonds
Officer Lloyd	Charles Brown
Officer Friezer	Arlen Dean
Officer Rollock	Pat McNamara
Willy Stepp	Cleavon Little
Bobby Foster	Dick Anthony Williams
Benjamin Hurspool	Moses Gunn
Charles Jefferson	Northern J. Calloway
Smiling Man	Dennis Tate

UNDERSTUDIES: Stepp, Hurspool, Arthur French; Foster, Charles Brown; DiSantis, Arlen Dean; Coyne, Heisenman, Frank Hamilton; Friezer, Rollock, Lowery, Steven Shaw; Jefferson, Lloyd, Turner, Charles Douglass

A drama in 2 acts and 10 scenes. The action takes place at the present time in a western state prison.

General Manager: Jose Vega
Press: Merle Debuskey, Leo Stern
Stage Managers: Robert St. Clair, Steven Shaw, Gene O'Neill
* Closed Jan. 11, 1976 after 5 performances and 2 previews.

Barry Kramer-Joseph Abeles Photos

**Right: Peter Masterson, Cleavon Little,
Dick Anthony Williams Top: Danny Meehan,
Daniel Barton, Gene O'Neill**

Cleavon Little, Northern J. Calloway
(top), Dick Anthony Williams

Moses Gunn, Peter Masterson,
Dick Anthony Williams, Cleavon Little

WINTER GARDEN

Opened Sunday, January 11, 1976.*
Harold Prince in association with Ruth Mitchell presents:

PACIFIC OVERTURES

Book, John Weidman; Music and Lyrics, Stephen Sondheim; Director, Harold Prince; Choreographer, Patricia Birch; Scenery, Boris Aronson; Costumes, Florence Klotz; Lighting, Tharon Musser; Orchestrations, Jonathan Tunick; Musical Direction, Paul Gemignani; Dance Music, Daniel Troob; Kabuki Consultant, Haruki Fujimoto; Make-up and Wigs, Richard Allen; Masks and Dolls, E. Taylor; Sound, Jack Mann; Wardrobe Supervisor, Adelaide Laurino; Assistant to director, Annette Brafman Meyers; Associate Conductor, Les Scott; Technical Supervisor, John J. Moore; Martial Arts Sequence, Soon-Teck Oh; Original Cast Album, RCA Records

CAST

Reciter/Shogun/Jonathan Goble	Mako
Abe, First Councillor	Yuki Shimoda
Manjiro	Sab Shimono
Second Councillor/Old Man/French Admiral	James Dybas
Shogun's Mother/Merchant/American Admiral	Alvin Ing
Third Councillor/Samurai's Daughter	Freddy Mao
Kayama	Isao Sato
Tamate/Samurai/Storyteller/Swordsman	Soon-Teck Oh
Servant/Commodore Perry	Haruki Fujimoto
Observers	Alvin Ing, Ricardo Tobia
Fisherman/Wrestler/Lord of the South	Jae Woo Lee
Son/Priest/Noble	Timm Fujii
Grandmother/Wrestler/Japanese Merchant	Conrad Yama
Thief/Samurai/Soothsayer/Warrior/ Russian Admiral	Mark Hsu Syers
Adams/Samurai/Noble	Ernest Abuba
Williams/Lord of the South	Larry Hama
Shogun's Wife	Freda Foh Shen
Physician/Madam/British Admiral	Ernest Harada
Priest/Boy	Gedde Watanabe
Shogun's Companion/Dutch Admiral	Patrick Kinser-Lau
Girls	Timm Fujii, Patrick Kinser-Lau, Gedde Watanabe, Leslie Watanabe
Imperial Priest	Tom Matsusaka
British Sailors	Timm Fujii, Patrick Kinser-Lau, Mark Hsu Syers
Musicians	Fusako Yoshida, Genji Ito

SERVANTS, SAILORS, TOWNSPEOPLE: Susan Kikuchi, Diane Lam, Kim Miyori, Freda Foh Shen, Kenneth S. Eiland, Timm Fujii, Joey Ginza, Patrick Kinser-Lau, Tony Marinyo, Kevin Maung, Ringo Secretario, Mark Hsu Syers, Ricardo Tobia, Gedde Watanabe, Leslie Watanabe

UNDERSTUDIES: Reciter, Jae Woo Lee; Tamate, Gedde Watanabe; Samurai, Storyteller, Freddy Mao; Swordsman, Abe, Ernest Abuba; Manjiro, Patrick Kinser-Lau; Kayama, Tom Matsusaka; Second Councillor, Ricardo Tobia; Third Councillor, Tony Marinyo

MUSICAL NUMBERS: "The Advantages of Floating in the Middle of the Sea," "There Is No Other Way," "Four Black Dragons," "Chrysanthemum Tea," "Poems," "Welcome to Kanagawa," "Someone in a Tree," "Lion Dance," "Please Hello," "A Bowler Hat," "Pretty Lady," "Next"

A musical in two acts. The action takes place in Japan in July of 1853, and from then on.

General Manager: Howard Haines
Company Manager: Leo K. Cohen
Press: Mary Bryant, Randy Kaplan
Stage Managers: George Martin, John Grigas, Carlos Gorbea

Closed June 27, 1976 after 193 performances and 13 previews. Winner of 1976 "Tony's" for Best Scenic Design, Best Costumes.

Van Williams, Martha Swope Photos

Top: Mako (c) Below: Patrick Kinser-Lau, Ernest Harada, Mark Hsu Syers, Yuki Shimoda, Alvin Ing, James Dybas

Soon-Teck Oh　　　　　Haruki Fujimoto

Katharine Hepburn, Paul Harding

BROADHURST THEATRE
Opened Tuesday, February 3, 1976.*
Robert Whitehead, Roger L. Stevens, Konrad Matthaei present:

A MATTER OF GRAVITY

By Enid Bagnold; Director, Noel William; Scenery, Ben Edwards; Costumes, Jane Greenwood; Lighting, Thomas Skelton; Production Assistants, Mark Potter, Katharine Allentuck; Wardrobe Supervisor, Colin Ferguson; Hairstylist, Charles Lo Presto

CAST

Dubois	Charlotte Jones
Estate Agent	Robert Moberly
Mrs. Basil	Katharine Hepburn
Nicky	Christopher Reeve
Shatov	Elizabeth Lawrence
Herbert	Paul Harding
Elizabeth	Wanda Bimson
Tom	Daniel Tamm

UNDERSTUDIES: Dubois, Shatov, Maggie Task; Herbert, Robert Moberly; Elizabeth, Kathleen Heaney; Estate Agent, Bill Becker

A comedy in three acts. The action takes place in a room in an old English country house at the present time.

General Manager: Oscar E. Olesen
Company Manager: David Hedges
Press: Seymour Krawitz, Patricia McLean Krawitz
Stage Managers: Ben Strobach, Bill Becker

* Closed Apr. 10, 1976 after limited engagement of 79 performances.

Sy Friedman Photos

40

Top: Christopher Reeve, Katharine Hepburn, Elizabeth Lawrence, Charlotte Jones, Wanda Bimson, Daniel Tamm, Paul Harding

MINSKOFF THEATRE
Opened Tuesday, February 17, 1976.*
Lester Osterman Productions and Joseph Kipness in Association with Martin Richards and Victor D'Arc, Marilyn Strauss present:

ROCKABYE HAMLET

By Cliff Jones; Based on Shakespeare's play "Hamlet"; Direction and Choreography, Gower Champion; Co-Choreographer, Tony Stevens; Scenery, Kert F. Lundell; Costumes, Joseph G. Aulisi; Lighting, Jules Fisher; Sound, Abe Jacob; Swordplay, Larry Carpenter; Hairstylist, Make-up, Ted Azar; Musical Direction and Vocal Arrangements, Gordon Lowry Harrell; Dance Music Arrangements, Douglas Katsaros; Assistant to director, Larry Carpenter; Special Effects, Robert Joyce; Wardrobe Master, Joe Busheme; Musical Coordinator, Eron Tabor; Associate Conductor, Bill Schneider

CAST

Horatio	Rory Dodd
Hamlet	Larry Marshall
Claudius	Alan Weeks
Gertrude	Leata Galloway
Priest	Meat Loaf
Polonius	Randal Wilson
Ophelia	Beverly D'Angelo
Laertes	Kim Milford
Rosencrantz	Christopher Chadman
Guildenstern	Winston DeWitt Hemsley
Player	Irving Lee
Playeress/Honeybelle Huckster	Judy Gibson

Standby: Philip Casnoff

ACOLYTES, SWORDSMEN, NOBLES, COURTESANS: Tommy Aguilar, Steve Anthony, Terry Calloway, Prudence Darby, George Giraldo, Larry Hyman, Kurt Johnson, Clinton Keen, Paula Lynn, Joann Ogawa, Sandi Orcutt, Merel Poloway, Joseph Pugliese, Yolanda Raven, Michelle Stubbs, Dennis Williams

SINGERS: James Braet, Judy DeAngelis, B. G. Gibson, Judy Gibson, Pat Gorman, Suzanne Lukather, Bruce Paine, William Parry

ROADIES: Chet D'Elia, David Fredericks, David Lawson, Jeff Spiman

MUSICAL NUMBERS: "Why Did He Have to Die?," "The Wedding," "That It Should Come to This," "Set It Right," "Hello-Hello," "Don't Unmask Your Beauty to the Moon," "If Not to You," "Have I Got a Girl for You," "Tis Pity, Tis True," "Shall We Dance," "All My Life," "Something's Rotten in Denmark," "Denmark Is Still," "Twist Her Mind," "Gentle Lover," "Where Is the Reason," "The Wart Song," "He Got It in the Ear," "It Is Done," "Midnight—Hot Blood," "Midnight Mass," "Hey!," "Sing Alone," "Your Daddy's Gone Away," "Rockabye Hamlet," "All by Yourself," "Rosencrantz and Guildenstern Boogie," "Laertes Coercion," "The Last Blues," "Didn't She Do It for Love," "If My Morning Begins," "Swordfight"

General Manager: Leonard Soloway
Press: Betty Lee Hunt, Maria Cristina Pucci, Bill Evans
Stage Managers: David Taylor, Bethe Ward, Tony Manzi

Closed Feb. 21, 1976 after 7 performances and 21 previews.

Kenn Duncan Photos

Top: Beverly D'Angelo, Larry Marshall
Below: Alan Weeks, Kim Milford

Judy Gibson, Larry Marshall

BILTMORE THEATRE
Opened Tuesday, February 24, 1976.*
Terry Allen Kramer and Harry Rigby by arrangement with
Circle Repertory Company present:

KNOCK KNOCK

By Jules Feiffer; Director, Marshall W. Mason; Setting, John Lee
Beatty; Costumes, Jennifer von Mayrhauser; Lighting, Dennis Pa-
richy; Sound, Charles London, George Hansen; Assistant Director,
John H. Davis; Production Assistant, Petder Lippman

CAST

Cohn	Daniel Seltzer
Abe	Neil Flanagan
Wiseman	Judd Hirsch†
Joan	Nancy Snyder
Messenger/Gambler/Judge/Joan's Voices	Judd Hirsch†

A comedy in three acts. The action takes place at the present time
in a small house in the woods.

General Manager: Leonard Soloway
Press: Henry Luhrman, Terry Lilly
Stage Managers: Dan Hild, Greg Taylor

*Closed May 23, 1976 after 104 performances. Opened Sunday, Jan.
18, 1976 at Circle Repertory Theatre with the same cast and played
48 performances before moving to Broadway. A new cast and
production opened at the Biltmore on Wednesday, June 2, 1976.
† Succeeded by Leonard Frey

Herbert Migdoll, Martha Swope Photos

Right: Judd Hirsch, Nancy Snyder,
Neil Flanagan, Daniel Seltzer
Top: Flanagan, Seltzer

Neil Flanagan, Daniel Seltzer

Nancy Snyder, Neil Flanagan, Daniel Seltzer

ANTA THEATRE

Opened Tuesday, March 2, 1976.*
J. Lloyd Grant, Richard Bell, Robert M. Cooper, Ashton Springer in association with Moe Septee, Inc., present the Media House Production of:

BUBBLING BROWN SUGAR

Book, Loften Mitchell; Based on a concept by Rosetta LeNoire; Director, Robert M. Cooper; Musical Direction, Danny Holgate; Choreography and Musical Staging, Billy Wilson; Sets, Clarke Dunham; Costumes, Bernard Johnson; Lighting, Barry Arnold; Projections, Lucie D. Grosvenor, Clarke Dunham; Sound, Joel S. Fichman; Additional Music, Danny Holgate, Emme Kemp, Lillian Lopez; Choral Arrangements, Chapman Roberts; Hairstylists, Gene Sheppard, Stanley James; Production Supervisor, I. Mitchell Miller; Production Coordinator, Sharon Brown; Assistant to director, Kathleen Stanford-Grant; Assistant to choreographer, Dyann Robinson; Wardrobe Mistress, Linda Lee; Original Cast Album by H & L Records

CAST

Skip/Young Checkers	Lonnie McNeil
Bill/Time Man/Bumpy/M. C.	Vernon Washington†
Ray/Young Sage	Newton Winters
Carolyn/Gospel Lady/Nightclub Singer	Carolyn Byrd
Norma	Karen Grannum
Gene/Gospel Lady's Son	Alton Lathrop
Helen	Dyann Robinson
Laura	Charlise Harris
Marsha/Young Irene	Vivian Reed
Tony/Waiter/Dutch	Anthony Whitehouse
Irene Paige	Josephine Premice
John Sage/Rusty	Avon Long
Checkers/Dusty	Joseph Attles
Jim/Nightclub Singer	Chip Garnett
Ella	Ethel Beatty
Judy/Dutch's Girl	Barbara Rubenstein
Charlie/Count	Barry Preston
The Solitunes	Alton Lathrop, Lonnie McNeil, Newton Winters
Chorus	Murphy Cross, Nedra Dixon, Emme Kemp, Stanley Ramsey

STANDBYS AND UNDERSTUDIES: Sage, Vernon Washington; Irene, Gospel Lady, Nightclub Singer, Emme Kemp; Marsha, Young Irene, Karen Grannum; Checkers, Bill, Bumpy, MC, David Bryant; Jim, Stanley Ramsey; Judy, Murphy Cross; Tony, Charlie, Dutch, Count, E. Lynn Nickerson; Gospel Lady's Son, Millard Hurley; Dance Alternates, Carol Pennyfeather, Millard Hurley.

MUSICAL NUMBERS: "Harlem '70," "Bubbling Brown Sugar," "That's What Harlem Is to Me," "Bill Robinson Specialty," "Harlem Sweet Harlem," "Nobody," "Goin' Back in Time," "Some of These Days," "Moving Uptown," "Strolling," "I'm Gonna Tell God All My Troubles," "His Eye Is on the Sparrow," "Swing Low, Sweet Chariot," "Sweet Georgia Brown," "Honeysuckle Rose," "Stormy Monday Blues," "Rosetta," "Sophisticated Lady," "In Honeysuckle Time When Emaline Said She'd Be Mine," "Solitude," "C'mon Up to Jive Time," "Stompin' at the Savoy," "Take the 'A' Train," "Harlem—Time," "Love Will Find a Way," "Dutch's Song," "Brown Gal," "Pray for the Lights to Go Out," "I Got It Bad," "Harlem Makes Me Feel!," "Jim, Jam, Jumpin' Jive," "There'll Be Some Changes Made," "God Bless the Child," "It Don't Mean a Thing"

A musical revue in 2 acts and 9 scenes. The action takes place in Harlem at the present time, and between 1920 and 1940.

General Managers: Ashton Springer, Susan Chase
Company Manager: Carolyne A. Jones
Press: Max Eisen, Barbara Glenn
Stage Managers: Sam Ellis, E. Lynn Nickerson

* Still playing May 31, 1976.
† Succeeded by David Bryant

Bert Andrews Photos

Right Center: Barbara Rubenstein, Barry Preston;
Vivian Reed, Newton Winters, Lonnie
McNeil
Top: Josephine Premice, Avon Long

Josephine Premice, Avon Long, Vivian Reed,
Joseph Attles, (top center) Chip Garnett

43

CIRCLE IN THE SQUARE THEATRE
Sundays, March 7 & 14, 1976.*
Circle in the Square (Theodore Mann, Artistic Director; Paul Libin, Managing Director) presents:

GERALDINE FITZGERALD
in
SONGS OF THE STREET

Directed by Richard Maltby; Musical Direction, Stanley Wietrzychowski; Vocal Consultant, Andy Anselmo
A one-woman "informal concert."

Press: Merle Debuskey, Susan L. Schulman
Stage Manager: Randall Brooks

* Presented for two performances only.

Left: Geraldine Fitzgerald

JOHN GOLDEN THEATRE
Opened Saturday, March 13, 1976.*
Adela Holzer presents:

ME JACK, YOU JILL

By Robes Kossez; Director, Harold J. Kennedy; Scenery and Costumes, Lawrence King, Michael H. Yeargan; Lighting, Jane Reisman; Special Effects, Ronald Vitelli, Neil Schatz; Hairstylist, Rosalba; Assistant to director, Skipp Lynch; Wardrobe Supervisor, Samuel Elterman

CAST

Bibi	Lisa Kirk
Annie	Barbara Baxley
Tessie	Sylvia Sidney
Young Man	Russ Thacker

Standbys: Donna Pearson, Jeffrey Danneman

A "play of suspense" in two acts and three scenes. The action takes place at the present time on the empty stage of a Broadway theatre.

General Manager: Leonard A. Mulhern
Company Manager: David Relyea
Press: Michael Alpert, Marilynn LeVine, Joshua Ellis
Stage Managers: Tom Porter, Jeffrey Danneman

* Closed March 14, 1976 after 2 performances and 14 previews.

Carl Samrock Photos

Above: Sylvia Sidney, also right with Lisa Kirk

Sylvia Sidney, Barbara Baxley, Russ Thacker

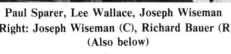

Paul Sparer, Lee Wallace, Joseph Wiseman
Right: Joseph Wiseman (C), Richard Bauer (R)
(Also below)

LYCEUM THEATRE
Opened Wednesday, March 17, 1976.*
Moe Septee presents:

ZALMEN OR THE MADNESS OF GOD

By Elie Wiesel; Stage Adaptation, Marion Wiesel; Director, Alan Schneider; Scenery, William Ritman; Costumes, Marjorie Slaiman; Lighting, Richard Nelson; Assistant Director, Susan Einhorn; Production Supervisor, Sander Hacker; Wardrobe Supervisor, Cindy Chock; Hairstylist, Nino Raffaello; Production Assistant, Lee Mastrodonato

CAST

Zalmen	Richard Bauer
The Rabbi	Joseph Wiseman
Chairman of the Synagogue Council	Paul Sparer
Members of Synagogue Council:	
Shmuel	Edwin Bordo
Srul	Sanford Seeger
Motke	Carl Don
Chaim	David Reinhardsen
Zender	Warren Pincus
The Doctor	David Margulies
Inspector from Ministry of Religious Affairs	Lee Wallace
Nina	Polly Adams
Mischa	Rodman Flender
Alexei	David Little
Cantor	John B. Jellison
Commissar	Jack Hollander
First Guard	Michael Haney
Second Guard	John B. Jellison
Third Guard	Irwin Atkins
Secretary	Nancy Dutton
Avron	Michael Gorrin
Feige	Zviah Igdalsky

UNDERSTUDIES AND STANDBYS: Mischa, Jonathan Weisgal; Zalmen, Srul, John B. Jellison; Rabbi, Irwin Atkins; Chairman, Doctor, Edwin Bordo; Inspector, Jack Hollander; Nina, Feige, Nancy Dutton; Alexei, David Reinhardsen; Avrom, Carl Don; Chaim, Michael Haney; Commissar, Sanford Seeger.

A drama in two acts. The action takes place in the late 1950's in a synagogue in a small town in Russia.

General Manager: Laurel Ann Wilson
Company Manager: Donald Tirabassi
Press: Max Eisen, Barbara Glenn, Judy Jacksina
Stage Managers: R. Derek Swire, Ted Harris, Michael Haney

* Closed April 5, 1976 after 22 performances and 5 previews.

Jack Hoffman Photos

David Little, Rodman Flender, Polly Adams,
Joseph Wiseman

CIRCLE IN THE SQUARE THEATRE
Opened Thursday, March 18, 1976.*
Circle in the Square (Theodore Mann, Artistic Director; Paul
Libin, Managing Director) presents:

THE LADY FROM THE SEA

By Henrik Ibsen; Translated by Michael Meyer; Director, Tony
Richardson; Scenery and Costumes, Rouben Ter-Arutunian; Light-
ing, Thomas Skelton; Music and Sound, Richard Peaslee; Produc-
tion Associate, Atsumi Kolba; Wardrobe Supervisor, Virginia
Merkel; Production Assistants, Gordon Bendall, Sandy Caltabiano,
Susan Elrod, Bernard Ferstenberg, Robin Groves, Sharon Kolberg,
Jolly Nelson, Susan Santiago, Tom Smith

CAST

Ballested	George Ede
Bolette	Kimberly Farr
Lyngstrand	Kipp Osborne
Hilde	Allison Argo
Dr. Wangel	Pat Hingle
Professor Arnholm	John Heffernan
Ellida	Vanessa Redgrave
The Stranger	Richard Lynch

A drama in two acts. The action takes place during the summer
in a small town by a fjord in northern Norway.

Company Manager: William Conn
Press: Merle Debuskey, Susan L. Schulman
Stage Managers: Randall Brooks, James Bernardi

* Closed May 23, 1976 after limited engagement of 77 performances
and 23 previews.

Inge Morath Photos

**Right: Vanessa Redgrave, Pat Hingle,
Richard Lynch Top: John Heffernan, Vanessa
Redgrave, Kipp Osborne**

George Ede, Kimberly Farr

Pat Hingle, Allison Argo, Kipp Osborne,
Kimberly Farr, John Heffernan, Vanessa Redgrav

ST. JAMES THEATRE

Opened Thursday, March 25, 1976.*
Herman Levin presents:

MY FAIR LADY

Book and Lyrics, Alan Jay Lerner; Adapted from Bernard Shaw's "Pygmalion"; Music, Frederick Loewe; Director, Jerry Adler; Based on the original by Moss Hart; Choreography and Musical Numbers, Crandall Diehl; Based on original by Hanya Holm; Scenery, Oliver Smith; Costumes, Cecil Beaton; Lighting, John Gleason; Special Costume Assistant, W. Robert Lavine; Musical Director, Theodore Saidenberg; Musical Arrangements, Robert Russel Bennett, Phil Lang; Dance Music Arrangements, Trude Rittman; Wardrobe Master, Joseph Busheme; Production Assistant, Anne Tomfohrde; Assistant Conductor, R. Bennett Benetsky; Hair Supervisors, Vincent Prestia, Michael Fisher; Hairstylist, Ray Iagnocco

CAST

Buskers	Debra Lyman, Stan Pincus, Ernie Pysher
Mrs. Eynsford-Hill	Eleanor Phelps
Freddy Eynsford-Hill	Jerry Lanning
Eliza Doolittle	Christine Andreas†1
Colonel Pickering	Robert Coote†2
Henry Higgins	Ian Richardson
First Cockney	Kevin Marcum
Second Cockney	Jack Starkey
Third Cockney/Flunkey	William James
Fourth Cockney/Footman	Stan Page
Bartender/Footman	Kevin Lane Dearinger
Harry/Lord Boxington/Zoltan Karpathy	John Clarkson
Jamie/Ambassador	Richard Neilson
Alfred P. Doolittle	George Rose
Mrs. Pearce	Sylvia O'Brien
Mrs. Hopkins/Lady Boxington	Margaretta Warwick
Butler/Bartender	Clifford Fearl
Servants	Sonja Anderson, Lynn Fitzpatrick, Karen Gibson, Vickie Patik, Kevin Lane Dearinger
Mrs. Higgins	Brenda Forbes
Chauffeur	Jack Karcher
Constable	Timothy Smith
Flower Girl	Dru Alexandrine
Queen of Transylvania	Karen Gibson
Mrs. Higgin's Maid	Sonja Stuart

SINGING ENSEMBLE: Sonja Anderson, Alyson Bristol, Lynn Fitzpatrick, Karen Gibson, Cynthia Meryl, Vickie Patik, Kevin Lane Dearinger, Clifford Fearl, William James, Kevin Marcum, Stan Page, Jack Starkey

DANCING ENSEMBLE: Dru Alexandrine, Sally Benoit, Marie Berry, Debra Lyman, Mari McMinn, Gina Ramsel, Catherine Rice, Sonja Stuart, Bonnie Walker, Richard Amron, Jeremy Blanton, David Evans, Jack Karcher, Richard Maxon, Stan Pincus, Ernie Pysher, Rick Schneider, Timothy Smith

MUSICAL NUMBERS: "Street Entertainers," "Why Can't the English?" "Wouldn't It Be Loverly?," "With A Little Bit of Luck," "I'm an Ordinary Man," "Just You Wait," "The Rain in Spain," "I Could Have Danced All Night," "Ascot Gavotte," "On the Street Where You Live," "Embassy Waltz," "You Did It," "Show Me," "Get Me to the Church on Time," "A Hymn to Him," "Without You," "I've Grown Accustomed to Her Face"

UNDERSTUDIES AND STANDBYS: Higgins, Patrick Horgan; Eliza, Vickie Patik; Doolittle, John Clarkson; Pickering, Richard Neilson; Mrs. Higgins, Eleanor Phelps; Freddy, William James; Mrs. Pearce, Margaretta Warwick; Harry, Kevin Marcum; Jamie, Stan Page; Mrs. Hopkins, Cynthia Meryl; Mrs. Eynsford-Hill, Karen Gibson; Karpathy, Kevin Marcum

A musical in 2 acts and 18 scenes. The action takes place in London.

General Manager: Philip Adler
Company Manager: Malcolm Allen
Press: Seymour Krawitz, Patricia McLean Krawitz
Stage Managers: Nicholas Russiyan, Alisa Jill Adler, Robert O'Rourke

* Still playing May 31, 1976. George Rose received a 1976 "Tony" for Best Actor in a Musical. Original production opened Mar. 15, 1956 at the Mark Hellinger Theatre with Rex Harrison, Julie Andrews, Stanley Holloway, and Cathleen Nesbitt and ran for 2715 performances. (See THEATRE WORLD, Vol. 12)
† During illness played by: 1. Vickie Patik, 2. Eric Brotherson

Sy Friedman Photos

George Rose   Christine Andreas

Top Right: Ian Richardson, Christine Andreas, also below with Robert Coote Center: Brenda Forbes, Jerry Lanning, Richardson, Andreas, Coote, Eleanor Phelps

47

THE MUSIC BOX

Opened Thursday, April 1, 1976.*
Ken Marsolais and James Scott Productions, Inc., in associa
tion with MPL, Ltd., present:

WHO'S AFRAID OF VIRGINIA WOOLF?

By Edward Albee; Directed by Mr. Albee; Setting and Lighting
William Ritman; Costumes, Jane Greenwood; Produced by arrange
ment with Richard Barr and Clinton Wilder; Assistant to producers
Jerry Sirchia; Assistant to director, Christopher Gore; Wardrobe
Supervisor, Fay Young

CAST

Martha	Colleen Dewhurst
George	Ben Gazzara
Honey	Maureen Anderman
Nick	Richard Kelton

STANDBYS: Martha, Betty Miller; George, James Karen; Honey
Katherine Bruce; Nick, Josef Warik

A comedy-drama in three acts. The action takes place at the
present time in the home of George and Martha in a university town

General Manager: Leonard Soloway
Company Manager: Terry Grossman
Press: Betty Lee Hunt, Maria Cristina Pucci
Stage Managers: Mark Wright, Wayne Carson

* Closed July 11, 1976 after 117 performances and three previews
Original production opened Oct. 13, 1962 at the Billy Rose The
atre and played 664 performances with Uta Hagen, Arthur Hill
George Grizzard and Melinda Dillon. (See THEATRE WORLD
Vol. 19)

**Left: Richard Kelton, Colleen Dewhurst
Top: Richard Kelton, Ben Gazzara, Maureen
Anderman, Colleen Dewhurst**

Colleen Dewhurst, Ben Gazzara

Ben Gazzara, Colleen Dewhurst, Richard Kelton

PALACE THEATRE
Opened Monday, April 19, 1976.*
HMT Associates present:

SHIRLEY MacLAINE
with
Shirley's Gypsies

Directed and Staged by Tony Charmoli; Musical Director, Donn Trenner; Music arranged or composed by Cy Coleman; Written by Fred Ebb; Additional Material, Bob Wells; Special Choreography, Alan Johnson; Lighting, Richard Winkler, Graham Large; Sound, Steve Wooley; Wardrobe Mistress, Sydney Smith; Recorded by Columbia Records

SHIRLEY'S GYPSIES: Jo Ann Lehmann, Gary Flannery, Adam Grammis, Larry Vickers

MUSICAL NUMBERS: "If My Friends Could See Me Now," "Personal Property," "Remember Me?," "Hey Big Spender," "I'm a Person Too," "Irma La Douce," "Gypsy in My Soul," "It's Not Where You Start," "Every Little Movement Has a Meaning All Its Own," "The Hustle," "Star," "I'm a Brass Band"

Performed without intermission.

General Management: Marvin A. Krauss Associates, David Wyler, Robert I. Goldberg
Company Manager: Bernard Lang
Press: Michael Alpert, Marilynn LeVine, Warren Knowlton, Carl Samrock, Jonas Halpern
Stage Manager: Earl Hughes

* Closed May 1, 1976 after 20 performances.

Robin Platzer Photos

Shirley MacLaine (also above and left)

BROADHURST THEATRE
Opened Tuesday, April 20, 1976.*
Steven Beckler and Thomas C. Smith present:

THE HEIRESS

By Ruth and Augustus Goetz; Based on Henry James' novel, "Washington Square"; Director, George Keathley; Setting, Oliver Smith; Costumes, Ann Roth; Lighting, David F. Segal; Associate Producer, Ken Morse; Produced for the Kennedy Center by Roger L. Stevens and Richmond Crinkley; Technical Supervisor, Mitch Miller; Wardrobe Supervisor, Colin Ferguson; Hairstylist, J. Roy Helland

CAST

Maria	Sharon Laughlin
Dr. Austin Sloper	Richard Kiley
Lavinia Penniman	Jan Miner
Catherine Sloper	Jane Alexander
Elizabeth Almond	Dorothy Blackburn
Arthur Townsend	Roger Baron
Marian Almond	Cecilia Hart
Morris Townsend	David Selby
Mrs. Montgomery	Toni Darnay
Coachman	William Gibberson

UNDERSTUDIES: Sloper, William Gibberson; Catherine, Marian, Sharon Laughlin; Lavinia, Diana Mathews; Morris, Roger Baron; Arthur, Coachman, Joe Lorden; Mrs. Almond, Mrs. Montgomery, Maria, Diana Mathews

A drama in 2 acts and 7 scenes. The action takes place in the front parlor of Dr. Sloper's house in Washington Square, New York City, in 1850.

General Manager: Theatre Now., Inc., Edward H. Davis, William C. Cohen
Press: Betty Lee Hunt, Maria Cristina Pucci
Stage Manager: Joe Lorden

* Closed May 9, 1976 after 23 performances and 5 previews. Original production opened Sept. 29, 1947 at the Biltmore and played 410 performances with Basil Rathbone, Wendy Hiller and Patricia Collinge. (See THEATRE WORLD, Vol. 4) Revived at City Center Jan. 25, 1950 for 15 performances with Basil Rathbone, Margaret Phillips, Edna Best and John Dall. (See THEATRE WORLD, Vol. 6)

Richard Braaten Photos

Top: Richard Kiley

50   **Right: David Selby, Jane Alexander**

Richard Kiley, Jane Alexander
Above: David Selby, Jan Miner

Opened Sunday, April 25, 1976.*
Richard Adler in association with Roger Berlind and Edward
R. Downe, Jr. presents:

REX

Book, Sherman Yellen; Music, Richard Rodgers; Lyrics, Sheldon
Harnick; Director, Edwin Sherin; Choreography, Dania Krupska;
Orchestrations, Irwin Kostal; Musical Director, Jay Blackton;
Dance Arrangements, David Baker; Scenery and Costumes, John
Conklin; Lighting, Jennifer Tipton; Hairstylist, Bert Anthony;
Werner Sherer; Technical Supervisor, Mitch Miller; Wardrobe Su-
pervisor, Mariana Torres; Assistant to director, Christopher Adler;
Assistant to producers, Giselle Steiker; Original Cast Album by
RCA Records

CAST

Norfolk	Charles Rule
Cardinal Wolsey	William Griffis
Will Somers	Tom Aldredge
Henry VIII	Nicol Williamson
Mark Smeaton	Ed Evanko
Princess Mary	Glenn Close
Queen Catherine of England	Barbara Andres
Lady Jane Seymour	April Shawhan
Francis, King of France	Stephen D. Newman
English Herald	Danny Ruvolo
French Herald	Jeff Phillips
Queen Claude of France/Lady Margaret/Queen Katherine Parr of England	Martha Danielle
Anne Boleyn/Princess Elizabeth	Penny Fuller
Dauphin	Keith Koppmeier
Comus	Merwin Goldsmith
First Guard	Ken Henley
Lady in Waiting	Melanie Vaughan
Young Princess Elizabeth	Sparky Shapiro
Nurse	Lillian Shelby
Second Guard	Dennis Daniels
Thomas Cromwell	Gerald R. Teijelo
Catherine Howard	Valerie Mahaffey
Prince Edward	Michael John

LADIES AND GENTLEMEN OF THE COURTS: Dennis Dan-
iels, Harry Fawcett, Paul Forrest, Pat Gideon, Ken Henley, Dawn
Herbert, Robin Hoff, Don Johanson, Jim Litten, Craig Lucas, Carol
Jo Lugenbeal, Valerie Mahaffey, G. Eugene Moose, Jeff Phillips,
Charles Rule, Danny Ruvolo, Lillian Shelby, Jo Speros, Gerald R.
Teijelo, Jr., Candace Tovar, John Ulrickson, Melanie Vaughan

SWORD AND MORRIS DANCERS: Dennis Daniels, Ken Henley, Don Johnson, Jim Litten, Jeff Phillips, Danny Ruvolo

UNDERSTUDIES: Henry, Stephen D. Newman; Anne Boleyn,
Martha Danielle; Somers, Jeff Phillips; Princess Elizabeth, Lady
Jane, Carol Jo Lugenbeal; Queen Catherine, Lillian Shelby; Princess
Mary, Lady Margaret, Pat Gideon; Queen Claude, Valerie Ma-
haffey; Queen Katherine Parr, Candace Tovar; Smeaton, Craig
Lucas; Comus, King Francis, Gerald R. Teijelo, Jr.; Wolsey, Charles
Rule; Prince Edward, Keith Koppmeier; Dauphin, Michael John

MUSICAL NUMBERS: "Te Deum," "No Song More Pleasing,"
"Where Is My Son?," "The Field of Cloth of Gold," "Basse Dance,"
"The Chase," "Away from You," "As Once I Loved You," "Eliza-
beth," "What Now?," "Christmas at Hampton Court," "Wee
Golden Warrior," "The Masque," "From Afar," "In Time"

A musical in 2 acts and 24 scenes. The action takes place during
the reign of Henry VIII of England until his death.

General Managers: Edward H. Davis, William C. Cohen
Company Manager: Leo K. Cohen
Press: Jeffrey Richards, James Storrow, Barbara Shelley
Stage Managers: Bob Bernard, Jack Timmers, Elise Warner

Closed June 5, 1976 after 48 performances and 14 previews.

Martha Swope Photos

Top: Nicol Williamson

Below: Ed Evanko, Penny Fuller

Stephen D. Newman, Michael John, Tom Aldredge,
Nicol Williamson, Penny Fuller, Glenn Close

HARKNESS THEATRE
Opened Tuesday, April 27, 1976.*
Frederick Brisson in association with The Harkness Organization and Wyatt Dickerson presents:

SO LONG, 174th STREET

Book, Joseph Stein; Based on his play "Enter Laughing"; From the novel by Carl Reiner; Music and Lyrics, Stan Daniels; Director, Bert Shevelove; Choreography, Alan Johnson; Scenery, James Riley; Costumes, Stanley Simmons; Lighting, Richard Nelson; Hairstylist, Ted Azar; Musical Direction, John Lesko; Orchestrations, Luther Henderson; Dance Music Arrangements, Wally Harper; Production Supervisor, Stone Widney; Wardrobe Supervisor, Agnes Farrell; Production Assistant, Kim Beaty; Assistant Conductor, Woody Kessler; Assistant to director, Patrick Horrigan; Assistant to choreographer, Graziela Daniele.

CAST

David	Robert Morse
Stage Manager	Joe Howard
Girl	Freda Soiffer
Barrymore/Waiter/Pike/Ziegfeld	Gene Varrone
Pope/Harry Hamburger	Robert Barr
King/Peabody	Richard Marr
Roosevelt	David Berk
Eleanor Roosevelt	Nancy Killmer
Mr. Foreman	Mitchell Jason
Wanda	Loni Ackerman
Marvin	Lawrence John Moss
Miss B	Sydney Blake
Don Baxter	Chuck Beard
Don Darwin	Michael Blue Aiken
Angela	Barbara Lang
Marlowe/Butler/Judge	George S. Irving
Papa	Lee Goodman
Soda Jerk/Man	James Brennan

ENSEMBLE: Jill Cook, Nancy Killmer, Meribeth Kisner, Denise Mauthe, Rita Rudner, Freda Soiffer, Michael Blue Aiken, Chuck Beard, David Berk, Joe Howard, Richard Marr, William Swiggard.

STANDBYS AND UNDERSTUDIES: David, James Brennan; Wanda, Rita Rudner; Swing Girl, Claudia Asbury; Swing Boy, Jack Magradey

MUSICAL NUMBERS: "David Kolowitz, the Actor," "It's Like," "Undressing Girls with My Eyes," "Bolero on Rye," "Whoever You Are," "Say the Words," "My Son the Druggist," "You Touched Her," "Men," "Boy Oh Boy," "Butler's Song," "Being with You," "If You Want to Break My Father's Heart," "So Long 174th Street," Finale

A musical performed without intermission. The action takes place at the present time and the late 1930's in New York City.

General Manager: Ralph Roseman
Company Manager: John A. Caruso
Press: Solters & Roskin, Bud Westman, Stanley F. Kaminsky, William Schelble
Stage Managers: Mortimer Halpern, Bryan Young, Jack Magradey

* Closed May 9, 1976 after 16 performances and 6 previews.

Martha Swope Photos

Robert Morse, also above with Loni Ackerman

Top: Lawrence John Moss, Robert Morse
Left: George S. Irving, Morse, Barbara Lang

LONGACRE THEATRE
Opened Wednesday, April 28, 1976.*
Mike Merrick and Don Gregory present:

THE BELLE OF AMHERST

By William Luce; Compiled by Timothy Helgeson; Director, Charles Nelson Reilly; Scenery and Lighting, H. R. Poindexter; Costumes, Theoni V. Aldredge; Hairstylist, Ray Iagnocco; Assistant to director, Timothy Helgeson; Assistants to producers, Rita Colecchio, Joan DeYoung

CAST

JULIE HARRIS

A play in two acts based on the life and works of Emily Dickinson. The action takes place in the Dickinson home in Amherst, Massachusetts, between 1845 and 1886.

General Manager: James Awe
Press: Seymour Krawitz, Patricia McLean Krawitz, Ted Goldsmith
Stage Managers: George Eckert, Berny Baker

* Closed Aug. 8, 1976 after 116 performances and 1 preview to tour.

Sy Friedman Photos

Julie Harris as Emily Dickinson

SAM S. SHUBERT THEATRE
Sunday, May 2, 1976
Friends of the Theatre and Music Collection of the Museum of
the City of New York present:

GEORGE ABBOTT
... A Celebration

Conceived and Produced by Anna Sosenko; Staged by Donald
Saddler; Lighting Design, Richard Winkler; Musical Direction, Co-
lin Romoff; Sound Design, Abe Jacob; Assistant to Miss Sosenko,
Donald Damask; Assistants to Mr. Saddler, Christopher Adler,
Mercedes Ellington; Wardrobe Supervisor, Marilyn Putnam; Pro-
duction Assistants, Paul Diaz, Merle Hubbard, Marvin Jenkins

CAST

Richard Adler, Christine Andreas, Desi Arnaz, Elizabeth Ashley,
Alexandra Borrie, David James Carroll, Tim Cassidy, Betty Com-
den, Donald Correia, Howard DaSilva, Fred Ebb, Ed Evanko, Joey
Faye, Arlene Francis, Martin Gabel, Jack Gilford, Ben Grauer,
Adolph Green, June Havoc, Will Holt, Del Horstman, George S.
Irving, Anne Jackson, John Kander, Maria Karnilova, Garson Ka-
nin, Sam Levene, Shirley MacLaine, Liza Minnelli, Sono Osato,
Maureen O'Sullivan, Julian Patrick, Eddie Phillips, Barry Preston,
Harold Prince, Jerome Robbins, Donald Saddler, Alan Sanderson,
Stanley Simmonds, Roy Smith, Tim Smith, Jean Stapleton, Maureen
Stapleton, Jule Styne, David Thome, Eli Wallach, Walter Willison

A gala tribute honoring George Abbott's 63 years as a Broadway
producer, director, playwright and actor.

Manager: Victor Samrock
Press: Bob Ullman
Stage Managers: Edward Preston, Robert Schear, Jerry
O'Connell

Robin Platzer Photos

**Right: Liza Minnelli, George Abbott,
Shirley MacLaine
Above: George Abbott, Maureen Stapleton**

Helen Hayes

George Abbott, Jean Stapleton

MARK HELLINGER THEATRE
Opened Tuesday, May 4, 1976.*
Roger L. Stevens and Robert Whitehead present:

1600 PENNSYLVANIA AVENUE

Book and Lyrics, Alan Jay Lerner; Music, Leonard Bernstein; Directed, Choreographed and Staged by Gilbert Moses and George Faison; Scenery, Kert Lundell; Costumes, Whitney Blausen, Dona Granata; Lighting, Tharon Musser; Musical Director, Roland Gagnon; Orchestrations, Sid Ramin, Hershy Kay; Sound, John McClure; Hairstylist, Werner Sherer; Produced by arrangement with Saint Subber; Assistant Choreographer, Renee Rose; Production Coordinator, Doris Blum; Production Assistants, Katharine Allentuck, Jim Beloff; Wardrobe Supervisor, Josephine Zampedri; Assistant Conductor, Robert Rogers

CAST

The President	Ken Howard
The President's Wife	Patricia Routledge
Lud	Gilbert Price
Seena	Emily Yancy
Little Lud	Guy Costley
Stage Manager	David E. Thomas

The Thirteen Delegates:

Massachusetts	Howard Ross
New York	Reid Shelton
Pennsylvania	Ralph Farnworth
New Hampshire	J. T. Cromwell
Rhode Island	Lee Winston
Connecticut	Richard Chappell
New Jersey	Walter Charles
Virginia	Edwin Steffe
North Carolina	John Witham
South Carolina	Richard Muenz
Delaware	Alexander Orfaly
Maryland	Raymond Cox
Georgia	Randolph Riscol

The Staff:

Henry	Raymond Bazemore
Rachel	Urylee Leonardos
Coley	Carl Hall
Joby	Janette Moody
Broom	Howard Ross
Jim	Cornel J. Richie
Sally	Louise Heath

The British:

Ordway	Walter Charles
Pimms	John Witham
Barker	Lee Winston
Glieg	Raymond Cox
Maitland	Alexander Orfaly
Ross	Edwin Steffe
Pratt	Richard Chappell
Scott	J. T. Cromwell
Budget	Richard Muenz
Cockburn	Reid Shelton
Rev. Bushrod	Bruce A. Hubbard
Auctioneer/Mr. Henry/Babcock	Lee Winston
James Hoban/Judge	Edwin Steffe
Royal Visitor	Randolph Riscol
Secretary of the Senate	Howard Ross
Senator Roscoe Condling	Reid Shelton

UNDERSTUDIES: President, Richard Chappell; President's Wife, Beth Fowler; Lud, J. Edwards Adams; Seena, Louise Heath; Little Lud, Karl M. Horton; Swing Dancers, Leah Randolph, Marial Roumain

SINGERS: Raymond Bazemore, Elaine Bunse, Nancy Callman, Richard Chappell, Walter Charles, Raymond Cox, J. T. Cromwell, Beth Fowler, Carl Hall, Louise Heath, Bruce A. Hubbard, Kris Karlowski, Urylee Leonardos, Joyce MacDonald, Janette Moody, Richard Muenz, Sharon Powers, Cornel J. Richie, Randolph Riscol, Martha Thigpen, Lee Winston

DANCERS: Jo-Ann Baldo, Clyde-Jacques Barrett, Joella Breedlove, Allyne DeChalus, Linda Griffin, Bob Heath, Michael Lichtefeld, Diana Mirras, Hector Jaime Mercado, Cleveland Pennington, Al Perryman, Renee Rose, Juliet Seignious, Thomas J. Stanton, Clayton Strange, Mimi B. Wallace

"A musical about the problems of housekeeping" in two acts. The action takes place at The White House in Washington, D. C.

General Manager: Oscar E. Olesen
Company Manager: James Walsh
Press: Seymour Krawitz, Patricia McLean Krawitz, Ted Goldsmith
Stage Managers: William Dodds, Marnel Sumner, Michael Turque

* Closed May 8, 1976 after 7 performances and 13 previews.

Sy Friedman Photos

Top Right: Patricia Routledge, Ken Howard
Below: Ken Howard (C)
Bottom: Gilbert Price, Emily Yancy

AMBASSADOR THEATRE

Opened Thursday, May 6, 1976.*

Under the sponsorship of L'Association Francaise D'Action Artistique of the Government of the French Republic, Le Treteau de Paris, Jean de Rigault in association with the French Institute/Alliance Francaise presents the Compagnie Renaud-Barrault in:

DAYS IN THE TREES
(Des Journees Entieres dans les Arbres)

By Marguerite Duras; Staged by Jean-Louis Barrault; Settings and Costumes, Atelier du Theatre d'Orsay; Lighting, Genevieve Soubirou; Sound, Carlos D'Alessio; Settings and Costumes Supervisor, Mason Arvold; Lighting Supervisor, Martin Aronstein; Wardrobe Master, Sam Elterman; Management, Seff Associates

CAST

The Mother	Madeleine Renaud
The Son (Jacques)	Jean-Pierre Aumont
Marcelle	Francoise Dorner
Bartender	Jean Martin

A drama in 3 acts and 4 scenes performed in French. The action takes place at the present time during spring in Paris in a two room apartment, on the street, and in a nightclub.

General Management: McCann & Nugent
Press: Michael Alpert, Marilynn LeVine, Warren Knowlton, Carl Samrock, Randi Cone
Stage Manager: Dominique Ehlinger

* Closed May 15, 1976 after limited engagement of 12 performances.

Ivan Farkas Photos

Madeleine Renaud, Jean-Pierre Aumont

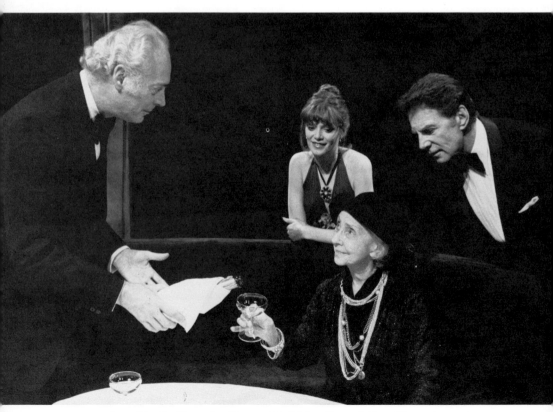

Jean Martin, Francoise Dorner, Madeleine Renaud, Jean-Pierre Aumont

ETHEL BARRYMORE THEATRE
Opened Thursday, May 13, 1976.*
Gladys Rackmil and Kennedy Center present:

LEGEND

By Samuel Taylor; Director, Robert Drivas; Settings, Santo Lo-quasto; Costumes, Florence Klotz; Lighting, Thomas Skelton; Original Music, Dan Goggin; Title Song, Ronee Blakely; Production Supervisor, Larry Forde; Produced for the John F. Kennedy Center for the Performing Arts by Roger L. Stevens; Assistant to director, Tony DeSantis; Wardrobe Supervisor, Warren Morrill; Hairstylist, Lyn Quiyou; Production Assistants, Elicia Rinaldi, Stacey Ralph

CAST

Quince	Robert Anthony
Tumbleweed	James Carrington
Alkali	Ben Slack
Barney-One-Ball	Ron Max
Mahogany Brown	Chev Rodgers
Muley	Munson Hicks
Kettle-Belly	Bill McIntyre
William F. P. Morgan	George Dzundza
"Doc" Jesse Lymburner	F. Murray Abraham
Judah Lymburner	George Parry
Betsy-No-Name	Elizabeth Ashley
Virgil Biggers (Colorado)	Stephen Clarke
Frankie Scruggs	Wayne Maxwell
Freddie Scruggs	Sebastian Stuart
Lacy Underwood/McNally	J. J. Quinn
Clarence/A Stranger	Tom Flagg

UNDERSTUDIES: Betsy, Tricia O'Neil; Doc, Robert Anthony; Virgil, James Carrington; Morgan, Ben Slack; Quince, Tumbleweed, Muley, Lacy Underwood, McNally, Clarence, Valentine Mayer; Alkali, Barney, Mahogany, Kettle-Belly, Frankie, Freddie, John Stewart; Stranger, J. J. Quinn; Judah, Donald Kehr

A romantic comedy in two acts. The action takes place somewhere in Western America, somewhere in the past.

General Management: Gatchell & Neufeld, Drew Murphy
Press: Betty Lee Hunt, Maria Cristina Pucci, Maurice Turet
Stage Managers: Valentine Mayer, John Stewart

* Closed May 16, 1976 after 5 performances and 18 previews.

Ron Reagan, Kramer-Abeles Photos

**Top: Stephen Clarke, (R) Elizabeth Ashley,
F. Murray Abraham**

Sebastian Stuart, Elizabeth Ashley
Above: Elizabeth Ashley

57

THE LITTLE THEATRE
Opened Tuesday, May 18, 1976.*
Wayne Adams and Willard Morgan by special arrangement
with the Hartman Theatre Company present:

THE RUNNER STUMBLES

By Milan Stitt; Director, Austin Pendleton; Set, Patricia Woodbridge; Costumes, James Berton Harris; Lighting, Cheryl Thacker

CAST

Amos	Morrie Piersol
Father Rivard	Stephen Joyce
Erna Prindle	Katina Commings
Toby Felker	James Noble
Sister Rita	Nancy Donohue
Mrs. Shandig	Sloane Shelton
Prosecutor	Craig Richard Nelson
Monsignor Nicholson	Joseph Mathewson
Louise	Marilyn Pfeiffer

UNDERSTUDIES: David Lile for male roles; Monica Guglielmina
for Erna, Louise, Mrs. Shandig; Marilyn Pfeiffer for Sister Rita

A drama in two acts. The action takes place in a cell and court-
room in Solon, Michigan, during April of 1911.

General Management: Dorothy Olim Associates, Thelma Cooper,
Amy Idell Gitlin
Press: Howard Atlee, Clarence Allsopp, Becky Flora
Stage Managers: Peggy Peterson, David Lile

* Still playing May 31, 1976.

Bert Andrews Photos

Above: Nancy Donohue, Stephen Joyce
Top: James Noble, Joyce,
58
(R) Katina Commings, Joyce

Craig Richard Nelson, Marilyn Pfeiffer
Above: Sloane Shelton, Stephen Joyce

LYCEUM THEATRE
Opened Thursday, May 27, 1976.*
Emanuel Azenberg, Dasha Epstein, John Mason Kirby present:

SOMETHING'S AFOOT

Book, Music, Lyrics by James McDonald, David Vos, Robert Gerlach; Additional Music, Ed Linderman; Directed and Choreographed by Tony Tanner; Scenery, Richard Seger; Costumes, Walter Watson, Clifford Capone; Lighting, Richard Winkler; Musical Director, Buster Davis; Orchestrator, Peter M. Larson; Production Associate, Peter Sanders; Music Coordinator, Earl Shendell; Sound, Robert Weeden; Wardrobe Supervisor, Sydney Smith

CAST

Lettie	Neva Small
Flint	Marc Jordan
Clive	Sel Vitella
Hope Langdon	Barbara Heuman
Dr. Grayburn	Jack Schmidt
Nigel Rancour	Gary Beach
Lady Grace Manley-Prowe	Liz Sheridan
Colonel Gillweather	Gary Gage
Miss Tweed	Tessie O'Shea
Geoffrey	Willard Beckham

STANDBYS: Miss Tweed, Lady Grace, Lu Leonard; Gillweather, Grayburn, Flint, Clive, Bryan Hull; Nigel, Geoffrey, Sal Mistretta; Hope, Lettie, Meg Bussert

MUSICAL NUMBERS: "A Marvelous Weekend," "Something's Afoot," "Carry On," "I Don't Know Why I Trust You But I Do," "The Man with the Ginger Mustache," "Suspicious," "Legal Heir," "You Fell Out of the Sky," "Dinghy," "I Owe It All," "New Day"

A musical mystery in two acts. The action takes place during the late spring of 1935 in Rancour's Retreat: a country estate in the English lake district.

General Manager: Marvin A. Krauss
Company Manager: Robert Frissell
Press: Merlin Group, Sandra Manley, Harriett Trachtenberg, Ron Harris
Stage Managers: Marilyn Witt, Sal Mistretta

* Closed July 18, 1976 after 61 performances and 13 previews.

Ken Howard Photos

Right: Willard Beckham, Barbara Heuman
Top: Marc Jordan, Liz Sheridan, Gary Gage,
Tessie O'Shea, Neva Small, Gary Beach,
Barbara Heuman, Willard Beckham, Sel Vitella,
Jack Schmidt

Neva Small, Gary Beach

Tessie O'Shea

EDEN THEATRE
Opened Monday, February 14, 1972*
(Moved June 7, 1972 to Broadhurst Theatre, November 21, 1972 to Royale Theatre) Kenneth Waissman and Maxine Fox in association with Anthony D'Amato present:

GREASE

Book, Music and Lyrics, Jim Jacobs, Warren Casey; Director, Tom Moore; Musical numbers and dances staged by Patricia Birch; Musical Supervision and orchestrations, Michael Leonard; Musical Direction-Vocal and Dance Arrangements, Louis St. Louis; Scenery, Douglas W. Schmidt; Costumes, Carrie F. Robbins; Lighting, Karl Eigsti; Sound, Bill Merrill; Hairstyles, Jim Sullivan; Assistant to Producers, Barbara Jean Block; Production Assistants, Pinocchio Madrid, Carolyn Ciplet; Original Cast Album, MGM Records; General Management, Theatre Now Inc.; Production Supervisor, T. Schuyler Smith.

CAST

Miss Lynch	Dorothy Leon†1
Patty Simcox	Ilene Kristen†2
Eugene Florczyk	Tom Harris†3
Jan	Garn Stephens†4
Marty	Katie Hanley†5
Betty Rizzo	Adrienne Barbeau†6
Doody	James Canning†7
Roger	Walter Bobbie†8
Kenickie	Timothy Meyers†9
Sonny LaTierri	Jim Borelli†10
Frenchy	Marya Small†11
Sandy Dumbrowski	Carole Demas†12
Danny Zuko	Barry Bostwick†13
Vince Fontaine	Don Billett†14
Johnny Casino	Alan Paul†15
Cha-Cha DiGregorio	Kathi Moss
Teen Angel	Alan Paul†15

UNDERSTUDIES: Shelley Barre, Adele Paige, John Fennessy, Ted Wass, Frank Piegaro

MUSICAL NUMBERS: "Alma Mater," "Summer Nights," "Those Magic Changes," "Freddy, My Love," "Greased Lightnin'," "Mooning," "Look at Me, I'm Sandra Dee," "We Go Together," "Shakin' at the High School Hop," "It's Raining on Prom Night," "Born to Hand-Jive," "Beauty School Dropout," "Alone at a Drive-in Movie," "Rock 'n' Roll Party Queen," "There Are Worse Things I Could Do," "All Choked Up," Finale.

A rock musical in two acts and twelve scenes. The action takes place in the late 1950's.

General Manager: Edward H. Davis
Press: Betty Lee Hunt, Maria Cristina Pucci
Company Managers: Robb Lady, Camille Ranson
Stage Managers: Lynne Guerra, Michael Martorella, John Fennessy
* Still playing May 31, 1976. For original production, see THEATRE WORLD, Vol. 28.
† Succeeded by: 1. Sudie Bond, Ruth Russell, 2. Joy Rinaldi, Carol Culver, 3. Barrey Smith, Stephen Van Benschoten, Lloyd Alann, 4. Jamie Donnelly, Randee Heller, Rebecca Gilchrist, Mimi Kennedy, 5. Meg Bennett, Denise Nettleton, Marilu Henner, Char Fontane, Diane Stilwell, 6. Elaine Petricoff, Randee Heller, Livia Genise, 7. Barry J. Tarallo, 8. Richard Quarry, John Driver, Ray DeMattis, Michael Tucci, 9. John Fennessy, Jerry Zaks, Michael Tucci, 10. Matt Landers, Albert Insinnia, 11. Ellen March, Joy Rinaldi, Jill P. Rose, 12. Ilene Graff, Candice Earley, 13. Jeff Conaway, John Lansing, Lloyd Alann, 14. Jim Weston, John Holly, Walter Charles, 15. Bob Garrett, Philip Casnoff, Joe Rifici, Philip Casnoff, Frank Piegaro

Top Right: Candice Earley (C)

Mimi Kennedy, Ellen March, Karren Dille

IMPERIAL THEATRE

Opened Monday, October 23, 1972.*
Stuart Ostrow presents:

PIPPIN

Book, Roger O. Hirson; Music and Lyrics, Stephen Schwartz; Direction and Choreography, Bob Fosse; Scenery, Tony Walton; Costumes, Patricia Zipprodt; Lighting, Jules Fisher; Musical Direction, Rene Wiegert; Orchestrations, Ralph Burns; Dance Arrangements, John Berkman; Sound, Abe Jacob; Hair Styles, Ernest Adler, James Amaral; Original Cast Album, Motown Records; Wardrobe Supervisor, A. T. Karniewich.

CAST

Leading Player	Ben Vereen†1
Pippin	John Rubinstein†2
Charles	Eric Berry
Lewis	Christopher Chadman†3
Fastrada	Leland Palmer†4
Musician/Swordbearer	John Mineo†5
The Head	Roger Hamilton
Berthe	Irene Ryan†6
Beggar	Richard Korthaze†7
Peasant	Paul Solen†8
Noble	Gene Foote†9
Field Marshall	Roger Hamilton
Catherine	Jill Clayburgh†10
Theo	Shane Nickerson†11

UNDERSTUDIES AND STANDBYS: Pippin, Dean Pitchford; Leading Player, Quitman Fludd III; Berthe, Dortha Duckworth; Catherine, Verna Pierce; Theo, Evan Turtz; Charles, Roger Hamilton; Gastrada, Patti D'Beck; Dance Alternates, Jill Owens, Roger Bigelow, Eileen Casey

MUSICAL NUMBERS: "Magic to Do," "Corner of the Sky," "Welcome Home," "War Is a Science," "Glory," "Simple Joys," "No Time at All," "With You," "Spread a Little Sunshine," "Morning Glow," "On the Right Track," "Kind of Woman," "Extraordinary," "Love Song," Finale

A musical in eight scenes, performed without intermission. The action takes place in 780 A.D. and thereabouts, in the Holy Roman Empire and thereabouts.

General Managers: Joseph Harris, Ira Bernstein
Company Manager: Nancy Simmons
Press: Solters/Roskin, Milly Schoenbaum, Nini Finkelstein
Stage Managers: Lola Shumlin, John H. Lowe III, Herman Magidson, Andy Keyser

* Still playing May 31, 1976. For original production, see THEATRE WORLD, Vol. 29.
† Succeeded by: 1. Northern Calloway, Samuel E. Wright, Irving Lee, Ben Harney, 2. Dean Pitchford, Michael Rupert, 3. Justin Ross, Jerry Colker, 4. Priscilla Lopez, Patti Karr, Antonia Ellis, 5. Ken Urmston, 6. Lucie Lancaster, Dorothy Stickney, Fay Sappington, 7. Larry Merritt, Roger Bigelow, Ken Miller, 8. Chet Walker, 9. Larry Giroux, Bryan Nicholas, 10. Betty Buckley, Joy Franz, 11. Douglas Grober

Michael Rupert (C)   **Michael Rupert, Joy Franz Top: Ben Harney (C)**

CORT THEATRE
Opened Tuesday, May 28, 1974.*
Edgar Lansbury, Joseph Beruh, Ivan Reitman present:

THE MAGIC SHOW

Book, Bob Randall; Songs, Stephen Schwartz; Magic, Doug Henning; Direction and Dances, Grover Dale; Setting, David Chapman; Costumes, Randy Barcelo; Lighting, Richard Nelson; Musical Director, Stephen Reinhardt; Dance Arrangements, David Spangler; Assistant to Director, Jay Fox; Associate Producer, Nan Pearlman; Audio Design, Phil Ramone; Assistant to Producers, Jo Marie Wakefield; Wardrobe Supervisor, Virginia Sylvain; Production Assistants, Sam Cristensen, Darrell Jonas, Walter Wood

CAST

Manny	Robert LuPone†1
Feldman	David Ogden Stiers†2
Donna	Annie McGreevey†3
Dina	Cheryl Barnes†4
Cal	Dale Soules
Doug	Doug Henning†5
Mike	Ronald Stafford
Steve	Loyd Sannes†6
Charmin	Anita Morris†7
Goldfarb	Sam Schacht

STANDBYS AND UNDERSTUDIES: Doug, Jeffrey Mylett; Cal, Donna, Bailie Gerstein; Charmin, Dina, Sharron Miller; Feldman, Goldfarb, Garnett Smith; Mike, Steve, Robert Brubach; Manny, Jay Fox, Christopher Lucas

MUSICAL NUMBERS: "Up to His Old Tricks," "Solid Silver Platform Shoes," "Lion Tamer," "Style," "Charmin's Lament," "Two's Company," "Goldfarb Variations," "Doug's Act," "A Bit of Villainy," "West End Avenue," "Sweet, Sweet, Sweet," "Before Your Very Eyes"

A magic show with music performed without intermission.

General Management: Marvin A. Krauss Associates
Company Manager: Gary Gunas
Press: Gifford/Wallace, Tom Trenkle, Glenna Freedman
Stage Managers: Herb Vogler, Jay Fox, John Actman

* Still playing May 31, 1976. For original production, see THEATRE WORLD, Vol. 30.
† Succeeded by: 1. Clifford Lipson, 2. Kenneth Kimmins, Timothy Jerome, 3. Lisa Raggio, 4. Lynne Thigpen, 5. Jeffrey Mylett, Joseph Abaldo, during vacation, 6. T. Michael Reed, Christopher Lucas, 7. Loni Ackerman

Doug Henning Top Right: Henning, Dale Soules, Timothy Jerome
Right Center: Cliff Lipson, Robert Brubach, Loni Ackerman, Ronald Stafford

PLYMOUTH THEATRE
Opened Thursday, October 24, 1974.*
Kermit Bloomgarden and Doris Cole Abrahams in association
with Frank Milton present:

EQUUS

By Peter Shaffer; Director, John Dexter; Scenery and Costumes,
John Napier; Lighting, Andy Phillips; Sound, Marc Wilkinson;
Mime, Claude Chagrin; American Supervision of Scenery and Lighting, Howard Bay; Costumes, Patricia Adshead; Production Assistant, Scott Rudin; Wardrobe Supervisor, Eric Harrison; Assistant to
the Director, Gabriel Oshen; American Supervision of Mime, Peter
Lobdell

CAST

Martin Dysart	Anthony Hopkins†1
Alan Strang	Peter Firth†2
Nurse	Mary Doyle†3
Hesther Salomon	Marian Seldes†4
Frank Strang	Michael Higgins†5
Dora Strang	Frances Sternhagen†6
Horseman/Nugget	Everett McGill†7
Harry Dalton	Walter Mathews†8
Jill Mason	Roberta Maxwell†9
Horses	Gus Kaikkoen, Philip Kraus, Gabriel Oshen, David Ramsey, John Tyrrell†10

STANDBYS AND UNDERSTUDIES: Dysart, Alan Mixon; Da-
vid Leary; Alan, Thomas Hulce, Jacob Milligan, Dennis Erdman;
Frank, Don Plumley, Page Johnson; Dora, Hesther, Mary Doyle;
Jill, Nurse, Dale Hodges, Betsy Beard; Harry, Horseman, Philip
Kraus, Jeffrey David Pomerantz, William Wright; Horses, Michael
Wieben, Terence Burk

A Drama in two acts. The action takes place in Rokeby Psychiatric Hospital in Southern England at the present time.

General Manager: Max Allentuck
Press: John Springer Associates, Louis Sica
Stage Managers: Robert L. Borod, Nicholas Russiyan, Michael
Wieben, Barry Kearsley, Peter Lobdell, Brent Peek, William
Schill, Terence Burk

* Closed Sept. 11, 1976 after 781 performances and 10 previews.
Winner of 1975 Best Play awards from New York Drama Critics
Circle, "Tony," Drama Desk, New York Outer Critics, also
"Tony" and Drama Desk awards for Best Director. For original
production, see THEATRE WORLD, Vol. 31.
† Succeeded by: 1. Anthony Perkins, Richard Burton, 2. Thomas
Hulce, Jacob Milligan, Keith McDermott, 3. Catherine Byers, 4.
Louise Troy, 5. Page Johnson, 6. Marian Seldes, 7. David Combs,
William Wright, 8. Don Plumley, Page Johnson, Richard Neilson,
9. Jeanne Ruskin, Betsy Beard, 10. John David, Peter Lobdell,
Gary Faga, Jeffrey David Pomerantz, Gregory Salata, William
Wright, Terence Burk

Van Williams Photos

**Top Right: Anthony Perkins, Thomas Hulce,
Everett McGill Below: Keith McDermott,
Richard Burton**

nces Sternhagen, Michael Higgins, Richard Burton

Anthony Perkins, Frances Sternhagen

MAJESTIC THEATRE
Opened Sunday, January 5, 1975.*
Ken Harper presents:

THE WIZ

Book, William F. Brown; Based on L. Frank Baum's "The Wonderful Wizard of Oz"; Music and Lyrics, Charlie Smalls; Direction and Costumes, Geoffrey Holder; Setting, Tom H. John; Lighting, Tharon Musser; Orchestrations, Harold Wheeler; Musical Direction and Vocal Arrangements, Charles H. Coleman; Dance Arrangements, Timothy Graphenreed; Choreography and Musical Numbers Staged by George Faison; Wardrobe Supervisor, Yvonne Stoney; Assistant to Choreographer and Dance Captain, John Parks; Music Coordinator, Earl Shendell; Wigs, Stanley James; Original Cast Album by Atlantic Records.

CAST

Aunt Em	Tasha Thomas†1
Toto	Nancy
Dorothy	Stephanie Mills
Uncle Henry	Ralph Wilcox†2
Tornado	Evelyn Thomas†3
Munchkins	Phylicia Ayers-Allen†4, Pi Douglass†5
	Joni Palmer†6, Andy Torres†7, Carl Weaver
Addaperle	Clarice Taylor
Yellow Brick Road	Ronald Dunham, Eugene Little,
	John Parks †8, Kenneth Scott
Scarecrow	Hinton Battle
Crows	Wendy Edmead, Frances Morgan, Thea Nerissa Barnes
Tinman	Tiger Haynes
Lion	Ted Ross†9
Kalidahs	Philip Bond†10, Pi Douglass†11,
	Rodney Green†12, Evelyn Thomas†13, Andy Torres†14
Poppies	Lettie Battle †15, Leslie Butler,
	Eleanor McCoy†16, Frances Morgan, Joni Palmer†17
Field Mice	Phylicia Ayers-Allen, Pi Douglass,
	Carl Weaver, Ralph Wilcox
Gatekeeper	Danny Beard†18
The Wiz	Andre De Shields†19
Evillene	Mabel King†20
Lord High Underling	Ralph Wilcox†2
Soldier Messenger	Carl Weaver
Winged Monkey	Andy Torres†21
Glinda	Dee Dee Bridgewater†22

EMERALD CITY CITIZENS: Thea Nerissa Barnes, Pat Estwick, Leslie Butler, Wendy Edmead, Lois Hayes, Keith Harris, Alvin McDuffie, Frances Morgan, Claudia Lewis, Ronald Dunham, Rodney Green, Eugene Little, Kenneth Scott, Alwin Taylor

PIT SINGERS: Robert Benjamin, DeMarest Grey, Sam Harkness, Jozella Reed, Hanyse M. Singleton

UNDERSTUDIES: Tin Man, Kwame Johnson; Lion, Toney Watkins; Scarecrow, Carl Weaver; Addaperle, Evelline, Ruth Brisbane; Wiz, Kenneth Scott; Glinda, Janyse M. Singleton; Aunt Em, Deborah Burrell; Dorothy, Renee Harris, Pat Estwick

MUSICAL NUMBERS: "The Feeling We Once Had," "Tornado Ballet," "He's the Wizard," "Soon as I Get Home," "I Was Born on the Day before Yesterday," "Ease on down the Road," "Slide Some Oil to Me," "Mean Ole Lion," "Kalidah Battle," "Be a Lion," "Lion's Dream," "Emerald City Ballet," "So You Wanted to Meet the Wizard," "To Be Able to Feel," "No Bad News," "Funky Monkeys," "Everybody Rejoice," "Who Do You Think You Are?", "Believe in Yourself," "Y'All Got It!", "A Rested Body Is a Rested Mind," "Home"

A musical in 2 acts and 16 scenes, with a prologue.

General Managers: Emanuel Azenberg, Eugene V. Wolsk
Manager: Jose Vega
Company Manager: Susan Bell
Press: The Merlin Group, Sandra Manley, Elizabeth Rodman, Ron Harris
Stage Managers: Christopher Kelly, Bob Burland, Steven Shaw

* Still playing May 31, 1976. For original production, see THEATRE WORLD, Vol. 31.
† Succeeded by: 1. Esther Marrow, 2. Al Fann, Toney Watkins, 3. Wendy Edmead, 4. Dyane Harvey, 5. Leslie Butler, 6. Lois Hayes, 7. Kwame Johnson, 8. Rodney Green, 9. James Wigfall, 10. Gregg Burge, 11. Keith Harris, 12. Alvin McDuffie, 13. Claudia Lewis, 14. Alwin Taylor, 15. Thea Nerissa Barnes, 16. Pat Estwick, 17. Lois Hayes, 18. Danny Beard, 19. Alan Weeks, 20. Edye Byrde, Theresa Merritt, 21. Keith Harris, 22. Deborah Burrell

Martha Swope Photos

Andre DeShields (c) Above: The Funky Monke,

Top Right: Stephanie Mills, Hinton Battle, James Wigfall, Tiger Haynes (top)

ALVIN THEATRE
Opened Tuesday, January 7, 1975.*
Philip Rose, Gloria and Louis K. Sher present:

SHENANDOAH

Book, James Lee Barrett, Peter Udell, Philip Rose; Music, Gary Geld; Lyrics, Peter Udell; Based on screenplay of same title by James Lee Barrett; Scenery, C. Murawski; Lighting, Thomas Skelton; Costumes, Pearl Somner, Winn Morton; Orchestrations, Don Walker; Musical Direction, Richard Parrinello; Dance Arrangements, Russell Warner; Choreography, Robert Tucker; Hairstylist, Werner Sherer; Wardrobe Supervisor, Lee Decker; Production Assistant, Rosemary Troyano; Original Cast Album by RCA Records

CAST

Charlie Anderson	John Cullum†7
Jacob	Ted Agress
James	Joel Higgins†1
Nathan	Jordan Suffin
John	David Russell
Jenny	Penelope Milford†2
Henry	Robert Rosen
Robert (The Boy)	Joseph Shapiro†3
Anne	Donna Theodore
Gabriel	Chip Ford†4
Rev. Byrd	Charles Welch
Sam	Gordon Halliday
Sgt. Johnson	Edward Penn
Lieutenant	Marshall Thomas
Tinkham	Charles Welch
Carol	Casper Roos
Corporal	Gary Harger
Marauder	Gene Masoner
Engineer	Ed Preble†5
Confederate Sniper	Craig Lucas†6

ENSEMBLE: Tedd Carrere, Dennis Cooley, Stephen Dubov, Richard Flanders, Kathleen Gordon, Gary Harger, David Cale Johnson, Robert Johanson, Sherry Lambert, Gene Masoner, Paul Myrvold, Dan Ormond, Casper Roos, J. Kevin Scannell, Emily Bindiger, E. Allan Stevens, Marshall Thomas, Matt Gavin.

UNDERSTUDIES: Charlie, Edward Penn, Casper Roos; Jacob, Gene Masoner; Nathan, James, Paul Myrvold; John, Matt Gavin; Jenny, Emily Bindiger; Henry, Dennis Cooley, Robert Johanson; Robert, Steve Grober; Anne, Kathleen Gordon; Gabriel, Donny Cooper; Byrd, Casper Roos; Sam, Richard Flanders; Johnson, Marshall Thomas; Lt., Tedd Carrere; Marauder, Tinkham, E. Allan Stevens; Carol, J. Kevin Scannell; Engineer, Dan Ormond

MUSICAL NUMBERS: "Raise the Flag of Dixie," "I've Heard It All Before," "Pass the Cross to Me," "Why Am I Me," "Next to Lovin' I Like Fightin'," "Over the Hill," "The Pickers Are Comin'," "Meditation," "We Make a Beautiful Pair," "Violets and Silverbells," "It's a Boy," "Freedom," "Papa's Gonna Make It Alright," "The Only Home I Know"

A musical in two acts with a prologue. The action takes place during the Civil War in the Shenandoah Valley of Virginia.

General Manager: Helen Richards
Press: Merle Debuskey, Leo Stern
Stage Managers: Steve Zweigbaum, Arturo E. Porazzi, Sherry Lambert

* Still playing May 31, 1976. For original production, see THEATRE WORLD, Vol. 31.
† Succeeded by: 1. Wayne Hudgins, 2. Maureen Silliman, 3. Mark Perman, 4. Bent Carter, David Vann, 5. E. Allan Stevens, 6. Dennis Cooley, 7. William Chapman during vacation

Friedman-Abeles Photos

Top Right: John Cullum, Donna Theodore

Donna Theodore, Chip Ford

BROOKS ATKINSON THEATRE
Opened Thursday, March 13, 1975.*
Morton Gottlieb, Dasha Epstein, Edward L. Schuman, Palladium Productions present:

SAME TIME, NEXT YEAR

By Bernard Slade; Director, Gene Saks; Scenery, William Ritman; Costumes, Jane Greenwood; Lighting, Tharon Musser; Hairstylist, Steve Atha; Associate producers, Ben Rosenberg, Warren Crane

CAST

Doris .... Ellen Burstyn†1
George .... Charles Grodin†2
Standbys: Rochelle Oliver, Peter DeMaio

A comedy in two acts and six scenes. The action takes place in a guest cottage of a country inn in Northern California from 1951 to 1975.

General Manager: Ben Rosenberg
Company Manager: Martin Cohen
Press: Solters & Roskin, Milly Schoenbaum
Stage Managers: Warren Crane, Kate Pollock

* Still playing May 31, 1976. For original production, see THEATRE WORLD, Vol. 31.
† Succeeded by: 1. Joyce Van Patten, Loretta Swit, Sandy Dennis, 2. Conrad Janis, Ted Bessell

Joyce Van Patten, Conrad Janis

Ted Bessell, Sandy Dennis
Top: Loretta Swit, Ted Bessell

BROADWAY PRODUCTIONS FROM OTHER YEARS THAT CLOSED THIS SEASON

Title	Opened	Closed	Performances
Raisin	10/18/73	12/8/75	847
Candide	3/8/74	1/4/76	740
Absurd Person Singular	10/8/74	3/6/76	591
Sherlock Holmes	1/12/75	1/4/76	479
The Ritz	1/20/75	1/4/76	398
All Over Town	12/29/74	7/20/75	233
Rodgers & Hart	5/13/75	8/16/75	108

OFF BROADWAY PRODUCTIONS

ELYSIAN PLAYHOUSE
Opened Sunday, June 1, 1975.*
The Mufson Company presents:

LAST OF THE RED HOT LOVERS

By Neil Simon; Director, Ken Mufson; Set, Shelly Gelfman; Lighting, Joel Levine

CAST

Barney Cashman	Douglas Andros
Elaine Navazio	Faye Cameron
Bobbi Michele	Elizabeth Sanders
Jeanette Fisher	Madlyn Cates

A comedy in three acts. The action takes place at the present time in New York's East Thirties.

Stage Manager: Jeff Buchman

* Closed June 15, 1975 after limited engagement of 15 performances.

"Last of the Red Hot Lovers" (also left)

Pamela Burrell

Christopher Reeve

STAGE 73
Opened Tuesday, June 17, 1975.*
The Company Stage presents:

BERKELEY SQUARE

By John L. Balderston; Director, Anthony Stimac; Set, David Sackeroff; Costumes, Sydney Brooks, Dean H. Reiter; Lighting, Clark W. Thornton; Music, Alan Rich; Coordinator, Joan M. Jeans; Technical Director, Michael LaCourse; Assistant to producer, Alice Gold; Wardrobe Supervisor, Virginia Merkel

CAST

Maid	Lynn Lobban
Tom Pettigrew	Munson Hicks
Kate Pettigrew	Robin Lane
Lady Anne Pettigrew	Beulah Garricks
Mr. Throstle	Peter Boyden
Helen Pettigrew	Claire Malis
Ambassador	Jonathan Moore
Mrs. Barwick	Lynne Hardy
Peter Standish	Christopher Reeve
Marjorie Frant	Joan Welles
Lord Stanley	Steve Lincoln
The Marquesa	Shanit Keter
Duchess of Devonshire	Pamela Burrell
Duke of Cumberland	James Brochu

A play in three acts and seven scenes. The action takes place in the morning room of a house of the Queen Anne period in Berkeley Square, London, in the years 1784 and 1928.

Press: Anne Marie Borger
Stage Managers: Leslie Leonelli, Zoe Oka

* Closed July 3, 1975 after limited engagement of 12 performances. No photos available.

JONES BEACH THEATRE
Opened Friday, June 27, 1975.*
Guy Lombardo presents:

OKLAHOMA!

Based on Lynn Riggs' play "Green Grow the Lilacs"; Book and Lyrics, Oscar Hammerstein 2nd; Music, Richard Rodgers; Director, John Fearnley; Choreographer, Robert Pagent; Scenery, John W. Keck; Costumes, Winn Morton; Lighting, Thomas Skelton; Musical Director, Jay Blackton; Entire production under the supervision of Arnold Spector; Wardrobe Mistress, Agnes Farrell; Assistant Conductor, Robert Stanley; Choral Director, Robert Monteil

CAST

Aunt Eller	Nancy Andrews
Curly	Thomas McKinney
Laurey	Judith McCauley
Ike Skidmore	Lee Cass
Slim	Stan Page
Will Parker	Harvey Evans
Jud Fry	Will Roy
Ado Annie Carnes	Patricia Masters
Ali Hakim	Bruce Adler
Gertie Cummings	Sherry Lambert
Andrew Carnes	John Dorrin
Cord Elam	Robert Pagent
Laurey in the ballet	Dru Alexandrine
Curly in the ballet	Jeremy Blanton
Jud in the ballett	Russell Anderson

COWBOYS, FARMERS, TOWNSPEOPLE: Jean Busada, Mary-Pat Carey, Mona Elgh, Doris Galiber, Mickey Gunnersen, Sherry Lambert, Joyce McDonald, Kathleen Robey, Irma Rogers, Laurie Ann Scadura, Renee Spector, Dixie Stewart, Sara Swanson, Marsha Tamaroff, Candace Tovar, Deborah Dean Walker, Lisa Berg (Swing)

Russell Anderson, Baruch Blum, Donald Bonnell, Lawrence Scott Cahn, Peter Clark, Eugene Edwards, Paul Flores, Robert Monteil, Dale Muchmore, Michael Page, Stan Page, George Pesaturo, Rick Schneider, Timothy Smith, Ralph Vucci, Arthur Whitfield, Kevin Wilson, Edward Zimmerman, Tony Slez (Swing)

UNDERSTUDIES: Curly, Stan Page; Jud, Lee Cass; Laurey, Deborah Dean Walker; Will, Donald Bonnell; Aunt Eller, Irma Rogers; Ali, Robert Monteil; Ado Annie, Sherry Lambert: Cord, Tony Slez; Carnes, Peter Clark; Ike, Ralph Vucci; Slim, Kevin Wilson; Gertie, Candace Tovar

MUSICAL NUMBERS: Overture, "Oh, What a Beautiful Mornin'," "Surrey with the Fringe on Top," "Kansas City," "I Cain't Say No," "Many a New Day," "It's a Scandal! It's an Outrage!," "People Will Say We're in Love," "Pore Jud," "Lonely Room," "Out of My Dreams," "The Farmer and the Cowman," "All er Nothin'," "Oklahoma!, Finale

A musical in two acts. The action takes place in the Indian Territory, now Oklahoma, just after the turn of the century.

Company Manager; Sam Pagliaro
Press: Saul Richman, Fred Nathan
Stage Managers: Mortimer Halpern, Bernard Pollock, Stan Page, Tony Slez

* Closed Aug. 31, 1975

Top: Harvey Evans (c)

Thomas McKinney, Judith McCauley
Above: Nancy Andrews, Patricia Masters

BILLY MUNK THEATRE
Opened Thursday, July 10, 1975.*
Moss Cooney and Pat Cooney present:

THE LOVE DEATH PLAYS OF WILLIAM INGE

Director, Barbara Loden; Assistant to director, Ellen Sullivan Casey; Associate Producer, Barry Moss; Set, Kurt Lundell, Ronald DuBois; Costumes, Bessie Lou Kazoo; Lighting, Brett Landow-Lewis; Original Music, George Quincy; Sound, Stephen Gabis

CAST

PART I
"Dialogue for Two Men"
Terry .... Jack Aaron
Joe .... Lane Smith
"Midwestern Manic"
George .... Morgan Donohue
Harley Ffoulkes .... Lane Smith
Marlene Ffoulkes .... Gayle Greene
Diane .... Judy Fields
"The Love Death"
Byron .... Lane Smith
    The action takes place at the present time in New York.

* Closed August 4, 1975 after limited engagement of 15 performances.
   Opened Thursday, July 17, 1975.**

PART II
"Venus and Adonis"
Nick/Gino .... Robert Giber
Mrs. Nell Fisher .... Janet Ward
"The Wake"
Al .... Al Herter
Esther .... Janet Ward
Fred .... Joe Jamrog
Ron .... Michael Nader
"The Star"
Julia Richards .... Janet Ward
Bea .... Molly McCarthy
    The action takes place at the present time in New York.

    Press: Michael Alpert, Anne Weinberg
    Stage Managers: Winnie Whipple, Frank Levan

* Closed August 4, 1975 after limited engagement of 12 performances.

    Peter Somogyi, Robertson Carricart Photos

Top Right: Judy Fields, Lane Smith
Below: Joe Jamrog, Michael Nader, Janet Ward

entire cast of "Ivanov"

CITY PLAYWORKS
Opened Thursday, August 14, 1975.*
ETC Theatre Company (Artistic Directors: Rae Allen, J. J. Barry, Frank Bongiorno) in association with City Playworks presents:

IVANOV

By Anton Chekhov; Translated by Alex Szogyi; Director, Gus Kaikkonen; Assistant Director, Linda Brumfield; Lighting, Richard Winkler; Technical Director, James Larkin; Scenery, David George

CAST

Nikolai Alexayevich Ivanov .... William Sadler
Anna Petrovna .... Patricia Johnson
Matvyey Semyonovich .... Warrington Winters
Pavel Kirilich Lyebedev .... Joe Endes
Zinaida Savishna .... Mary Ed Porter
Sasha .... Marilyn Pfeiffer
Yevgeny Kostantinovich Lvov .... Ted Kubiak
Marfa Yegorovna Babakina .... Susan Krebs
Dmitri Nikitich Kosich .... Christopher Cara
Mikhail Mikhailovich Borkin .... Robb Webb
Avdotya Nazarovna .... Parker McCormick

    A drama in four acts. The action takes place in 19th Century Russia.

    Press: Joshua Ellis
    Stage Manager: David Semonin

* Closed Sept. 7, 1975 after 20 performances.

    Robb Webb Photos

ST. JOHN'S IN THE VILLAGE

Opened Thursday, August 14, 1975.*
Theater QED presents:

MIME FOR A SUMMER NIGHT
RICHARD MORSE
PILAR GARCIA

Set, Carlos Delgado; Lighting, Lyn Corno; Technical Director, Mitchell Bogard; Costumes, Pamela Scofield; Assistant to Mr. Morse, Barbara Marks

Stage Manager: Mitchell Green

* Closed September 21, 1975 after limited engagement of 13 performances.

Opened Thursday, August 21, 1975.*
Theatre QED presents:

SHAW FOR A SUMMER NIGHT

Director, Edward Townley; Assistant to director, Barbara Marks; Set, Carlos Delgado; Costume Coordinator, Shelly Friedman; Lighting and Technical Direction, Mitchell Bogard

CAST

"Overruled"
Mrs. Juno .... Christine Lahti
Mr. Lunn .... Thomas Wagner
Mrs. Lunn .... Rasa Allen
Mr. Juno .... Saylor Creswell

The action takes place in 1912 in the garden of a seaside hotel.

"Village Wooing"
A .... Richmond Hoxie
B .... Mary Shelley

The action takes place aboard the Empress of Patagonia in January of 1932, and in a village shop in the Wiltshire Downs.

Press: Bud Westman, Sheldon Jacobs, Lyn Corno
Stage Manager: Mitchell Green

* Closed Sept. 20, 1975 after limited engagement of 12 performances

Pilar Garcia, Richard Morse

ACTORS PLAYHOUSE

Opened Wednesday, September 17, 1975.*
Edith O'Hara in association with Lee Barton and Christopher Larkin presents:

BOY MEETS BOY

Book, Bill Solly and Donald Ward; Music and Lyrics, Bill Solly; Director, Ron Troutman; Scenery and Lighting, David Sackeroff; Musical Direction and Vocal Arrangements, David Friedman; Music and Dance Arrangements, James Fradrich; Costumes, Sharon Buchs; Musical Numbers Staged by Robin Reseen; Piano, Jim Fradrich; Electric Keyboards, Dylan Hartman

CAST

Casey O'Brien .... Joe Barrett
Andrew .... Paul Ratkevich
Guy Rose .... David Gallegly
Bellboy/Alphonse .... Bobby Bowen
Reporters .... Richard King, Bobby Reed, Dan Rounds
Photographers .... Jan Crean, Monica Grignon
The Van Wagners .... Bobby Bowen, Kathy Willinger
Clarence Cutler .... Raymond Wood
Lady Rose/Josephine LaRosa .... Rita Gordon
Bruce .... Bobby Reed
Head Waiter .... David Guinn
Assistant Hotel Manager/Porter .... Richard King
Rosita .... Kathy Willinger
Lolita .... Mary-Ellen Hanlon
Pepita .... Jan Crean

MUSICAL NUMBERS: "Boy Meets Boy," "Giving It Up for Love," "Me," "English Rose," "Marry an American," "It's a Boy's Life," "Does Anybody Love You?," "You're Beautiful," "Let's Dance," "Just My Luck," "It's a Dolly," "What Do I Care?," "Clarence's Turn," Finale

A musical in two acts. The action takes place in London and Paris during December of 1936.

General Manager: Jim Payne
Press: Sol Jacobson, Lewis Harmon
Stage Managers: Gene Borio, David Guinn

* Still playing May 31, 1976.

Joe Neumeyer Photos

Joe Barrett, David Gallegly

VANDAM THEATRE
Opened Thursday, September 11, 1975.*
Bari & Bennett Productions presents:

M. GORKY: A PORTRAIT
by
MICHAEL A. DEL MEDICO

Written and Directed by Michael A. Del Medico; Production and Costume Design, L. Bari; Lighting, Joy Lilly; Sound Technician, P. Brandstein

Presented in four parts, each depicting another aspect of Gorky's life from early childhood to his last years.

General Manager: J. Bennett

* Closed Oct. 5, 1975 after limited engagement of 16 performances.
Irene Fertik Photos

MARYMOUNT MANHATTAN COLLEGE
Opened Friday, September 19, 1975.*
Marymount Manhattan College in association with BPS presents:

THE CAST AWAYS

Book and Direction, Anthony J. Stimac; Music, Don Pippin; Lyrics, Steve Brown; Sets and Lighting, Clarke W. Thornton; Costumes, Dean Reiter; Choreography, Gene Kelton; Musical Director, D. Bishop; Hairstylist, Vincent Prestia; Technical Director, Ken Merkel; Production Assistant, Rick Ladson

CAST

Mr. Warren/Jasper/Indian	Reid Shelton
Mrs. Warren/Christine	Marie Santell
Mr. Cooke/Jerry/Pendragon/General	Peter Boyden
Mrs. Cooke/LaRole	Patti Perkins
Mr. Lewis/Capt. Lenox	Dennis Howard
Mrs. Lewis/Adela	Sydney Blake
The Mate	Gibby Brand
Pirate Captain	Hank Berrings

MUSICAL NUMBERS: "All the World's a Hold," "I Won't Love a Soldier Boy," "The Chase," "Let's Mop Up These Yankees and Go Back Home," "Bring Out Old Glory," "My Love," "She Would Be a Soldier," "Whipperwill," "Call Back the Times," "If I Had Wings," "Isn't She," "This Dawn"

A pirate musical in two acts. The action takes place in 1819 in the hold of a Barbary pirate ship somewhere in the Mediterranean.

Stage Managers: Clarke W. Thornton, Michael LaCourse

* Closed Sept. 28, 1975 after limited engagement of 12 performances.

Michael A. Del Medico

THEATRE DE LYS
Opened Monday, September 29, 1975.*
Rudi Golyn and Lee D. Sankowich present:

FINN MACKOOL THE GRAND DISTRACTION

By Frank Hogan; Director, Lee D. Sankowich; Scenery, David Chapman; Costumes, Jane Greenwood; Lighting, Richard Nelson; Sound, Abe Jacob; Visual Projections, Jack Coddington; Wardrobe Mistress, Evelyn Seubert; Technical Director, Jack Magnifico

CAST

Ossian	Michael J. Hume
Dark Marion	Valerie French
Mother Finn MacKool	Eulalie Noble
Vonner	Peter MacLean
Janna	Patti Walker
Father Finn MacKool	William Hickey

A play in two acts and eight scenes.

General Manager: Leonard A. Mulhern
Company Manager: David Relyea
Press: Howard Atlee, Clarence Allsopp, Meg Gordean, Becky Flora
Stage Managers: Paul Bennett, Lynn Gutter

* Closed Sept. 29, 1975 after one performance.

Ken Howard Photos

Peter MacLean, Valerie French, Eulalie Noble

EDEN THEATRE
Opened Sunday, October 12, 1975.*
Harry Rothpearl and Jewish Nostalgic Productions, Inc.,-
present:

THE FIFTH SEASON

Adapted by Luba Kadison from the play of the same name by Sylvia Regan; Music and Lyrics, Dick Manning; Director, Joseph Buloff; Musical Director, Renee Solomon; Sets and Costumes, Jeffrey B. Moss; Lighting, Bob McCarthy; Yiddish Adaptation of Lyrics, Isaac Dogim; Wardrobe Supervisor, Sylvia Friedlander; Hairstylist, Jerry of Bergdorf's.

CAST

Mr. Katz	Elias Patron
Shelly	Gerri-Ann Frank
Laurie	Raquel Yossiffon
Perl	David Carey
Max Pincus	Joseph Buloff
Benny Goodwin	Stan Porter
Frances Goodwin	Evelyn Kingsley
Marty Goodwin	Gene Barrett
Miriam Oppenheim	Miriam Kressyn
Mr. Lewis	Jack Rechtzeit
Models	Franceska Fishler, Cathy Carnevale, Barbara Joan Frank

MUSICAL NUMBERS: "Believe in Yourself," "My Son, the Doctor," "Goodbye," "The Fifth Season," "Friday Night," "Mom! You Don't Understand!," "How Did This Happen to Me," "From Seventh Avenue to Seventh Heaven"

A musical in two acts and six scenes. The action takes place at the present time in a Seventh Avenue fashion showroom.

General Manager: Seymour Rexite
Press: Max Eisen, Judy Jacksina, Barbara Glenn
Stage Manager: Jay S. Hoffman

Top Right: Joseph Buloff, Miriam Kressyn
Below: Joseph Buloff, Stan Porter, Evelyn Kingsley

THEATRE AT MAMA GAILS
Opened Wednesday, October 22, 1976.*
Theatre at Mama Gails presents:

MEN WOMEN
and Why It Won't Work

Book, June Siegel, Miriam Fond; Music, David Warrack; Lyrics, June Siegel; Direction and Choreography, Miriam Fond; Musical Direction and Arrangements, John R. Williams; Set, Dan Leigh; Costumes, Danny Morgan; Lighting, Deanna Greenwood; Producer, Charles Leslie; Pianist, John R. Williams

CAST

Elaine Desmond	Ann Hodapp
Art Desmond	Arne Gundersen
Jill Callen	Leila Holiday
Al Callen	Charles Maggiore
Phyllis Gelman	Gail Oscar
Herb Kessler	Garrett M. Brown
Kay Windsor	Barbara Lea

MUSICAL NUMBERS: "What Do We Do?," "Weekend at the Club," "Brand New Wall-to-Wall Day," "Desire under the Elmsford Country Club Oaks," "Temporary Woman Blues," "Let's Spend an Hour," "Have a Career," "It's Great to Be Single Again," "Background Music," "Morris," "Wild Kingdom," "Capitalist Beguine," "Lonely Woman," "Men Are Never Lonley," "It's Love! So What?," "It's Really Easy Baking Bread," "Best of Both Possible Worlds," "People Are Up for Grabs," "Faceless Clock," "Milles Fountain," "Take Me—Find Me," Finale

A musical in 2 acts and 15 scenes. The action takes place at the present time in the city and the suburbs.

Stage Managers: Greg Husinko, Walter Ditman

* Closed Nov. 8, 1975 after limited engagement of 12 performances.

Barbara Lea, Leila Holiday, Garrett M. Brown,
Ann Hodapp, Charles Maggiore, Gail Oscar,
Arne Gundersen

TOP OF THE GATE
Opened Wednesday, October 29, 1975.*
Elliot Martin presents the Playhouse Square Production of:

CONVERSATIONS WITH AN IRISH RASCAL

Adapted from the works of Brendan Behan by Kathleen Kennedy with David O. Frazier; Director, Joseph J. Garry

CAST
DAVID O. FRAZIER
GUSTI

"A musical biography" of Brendan Behan performed in two parts.

General Manager: Leonard A. Mulhern
Associate Manager: David Relyea
Press: Frank Goodman, Seymour Krawitz, Arlene Wolf Goodman, Barbara Carroll
Stage Manager: Paul Bennett

* Closed Nov. 9, 1975 after 13 performances.

Foto Arts Photo

Right: Gusti, David O. Frazier

NEW YORK THEATER ENSEMBLE
Opened Wednesday, November 5, 1975.*
The New York Theater Ensemble (Lucille Talayco, Artistc Director) presents:

TANIA

Book, Mario Fratti; Music and Lyrics, Paul Dick; Director, Ron Nash; Assistant Director, Rudy Garza; Lighting, David Andrews; Costumes, John Reid, Dianne Charbonneau; Piano, Zelig Sokoll

CAST

Walter	Walter George Alton
Ann	Marcy Olive
Mizzie	Norah Foster
Cynthia	Cynthia Haynes
Helen	Lee Torchia
Cinque	Dennis Jones
Bob	Norman Lewis
Akki	Akki Onyango
Diana	Jane Kerns
Lee	Marsha Bonine

MUSICAL NUMBERS: "To Start a Revolution," "There'll Come a Day," "Fire and Joy," "The American Dream," "I Sing Woman," "Man in a Cage," "Hail Alma Mater," "The Wall," "The Shoot Out"

A musical in two acts.

Stage Manager: John Wickman

* Closed Dec. 14, 1975 after 30 performances,

Elise Sokoll Photo

**Cynthia Haynes (top), Dennis Jones,
Walter George Alton, Marsha Bonine**

STAGE 73

Opened Wednesday, November 5, 1975.*
Catherine Ellis presents:

AND SO TO BED

By J. B. Fagan; Director, Eugenie Leontovich; Sets, Kristine Haugan; Costumes, Patricia Britton; Lighting, Barry Arnold; Musical Arrangements and Supervision, Jason McAuliffe; Hairstylist, Louis Guarascio; Assistant to director, Nora Peterson

CAST

Jacke	Michael Oakes
Samuel Pepys	David MacEnulty
Doll	Pawnee Sills
Mrs. Knight	Ellen Farran
Julia	Jane Altman
Pelling	Christopher Wynkoop
Pelham Humfrey	Jason McAuliffe
Mrs. Pierce	Laura May Lewis
Mrs. Knepp	Sharon Talbot
Mrs. Pepys	Catherine Ellis
Lettice	Cam Kornman
Prodgers	Randall Robbins
Charles II	John Bergstrom

A comedy in three acts. The action takes place in London a few days after the close of the Diary in June of 1669.

General Manager: Ashton Springer
Press: David Powers, William Schelble
Stage Managers: Peter Lawrence, Michael Oakes

* Closed Nov. 9, 1975 after 7 performances and 9 previews.

Bert Andrews Photo

David MacEnulty, Ellen Farran

Gail Cook, John Neville-Andrews, Darrell Ziegler

WONDERHORSE

Opened Thursday, November 6, 1975.*
Wayne Adams in association with Willard Morgan and Michael Condon presents the Alive Theatre Production of:

THE HOMECOMING

By Harold Pinter; Directed and Designed by Jack Chandler; Lighting, Darrell Ziegler; Costumes, Betty Martin; Music Designed by Gary Burke, Dede Washburn; Production Coordinator, Ken Shelby

CAST

Lenny	John Neville-Andrews
Max	Jack Eric Williams
Sam	Tim Cahill
Joey	Darrell Ziegler
Teddy	Brad Russell
Ruth	Gail Cook

A play in two acts. The action takes place at the present time in an old house in the north of London in late summer.

Press: Howard Atlee, Clarence J. Allsopp, Meg Gordean, Becky Flora
Stage Manager: Victor Amerling

* Closed Nov. 14, 1975 after 8 performances and 7 previews.

Bill McDonough Photo

WESTSIDE THEATER

Opened Wednesday, November 12, 1975.*
The Chelsea Theater Center of Brooklyn (Robert Kalfin, Artistic Director; Michael David, Executive Director; Burl Hash, Productions Director) and Peter Witt present:

THE FAMILY

By Lodewijk de Boer; Translated by Albert Maurita; Director, Barry Davis; Scenery, Lawrence King; Costumes, Jeanne Button; Lighting, Daniel Flannery; Videography, Alan Shulman and Mediatrics; Assistant to director, Eric Bogosian; Video and Sound, Michael Schaefer; Original Theme composed and performed by L. Joyce Hitchcock; Wardrobe Mistress, Melissa Adzima

CAST

Play 1
Doc .... David Selby
Kil .... Brent Spiner
Gina .... Dale Soules
Cabot .... Joe Palmieri
Brigit .... Diane Kagan

In 2 acts and 4 scenes.

Play 2
Gina .... Dale Soules
Kil .... Brent Spiner
Brigit .... Diane Kagan
Doc .... David Selby
Man .... Ed Preble

In 2 acts and 5 scenes.

UNDERSTUDIES: Doc, Kil, Richmond Hoxie; Brigit, Gina, Lynn Ritchie; Man, Edward Seamon

The action takes place in Amsterdam, Holland, a few years ago.

Press: Betty Lee Hunt Associates, Bill Evans
Stage Managers: Julia Gillett, M. S. Andrews

* Closed Nov. 30, 1975 after 23 performances and 14 previews.

Laura W. Pettibone Photos

David Selby, Dale Soules, Brent Spiner

Ed Kuczewski, Prima Stephen

ELYSIAN PLAYHOUSE
Opened Friday, November 14, 1975.*
The Fantasy Factory presents:

A MASS MURDER IN THE BALCONY OF THE OLD RITZ-RIALTO

Book, Ed Kuczewski; Music and Lyrics, Bill Vitale; Musical Direction, Vocal Arrangements, Orchestrations, Dance Music, Leon Odenz; Director, Bill Vitale; Choreography, Martin Rivera; Additional Staging, Teddy Kern; Setting, Elmon Webb, Virginia Dancy; Lighting, Rick Claflin; Costumes and Hairstyles, Reve Richards; Additional Orchestrations, James Fradrich; Sound, Danny O'Neil, Richard Foltz

CAST

Joseph Adorante, Linda Andrews, Marc Castle, Louise Claps, Bruno Damon, Joyce Griffen, Michael Kemmerling, Ed Kuczewski, Ethel A. Morgan, Joy Venus Morton, Joan Neuman, David Noh, Oliver Rish, Martin Rivera, Bob Santucci, Ray Shelton, Prima Stephen, Claudia Tompkins, LizaGrace Vachon-Coco, Paul Vanase, Steve Wadley, Louis Zippin

MUSICAL NUMBERS: "Shadow Song," "Slumming," "Homely Woman," "42nd Street," "Popcorn and Piss," "Dope," "Dope Rag," "Dope Double Time," "Let's All Go to the Lobby," "Musical Chairs," "I Got Rhythm Too," "The Old Days," "Sung-Fu," "Pictures and an Exhibition," "Savin' Souls," "Time to Go Home, Vernon," "Anybody Wanna Buy a Little Love," "Pink Lady," "The Comic," "When You're Shot in the Movies"

A musical performed without intermission.

Stage Managers: Theodore Pappas, Garry Cavanagh, Larry Brumer

* Closed Dec. 21, 1975 after 20 performances.

Ken Howard Photo

WESTSIDE THEATER

Opened Sunday, November 23, 1975.*
The Chelsea Theater Center of Brooklyn (Robert Kalfin, Artistic Director; Michael David, Executive Director; Burl Hash, Productions Director) presents:

BY BERNSTEIN

Conceived by Betty Comden and Adolph Green with Michael Bawtree, Norman L. Berman and the Chelsea Theater Center; Music, Leonard Bernstein; Lyrics, Leonard Bernstein, Comden and Green, John Latouche, Jerry Leiber, Stephen Sondheim; Written by Betty Comden and Adolph Green; Director, Michael Bawtree; Scenery and Costumes, Lawrence King, Michael H. Yeargan; Lighting, Marc B. Weiss; Vocal Arrangements and Musical Direction, Clay Fullum; Orchestrations, Thomas Pierson; Assisting Director, Norman L. Berman; Production Assistants, Amy Fripp, Cindee Mayfield

CAST

Jack Bittner
Margery Cohen
Jim Corti
Ed Dixon
Patricia Elliott
Kurt Peterson
Janie Sell
Understudy: David Horwitz

MUSICAL NUMBERS: "Welcome," "Gabey's Comin'," "Lonely Me," "Say When," "Like Everybody Else," "I'm Afraid It's Love," "Another Love," "I Know a Fellow," "It's Gotta Be Bad to Be Good," "Dream with Me," "Ringaroundarosy," "Captain Hook's Soliloquy," "The Riobamba," "The Intermission's Great,""Story of My Life," "Ain't Got No Tears Left," "The Coolie's Dilemma," "In There," "Spring Will Come Again," "Here Comes the Sun"

A musical entertainment in two parts.

Press: Betty Lee Hunt Associates, Bill Evans
Stage Managers: Fred Reinglas, David Horwitz

* Closed Dec. 7, 1975 after 17 performances and 40 previews.

Laura W. Pettibone Photos

Margery Cohen, Ed Dixon, Jim Corti, Janie Sell, Patricia Elliott, Kurt Peterson

PLAYERS THEATRE

Opened Monday, December 1, 1975.*
Wayne Clark and Joseph Tiraco in association with Larry J Pontillo present:

GIFT OF THE MAGI

Based on O. Henry's short story; Book, Music and Lyrics by Ronnie Britton; Director, M. T. Knoblauh; Musical Direction and Arrangements, James Fradrich; Setting, Michael Dulin; Costumes Neil Cooper; Lighting, Jerryn Michaels; Production Coordinator David M. Clark; Musical Supervisor, Tom Roberts; Hairstylist Wendy Kaplan

CAST

Her	Mary Saunder
Della	Paige O'Har
Jim	Bill Marc
Him	William Brockmeie

MUSICAL NUMBERS: "Magi Waltz," "There You Go Again," "The Gift," "Della's Desire," "Mr. James Dillingham Young: "Day after Day," "Kids Are Out," "Sullivan Street Flat," "Beautiful Children," "You'd Better Tell Her," "Washington Square," "Til Tomorrow," "Quiet Morning," "Brave You," "A Penny Saved," "I've Got Something Better," "Pretty Lady," "He Did It, She Di It!," "Make Him Think I'm Still Pretty," Finale

A musical in two acts. The action takes place in Greenwich Village, New York City, during December of 1906.

General Manager: Wayne Clark
Press: Betty Lee Hunt Associates, Ted Goldsmith
Stage Manager: Schorling Schneider

* Closed Jan. 4, 1976 after 40 performances and 16 previews.

Kenn Duncan Photo

Paige O'Hara, Mary Saunders, William Brockmeier, Bill March

TOP OF THE GATE

Opened Monday, December 1, 1975.*
(Moved Friday, December 26, 1975 to Westside Theater) Jerry Schlossberg, Arch Lustberg, Bruce Nelson present:

TUSCALOOSA'S CALLING ME ...
but I'm not going!

Written by Bill Heyer, Hank Beebe, Sam Dann; Music, Hank Beebe; Lyrics, Bill Heyer; Costumes, Rome Heyer; Musical Director, Jeremy Harris; Audio, Donald P. Smith; Designed by Charles E. Hoefler; Staged and Directed by James Hammerstein and Gui Andrisano; Associate Manager, David Relyea; Associate Production Manager, Dave Okarski

CAST
Len Gochman †1
Patti Perkins
Renny Temple†2

MUSICAL NUMBERS: "Only Right Here in New York City," "I Dig Myself," "Cold Cash," "Things Were Out," "Central Park on a Sunday Afternoon," "New York from the Air," "The Old Man," "Backwards," "Delicatessen," "Out of Towner," "Everything You Hate Is Right Here," "Suburban Fugue," "Purse Snatch," "Poor," "Grafitti," "Singles Bar," "New York '69," "Tuscaloosa's Calling Me, But I'm Not Going."

A musical in two acts. The action takes place at the present time in New York City.

General Manager: Leonard A. Mulhern
Press: Michael Alpert Associates, Warren Knowlton

* Still playing May 31, 1976.
† Succeeded by: 1. Ted Pritchard, Paul Kreppel, 2. Chip Zien

Ken Howard Photos

Right: Patti Perkins, Renny Temple, Len Gochman

Paul Kreppel, Patti Perkins

Patti Perkins, Chip Zien, Ted Pritchard

GOOD SHEPHERD-FAITH PRESBYTERIAN CHURCH
Opened Thursday, December 4, 1975.*
The Comedy Stage Company presents:

EVERYMAN
and
ACT WITHOUT WORDS i

Director, Tim Ward; Choreography, Hedy Weiss; Scenery, Alyse Newman; Costumes and Sculpture, Wendy Moore; Lighting, Tony Thompson

CAST

"Everyman" (Anonymous)
Messenger .... Betsy Julian Robinson
God/Confession .... Amandina Lihamba
Death .... Anne O'Sullivan
Everyman .... Michael Sears
Fellowship/Strength/Angel .... James-Ivers O'Connor
Cousin/Five Wits .... Alice Barrett
Kindred/Discretion .... Otis Gustafson
Goods/Beauty .... Matthew Schuster
Good Deeds .... Sheila Ward
Knowledge .... John J. Barilla

The action takes place at the present time in Times Square, New York City.

"Act without Words I" by Samuel Beckett
Performed by Will Lebow
The Action takes place at the present time on a desert.

Press: Sheila Ward
Stage Manager: Paula Cohen

* Closed Dec. 21, 1975 after limited engagement of 12 performances.

Susan Cook Photos

Mike Scott, Corie Sims

TOWN HALL
Opened Tuesday, January 6, 1976.*
Town Hall by arrangement with Arthur Cantor presents:

EMLYN WILLIAMS
AS
CHARLES DICKENS

Mr. Williams, made up as Charles Dickens, reads from the works of Mr. Dickens.

Press: Dan Langan
Production Supervisor: Robert Crawley

* Closed Jan. 10 after limited engagement of 6 performances.

"Everyman"

CITY PLAYWORKS THEATRE
Opened Thursday, December 18, 1975.*
City Playworks presents:

IN THE BOOM BOOM ROOM

By David Rabe; Director, Terry Grossman; Designed by Michael Hotopp and Paul DePass; Musical Supervisor, Marty Silvestri; Dance Sequences, Lynn Gannaway; Associate Producer, Christopher Cara; Executive Producer, Jonathan Sand

CAST

Chrissy .... Corie Sims
Susan .... Randy Danson
Harold/Eric/Guy/Al/The Man .... Mike Scott
Ralphie .... Mark Kologi
Helen .... Gloria Lord
Girls ...... Mary Ed Porter, Marilyn Pfeiffer, Linda Brumfield

A play in two acts. The action takes place in Philadelpbia in the mid 1960's.

Press: Joshua Ellis
Stage Managers: Harold Apter, Kathy Spear, Janie Maxwell

* Closed Dec. 28, 1975 after limited engagement of 8 performances.

Robb Webb Photo

Emlyn Williams

MARYMOUNT MANHATTAN THEATRE
Opened Wednesday, January 7, 1976.*
Charles Woodward presents:

FROM SHOLOM ALEICHEM WITH LOVE

Adapted and Staged by Elliot Levine; Lighting, Rick Claflin; Technical Director, Terrence Byrne; Associate Producer, Jerry Sirchia

with
ELLIOTT LEVINE

An evening in English with the Jewish Mark Twain during 1915 in New York City. Performed in two acts.

Press: Betty Lee Hunt Associates

* Closed Feb. 1, 1976 after 32 performances.

Elliot Levine

Pat Daniel

WOOD THEATRE
Opened Monday, January 12, 1976.*
Wood Theatre presents:

ALLEY CATS

Written, Directed and Designed by Tom Coble.

with
PAT DANIEL

A Dramatic monologue without intermission.

Press: Max Eisen
Stage Manager: Margie A. Phillips

Charles Livingston Photo

ALL SOULS UNITARIAN CHURCH
Opened Thursday, January 22, 1976.*
The All Souls Players present:

SOMEONE SORT OF GRANDISH

Conceived and Directed by Tran William Rhodes; Choreography, Kirby Lewellen; Lighting, Bill Pietrucha, Harry Blum; Projections-Photography, Mary Lumsden; Costumes, Hank Laurencelle

CAST

Dana Coen	Kathleen Roche-Zujko
Hester Lewellen	Monona Rossol
Kirby Lewellen	Allan Smith
Linda Lipson	Tina Tymus
Dick Pohlers	Gyle Waddy
Tran William Rhodes	Roger Whitmarsh

A Musical Tribute to E. Y. (Yip) Harburg consisting of 59 songs spanning the career of the Broadway and Hollywood lyricist-librettist.

Stage Manager: Lou Pavone

* Closed January 26, 1976 after limited engagement of 6 performances.

"Someone sort of Grandish"

HUNTER COLLEGE PLAYHOUSE
Saturday & Sunday, January 24–25, 1976.*
Frank Wicks and Hunter Arts Concert Bureau present:

JUST BETWEEN US
with
PEGGY COWLES

Conceived and Adapted by Daniel Stein; Material by Daniel Stein, Ruth Draper, Thomas Hardy, Guy de Maupassant, Marietta Holley, and Vachel Lindsay

* Presented for two performances only.

Peggy Cowles

Mike Kellin, Michael Egan, J. T. Walsh
(also above)

ST. CLEMENT'S THEATRE
Opened Monday, January 26, 1976.*
St. Clement's Theatre (Brian Murray, Artistic Director; Lawrence Goossen, Executive Producer) presents:

AMERICAN BUFFALO

By David Mamet; Director, Gregory Mosher; Set, Leo Yoshimura; Lighting, Gary Porto; Costumes, Danny Mizell; Technical Coordinator, Jeffrey M. Jones; Coordinator, Jean Halbert; Wardrobe Mistress, Terry Rosario

CAST

Donny Dubrow	Michael Egan
Walter Cole, "Teach"	Mike Kellin
Bobby	J. T. Walsh

A play in two acts.

Press: Jean Halbert
Stage Managers: Lynn Gutter, Vicki Paul

* Closed Feb. 7, 1976 after limited engagement of 16 performances.

Rena Hansen Photos

80

PROVINCETOWN PLAYHOUSE
Opened Thursday, January 29, 1976.*
The Peoples Performing Company presents:

FIRE OF FLOWERS

Words and Lyrics, Peter Copani; Music, Christian Staudt, Bob Tuthill, Lawrence Pitilli, David McHugh, Ed Vogel, Peter Copani; Musical Director, Ed Vogel; Director, Don Signore; Set and Lighting, Richard Harper; Production Assistants, Bill Barry, Colleen DeBlaise, Denise Bonenfant, Rafael Diaz, Al Simonds, Norma Signore

CAST

Larry Campbell
Sylvia Miranda
Val Reiter
Gwen Sumter

MUSICAL NUMBERS: "Today Will Be," "Keep Hope Alive," "Poppy Fields," "A Special Man," "If Jesus Walked," "Instant Hate," "One of Us," "I Need to Know," "In the Name of Love," "I'm Afire," "God Is in the People," "A Lover's Dream," "Who Can Say?," "Strawberries, Pickles and Ice Cream," "Down on Me," "Blind Junkie," "Riot," "I Love the Sun," "Pairs of One," "Verily, Verily," "More Than Love," "Make Them Hate," "Street Jesus," "L'America Ha Fato Per Te," "Love Comes and Goes," "Drug Free," "Wait and See," "When We Are Together"

Press: Lewis Harmon
Stage Manager: John Copani

* Closed Feb. 29, 1976 after 38 performances and 17 previews.

Gary Wheeler Photo

**Top Right: (front) Larry Campbell, Sylvia Miranda
(back) Gwen Sumter, Val Reiter**

**nt) Christopher Lloyd, Gale Garnett, Jeremy Lucas,
Louis Giambalvo, (back) Jane Lowry, Meg Myles,
Victor Garber, Mary Elaine Monti, Donald Linahan**

THEATRE DE LYS
Opened Tuesday, February 10, 1976.*
Adela Holzer presents:

CRACKS

By Martin Sherman; Director, Tony Giordano; Music, Carlos Holzer; Scenery, Peter Larkin; Costumes, Randy Barcelo; Lighting, Marc B. Weiss; Associate Manager, David Relyea; Production Assistant, Rosemarie Schieffer; Wardrobe Supervisor, Judy Mauer; Hairstylist, Karol Coeyman

CAST

Gideon	Christopher Lloyd
Maggie	Meg Myles
Sammy	Victor Garber
Nadine	Gale Garnett
Clay	Donald Linahan
Jade	Mary Elaine Monti
Roberta	Louis Giambalvo
Irene	Jane Lowry
Rick	Jeremy Lucas

UNDERSTUDIES: Gideon, Jeremy Lucas; Irene, Maggie, Nadine, Susanne Wasson

A comedy performed without intermission. The action takes place at the present time in Rick's house in Southern California on a summer evening.

General Manager: Leonard A. Mulhern
Company Manager: Paul B. Berkowsky
Press: Michael Alpert, Marilynn LeVine, Warren Knowlton, Joshua Ellis, Randi Cone

* Closed Feb. 10, 1976 after one performance.

Sy Friedman Photo

PERFORMING GARAGE

Opened Tuesday, February 10, 1976.*
(Moved April 15, 1976 to Provincetown Playhouse)
The Ridiculous Theatre Company presents:

CAPRICE

Written and Directed by Charles Ludlam; Set, Bobjack Callejo; Lighting, Richard Currie; Costumes, Edward Avedisian, Arthur Brady, Mario Montez, Suzanne Peters, Roy Finamore, Georg Osterman, Mary Brecht; Choreography, Ethyl Eichelberger

CAST

Claude Caprice	Charles Ludlam
Adrian	John D. Brockmeyer
TaTa	Adam MacAdam
Harry Feinschmecher	Lola Pashalinski
Zuni Feinschmecher	Black-Eyed Susan
Twyfford Adamant	Bill Vehr
Copelias	Georg Osterman
Scrub Woman/La Fleur/Bertha	Ethyl Eichelberger
Ballerinas	Ekathrina Sobechanskaya, Tamara Karpova, Claudette Caprichovna, Flossie Flanagan

A comedy in two acts.

General Management: New Arts Management
Press: Alan Eichler
Stage Manager: Richard Gibbs

* Closed April 25, 1976 after 45 performances.

John Stern Photo

Black-Eyed Susan, Charles Ludlam

Sandra Seacat, Geoffrey Horne

ACTORS STUDIO

Opened Thursday, March 18, 1976.*
The Actors Studio presents:

ECONOMIC NECESSITY

By John Hopkins; Director, Arthur Sherman; Executive Producer, Carl Schaeffer; Technical Director, Eric R. Cowley; Coordinator, Alan Mandell; Lighting, Paul Kaine; Set, Sally Lock; Costumes, Francie Trotta; Assistant to director, Heather Gubner

CAST

Audrey	Sandra Seac.
Barry	Michael Ha
Christine	Maxmillia Scheid
Dennis	Geoffrey Hor
Eric	Joseph Ragi
Frank	J. J. Quir
Gerry	Nick La Padu
Harriet	Carlin Gly
Ian	Paul Gleas
Jessica	Ann Wedgewo
Ken	Michael Ha

A play in two acts.

Production Manager: Deedee Wehle
Press: Lee Pucklis
Stage Manager: Howard Meadow

* Closed April 4, 1976 after limited engagement of 12 performanc

Mallory Jones Photo

Opened Monday, February 16, 1976.*
Jack Schlissel, Joseph Kipness, Steven Steinlauf present:

THE PRIMARY ENGLISH CLASS

By Israel Horovitz; Director, Edward Berkeley; Associate Pro-
ucer, Irving Welzer; Scenery, Fredda Slavin; Lighting, Andrea
'ilson; Costumes, Patricia McGourty; Production Supervisor,
nna Antaramian; Production Assistant, Alan Lifschitz

CAST

miednik . . . . Tom Kubiak
atumiera. . . . . Richard Libertini
aPoubelle . . . . Jean-Pierre Stewart
ranslator . . . . Rogert Picardo
Iulleimer . . . . Sol Frieder
Irs. Pong . . . . Lori Tan Chinn
ranslator . . . . Christine Von Dohln
oko Kazukago . . . . Atsumi Sakato
ebbie Wastba . . . . Diane Keaton†

NDERSTUDIES: Debbie, Christine Von Dohln; Patumiera, La
oubelle, Mulleimer, Robert Picardo

A comedy performed without intermission. The action takes place
t the present time in a classroom at night.

General Manager: Jay Kingwill
Assistant General Manager: Mark Bramble
Press: Solters & Roskin, Milly Schoenbaum, Bud Westman
Stage Manager: Robert Schear

Closed May 16, 1976 after 104 performances.
Succeeded by Jill Eikenberry

Ken Howard Photos

**Atsumi Sakato, Jean-Pierre Stewart, Diane Keaton, Richard Libertini, Sol Frieder
Top Right: Jill Eikenberry**

THE THEATRE

Opened Thursday, March 20, 1976.*
New York Theater Strategy presents:

SHE WHO WAS HE

By Rosalyn Drexler; Director, William Prosser; Music, John Herbert McDowell; Choreographer, Joe Goode; Set, Robert Franklin; Costumes, Carole Steinke, Kathi Horne; Lights, Michael Watson; Technical Director, Gary Grill

CAST

Tumbler/Dancer	Edward Bartonn
Amon Ra/Tutmose I	Lawrence Gallegos
Ahmose	Gretel Cummings
Priest	Dale Fuller
Hathor	Yvonne Dell
Hatshepsut	Roxana Stuart or Margaret Harrington
Nemra/Dancer	Richard Thorne
Sheeshonk/Dancer/Set	Bill Kirkpatrick
Tutmose II	Tazewell Thompson
Kinnor	Ken Fitch
Singer	Carol Grant
Senmut	Amlin Gray
Sekmet/Dancer	Andrea Borak
Isis	Ann Freeman
Tutmose III	Gabriel Gribetz
Young Soldier	Cameron Duncan
Hand Maidens	Jana Fontana, Lenora May
Dancers	Candice Christakos, Mary Dunnavant
Percussionist	Daniel Wallack

A drama in two acts. The action takes place in Egypt.

Press: Alan Eichler
Stage Managers: Timothy Gabbert, John Buonassissi, Dorothy Silver

* Closed April 4, 1976 after limited engagement of 12 performances.

Roxana Stuart

David Clennon, Howard E. Rollins, Jr.

THEATRE DE LYS

Opened Sunday, March 28, 1976.*
Paul B. Berkowsky, Woodie King, Jr. and Lucille Lortel present:

MEDAL OF HONOR RAG

By Tom Cole; Director, David Chambers; Setting, Raymond C. Recht; Lighting, Marshall S. Spiller; Costumes, Carol Oditz; Wardrobe Mistress, Rebecca Howard; Assistant to director, Clay Stevenson; Production Assistant, Kevin B. Berkowsky

CAST

Doctor	David Clennon
Dale Jackson (D.J.)	Howard E. Rollins, Jr.
Military Guard	John Robert Yates

A drama performed without intermission. The action takes place in an office of the Valley Forge Army Hospital, Valley Forge, PA, on the afternoon of April 23, 1971.

General Manager: Paul B. Berkowsky
Press: Merlin Group, Sandra Manley, Elizabeth Rodman
Stage Managers: Dan Early, John Robert Yates

* Closed May 2, 1976 after 41 performances.

Arlene Spiller Photo

WESTSIDE THEATER
Opened Monday, March 22, 1976.*
The Chelsea Theater Center, The Lion Theatre Company, and
Playwrights Horizons present:

VANITIES

By Jack Heifner; Director, Garland Wright; Scenery, John Arnone; Lighting, Patrika Brown; Costumes, David James; Wardrobe Mistress, Gertrude Sloan

CAST

Kathy.....................................Jane Galloway
Mary......................................Susan Merson
Joanne....................................Kathy Bates

A play in three acts. The action takes place in a gymnasium in 1963, a sorority house in 1968, and a garden apartment in 1974.

Press: Betty Lee Hunt, Maria Cristina Pucci
Stage Manager: Ginny Freedman

* Still playing May 31, 1976.

Laura W. Pettibone Photos

Right: Jane Galloway, Susan Merson, Kathy Bates

Kathy Bates, Jane Galloway, Susan Merson

DIPLOMAT CABARET THEATRE
Opened Friday, April 2, 1976.*
Jolandrea Music Inc. in association with Gail Davis, Parker
Willson, Edmund Gaynes presents:

LE BELLYBUTTON

Book, Music, Lyrics, and Direction by Scott Mansfield; Choreography, Katherine Hull, Louise Quick; Designed by David Chapman; Lighting Associate, Richard Winkler; Costume Associate, Ben Gutiérrez-Soto; Orchestrations and Musical Direction, Ken Werner; Additional Sketch Material, Johnathan Copley, Joel Scott; Assistant Director, Alan Fox; Production Consultant, Gail Davis; Assistant to producers, Jane Hershcopf; Assistant Musical Director, Donald Oliver; Wardrobe Mistress, Fern Laurie

CAST

Marilyn Chambers	Alan Lee Kootsher
Thommie Bush	Billy Padgett
Jessie Hill	Paulette Sanders
Adrienne Frimet	Jim Sbano
Larry Kingery	Alan Scott
Debbie Kinney	Suzanne Walker

A musical in two acts.

General Manager: Malcolm Allen
Press: Henry Luhrman, Terry Lilly
Stage Managers: Alan Fox, Lee Triplett

* Closed April 25, 1976 after 28 performances.

Jerome Yulesman Photos

**Right: Marilyn Chambers, Thommie Bush,
Adrienne Frimet, Larry Kingery, Suzanne Walker
Above: Debbie Kinney, Marilyn Chambers,
Suzanne Walker**

**Lisa Hall, Norman Weiler, William Fredericks,
Margo Lacey, Jonathan Jones**

BILLY MUNK THEATRE
Opened Monday, April 12, 1976.*
Marc Hamerman presents:

I KNOCK AT THE DOOR

By Sean O'Casey; Adapted by Paul Shyre; Music and Lyrics, Pa
Dick; Director, Ron Nash; Music Director, Sal Sicari; Costum
John Reid; Associate Producer, Robert Pace

CAST

Mother	Margo Lac
Johnny	Jonathan Howard Jon
Narrator/Cabman	Richard Iar
Nurse/Ella	Lisa H
Doctor/Conductor/Archie/Mr. Story/Cabman/	
Harry Tait	William Frederi
Father/Old Man/Clergyman/Slogan	Kevin Hun
Narrator/Aunt/Woman in hospital/Woman at	
Wake/Jenny	Susan J. Ba
One-eyed	Man/Murphy/Cabman/Mich.
George Middleton/Rev. Hunter	Norman Wei

MUSICAL NUMBERS: "The Last Shake o' the Bag," "At
Annual Vice-Regal Ball," "Ounce of Cavendish Cut Plug," "
Love Goes Down," "Prepare Ye Now for the World to Com
"Same Way Home," "Little Boy Blue," "Cock Robin," "There
a Funny Man," "White Bum," "An Irish Ireland," "Why Are Y
Weepin', Jenny?," "My Country's Call," "Ay, Michael, O, M
chael," "Soliloquy on a Sunny Wedding Morn," "The Brook"

A musical in two acts.

Stage Managers: JW Roberts, Pat Sullivan

* Closed April 14, 1976 after limited engagement of four perf
mances.

CITY CENTER 55th STREET THEATER
Opened Thursday, April 15, 1976.*
Artists Consultants presents:

MONTY PYTHON LIVE!

American Scenic Supervision, Karl Eigsti; Sound, Abe Jacob;
Lighting Designer, John Gleason; Wardrobe Supervisor, Ann Goodson; Production Coordinators, Charles Knode, Anne Henshaw

CAST

Terry Gilliam
Terry Jones
John Cleese
Eric Idle
Graham Chapman
Michael Palin
with Neil Innes, Carol Cleveland

A British comedy revue in two acts.

General Manager: Theatre Now, Inc.
Company Manager: Robert Frissell
Press: Wartoke Concern, Jane Friedman
Stage Managers: Molly Kirkland, Frank Marino

* Closed May 2, 1976 after limited engagement of 22 performances and 2 previews.

Martha Swope Photos

ASTOR PLACE THEATRE
Opened previews Tuesday, April 20, 1976.*
Labor Arts Community Services Committee in association with
Stuart White presents:

I PAID MY DUES

Book and Lyrics, Eric Blau; Music Arrangements, Musical Direction, David Frank; Director, George Allison Elmer; Sets and Costumes, Don Jensen; Lighting, Jeff Davis; Assistant Conductor, Bob
Stecko; Production Assistant, Dell Setzer

CAST

Joe Morton

Christopher Cable	James Robinson
Tom Demenkoff	Edward Rodriguez
Jacqueline Reilly	Wendy Wolfe
Linda Rios	Zenobia

Alternates: Lynnie Godfrey, Alphanzo Harrison

MUSICAL NUMBERS: "I Paid My Dues," "In Good Old Colony
Times," "Whiskey in the Jar," "Yankee Doodle," "Fate of John
Burgoyne," "Battle of Trenton," "Young Ladies in Town," "Yankee
Doodle Dandy-O," "Johnny Has Gone for a Soldier," "Blow Ye
Winds," "Cape Cod Girls," "Haul on the Bow Line," "Erie Canal,"
"Frozen Logger," "Santy Anno," "Praties They Grow Small,"
"Shenandoah," "John Henry," "Doney Gal," "Red Iron Ore," "My
Sweetheart's the Mule in the Mine," "Railroad Bill," "A Cowboy's
Life," "The Cowboys," "Zum Gali, Gali," "Drill Ye Tarriers,
Drill," "Wade in the Water," "Hushabye," "Go Down Moses,"
"This Train," "Oh! Freedom," "Take This Hammer," "When I'm
Gone," "Pick a Bale of Cotton," "Many Thousands Gone," "Tent-
ing Tonight," "John Brown's Body," "Battle Hymn of the Repub-
lic," "Solidarity Forever," "Dark as a Dungeon," "Sixteen Tons,"
"Union Maid," "Which Side Are You On," "Talking Union," "The
Scabs Crawl In," "Hinky Dinky Parlez Vous," "On the Line,"
"You've Got to Go Down," "Roll the Union On," "Casey Jones,"
"Hold the Fort," "We Shall Not Be Moved," "Goin' Down the
Road," "Beans, Bacon and Gravy," "Soup Song," "Brother Can
You Spare a Dime?," "Let's Have Another Cup of Coffee," "When
the Red Red Robin," "I Want to Be Happy," "Agent 008," "Violet
Eyes," "Ballad of Mervyn Schwartz," "Nosotros Venceremos," "A
Man's a Man for All That"

A musical celebration of labor in two acts.

General Manager: Lily Turner
Press: Seymour Krawitz, Ted Goldsmith, Patricia McLean
Krawitz
Stage Manager: James Nisbet Clark

* Closed May 23, 1976 after 20 performances.

Bert Andrews Photos

Christopher Gable, Jacqueline Reilly, James Robins
Edward Rodriguez, Tom Demenkoff,
Wendy Wolfe, Linda Rios, Zenobia
Above: Linda Ross, Joe Morton

TRUCK AND WAREHOUSE THEATRE
Opened Tuesday, April 20, 1976.*
R. Paul Evans and Otto Grun, Jr. present:

· WOMEN BEHIND BARS

By Tom Eyen; Director, Ron Link; Designed by Sturgis Warn
Lighting, Michael Lodick; Production Assistant, Trey Luckenba
Title Song, Tom Eyen; Sung by Larry Paulette

CAST

Matron	Div
Louise	Sweet Willi
Blanche	Lori Saveria
Jo-Jo	Beverly Bon
Cheri	Brenda Bergm
Gloria	Ellie Sch
Ada	Jana Schnei
Guadalupe	Vira Colora
Mary-Eleanor	Lisa Jane Pers
Granny	Virginia Bar

A comedy performed without intermission. The action takes pl
in the Women's House of Detention between 1952 and 1960.

Company Manager: Jerry Sandusky
Press: Alan Eichler, Tony Kavanaugh

* Still playing May 31, 1976.

Glenn Capers Photos

Ellie Schadt, Jana Schmeider, Divine,
Brenda Bergman, Lisa Jane Persky

Opened Monday, April 26, 1976.*
Norman Stephens and Primavera Productions Ltd. in association with Max Weitzenhoffer present:

TICKLES BY TUCHOLSKY

Original Material, Kurt Tucholsky; Translated and Adapted by Louis Golden, Harold Poor; Conceived and Directed by Moni Yakim; Music Arranged and Conducted by Wolfgang Knittel; Sets, Don Jensen; Lights, Spencer Mosse; Costumes, Christina Giannini; Production Coordinator, George Allison Elmer; Assistant to director, Kathleen Gargan; Wardrobe Mistress, Betty Martin

CAST
Helen Gallagher
Joe Masiell
Jana Robbins
Joseph Neal
Jerry Jarrett
Understudy: Susan Waldman

MUSICAL NUMBERS AND SKETCHES: "The Song of Indifference," "Rising Expectations," "Tickles," "Christmas Shopping," "Brown Shirted Cowboy," "German Evening," "Transition," "Lovers," "Waldemar," "Compromise Soft Shoe," "Come Avec!," "How to Get Rich," "King's Regiment," "Lullaby," "Verdun," "War against War," "Waiting," "Follow Schmidt," "Anna Louisa," "Lamplighters," "Heartbeat," "It's Your Turn," "25 Points," "I'm Out," "General! General!," "To You I Gave My All," "Now That Things Are Rough," "Testimony," "Over the Trenches," Epilogue

A "cabaret musical" in two acts.

General Manager: Lily Turner
Company Manager: Donald Joslyn
Press: Merlin Group, Sandra Manley, Harriett Trachtenberg, Ron Harris
Stage Managers: Phillip Price, Steve Helliker

* Closed May 9, 1976 after 16 performances and 24 previews.

Bert Andrews Photos

Jerry Jarrett,
Helen Gallagher

Joe Masiell, Jana Robbins
Top: Jerry Jarrett,
Joseph Neal,
Helen Gallagher, Joe Masiell

Dolly Jonah, Will Holt

EDISON THEATRE
Opened Tuesday, May 4, 1976.*
Norman Kean presents:

A KURT WEILL CABARET

Conceived and Directed by Will Holt; Musical Direction, William Cox

CAST
WILL HOLT & DOLLY JONAH

MUSICAL NUMBERS: "Alabama Song," "Ballad of the Easy Life," "Barbara Song," "Moritat, "Mahagonny Duet," "Tango Ballade," "Pirate Jenny," "Recruiting Song," "Benares Song," "Denn Wie Man Sich Bettet," "Caesar's Death," "Johnny Johnson," "My Ship," "Speak Low," "Jenny Made Her Mind Up," "September Song," "It Never Was You," "Mandalay Song," "Sailor's Tango," "Surabaya Johnny," "Bilboa Song," Finale

A musical cabaret in two acts.

Company Manager: Maria Di Dia
Press: Les Schecter Associates
Stage Manager: Sam Stickler

* Closed May 25, 1976 after limited engagement of 3 performances.

Bert Andrews Photos

VAN DAM THEATRE
Opened Monday, May 10, 1976.*
John Rothman Productions Ltd. in association with the Direct
Theatre and Dorothy Ames presents:

TITANIC
and
DAS LUSITANIA SONGSPIEL

Director, Peter Mark Schifter; Sets and Costumes, Ernie Smith;
Lighting, Mitchell Kurtz; Accompanist, Jack Gaughan; Production
Associate, David Geronemus

CAST

"Das Lusitania Songspiel":
The Theatre Songs of Bertolt Breck
Christopher Durang
Sigourney Weaver

"Titanic" by Christopher Durang
Victoria Tammurai . . . . Kate McGregor-Stewart
Richard Tammurai . . . . Stefan Hartman
Teddy Tammurai . . . . Richard Peterson
Lidia . . . . Sigourney Weaver
The Captain . . . . Jeff Brooks
Higgins . . . . Ralph Redpath

Manager: Jerry Arrow
Press: Betty Lee Hunt, Maria Cristina Pucci, Fred Hoot
Stage Managers: Peter Schifter, Chris Durang, Anne Hoffman,
Kimberly Meyers

* Closed May 16, 1976 after 7 performances and 7 previews.

Laura W. Pettibone Photos

**Right: Kate McGregor-Stewart, Richard Peterson,
Ralph Redpath, Sigourney Weaver, Stefan
Hartman in "Titanic" Top: Sigourney Weaver,
Christopher Durang in "Das Lusitania
Songspiel"**

Lee Nagrin, Margaret Beals, Brook Myers

THERESA L. KAUFMANN CONCERT HALL
Opened Sunday, May 23, 1976.*
Impulses Arts Inc. in association with the 92 Street Y
YWHA presents:

STINGS

Based on "Ariel," the final poems of Sylvia Plath; Created,
rected and Choreographed by Margaret Beals; Scenery, Jim Mea
Costumes, Sally Ann Parsons; Lighting, Edward M. Greenbe
Sound, Antony Giovanetti

CAST

Margaret Beals
Brooke Myers
Lee Nagrin

POEMS: "Tulips," "Elm," "Couriers," "Applicant," "Lady La
rus," "Duet," "Ariel," "Trio," "Lesbos," "A Birthday Prese
"Daddy," "Edge," "Words."

Performed without intermission.

Management: Bruce Michaels, Neil Fleckman
Stage Manager: Richard Tauber

* Closed May 27, 1976 after limited engagement of 4 performan

Suzanne Opton Photo

THE ACTING COMPANY

John Houseman, Artistic Director
Margot Harley, Producing Director
Porter Van Zandt, Executive Director

ARKNESS THEATRE
Opened Tuesday, October 7, 1975.*
The Acting Company presents:

THE ROBBER BRIDEGROOM

Book and Lyrics, Alfred Uhry; Based on novella by Eudora
'elty; Composed and Arranged by Robert Waldman; Director,
erald Freedman; Choreography, Donald Saddler; Settings, Doug-
s W. Schmidt; Costumes, Jeanne Button; Lighting, David F. Segal;
echnical Director, Richard Elkow; Wardrobe Supervisor, Karen L.
fert; Hairstylist, Steve Atha

CAST

mie Lockhart	Kevin Kline
like Fink	Norman Snow
lemment Musgrove	David Schramm
oat	Robert Bacigalupi
ittle Harp	J. W. Harper
g Harp	Anderson Matthews
yle Nunnery	Brooks Baldwin
om Plymale	Richard Ooms
lly Brenner	Nicolas Surovy
hn Oglesby	Roy K. Stevens
rnie Summers	Peter Dvorsky
erman McLaughlin	Michael Tolaydo
alome	Mary Lou Rosato
osamund	Patti LuPone
oat's Mother	Glynis Bell
irie	Sandra Halperin
aven	Elaine Hausman
ueenie Sue Stevens	Cynthia Dickason
iddler	Alan Kaufman

NDERSTUDIES: Jamie, Mike, Nicolas Surovy; Little Harp, Nor-
an Snow; Clemment, Richard Ooms; Goat, Brooks Baldwin;
alome, Glynis Bell; Rosamund, Sandra Halperin; Goat's Mother,
laine Hausman; Airie, Raven, Cynthia Dickason; Alternate Big
arp, Benjamin Hendrickson

IUSICAL NUMBERS: "With Style," "The Real Mike Fink,"
The Pricklepear Bloom," "Nothin' Up," "Deeper in the Woods,"
Riches," "Love Stolen," "Poor Tied Up Darlin'," "Goodbye
alome," "Sleepy Man"

A country-folk musical performed without intermission. The ac-
on takes place in legendary Mississippi.

Company Manager: Mannie Kladitis
Press: Gifford/Wallace, Tom Trenkle
Stage Managers: Howard Crampton-Smith, San Clester, Jo
Mayer

Closed Oct. 18, 1975 after limited engagement of 15 performances
and 1 preview.

Diane Gorodnitzki Photos

**Top Right: David Schramm, Patti LuPone,
Kevin Kline Below: Kevin Kline, Nicolas Surovy,
Patti LuPone**

Patti LuPone, Kevin Kline

Norman Snow, Patti LuPone, Mary-Joan Negro

HARKNESS THEATRE
Opened Tuesday, October 21, 1975.*
The Acting Company presents:

EDWARD II

By Christopher Marlowe; Director, Ellis Rabb; Music and Sour
Bob James; Costumes, Nancy Potts; Settings, Douglas W. Schmi
Lighting, David F. Segal

CAST

Gaveston	Peter Dvors
Beggar I	Anderson Matthe
Beggar II	Cynthia Dickas
Beggar III	Roy K. Steve
King Edward II	Norman Sn
Lancaster	Benjamin Hendrickson or Kevin Kli
Elder Mortimer	Richard Oor
Young Mortimer	Sam Tsoutsou
Kent, brother of Edward II	David Schram
Warwick	Brooks Baldw
Bishop of Coventry	Michael Tolay
Archbishop of Canterbury	Nicolas Suro
Queen Isabella	Mary-Joan Neg
Lady Margaret	Elaine Hausm
Baldock	J. W. Harp
Spencer	Robert Bacigalu
Leicester	Michael Tolay
Price Edward, later Edward III	Patti LuPo
Abbott	Richard Oor
Matrevis	Roy K. Steve
Berkeley	Brooks Baldw
Gurney	Anderson Matthe
Lightborn	Kevin Kline or Benjamin Hendricks
Ladies-in-waiting	Cynthia Dickason, Sandra Halper
Attendants	Cynthia Dickason, Peter Dvorsk

Sandra Halperin, J. W. Harper, Elaine Hausman, Anders
Matthews, Richard Ooms, Roy K. Stevens, Micha
Tolay

UNDERSTUDIES: Prince Edward, Sandra Halperin; Margare
Cynthia Dickason; Isabella, Mary Lou Rosato; Leicester, Cante
bury, Matrevis, Gurney, Bishop, Beggar, Attendant, Gerald G
tierrez; Young Mortimer, Lancaster, Lightborn, J. W. Harpe
Gaveston, Attendant, Kevin Kline; Spencer, Anderson Matthew
Edward II, David Schramm; Baldock, Roy K. Stevens; Elder Mor
mer, Warwick, Abbott, Alternate Lancaster, Lightborn, Kev
Kline

Performed with one intermission.

Company Manager: Mannie Kladitis
Press Gifford/Wallace, Tom Trenkle
Stage Managers: Howard Crampton-Smith, Sam Clester, Jo
Mayer

* Closed Oct. 25, 1976 after limited engagement of 8 performanc
and 1 preview in repertory.

Diane Gorodnitzki Photos

**Top Left: Mary-Joan Negro,
Norman Snow, Peter Dvorsky**

HARKNESS THEATRE
Opened Tuesday, October 28, 1975.*
The Acting Company presents:

THE TIME OF YOUR LIFE

By William Saroyan; Director, Jack O'Brien; Settings, Douglas W. Schmidt; Costumes, Nancy Potts; Lighting, David F. Segal; Technical Director, Richard Elkow; Wardrobe Supervisor, Karen L. Eifert; Lighting Associate, Timmy Harris; Hairstylist, S. A. Moore

CAST

Newsboy	Elaine Hausman
Joe	Nicolas Surovy
Arab	Richard Ooms
Drunkard	Anderson Matthews/Michael Tolaydo
Nick	Benjamin Hendrickson
Willie	Michael Tolaydo/Sam Tsoutsouvas
Tom	Norman Snow
Kitty Duval	Patti LuPone
Harry	Brooks Baldwin
Dudley	Robert Bacigalupi
Wesley	Gerald Gutierrez
Lorene/Killer's Sidekick	Glynis Bell
Blick	J. W. Harper
Mary L	Mary Lou Rosato
Krupp	Roy K. Stevens
McCarthy	Kevin Kline
Kit Carson	David Schramm
Sailor	Anderson Matthews
Killer	Cynthia Dickason
Elsie	Sandra Halperin
Society Lady	Mary-Joan Negro
Society Gentleman	Peter Dvorsky

UNDERSTUDIES: Joe, David Schramm; Kitty, Sandra Halperin; Nick, Roy K. Stevens; Kit, J. W. Harper; Arab, Dudley, Michael Tolaydo; Krupp, Harry, Anderson Matthews; Elsie, Cynthia Dickason; Blick, Sam Tsoutsouvas; McCarthy, Peter Dvorsky; Mary L, Mary-Joan Negro; Tom, Wesley, Kevin Kline; Society Lady, Killer, Glynis Bell

A drama in three acts. The action takes place in Nick's Pacific Street Saloon, Restaurant and Entertainment Palace at the foot of Embarcadero in San Francisco during an afternoon and night in October of 1939.

Company Manager: Mannie Kladitis
Press: Gifford/Wallace, Tom Trenkle
Stage Managers: Howard Crampton-Smith, Sam Clester, Jo Mayer

* Closed November 1, 1975 after limited engagement of 8 performances and 1 preview in repertory.

Patti LuPone

Top Right: Patti LuPone, Norman Snow

93

HARKNESS THEATRE
Opened Tuesday, November 4, 1975.*
The Acting Company presents:

THE THREE SISTERS

By Anton Chekhov; Translated by Tyrone Guthrie and Leonard
Kipnis; Director, Boris Tumarin; Musical Direction, Gerald G
tierrez; Dances Staged by Elizabeth Kee; Settings, Douglas V
Schmidt; Costumes, John David Ridge; Lighting, David F. Sega
Hairstylist, Jonn Quaglia

CAST

Olga	Mary Lou Rosa
Masha	Mary-Joan Neg
Irina	Patti LuPo
Baron Tusenbach	Norman Sno
Chebutykin, Military Doctor	David Schram
Captain Solyony	Sam Tsoutsouv
Dounyasha	Elaine Hausm
Anfisa (Nyanya)	Glynis B
Ferapont	Roy K. Steve
Colonel Vershinin	Peter Dvors
Andrey Prozorov	Benjamin Hendricks
Fyodor Kulygin	Richard Oo
Natasha	Sandra Halpe
Lt. Fedotik	Nicolas Suro
Lt. Rode	Michael Tolay
Members of the Prozorov Household	Brooks Baldw

Cynthia Dickason, Anderson Matthews, J. W. Har

UNDERSTUDIES: Olga, Glynis Bell; Natasha, Dounyas
Cynthia Dickason; Masha, Mary Lou Rosato; Irina, Anfisa, Ela
Hausman; Rode, Solyony, Robert Bacigalupi; Fedotik, Gerald G
tierrez; Chebutykin, J. W. Harper; Baron, Colonel, Kevin Kli
Fyodor, Nicolas Surovy; Ferapont, Michael Tolaydo; Andrey, S
Tsoutsouvas

A drama in four acts performed with one intermission. The act
takes place in the Prozorov home in a provincial town of Russi
the turn of this century.

Company Manager: Mannie Kladitis
Press: Gifford/Wallace, Tom Trenkle
Stage Managers: Howard Crampton-Smith, Sam Clester, Jo
Mayer

* Closed Nov. 8, 1975 after 8 performances and 1 preview in rep
tory.

Mary-Joan Negro, Patti LuPone, Mary Lou Rosato

Top: David Schramm, Patti LuPone,
Gerald Gutierrez, Benjamin Hendrickson, Norman

AMERICAN PLACE THEATRE

Wynn Handman, Director
Julia Miles, Associate Director
Twelfth Season

AMERICAN PLACE THEATRE
Opened Sunday, November 16, 1975.*
The American Place Theatre presents:

GORKY

By Steve Tesich; Director, Dennis Rosa; Music, Mel Marvin;
Lyrics, Steve Tesich; Scenery, David Jenkins; Costumes, Shadow;
Lighting, Roger Morgan; Orchestrations, Mel Marvin, Ken Guil-
martin; Technical Director, Henry Millman; Wardrobe Mistress,
Ula III; Assistant Director, Douglas Cloud; Production Assistant,
Michael St. John; Costume Associate, Hugh Sherrer

CAST

Gorky	Philip Baker Hall
Doctor/Gypsy/Matthew	Richard Ramos
Grandma/Peasant	Lilia Skala
Grandpa/Peasant	Fyvush Finkel
Offstage Speaking Patient/Gavrillo	Stuart Pankin
Alex (Gorky as a boy)	John Gallogly
Mother/Peasant/Electric Lady	Tanny McDonald
Lucky	Caroline Kava
Priest/Nikita/Stalin	Lloyd Battista
Maxim (Gorky as a young man)	Douglas Clark
Peasant/Party Man	J. Kevin Scannell
Chaliapin/Cement Man	Monte Jaffe
Peasant Woman	Jacque Dean
Peasant Girl/Dancer	Diane Duffy
Young Peasant/Dancer	Robert Petersen

A play in two acts. The action takes place in Old Russia during
the-revolution days and into Soviet Union.

Press: David Roggensack
Stage Managers: Franklin Keysar, Mary E. Baird

Closed Nov. 30, 1975 after 48 performances.

Martha Holmes Photos

**Top Right: Tanny McDonald, J. Kevin Scannell,
Monte Jaffe, Douglas Clark, John Gallogly**

**Philip Baker Hall, John Gallogly,
Lloyd Battista, Douglas Clark**

John Gallogly, Philip Baker Hall, Douglas Clark

AMERICAN PLACE THEATRE
Opened Monday, December 8, 1975.*
Seff Associates Limited presents Le Treteau de Paris (Jea
Rigault, Executive Director) Production of:

PHEDRE

By Racine; Director, Michel Hermon; Scenery, Michel Hart
tumes, Michel Hermon; Masks, Jean Herbin; Lighting, Pollux;
Administrator, Francisco De Castro

CAST

Hippolyte	Didier S
Theramene	Olivie
Oenone	Anita Plessner or Miche
Phedre	Jeanne
Aricie/Ismene	Lawrence F
Thesee	Michel He

A tragedy in five acts performed with one intermission. The
takes place in Trezene, city of Peloponnesus.

Stage Manager: Roland Hergault

* Closed Dec. 14, 1975 after limited engagement of 8 perform
in French.

AMERICAN PLACE THEATRE
Opened Sunday, February 15, 1976.*
The American Place Theatre presents:

EVERY NIGHT WHEN THE SUN GOES DOWN

By Phillip Hayes Dean; Director, Gilbert Moses; Scenery, Kert
Lundell; Lighting, Richard Nelson; Costumes, Judy Dearing;
Sound, Jerry Kornbluth; Music Arranged and Adapted by Howard
Roberts; Hymns performed by the Metropolitan AME Church
Choir; Technical Director, Henry Millman; Wardrobe Mistress,
Lula III

CAST

Rocky Pete	Joe Seneca
Wood	Frank Adu
Caledonia	Marge Eliot
Pretty Eddie	Roscoe Orman
Ballerina	Marki Bey
Clean Sam	Les Roberts
Sancho	Norman Matlock
Buckeyed Rose	Billie Allen

A drama in two acts. The action takes place in the recent past in
Antioch, Michigan.

Press: David Roggensack
Stage Managers: Franklin Keysar, Mary E. Baird

Closed Feb. 22, 1976 after 46 performances.

Martha Holmes Photos

Right: Frank Adu, Marki Bey

**Richard Ward, Roscoe Orman, Marge Elliot, Marki Bey, Joe Seneca, Billie Allen,
Norman Matlock**

AMERICAN PLACE THEATRE
Opened Sunday, April 18, 1976.*
The American Place Theatre presents:

THE OLD GLORY
A Trilogy

By Robert Lowell; Scenery, John Wulp; Costumes, Willa Kim;
Lighting, Neil Peter Jampolis; Technical Director, Henry Millman;
Wardrobe Mistress, Jody Mayer

CAST

ENDECOTT AND THE RED CROSS
Directed by Brian Murray; Music, Herbert Kaplan; Choreography,
Eileen Lawlor

Assawamset	Manu Tupou
Thomas Morton	Jerome Dempsey
Merry Mount Men	James Cromar, George Hall, Rene Mainguy, Colter Rule
Indians	Frank Askin, George Simson, Gerard Wagner
Assawamset's Daughter	Joan Jacklin
Mr. Blackstone	Richard Clarke
Man with stag's head	Andre Bishop
Edward	Noah Manne
Edith	Elisabeth Price
Indian Whore	Gloria Rossi
Sergeant	Thomas O'Rourke
Private	Bruce Bouchard
Soldiers	James Cromar, Rene Mainguy, Robert Rigley
Drummer	George Simson
Governor Endecott	Kenneth Harvey
Standard Bearer	Josh Clark
Man with wolf's head	Colter Rule
Palfrey	J. T. Walsh
Man dressed as witch	George Hall
Merry Mount Woman	Barbara Le Brun
Bear	Rene Mainguy
Merry Mount Girl	Sallyanne Tackus
Executioner	Frank Askin

The action takes place in the 1630's at Merry Mount, the settlement of Thomas Morton, near Wollaston, Massachusetts.

MY KINSMAN, MAJOR MOLINEUX
Director, Brian Murray; Music, Herbert Kaplan

Ferryman	Manu Tupou
Boy	Scott Sorrell
Robin	Josh Clark
First Redcoat	Rene Mainguy
Second Redcoat	Colter Rule
First Barber	Thomas O'Rourke
Tavern Keeper	J. T. Walsh
Second Barber	Bruce Bouchard
Clergyman	George Hall
Prostitute	Gloria Rossi
Colonel Greenough	Jerome Dempsey
Man in periwig	Richard Clarke
Watchman	J. T. Walsh
Major Molineux	Kenneth Harvey
Citizens of Boston	Frank Askin, Andre Bishop, James Cromar, Joan Jacklin, Barbara LeBrun, Noah Manne, Elisabeth Price, Robert Rigley, George Simson, Sallyanne Takcus, Gerard Wagner

The action takes place in Boston just before the American Revolution.

**Top Right: Paul Benjamin, John Getz,
Roscoe Lee Browne, Nicolas Coster in "Benito
Cereno"**

BENITO CERENO
Director, Austin Pendleton
Associate Director, John Parks

Captain Amasa Delano	Nicolas Cos...
John Perkins	John G...
Don Benito Cereno	Alan Mi...
Babu	Roscoe Lee Brow...
Arufal	Paul Benjan...
Francesco	Darryl Crox...
American Sailors	Bill Conway, Mark A. Fren... Steven Pally, Stephen Lawrence Smith, Daniel Stern, Peter Gelblum, Peter Low...
Negro Slaves	Make Bray, Edythe Davis, Sandra Har... Gregory Jackson, Llewellyn Jones, Bob Long, Gavin Mos... Jarett Smithwrick, Sidney Strong, Anthony Wa...

The action takes place about the year 1800, aboard the ships
President Adams and the San Domingo.

Press: David Roggensack
Stage Managers: Franklin Keysar, Mary E. Baird, Peter
Schneider, Samuel Miller

* Closed May 23, 1976 after 54 performances to appear in Ams...
dam and Paris.

Martha Holmes Photos

Noah Manne, Kenneth Harvey, Elisabeth Price, Thomas O'Rourke, Bruce Bouchard in
"Endecott and the Red Cross" Top: "My Kinsman, Major Molineux"

BIL BAIRD THEATER

Opened Sunday, November 2, 1975.*

The American Puppet Arts Council (Arthur Cantor, Executive Producer) presents:

BIL BAIRD'S MARIONETTES
Tenth Season

ALICE IN WONDERLAND: Book, A. J. Russell; Music, Joe Raposo; Lyrics, Sheldon Harnick; Scenery, Howard Mandel; Lighting, Peggy Clark; Designed and Produced by Bil and Susanna Baird; Artistic Associate, Frank Sullivan; Director, Paul Leaf; Based on the book by Lewis J. Carroll

PUPPETEERS

Olga Felgemacher	Rebecca Bondor
William Tost	Steven Widerman
Peter Baird	Brian Stashick

and the singing voices of Mary Case, George S. Irving, Sheldon Harnick, Rose Marie Jun, Ivy Austin, Margery Gray, William Tost, Bil Baird

* Closed January 18, 1976 after 87 performances. On January 24, 1976 "Winnie the Pooh" opened and played 111 performances, closing April 30, 1976.

WINNIE THE POOH: By A. A. Milne; Adapted by A. J. Russell; Music, Jack Brooks; Lyrics, A. A. Milne, Jack Brooks; Director, Bil Baird; Scenery, Howard Mandel; Lighting, Peggy Clark; Musical Director, Arranger, Alvy West; Designed and Produced by Bil and Susanna Baird; Production Manager, Douglas Gray

General Manager: Henry Senber
Assistant General Manager: Debbie Lepsinger
Press: C. George Willard

Nat Messik Photos

Fish Footman in "Alice in Wonderland"
Top: "Winnie-the-Pooh"

BROOKLYN ACADEMY OF MUSIC

Harvey Lichtenstein, Executive Director
Judith E. Daykin, General Manager

BROOKLYN ACADEMY PLAYHOUSE
Opened Wednesday, December 3, 1975.*
The Brooklyn Academy of Music presents the Kennedy Center-
Xerox Corporation American Bicentennial Theatre Production
of:

SWEET BIRD OF YOUTH

(see Broadway Calendar page 31)
Closed December 14, 1975 after limited engagement of 16 performances. Re-opened on Broadway Monday, Dec. 29, 1975.

BROOKLYN ACADEMY PLAYHOUSE
Opened Tuesday, December 16, 1975.*
The Brooklyn Academy of Music presents the Kennedy Center-
Xerox Corporation American Bicentennial Theatre Production
of:

THE ROYAL FAMILY

(see Broadway Calendar page 32)
Closed Dec. 18, 1975 after limited engagement of 16 performances. Re-opened on Broadway Tuesday, December 30, 1975.

Richard Bratten Photos

Christopher Walken, Irene Worth in "Sweet Bird of Youth" Top: Mary Layne, Rosemary Harris, Sam Levene, Eva LeGalliene, Joseph Maher, Mary Louise Wilson, George Grizzard

BROOKLYN ACADEMY OPERA HOUSE
Opened Wednesday, January 28, 1976.*
The Brooklyn Academy of Music presents the Kennedy Center-
Xerox Corporation American Bicentennial Theatre Production
of:

LONG DAY'S JOURNEY INTO NIGHT

By Eugene O'Neill; Director, Jason Robards; Scenery, Ben Edwards; Costumes, Jane Greenwood; Lighting, Ken Billington; Production Supervisor, Jack Hofsiss; Wardrobe Supervisor, Walter
Rivera; Hairstylist, Steve Atha; Assistant Director, Lois O'Connor

CAST

James Tyrone	Jason Robards
Mary Cavan Tyrone	Zoe Caldwell
James Tyrone, Jr	Kevin Conway
Edmund Tyrone	Michael Moriarty
Cathleen	Lindsay Crouse

STANDBYS AND UNDERSTUDIES: Tyrone, Ernest Graves;
Mary, Carol Teitel; Tyrone, Jr., Paul Thomas; Edmund, W. T.
Martin; Cathleen, Dyanne Hochman

A drama in three acts and five scenes. The action takes place in
the living room of the Tyrones' summer home on an August day and
night in 1912.

General Manager: Edmonstone Thompson, Jr.
Company Manager: Bill Liberman
Press: Charles Ziff, Kate MacIntyre, Deborah Ann Williams
Stage Managers: Murray Gitlin, Dyanne Hochman, W. T.
Martin

* Closed Feb. 8, 1976 after limited engagement of 16 performances.

Richard Braaten Photos

Kevin Conway, Michael Moriarty, Zoe Caldwell, Jason Robards
Top Right: Jason Robards, Zoe Caldwell

BROOKLYN ACADEMY OPERA HOUSE
Opened Wednesday, April 21, 1976.*
The Brooklyn Academy of Music by arrangement with the
Governors of the Royal Shakespeare Theatre, Stratford-upon-
Avon, England, presents the Royal Shakespeare Company
(Trevor Nunn, Artistic Director and Chief Executive) in:

HENRY V

By William Shakespeare; Director, Terry Hands; Designed by
Farrah; Music, Guy Woolfenden; Lighting, Stewart Levition;
Sound, Keith Clarke; Wardrobe Mistress, Carol Deary; Wardrobe
Supervisor, Walter Rivera; Assistant to director, Ian Judge

CAST

Chorus	Emrys James
The English:	
Archbishop of Canterbury	Jeffery Dench
Bishop of Ely	Trevor Peacock
King Henry V	Alan Howard
Humphrey Duke of Gloucester	Stephen Jenn
Thomas Duke of Clarence	Anthony Naylor
Duke of Exeter	Philip Brack
Earl of Cambridge	Barrie Rutter
Lord Scroop	Charles Dance
Sir Thomas Grey	Arthur Whybrow
Earl of Westmoreland	Reginald Jessup
Corporal Bardolph	Tim Wylton
Corporal Nym	Philip Dunbar
Ancient Pistol	Richard Moore
Boy	Peter Bourke
Mistress Quickly	Brenda Bruce
Gower	Jeffrey Dench
Fluellen	Trevor Peacock
Macmorris	Barrie Rutter
Jamy	Ken Stott
Williams	Charles Dance
Bates	Arthur Whybrow
Court	Richard Derrington
Sir Thomas Erpingham	Reginald Jessup
The French:	
King Charles VI	Clement McCallin
Dauphin	Geoffrey Hutchings
Katharine	Carolle Rousseau
Duke of Orleans	Philip Dunbar
Constable of France	Bernard Brown
Montjoy	Oliver Ford-Davies
Monsieur le Fer	Tim Wylton
Alice	Yvonne Coulette
French Bishop	Oliver Ford-Davies

Presented in two acts.

Stage Managers: Tim Richards, Anne Bonehill, David Hendry
Press: Charles Ziff, Kate MacIntyre, Kay Green

Closed May 9, 1976 after limited engagement of 23 performances.
Two performances of "Hollow Crown" were given at matinees
May 1 and May 8, 1976. The cast consisted of Jeffery Dench,
Oliver Ford-Davies, Brenda Bruce, Richard Moore, Bill Home-
wood. (No photos available)

**Top Right: Alan Howard Below: Philip Brack,
Stephen Jenn, Alan Howard, Anthony Naylor**

Richard Moore, Tim Wylton, Philip Dunbar

BROOKLYN ACADEMY/LEPERCQ SPACE
Opened Thursday, May 6, 1976.*
The Brooklyn Academy of Music presents the Mabou Mines production of:

THE RED HORSE ANIMATION

Text and Direction by Lee Breuer; Music, Philip Glass; Lighting Design, Jene Highstein

CAST

JoAnne Akalaitis
Ruth Maleczech
David Warrilow

The process and procedure of a creative act—animating an image of a red horse.

Press: Charles Ziff, Kate MacIntyre, Clint Brownfield

* Closed May 9, 1976 after limited engagement of 4 performances.

Top Right: David Warrilow, JoAnne Akalaitis, Ruth Maleczech in "The Red Horse Animation"

"Dante"

BROOKLYN ACADEMY/OPERA HOUSE
Opened Tuesday, May 25, 1976.*
The Brooklyn Academy of Music presents the Warsaw Slavic Cultural Center (E. J. Czerwinski, Artistic Director) production of:

DANTE

Written, Directed and Designed by Jozef Szajna; Based on Dante's "The Divine Comedy"; Music, Krzysztof Penderecki; Projections, Kazimierz Urbanski

CAST

Dante	Tomasz Marzecki
Beatrice	Anna Milewska
Charon	Antoni Pszoniak
Maria	Aleksandra Karzynska
Magdalene	Ewa Szykulska
Francesca	Ewa Kozlowska
Jacob	Zygmunt Maciejewski
John/The Damned	Tadeusz Wludarski
Judas	Jozef Wieczorek
Pope/Clotho	Wanda Lothe-Stanislawska
Cardinal/Atropos	Helena Norowicz
Monk/Lachesis/Megaera	Krystyna Kolodziejczyk
Medusa	Ewa Poka
Megaera	Krystyna Kolo
Fury/Monk II	Krystyna Chmielewska
Cerberus	Gustaw Kron
Penitent	Stanislaw Brudny
The Chosen	Eugeniusz Priwieziencev

* Closed May 30, 1976 after limited engagement of 7 performances.

Opened Tuesday, June 1, 1976.*

REPLIKA

Conceived and Directed by Jozef Szajna; Music, Boguslaw Schaffer

CAST

Ewa Kozlowska
Irena Jun
Stanislaw Brudny
Antonia Pszoniak
Jozef Wieczorek

A wordless odyssey through the holocaust, depicting the indomitable spirit of man, tempered by the inhumanity directed against him by himself.

Press: Charles Ziff, Kate MacIntyre, Clint Brownfield

* Closed June 6, 1976 after limited engagement of 7 performances.

CHELSEA THEATER CENTER OF BROOKLYN

Robert Kalfin, Artistic Director
Michael David, Executive Director
Burl Hash, Productions Director

BROOKLYN ACADEMY OF MUSIC
Opened Wednesday, November 26, 1975.*
Chelsea Theater Center of Brooklyn presents:

ICE AGE

By Tankred Dorst in cooperation with Ursula Ehler; English version, Peter Sander; Director, Arne Zaslove; Setting, Wolfgang Roth; Costumes, Ruth Morley; Lighting, Daniel Flannery; Technical Director, James Burke; Production Coordinator, Ginny Freedman

CAST

Old Man	Roberts Blossom
Fragile Lady	Anne Ives
Cleaning Lady/Diva	Sonia Zomina
Gardener/Man with camera	Curt Williams
Spinster	Eleanor Cody Gould
Major's Widow	Frances Pole
Oswald	Nicholas Hormann
Prof. Jenssen	Jerrold Ziman
Male Assistant	Robert Einenkel
Female Assistant	Janice Fuller
Paul	George Morfogen
Holm/Man in mask	Larry Swansen
Reich/Fat Man in mask	K. Lype O'Dell
Bank Director/Blind Man	Gary Allen
Vera	Ruth Hunt
Woman in wheelchair	Frances Bay
Old Soldier	William Robertson
Berend	Charles Mayer
Cook	Renos Mandis
Cristian	Roger DeKoven

UNDERSTUDIES: Frances Bay (Vera, Fragile Lady, Major's Widow, Cleaning Lady), Roger DeKoven (Old Man), Robert Einenkel (Reich, Paul, Oswald); K. Lype O'Dell (Cook), Curt Williams (Kristian, Jenssen, Berend), Jerrold Ziman (Bank Director, Holm), Sonia Zomina (Spinster)

A drama in two acts. The action takes place at an old people's home and the adjoining park in Norway during 1947 and 1948.

General Manager: William Craver
Press: Joel Wald, Betty Lee Hunt Associates
Stage Managers: Sherman Warner, Bob Jaffe

Closed Dec. 14, 1975 after 32 performances.

Laura W. Pettibone Photos

Top Right: Gary Allen, Larry Swansen, K. Lype O'Dell, Roberts Blossom

Roger DeKoven, Roberts Blossom

BROOKLYN ACADEMY OF MUSIC
Opened Thursday, March 4, 1976.*
Chelsea Theater Center of Brooklyn presents:

THE BOSS

By Edward Sheldon; Director, Edward Gilbert; Settings, Lawrence King; Costumes, Carrie F. Robbins; Lighting, William Mintzer; Assistant to director, Charles Conwell; Music Consultant, Mel Marvin; Hairstylist, Paul Huntley

CAST

James D. Griswold	Allan Frank
Donald Griswold	Gregory Abels
Emily Griswold	Louise Shaffer
Mitchell	John Genke
Lawrence Duncan	Dennis Lipscomb
Michael R. Regan	Andrew Jarkowsky
Davis	Richard K. Sanders
Mrs. Cuyler	Pamela Burrell
Gates	John Eames
"Porky" McCoy	Tom-Patrick Dineen
Scanlan	Chris Carrick
Archbishop Sullivan	Igors Gavon
A Cook	Pamela Burrell
French Maid	Catherine Henry Lamm
Lieutenant of Police	John Genke
Police Officers	Chris Carrick, Chip Lucia

UNDERSTUDIES: Allan Frank (Gates), Igors Gavon (Inspector), John Genke (Davis, Regan, Archbishop), Catherine Henry Lamm (Emily, Mrs. Cuyler), Dennis Lipscomb (Scanlan), Chip Lucia (Donald, Duncan, Porky), Richard K. Sanders (Mitchell)

A drama in four acts performed with one intermission. The action takes place in one of the Eastern lake-ports during 1910 and 1911.

General Manager: William Craver
Press: Joel Wald
Stage Managers: Bob Jaffe, Joseph Kavanagh

* Closed March 14, 1976 after 24 performances. Re-opened in Queens Playhouse for 16 performances.

Laura W. Pettibone Photos

Louise Shaffer, Andrew Jarkowsky

**Tom-Patrick Dineen, Andrew Jarkowsky
Top: Louise Shaffer, Chris Carrick, Andrew Jarkowsky**

CIRCLE REPERTORY COMPANY

Marshall W. Mason, Artistic Director
Jerry Arrow, Executive Director
Seventh Season

CIRCLE REPERTORY COMPANY THEATRE
Opened Thursday, June 12, 1975.*
Circle Repertory Company presents:

SPRING'S AWAKENING

By Frank Wedekind; Director, Jan P. Eliasberg; Set, Tracy Killam; Costumes, Faye Fingesten; Lighting, David Kissel; Original Music, Tom Aronis; Technical Director, Bob Yanez

CAST

Wendla	Lisa Pelikan
Mrs. Bergmann	Jo-Anne Belanger
Melchior	Arthur Marcus
Lammermeier	Kevin Geer
Moritz	Kenneth Norris
Ernst	Van Gosse
Hans	Charles T. Harper
Martha	Kate Schaefer
Thea	Cynthia Crumlish
Mrs. Gabor	Natalie Priest
Ilse	Deborah Offner
Rev. Sonnenstich	William Robertson
Judge Gabor	Thomas Barbour
Man in the mask	Roger McIntyre

A play in three acts. The action takes place in Germany in 1892

Company Manager: Barbara Darwall
Press: Sharon Madden
Stage Managers: Susana Meyer, Anne Fishel

* Closed June 15, 1975 after limited engagement of 5 performances. No photos available.

CIRCLE REPERTORY COMPANY THEATRE
Opened Wednesday, June 25, 1975.*
Circle Repertory Company presents:

NOT TO WORRY

By A. E. Santaniello; Director, Lanford Wilson; Setting, John Lee Beatty; Costumes, Jennifer von Mayrhauser; Lighting, Dennis Parichy; Sound, Chuck London, George Hansen; Technical Director, Bob Yanez; Production Coordinator, Marshall Oglesby

CAST

Larry	Brad Dourif
Tony	Rob Thirkield
Ruth	Teri Keane

A play in two acts and five scenes. The action takes place at the present time in a garden apartment in the French Quarter of New Orleans, LA.

Company Manager: Barbara Darwall
Press: Sharon Madden
Stage Managers: Walter Wood, Cathy Rennich, Sarah Rodman

* Closed July 13, 1975 after limited engagement of 20 performances.

Michael Zettler Photo

Top Right: Rob Thirkield, Brad Dourif in "Not to Worry" Below: Lisa Pelikan, Neil Flanagan, Helen Stenborg in "The Elephant in the House"

CIRCLE REPERTORY COMPANY THEATRE
Opened Sunday, November 2, 1975.*
Circle Repertory Company presents:

THE ELEPHANT IN THE HOUSE

By Berrilla Kerr; Director, Marshall W. Mason; Setting, John Lee Beatty; Costumes, Jennifer von Mayrhauser; Lighting, Dennis Parichy; Original Music, Jonathan Hogan; Sound, Charles London, George Hansen; Assistant Director, Steven Gomer; Technical Director, Earl R. Hughes

CAST

Mary Elizabeth Adams	Helen Stenborg
Francesca	Lisa Pelikan
Mr. Johnson	Neil Flanagan
Timothy	Terence Foley
Molly	Conchata Ferrell
Jenny	Stephanie Gordon
Horace	Rob Thirkield
Gwenyth	Henrietta Bagley

and Sugar, Cowboy, Cha-Cha and Apache

A play in two acts. The action takes place at the present time in Mary Elizabeth Adams' house in New York City.

Company Manager: Dennis Purcell
Press: Rima Corben
Stage Managers: Susana Meyer, Dave Clow

* Closed Nov. 23, 1976 after limited engagement of 25 performances and 7 previews.

Marc Sadoux Photos

107

CIRCLE REPERTORY COMPANY THEATRE
Opened Sunday, December 14, 1975.*
Circle Repertory Company presents:

DANCING FOR THE KAISER

By Andrew Colmar; Director, Marshall Oglesby; Settings, Atkin Pace; Costumes, Jennifer von Mayrhauser; Lighting, Dennis Parichy; Choreography, Gilda Mullette; Sound, George Hansen, Charles London; Assistant Director, Carla Granat;

CAST

Douglas North Wicksteed	Douglass Watson
Walter Skendal	Peter Burnell
Willimot	Hy Mencher
Lional Buckmaster	Tom McDermott
Erica Kroonenberg	Jacqueline Bertrand
Martha Willow	Joanna Miles
Mrs. Willow	Maryellen Flynn
Rev. Father Bernard Buller	George Hall
Leo Kroonenberg	Peter Walker
Sir Osmon Pryor	Peter Murphy
Maurice	Hy Mencher
Annie	Patricia Roberts
Judge Sweet	George Hall
Court Clerk	Hy Mencher
Dr. Alfred Brey	Tom McDermott
The Man	Jean-Pierre Stewart

A drama in two acts. The action takes place in London in 1918.

Company Manager: Dennis Purcell
Press: Rima Corben
Stage Managers: Richard Kilberg, Robin Tagliente

* Closed Jan. 4, 1976 after limited engagement of 25 performances and 7 previews.

Marc Sadoux Photos

Top Right: Peter Murphy, Peter Burnell

Peter Walker, Joanna Miles

Nancy Snyder, Daniel Seltzer

CIRCLE REPERTORY COMPANY THEATRE
Opened Sunday, January 18, 1976.*
Circle Repertory Company presents:

KNOCK KNOCK

By Jules Feiffer; Director, Marshall W. Mason; Setting, John L Beatty; Costumes, Jennifer von Mayrhauser; Lighting, Dennis P. richy; Sound, Charles London, George Hansen; Technical Directors, Earl Hughes, Robert Yanez; Assistant to director, Steve Gomer

CAST

Cohn	Daniel Seltzer
Abe	Neil Flanag
Wiseman	Judd Hirsc
Joan	Nancy Snyd
Joan's Voices and other apparitions	Judd Hirsc

A comedy in three acts. The action takes place at the present tim in a small house in the woods.

Company Manager: Dennis Purcell
Press: Rima Corben
Stage Manager: Dan Hild

* Closed Feb. 22, 1976 after 41 performances and 7 previews move to Broadway. (See Broadway Calendar page 37)

Herbert Migdoll Photos

CIRCLE REPERTORY COMPANY THEATRE
Opened Wednesday, March 10, 1976.*
Circle Repertory Company presents:

WHO KILLED RICHARD CORY?

By A. R. Gurney, Jr.; Director, Leonard Peters; Setting, Joan
renchak; Costumes, Gary Jones; Lighting, Arden Fingerhut; Mu-
al Director, Charles L. Greenberg; Choreography, Bridget Leices-
; Assistant to director, Steve Steisel; Wardrobe Mistress, Cathy
mey

CAST

chard Cory	Bruce Gray
ward/Joe/Chip	Roger Chapman
ostitute/Librarian/Emily	Jane Hallaren
ice/Louise/Bessie	Sharon Madden
se/Charlotte/Grandmother	Patricia O'Connell
sie/Mrs. Baker/Richard's Mother	Joyce Reehling
die/Richard's Father/Anarchist	Larry Rosler
octor/William/Chester	M. Jonathan Steele
ank/Rev. Davis/Ted Babcock	Robb Webb

A drama in two acts.

Company Manager: Dennis Purcell
Press: Rima Corben, Marlyn Baum
Stage Managers: Marjorie Horne, Amy Schecter

Closed March 18, 1976 after 23 performances and 9 previews.

Ken Howard Photo

Bruce Gray (c)

CIRCLE REPERTORY COMPANY THEATRE
Opened Wednesday, May 5, 1976.*
Circle Repertory Company presents:

SERENADING LOUIE

By Lanford Wilson; Director, Marshall W. Mason; Setting, John
Lee Beatty; Costumes, Jennifer von Mayrhauser; Lighting, Dennis
Parichy; Assistant to Director, John Sheehan; Artistic Staff Assis-
tant, Daniel Irvine; Administrative Staff Assistant, Marlyn Baum

CAST

Mary	Tanya Berezin
Carl	Edward J. Moore
Gabrielle	Trish Hawkins
Alex	Michael Storm

A play in two acts. The action takes place at the present time in
a suburban home north of Chicago during late October.

Company Manager: Dennis Purcell
Press: Rima Corben, Marlyn Baum
Stage Managers: Dave Clow, Amy Schecter

* Closed May 30, 1976 after limited engagement of 33 performances
and 7 previews.

Gerry Goodstein Photos

nya Berezin, Trish Hawkins, Edward J. Moore,
Michael Storm, also Right Center

THE CLASSIC THEATRE

Nicholas John Stathis, Producer

CENTRAL PRESBYTERIAN CHURCH
November 12–30, 1975 (16 performances)

MARY TUDOR by Victor Hugo; Director, Maurice Edwards; Sets, James Cuomo; Costumes, Maryanne White; Music, George Prideaux; Lights, Howard Wallowitz; Technical Director, Terry Hunter; Stage Managers, Valerie Laura Imbarrato, Ron Cappa. CAST: Linda Barnhurst, Russell Costen, John Getz, Elek Hartman, Toni Kalem, Robert Milton, Norman Sample, Ron Cappa, Dan Hall, Tom Jarus, Lloyd Kay, Ron Piretti

HAIK & ALICE KAVOOKJIAN AUDITORIUM
January 18–February 3, 1976 (12 performances)

BADVI HAMAR (For the Sake of Honor) by Alexandre Shirvanzade; Translation, Nishan Parlakian; Director, Maurice Edwards; Sets, Tony Giovanetti; Costumes, Ruth Thomason; Lights, Annie Rech, Diana Conkling, Betsey McKearnan; Props, Renee Dodge; Stage Manager, Valerie L. Imbarrato. CAST: David Kerman, Elia Braca, Dan Lutzky, Michael Hardstark, Wende Sherman, Miriam Guttman-Iranyi, Dan Rubinate, Vincent Millard, Lawrence Harbison, Annie Rech

CENTRAL PRESBYTERIAN CHURCH
March 28–April 11, 1976 (12 performances)

THE APOCALYPSE ACCORDING TO J - J (ROUSSEAU) by Mario Apollonio (World Premiere); Translated by Anne Paolucci; Director, Maurice Edwards; Sets and Lights, Tony Giovanetti; Costumes, John Ahrens; Music, Joseph Albano; Choreography, Carin Molnar; Technical Assistants, Renee Dodge, Anthony Borovicka; Stage Manager, D. Jule Oliver. CAST: John Michalski (Jean-Jacques Rousseau), Joseph Frisari, Annette Hunt, Tom Jarus, Ellen Kelly, Jillian Lindig, Robert Milton, Wendy Nute, Emile Van der Noot, Craig Wyckoff, Loyola Boys Choir (Rona Klinghoffer, Director)

CLASSIC THEATRE
April 22–May 9, 1976 (12 performances)

A REPORT TO AN ACADEMY by Franz Kafka; Adapted, Designed and Directed by Gerd Staub; Lighting, Technical Adviser, Anthony Borovicka; Assistant to director, Matthias Boettrich; Stage Manager, Terry Hunter; Press, Alan Eichler. CAST: Henry Bal Robert Milton, Linda Barnhurst

Ann Blackstock Photos

Ron Piretti, Lloyd Kaye in "Mary Tudor"

Henry Bal in "A Report to the Academy"

Robert Milton, John Merensky, and above:
Wendy Nute in "The Apocalypse according to J. J

110

COLONNADES THEATRE LAB

Michael Lessac, Artistic Director-Producer
Tom V. V. Tammi, Associate Artistic Director
Louisa Anderson, Administrative Director

COLONNADES THEATRE LAB
Opened Tuesday, December 2, 1975.*
Colonnades Theatre Lab presents;

SECOND WIND

By David Morgan; Director, Michael Lessac; Composer, Joseph
unt; Sets and Projections, Robert U. Taylor; Lighting, Joe Ka-
insky; Costumes, Joan Ferenchak, Donato Moreno; Sound, Gary
arris; Technical Director, Robert H. Rickner; Wardrobe Master,
yke Fiorentine

CAST

ene	Jacqueline Cassel
evor	Louis Giambalvo
ish	Charlie Stavola
rs. Galbraith	Sherrill Wainer

Stage Managers: Michael Boonstra, Patricia Hannigan

Closed Jan. 18, 1976 after limited engagement of 15 performances
in repertory.

Opened Tuesday, December 2, 1975.*

CINEMA SOLDIER

By Paavo Tammi; Director, Tom Tammi; Musical Arrangements,
lexandra O'Karma, Miriam Moses; Lighting, Joe Kaminsky;
raphics, Carol Banever

CAST

ldier	Rhea Perlman
nes	Ruth Wallman
oltz	Ellene Winn
anist	Alexandra O'Karma

Press: Ruth Wallman
Stage Managers: Michael Boonstra, Louisa Anderson

Closed Jan. 18, 1976 after limited engagement of 14 performances
in repertory.

**Top Right: Ruth Wallman, Rhea Perlman,
Ellene Winn in "Cinema Soldier"**

**Jacqueline Cassel, Edward Edwards
in "A Month in the Country"**

COLONNADES THEATRE LAB
Opened Thursday, December 4, 1975.*
Colonnades Theatre Lab presents:

A MONTH IN THE COUNTRY

By Ivan Turgenev; Adaptation, David Morgan; Director, Michael
Lessac; Music Coordinator, Joseph Blunt; Sets, Robert U. Taylor;
Costumes, Donato Moreno, Joan Ferenchak; Sound, Gary Harris

CAST

Adam Ivanitch Schaff	Bob Byrd
Anna Semyonovna	Marian Baer
Lizaveta Bogdanovna	Sherrill Wainer
Natalya Petrovna	Alexandra O'Karma
Mihail Alexandritch Rakitin	Tom V. V. Tammi
Kolya	Sima Chalfy
Alexei Nicolaitch Beliayev	Edward Edwards
Mattvei	Charlie Stavola
Ignaty Illyitch Shpigelsky	Bill E. Noone
Vera Alexandrovna	Jacqueline Cassel
Arkady Sergeitch Yslaev	John Hammil
Katya	Linda Swenson
Afanasy Ivanitch Bolshintsov	Louis Giambalvo

Press: Ruth Wallman
Stage Managers: Michael Boonstra, Patricia Hannigan

* Closed Jan. 14, 1976 after 14 performances in repertory.

COLONNADES THEATRE LAB
Opened Tuesday, December 9, 1975.*
Colonnades Theatre Lab presents:

REFLECTIONS

By David Morgan; Based on story by Oscar Wilde; Director,
Michael Lessac; Music, Miriam Moses; Sets, Robert U. Taylor;
Lighting, Joe Kaminsky; Costumes, Joan Ferenchak; Sound, Gary
Harris; Choreographic Assistant, Bill E. Noone; Pianist, Elvira
Steinberg

CAST

The Reflection	Jacqueline Cassel
The Narrator	Peter Scolari
The Infanta	Deborah Davison
The Duchess	Sherrill Wainer
The King	Tom V. V. Tammi
Yuval	John Hammil
Nada	Portia Patterson
Vita	Rhea Perlman
The Hunter	Charlie Stavola
The Dwarf	Louis Giambalvo

Press: Ruth Wallman
Stage Managers: Michael Boonstra, Jim Palmer

* Closed Jan. 16, 1976 after 16 performances in repertory.

Diane Gorodnitzki Photos

COUNTERPOINT THEATRE COMPANY

Howard Green, Artistic Director
Gonzalo Madurga, Associate Artistic Director
Paulene Reynolds, Managing Director

COUNTERPOINT THEATRE

October 3 - 20, 1975 (12 performances)

MISS JULIE and THE STRONGER by August Strindberg; Director, Gonzalo Madurga; Costumes, Ernesto Leston; Scenery, Minda Chipurnoi; Lighting, James Singlar; Stage Managers, Fred Berry, Darleen Bever. CAST: "The Stronger" - Paulene Reynolds (Miss Y), Linda Geiser (Mrs. X) Howard Green (Waiter), "Miss Julie" - Howard Green (Jean), Linda Geiser (Kristin), Paulene Reynolds (Julie)

November 21 - December 15, 1975 (16 performances)

CHILDREN OF DARKNESS by Edwin Justus Mayer; Director, Howard Green; Scenery, Minda Chipurnoi; Costumes, Ernesto Leston; Lighting, Ronald Daley; Assistant to director, Darleen Bever; Technical Director, George Coleman; Sound, Gary Tims. CAST: George Salerno (Mr. Snap), George Coleman (First Bailiff), Carl Brown (Cartwright), Don Marletto (Fierce), Tom Leo (Jonathan), Donald Berry (Count), Marina Stefan (Laetitia), Fred Berry (Second Bailiff), Jeremy Brook (Wainwright)

January 16 - February 2, 1976 (12 performances)

A CHEKHOV PORTFOLIO by Anton Chekhov; Director, Howard Green; Scenery, Lighting, George Coleman; Costumes, Carol D. Wahlquist; Production Assistant, Darleen Bever; Stage Managers, Fred Berry, Rawle Brome, Cindy Russell, Gary Tims. CAST: "The Harmfulness of Tobacco" - Ed Crowley (Lecturer), "The Brute" - Tom Leo (Luka), Annie Kravat, Paulene Reynolds (Mrs. Popov), James Himelsbach (Smirnov), "Summer in the Country" - Tom Leo (Murashkin), Don Marlette (Tolkachov), "Swan Song" - Sam Gray (Vassily), Don Marlette (Nikita)

March 5-22, 1976 (12 performances)

ROCKET TO THE MOON by Clifford Odets; Director, Joel Friedman; Lighting, Deborah Lynne Helitzer; Costumes, Ernesto Leston; Technical Director, George Coleman; Company Manager, Fred Berry; Stage Managers, Rawle Brome, Gareth Tims. CAST: Howard Green (Ben), Sylvia Gassell (Belle), Tanny McDonald (Cleo), John J. Martin (Phil), Sam Gray (Prince), Len Auclair (Frenchy), Elek Hartman (Wax)

April 23 - May 10, 1976 (12 performances)

THE REHEARSAL by Jean Anouilh; Director, Howard Green; Scenery and Lighting, George L. Coleman; Costumes, Ernesto Leston; Stage Manager, Cindy Russell. CAST: Elek Hartman (Damiens), Linda Geiser (Countess), Geoffrey Webb (Count), Rebecca Darke (Hortensia), Gonzalo Madurga (Hero), Rod Britt (Villebosse), Elaine Kilden (Lucile)

Right: Sam Gray, Donald Marlette in "A Chekhov Portfolio" Above: Marina Stefan, Carl Brown, Donald Berry, George Salerno, Tom Leo in "Children of Darkness"

Linda Geiser, Paulene Reynolds in "Miss Julie"

Gonzalo Madurga, Elaine Kilden in "The Rehearsal"

Howard Green, Tanny McDonald in "Rocket to the Moon"

THE CUBICULO

Philip Meister, Artistic Director
Elaine Sulka, Managing Director
John Dudich, Publicity Director

THE CUBICULO
September 18 - October 11, 1975 (12 performances)

THE MEMOIRS OF CHARLIE POPS by Joseph Hart; Director, John Bettenbender; Scenery, Joseph Miklojcik; Lighting and Projections, Michael Tomko; Sound, William Motyka; Costumes, Vickie McLaughlin; Technical Adviser, Priscilla Travis; Stage Managers, Donna Miklojcik, Tom Iovanne. CAST: Frank Ammirati (Charlie Pops), Keith Kermizian (Robert), Ann Rottman (Anna), Robin Siegel (Mary), Fred Sirasky (Coolie), Edward Yanowitz (John), Rita Bascari (Jeannie), Brian Connors, William Mastrosimone (Two Men), Italian Ladies: Sherry Akselrod, Esther Blanchford, Mary Ann Michaels, Wendy Lyon, Yasmin Vargas

September 25 - 28, 1975 (4 performances)

WEEKS by Nancy Heikin; Songs, Nancy Heikin; Lighting, Tammy Temptation; Stage Manager, Nicki Nelki. CAST: Susan Topping (Inner), Michael Haynes (Herr Guitar), Nancy Heikin (Outer)

October 23 - November 8, 1975 (12 performances)

SURVIVING THE BARBED WIRE CRADLE by Francine Storey; Director, Dana Roberts; Stage Manager, Lawrence Harbison; Lighting, Curt Ostermann; Assistant Stage Manager, Geraldine Kedrick; Art Director, Kenneth G. Beck. CAST: Janice Kay Young (Maureen), Jen Jones (Nanna), John Camera (The Man)
TERRIBLE JIM FITCH by James Leo Herlihy; Director, Dana Roberts; Stage Manager, Lawrence Harbison CAST: Mary Ed Porter (Sally), Richard Zobel (Jim)

November 12 - 22, 1975 (8 performances)

A GOOD OLD-FASHIONED REVUE conceived and directed by Les Barkdull; Scenery, Michael Hotopp, Paul dePass; Lighting, Randy Becker; Costumes, Al Sardella; Musical Direction, John Franceschina; Musical Staging, Judy Haskell; Stage Managers, Lee Cotterell, Barbara Ramsey; Press, Alan Eichler. CAST: Carleton Carpenter, Sue Lawless, Gordon Ramsey, Harold Davis Ann Hodapp

November 14 - 30, 1975 (12 performances)

PEOPLE FROM DIVISION STREET by Studs Terkel; Adapted by Alexandra Devon; Director, MacIntyre Dixon; Assistant to director, Philip Visco; Producer, Pegasus Productions; Associate Producer-Stage Manager, Carole McPhee; Lighting, Howard Kessler; Scenery, Michael deSouza. CAST: MacIntyre Dixon, Saundra MacDonald, Gail Ryan, Jay Bonnell, Owen Hollander, Beverly Wideman, Jeanne Schlegel, Philip Visco

December 4 - 21, 1975 (12 Performances)

BOXES by Gary Martin; Director, Gene Becker; Sets, Leon Munier; Lighting, Rafe Scheinblum; Costumes, Dianne Huffman; Assistant Director, Ronnie Asbell; Technical Director, Randy Becker; Stage Managers, Jill Harwood, Geri Silk. CAST: "Benson and Cissy" - Darrie Lawrence (Cissy), Mark Curran (Benson), Ron Harrington (Moriarity), Bilo Bryant (Wanda), "Boxes Going to Salem" - Margot Hastings (Annette), Michael Kolba (Sam), Ron Harrington (Carlos), "Two See beside the Sea"-Don Welch (Jon), Ron Welch (Don)

Conrad Ward Photos

**Top Right: Carleton Carpenter in
"Good Old-Fashioned Revue"
Below: Raymond Stough,
Mary Ellen Mathews in "Holy Ghosts"**

Sally Mercer, Jeffrey DeMunn in "Founding Father"

113

THE CUBICULO

January 28 - February 8, 1976 (12 performances)

THE HOME by Kent Anderson and Bengt Bratt; Translated from the Swedish by Yvonne Sandstroem; Adapted and Directed by Bob Horen; Choreography, Louanna Gardner; Music, Don Arrington; Designed by Jay B. Keene; Stage Managers, David Rosenberg, Philip Hirsch, Mary Jo Robertiello. CAST: Pat Carmichael (Dagny), Suzanne Granfield (Jenny), Gwendolyn Brown (Matilda), Ann Freeman (Svea), Lee Billington (Charlotte), Fred Carmichael (Hjalmar), Peter Murphy (Nils), Kenneth L. Chomont (Albin), Edwin Young (Johan), John Merensky (Nurse Siv), Gary Swartz (Nurse Gunnel), K. T. Baumann (Anette).

January 28, 1976 (1 performance)

DUETS OF DRAMA PRESENTED BY the Inscape Company, (Jacqueline Berger, Roseann Sheridan, Artistic Directors); Technical Director, Randy Becker; Art Design, Lighting, Marian Bruhns; Poetry and Narration, Marianne Wrobleski. CAST: "I Hate the Situation More Than I Love You" by Jacqueline Berger: William Van Hunter (Burt), Roseann Sheridan (Norma) "Kiss the World Goodbye" by Jack Hollander; Director, William Van Hunter: Michael McCarthy (Charles), Roseann Sheridan (Violet), Jacqueline Berger (Joanne), William Van Hunter (George), Tim Silver (Milton), Gil Tores (Leo)

February 19- March 7, 1976 (12 performances)

HOLY GHOSTS by Romulus Linney; Director, John Olon-Scrymgeour; Scenery and Lighting, Jane Thurn; Music Coach, Janet Siegal; Stage Manager, Deborah Teller. CAST: Susan Berger (Nancy), Guy Boyd (Coleman), Robert Baines (Rogers), John Wilkerson (Obediah), Charles Harper (Virgil), Frank Rohrbach (Orin), Martin Treat (Howard), Dolores Kenan (Lorena), Josephine Nichols (Mrs. Wall), Mary Ellen Mathews (Muriel), Curt May (Billy), Ric Lavin (Obediah Sr.), Robert Milton (Carl), Elaine Sulka (Bonnie), Raymond Stough (Cancer Man)

THE BEDBUG by Vladimir Mayakovsky; Adapted and Directed by John Merensky; Designed by Joe Phillips; Lighting, Paul Harkins; Music, Joseph Hardin; Movement, Francine Storey; Artistic Director, Philip Meister; Stage Manager, Jim Singlar; Presented by The Cubiculo Playmakers. CAST: Karen Bernhard, Kenneth Freeman, Joseph Hardin, Dolores Kenan, Ron Klein, Bill Maloney, Sally Mercer, John Merensky, Jim Singlar, Francine Storey

"The Bedbug"   Pictures of People Ph

April 5 - 25, 1976 (12 performances)

DR. HERO by Israel Horovitz; Director, Lee Rachman; Scen Trueman Kelley; Lighting, Bradley G. Richart; Sound, Bob J Program Coordinators, John Dudich, Dinah Carlson; Stage M ager, Barbara Alpert. CAST: Anthony Mark, Leah Brecher, M Keeler, Nancy Mette, Bob Perry, Alan Rosenberg

April 22 - May 9, 1976

FOUNDING FATHER by Amlin Gray; Director, Consta Clarke; Set, Ted Enik; Lighting, Paul Harkins; Costumes, C Franks; Technical Director, John Moran; Stage Manager, C. Kuypers; Special Consultant, Mary E. Devine. CAST: Jeffrey Munn (Aaron Burr), Karen Bernhard (Margaret), Perrin Fe (Leroy), Ed Powell (Robinson), Ed Crowley (Harmon), Irving M man (James), Sally Mercer (Theodosia), John Merensky (Gide Jeffrey Herman (Marques), Ed Powell (John Marshall), Richm

Hoxie (George Hay)

May 11 - 16, 1976 (5 performances)

CLYTEMNESTRA by Elaine Sulka; Director, Philip Meister; C tumes, Sharon Hollinger; Setting, Marie McKim; Music and So John Franceschina; Movement, Francine Storey; Lighting, Wil Lambert; Stage Manager, Kirk Wolfinger; Technical Director, B ley G. Richart. CAST: Joanna Merlin (Clytemnestra), Cynthia D low (Electra), Irene Frances Kling, Darrie Lawrence, Jea Schlegel (Voci/Furies), Women: Eliza DeCroes, Ann Freem Willi Kirkham, Amy Margaret Samuelson, Marilynn Winb Grace Woodard

May 20 - 30, 1976 (8 performances)

OH SPEAKIES by Sandro Key-Aberg; Translated from Swedish Goran Prinyz-Pahlson and Brian Rothwell; Adapted and Dire by Bob Horen; Choreography, Louanna Gardner; Lights and V als, Jay Keene; Production Supervisor, David Rosenberg; St Manager, Carmalita Fuentes. CAST: K. T. Baumann, Julia Cu Suzanne Granfield, Douglas Maxwell, Frank Vohs, Edwin Yo

May 25 - 30, 1976 (8 performances)

STAUF by Michael Sahl and Eric Salzman; Composed and Dire by Mr. Sahl and Mr. Salzman; Presented by the Quog Music The (Eric Salzman, Artistic Director; Richard Green, Executive D tor; Choreography, Anne Sahl; Scenery, Christina Weppner; C tumes, Sally Ann Parsons; Tape, Laurie Spiegel; Lighting, Winberry; Stage Manager, Andrew Bates; Keyboards, Michael S Jordan Kaplan. CAST: William Parry (Stauf), Denise Delape (Margarita), Gerrianne Raphael (Kali), Michael Best (Dr. Jo Peggy Levine, David Barney (Dancers)

Joanna Merlin, Cynthia Darlow in "Clytemnestra"

114

DUME SPANISH THEATRE

Herberto Dume, Producer-Artistic Director
Enrique Gomez, Public Relations

DUME SPANISH THEATRE
June 13 - 29, 1975 (15 performances)

EL MALENTENDIDO by Albert Camus; Produced and Directed
by Herberto Dume; Sets, Guido Betancourt; Costumes, Serge Pinckney; Lighting, Wilfredo Zagal; Hairstylist, Julio Ambros; Make-up, Rolando Zaragoza; Assistant Director, Wilfredo Zagal. CAST: Enrique Gomes (Jesus), Isabel Segovia (Marta), Sol (La Madre), Idalia Diaz (Maria), Rafael Delgado (El Viejo)

October 10 - November 9, 1975 (23 performances)

SANTA CAMILA DE LA HABANA VIEJA by Jose R. Brene; Produced and Directed by Herberto Dume; Sets, Guido Betancourt; Costumes, Serge Pinckney; Assistant Director, Juan Carlos Gimenez. CAST: Mercedes Enriquez (Camila), Antonieta Blanco (Cuca), William Perez (Nico), Emma Vilvas (Antonia), Mateo Gomez (Pirey), Israel Ramos (Bocachula), Esther Rivera (Madrina), Idalia Diaz (Leonor), Teresa Pernas (Jacinta), Emilio Rodriguez (Teodoro)

November 19 - December 7, 1975 (15 performances)

LA SENORITA JULIA by August Strindberg; Produced and Directed by Herberto Dume; Sets, Guido Betancourt; Costumes, Serge Pinckney; Assistant Director, Juan Carlos Gimenez; Make-up, Rolando Zaragoza. CAST: Teresa Yenque (Cristina), Manuel Yesckas (Juan), Isabel Segovia (Julia), Belinda Roger (Criada), Juan Carlos Gimenez (Criado)

January 30 - February 29, 1976 (15 performances)

BURLESQUE and LA RELACION by Lorenzo Piriz-Carbonell; Sets, Guido Betancourt; Costumes, Serge Pinckney; Assistant Director, Juan Carlos Gimenez; General Director, Herberto Dume. CAST: "Burlesque" Patricia Rodriguez (Lina), Manuel Yesckas (Tony), "La Relacion" Teresa Yenque (Rosa), Freddy Valle (Brian)

April 2 - May 30, 1976 (29 performances)

LA NOCHE DE LOS ASESINOS by Jose Triana; Director, Herberto Dume; Sets, Guido Betancourt; Costumes, Serge Pinckney; Make-up Rolando Zaragoza; Stage Manager, Mario Castillo. CAST: Silvia Brito (Cuca), Manuel Yesckas (Lalo), Teresa Yenque (Beba)

Rafael Llerena Photos

**Top Right: Mercedes Enriquez,
William Perez in "Santa Camila ..."
Below: Teresa Yenque,
Freddy Valle in "Le Relacion"**

**Sol, Enrique Gomez,
Isabel Segovia in "El Malentendido"**

Isabel Segovia, Manuel Yesckas in "La Senorita Julia"

115

EQUITY LIBRARY THEATRE

George Wojtasik, Managing Director
Lynn Montgomery, Production Director
Ann B. Grassilli, Producer ELT Informals

EQUITY LIBRARY THEATRE
Opened Thursday, October 16, 1975.*
Equity Library Theatre presents:

THE PURSUIT OF HAPPINESS

By Lawrence Langner and Armina Marshall Langner; Director, Tisa Ching; Costumes, Susan Sigrist; Set, John Barker; Music, Louis Stewart; Lighting, Pat Stern; Hairstylist, J. Alexander

CAST

Meg	Grace Woodard
Mose	Peter Yoshida
Capt. Aaron Kirkland	Alvin Lum
Colonel Sherwood	Gus Fleming
Prudence	Deborah Moldow
Comfort	Lilah Kan
Max	Peter Julian
Thad	Dennis Sakamoto
Rev. Banks	Stan Kahn

A comedy in 2 acts and 4 scenes. The action takes place in the parlor of the Kirkland farm in Westville, Connecticut.

Press: Lewis Harmon, Sol Jacobson
Stage Managers: Laurence Rothenberg, Nancy T. Finn

* Closed Oct. 26, 1975 after limited engagement of 14 performances.

**Top Right: Dennis Sakamoto,
Stan Kahn, Alvin Lum, Deborah Moldow**

EQUITY LIBRARY THEATRE
Opened Thursday, November 6, 1975.*
Equity Library Theatre presents:

TENDERLOIN

Book, George Abbott, Jerome Weidman; Based on novel by Samuel Hopkins Adams; Music, Jerry Bock; Lyrics, Sheldon Harnick; Director, Robert Brink; Choreographer, Rick Atwell; Musical Direction and Dance Arrangements, Bill Grossman; Vocal Arrangements, Bill Grossman, Thomas Helm; Assistant Musical Director, Thomas Helm; Settings, James Steere; Lighting, Jeffrey Schissler; Costumes, Mimi Berman Maxmen

CAST

Tommy	Brad Blaisdell
Nita	Sherry Rooney
Lt. Schmidt	Jim Hillgartner
Rev. Brock	Stan Page
Gertie	Beverly Hartz
Maggie	Sally Mitchell
Margie	Adrienne Del Monte
Bridget	Elaine Rinehart
Terence	Steven Rotblatt
Richard	Craig Schaefer
Angela	Amanda Castle
Jessica	Suzanne Ford
Laura	Pamela McLernon
Ellington	William Perley
Purdy	Richard Rossomme
Joe Kovack	Alan Abrams
Martin	Michael Makman
Rooney	Marcus Smythe
Nellie	Deborah Geffner
Sgt. Becker	Douglass Wenrich
Jake	Jerry Colker
Frye	Neal Thompson
Liz	Janice Ehrlich
Deacon	Michael Zeke Zaccaro
Lillie	Betsy Lapka

MUSICAL NUMBERS: "Bless This Land," "Little Old New York," "Dr. Brock," "Artificial Flowers," "What's in It for You," "Reform," "I Wonder What It's Like," "Tommy, Tommy," "Lovely Laurie," "Picture of Happiness," "Shame Dance," "Dear Friend," "Army of the Just," "Money Changes Hands," "Good Clean Fun," "My Miss Mary," "My Gentle Young Johnny," "The Trial," "Tenderloin Celebration," "Nobody Cares," Epilogue

A musical in 2 acts and 18 scenes. The Action takes place on the Island of Manhattan in the latter part of the 19th Century.

Press: Lewis Harmon, Sol Jacobson
Stage Managers: Robert Bennett, Nancy Harrington, Amy F. Leveen

* Closed Nov. 23, 1975 after limited engagement of 22 performances.

Gary Wheeler Photo

**Adrienne Del Monte, Sherry Rooney,
Beverly Hartz, Sally Mitchell**

ANOTHER LANGUAGE

By Rose Franken; Director, Leonard Peters; Set, Calvin Churchman; Lighting, Todd Lichtenstein; Costumes, Dennis O'Connor; Assistant to director, Bob Dixon; Hairstylist, J. Alexander; Wardrobe Mistress, Linda Kavy

CAST

Mrs. Hallam	Mildred Dana
Mr. Hallam	Warrington Winters
Harry Hallam	James Doerr
Helen Hallam	Nicki Kaplan
Walter Hallam	Mel Boudrot
Grace Hallam	June Squibb
Paul Hallam	Robert Bonds
Etta Hallam	Marjorie Lovett
Victor Hallam	Ron Frazier
Stella Hallam	Margaret Whitton
Jerry Hallam	Dennis Boutsikaris

A play in 3 acts. The action takes place in the Hallams' home during October in the early 1930's.

Press: Lewis Harmon, Sol Jacobson
Stage Managers: Mary Burns, Marge Pfleiderer

* Closed Dec. 14, 1975 after limited engagement of 14 performances.

Gary Wheeler Photo

Marjorie Lovett, Nicki Kaplan, June Squibb

PANAMA HATTIE

Music and Lyrics, Cole Porter; Book, Herbert Fields, B. G. DeSylva: Adaptation, Charles Abbott, Fredric Dehn; Director, Charles Abbott; Musical Direction, Eileen LaGrange; Choreography, Roger Braun; Musical Numbers Staged by Charles Abbott, Roger Braun; Vocal and Dance Arrangements, Eileen LaGrange; Sets, Philipp Jung; Lighting, Emily Jefferson; Costumes and Hairstyles, Mimi Berman Maxmen; Assistant Musical Director, Thomas Helm

CAST

Skat	Robert Browning
Windy	Terrance McKerrs
Woozy	Michaeljohn McGann
Mac	Christopher Wynkoop
Florrie	May Keller
Hattie Maloney	Mary Ellen Ashley
Leila Tree	Lynn Martin
Nick Bullett	Michael Davis
Geraldine Bullett	Diana Barrows
Vivien Budd	Douglas Hayle
Whitney Randolph/Admiral Tree	Christopher Wynkoop
Sea Biscuit	Nick

PANAMANIANS, GUESTS, SAILORS: Robert Longbottom (Bootblack/M.P.), Vernon Spencer (Bootblack/Captain/Conga Drummer), Donn Hollander (Father/Announcer), Martha Deering (Mother/Senorita), Mark Barrows (Son), K. K. Preece (Vendor/-Girl with ice cubes), Steve Belin (Newsboy/Messenger/Henry), Robert Lintner (Waiter), Sue Anne Gershenson (Girl on beach/Girl with leis), J. Thomas Wierney (Boy on beach/Conga Drummer), Rick DeFilipps (Stranger/Guard), Karen Keller (Mrs. Foxcroft-/Girl with Cards), Marilyn Firment (Guest/Girl with smile), Linda Madama (Senorita/Girl with pinatas), Dione Messina (Girl with two ribs)

MUSICAL NUMBERS: "A Stroll on the Plaza," "Visit Panama," "My Mother Would Love You," "I've Still Got My Health," "Make It Another Old Fashioned," "Let's Be Buddies," "Don't Look at Me That Way," "Who Would Have Dreamed Dance," "I'm Throwing a Ball Tonight, "Fiesta," "So Near and Yet So Far," "I've Got You under My Skin," "Fresh as a Daisy," "You Said It," "Join It Right Away," Finale

A musical in 2 acts and 12 scenes. The action takes place in Panama City

Press: Sol Jacobson, Lewis Harmon
Stage Managers: Eve Sorel, Rona Cappa, P. Steven Shlansky

* Closed February 1, 1976 after limited engagement of 22 performances.

**Douglas Hayle, Diana Barrows,
Michael Davis, Mary Ellen Ashley**

EQUITY LIBRARY THEATRE
Opened Thursday, February 12, 1976.*
Equity Library Theatre presents:

MISSOURI LEGEND

By E. B. Ginty; Director, Thom Molyneaux; Scenery, Marla Schweppe; Lighting, Timothy Galvin; Costumes, Paula Davis; Musical Direction, Earl Wentz; Additional Music and Lyrics, Earl Wentz, Thom Molyneaux

CAST

Billy Gashade	Earl Wentz
Aunt Belle	Jeanne Schlegel
Frank Howard	Todd Drexel
Jim Cummins	Peter Looney
Charlie Johnson	Michael Cutt
Bob Johnson	Michael Oakes
Mrs. Howard	Sofia Landon
Thomas Howard	Bill Tatum
Martha	Jody Hingle
Widow Weeks	Susanne Marley
Hosea "Pop" Hickey	Bill Wiley
Sam	James Galvin
George	Ray Rantapaa
Asa	Michael Zeke Zaccaro
Jenny	Annie O'Neill
Trapper's Wife	Georgia Southcotte
Police Commissioner Gregg	Harry Carlson
The Reverend	Ray Rantapaa

A play in 2 acts and 6 scenes. The action takes place in Missouri in March in the past.

Press: Sol Jacobson, Lewis Harmon
Stage Managers: Ed Oster, Amy F. Leveen, Tom Nagle

* Closed Feb. 22, 1976 after limited engagement of 14 performances.

Gary Wheeler Photo

Sofia Landon, Harry Carlson, Bill Tatum

EQUITY LIBRARY THEATRE
Opened Thursday, March 4, 1976.*
Equity Library Theatre presents:

MAGGIE FLYNN

Book, Music, Lyrics, Hugo Peretti, Luigi Creatore, George D. Weiss; Book in collaboration with Morton DaCosta; Based on idea by John Flaxman; Conceived, Directed, Staged by William Koch; Musical Concept and Direction, Thomas Helm; Scenery and Lighting, Richard B. Williams; Costumes, Susan Tsu; Assistant to director, Joanne Benson; Wardrobe Mistress, Shelly Friedman

CAST

Austin Colyer (O'Brian, Ed Waters, Jenkins, Ambassador), Deborah Combs (Mary O'Cleary, Mrs. Schultz), Paul A. Corman (Timmy, Schultz), Mike Dantuono (Farraday, Chauncey), Bette Glenn (Maggie Flynn), Richard Halpern (Carter, O'Rourke, William, Piedmont, Opdyke), Mark Hattan (O'Reilly, Mulligan, Sgt. Andrew, Efram, O'Shaughnessy), Parks Hill (Walter, Logan, Will Jefferson, Senator Savage), Linda Kampley (Hyacinth, Molly, Mrs. Van Horn, Mrs. Parkington), Nita Novy (Jenny, Violet, Mrs. Van Stock, Mrs. Opdyke), Ian O'Connell (O'Leary, O'Shea, Sebastian, Bob Jefferson, Gen. Parkington), Paula Parker (Tessie, Pansy, Mrs. Humperdink, Bearded Lady, Mrs. Savage), Ross Petty (Phineas Flynn), Bill Roberts (Sprague Sgt., Suggins, Erasmus, Donnelly), Cathy Roskam (Gladys, Chrysanthemum, Mrs. Vanderhoff)

MUSICAL NUMBERS: "Overture of Coming Attractions," "Cold Morning Montage," "Nice Cold Morning," "Hot Morning Montage," "Any Other Way," "Maggie Flynn," "Learn How to Laugh," "Look around Your Little World," "Thank You Song," "I Won't Let It Happen Again," "Homeless Children," "How about a Ball," "They're Never Gonna Make Me Fight," "Pitter Patter," "It Works!," "Why Can't I Walk Away?," "Game of War," "Let's Drink to That," "Mr. Clown"

A musical in 2 acts and 14 scenes. The action takes place in the Irish Bowery of New York City in 1863.

Press: Lewis Harmon, Sol Jacobson
Stage Managers: Ellen Zalk, R. Bruce Martin, Camille Monte

* Closed March 21, 1976 after limited engagement of 22 performances.

Gary Wheeler Photo

Mark Hattan, Richard Halpern, Bette Glenn, Ian O'Connell, Paul Corman, Parks Hill

EQUITY LIBRARY THEATRE
Opened Thursday, April 1, 1976.*
Equity Library Theatre presents:

THE RIMERS OF ELDRITCH

By Lanford Wilson; Director, Cyprienne Gabel; Scenery, John C. Jackson; Costumes, Joyce Aysta; Lighting, Patrika Brown; Associate Scenic Designer, Kenneth A. Shewer; Wardrobe Mistress, Maggie Raywood

CAST

Judge-Preacher	Kender Jones
Wilma Atkins	Virginia Downing
Martha Truit	Joan G. Gilbert
Nelly Windrod	Martha Miller
Mary Windrod	Rose Lischner
Robert Conklin	Daniel Landon
Trucker	Robert Einenkel
Cora Groves	Ruth Livingston
Walter	Richard Harmel
Eva Jackson	Amy Wright
Josh Johnson	Timothy Wallace
Skelly Mannor	William Robertson
Peck Johnson	Wally Duquet
Evelyn Jackson	Edith Greenfield
Mavis Johnson	Shirley Bodtke
Patsy Johnson	Valli Hanley
Lena Truit	Deborah Savadge

A play in two acts. The action takes place at the present time in Eldritch, a small former mining town in the Middle West with a population of about 70.

Press: Lewis Harmon, Sol Jacobson
Stage Managers: Amy Pell, David Rosenberg

* Closed April 11, 1976 after limited engagement of 14 performances.

Gary Wheeler Photo

**Top Right: Amy Wright, Daniel Landon
in "The Rimers of Eldritch"**

**Randy Hugill, Kaylyn Dillehay, Nancy Salis,
George F. Maguire, Eleanor Barbour in
"Follies"**

EQUITY LIBRARY THEATRE
Opened Thursday, May 6, 1976.*
Equity Library Theatre presents:

FOLLIES

Book, James Goldman; Music and Lyrics, Stephen Sondheim; Director, Russell Treyz; Musical Direction, Jim Coleman; Choreography, John Montgomery; Scenery, John M. Falabella; Costumes, Donna Meyer; Lighting, Victor En Yu Tan; Hairstylist, J. Alexander Scafa; Wardrobe Mistresses, Shelly Friedman, Lynda Kavy; Assistant Choreographer, Barbara Beck; Headdresses, J. Douglas James

CAST

Sally Durant Plummer	Lois Ann Saunders
Roscoe	Andrew Roman
Phyllis Rogers Stone	Joan Ulmer
Benjamin Stone	George F. Maguire
Buddy Plummer	Jack Finnegan
Dimitri Weissman	Donald C. Moore
Stella Deems	Ileane Gudell
Max Deems	Joshua Michaels
Hattie Walker	Sarah Philips Felcher
Solange La Fitte/Vanessa	Lucille Patton
Young Phyllis	Eleanor Barbour
Young Sally	Sara Louise
Young Buddy	Randy Hugill
Young Ben	Richard Cooper Bayne†1
Vincent	Alan Gilbert
Heidi Schiller	Lynn Archer †2
Carlotta Campion	Barbara Lea
Emily Whitman	Virginia Barton
Theodora Whitman	Emile Julian
Young Heidi	Robbi Curtis
Kevin/Young Vincent	Michael Perrier
Young Vanessa	Nancy Salis
Young Stella	Kaylyn Dillehay†3

MUSICAL NUMBERS: "Beautiful Girls," "Don't Look at Me," "Waiting for the Girls Upstairs," "Listen to the Rain on the Roof," "Ah Paris!," "Broadway Baby," "The Road You Didn't Take," "Bolero D'Amour," "In Buddy's Eyes," "Who's That Woman," "I'm Still Here," "Too Many Mornings," "The Right Girl," "One More Kiss," "Could I Leave You?," "Loveland," "You're Gonna Love Tomorrow," "Love Will See Us Through," "The God-God-Why-Don't-You-Love-Me Blues," "Losing My Mind," "The Story of Lucy and Jessie," "Live, Laugh, Love"

A musical in two acts. The action takes place at a party on the stage of the Weissman Theatre on an evening in May of 1971.

Press: Lewis Harmon, Sol Jacobson
Stage Managers: Joel Grynheim, Victor A. Gelb, Mark Dennis Mellender

* Closed May 30, 1976 after limited engagement of 30 performances.
† Succeeded by: 1. Kurt Johnson, 2. Margaret Goodman, 3. Spence Ford

Gary Wheeler Photo

LINCOLN CENTER LIBRARY & MUSEUM
Monday, Tuesday Wednesday, October 20 - 22, 1975.
Equity Library Theatre presents:

BRAINWASHED
and
WITNESS

By Florence Stevenson; Director, Michael Dennis Moore; Scenery, John Schak; Lighting, Candy Dunn; Stage Manager, Cindy Horton

CAST

"Brainwashed"
Carol	Patricia Carter
Eb	Dana Gladstone
Harry	Franz Jones
Agnes	Lee Kheel
Bunny	Madonna Young

"Witness"
Freddie	Hattie Crystal
Ursula	Julia Curry
Dave	Dana Gladstone
Ziggy	Wayne Harding
Betty	Joelle Pacht
Joe	Bill Weylock

LINCOLN CENTER LIBRARY & MUSEUM
Monday, Tuesday, Wednesday, December 8 - 10, 1975
Equity Library Theatre Presents:

THANKSGIVING
and
JULY 2

By Stan Kaplan; Director, Francis Carmine Miazga; Lighting, Dan Bartlett; Stage Manager, Jaqui Oringer

CAST

"Thanksgiving"
Maryanne	Suzanne Foster
Martin	Paul Meacham
Max	Lou Miranda
Mother Huff	Valerie Morrell
Father Huff	Sid Paul
Johnny	Alan Spitz

"July 2"
Tony	Robert Coluntino
Ben	Paul Meacham
Monk	Lou Miranda
Mike	Sid Paul
Big Al	Nick Quinault
Sammy	Alan Spitz
Tommy	Bill Tatum

LINCOLN CENTER LIBRARY & MUSEUM
Monday, Tuesday, Wednesday, January 26 - 28, 1976
Equity Library Theatre Informals presents:

SEPARATE CHECKS, PLEASE

By Harry Cauley, Sally-Jane Heit; Music and Lyrics, Shirley Grossman

CAST

Sally-Jane Heit
Harry Cauley

LINCOLN CENTER LIBRARY & MUSEUM
Monday, Tuesday, Wednesday, February 23 - 25, 1976
Equity Library Theatre Informals presents:

THE LILY AND THE ROSE

Arranged by Nina Polan; Director, Steven D. Nash; Stage Managers, Judy Goldstein, Annabel Brigleb, Sunny Baker

CAST

James Higgins	Nina Polan
Tom Jarus	Forbesy Russell
Heidi Mefford	Neil Semer

LINCOLN CENTER LIBRARY & MUSEUM
Monday, Tuesday, Wednesday, March 22–24, 1976
Equity Library Theatre Informals presents:

HOLE IN THE WALL
and
CLICK

By Stan Hart; Director, Richard Harden; Designed by Patrick Mann; Stage Manager, Robert Foose

CAST

"Hole in the Wall"	"Click"
Sam Assaid	Sam Assaid
Tony Aylward	Beth Dixon
Linda Cook	Woody Eney
Andy Rohrer	Toby Nelson

LINCOLN CENTER LIBRARY & MUSEUM
Monday, Tuesday, Wednesday, April 19–21, 1976
Equity Library Theatre Informals presents:

THE VIRGIN AND THE UNICORN

By Oscar Mandel; Director, Michael Martorella; Set, David Murdock; Costumes, Karen Seitz; Music, Jack Biser; Stage Managers, Jim Pentecost, Anabel Brigleb

CAST

Sir Ralf	Norman Beim
Baron	Avrom Berel
Peter	Jack Biser
Earl	John Edward Daley
Margaret	Kathleen Huber
Clotilda	Gwen Humble
Leofa	Leon Spelman

LINCOLN CENTER LIBRARY & MUSEUM
Monday, Tuesday, Wednesday, May 17–19, 1976
Equity Library Theatre present:

NAOMI

By Nell Branyon; Directed by the author; Set, Jerry Simeone; Lighting, Anne L. Peters; Costumes, Sally Krell; Stage Manager, Joanne Benson

CAST

Michael	Jim Burnett
Naomi	Gina Collens
Sheriff	Bill DaPrato
Harold Burns	John Fowler
Floosie	Marian Haraldson
Sally	Margaret Kitchings
Luanna	Meg Sargent
Mrs. Bonely	Louise Shelton
Grandma	Marion Wells

120

JOSEPH JEFFERSON THEATRE COMPANY

Cathy Roskam, Executive Director
Connie Alexis, General Manager

LITTLE CHURCH AROUND THE CORNER
October 23–November 8, 1975 (12 performances)

THUNDER ROCK by Robert Ardrey; Director, William Koch; Set, Richard Williams; Lighting, Robby Monk; Costumes, John Scheffler; Sound, Gerald Weinstein; Assistant to director, Paul Terry; Stage Manager, Joanne Benson. CAST: Bill Tatum (Streetcar), Tracey Walter (Nonny), Richard Marr (Inspector), Reathel Bean (Charleston), Paul Meacham (Captain), William Koch (Briggs), Frank Miazga (Dr. Kurtz), Nita Novy (Melanie), Suzanne Osborne (Miss Kirby), Madeleine Gorman (Anne Marie), Peter Alzado (Cassidy).

December 2–13, 1975 (12 performances)

THE WOOING OF LADY SUNDAY by Ted Pezzulo; Set, Cliff Simon; Lighting, Francis Roefaro; Costumes, A. Christina Giannini; Stage Managers, David Rosenberg, Karen E. Nothmann. CAST: Henry Ferrentino (Briglio), Marjorie Austrian (Concetta), Susan Walker (Domenica), Frank Cascio (Benvenuto), Jason Howard (Agnello), Josh Milder (Giuseppe), Jennifer Thompson (Tommasino), Rachael Milder (Chiarina), Rifka Milder (Giuseppina), Kate Schapiro (Iolanda), Justine Grubar (Carmela), Jevan Damadian (Antonio)

APRIL FISH by Ted Pezzulo; other credits above. CAST: Jason Howard (Anselmo), Jo Flores Chase (Assunta), Richard Zavaglia (Fortunato), Dwight Marfield (Umberto), Marianne Muellerleile (Sabbatella), Rachael Milder (Giovannina), Stephanie Satie (Nicolina), Michael Brindisi (Pasquale), Antonio Pandolfo (Pietro), Hope W. Sacharoff (Filomena), Maurice Braddell (Padre)

February 11–28, 1976 (12 performances)

MORNING'S AT SEVEN by Paul Osborn; Director, Cathy Roskam; Sets, Gerald Weinstein, Costumes, Cindy Polk; Lighting, Robby Monk; Sound, Fred Garrett, Bill Stallings; Press, Marion Gredi Towbin; Stage Managers, Evan Canary, Joanne Benson; Wardrobe Mistress, Rachael Milder; Production Coordinator, Evan Canary. CAST: William Robertson (Theodore), Anita Bayless (Cora), Rose Lischner (Aaronetta), Frances Pole (Ida), William DaPrato (Carl), I. W. Klein (Homer), Melanie Hill (Myrtle), Eleanor Cody Gould (Esther), George Lloyd (David)

May 5–22, 1976 (12 performances)

JOHN by Philip Barry; Director, Cyril Simon; Set, Kenneth Shewer; Lighting, Jennifer Herrick Jebens; Costumes, Susan Hilferty; Hairstylist, Patrik D. Moreton; Music, Wendy Erdman; Costume Mistress, Cindy Polk; Sound, Debbie Carter; Assistant to director, Missy Powell; Press, Marion Fredi Towbin; Stage Managers, Evan Canary, Toby Bellin, Marilyn Modlin. CAST: David Rasche (Joel), Richard Cox (Hanan), James Carruthers (Antipas), Elizabeth Hubbard (Herodias), Oz Tortora (Pete), Stanton Coffin (Nathaniel), Duane Morris (Simon), Robert Shockley (Andrew), Paul Ruben (Dan), Armand Assante (John), Joel Parsons (James), Tom Bair (Ethan), Sylvester Rich (Zebedee), Natalia E. Chuma (Salome), Charles C. Timm (Dancing Master), Davidson Garrett (Servant), Allan Warren (Warden)

Ambur Hiken, Mike Uffer Photos

**Top Right: Bill Tatum, Reathel Bean in
"Thunder Rock" Below: "April Fish" and "The
Wooing of Lady Sunday"
Right Center: Rose Lischner,
William Robertson in "Morning's at Seven"**

**Elizabeth Hubbard, Armand Assante
in "John"**

121

MANHATTAN THEATRE CLUB

Lynne Meadow, Artistic-Executive Director
Managing Director, Barry Grove; Associate Director, Thomas Bullard; Press, Daniel Caine; Technical Director, William D. Anderson; Assistant to Managing Director, Pat Bartolotta; Administrative Assistant, Lorie Barber; Technical Assistants, Ron Woods, Frank Kelly; Staff Assistants, Sylvia Hollander, Frances Burdock; Cabaret Directors, Thomas Bullard, Stephen Pascal

MANHATTAN THEATRE CLUB
October 23–November 9, 1975 (12 performances)

RUBY'S PLACE with Book by Richard Beeson Johnson; Music and Lyrics, Elli Faye; Musical Direction and Arrangements; Staged by Andre De Shields. CAST: Sarah Harris, Lawrence John Moss, Alaina Reed, Andre De Shields

October 23–November 9, 1975 (12 performances)

SEA MARKS by Gardner McKay; Director, Steven Robman; Scenery, Marjorie Kellogg; Costumes, Kenneth M. Yount; Lighting, Arden Fingerhut. CAST: Edwin J. McDonough (Colm Primrose), Veronica Castang (Timothea Stiles)

October 24–November 9, 1975 (12 performances)

GOLDEN BOY by Clifford Odets; Director, Lynne Meadow; Settings, John Lee Beatty; Costumes, Vittorio Capecce; Lighting, William D. Anderson; Sound, George Hansen, Charles London; Assistant to director, Zane Weiner; Stage Manager, Michael Heaton. CAST: Dick Latessa (Tom), Laura Esterman (Lorna), Jerry Zaks (Joe), Dan Hedaya (Tokio), Frank Hamilton (Carp), Michael Kell (Siggie), Paul Lipson (Bonaparte), Erica Weingast (Anna), Joel Colodener (Frank), Jerrold Ziman (Roxy), Clarence Felder (Eddie), Larry Guardino (Pepper), Bob DeFrank (Mickey), Danny Sewell (Drake), Vic Polizos (Barker)

November 13–30, 1975 (12 performances)

MARVIN'S GARDEN with Music by Mel Marvin; Director, David Chambers; Lyrics, Moose 100, Ron Whyte, David Chambers. CAST: Donna Emmanuel, Robert Montgomery, Richard Ryder, Dale Soules, Donovan Sylvest, Mary Wright

November 13–23, 1975 (12 performances)

THE BASEMENT by Harold Pinter; Director, David Kerry Heefner; Settings, Sandi Marks; Lighting, Patricia Moeser; Costumes, Louis Pshena; Sound, George Hansen; Stage Managers, Katherine Talbert, Neil Broat; Production Assistant, Lee Pucklis. CAST: John C. Vennema (Law), James Hummert (Stott), Patricia Gorman (Jane); A SLIGHT ACHE by Harold Pinter; Same staff as preceding. CAST: Kathleen Betsko (Flora), James Hummert (Edward), John C. Vennema (Matchseller)

December 4–21, 1975 (12 performances)

LIFE CLASS by David Storey; Director, Robert Mandel; Setting, Marjorie Kellogg; Lighting, Arden Fingerhut; Costumes, Jennifer von Mayrhauser; Stage Managers, Marjorie Horne, Amy Schecter. CAST: Kevin Conway (Allott), David Wilson (Warren), William Carden (Saunders), Veronica Castang (Stella), Lenny Baker (Mathews), Dale Hodges (Brenda), Christopher Curry (Carter), Swoosie Kurtz (Catherine), Keith McDermott (Mooney), Toni Kalem (Gillian), John Ramsey (Abercrombie), William Roerick (Foley), Peter DeMaio (Phillips)

December 4–21, 1975 (11 performances)

A MUSICAL EVENING WITH FRED COFFIN AND DOROTHEA JOYCE

December 4–21, 1975 (15 performances)

GEOGRAPHY OF A HORSE DREAMER by Sam Shepard; Director, Jacques Levy; Settings, T. Winberry; Costumes, Kenneth M. Yount; Lighting, Frank R. Kelly; Sound, Carol Waaser; Assistant to director, Nancy Tribush; Stage Managers, Sari Weisman, Stephen Radosh. CAST: Rick Warner (Cody), Robert Lesser (Santee), J. Zakkai (Beaujo), John Mitchell (Fingers), Gordon Hammett (Doctor), Paul Andor (Walter), Ronald F. Toler (Jasper), Lee Jines (Jason)

Ken Howard Photos

**Right Center: David Leary,
Robert Christian in "The Blood Knot"**

**Laura Esterman, Dick Latessa,
Dan Hedaya in "Golden Boy"**

**Keith McDermott, Lenny Baker,
Kevin Conway in "Life Class"**

MANHATTAN THEATRE CLUB

December 19, 1975 (1 performance)

GOOD TIME DOLLY DEE by John Vari; Director, Alfred Christie. CAST: Alan Fleisig (Narrator), Jo Flores Chase (Dolly Dee), Don Nute (Sonny), Madeleine Gorman (Fitzy), Dennis Drew (Judge), Tom Coppola (Little Willie)

February 4–21, 1976 (12 performances)

A KANDER & EBB CABARET: An evening of songs by John Kander and Fred Ebb; Conceived and Directed by Seth Glassman; Musical Director, Richard DeMone. CAST: Carl Barone, Tommy Breslin, Channing Case, Kay Cummings, Linda Glick, Suzanne Oberjat

February 4–22, 1976 (15 performances)

PATRICK HENRY LAKE LIQUORS by Larry Ketron; Director, Ronald Roston; Set and Costumes, Ernie Smith; Lighting, John Gisondi; Sound, George Hansen, Charles London; Stage Managers, Amy Schecter, Frances Murdock; Production Assistant, Kevin Constant. CAST: Jay Devlin (James), James Hilbrandt (Horace), Ed Seamon (Mickey), Regina Baff (Sandra), Christine Lavren (Louise), Donna Emmanuel (Ann), Vic Polizos (Gary), Mark Metcalf (Leif), Toni Kalem (Floral), George Brice (Customer), Frank Saracino (Customer)

February 12–March 6, 1976 (18 performances)

THE BLOOD KNOT by Athol Fugard; Director, Thomas Bullard; Scenery, Pat Woodbridge; Costumes, Kenneth M. Yount; Lighting, Arden Fingerhut; Stage Managers, Katherine Talbert, Joe Millett; Production Assistant, Kevin Constant. CAST: David H. Leary (Morris), Robert Christian (Zachariah)

February 26–March 14, 1976 (12 performances)

SONGS FROM PINS AND NEEDLES by Harold Rome; Directed and Choreographed by Marc Gass; Musical Director, Jez Davidson. CAST: Scott Bodie, Cynthia Bostick, Margery Cohen, Jonathan Hadary, Margaret Warncke

March 3–21, 1976 (15 performances)

THE VOICE OF THE TURTLE by John van Druten; Director, Julianne Boyd; Scenery, Bill Groom; Costumes, Danny Mizell; Lighting, Patricia Moeser; Stage Managers, Ian McColl, Stacy Scott. CAST: Susan Sharkey (Sally), Julie Garfield (Olive), Munson Hicks (Bill)

March 3–21, 1976 (15 performances)

AN EVENING OF SHOLOM ALEICHEM: Stories from the works of Sholom Aleichem; Director, Richard Maltby, Jr.; Costumer, Pegi Goodman. CAST: Murray Horwitz in a solo performance.

March 18–April 4, 1976 (12 performances)

THE SON by Gert Hofmann; Translated by Jon Swan; Director, Stephen Pascal; Set and Lighting, Raymond Recht; Costumes, Vittorio Capecce; Stage Managers, Kevin Constant, Robert Epstein. CAST: Tanya Berezin (Mrs. Nickel), Andrew Bloch (Karlemann), J. Zakkai (Councilman, Station Attendant, Shopkeeper, Landlord), Diane Barry (Secretary, Shopkeeper's Wife, Fanny), Gail Kellstrom (Traveler, Monika), Reed Birney (Traveler, Customer), Robert Epstein (Traveler), Elaine Bromka (Waitress, Lucretia)

March 31–April 18, 1976 (15 performances)

DEARLY BELOVED by John Raymond Hart; Director, Paul Schneider; Scenery, Vittorio Capecce; Costumes, Margo Bruton Elkow; Lighting, Paul Kaine; Sound, George Hansen, Charles London; Dialect Coach, Gordon A. Jacoby; Stage Managers, David M. Everard, Nona Pipes. CAST: Margaret Ladd (Nora), Suzanne Collins (Cathleen), Barbara eda-Young (Joanna), Judith L'Heureux (Deirdre), Robert B. Silver (David), Larry Bryggman (Christian), Robert McIlwaine (Peter), James Rebhorn (Frank), Nancy Reardon (Bridget), Joseph Daly (Owen)

April 8–18, 1976 (12 performances)

DEVILS AND DIAMONDS: a one-woman show of song and poetry by Stephanie Cotsirilos.

April 21–May 16, 1976 (28 performances)

IN THE WINE TIME by Ed Bullins; Director, Robert Macbeth; Settings, Steven Rubin; Costumes, Grace Williams; Lighting, Spencer Mosse; Sound, Sonny Morgan; Stage Managers, Mark Paquette, Ivy McCray. CAST: Robert Christian (Cliff), Loretta Greene (Lou), Alvin Alexis (Ray), Marilyn Randall (Bunny), Flow Wiley (Doris),

John Heard, Laura Esterman in "The Pokey"

Martha Short-Goldsen (Miss Minny), Otis Young-Smith (Red), Walter Steele (Bama), Dana Manno (Beatrice), Jenny Gooch (Tiny), Richard Gant (Silly Willy), Steve Sheahan (Policeman)

April 21–May 1, 1976 (9 performances)

CRACKED TOKENS: a comedy-improvisation group featuring Robert Fraina, Joanna Lipari, Pam Moller, John Slavin, Mary Steenburgen

April 22–May 9, 1976 (10 performances)

SONGS OF QUINCY-BURCH with Lynn Gerb

MANHATTAN THEATRE CLUB

May 5–23, 1976 (14 performances)

A NOEL COWARD CABARET: Conceived and Directed by Gary Pearle; Musical Director, Steven Blier. CAST: George Lee Andrews and Marti Morris

May 5–22, 1976 (15 performances)

THE POKEY by Stephen Black; Director, Lynne Meadow; Settings, Raymond Recht; Costumes, Margo Bruton Elkow; Lighting, William D. Anderson; Stage Managers, David M. Everard, Robert Epstein. CAST: Laura Esterman (Young Woman), John Heard (Young Man)

May 13–June 6, 1976 (16 performances)

JAZZ BABIES: Written, Directed and Choreographed by Marc Jordan Gass; Musically Arranged and Directed by Jez Davidson; Conceived by Marc Gass and Jez Davidson; Stage Manager, Christopher Pitney. CAST: Cynthia Bostick, Herb Downer, Joel Eagon, Susan Edwards, Frank Juliano

May 18–June 6, 1976 (15 performances)

TRANSFORMATIONS by Anne Sexton; Music, Conrad Susa; Director, David Shookhoff; Musical Director, Benton Hess; Scenery, Pat Woodbridge; Costumes, Ken Holamon; Lighting, Spencer Mosse; Stage Manager, David S. Rosenkak. CAST: Karen Clauss, Patricia Deckert, Tonio Di Paolo, Jonathan Rigg, Thomas A. Rowe, Raymond Sambolin, John Shackelford, Carolyn Weber

May 26–June 6, 1976 (15 performances)

LIFE IS LIKE A MUSICAL COMEDY: Songs by George M. Cohan; Conceived and Directed by Jack Allison; Musical Director, Anthony Zaleski; Stage Manager, Liz Plonka. CAST: Alice Cannon, Melanie Chartoff, David Dyer, Wayne Scherzer, Barbara Worthington

May 28–June 12, 1976 (13 performances)

THE HUMAN VOICE: Music by Francis Poulenc; Text, Jean Cocteau; English Version, Joseph Machlis; Director, Thomas Bullard; Musical Director, Ethan Mordden; Sets, Vittorio Capecce; Costumes, Ann Wolff; Lights, John Gisondi; Stage Manager, Rena Rockoff. CAST: Linda Phillips or Judith James

123

THE NEGRO ENSEMBLE COMPANY

Dougals Turner Ward, Artistic Director
Robert Hooks, Executive Director
Frederick Garrett, Administrative Director

ST. MARK'S PLAYHOUSE
Opened Wednesday, March 3, 1976.*
The Negro Ensemble Company presents:

EDEN

By Steve Carter; Director, Edmund Cambridge; Scenery, Pamela S. Peniston; Costumes, Edna Watson; Lighting, Sandra L. Ross; Technical Director, Dik Krider; Assistant, George Scott; Wardrobe Mistress, Marzetta Jones

CAST

Eustace	Samm-Art Williams
Nimrod	Nate Ferrell
Solomon	Laurence Fishburne 3d
Aunt Lizzie	Barbara Montgomery
Agnes	Ramona King
Annetta	Shirley Brown
Florie	Ethel Ayler
Joseph Barton	Graham Brown

UNDERSTUDIES: George Campbell, Dean Irby, Sheryl-Lee Ralph, Lea Scott

A drama in 3 acts and 9 scenes. The action takes place in the Bartons' apartment on the upper West Side of New York City during 1927.

Company Manager: Frederick Garrett
Press: Howard Atlee, Clarence Allsopp
Stage Manager: Clinton Turner Davis

* Closed May 9, 1976 after 79 performances. Moved May 16, 1976 to Theatre DeLys and still playing May 31, 1976. Laurence Fishburne 3d was succeeded by George Campbell, James Warden, Jr.

Bert Andrews Photos
Right: Ramona King, Shirley Brown
Top: Ethel Ayler, Graham Brown

Shirley Brown, Samm-Art Williams

James Warden, Jr., Graham Brown

ST. MARK'S PLAYHOUSE
Opened Wednesday, May 19, 1976.*
The Negro Ensemble Company presents:

LIVIN' FAT

By Judi Ann Mason; Director, Douglas Turner Ward; Scenery and Costumes, Mary Mease Warren; Lighting, Sandra L. Ross; Title Song Composed and Arranged by Jothan Callins; Lyrics, Douglas Turner Ward; Sung by Hattie Winston; Production Assistant, Ron Lewis; Technical Director, Dik Krider; Assistant, George Scott; Wardrobe Supervisor, Ali Davis.

CAST

Big Mama	Minnie Gentry
Mama	Frances Foster
Daddy	Wayne Elbert
Candy	Joyce Sylvester
David Lee	Dean Irby
Boo	Frankie Faison

Understudies: Charles Brown, Rosanna Carter

A comedy in 2 acts and 5 scenes. The action takes place at the present time in the front room of the Carter family in the black quarters section of a southern city.

Company Manager; Frederick Garrett
Press: Howard Atlee, Clarence Allsopp
Stage Manager: Horacena J. Taylor

* Closed July 18, 1976 after 69 performances.

Bert Andrews Photos

Top: Frances Foster, Wayne Elbert, Dean Irby
Below: Dean Irby, Joyce Sylvester, Frankie Faison

Frankie Faison, Dean Irby
Top: Wayne Elbert, Frances Foster

125

THE NEW DRAMATISTS INC.

Chairman, L. Arnold Weissberger; President, Mary K. Frank; Program Director, Jeff Peters; Workshop Coordinator, Stephen Harty; Administrative Assistant, Kathleen Mucciolo; Technical Director, Clay Coyle

Thursday, June 5, 1975

THE WOLVES AND THE LAMBS by Frieda Lipp. CAST: Roger Serbagi (Wayne), Nancy Franklin (Cynthia), Douglas Cowgill (Steven), Eren Özker (Louise), Kate Williamson (Amy), Bill Weylock (Joseph), Arthur Hammer (Prosecutor), Bette Howard (Marianne), Lawrence Watson (Lester), Jim Horn (Deputy/Guard/Officer/-Judge)

June 11 & 12, 1975

HALFWAY TREE BROWN by Clifford Mason; Director, Stan Lachow; Stage Manager, Everett Johns; Technician, Maureen Bryan. CAST: Robin Braxton (Elizabeth), Sandi Franklin (Hyacinth), Richard Ward (Edward), Wendell Brown (Winston), Jorge Johnson (Derrick), Ingrid Wang (Yvonne), Clifford Mason (Richard), Dorothi Fox (Enid), Herb Rice (Buddu/Photographer), Roy Thomas (Calypsonian/Governor General), Sundra Jean Williams (Mae), Ernest Thomas (Rastus), Faizul Khan (Babu/Isaacs), Derrel Edwards (David), Arthur Hammer (Englishman), Sam Singleton (Minister)

June 19 & 20, 1975

THE CORRIDOR by Diane Kagan; Production and Lighting Design, Meryl Joseph; Music Direction, Herbert Kaplan; Stage Manager, Peter Abode; Sound, Bruce Lazarus. CAST: Anna Minot (Woman), Joseph Warren (Man), Lisa Richards (Emissary)

September 14, 1975

THE ENCHANTED HUDSON by Eric Thompson. CAST: Edmond Lyndeck (Paul), Joan Shepard (Mary), Jeanne Ruskin (Ann)

September 23–27, 1975 (5 performances)

NEVER A SNUG HARBOUR by David Ulysses Clarke; Director, Tom Ligon; Lighting, Gregg Marriner; Sound, Katharine Clarke; Costumes, David James; Stage Manager, Roger Pippin. CAST: Joseph Regalbuto (Will), Richard Brestoff (Gwylim), Robert Boardman (Teddy), Paul Andor (Simon), Nora Dunfee (Mary), Peter Dee (Charlie), Tom Bair (Joe), Katherine Clark (Ellen), Joseph Jamrog (Jack)

Jeff Peters Photos

Barbara Coggin in "Father Uxbridge Wants to Ma

**Joseph Daly, Lillah McCarthy, Robert Lydiard,
Steve Vinovich, Diana Stilwell in "The Last Christians"**

THE NEW DRAMATISTS INC.

October 7–11, 1975 (5 performances)

THE LAST CHRISTIANS by Jack Gilhooley; Director, Clinto Atkinson; Set, Kevin Golden; Lighting, Stephen Ommerle; St Managers, Stephen Ommerle, Peter Abode; Production Assist Barbara Nivelt. CAST: Alan Brasington (Caiaphas), Robert Lydi (Herod), Steve Vinovich (Rev. Sykes), Marianne Muellerleile (N Trudy), Libby Lyman (Mrs. Young), Joseph Alaskey (Harris Nick Francesco (P. P.), William Russ (J. J.), Nancy Bar (Veronica), Terrence Hopkins (Judas), Joseph Daly (Jedediah), ane Stilwell (Dummy), Lillah McCarthy (Aurelia)

October 21–25, 1975 (5 performances)

THE WOLVES AND THE LAMBS by Frieda Lipp; Direc Christopher Adler; Lighting, Gregg Marriner; Stage Manag Roger Pippin, Barbara Alpert. CAST: Mervyn Gaines, Jr. (Way Edith Greenfield (Cynthia), Peter Anlyan (Steven), Lane Bink (Louise), Beth Holland (Amy), Stephan Weyte (Caravella), Da Clarke (Alexander), Lawrence Wall (Authority), Beatrice Wi (Marianne), Laurence Watson (Lester)

November 4–7, 1975 (5 performances)

SISTER SADIE by Clifford Mason; Director, Mr. Mason; Assis to director, Angela Lee; Set and Lighting, Guy J. Smith; St Manager, Haskell V. Anderson III; Production Assistant, Barl Nivelt. CAST: Virginia Capers (Sadie), Ernest Harden, Jr. (Bi Fred Morsell (Fish), Ellwoodson Williams (Horse), Henry Hayw (Moe), Maurice Watson (Blue), Maurice Sneed (Squeeze), Ja Smithwrick (Popsey), Dorothi Fox (Lula), Andrea Frierson (metta)

November 18–22, 1975 (5 performances)

FATHER UXBRIDGE WANTS TO MARRY by Frank Gagli Director, Mr. Gagliano; Set, Robert Steinberg; Lighting, C Porto; Sound and Music, James Reichert; Costumes, Ariel; St Manager, Gary Porto; Sound, George Patterson. CAST: Bar Coggin (Mrs. Green), Steve Vinovich (Norden), Bill McIntyre ther Uxbridge), Valerie Mahaffey (Angel), Robert Christian (On

NEW DRAMATISTS INC.

December 9–13, 1975 (5 performances)

THE ENCHANTED HUDSON by Eric Thompson; Director, Thom Molyneaux; Set, Clay Coyle; Lighting, Chuck Ferrand; Stage Managers, Larry Lorberbaum, Mike Maines. CAST: Ellen Cameron (Mary), Bernard Pollock (Paul), Marina Thompson (Child), Barbara Cohen (Ann), Carrie Rubio (Mimu), Haskell V. Anderson III (Kabari), William Preston (Grandfather), Rocko Cinelli (Chief), Jeanne Ruskin (Organist), Natives: Jamie Farbman, Nick Francesco, Jody Hingle, Nicki Stephens

January 14–16, 1976 (3 performances)

THE BEACH CHILDREN by John von Hartz; Director, Ronald Roston; Stage Manager, Sari Weisman. CAST: Maia Danziger (Sherry), Mark Metcalf (Jimmy), Roger Omar Serbagi (Max), Nancy Franklin (Margaret), Martin Marinaro (Domingo), Tanny McDonald (Alma), Gil Rogers (Antonio)

January 19, 1976

AMOUREUSE by Anne and Stuart Vaughan; From the French play by Georges de Porto-Riche. CAST: Donald Madden (Dr. Feriaud), Sharon Laughlin (Germaine), Louis Turenne (Pascal), Laurinda Barrett (Catherine), Barbara Caruso (Mme. de Chazal), Angela Wood (Mme. Henriet), Ann Thompson (Madelein)

January 28, 1976

A NICE GIRL LIKE YOU by Aldo Giunta; Stage Manager, Peter Kozik. CAST: Tony Wein (Anne), Ben Slack (Fatso), Bob Resnikoff (Sam), Joe Ragno (Charley), Tucker Smallwood (Wade)

February 17–19, 1976 (3 performances)

THE ELUSIVE ANGEL by Jack Gilhooley; Director, Peter Maloney; Stage Manager, Mark Oberman. CAST: Tracey Walter (Carlton), Amy Wright (Mary), Graham Beckel (Slick), Jayne Haynes (Bo Peep), Lillah McCarthy (Lucy), James Handy (Ken)

February 27, 1976

APRIL by John Wolfson; Stage Directions read by John Yates. CAST: Laura Ilene (Melody), Norman Evans (Mankowitz), Sam Affoumado (Arnold), Harry Browne (Buddy), Gladys Smith (April), John Yates (Val), Richie Allan (Waldo), Richard Niles (Steve), Ozzie Tortora (Poletti), John LaGioia (Dominick), Faith Catlin (Diane), Bill Roulet (Huong)

Amy Wright, Tracey Walter in "The Elusive Angel"

March 5, 1976

THE FAR-OFF SWEET FOREVER by Conn Fleming; Stage Manager, John Mintun. CAST: Maurice Copeland (Patton), Mark Metcalf (Banner), Karen Shallo (Mable), Ed Genest (Dr. Phipps/Preacher), Barbara Coggin (Oma), Townspeople: Sharon Brewer, Tom Keever, Katie Mucciolo, Greg Willis

March 8–11, 1976 (3 performances)

THE MAN WHO DREW CIRCLES by Barry Berg; Director, Cliff Goodwin. CAST: David Dukes (Harold), Elizabeth Reavey (Vanessa), Richard Greene (Norman), Nancy Franklin (Brenda), Richard DeFabees (Ted), Anna Minot (Miriam)

March 16 & 17, 1976 (2 performances)

A SAFE PLACE by C. K. Mack. CAST: Douglas Stark (Arthur), Bette Marshall (Elizabeth), Toni Kalem (Nadia), Beatrice Winde (Besse), Stuart Vaughan (Henry), Amy Wright (Jennifer), Jayne Haynes (Heidi), Linda Lodge (Charlie), Donna Gabel (Anna/Florence)

April 2, 1976

EVEN THE WINDOW IS GONE by Gene Radano; Director, Shan Covey CAST: Jack Aaron (Paul), Julia Barr (Bonnie), Laura Esterman (Shirley), Jeanne Kaplan (Mother), Susan Marshall (Carmella), Mary Moon (Florence), Harvey Siegel (Mel), Lou Tiano (Sal)

April 20–24, 1976 (6 performances)

THE RESURRECTION OF JACKIE CRAMER by Frank Gagliano; Music, Raymond Benson; Director, J. Ranelli; Set and Lighting, Robert Steinberg; Musical Direction and Performed by Raymond Benson; Stage Manager, Gary Porto. CAST: David Berman (Jackie Cramer), Mary Testa (Mom), Jerry McGee (Pop), Kenith Bridges (Father Bodoni), Nancy Foy (Susie), Joseph White (Remo), Jane MacDonald, John Canary (Chorus), Phylis Frelich (Benjy), Board of Directors: Joel Brooks, Mike Dantuono, Doug Holsclaw, Marion Lindell

May 5, 1976

THE HOUSE OF SOLOMON by Allen Davis III. CAST: Paul Lipson (Joseph Solomon), Ruth Jaroslow (Rachel), Nancy Marchand (Esther), Wil Albert (Ted) Paul Sparer (Danny), Alba Oms (Felicia)

May 13, 1976

LUST by Steven Somkin; Director, Rhoda Feuer. CAST: Betty Russell, (Madeleine), Linda Bernstein (Adele), Frederic Major (Bernard), Peter Flood (Richard), Myra Turley (Dora), Paul Merrill (Charles), Victor DeRose (Bobby), Nicholas Levitin (Auctioneer), Bidders: Murray Cantor, Belle Weiss

Virginia Capers, Fred Morsell in "Sister Sadie"

NEW YORK SHAKESPEARE FESTIVAL AT LINCOLN CENTER

Joseph Papp, Producer
Bernard Gersten, Associate Producer

VIVIAN BEAUMONT THEATER
Opened Wednesday, October 15, 1975.*
The New York Shakespeare Festival presents:

TRELAWNY OF THE 'WELLS'

By Sir Arthur Wing Pinero; Director, A. J. Antoon; Scenery, David Mitchell; Costumes, Theoni V. Aldredge; Supervised by Hal George; Lighting, Ian Calderon; Music, Peter Link; Wardrobe Supervisor, James McGaha; Production Assistants, Daniel Koetting, Bonnie Christensen; Assistant to director, Jane Paley; Hairstylist, J. Roy Helland

CAST

Mrs. Mossop	Helen Verbit
Mr. Ablett	Merwin Goldsmith
Mr. Tom Wrench	Michael Tucker
Miss Imogen Parrot	Meryl Streep
Mr. James Telfer	Jerome Dempsey
Mr. Ferdinand Gadd	John Lithgow
Mr. Augustus Colpoys	Ben Slack
Mrs. Telfer (Violet Sylvester)	Anita Dangler
Miss Avonia Bunn	Sasha von Scherler
Miss Rose Trelawny	Marybeth Hurt
Mr. Arthur Gower	Mandy Patinkin
Sarah	K. T. Baumann
Clara De Foenix	Ann McDonough
Captain DeFoenix	Jeffrey Jones
Justice William Gower	Walter Abel
Miss Trafalger Gower	Aline MacMahon
Charles	Walt Gorney
O'Dwyer (Stage Manager)	Christopher Hewett
Mr. Denzil	Jerry Mayer
Miss Brewster	Suzanne Collins
Mr. Hunston	Tom Blank

UNDERSTUDIES: Wrench, Arthur, Tom Blank; Justice, Telfer, Charles, Thomas Barbour; Clara, K. T. Baumann; Avonia, Imogen, Sara, Suzanne Collins; Gadd, O'Dwyer, Jeffrey Jones; Augustus, Ablett, Captain, Jerry Mayer; Rose, Ann McDonough; Trafalgar, Mrs. Telfer, Mrs. Mossop, Elsa Raven

A comedy in four acts performed with one intermission. The action takes place in New York City around the turn of the century.

Press: Merle Debuskey, Faith Geer
Stage Managers: Louis Rackoff, Richard S. Viola

* Closed Nov. 23, 1975 after 47 performances and 14 previews.

Barry Kramer-Joseph Abeles Photos

Walter Abel, Aline MacMahon

Marybeth Hurt, Michael Tucker, Sasha von Sche[r]
John Lithgow Top: Mandy Patinkin,
Michael Tucker, Marybeth Hurt

VIVIAN BEAUMONT THEATER
Opened Wednesday, December 17, 1975.*
New York Shakespeare Festival presents:

HAMLET

By William Shakespeare; Director, Michael Rudman; Scenery, Santo Loquasto; Costumes, Hal George; Lighting, Martin Aronstein; Music, John Morris; Production Assistant, Frank Di Filia; Fight Sequences, Erik Fredricksen

CAST

Claudius	Charles Cioffi
Gertrude	Jane Alexander
Hamlet	Sam Waterston
Polonius/First Gravedigger	Larry Gates
Laertes	James Sutorius
Ophelia	Maureen Anderman
Horatio	George Hearn
Voltmand	James Gallery
Rosencrantz	David Ackroyd
Guildenstern	John Heard
Marcellus/ A. Murderer	Richard Brestoff
Francisco/Player Queen;	David Naughton
Bernardo/Priest/Dumb Show Murderer	Stephen Lang
Reynaldo	Erik Fredricksen
Second Gravedigger	Jack R. Marks
Fortinbras/Dumb Show King	Mandy Patinkin
Captain to Fortinbras/Dumb Show Queen	Hannibal Penney, Jr
Ghost of Hamlet's Father	Robert Burr
Osric	Bruce McGill
Player King	James Hurdle
Player Queen	David Naughton
Prologue/Apprentice Actor	Nancy Campbell
Company Manager	Vance Mizelle
Technical Director	Ernest Austin
Stagehands	Michael Cutt, Ronald Hunter, Reginald Vel Johnson, Jack R. Marks, David Howard

ENSEMBLE: Ernest Austin, Richard Brestoff, Michael Cutt, Erik Fredricksen, David Howard, Ronald Hunter, Reginald Vel Johnson, Henson Keys, Stephen Lang, Jack R. Marks, Vance Mizelle, Bruce McGill, David Naughton, Richard Sanders

A drama in two acts.

General Manager: Robert Kamlot
Press: Merle Debuskey, Faith Geer
Stage Managers: D. W. Koehler, Michael Chambers

Closed Jan. 25, 1976 after 47 performances and 14 previews.

George E. Joseph Photos

**Right: Sam Waterston,
and top with Jane Alexander**

George Hearn, Sam Waterston

Maureen Anderman, Larry Gates

129

MITZI E. NEWHOUSE THEATER
Opened Thursday, January 22, 1976.*
New York Shakespeare Festival presents:

THE SHORTCHANGED REVIEW

By Michael Dorn Moody; Director, Richard Southern; Scener
Marsha L. Eck; Costumes, Hilary M. Rosenfeld; Lighting, Cher;
Thacker; Sound, Samuel E. Platt; Music, Clouds; Assistant to dire
tor, Gwen Jennings; Wardrobe Master, Al Calamoneri

CAST

Ed Squall	Herbert Brah
Nicky Shannigan	Mason Adan
Vanessa Sloat	Tricia Boy
Jane Sloat Shannigan	Virginia Vesto
Darrell Shannigan	T. Mira
Peter Cope	William Ru

UNDERSTUDIES: Raleigh Bond (Nicky, Ed), Robert Burke (Da
rell, Peter), Mia Dillon (Vanessa), Janet Sarno (Jane)

A drama in two acts. The action takes place during 1975
suburban New York.

Production Manager: Andrew Mihok
Press: Merle Debuskey, Faith Geer
Stage Managers: Louis Rackoff, Zoya Wyeth

* Closed Feb. 29, 1976 after 46 performances.

Kramer-Abeles Photos

Left: Virginia Vestoff, Herbert Braha, Mason Ad:

Virginia Vestoff, Mason Adams

T. Miratti, Tricia Boyer

Ron Randell, Lynn Redgrave, Philip Bosco,
Ruth Gordon, Milo O'Shea, Edward Herrmann

VIVIAN BEAUMONT THEATER
    Opened Wednesday, February 18, 1976.*
New York Shakespeare Festival presents:

MRS. WARREN'S PROFESSION

By Bernard Shaw; Director, Gerald Freedman; Settings, David
Mitchell; Costumes, Theoni V. Aldredge; Lighting, Martin Aronstein; Assistant to director, John Seidman; Hairstylist, J. Roy Helland; Technical Director, Mervyn Haines, Jr.

CAST

Vivie Warren	Lynn Redgrave
Praed	Ron Randell
Mrs.Kitty Warren	Ruth Gordon
Sir George Crofts	Philip Bosco
Frank Gardner	Edward Herrmann
Rev. Samuel Gardner	Milo O'Shea

UNDERSTUDIES: John Carpenter (Gardner, Crofts), Donna
Isaacson (Vivie), Edmund Lyndeck (Praed), John Schak (Frank)

A drama in four acts, performed with one intermission. The action
takes place during 1894 in a summer cottage garden in Haslemere,
Surrey, England, in the rectory garden, and Honoria Fraser's chambers in Chancery Lane, London.

Press: Merle Debuskey, Faith Geer
Stage Managers: Mary Porter Hall, John Beven

Closed Apr. 4, 1976 after 55 performances and 14 previews.

Sy Friedman Photos

Edward Herrmann, Lynn Redgrave

131

Dorian Harewood, Paul Rudd

MITZI E. NEWHOUSE THEATER
Opened Wednesday, April 21, 1976.*
New York Shakespeare Festival presents:

STREAMERS

By David Rabe; Director, Mike Nichols; Setting, Tony Walt
Costumes, Bill Walker; Lighting, Ronald Wallace; Production ·
sistant, Kathy Talbert; Wardrobe Master, Al Calamoneri; Prod·
tion Supervisor, Jason Steven Cohen

CAST

Martin	Michael K
Richie	Peter Ev·
Carlyle	Dorian Harewoo·
Billy	Paul Rud·
Roger	Terry Alexan·
Sgt. Rooney	Kenneth McMil·
Sgt. Cokes	Dolph Sw·
M. P. Officer	Arlen Dean Sny·
Hinson	Les Rob·
Clark	Mark Met·
M. P.	Miklos Horv·

UNDERSTUDIES: Miklos Horvath (Clark, Hinson, M.P.),
chael Kell (Richie), Mark Metcalf (Billy), Les Roberts (Carl·
Roger), Arlen Dean Snyder (Rooney, Cokes)

A drama in two acts. The action takes place in 1965 in an a·
barracks in Virginia.

General Manager: Robert Kamlot
Production Manager: Andrew Mihok
Press: Merle Debuskey, Faith Geer
Stage Managers: Nina Seely, Miklos Horvath

* Still playing May 31, 1976.
† Succeeded by: 1. Kene Holliday, 2. Mark Metcalf, Peter We·
Martha Swope Photos

Top: Kenneth McMillan, Dolph Sweet,
Terry Alexander, Peter Evans, Paul Rudd

IVIAN BEAUMONT THEATER
Opened Saturday, May 1, 1976.*
New York Shakespeare Festival presents:

THREEPENNY OPERA

By Bertolt Brecht and Kurt Weill; Translated by Ralph Manheim
nd John Willett; Director, Richard Foreman; Scenery, Douglas W.
chmidt; Costumes, Theoni V. Aldredge; Lighting, Pat Collins;
Wardrobe Supervisor, Elonzo Dann; Sound, Joseph Dungan; Hairs-
lists, J. Roy Helland, Kathy Jones; Assistant to producers, Mari-
n Lebowitz, Peggy Marks

CAST

allad Singer	Roy Brocksmith
Mack the Knife	Raul Julia
enny Towler	Ellen Greene
onathan Peachum	C. K. Alexander
amuel	Tony Azito
harles Filch	Ed Zang
Mrs. Peachum	Elizabeth Wilson
Matt	Ralph Drischell
olly Peachum	Caroline Kava
ake	William Duell
ob	K. C. Wilson
ed	Rik Colitti
immy	Robert Schlee
Walt	Max Gulack
iger Brown	David Sabin
mith	Glenn Kezer
ucy Brown	Blair Brown
Whores	Penelope Bodry, Nancy Campbell,
	Gretel Cummings, Brenda Currin, Mimi Turque

BEGGARS AND POLICEMEN: Pendleton Brown, M. Patrick
Hughes, George McGrath, Rick Petrucelli, John Ridge, Craig
Rupp, Armin Shimerman, Jack Eric Williams, Ray Xifo.

UNDERSTUDIES: Keith Charles (Mack), Tony Azito (Ballad
inger), Penelope Bodry (Polly, Lucy), Pendleton Brown (Walt),
Gretel Cummings (Mrs. Peachum), Ralph Drischell (Peachum),
rank di Filia (Ensemble Swing), Glenn Kezer (Tiger), Liza
Kirchner (Ensemble Swing), George McGrath (Samuel, Bob), John
Ridge (Matthew), Craig Rupp (Jimmy, Smith), Armin Shimerman
Filch, Ned), Mimi Turque (Jenny), Jack Eric Williams (Ballad
inger), Ray Xifo (Jake)

A musical in three acts. The action takes place in London at the
me of Queen Victoria's Coronation, re-arranged in Brecht's imagi-
ation.

General Manager: Robert Kamlot
Production Manager: Andrew Mihok
Press: Merle Debuskey, Faith Geer
Stage Managers: D. W. Koehler, Michael Chambers, Frank Di
Filia

Still playing May 31, 1976

Kramer-Abeles Photos

ht: Raul Julia, Ellen Greene Top: C. K. Alexander,
Elizabeth Wilson, Caroline Kava

Raul Julia, Caroline Kava, David Sabin

Raul Julia, Blair Brown

133

NEW YORK SHAKESPEARE FESTIVAL
PUBLIC THEATER

Joseph Papp, Producer
Bernard Gersten, Associate Producer

PUBLIC THEATER/OTHER STAGE
Opened Sunday, November 2, 1975.*
The New York Shakespeare Festival presents:

JESSE AND THE BANDIT QUEEN

By David Freeman; Director, Gordon Stewart; Setting, Richard J. Graziano; Costumes, Hilary M. Rosenfeld; Lighting, Arden Fingerhut; Wardrobe Mistress, Sue Gandy

CAST

Belle .... Pamela Payton-Wright†1
Jesse .... Kevin O'Connor†2
Understudies: Judith Light, Tracey Walter

The play takes place in Missouri, Kansas, and the Indian Territories from just after the Civil War until the early 1880's.

Press: Bob Ullman, Bruce Cohen, Eileen McMahon
Stage Managers: Penny Gebhard, Miklos Horvath

* Closed Feb. 29, 1976 after 155 performances.
† Succeeded by: 1. Dixie Carter, 2. Barry Primus

Barry Kramer-Joseph Abeles Photos

Dixie Carter, Barry Primus Top Right:
Kevin O'Connor, Pamela Payton-Wright

Dixie Carter, Barry Primus, also above

PUBLIC/OTHER STAGE
Opened Friday, December 26, 1975.*
New York Shakespeare Festival presents:

SO NICE, THEY NAMED IT TWICE

By Neil Harris; Director, Bill Lathan; Scenery, Lighting and Visual Format, Clarke Dunham; Projections, Lucie D. Grosvenor; Sound, Gerald Dellasala; Wardrobe, Saidah Nelson

CAST

Abe	Bill Jay
Betty	Veronica Redd
Doris	Dianne Kirksey
Dr. Harris	Nick Smith
Mrs. Jones	Joanna Featherstone
Go Go Dancer	Nadyne Spratt
Reggie	Neil Harris
Gunn	J. W. Smith
Henrietta	Starletta DuPois
Kitty	Robbie McCauley
Larry	Brent Jennings
Lee	Taurean Blacque
Terry	Alfre Woodard
Miji	Allen Ayers
Country Bill	Hank Ross
Passersby	War Hawk Tanzania, Cheryl Jones, Hank Frazier

UNDERSTUDIES: Gerry Black (Abe), Hank Frazier (Gunn, Miji, Country Bill), Nadyne Spratt (Kitty, Terry), War Hawk Tanzania (Reggie, Lee, Larry), Cheryl Jones (Doris, Henrietta), Sundra Jean Williams (Betty, Mrs. Jones)

A play in two acts. The action takes place at the present time in New York City.

General Manager: Robert Kamlot
Press: Merle Debuskey, Bob Ullman, Bruce Cohen
Stage Managers: Martha Knight, Toby MacBeth

* Closed Jan. 4, 1976 after 8 performances.

Kramer-Abeles Photo

Neil Harris, Dianne Kirksey

**John Ferraro, Michael Moran,
David Laden, Larry Pine**

PUBLIC THEATER/MARTINSON HALL
Opened Wednesday, January 21, 1976.*
New York Shakespeare Festival presents:

JINXS BRIDGE

By Michael Moran; Conceived, Directed and Designed by members of The Manhattan Project (Andre Gregory, Artistic Director); Lighting, Victor En Yu Tan; Special Effects, Arthur Muhleisen

CAST

Ghost of Capt. Ogden Leroy Jinxs	Tom Costello
Charlie	John P. Holms
Mendelsohn Wilkes Jinxs	Tom Costello
Alvin Dimple	Himself
Carl	Michael Moran
Maeve Zant	Kate Weiman
Vito Benelli	John Ferraro
Elmo Durke	Larry Pine
Fred E. Metzman	David Laden
Maria Louise Bianci	Angela Pietropinto

A play in 2 acts and 5 scenes. The action takes place in a room under a bridge over the Harlem River at the present time.

Production Manager: Carlos Esposito
Company Manager: Victoria Berning

Press: Bob Ullman, Bruce Cohen, Eileen McMahon

* Closed Feb. 15, 1975 after 31 performances.

PUBLIC/NEWMAN THEATER
Opened Thursday, February 19, 1976.*
New York Shakespeare Festival presents:

RICH AND FAMOUS

By John Guare; Director, Mel Shapiro; Musical Direction and Arrangements, Herbert Kaplan; Music and Lyrics, John Guare; Setting, Dan Snyder; Costumes, Theoni V. Aldredge; Lighting, Arden Fingerhut; Production Assistant, Jory Johnson; Wardrobe Mistress, Melissa Adzima; Production Supervisor, Jason Steven Cohen; Technical Director, Mervyn Haines, Jr.

CAST

Bing Ringling . . . . William Atherton
All Other Characters . . . . Ron Leibman, Anita Gillette

A comedy performed without intermission. The action takes place on the opening night of Bing Ringling's first produced play.

General Manager: Robert Kamlot
Production Manager: Andrew Mihok
Press: Merle Debuskey, Bob Ullman, Bruce Cohen
Stage Managers: Peter von Mayrhauser, Jean Weigel

* Closed April 25, 1976 after 120 performances.

Martha Swope Photos

**Ron Leibman, William Atherton,
Anita Gillette (also above)**

PUBLIC/ANSPACHER THEATER

Opened Thursday, February 12, 1976.*
New York Shakespeare Festival presents:

APPLE PIE

Libretto, Myrna Lamb; Music, Nicholas Meyers; Director, Joseph Papp; Design, David Mitchell; Costumes, Timothy Miller; Lighting, Pat Collins; Musical Direction, Liza Redfield; Paintings, Richard Lindner; Visuals, Thom Lafferty, David Mitchell; Movement, Lynne Weber; Associate Producer, Bernard Gersten; Assistant to director, Andy Lopata; Production Assistant, Jonathan Sheffer; Assistant Conductor, Bill Grossman; Wardrobe Mistress, Jackie Carhart

CAST

Lise	Stephanie Cotsirilos
The Mirror	Ilsebet Anna Tebesli
Mother Marlene	Lucille Patton
Streicher	Spain Logue
American	Robert Polenz
Doctor	Joseph Neal
Boss	John Watson
Marshall	Robert Guillaume†
Harry/Father	Lee Allen

UNDERSTUDIES: Harry/Father, Virgil Curry; Streicher, Will Sharpe Marshall; Marshall, Ra Joe Darby; Lise, Marlene, Mirror, Dorothea Joyce

MUSICAL NUMBERS: "Yesterday Is Over," "I'm Lise," "Waltz of Lise's Childhood," "Father's Waltz," "Men Come with Guns," "Hundsvieh," "Mother's March," "The Trial," "Marshall's Blues," "Counterman," "America, We're in New York," "Victim Dream," "Stockboy Blues," "Too Much Motet," "Mating Dance," "Love Scene," "The Doctor," "Lise Dear," "The Wedding," "Gun Scene," "Harry's Rag," "Freedom Anthem," "Reified Expression," "Break-up Rag," "Marshall's Reply," "Survival Song," "Final Judgment"

A musical work performed without intermission.

General Manager: Robert Kamlot
Press: Bob Ullman, Bruce Cohen, Eileen McMahon
Stage Managers: Richard S. Viola, Jane E. Neufeld

* Closed March 21, 1976 after 72 performances.
† Succeeded by Alan Weeks

Sy Friedman Photos

**Stephanie Cotsirilos, Lee Allen, Robert Guillaume
Top: Spain Logue, Stephanie Cotsirilos,
Lucille Patton, John Watson, Ilsebet Anna Tebesli,
Joseph Neal, Robert Rolenz, Lee Allen**

**Maria Zakrzewski, Joseph Chaikin, Ray Barry,
Jake Dengel, Ron Faber, Arthur Strimling**

PUBLIC/MARTINSON THEATER

Opened Wednesday, March 24, 1976.*
The New York Shakespeare Festival presents:

WOYZECK

By Georg Buchner; Completed by Mira Rafalowicz; Director, Leonardo Shapiro; Lighting, Nicholas Wolff Lyndon; Costumes, Patricia McGourty; Design Coordinator, Ronald Antone; Music, Peter Golub; Production Manager, DeLoss Brown

CAST

Drum Major/Grandmother/Cop	Ray Barry
Idiot	James Carrington
Woyzeck	Joseph Chaikin
Child/Doctor/Soldier	Jake Dengel
Captain/Barker/Soldier/Student/Pawnbroker	Ron Faber
Andres/Old Man/Soldier/Student/Child	Christopher McCann
Marie	Jane Mandel
Announcer/Servant/Soldier/Student	Arthur Strimling
Margaret/Monkey/Horse/Kathy/Child	Maria Zakrzewski

* Closed Apr. 25, 1976 after 35 performances.

Nathaniel Tileston Photo

PHOENIX THEATRE

T. Edward Hambleton, Managing Director
Marilyn S. Miller, Executive Director
Daniel Freudenberger, Producing Director

THE PLAYHOUSE
Opened Monday, January 26, 1976.*
The Phoenix Theatre presents

27 WAGONS FULL OF COTTON

by Tennessee Williams
and

A MEMORY OF TWO MONDAYS

by Arthur Miller
Scenery and Lighting, James Tilton; Costumes, Albert Wolsky;
Production Manager, Robert Beard; Production Assistant, Barbara
Carrellas

CAST

"27 Wagons Full of Cotton"
Jake Meighan .... Roy Poole
Flora Meighan .... Meryl Streep
Silva Vicarro .... Tony Musante

UNDERSTUDIES: Jake, Rex Robbins; Flora, Fiddle Viracola;
Silva, Joel Colodner

The action takes place on the front porch of the Meighan's cottage
near Blue Mountain, Mississippi.

"A Memory of Two Mondays"
Bert .... Thomas Hulce
Raymond .... Pierre Epstein
Agnes .... Alice Drummond
Patricia .... Meryl Streep
Gus .... Roy Poole
Jim .... Leonardo Cimino
Kenneth .... John Lithgow
Larry .... Tony Musante
Frank .... Joe Grifasi
Jerry .... Joel Colodner
William .... Calvin Jung
Tom .... Rex Robbins
Mechanic .... Clarence Felder
Mr. Eagle .... Ben Kapen

UNDERSTUDIES: Bert, Kenneth, Joel Colodner; Gus, Jim, Ben
Kapen; Raymond, Larry, Clarence Felder; Patricia, Linda Carlson;
Agnes, Fiddle Viracola; Tom, Joe Grifasi

The action takes place in the shipping room of a large auto parts
warehouse in Manhattan.

General Manager: Marilyn S. Miller
Press: Gifford/Wallace, Tom Trenkle
Stage Managers: Jonathan Penzner, Peter DeNicola

* Closed March 21, 1976 after 40 performances in repertory and 7
previews.

Van Williams Photos

Top Left: Roy Poole, Meryl Streep

Tony Musante, Roy Poole, Meryl Streep

Roy Poole, Joel Colodner, Calvin Jung, Pierre Epstein, John Lithgow, Tony Musante, Thomas Hulce, Rex Robbins Top: (L) Meryl Streep, Tony Musante (R) Tony Musante, Thomas Hulce, John Lithgow, Clarence Felder

THEY KNEW WHAT THEY WANTED

By Sidney Howard; Director, Stephen Porter; Production Manager, Robert Beard; Production Assistant, Barbara Carrellas; Wardrobe Supervisor, Helen McMahon; Hairstylist, J. Roy Helland

CAST

Joe	Barry Bostwick
Father McKee	Leonardo Cimino
Ah Gee	Calvin Jung
Tony	Louis Zorich
The R. F. D.	Ben Kapen
Amy	Lois Nettleton
Angelo	Clarence Felder
Giorgio	Joel Colodner
The Doctor	Rex Robbins

UNDERSTUDIES: Tony, Clarence Felder; Amy, Linda Carlson; Joe, Joel Colodner; Father McKee, Doctor, Pierre Epstein

A drama in three acts. The action takes place in Tony's farmhouse in the Napa Valley, California.

General Manager: Marilyn S. Miller
Press: Gifford/Wallace, Tom Trenkle
Stage Managers: Jonathan Penzner, Peter DeNicola

* Closed March 6, 1976 after 23 performances in repertory.

Van Williams Photos

Barry Bostwick, Lois Nettleton, Louis Zorich Top Right: Lois Nettleton, Louis Zorich

THE PLAYHOUSE
Opened Monday, April 12, 1976.*
The Phoenix Theatre presents:

SECRET SERVICE

By William Gillette; Director, Daniel Freudenberger; Scenery and Lighting, James Tilton; Costumes, Clifford Capone; Audio, David Rapkin; Musical Director, Arthur Miller; Hairstylist, Lyn Quiyou; Production Assistant, Barbara Carrellas; Wardrobe Supervisor, Helen McMahon

CAST

Wilfred Varney	Don Scardino
Martha	Louise Stubbs
Mrs. Varney	Alice Drummond
Edith Varney	Meryl Streep
Jonas	David Harris
Lt. Maxwell	Frederick Coffin
Capt. Thorne	John Lithgow
Caroline Mitford	Marybeth Hurt
Benton Arrelsford	Charles Kimbrough
Cpl. Matson	Joe Grifasi
Pvt. Eddinger	Stuart Warmflash
Cavalry Orderly	Moultrie Patten
Henry Dumont	Lenny Baker
Lt. Allison	Jonathan Penzner
Lt. Foray	Rex Robbins
Telegraph Messenger	Hansford Rowe
Sgt. Wilson	Jeffrey Jones
Maj. Gen. Harrison Randolph	Roy Poole
Banjo, Autoharp, Harmonica	Arthur Miller

UNDERSTUDIES: Gwendolyn Brown (Mrs. Varney, Edith), Stuart Warmflash (Wilfred), Ann McDonough (Caroline), Rex Robbins (Thorne), Frederick Coffin (Benton), Jeffrey Jones (Maxwell, Dumont), Joe Grifasi (Foray), Moultrie Patten (Randolph, Allison)

A play in 2 acts and 4 scenes. The action takes place during 1864 in General Varney's house on Franklin Street in Richmond, VA, and in the War Department's telegraph office.

General Manager: Marilyn S. Miller
Production Manager: Robert Beard
Press: Gifford/Wallace, Tom Trenkle
Stage Managers: Jonathan Penzner, Peter DeNicola

* Closed May 2, 1976 after 13 performances in repertory with "Boy Meets Girl."

Van Williams Photos

John Lithgow, Meryl Streep

Top: Marybeth Hurt, John Lithgow
ght: Meryl Streep, Alice Drummond, Charles Kimbrough

THE PLAYHOUSE
Opened Tuesday, April 13, 1976.*
The Phoenix Theatre presents:

BOY MEETS GIRL

By Bella and Sam Spewack; Director, John Lithgow; Scenery and Lighting, James Tilton; Costumes, Clifford Capone; Audio, David Rapkin; Musical Director, Arthur Miller

CAST

Robert Law	Lenny Baker
Larry Toms	Frederick Coffin
J. Carlyle Benson	Charles Kimbrough
Rosetti	Rex Robbins
Mr. Friday (C. F.)	Roy Poole
Peggy	Ann McDonough
Miss Crews	Alice Drummond
Rodney Bevan	Don Scardino
Green/Announcer	Joe Grifasi
Slade	Moultrie Patten
Susie	Marybeth Hurt
Studio Nurse	Gwendolyn Brown
Young Man	Stuart Warmflash
Studio Officer	David Harris
Cutter	Arthur Miller
Hospital Nurse	Louise Stubbs
Major Thompson	Jeffrey Jones

UNDERSTUDIES: Joe Grifasi (Law), Moultrie Patten (Larry, Thompson), Jeffrey Jones (Benson, Rosetti), Stuart Warmflash (Bevan, Slade), Ann McDonough (Susie), Gwendolyn Brown (Miss Crews), Louise Stubbs (Peggy), David Harris (Green), Hansford Rowe (Friday)

A comedy in 3 acts and 7 scenes. The action takes place in the Royal Studios in Hollywood, CA, in the past.

Production Manager: Robert Beard
Press: Gifford/Wallace, Tom Trenkle
Stage Managers: Jonathan Penzner, Peter DeNicola

* Closed May 1, 1976 after 10 performances in repertory with "Secret Service."

Van Williams Photos

Top: Charles Kimbrough, Lenny Baker, also Right with Rex Robbins, Frederick Coffin

142

Alice Drummond, Charles Kimbrough, Marybeth Hurt, Lenny Baker, Roy Poole Above Baker, Kimbrough, Joe Grifasi

PLAYWRIGHTS HORIZONS, INC.

Robert Moss, Executive Director
Philip Himberg, Producing Director
Associate Producer, Joan Lowell; Fiscal Manager, Jim Swaine; Technical Directors, Charles Tyndall, Mary Calhoun; Associate Technical Director, Christie Heiss; Program Administrator, Ira Schlosser; Literary Manager, Andre Bishop

PLAYWRIGHTS HORIZONS

June 19–22, 1975 (4 performances)

TWELFTH NIGHT by William Shakespeare; Director, Garland Wright; Set, Jemima; Stage Managers, Robert Tomlin, Eric Segal; Produced in association with The Lion Theatre Company. CAST: Garland Wright, Jack Heifner, John Arnone, William Metzo, Robert Machray, Gene Nye, John Guerrasio, Sharon Laughlin, Wanda Bimson, Janice Fuller, Bill Karnowsky, Randy Goldsborough

June 22–29, 1975 (10 performances)

MISSISSIPPI MOONSHINE by Jim Magnuson; Director, Leland Moss; Set, Jim Stewart; Costumes, Susan Dennison; Lights, Jeremy Lewis; Stage Manager, Christie Heiss. CAST: Mike Burke, Mary Carter, Kathleen Chalfant, Kelly Fitzpatrick, David Gallagher, Jane Galloway, Laurie Heinemann, Gil Robbins, John Ross, Ken Tigar, Ron Van Lieu, Horton Willis

June 24–27, 1975 (3 performances)

SWAN DIVE by Frederick Kirwin; Director, Caymichael Patten; Lights, Charles Tyndall; Stage Manager, Georgie Fleenor. CAST: Maria Cellario, Christopher Pitney, Rozanne Ritch

June 27–30, 1975 (4 performances)

GETTING GERTIE'S GARTER by Willson Collison and Avery Hopwood; Director, Robert Moss; Sets and Lights, Richard Williams; Costumes, Hugh Sherrer; Stage Manager, Connie Alexis; Produced in association with the Joseph Jefferson Theatre Company. CAST: Carole Doscher, Peter Simpson, Cathy Roskam, Maria Cellario, Robert McFarland, Dana Gladstone, Douglas Travis, Linda Robbins, Dameon Fayad

September 25–October 12, 1975 (14 performances)

CLAIR AND THE CHAIR by Marsha Sheiness; Director, Hillary Wyler; Lights, Arden Fingerhut; Stage Manager, Kent Rigsby. CAST: Linda Barry, Jane Cook, Lisa Bryon, Arthur DeMaio
PROFESSOR GEORGE by Marsha Sheiness; Director, Miss Sheiness; Stage Manager, David Rosenberg. CAST: Steve Pomerantz, Alice Elliott, Maria Callario, Paul Lieber, Robert Burke, Victoria Boothby

October 2–9, 1975 (7 performances)

THE IMPORTANCE OF BEING EARNEST by Oscar Wilde; Director, Paul Cooper; Sets, Hope Auerbach; Costumes, Lorri Schneider; Lights, Cheryl Thacker; Stage Manager, Christie Heiss. CAST: Ron Johnston, Peter Bartlett, Gene Nye, Margaret Gwenver, Jayne Haynes, Kathleen Gray, Alice White, Robert Einenkel

"A Report to the Stockholders"

PLAYWRIGHTS HORIZONS

October 16–November 2, 1975 (13 performances)

A QUALITY OF MERCY by Roma Greth; Director, Anita Khanzadian; Sets, Cliff Simon; Costumes, Louise Herman; Lights, James Chaleff; Sound, Joe Lazarus; Stage Manager, Ian McColl. CAST: Andy Backer, Sheila Coonan, Elizabeth Perry, Fran Myers, Kathy Bates, John Martinuzzi

October 23–30, 1975 (7 performances)

THE MIKADO by Gilbert and Sullivan; Director, Barry Keating; Musical Director, Larry Garner; Associate Director, Pat LaVelle; Sets, Frank Kelly; Costumes, Bosha Johnson, Cynthia Ann Geis; Lights, James Chaleff; Stage Manager, Adrien Birnbaum. CAST: Sebastian Russ, Ira Siff, Barry Keating, Tom Cipolla, Vance Mizelle, Chuck Richie, Martha Thigpen, Leslie Middlebrook, Cyndee Szymkowicz, Marjorie Minnis, Lauren Shub, Maura Stevens, Deborah Packard, Linda Creamer, Bernard Mantel, Robert B. Whittemore, Craig Sturgis, Charles Ryan

November 6–23, 1975 (14 performances)

THE LYMWORTH MILLIONS by David Shumaker; Director, Alfred Gingold; Sets, Joe Lazarus; Costumes, Louise Herman; Lights, John Gisondi; Stage Manager, Marjie Klein. CAST: George Mirabella, Mary Jennings Dean, Cathy Roskam, Peter Coffeen, Brian Meister, Lynda Myles, Andy Backer

November 17–21, 1975 (5 performances)

GLANCE OF A LANDSCAPE by Stephen Yaffee; Director, William Shorr; Set, Tony Straiges; Lights, Tony Santoro; Stage Manager, Barbara Murphy. CAST: Kent Rigsby, Tom Cuff, Robert J. Herron, Peter Evans, Lee Wilkof, Randall Merrifield, Alan Rosenberg, Christine Jansen, Frank Spencer

November 25–December 14, 1975 (13 performances)

REPORT TO THE STOCKHOLDERS by Kevin O'Morrison; Director, Robert H. Livingston; Music, Louis Schere; Set and Lighting, Clarke Dunham; Costumes, Allen Munch; Stage Manager, Lewis Pshena. CAST: Ron Comenzo, Peter Dompe, Hugh L. Hurd, Robbee Jones, Dolores Kenan, John Lack, J. Frank Lucas, James Pritchett, Michael Sklaroff, Paulette Sinclair, Chris Weatherhead

December 4–11, 1975 (8 performances)

JULIUS CAESAR by William Shakespeare; Director, Paul Schneider; Sets, David Sackeroff; Costumes, Greg Etchison; Lights, Paul Kaine; Stage Managers, Katherine Mylenki, Ellen Zalk. CAST: John Archibald, Neal Arluck, Ralph Byers, Pierre Epstein, Steven Gilborn, Tony Giardina, Robert Grillo, Charles Harper, Steven Pamela Lewis, Pinocchio Madrid, Jeff Maron, Tom McCready, Charles Morey, Claude Peters, Jack Pettey, Peter Reznikoff, John Shearin, James Shearwood, Robert Silver

December 4–6, 1975 (5 performances)

MATT, THE KILLER by Howard Pflanzer; Director, Paul Cooper; Stage Manager, Cindy S. Tennenbaum. CAST: Dan Deitch, Richard Allert, Alison Mills, Janis Dardaris, Elliot Burtoff, Harold Cherry, Stan Edelman

Douglas Travis, Maria Cellario in
"Getting Gertie's Garter"

PLAYWRIGHTS HORIZONS

December 17, 1975–January 4, 1976 (10 performances)

WINNER TAKE ALL by Meir Zvi Ribalow; Director, Michael Heaton; Stage Manager, Marjie Klein. CAST: Linda Carlson, Paul Geier, Lin Shaye

December 18–28, 1975 (9 performances)

GUY GAUTHIER'S EGO PLAY by Guy Gauthier; Director, Kent Wood; Sets, Minda Chipurnoi; Costumes, Danny Morgan; Lights, Gail Kennison; Stage Manager, Ira Schlosser. CAST: Robert Burke, Laurie Copland, Sheldon Feldner, Paul Lieber

January 8–18, 1976 (8 performances)

MISALLIANCE by George Bernard Shaw; Director, Robert Moss; Sets, Frank Kelly; Costumes, Susan Sudert; Lights, John Gisondi; Stage Manager, Amy Chase. CAST: Richard Ryder, Peter Simpson, Carolyn Kruse, Victoria Boothby, Gil Robbins, Douglas Fisher, Peter Brouwer, Jane Sanford, Keith McDermott

January 15–February 1, 1976 (13 performances)

VANITIES by Jack Heifner; Director, Garland Wright; Sets, John Arnone; Costumes, David James; Lights, Tony Santoro; Stage Manager, Charles Kopelman; Produced in association with the Lion Theatre Co. CAST: Jane Galloway, Susan Merson, Kathy Bates

January 29–February 7, 1976 (11 performances)

OCEAN WALK by Philip Magdalany; Director, Michael Flanagan; Sets, John Gisondi; Costumes, Marya Ursin; Lights, Paul Kaine; Stage Managers, Ted Snowdon, Steve Burdick. CAST: Geraldine Court, Claire Malis, T. Richard Mason, John Martinuzzi, Rex Stallings, John Shearin

February 6–15, 1976 (9 performances)

THE CHEKHOV COMEDIES by Anton Chekhov; Directors, Jonathan Alper, Dennis Pearlstein, Kent Wood, Robert Moss, Philip J. Himberg; Composer, Jeremiah Murray; Sets, Chris Thomas; Lights, David George; Costumes, Louise Herman; Stage Managers, Ian McColl, Marjie Klein. CAST: Anthony Baksa, Patrick Beatey, Kenneth Bell, Victoria Boothby, Jim Broaddus, Mary Louise Burke, Larry Carr, Mike Champagne, Samuel Chapin, Richert Easley, Dameon Fayad, Lucy Lee Flippen, Donna Gabel, Madeline Gorman, Ron Lindbloom, Tony Pandolfo, Don Paul, Linda Phillips, Susan Varon, David Washburn

February 11–15, 1976 (7 performances)

THE TEACHER'S ROOM by Howard Pflanzer; Director, Carol Corwen; Stage Manager, Cindy Tennenbaum. CAST: Leonard Di Sesa, Robert McFarland, Sharon Spitz, William Hart, Robert Barger, Hal Studer, Rick Petrucelli, Billie Lou Watt

"Misalliance" Top Right: **"The Teacher's Room"**
Below: **"Guy Gauthier's Ego Play"**

"Winner Take All"
Above: **"Oceanwalk"**

PLAYWRIGHTS HORIZONS

February 19–28, 1976 (13 performances)

THE PUBLIC GOOD by Susan Dworkin; Director, Leonard Peters; Sets, Steve Duffy, Costumes, Ruth A. Wells; Lights, John Gisondi; Stage Managers, Patricia Wingerter, Steven Steisel, Mary Burns. CAST: Patricia Triana, Robert Bonds, Earl Hindman, Dennis Tate, Martin Shakar, Andrew Bloch, Robert Manuel, Jim Weiss, June Squibb, Marsha Wischhusen, Anne Murray, Sharron Shayne, Rise Cherylyn Collins, Avner Reyer, A. D. Cannon

February 26–March 13, 1976 (13 performances)

THE SPELLING BEE by Marsha Sheiness; Director, Harold Scott; Sets, John Scheffler; Costumes, Kenneth M. Yount; Lights, Arden Fingerhut; Stage Managers, David Rosenberg, Linda Robin Morris. CAST: Joel Brooks, Chevi Colton, Robyn Goodman, Patricia Stewart, Christopher Curry, McLin Crowell, Amelia Haas, John Wylie

March 17–28, 1976 (14 performances)

THE BOSS by Edward Sheldon; Director, Edward Gilbert; Set, Lawrence King; Costumes, Carrie F. Robbins; Lights, William Mintzer; Stage Manager, Bob Jaffe. CAST: Allan Frank, Gregory Abels, Louise Shaffer, John Genke, Dennis Lipscomb, Andrew Jarkowsky, Richard K. Sanders, Pamela Burrell, John Eames, Tom-Patrick Dineen, Chris Carrick, Igors Gavon, Chip Lucia, Catherine Henry Lamm

March 17–21, 1976 (6 performances)

PUP by Iris Rosofsky; Director, Anita Khanzadian; Stage Manager, David Thalenberg. CAST: Edwin Owens, Janice Fuller, Mary Carter, Eddy Jones, Cynthia Frost

April 1–18, 1976 (13 performances)

PERCHED ON A GABARDINE CLOUD by Steven Braunstein; Director, Frank Cento; Sets and Lights, David George; Costumes, Greg Etchison; Stage Manager, Ian McColl. CAST: Rex D. Hays, Alan Braunstein, K. T. Baumann, Liesha Gullison, Geena Goodwin, Don Paul, Joel Simon, Robert C. Brandt, Kate Weiman

April 1–25, 1976 (12 performances)

TWO FOR THE SEESAW by William Gibson; Director, Michael Heaton; Set, John Gisondi; Costumes, Louise Klein; Lights, William D. Anderson; Stage Manager, Marjie Klein. CAST: Lin Shaye, John Cunningham

April 22–May 1, 1976 (11 performances)

MAGRITTE SKIES by Yale M. Udoff; Director, Richard Place; Sets, John W. Jacobsen; Costumes, Greg Etchison; Lights, Spencer Mosse; Stage Manager, Iris Olshin. CAST: Chevi Colton, Mark Lenard, Tobias Haller, Faith Catlin

PLAYWRIGHTS HORIZONS

April 29–May 9, 1976 (11 performances)

GEORGE WASHINGTON SLEPT HERE by George S. Kaufman and Moss Hart; Director, Paul Cooper; Lights, William J. Plachy; Costumes, Louise Klein; Stage Managers, Ellen Zalk, Camille Monte. CAST: Elaine Bromka, Michael Burke, Mary Carter, Jerome Collamore, Louis Cruz, Carmelita Fuentes, Margaret Gwenver, Bob Horen, Greg Johnson, Joan Lowell, Bob Luciano, William Robertson, Douglas Stark, Dai Stockton, Louise Williams, Ellen Murray

May 13–22, 1976 (12 performances)

THE CASEWORKER by George Whitmore; Director, Leland Moss; Sets, Christopher Hacker; Costumes, Susan Dennison; Lights, Jeffrey Schissler; Sound, Harry Itkowitz; Stage Manager, Bruce Conner. CAST: William Schilling, Tony Campisi, Chuck McCaughan, Mary Carter

May 27–June 5, 1976 (12 performances)

CAKES WITH THE WINE by Edward M. Cohen; Directed by the author; Sets, Greg Etchison; Costumes, Louise Herman; Lights, Tony Santoro; Stage Manager, Peter DeLaurier. CAST: Nita Reiter, Helen Hanft, Jake Dengel, Anna Shaler, Rodman Flender, Willy Switkes, Arn Weiner, Warren Pincus, Stan Edelman, Charles Kopelman

Top Right: "Perched on a Gabardine Cloud"
Below: "Magritte Skies"

"Cakes with the Wine"
Above: "George Washington Slept Here"

PUBLIC PLAYERS, INC.

J. Perry McDonald, Producer-Director

CENTRAL ARTS THEATRE
Saturday, September 20, 1975

ONCE IN A LIFETIME by Moss Hart and George S. Kaufman; Director, J. Perry McDonald; Assistant Director, Gary Knight; Music John Kander, Stephen Sondheim, Guiseppe Verdi; Sound, Joseph Bly; Sets and Lighting, Charles McDonough. CAST: Jim Hackett (George), Nancy Frangione (May), Rod Britt (Jerry), Andrew C. Dinan (Porter/Ernest), Dana Smith (Helen), Erika Fox (Susan), Candace Coulston (Phyllis), Jo Ann Havrilla (Florabel), Peggy Cooper (Mrs. Walker), Dolph Browning (Herman)

December 4–7, 1975 (4 performances)

RING ROUND THE MOON by Jean Anouilh; Director, J. Perry McDonald; Pianist, Eliott Finkle. CAST: Charles McDonough (Hugo), Dolph Browning (Joshua), John Sheehan (Frederic), Jamy Rand (Diana), J. R. Horne (Messerschmann), Nancy L. Green (Lady India), Andrew C. Dinan (Patrice), Marguerite Hunt (Mme. Desmortes), Carol de Onis (Capulet), Andrew Natzke (Romainville), Nancy Frangione (Isabelle), Peggy Cooper (Her Mother)

January 22–February 1, 1976 (8 performances)

LA RONDE by Arthur Schnitzler; English Version, Eric Bentley; Producer-Director, J. Perry McDonald; Associate Producer, Iris Grossman; Assistant to producers, Ellen Kaplan; Lighting, Ricki Klein; Set, Charles McDonough; Costumes, Max Navarre; Stage Manager, Andrea Larson. CAST: Nancy Frangione (Whore), Gerard Surerus (Soldier), Nancy L. Green (Parlor Maid), John Sheehan (Young Gentleman), Barbara Myers (Young Wife), Jim Hackett (Husband), Mary Ann Renz (Little Miss), Bernard Tato (Poet), Peggy Cooper (Actress), Mark M. Kelly (Count)

March 11–21, 1976 (12 performances)

A MIDSUMMER NIGHT'S DREAM by William Shakespeare; Director-Producer, J. Perry McDonald; Assistant Director, Iris Grossman; Lighting, Ricki Klein; Set, Charles McDonough; Costumes, Max Navarre; Audio, Joe Bly; Press, Fern Alvins; Stage Manager, Amy Corenthal. CAST: Peggy Cooper (Hippolyta), Alan Coates (Theseus), Edward Sager (Egeus), Mary Ann Renz (Hermia), John Sheehan (Demetrius), Gerard Surerus (Lysander), Nancy Frangione (Helena), Andrew C. Dinan (Peter Quince), Jim Hackett (Bottom), Mark M. Kelly (Flute), Bobby Sheridan (Snout), Elbert Dinkins (Snug), K. W. Geoffries (Starveling), Pat Pell (Puck), Dorothy Fielding (Titania), Richard Ryder (Oberon)

Frank Derbas, Ron Schwinn Photos

Top Right: cast of "La Ronde"
Below: "Ring Round the Moon"

Dorothy Fielding

"A Midsummer Night's Dream"

ROUNDABOUT THEATRE COMPANY

Gene Feist, Producing Director
Michael Fried, Executive Director
Tenth Season

ROUNDABOUT THEATRE/STAGE TWO
Opened Wednesday, June 4, 1975.*
The Roundabout Theatre Company presents:

A MUSICAL MERCHANT OF VENICE

Book, William Shakespeare; Music, Jim Smith; Lyrics, Tony Tanner; Director, Tony Tanner; Set, Sandro LaFerla; Costumes, Dwayne Moritz; Lights, Lewis Mead; Associate Producer, David Guc; Production Associates, Diane Factor, Mark McKenna; Manager, Leslie H. Magerman

CAST

Lorenzo .... Gary Beach
Antonio .... Rudy Hornish
Portia .... Cara-Duff McCormick
Jessica .... Mary Ann Robbins
Shylock .... Danny Sewell
Duke .... Albert Verdesca
Arragon .... Sel Vitella
Gratiano .... John Thomas Waite
Nerissa .... Phylis Ward
Bassanio .... Mark Winkworth
Chorus ..... Michael Bright, Linda diDario, Nancy Donovan, Jack Godby, Sara Maylond, Theresa Saldana

Press: Gerald Siegal
Stage Manager: Charles Repole

* Closed June 13, 1975 after limited engagement of 12 performances.

Sara Lou Cooper, Wyman Pendleton, Deborah Mooney, Bill Newman, Katharine Stanton, Robin Rose, Michael Storm, Livia Genise, Lou Meade, Eda Reiss Merin, Nancy Donovan in "Summer and Smoke"

Deborah Mooney, Michael Storm

ROUNDABOUT THEATRE/STAGE ONE
Opened Monday, October 6, 1975.*
Roundabout Theatre Company presents:

SUMMER AND SMOKE

By Tennessee Williams; Director, Gene Feist; Set, Holmes Easley; Lighting, Ian Calderon; Costumes, Christina Giannini; Sound, T. Richard Fitzgerald; Score, Philip Campanella; Sculpture, Debra Schechter; Hairstylist, Paul Huntley; Technical Director, Lewis Mead; Production Supervisor, Ian Calderon; Assistant Producers, Steve Evans, David Guc

CAST

Mrs. Winemiller .... Sara Lou Cooper
Rev. Winemiller .... Wyman Pendleton
Alma Winemiller .... Debra Mooney
Dr. John Buchanan, Jr. .... Michael Storm
Rosa Gonzales .... Livia Genise
Nellie Ewell .... Robin Pearson Rose
Chloe .... Katharine Stanton
Roger Doremus .... William Newman
Dr. John Buchanan, Sr. .... Edward Holmes
Mrs. Bassett .... Eda Reiss Merin
Rosemary .... Nancy Donovan
Dusty .... Lewis Mead
Gonzales .... John Seitz
Archie Kramer .... Howard Schechter

A drama in two acts. The action takes place in the town of Glorious Hill, Miss., at the turn of the century.

General Manager: Mary Beth Carroll
Company Manager: Barbara Price
Production Manager: James Grant
Press: Gerald Siegal, Valerie Warner
Stage Manager: Douglas F. Goodman

* Closed Oct. 9, 1975 after 40 performances and 24 previews.

Martha Swope Photos

ROUNDABOUT THEATRE/STAGE TWO
Opened Thursday, December 4, 1975.*
Roundabout Theatre Company and McGraw-Lyttle Productions present:

DEAR MR. G

By Donna de Matteo; Director, Gene Feist; Set, Holmes Easley; Costumes, Christina Giannini; Lighting, Dan Koetting, Ian Calderon; Assistant to director, Diane Factor; Wardrobe, Samantha S. Hamilton

CAST

Tommy Giordano	Antony Ponzini
Marlene Giordano	Karen Leslie
Louis "Squint" Polaski	Chip Zien
Roscoe Nigera	Frank Nastasi
Carmella Giordano	Mildred Clinton

A comedy in two acts. The action takes place at the present time in the home of Mr. and Mrs. Thomas Giordano in a suburban town in Queens, N. Y.

Company Manager: Barbara Price
Press: Gerald Siegal, Valerie Warner
Stage Manager: J. R. Grant

* Closed Jan. 4, 1976 after 37 performances and 9 previews.

Martha Swope Photos

Right: Mildred Clinton, Frank Nastasi, Anthony Ponzini, Karen Leslie, Chip Zien Top: Karen Leslie, Chip Zien, Anthony Ponzini

Anthony McKay, Sam McMurray, Sonny Fox, Stephen Keep, Nancy Addison, Barbara Britton, Marian Clarke

ROUNDABOUT THEATRE/STAGE ONE
Opened Tuesday, January 6, 1976.*
Roundabout Theatre Company presents:

CLARENCE

By Booth Tarkington; Director, Gene Feist; Set, Holmes Easle; Costumes, Christina Giannini; Lighting, Ian Calderon; Musical S; pervision, Philip Campanella; Hairstylist, Paul Huntley; Technic Director, Lewis Mead; Wardrobe, Rozanne Myers

CAST

Mrs. Martyn	Lorraine Spritz
Mr. Wheeler	Sonny F.
Mrs. Wheeler	Barbara Britt
Bobby Wheeler	Sam McMurr
Cora Wheeler	Nancy Addis
Violet Pinney	Marian Clar
Clarence	Stephen Ke
Della	Carolyn Lagerf
Dinwiddie	John Neville-Andre
Hubert Stem	Anthony McK

A comedy in four acts, presented with two intermissions. T action takes place during 1919 in Mr. Wheeler's office in New Yo and the living room of his home in Englewood, N.J.

Production Manager: James Grant
Press: Gerald Siegal, Valerie Warner
Stage Manager: Douglas F. Goodman

* Closed Feb. 15, 1976 after 48 performances and 16 previews.

Martha Swope Photos

ROUNDABOUT THEATRE/STAGE ONE
Opened Monday, April 26, 1976.*
Roundabout Theatre Company presents:

THE CHERRY ORCHARD

By Anton Chekhov; Director, Robert Mandel; Set, Holmes Easley; Costumes, Christina Giannini; Lighting, Arden Fingerhut; Music, Robert Dennis; Choreography, Pennye Stahlnecker; Hairstylist Robert Baker; Technical Director, Lewis Mead; Technical Coordinator, James Grant; Assistant to director, Craig LaPlount; Wardrobe Mistress, Nette Reynolds.

CAST

Lopahin	Paul Benedict
Dunyasha	Regina Baff
Epihodov	Roy K. Stevens
Firs	Fred Stuthman
Madame Ranevskaya	Kim Hunter
Anya	Patricia Conwell
Varya	Verna Bloom
Charlotta	Sudie Bond
Gaev	William Roerick
Pishtchik	Kurt Knudson
Yasha	Christopher Curry
Trofimov	Stephen Keep
A Wayfarer	Michael Kolba
Station Master	Paul Pape
Post Office Clerk	Mark Blum

A drama in four acts performed with one intermission. The action takes place in Russia during 1904 on the country estate of Madame Ranevskaya.

General Manager: Mary Beth Carroll
Stage Manager: Douglas F. Goodman

* Closed May 23, 1976 after 32 performances and 24 previews.

Martha Swope Photos

ight: **Paul Benedict, William Roerick, Stephen Keep, Fred Stuthman, Verna Bloom, Kim Hunter, Patricia Conwell** Top: **Verna Bloom, Kim Hunter, William Roerick**

Jon Benson, William Preston, Georgia Southcotte

ROUNDABOUT THEATRE/STAGE TWO
Opened Thursday, May 6, 1976.*
Roundabout Theatre Company presents:

LOVE AND INTRIGUE

By Friedrich von Schiller; Translated by Frederick Rolf; Director, Gavin Cameron-Webb; Costumes, Carol David; Technical Advisers, Ron Antone, James R. Grant, Dan Koetting, Lewis Mead

CAST

Miller	William Preston
Mrs. Miller	Georgia Southcotte
Worm	Jon Benson
Louisa Miller	Shelley Wyant
Baron Ferdinand Walter	John Shearin
Chancellor, Baron Walter	Frank Hamilton
Lord Chamberlain Stork	Chris Tenney
Sophy	Carol David
Lady Milford	Kate Weiman
Steward	Roger DeKoven
Attendants	Chip Keys, Steve Satterfield

A play in three acts. The action takes place during 1784 in a dukedom in Germany in the Millers' house, the chancellor's palace, and Lady Milford's mansion.

Stage Manager: Cameron A. Thompson

* Closed May 23, 1976 after 12 performances.

Anastasia Nicole Photo

SPANISH THEATRE REPERTORY COMPANY

Gilberto Zaldivar, Producer

GRAMERCY ARTS THEATRE
May 29, 1975–May 31, 1976 (49 performances)

LOS SOLES TRUNCOS by Rene Marques; Director, Rene Buch; Designs, Robert Federico; Production Assistant, Braulio Villar. CAST: Mirtha Cartaya, Vivian Deangelo, Haydee Zambrana

July 20, 1975–May 25, 1976 (53 performances)

PASOS Y ENTREMESES: 4 one-act plays directed by Francisco Morin; Designer, Robert Federico; Costumes, Ofelia Gonzalez; Technician, William Stiegel. "La Caratula" by Lupe de Rueda, with Tony Diaz, Sadel Alamo, Jean Cacharel, "Las Aceitunas" by Lupe de Rueda, with Braulio Villar, Phyllis Balzaretti, Maria Norman, Vivian Deangelo, Ofelia Gonzalez, Sadel Alamo, Tony Diaz, "Los Habladores" by Miguel de Cervantes, with Sadel Alamo, Tony Diaz, Jean Cacheral, Raoul Alphonse, Braulio Villar, Rene Sanchez, Regina Suarez, Ofelia Gonzalez, Eduardo Barrios, Omar Restrepo, "El Viejo Celoso" by Miguel de Cervantes, with Phyllis Balzaretti, Regina Suarez, Maria Norman, Rene Sanchez, Alfonso Manosalvas, Braulio Villar, Sadel Alamo, Tony Diaz

October 9–19, 1975 (10 performances)

LA REVOLUCION by Isaac Chocron; Director, Roman Chalbaud; Lighting and Assistant to director, Elias Perez Borjas; Costumes, Anibal Soto, Afiche, John Lange. CAST: Rafael Briceno, Jose Ignacio

November 13, 1975–May 31, 1976 (44 performances)

DONA ROSITA, LA SOLTERA by Federico Garcia Lorca; Director, Rene Buch; Designer, Robert Federico; Costumes, Maria Ferreira; Assistant Director, Tony Diaz; Musical Director, Juan Viccini; Visual Effects, Skip Ronglin; Pianist, Zenaida Manfugas. CAST: Alfonso Manosalvas, Lolina Gutierrez, Ofelia Gonzalez, Amelia Bence, Virginia Rambal, Tony Diaz, Raoul Alphonse, Phyllis Balzaretti, Luisa Leschin, Nereida Mercado, Braulio Villar, Graciela Mas, Xonia Benguria, Vivian Deangelo, Maria Norman, Haydee Zambrana, Nidia Pulles, Jose Rodriguez, Rene Sanchez, Orlando Nunez, Felipe Paredes, Rafael Gorbea, Tony Diaz

Top Right: Virginia Rambal, Maria Norman in "Los Soles Truncos" Below: Tony Diaz, Sadel Alamo in "La Caratula"

December 5–22, 1975 (9 performances)

LA COMPANIA DE MARIONETAS DE BOGOTA directed b Jaime Manzur, with Alfonso Aranguren, Francisco Piedrahita, Ma tha Ulloa, Pedro Nel Lopez, Victoria Londono, Esther Giraldo

February 18–April 25, 1976 (6 performances)

LOS SOLES TRUNCOS by Rene Marques; Translated by Char Pilditch; Designer, Robert Federico; Director, Rene Buch; Produ tion Assistant, Braulio Villar. CAST: Virginia Rambal, Luisa L chin, Phyllis Balzaretti, Maria Norman

GRAMERCY ARTS THEATRE
March 13–May 31, 1976 (53 performances)

LA MALQUERIDA by Jacinto Benavente; Director, Rene Buc Scenery and Lights, Robert Federico; Costumes, Maria Ferrei Rafael Martinez. CAST: Ofelia Gonzalez, Alfonso Manosalvas, V ian Deangelo, Maria Norman, Rene Sanchez, Jose Rodriguez, To Diaz, Alberto Tore, Regina Suarez, Braulio Villar, Sadel Alam Tony Diaz, Lolina Gutierrez, Bela Aguirre, Maria Meulener, Phy Balzaretti, Luisa Leschin, Haydee Zambrana, Jean Cacharel, Raf Gorbea, Tony Diaz, Eduardo Aranco, Jorge Amud

April 4–12, 1976 (5 performances)

NINO ROGER IN HOMBRE, GRITO Y GUITARRA Rodolfo C. Quebleen; Music, Gaudencio Thiago de Mello.

April 24–May 31, 1976 (12 performances)

AMOR DE DON PERLIMPLIN CON BELISA EN SU JARD by Federico Garcia Lorca; Director, Christopher Martin; Assis to director, Tony Diaz; Production Assistant, Braulio Villar; C tume Coordinator, Ofelia Gonzalez; Lighting, Robert Feder CAST: Alfonso Manosalvas, Vivian Deangelo, Ofelia Gonza Lolina Gutierrez, Tony Diaz, Sadel Alamo, Raoul Alpho Braulio Villar, Omar Restrepo

Gerry Goodstein Photos

Amelia Bence, Alfonso Monosalvas in "Dona Rosita, la Soltera"

THEATRE OFF PARK

Martin deMaat, Executive Director
Patricia Peate, Associate Director
Monica May, Artistic Consultant

COMMUNITY CHURCH

September 23–October 4, November 10–23, 1975 (24 performances)

SMOKING PISTOLS by Don Kvares; Director, Ernest Martin; Set, Cliff Simon; Lighting, Robby Monk; Sound, Jerry Kornbluth, A & J Audio Visual; Stage Managers, Zoa and Phillip Becker. CAST: Douglas Andros (Woody), Monica May (Edie)

January 12–26, 1976 (12 performances)

DIARIES OF ADAM AND EVE adapted from Mark Twain by Mary Allyn-Raye; Director, Miss Allyn-Raye; Costumes, Ann Gehrt; Stage Manager, Laurie Leffingwell. CAST: Eve Packer (Eve), Roy Sorrels (Adam)

March 7–20, 1976 (12 performances)

THE PIMIENTA PANCAKES by Sally Dixon Wiener; Adapted from O. Henry; Director, Monica May; Designer, Gary Weathersbee; Associate Producer, Evelyn Bunn; Assistant to director, Sylvia Radford; Stage Managers, Alvin Ho, David Bosboom, Lee Pucklis, Linda Harris; Production Assistant, Susan Greenbaum; Music and Lyrics, Sally Dixon Wiener; Musical Arrangements, Vernon Jernigan. CAST: Ned Austin (Uncle Emsley), Vernon Jernigan (Vern), Eric Marshall (Judson), Don Paul (Jackson), Celia Weston (Wilella)

COWBOYS #2 by Sam Shephard; Director, David Avcollie; Associate Producer, Phillip Becker. CAST: Vincent Ferro (Chet), Marty Levy (Stu)

May 23–June 13, 1976 (12 performances)

SMALL WAR ON MURRAY HILL by Robert Sherwood; Director, Frank Marino; Set, Bill Michaelovitch; Lighting, John Gleason; Costumes, Anne deVelder; Stage Managers, Judy Binus, Mark Sick. CAST: Keith Aldrich (Judah), Michael Clarke (Mullet), Dottie Dee Susan), Woody Eney (Robert), James A. Farley III (Soldier), Wayne Flower (Messenger), Paul Haskins (Gen. Howe), Wanda Jean Jones (Amelie), Lars Kampmann (Von Donop), Anna Lawrence (Daisy), Lou Miranda (Maj. Clove), Robert E. Quigley (Frederick), Linda Selman (Mary), Richard Vernon (Galway)

Mike Uffer, Gerard Barnier Photos

Monica May, Douglas Andros in "Smoking Pistols"

Eric Marshall, Don Paul, and right center, Celia Weston, Ned Austin, Eric Marshall in "The Pimienta Pancakes"

SULLIVAN STREET PLAYHOUSE
Opened Tuesday, May 3, 1960.*
Lore Noto presents:

THE FANTASTICKS

Book and Lyrics, Tom Jones; Suggested by Edmond Rostand's "Les Romanesques"; Music, Harvey Schmidt; Director, Word Baker; Original Musical Direction and Arrangements, Julian Stein; Designed by Ed Wittstein; Associate Producers, Sheldon Baron, Dorothy Olim, Robert Alan Gold; Assistant to the producer, Thad Noto; Production Assistant, John Krug; Original Cast Album, MGM Records

CAST

The Narrator............................David Brummel†1
The Girl.................................... Sarah Rice†2
The Boy................................. Ralph Bruneau†3
The Boy's Father .... Lore Noto
The Girl's Father .... Sy Travers†4
The Actor .... Evan Thompson†5
The Man Who Dies .... Jack Fogarty†6
The Mute............................. Paul W. Francis†7
At the piano .... William F. McDaniel
At the harp .... Pattee Cohen

MUSICAL NUMBERS: Overture, "Try to Remember," "Much More," "Metaphor," "Never Say No," "It Depends on What You Pay," "Soon It's Gonna Rain," "Rape Ballet," "Happy Ending," "This Plum Is Too Ripe," "I Can See It," "Plant a Radish," "Round and Round," "They Were You," Finale

A musical in two acts.

Press: David Powers
Stage Managers: Ned Levy, Anthony Rasemus

* Still playing May 31, 1976. For original production see THE-

† Succeeded by: 1. David Rexroad, Roger Brown, 2. Cheryl Horne, Betsy Joslyn, 3. Bruce Cryer, 4. Arthur Anderson, David Vogel, 5. Seamus O'Brien, Anthony Rasemus, 6. James Cook, 7. Tom Flagg, John Thomas Waite

Top Right: Roger Brown (top), Arthur Anderson, Betsy Joslyn, Lore Noto, John Thomas Waite, Bruce Cryer, James Cook

Seamus O'Brien, James Cook

Arthur Anderson, Bruce Cryer, Betsy Joslyn, Lore Noto

VILLAGE GATE
Opened Tuesday, January 8, 1974.*
Phil Oesterman presents:

LET MY PEOPLE COME

Music and Lyrics, Earl Wilson, Jr.; Music Arranged and Conducted by Billy Cunningham; Choreography, Ian Naylor; Lighting, Centaur Productions; Produced and Directed by Phil Oesterman; Production Assistant, Neal Haynes; Wardrobe Coordinator, Dianemarie Lemon; Associate Music Director, Norman Bergen; Original Cast Album by Libra Records

CAST

Joanne Baront†	Judy Gibson
Robin Charin	Jo Ann Lehmann
Ray Colbert	Edwina Lewis
Steven Alex-Cole	James Morgan
Lorraine Davidson	Michael Poulos
Carl Deese	Jim Rich
Marty Duffy	Tuesday Summers

ACT I: "Opening Number," "Mirror," "Whatever Turns You On," "Give It to Me," "Giving Life," "The Ad," "Fellatio 101," "I'm Gay," "Linda Georgina Marilyn & Me," "Dirty Words," "I Believe My Body"
ACT II: "The Show Business Nobody Knows," "Take Me Home with You," "Choir Practice," "And She Loved Me," "Poontang," "Come in My Mouth," "The Cunnilingus Champion of Company C," "Doesn't Anybody Love Anymore," "Let My People Come"

General Management: Jay Kingwill
Company Manager: Mark Bramble
Press: Saul Richman, Fred Nathan
Stage Managers: Duane F. Mazy, Ray Colbert

* Closed July 4, 1976 after 1167 performances to move to Broadway. For original production, see THEATRE WORLD, Vol. 30.
† During the season, the following succeeded various members of the cast: James Bryan, Scott Farrell, Yvette Freeman, Bob Jockers, Empress Kilpatrick, Barry Pearl, Rocky Suda, Dean Tait, Terri White, Irma Kaye

Ken Howard Photos

Top Right: Carl Deese, Joanne Baron, Jim Rich

Terry White, Edwina Lewis

Scott Farrell, Empress Kilpatrick

CHERRY LANE THEATRE
Opened Monday, May 17, 1971.*
(Moved August 10, 1971 to Promenade Theatre)
Edgar Lansbury, Stuart Duncan, Joseph Beruh present:

GODSPELL

Based on the Gospel according to St. Matthew; Music and Lyrics, Stephen Schwartz; Conceived and Directed by John-Michael Tebelak; Lighting, Barry Arnold; Costumes, Susan Tsu, Reet Pell; Production Supervisor, Nina Faso; Musical Director, Bob Christianson; Associate Producer, Charles Haid; Musical Arrangement and Direction, Stephen Schwartz; Musical Supervision, Steve Reinhardt; Set, Fred Gallo; Original Cast Album by Bell Records

CAST

Kerin Blair	Howard Sponseller
Bruce Connelly	Melinda Tanner
Elizabeth Lathram	Ed Trotta
Bobby Lee	Jaison Walker
Marilyn Pasekoff	Valerie Williams

Alternates: Nancy McCall, Douglas Walker

MUSICAL NUMBERS: "Tower of Babble," "Prepare Ye the Way of the Lord," "Save the People," "Day by Day," "Learn Your Lessons Well," "Bless the Lord," "All for the Best," "All Good Gifts," "Light of the World," "Turn Back, O Man," "Alas for You," "By My Side," "We Beseech Thee," "On the Willows," Finale

A musical in two acts and sixteen scenes.

General Manager: Al J. Isaac
Company Manager: Gail Bell
Press: Gifford/Wallace, Tom Trenkle
Stage Managers: Michael J. Frank, Tom Demenkoff

* Closed June 13, 1976 after 2118 performances to move to Broadway.

OFF-BROADWAY PRODUCTIONS FROM OTHER YEARS THAT CLOSED THIS SE.

Title	Opened		Closed	Perform
The Hot l Baltimore	3/22/73	....	11/30/75	....
Diamond Studs	1/14/75	....	8/3/75	....
National Lampoon Show	2/21/75	....	6/29/75	....
Rubbers/Yanks 3 Detroit 0				
Top of the Seventh	5/16/75	....	9/21/75	....
Be Kind to People Week	3/23/75	....	6/14/75	....
Bluebeard	4/18/75	....	6/22/75	....
The Taking of Miss Janie	5/4/75	....	6/15/75	....
Harry Outside	5/11/75	....	6/8/75	....

THE RED DEVIL BATTERY SIGN

...y Tennessee Williams; Director, Edwin Sherin; Scenery, Robin
...gner; Costumes, Ruth Wagner; Lighting, Marilyn Rennagel;
...sic, Sidney Lippman; Musical Arrangements and Supervision,
...race Diaz, Robert Colby; Sound, Robert Maybaum; Wardrobe
...ervisor, Kathleen Foster; Hairstylist, Tony Marrero; Production
...sistant, Penny Franks; Presented by David Merrick, Doris Cole
...rahams, Robert Colby; Opened at the Shubert Theatre in Boston,
...A., Monday, June 16, 1975 and closed there June 28, 1975.

CAST

...man downtown	Claire Bloom
...n at the bar	Pat Corley
...arlie the barman	John Ramsey
...g Del Rey	Anthony Quinn
...o	Frank C. Martinez
...Nina	Annette Cardona
...la	Katy Jurado
...Cabe	Stephen McHattie
...ummer	Alfred Karl
...tel Manager	Tom Noel
...armacist	Will Hussung
...st Policeman	Pat Corley
...ond Policeman	John Ramsey

...E KING'S MEN: Agustin Bustamente, Paul Cohen, Juan De
...ictis, Dick Dia, Ford Harrison, Paul La Tirenta, Frank C. Marti-
..., Emilio Prados, San Rainone

...NDERSTUDIES: King, Alfred Karl; Woman, Lee Terry; Perla,
...nne Kaplan; McCabe, Drummer, Charlie, Mitchell McGuire; La
...na, Sandra Gallardo; Man, Manager, Pharmacist, Eugene Stuck-
...nn

...A drama in two acts and ten scenes. The action takes place in
...llas, Texas, shortly after the John F. Kennedy assassination.

General Manager: Helen L. Nickerson
Company Manager: Gino Giglio
Press: Solters & Roskin, Stanley F. Kaminsky
Stage Managers: Marnel Summer, Eugene Stuckmann

No production photographs taken.

TRUCKLOAD

Music, Louis St. Louis; Lyrics, Wes Harris; Book, Hugh Wheeler;
Direction and Choreography, Patricia Birch; Scenery, Douglas W.
Schmidt; Costumes, Carrie F. Robbins; Lighting, John Gleason;
Sound, Robert Minor; Orchestrations, Michael Gibson, Bhen Lan-
zaroni; Vocal Arrangements, Flamin' Mama Music/Carl Hall; As-
sistant to director, James Dybas; Wardrobe Supervisor, Josephine
Zampedri; Production Assistants, Francis Tobin, Roz Monahan;
Associated Conductor, Richard Weinstock; Music Coordinator,
Earl Shendell; Presented by Adela Holzer, The Shubert Organiza-
tion, Dick Clark. Opened Saturday, September 6, 1975 at the Lyceum Theatre, NYC, and closed there Sept. 11, 1975.

CAST

Driver	Louis St. Louis
Heustis	Kelly Ward
Bonnie	Ilene Graff
Horace	Donny Burks
Amelia	Laurie Prange
Glory	Cheryl Barnes
Darleen	Sherry Mathis
Leon	Doug McKeon
Lee Wu	Kenneth S. Eiland
Whitfield	Ralph Strait
Rosa	Deborah Allen
Ricardo	Jose Fernandez
Carlos	Rene Enriquez

and The All Nite Drivers

UNDERSTUDIES: Darleen, Rosa, Chris Callan; Driver, Bob
Christianson; Leon, Fred Fields; Glory, Andrea Frierson; Amelia,
Bonnie, Laura Michaels; Horace, Anthony William Perkins; Heus-
tis, Whitfield, John Scoullar

MUSICAL NUMBERS: "Truckload," "Find My Way Home:"
"Cumbia/Wedding Party:" "Step-Mama," "Look at Us," "Standing
in this Phonebooth," "Amelia's Theme," "I Guess Everything Will
Turn Out All Right," "Rest Stop," "Boogie Woogie Man," "Ricardo's Lament," "Hash House Habit," "Dragon Strikes Back," "Bonnie's Song," "Our Out Your Soul," "There's Nothing Like Music,"
"Hello Sunshine."

A musical performed without intermission. The action takes place
last night on any open road.

General Manager: Emanuel Azenberg
Managers: Jose Vega, John M. Kirby
Press: Betty Lee Hunt Associates, Maria Cristina Pucci, Bill
Evans, Maurice Turet
Stage Managers: T. Schuyler Smith, William H. Batchelder, Lani
Sundsten

**Sherry Mathis, Louis St. Louis, and top right,
Donny Burks in "Truckload"**

SOUVENIR

By George Axelrod and Peter Viertel; Director, Gerald Freedman; Scenery, William Pitkin; Costumes, Theoni V. Aldredge; Lighting, Martin Aronstein; Sound, Pia Gilbert; Production Manager, Mitchell Erickson; Production Assistants, William R. Goulding, Peter T. Kulok; Wardrobe Master, Elonzo Dann; Presented by Arthur Cantor and E. E. Fogelson in association with Eric Friedheim. Opened Wednesday, Oct. 29, 1975 at the Shubert Theatre in Century City, CA., and closed there Nov. 9, 1975.

CAST

Julie's Stand-in	Jillian Lindig
Jack's Stand-in	Bryce Holman
Fritz Tauber	John Carpenter
Mark Sanders	Tony Musante
Assistant Director	Joseph Hill
Camera Operator	Bruce Brighton
Jack Robson	Edward Easton
Eunice Blaustein	Donna Isaacson
Julie Stevens	Deborah Kerr
William (Swanee) Swanson	Edmund Lyndeck
Ben	Laurence Hugo
Larry Stevens	Reno Roop
Edith	Emmy Nance Grise
French Bellboy	Gary Farr
Italian Bellboy	John Michalski
Guy Holstein	Arthur Ed Forman
Rick Townsend	Art Burns

STANDBYS AND UNDERSTUDIES: Julie, Jillian Lindig; Mark, Art Burns; Ben, Joseph Hill; Swanee, John Carpenter; Larry, John Michalski; Jack, Bryce Holman; Fritz, Arthur Ed Forman; Rick, Gary Farr; Guy, Bruce Brighton

A romantic comedy in two acts. The action takes place at the present time in Hollywood.

Company Manager: Ronald Bruguiere
Press: Stanley F. Kaminsky, C. George Willard
Stage Managers: Charles Kindl, Richard Delahanty

Eric Skipsey Photos

Tony Musante, Deborah Kerr

Deborah Kerr, Laurence Hugo
Top: Tony Musante, Deborah Kerr

WEEKEND WITH FEATHERS

By Romeo Muller; Director, Morton DaCosta; Scenery, James Hamilton; Costumes, Gloria Gresham; Lighting, Thomas Skelton; assistant to director, Janet O'Morrison; Wardrobe Supervisor, Thelma Davis; Presented by Don Saxon, Don Kaufman, Lesley Savage. Opened Saturday, April 10, 1976 at the Shubert Theatre in New Haven, CT., and closed at the Playhouse Theatre, Wilmington, DE., Apr. 24, 1976.

CAST

Hotel Bellhop	Nick Malekos
Millie Burroughs	Cara Duff-MacCormack
Danny Stone	Donald O'Connor
Hotel Maid	Gloria Irizarry
Sparky	Robert R. Kaye
Mr. Warhol	Truman Gaige
Mary "Feathers" Jones	Lee Meredith

Understudies: Vince O'Brien, Jeramie Rain

A comedy in two acts and four scenes. The action takes place at the present time in a large over-priced hotel suite in midtown Manhattan, N.Y.

General Manager: Hal Grossman
Company Manager: Morry Efron
Press: Marvin Kohn, Michael Sean O'Shea
Stage Managers: Ben D. Kranz, Jeramie Rain

Sy Friedman Photos

Right: Donald O'Connor, Lee Meredith

Donald O'Connor, Cara Duff-MacCormick

Donald O'Connor, Truman Gaige

ALL OVER TOWN

By Murray Schisgal; Director, Dustin Hoffman; Scenery, Oliver Smith; Costumes, Albert Wolsky; Lighting, John Gleason; Production Supervisor, Frank Marino; Wardrobe Supervisor, Carl Rosenthal; Assistant to director, Theresa Curtin; Hairstylist, Pat Huntley; Presented by Adela Holzer; Opened Tuesday, August 1, 1975 at the Shubert in Chicago, IL., and closed Sept. 27, 1975 at the Fisher in Detroit, MI. For original NY production, see THEATRE WORLD, Vol. 31.

CAST

Sybil Morris	Mary Neal
Dr. Lionel Morris	Thomas Toner
Beebee Morris	Constance Bacc
Millie	Beth Hattub
Charles Kogan	Philip Polit
Col. Martin Hopkins	William LeMassena
Lewis	Ron O'Neal
Louie	Chip Zien
Michael Boyssan	Arn Weine
Jackie Boyssan	Marie Tommo
Laurent	Albert Sande
Philomena Hopkins	Sarah Saltu
Demetrius	Leon Spelma
Harold P. Hainesworth	Pi Douglas
Francine	Barbara Slotnic
Maharishi Bahdah	Kurt Knudso
Detective Peterson	Arn Weine
Detective Kirby	Fredric Ston

UNDERSTUDIES: Lewis, Hainsworth, Mel Johnson, Jr.; Louie, Charles, Laurent, Fredric Stone; Sybil, Millie, Jackie, Barbara Slotnick; Beebee, Philomena, Kate Webster; Dr. Morris, Hopkins, Michael, Kurt Knudson

A comedy in 2 acts and 5 scenes. The action takes place at the present time in the Morris family's duplex apartment on Manhattan's Upper East Side.

General Management: Theatre Now, Inc., Edward H. Davis, William Court Cohen
Company Manager: Donald Antonelli
Press: Michael Alpert, Fred Weterick
Stage Managers: Michael Mortorella, Leon Spelman, Mel Johnson, Jr.

Chip Zien, Ron O'Neal, Beth Hattub, Thomas Toner, William LeMassena
Top Left: Ron O'Neal, Beth Hattub, Thomas Toner

CHARLEY'S AUNT

By Brandon Thomas; Director, James Higgins; Settings and
Lighting, Leo B. Meyer; Presented by Jane Friedlander, Saul Nock; Opened Monday, May 10, 1976 at Power Center, Ann Arbor,
MI, and closed June 26, 1976 at the Performing Arts Center, Milwaukee, WI.

CAST

Jack Chesney	Robert Doyen
Brassett	Carle Bensen
Charley Wykeham	Paul Anderson
Lord Fancourt Babberley	Roddy McDowall
Kitty Verdun	Joanna Hall
Amy Spettigue	Ann Potts
Col. Sir Francis Chesney	James Higgins
Stephen Spettigue	Vincent Price
Donna Lucia d'Alvadorez	Coral Browne
Ela Delahay	Isabel Grandin

UNDERSTUDIES: Spettigue, Carle Bensen; Babberley, Charley,
Jack Brassett, Barry Smith; Donna Lucia, Amy, Ela, Kitty, Liz
Bolick

A comedy in three acts. The action takes place at Oxford in 1892,
and in the drawing room of Spettigue's house.

Company Manager: Irving Sudrow
Press: Howard Atlee, Clarence Allsopp, Meg Gordean, Becky
Flora
Stage Managers: Mark Krause, Barry Smith

Vincent Price, Coral Browne, Roddy McDowall (also top right)

A CHORUS LINE

Conceived, Choreographed and Directed by Michael Bennet; Book, James Kirkwood and Nicholas Dante; Music, Marvin Ham lisch; Lyrics, Edward Kleban; Setting, Robin Wagner; Costume Theoni V. Aldredge; Lighting, Tharon Musser; Sound, Abe Jacol Co-Choreographer, Bob Avian; Orchestrations, Bill Byers, Hersh Kay, Jonathan Tunick; Music Coordinator, Robert Thomas; Musi Direction and Vocal Arrangements, Don Pippin; Internation Company Music Director, Ray Cook; Associate Producer, Bernar Gersten; Presented by the New York Shakespeare Festival in assoc ation with Plum Productions; Assistant Conductor, Patrick Ho land; Wardrobe Master, Darrell Reed. Opened Monday, May 1976 at the Royal Alexandra Theatre, Toronto, Canada, and st playing May 31, 1976.

CAST

Paul	Tommy Aguila
Kristine	Christine Barke
Al	Steve Bauman
Vicki	Nancy Dafgo
Tom	Mark Dove
Maggie	Jean Frase
Frank	Troy Garz
Val	Mitzi Hamilto
Zach	Eivind Haru
Mike	Jeff Hyslo
Diana	Loida Iglesi
Greg	Andy Keys
Bobby	Ron Kurows
Connie	Jennifer Ann L
Lois	Wendy Mansfie
Judy	Yvette Mathev
Richie	A. William Perkir
Larry	T. Michael Re
Butch	Ken Roge
Cassie	Sandy Rove
Mark	Timothy Sc
Roy	Donn Simior
Sheila	Jane Summerha
Bebe	Miriam Wel
Tricia	Nancy Woo
Don	Ronald Your

For musical numbers, see Broadway Calendar, page 14.

General Manager: Emanuel Azenberg
Company Manager: Maurice Schaded
Press: Gino Empry
Stage Managers: Martin Herzer, David Taylor, Michael Austir

Jean Fraser, Mark Dovey, Miriam Welch, Ronald Young, Jane Summerhays, Eivind Harum, Sandy Roveta, Ron Kurowski, Yvette Mathews, Troy Garza, Christine Barker, A. William Perkins Top Left: Sandy Roveta, Jane Summerhays, Ron Kurowski, Miriam Welch, Yvette Mathews, A. William Perkins Below: Steve Baumann, Christine Barker, Wendy Mansfield, Timothy Scott, Tommy Aguilar, Loida Iglesias

A CHORUS LINE

Conceived, Choreographed and Directed by Michael Bennett; Book, James Kirkwood, Nicholas Dante; Music, Marvin Hamlisch; Lyrics, Edward Kleban; Setting, Robin Wagner; Costumes, Theoni V. Aldredge; Lighting, Tharon Musser; Sound, Abe Jacob; Co-Choreographer, Bob Avian; Orchestrations, Bill Byers, Hershy Kay, Jonathan Tunick; Music Coordinator, Robert Thomas; Music Direction and Vocal Arrangements, Don Pippin; Musical Direction, Arthur Rubinstein; Associate Conductor, Tom Hancock; Associate Producer, Bernard Gersten; Presented by the New York Shakespeare Festival in association with Plum Productions; Opened Wednesday, July 7, 1976 at the Shubert in Los Angeles.

CAST

Kristine	Renee Baughman
Val	Pamela Blair
Roy	Tim Cassidy
Mark	Paul Charles
Maggie	Kay Cole
Mike	Don Correia
Richie	Ronald Dennis
Judy	Patricia Garland
Greg	Andy Keyser
Don	Ron Kuhlman
Bebe	Nancy Lane
Connie	Baayork Lee
Diana	Priscilla Lopez
Zach	Robert LuPone
Cassie	Donna McKechnie
Vicki	Mary Ann O'Reilly
Bobby	Scott Pearson
Al	Don Percassi
Sheila	Charlene Ryan
Larry	Roy Smith
Butch	Sam Tampoya
Tom	Danny Taylor
Frank	Claude R. Tessier
Paul	Sammy Williams
Lois	Lee Wilson
Tricia	Rebecca York

For musical numbers, see Broadway Calendar, page 14.

General Manager: Emanuel Azenberg
Company Managers: Peter Neufeld, Douglas C. Baker
Press: Merle Debuskey, Judi Davidson
Stage Managers: Jeff Hamlin, Patricia Drylie, Frank Hartenstein, Andy G. Bew

Donna McKechnie, Charlene Ryan Top Right:
Pamela Blair, Sammy Williams, Donna
McKechnie, Robert LuPone, Charlene Ryan, Priscella Lopez

Don Correia Above: Donna McKechnie

DON'T BOTHER ME, I CAN'T COPE

By Micki Grant; Conceived and Directed by Vinnette Carroll; Choreography, Edmond Kresley; Choral Director, Micki Grant; Musical Director, George Broderick; Producer, Tom Mallow; Associate Producer, James Janek; Musical Arrangements, Danny Holgate; Production Supervisor, Roger Franklin; Presented by American Theatre Productions; Opened Sept. 17, 1975 in Hamilton, Ont., Can., and closed Feb. 1, 1976 in Brockville, Ont., Can. For original NY production, see THEATRE WORLD, Vol. 28.

CAST

Bardell Conner	Bobby London
Clinton Derricks	Robert Melvin
Michel DeSilva	Nat Morris
Sheila Ellis	Steiv Semien
Elaine Holloman	Jacqueline Smith-Lee
Sally Johnson	Charlaine Woodard

MUSICAL NUMBERS: "I Gotta Keep Movin'," "Harlem Intro," "Lock Up the Dog," "Harlem Street," "Lookin' Over from Your Side," "Don't Bother Me, I Can't Cope," "Children's Rhymes," "Billie Holliday Blues," "Ghetto Life," "You Think I Got Rhythm?," "Time Brings about a Change," "So Little Time," "Thank Heaven for You," "Show Me That Special Gene," "My Love's So Good," "Men's Dance," "They Keep Comin'," "My Name Is Man," "All I Need," "Questions," "Love Mississippi," "It Takes a Whole Lot of Human Feeling," "Good Vibrations," "Prayer," "Sermon," "Fighting for Pharoah," "Universe in Mourning," "We Gotta Keep Moving'"

A "musical entertainment" in two acts.

General Manager: James Janek
Company Manager: Robert Ossenfort
Press: Howard Atlee, Clarence Allsopp
Stage Managers: Robert Bruce Holley, Steiv Semien

Bert Andrews Photos

Prudence Darby (C) Top Right: Elaine Holloman

EQUUS

By Peter Shaffer; Director, John Dexter; Scenery and Costumes, John Napier; Lighting, Andy Phillips; Sound, Marc Wilkinson; Mime, Claude Chagrin; Production Supervisor, Robert Borod; Presented by Kermit Bloomgarden, Doris Cole Abrahams in association with Frank Milton; Opened Tuesday, Nov. 18, 1975 at the Wilbur in Boston, MA, and still playing May 31 1976. For original NY production see THEATRE WORLD, Vol. 31.

CAST

Martin Dysart	Brian Bedford
Alan Strang	Dai Bradley
Nurse	Mary Hara
Hesther Salomon	Sheila Smith
Frank Strang	Humbert Allen Astredo
Dora Strang	Delphi Lawrence
Horseman/Nugget	Richard Marshall
Harry Dalton	Danny Sewell
Jill Mason	Penelope Willis
Horses	Joseph Capelli, Mark Hanks, Tom Rolfing, Patrick Watkins, Mark Shannon†

UNDERSTUDIES: Dysart, Humbert Allen Astredo; Alan, Dennis Erdman; Frank, Danny Sewell; Dora, Hesther, Mary Hara; Jill, Nurse, Dorothy French; Harry, Joseph Cappelli; Horseman/Nugget, Tom Rolfing

A drama in two acts. The action takes place in Rokeby Psychiatric Hospital in Southern England at the present time.

General Manager: Max Allentuck
Company Manager: John Bloomgarden
Press: John Springer, Louis Sica, Harry Davies
Stage Managers: Nicholas Russiyan, Robert L. Borod, Mark Shannon, Dorothy French

Succeeded by Michael Paliotti

Van Williams Photos

Top: Brian Bedford, Dai Bradley, Richard Marshall Right: Dai Bradley, Delphi Lawrence, Humbert Allen Astredo

**Dai Bradley, Penelope Willis
Above: Brian Bedford, Sheila Smith**

Ed Nelson as Harry S. Truman

GIVE 'EM HELL HARRY!

By Samuel Gallu; Director, Peter H. Hunt; Scenic Design, Jam
Hamilton; Presented by Samuel Gallu and Thomas J. McErla
Technician, John Lucas; Coordinator, Bambi Dudley; Opened Se
17, 1975 at the Robinson Auditorium in Little Rock, AR., a
closed Apr. 27, 1976 in Portland, OR.

CAST

ED NELSON

A play in two acts, based on the life and times of President Ha
S. Truman.

Company Manager: Jo Rosner
Press: Robert W. Jennings
Stage Manager: Martha Knight, succeeded by Leanna Lenha

KENNEDY'S CHILDREN

By Robert Patrick; Director, Clive Donner; Designed by Santo
.quasto; Lighting, Martin Aronstein; Presented by Michael Har-
y in association with Robert Colby; Associate Producer, Ramon
.etzov; Tour Direction, Theatre Now, Inc.; Opened Friday, March
. 1976 in San Francisco, CA, in Marines' Memorial Theatre, and
.sed May 29, 1976 in the Studebaker Theatre in Chicago, IL.

CAST

.anda	Bobo Lewis†1
.rtender	K. C. Kelly
.arger	Don Parker†2
.ark	Michael Sacks†3
.na	Kaiulani Lee†4
.rla	Shirley Knight†5

.NDERSTUDIES: Jane Sanford (Wanda, Rona, Carla), K. C.
.lly (Mark, Sparger), Ernest Austin (Bartender)

A drama in two acts. The action takes place in a bar on the lower
.st Side of New York City on a rainy February afternoon in 1974.

General Manager: Jay Kingwill
Company Manager: Donald Antonelli
Press: Alan Edelson, Beverly Snyder
Stage Managers: Murray Gitlin, Ernest Austin

Succeeded by: 1. Barbara Rush, Shelley Winters, 2. Farley
Granger, 3. Al Freeman, Jr., 4. Sally Kirkland, 5. Ann Wedgeworth

Ken Howard Photos

**Right: Al Freeman, Jr., Farley Granger,
Shelley Winters**

Sally Kirkland, Shelley Winters, Ann Wedgeworth

MAN OF LA MANCHA

Book, Dale Wasserman; Music, Mitch Leigh; Lyrics, Joe Dario
Direction and Choreography, Joe Lorden; Musical Director, Mi
Setzer; Associate Producer, James Janek; Designed by Associ
Theatrical Designers, Ltd.; Costume Coordinator, Darrell R
Producer, Tom Mallow; Assistant Conductor, Jene Citronba
Wardrobe Supervisor, Darrell Reed; Production Assistant, Ricl
Martini; Opened Tuesday, Jan. 15, 1976 in Kalamazoo, MI,
closed Apr. 4, 1976 in Paramus, NJ. For original NY product
see THEATRE WORLD, Vol. 22.

CAST

Don Quixote (Cervantes)	David Atkir
Sancho	Mark I
Aldonza	Alice E'
Innkeeper	Frederic M
Padre	Walter Blo
Dr. Carrasco	Christopher N
Antonia	Melanie Le
Barber/Paco	Donald Ta
Pedro, Head Muleteer	David Brum
Anselmo	Richard R
Housekeeper/Maria	Louise Armstr
Jose/Mule	Hector Merc
Tenorio/Horse	Luis Mor
Juan	Mark Holl
Fermina	Donna N
Captain of Inquisition	Michael J. S'
Moorish Dancer	Donna N
Guitarist	Robin Pol:
Guards and Inquisitors	John Hemmer, Jacqu
	Rohrbacker, Charles Sh

UNDERSTUDIES: Quixote, Michael Stone; Aldonza, Mel
Lerner; Sancho, Donald Tango; Innkeeper, David Brummel; Bar
Richard Reece; Padre, Anselmo, Mark Holliday; Captain, Pe
John Hemmer; Antonia, Housekeeper, Maria Fermina, Moc
Dancer, Jacquiline Rohrbacker; Swing, Glen McClaskey; Carra
David Brummel

MUSICAL NUMBERS: "Man of La Mancha," "It's All the Sai
"Dulcinea," "I'm Only Thinking of Him," "I Really Like H
"What Does He Want of Me," "Little Bird," "Barber's So
"Golden Helmet of Mambrino," "To Each His Dulcinea," "
Quest," "The Combat," "The Dubbing," "The Abduction," "M
ish Dance," "Aldonza," "Knight of the Mirrors," "A Little (
sip," "The Psalm"

A musical performed without intermission. The action takes p
in a dungeon in Seville at the end of the 16th Century, and in
imagination of Cervantes.

General Manager: James Janek
Company Manager: L. Liberatore
Press: Fred Weterick
Stage Managers: Jack Welles, Charles Shores, John Hemm

Bert Andrews Photos

**Top Left: David Atkinson
Below: Alice Evans, Mark Ross**

David Atkinson, Mark Ross

NATIONAL SHAKESPEARE COMPANY

Artistic Director, Philip Meister; Managing Director, Elaine Sulka; Tour Director, Mary Spector; Scenery, Jane Thurn; Costumes, Sharon Hollinger; Lighting, Bob Lampel; Technical Director, Mustafa Kadaster; Opened Friday, Oct. 3, 1975 in Glen Falls, NY, and closed Apr. 22, 1976 in West Long Branch, NJ.

CAST

"Much Ado about Nothing" by William Shakespeare; Directed by Philip Meister

Leonato	William A. Leone
Borachio	Bert Kruse
Beatrice	Vivienne Lenk
Hero	Nancy Hammill
Don Pedro	Richard Boddy
Benedick	John Camera
Don John	Julian Bailey
Claudio	K. C. Kizziah
Dogberry	Philip W. Shaw
Verges	Granvill Marsh
Francis Seacole	Peter Umbras
Friar Francis	Julian Bailey

"Macbeth" by William Shakespeare; Directed by Neil Flanagan

Witch	Nancy Hammill
Duncan	Philip W. Shaw
Malcolm	Bert Kruse
Seyton	Granvill Marsh
Donalbain	K. C. Kizziah
Ross	William A. Leone
Macbeth	T. Louis Weltz, Julian Bailey
Banquo	Julian Bailey, Peter Umbras
Macduff	John Camera
Old Siward	Richard Boddy
Lady Macbeth	Vivienne Lenk

"The Tempest" by William Shakespeare; Directed by Mario Siletti

Miranda	Nancy Hamill
Prospero	Richard Boddy
Ariel	Vivienne Lenk
Caliban	Joe Dalton Lauck, John Camera
Ferdinand	K. C. Kizziah
Gonzalo	William A. Leone
Alonso	Julian Bailey
Sebastian	Philip W. Shaw, Bert Kruse
Antonio	Peter Umbras
Trinculo	Granvill Marsh
Stephano	Philip W. Shaw
Mariner	Mustafa Kadaster

Company Manager: Richard Boddy
Press: John Dudich
Stage Managers: Peter Umbras, K. C. Kizziah, Mustafa Kadaster

Top Right: Nancy Hammill, Richard Boddy in "Much Ado about Nothing" Below: T. Louis Weltz, Nancy Hammill, Julian Bailey in "Macbeth"

Vivian Lenk, Philip W. Shaw, Joe Dalton Lauck in "The Tempest"

NEW YORK THEATRE COMPANY

Artistic Director, Philip Meister; Managing Director, Elaine Sulka; Tour Director, Mary Spector; Assistant Tour Director, Ellen Davidow; Sets, Joan Ferncheck; Costumes, Sharon Hollinger; Musical Director, Ross Allen; Stage Manager, Kirk Wolfinger

CAST

"The Fantasticks"—Book and Lyrics, Tom Jones; Music, Harvey Schmidt

Mute .... Kirk Wolfinger
Hucklebee .... David Clark
Amy Bellamy .... Mary Helen Fisher
Luisa .... Marilynn Winbush
Matt .... Gary T. Colombo
El Gallo .... Lawrence Raiken
Henry .... Kirk Wolfinger

Opened Jan. 28, 1976 in Kings Point, NY, and closed Apr. 6, 1976 in Lawrenceville, NJ

"Spoon River Anthology"
Book and Music, John Franceschina

David Clark
Gary T. Colombo
Mary Helen Fisher
Lawrence Raiken
Marilynn Winbush
Kirk Wolfinger

Opened Feb. 1, 1976 in Marion, IL., and closed Apr. 13, 1976 in Washington, PA.

Gary T. Colombo, Kirk Wolfinger, Marilynn Winbush, Lawrence Raiken, David Clark, Mary Helen Fisher in "Spoon River Anthology" Top Right: David Clark, Mary Helen Fisher in "The Fantasticks"

168

RAISIN

Based on Lorraine Hansberry's "A Raisin in the Sun"; Book, Robert Nemiroff, Charlotte Zaltzberg; Music, Judd Woldin; Lyrics, Robert Brittan; Directed and Choreographed by Donald McKayle; Assistant, Dorene Richardson; Scenery, Robert U. Taylor; Costumes, Bernard Johnson; Lighting, William Mintzer; Musical Director-Conductor, Margaret Harris; Orchestrations, Al Cohn, Robert Freedman; Vocal Arrangements, Howard Roberts, Joyce Brown; Dance Arrangements, Judd Woldin; Incidental Arrangements, Dorothea Freitag; Production Supervisor, Nate Barnett; Dance Supervisor, Zelda Pulliam; Producer, Robert Nemiroff; Associate Producers, Sydney Lewis, Jack Friel; Executive Associates, Irving Welzer, Will Mott, Charles Briggs; Technical Adviser, Mitch Miller; Wardrobe Supervisor, Betty D'Aloia; Hairstylists, Stanley James, Michael Smith; Associate Conductor, Frank Anderson; Opened Tuesday, Dec. 9, 1975 at the Playhouse, Wilmington, DE, and still touring May 31, 1976. For original NY production, see THEATRE WORLD, Vol. 30.

CAST

Pusher	Le-Von Campbell
Victim	Loretta Abbott
Ruth Younger	Mary Seymour
Travis Younger	Darren Green
Mrs. Johnson	Sandra Phillips
Walter Lee Younger	Autris Paige
Beneatha Younger	Arnetia Walker
Lena "Mama" Younger	Virginia Capers
Bar Girl	Zelda Pulliam
Bobo Jones	Irving Barnes
Willie Harris	Walter P. Brown†1
Joseph Asagai	Milton Grayson
Pastor	Roderick Sibert†2
Pastor's Wife	Kay Barnes
Karl Lindner	Stacy McAdams

PEOPLE OF THE SOUTHSIDE: Eddie Jordan, Le-Von Campbell, Renee Warren, Zelda Pulliam, Irving Barnes, Lacy Phillips, H. Douglas Berring, Vanessa Shaw, Corliss Taylor, Kay Barnes, Charles E. Grant, Bonita Jackson, Cleveland Pennington, Roderick Sibert

UNDERSTUDIES: Walter, Asagai, Nate Barnett; Ruth, Vanessa Shaw; Beneatha, Zelda Pulliam; Lena, Sandra Phillips; Mrs. Johnson, Kay Barnes; Lindner, Will Mott; Willie, Bobo, Roderick Sibert; Travis, Lacy Phillips; Pastor, Irving Barnes; Walter, Asagai, H. Douglas Berring

MUSICAL NUMBERS: Prologue, "Man Say," "Whose Little Angry Man," "Runnin' to Meet the Man," "A Whole Lotta Sunlight," "Booze," "Alaiyo," "African Dance," "Sweet Time," "You Done Right," "He Come Down This Morning," "It's A Deal," "Sidewalk Tree," "Not Anymore," "Measure the Valleys"

A musical in two acts. The action takes place in the 1950's in Chicago, Illinois.

General Manager: John Corkill
Company Manager: Kimo Gerald
Press: Arlene Shattil, Max Eisen
Stage Managers: Anthony Neely, Bert Wood, Stacy McAdams

Succeeded by: 1. Gregg Baker, 2. Isaac Clay

Top Right: Darren Green, Autris Paige, Mary Seymour, Virginia Capers, Arnetia Walker Below: Clinton Keen, Loretta Abbott, Irving Barnes, Zelda Pulliam, Autris Paige, Renee Warren, Chuck Thorpes

Sandra Phillips, Virginia Capers, Mary Seymour

THE ROCKY HORROR SHOW

Book, Music and Lyrics, Richard O'Brien; Director, Michael Amarino; Musical Director, Steven Applegate; Set, George Barcos; Costumes, Mary Piering; Lighting, Fred Kopp; Presented by D. J. Enterprises; Opened Tuesday, February 3, 1976 at Montgomery Playhouse, San Francisco, CA, and still touring May 31, 1976. For original NY production, see THEATRE WORLD, Vol. 31.

CAST

Dr. Frank N. Furter	David James
Rocky Horror	Bill Tackey
Janet Weiss	Sharon Widman
Brad Majors	Robert Reynolds
Riff-Raff	Buddy King
Magenta/Trixie	Vikki D'Orazzi
Columbia	Kelli Whitehil
Eddie/Dr. Scott	Emil Borell
Narrator	Richard Gee
Back-up Singer	Kelly St. John

MUSICAL NUMBERS: "Science Fiction," "Wedding Song," "Over at the Frankenstein Place," "Sweet Trnasvestite," "Time Warp," "Sword of Damocles," "Charles Atlas Song," "What Eve Happened to Saturday Night," "Eddie's Teddy," "Once in Awhile," "Planet Shmanet Janet," "It Was Great When It All Began," "Super Heroes," Finale

A rock musical in 2 acts and 17 scenes.

Press: Carol Orsborn
Stage Managers: David Rubin, Richard Gee

Barry Kelsall Photos

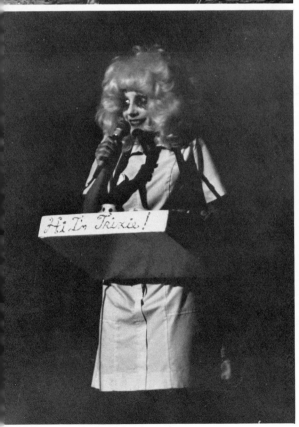

Vikki D'Orazzi Top: David James, Emil Borelli

Bill Tackey

SHERLOCK HOLMES

By Arthur Conan Doyle and William Gillette; Director, Warren [nters]; Scenery and Costumes, Carl Toms; Lighting, Neil Peter [mpolis]; Music Arranged by Michael Lankester; Production Asso-[ates], Cathy Blaser, Sandra Mandel; Wardrobe Supervisor, Billie [hite]; Hairstylist, Tiv Davenport; Scenery and Costumes super-sed by Mason Arvold; Theme Music, Irving Joseph; The Royal [hakespeare] Company's Production is presented by James Neder-nder, Shubert Organization, Kennedy Center Productions, Adela [olzer], Eddie Kulukundis and Victor Lurie; Opened Jan. 14, 1976 [at] the O'Keefe Center, Toronto, Can., and closed May 22, 1976 at [the] Shubert in Chicago, IL. For original NY production, see THE-[A]TRE WORLD, Vol. 31.

CAST

[M]adge Larrabee	Valerie French
[Jo]hn Forman	Neil Hunt
[Ja]mes Larrabee	Dalton Dearborn
[Th]erese	Alexandra Stoddart
[Si]dney Prince	Geoff Garland
[A]lice Faulkner	Diana Kirkwood
[S]herlock Holmes	Robert Stephens†
[P]rofessor Moriarty	Alan Sues
[Jo]hn	Richard Lederer
[A]lfred Bassick	Charles Berendt
[Bi]lly	Jeffrey Hillock
[D]r. Watson	Ronald Bishop
[Ji]m Craigin	Alvah Stanley
[T]homas Leary	Henry Leon Baker
[Li]ghtfoot" McTague	John Seitz
[P]arsons	Richard Lederer
[Si]r Edward Leighton	John C. Vennema
[C]ount von Stalburg	George Ebeling
[N]ewsboy	Brian Brownlee
[L]ondoners ... Michael Connolly, Tiv Davenport, Vivien Ferrara	
[Vi]olin	Paul Childs

A mystery in 2 acts and 5 scenes. The action takes place in London [in] 1891.

General Manager: Nelle Nugent
Company Manager: Fred J. Cuneo
Press: Michael Alpert, Horace Greeley McNab, Marilynn
LeVine, Joshua Ellis
Stage Managers: Paul Bengston, Elizabeth Caldwell, Jeffrey
Hillock, Brian Brownlee

**Top: Leonard Nimoy, Diana Kirkwood
Right: Leonard Nimoy, Alan Sues**

Robert Stephens

SNOOPY!!!

Based on the comic strip "Peanuts" by Charles M. Schulz; Book, Warren Lockhart, Arthur Whitelaw, Michael L. Grace; Music, Larry Grossman; Lyrics, Hal Hackady; Director, Arthur Whitelaw; Choreography, Marc Breaux; Designed by David Graden; Lighting, Ken Billington; Musical Direction and Vocal Arrangements, Lawrence J. Blank; Production Assistant, Richard Otto; Pianists, Larry Blank, Jon Olson; Wardrobe Supervisor, Rita Yovino; Presented by Arthur Whitelaw, Michael L. Grace, Susan Bloom, Warren Lockhart in association with Charles M. Schulz Creative Associates; Opened Tuesday, Dec. 9, 1975 at the Little Fox Theatre, San Francisco, CA, and closed July 5, 1976 in Marin County, CA.

CAST

Charlie Brown	James Gleason
Linus	Jimmy Dodge
Sally	Randi Kallan
Lucy	Janell Pulis
Peppermint Patty	Pamela Myers
Snoopy	Don Potter
Woodstock	Cathy Cahn

Understudies; Rhoda Butler Blank, John Forman

MUSICAL NUMBERS: "The World according to Snoopy," "Sit Up! Lie Down! Roll Over! Play Dead!," "Woodstock's Theme," "Edgar Allan Poe," "I Know Now," "The Vigil," "Clouds," "Where Did That Little Dog Go?," "Daisy Hill," "Friend," "It was a Dark and Stormy Night," "Wishy-Washy," "Poor Sweet Baby," "Don't Be Anything Less Than Everything You Can Be," "The Big Bow-Wow!," "Just One Person"

"A musical entertainment" in two acts.

General Manager: Peter H. Russell
Press: Suzy Strauss, Kevin Kaiser
Stage Managers: John Anderson, John Forman

Right: Jimmy Dodge Top: Don Potter

Sammy Cahn

WORDS AND MUSIC

Director, Jerry Adler; Musical Director, Richard Leona[ ] Gowns, Anne Fogarty; Associate Producer, James Janek; Prod[ ] tion Supervisor, Jack Welles; Production Assistant, Mary Be[ ] Tour Management, American Theatre Productions; Opened Fri[ ] September 26, 1975 in Ann Arbor, MI, and closed January 11, 1[ ] in Los Angeles, CA. For Original NY production, see THEAT[ ] WORLD, Vol. 30.

CAST

SAMMY CAHN
Martha Danielle
Sydnee Devitt
Paul Eichel
Standby: William James

An evening of songs written by Sammy Cahn. Presented in [ ] parts.

General Manager: James Janek
Company Manager: Stanley J. Brody
Press: Horace Greeley McNab
Stage Manager: William James

Bert Andrews Photos

ANNUAL SHAKESPEARE FESTIVALS

LABAMA SHAKESPEARE FESTIVAL

Anniston, Alabama
July 18–August 23, 1975

Artistic Director, Martin L. Platt; Associate Director, Bruce
ard; Stage Managers, Melissa Taylor, Lissa LeGrand; Assistant
Director, Kathryn Dell; Set Design and Technical Direction, Joel
ehr; Costume Design, Alan Armstrong; Costumer, Lynn Em-
rt; Assistant Technical Director, Alan Prendergast; Property
stress, Paula Drucker; Lighting, Alan Prendergast; Production
sistants, Margaret Jones, Kathy Chandler, Sam Hitchcock, Jack
riakos, Laurence Feldman, Michael Stedham, Mary Ann O'Neal,
my Hensleigh; Wardrobe, Rose Mary Etheridge, Hi Bedford,
dra Fuller, Barry Sellers, Deborah Bunson; Original Music com-
ed and conducted by Martin L. Platt and Bruce Hoard

COMPANY

arles Antalosky, Michael Burt, Kathryn Dell, Bruce Hoard,
ckson Lane, Joseph Larrea, Lissa LeGrand, Randye Lordon,
ster Malizia, Joseph Mauck, William F. Miller, Norman Neil,
d Osterhoff, Sebastian Richards, Robert Rieben, Robin Robinson,
egory Schroeder, Elizabeth Schuette, Ronald S. Sopyla, Michael
dham, Beth Taffee, Melissa Taylor, Mark Varian, Jennifer
rner, Ronald Wainscott, Steve Wise

PRODUCTIONS

he Tempest," "Richard II," "Twelfth Night," "Fitting for La-
s" by Feydeau translated by Peter Meyer, "Ralph Roister Dois-
"

Glenn Andrews, Jr. Photos

"Richard II"

AMERICAN SHAKESPEARE THEATRE

Stratford, Connecticut
May 17–August 31, 1975
Twenty-first Season

Artistic Director, Michael Kahn; Managing Director, William Stewart; Production Manager, Lo Hardin; Stage Managers, Stephen Nasuta, Arthur Karp; Assistant Director, Larry Carpenter; Wardrobe Mistress, Helen McMahon; Hairstylist, Steve Atha; Production Assistant, Michael Novak; Music Director and Conductor, Allan Lewis; Press, Thomas O'Connor, Seymour Krawitz; President of the Board, Konrad Matthaei; Directors, Anthony Page, Michael Kahn; Scenery, David Jenkins, John Conklin; Costumes, Jane Greenwood, Lawrence Casey; Lighting, Ken Billington; Movement, Liz Thompson; Fights Staged by Rod Colbin; Choreography, Elizabeth Keen; Business Manager, Donald Bundock.

COMPANY

Gregg Almquist, David Arnstein, Richard Backus, Sally Backus, Laurinda Barrett, Robert Beseda, Powers Boothe, Frank Borgman, Morris Carnovsky, Richard Dix, Tom Everett, Geraldine Fitzgerald, John Glover, Grayce Grant, Fred Gwynne, Eileen Heckart, Bette Henritze, Michael Houlihan, William Larsen, Julia MacKenzie, Donald Madden, Kate Mulgrew, E. E. Norris, Wyman Pendleton, Briain Petchey, Sarah Peterson, Lee Richardson, Jack Ryland, Michele Shay, Marshall Shnider, Theodore Sorel, Alvah Stanley, Charles Sweigart, Maria Tucci, Janet White, Luke Yankee

REPERTOIRE

"King Lear" by William Shakespeare; Director, Anthony Page; "The Winter's Tale" by William Shakespeare; Director, Michael Kahn; "Our Town" by Thornton Wilder; Director, Michael Kahn

Martha Swope Photos

William Larsen, Eileen Heckart, Richard Backus, Kate Mulgrew, Lee Richardson, Geraldine Fitzgerald, (front), Victoria Nuland, Todd Alechnowicz in "Our Town" Top Left: Morris Carnovsky, Michele Shay in "King Lear" Below: Bette Henritze, Maria Tucci, Donald Madden in "The Winter's Tale"

Gerard E. Moses in "Timon of Athens"

CHAMPLAIN SHAKESPEARE FESTIVAL

Burlington, Vermont
July 9–August 30, 1975
Seventeenth Season

Director, Edward J. Feidner; Associate Producer, George B. Bryan; Stage Manager, Andrew Mack; Costumes, Polly Smith; Designer, Lisa M. Devlin; Technical Director, Alan Campbell; Assistant Director, James Wimsatt; Business Manager, Barbara Phillips; Press, Peter Kurth; Sound, Nadine Maleski; Musical Director, Steven A. Freeman; Technical Assistants, W. Bradford Walker, John Patton; Choreographer, Ruthmary O'Brien.

COMPANY

Tom Carlisle, Jeffrey DeMunn, Jon Farris, Dennis Lipscomb, Rita Litton, Gerard E. Moses, Robert Odsley, Armin Shimerman, Marcus Smythe, Sarah Brooke, Susan Dunlop, Margaret Klenck, Sara O'Neil, Claude Albert Saucier, Susan Selig, Charles Touers, Jonathan Bourne, Peter DeLorenzo, Brooke Gladstone, David S. Godkin, Kevin Meconi, Ciel Metoyer, Greg Patnaude, John Patton, Craig Purinton, Sally Faye Reit, Jose Angel Santana, Ed Tracy

REPERTOIRE

"Timon of Athens" by William Shakespeare; Director, Edward J. Feidner; "Much Ado about Nothing" by William Shakespeare; Director, John Milligan; "Our Town" by Thornton Wilder; Director, Edward J. Feidner

Robert Ousley, Thomas Carlisle, Marcus Smythe
in "Much Ado about Nothing"

GLOBE OF THE GREAT SOUTHWEST

Odessa, Texas
June 20–August 24, 1975

Seventh Season

Founder-Producer-Director, Charles David McCally; Business Manager, Bert Coleman; Technical Director, Gregory Wurz; Press, Wanda Snodgrass; Chairman of the Board, Jim Reese; Costumes, Cathleen Gregory Runge; Sets, D. Arthur Runge; Stage Managers, Steve Linn, Michael Ward, Evan Lee, Gwen Griffith, Michael Rowan, Greta Reese, Ruthmary Turnham; Original Music, Michael Morrison; Choreographers, James Kelley, Chikita Wallace; Guest Director, Michael Finlayson.

COMPANY

Wayne Alexander, James Bottom, Dennis Arthur Runge, Steven Linn, Michael Ward, James Kelley, Jeffrey G. Forward, Barry S. Eisenberg, Evan Lee, Criss Bramlet, Matthew Pearl, Alice Altvater, Michael Morrison, Chikita Wallace, Kathleen Gregory Runge, Morris Brown, Charles Benton, Casey Childs, Ruthmary Turnham, Thomas Taylor, Veronica Newell, Peggy McCracken, Jon Shapiro, James M. Rymer, Jr., Steve Bland, Art Berggren, Greta Reese, Joe Durham, Gwendolyn Griffith, Steve McGuire, Lindie Nichols, Brett Elise McCally, Fred Cowles

REPERTOIRE

"Much Ado about Nothing" by William Shakespeare; Director, Michael Finlayson; "Dames at Sea" by George Haimsohn and Robin Miller; Director, Charles David McCally; "Troilus and Cressida" by William Shakespeare; Director, Michael Finlayson; "The Life of Christ" by Regina Walker McCally; Adapted from the Four Gospels; Director, Charles David McCally

"As You Like It" Top Right: "Dames at Sea"

THE GLOBE PLAYHOUSE

Los Angeles, California
August 22, 1975–May 16, 1976
Producing Organization, The Shakespeare Society of America; Executive Producer-Founder, R. Thad Taylor; Artistic Director, DeVeren Bookwalter; Associate Producers, Robert Epstein, James Farquharson, Thom Shields; Directors, DeVeren Bookwalter, Shannon Eubanks, Martin Platt; Sets, Roger Hampton, Steven Sassen; Costumes, Alan Armstrong, Kathleen Bishop, Shannon Eubanks, Gerri Grammer, B. Jaye Schooley; Lighting, Rob Esselstein, Lewis Martin, Douglas J. Oliver; Music and Sound, James Farquharson, Chris Kuhni

PRODUCTIONS AND CASTS

CYRANO DE BERGERAC with DeVeren Bookwalter (Cyrano), Adair Jameson (Roxana), Jefferson Watts (Christian), Gary Bass, Paul Bordman, James Boller, Stefan Cotner, Alfred Dennis Shannon Eubanks, Herb Fitch, Frank Geraci, Charles Goldman, Richard Grady, William Gunther, Roger Hampton, Patricia Harvey, Colin Jameson, David Kinne, Jerry Marymont, Karen McLaughlin, Norrine Philips, Gloria Reese, Augie Tribach. This production was the recipient of three awards from the Los Angeles Drama Critics Circle: Distinguished Production, Distinguished Direction, Distinguished Performance (DeVeren Bookwalter). During the season it was returned to the repertoire with the following replacements in the cast: Gloria Dorcy, Ann Driscoll, Edward Dullaghan, B. J. Grogan, Stevie Ann Mitchell, Jon Palo, Michael Ross-Oddo, Raynor Scheine, Steven Schwartz, Bradley Thrush

HAMLET with DeVeren Bookwalter (Hamlet), Shannon Eubanks (Ophelia), Amelia Lauren (Gertrude), Herb Fitch (Claudius), Charles Goldman (Polonius), Stefan Cotner, Gloria Dorcy, Edward Dullaghan, Ray Van Goeye, Richard Grady, William Gunther, Roger Hampton, Odysseus Llowell, Jerry Marymont, Norrine Philips, Robert Redding, Michael Ross-Oddo, Raynor Scheine, Steven Schwarts, Bradley Thrush, Jefferson Watts

LOVE'S LABOURS LOST with James Scott (Berowne), Kres Mersky (Rosaline), Daniel Arden, Richard Baker, Kathleen Bishop, David Bulasky, Stefan Cotner, Michael Endy, William Frankfather, Paul Fredrix, Dan Gilvezan, Ann Greer, Charles Hutchins, Thomas Mahard, Kim Sudol, Jennifer Varner, Erik White

KING RICHARD III with DeVeren Bookwalter (Richard), Alfred Rossi (Buckingham), Sarah Boulton, Bronia Dearle, Craig Fisch, John Flynn, Ann Greer, Richard Guilfoyle, William Gunther, Roger Hampton, Don Higdon, Jerry Marymont, John Megna, Karen McLaughlin, Norrine Philips, Mark Pint, Anne Potts, Michael Ross-Oddo, Raynor Scheine, Robert Schenk, Steven Schwartz, John Sherwood, Cal Thomas, Bradley Thrush

CYMBELINE with Anne Potts (Imogen), Richard Baker (Posthumus), Steven Schwartz (Cloten), Jay Bell, Sarah Boulton, Christiana Bramlet, Robert Chapel, Tina Deane, Gregory Elliot, William Forward, William Frankfather, Ed Garrabrandt, Frank Geraci, Richard Guilfoyle, William Hargreaves, David Meyers, James O'Kleshen, James Ralston

James Saterlie, Ralph Bien Photos

Karen McLaughlin, Deveren Bookwalter in "Richard III" Top Right: Bookwalter, Charles Goldman, Adair Jameson in "Cyrano de Bergerac"

Shannon Eubanks, Deveren Bookwalter in "Hamlet"

GREAT LAKES SHAKESPEARE FESTIVAL

Lakewood, Ohio
Lawrence Carra, Producer-Director
July 3–October 11, 1975
Administrative Director, Mary Bill; Press, William Rudman; Sets,
Warner Blake; Costumes, Michael Olich; Lighting, Frederic You-
ens; Stage Managers, J. P. Valente, Harold Warren; Guest Directors,
Jean Gascon for "The Miser," Tad Danielewski for "The Winter's
Tale"

COMPANY

Robert Allman, Michael R. Boyle, Gregory Lehane, Keith Mackey
Tom Mardirosian, Erika Petersen, James Selby, Billie Anita Stewart
Edward Stevlingson, John Straub, Patrick Watkins, David Williams
Susan Willis, Kate Young

PRODUCTIONS

"As You Like It" and "The Winter's Tale" by William Shakespeare
"The Miser" by Moliere, "Our Town" by Thornton Wilder, "The
Frogs" by Shevelove/Sondheim, freely adapted from Aristophanes

Joseph Karabinus, William Goddard Photos

Left: Robert Allman, John Straub in "The Frogs"
Top: Patrick Watkins, Kate Young, James
Selby, Billie Anita Stewart in "As You Like It"

Erika Petersen, Keith Mackey, Gregory
Lehane in "The Frogs"

Edward Stevlingson, Tom Mardirosian
in "The Miser"

NATIONAL SHAKESPEARE FESTIVAL

Old Globe Theatre
San Diego, California
June 3–September 14, 1975
Twenty-sixth Season

Producing Director, Craig Noel; General Manager, Robert McGlade; Art Director, Peggy Kellner; Press, William B. Eaton; Stage Directors, Ellis Rabb, Jack O'Brien, Diana Maddox; Costumes, Edguard Johnson, Steven Rubin; Lighting, John McLain; Composers, Cathy MacDonald, Conrad Susa; Sound, Charles Richmond, Dan Dugan; Stage Managers, Tom Corcoran, Diana Clarke

COMPANY

Frank Adams, Ronnie B. Baker, Joseph Bird, Katherine Donohoe Brecka, Forrest Buckman, Patrick Carroll, Hal Chidnoff, Andrew Cole, Tom DeMastri, Patrick Ferguson, Christopher Foster, Lew Horn, David Jensen, Mary Ann Jensen, John-Frederick Jones, Toni Joy, Barry Kraft, Mary Layne, Jason Lee, Ronald Long, Sindy McKay, Richard Marion, Patrick McMinn, Marian Mercer, David Meyers, Danna Mongoven, Susan Mosher, Thomas M. Nahrwold, Pam Navarre, D. Michael Nowicki, Terrence O'Connor, Ellis Rabb, Tom Ramirez, Larry St. John, Patrick B. Sammon, Susan Saunders, Holly Schoonover, Norman Simpler, Mimi Smith, Michael Staetter, David Ogden Stiers, Valeda Turner, Carl Weintraub, G Wood, Vikki Young

PRODUCTIONS

"The Tempest," "Much Ado about Nothing," "Measure for Measure" by William Shakespeare, "Godspell" by Stephen Schwartz

Bill Reid Photos

Top: Tom DeMastri, Ellis Rabb in "The Tempest"

Right: Barry Kraft, Mary Layne, G Wood, Marian Mercer, John Frederick Jones in "Much Ado about Nothing" Below: Terrence O'Connor, Patrick Duffy in "Measure for Measure"

David Meyers, Larry St. John in "Godspell"

179

NEW JERSEY SHAKESPEARE FESTIVAL

Madison, N. J.
June 24–November 16, 1975
Eleventh Season

Artistic Director, Paul Barry; Guest Director ("Uncle Vanya"). Davey Marlin-Jones; Press, Ellen Barry; Stage Managers, John Starr, Gary C. Porto; Scenery, David M. Glenn; Costumes, Gay Beale Smith, Dean H. Reiter; Lighting, Gary C. Porto; Assistant Producer, Tom Borsay; Administrative Assistant, Rose Pancirov; Musical Director, Brian Lynner; Press Assistants, Pam Wright, Carol Saville

COMPANY

Humbert Allen Astredo, Ellen Barry, Paul Barry, Robertson Carricart, Kevin Cotter, Kathy Dyas, Robert Foley, Clarence Felder, Richard Graham, David Howard, J. C. Hoyt, Alan Jordan, Lloyd Kay, Daryn Kent, Tarina Lewis, Robert Machray, Ron Mangravite, Susanne Marley, William Preston, Naomi Riseman, Dale Robinette, Edward Rudney, Margery Shaw, Ronald Steelman, Eric Tavaris, Y Yve York

Barbara Adinaro, Barbi Alison, Sue Arsenault, Dean Barclay, Sue Barr, Geoffrey M. Brandt, Jim Bender, Alexander H. Berkeley, Leona Beth, Susan Bewley, Susan Bloodworth, Vincent Borelli, Bettina R. Carter, Mark L. Churchill, Carol Craddock, Patrick Crea, Matthew Connors, Anne-Marie Czaykowski, Robert D'Aprile, Linda Ann Davis, Bethany DeCof, Linda Della-Grotte, Robert Desiderio, Jeffrey Dighton, Richard H. Dorfman, Camelia Drew, Debra L. Dumas, Ted Gargiulo, Gail Gordon, Michael Hegedus, Mark S. Herb, Cynthia Hodin, Sheri L. Johnson, Rose H. Jung, Stephen P. Katz, Rick Kirsch, Douglas Kisley, Jeffrey H. Klotz, David Krafchick, Perry Kroeger, Sarah Fairfax Lansden, William LaRosa, James Lawrence, Susan Levine, Robert Jeffrey Levitt, Brian Lynner, Druce McDaniel, Carol Millstein, Garry Morris, Scott Nangle, Sasha Nanus, Gary Pannullo, Rush Pearson, Roger I. Pellaton, Faye Pollock, David Porter, Deborah Putnam, Leslie H. Raff, Ramon Ramos, John Rathburn, Bruce Rayvid, Douglas E. Richardson, Nancy K. Rieth, Jose Rivera, Amy Rosenberg, Tiana Jo Schlitten, Mary Schmidt, Jan Ian Schwartz, Jo Sennett, S. R. Serafin, Camille Shawnasey, John Shepherd, Ronald Skorton, Dick St. George, Neil Stadtmore, Artie Stern, Rawle Titus, Stewart Turner, Debbie Waxman, R. E. Wertheim, Haig Zakian

PRODUCTIONS

"Henry IV, Part I," "Henry IV, Part II," "Two Gentlemen of Verona" by William Shakespeare, "John Brown's Body" by Stephen Vincent Benet, "That Championship Season" by Jason Miller, "Uncle Vanya" by Anton Chekhov, "Sweet Bird of Youth" by Tennessee Williams, "The Lady's Not for Burning" by Christopher Fry

Blair Holley, Rich Towlen, Lee Tanner Photos

Right: "Sweet Bird of Youth"
Above: "Uncle Vanya" Top: "Henry IV, Part II"

Margery Shaw, Paul Barry in "The Lady's Not for Burning"

Eric Tavaris in "Two Gentlemen of Verona"

NEW YORK SHAKESPEARE FESTIVAL

Delacorte Theater-Central Park
New York, N.Y.
June 18–August 24, 1975
Nineteenth Season
Producer, Joseph Papp; Associate Producer, Bernard Gersten; Produced in association with the City of New York; Production Manager, Andrew Mihok; Assistant to producer, Gail Merrifield; Press, Merle Debuskey, Bob Ullman, Norman L. Berman; Production Associate, Meir Zvi Ribalow; Music Coordinator, Herbert Harris

June 18–July 19, 1975

HAMLET

By William Shakespeare; Director, Michael Rudman; Setting, Santo Loquasto; Costumes, Albert Wolsky; Lighting, Martin Aronstein; Fight Sequences, Erik Fredericksen; Percussion Score, Herbert Harris; Danish Anthem, Norman L. Berman; Stage Managers, Jason Steven Cohen, Louis Rackoff; Technical Coordinator, David Manwaring; Wardrobe Master, James McGaha; Production Assistant, Frank Difilia

CAST

Robert Burr (Claudius/Ghost), Ruby Dee (Gertrude), Sam Waterston (Hamlet), Larry Gates (Polonius/First Gravedigger), John Lithgow (Laertes/Player King), Andrea Marcovicci (Ophelia), James Cahill (Horatio), James Gallery (Voltemand), Douglas Stender (Rosencrantz/2nd Gravedigger), John Heard (Guildenstern/Priest), Mark Metcalf (Marcellus/Dumb Show King), Richard Brestoff (Francisco), Bruce McGill (Reynaldo), Franklyn Seales (Fortinbras/Player Queen), Hannibal Penney, Jr. (Captain/Dumb Show Queen), Stephen Lang (Prologue), Vance Mizelle (Company Manager), Ernest Austin (Technical Director), Aides to the King: Richard Brestoff, Graham Beckel, Ray Munro, Cleveland O'Neal III, John Rowe, Stage Hands: Michael Cutt, Reggie Johnson, Jack R. Marks, Ken Marshall, Peter Van Norden, Nancy Campbell (Apprentice Actor)

Friedman-Abeles Photos

August 6–24, 1975

THE COMEDY OF ERRORS

By William Shakespeare; Director, John Pasquin; Music, Peter Link; Setting and Costumes, Santo Loquasto; Lighting, Martin Aronstein; Choreography, Elizabeth Keen; Stage Managers, Richard S. Viola, Peter von Mayrhauser; Technical Coordinator, David Manwaring; Wardrobe Master, Alfred Calamoneri; Production Assistant, Frank DiFilia

CAST

Ted Danson (Bodyguard), Peter Iacangelo (Bodyguard), Leonardo Cimino (Egeon), John Seitz (Solinus), Laurie Faso (Merchant), Paul Kreppel (Merchant), Don Scardino (Antipholus), Michael Tucker (Dromio of Syracuse), Larry Block (Dromio of Ephesus), June Gable (Adriana), Blair Brown (Luciana), John Christopher Jones (Antipholus of Ephesus), Danny DeVito (Balthazar), Susan Peretz (Luce), Pierre Epstein (Angelo), Linda Lavin (Courtesan), Jeffrey Jones (Dr. Pinch), Anita Dangler (Emilia), Townspeople: Maggie Askew, Roxanne Hart, Terri King, Charles McCaughan, Thom McCleister, Harlan Schneider, Kas Self

Friedman-Abeles Photos

Top Right: Robert Burr, Ruby Dee, Sam Waterston in "Hamlet" Below: Sam Waterston, Andrea Marcovicci in "Hamlet"

Don Scardino, June Gable, John Christopher Jones in "Comedy of Errors"

OREGON SHAKESPEARE FESTIVAL

Ashland, Oregon
February 14–April 12, June 14–September 21, 1975
Fortieth Season

Founder-Consultant, Angus L. Bowmer; Producing Director Jerry Turner; General Manager, William Patton; Scenery, Richard L. Hay; Costumes, Jeannie Davidson; Lighting, Steven A. Max; Directors, James Edmondson, Will Huddleston, Jon Jory, Andrew Stanley; Production Coordinator, Pat Patton; Technical Director, Duncan MacKenzie; Choreographer, Judith Kennedy; Music Director, Jack Ashworth; Stage Managers, James Verdery, Peter Allen, Dennis Bigelow, Jeffrey Hirsch; Hairstylists, Candy Neal, Dian Gates; Press, Joan Olson, Kathy Glaser, Sally White

COMPANY

Bruce Abbott, Adrienne Alexander, Denis Arndt, Jack Ashworth, Larry R. Ballard, Alan Blumenfeld, Carmi Boushey, David L. Boshey, Jeff Brooks, John A. Caldwell, Joseph De Salvio, James Daniels, Ted D'Arms, Randi Douglas, le Clanche du Rand, James Edmondson, Joseph H. Feldman, Michael Keys Hall, David Hart, Christine Healy, Keith Herritt, Michael J. Hill, Michael Horton, Will Huddleston, William M. Hurt, Katherine James, Philip Jones, Wayne Lee, E. Bonnie Lewis, David Marston, Eric Booth Miller, Michael Kevin Moore, William Moreing, Barry Mulhollan, Mark D. Murphey, Allen Nause, Gayle Stuwe Neuman, Steve Newcomb, Todd Oleson, Brad O'Neil, Judd Parkin, JoAnn Johnson Patton, Kristin Ann Patton, Pat Patton, Shirley Patton, Mack Ramsey, Todd Reichenbach, Rebecca Robbins, Neil A Savage, Peter Silbert, Jean Smart, Mary Turner, William Turner, Leslie Velton, Mark Wardenburg, Cal Winn

PRODUCTIONS

"Winter's Tale," "Charley's Aunt," "Oedipus the King," "The Petrified Forest," "Romeo and Juliet," "All's Well That Ends Well," "Henry VI," "Long Day's Journey into Night"

Hank Kranzler Photos

Top: Christine Healy, Mark Murphey in "Romeo and Juliet" Left: "All's Well That Ends Well"

**"The Winter's Tale"
Above: "Romeo and Juliet"**

SHAKESPEAREAN THEATER OF MAINE

Monmouth, Maine
June 26–August 31, 1975
Artistic Director, Earl McCarroll; Guest Director, Beatrice MacLeod; Sets, Ursula Beldon; Costumes, Joyce Aysta; Lighting, Paul Gallo; Business Manager, Paul Wycisk; Stage Manager, James J. Thesing

COMPANY

Lee McClelland, Robert De Lany, Laverne Light, William Meisle, Ronald Parady, Bob Burrus, John H. Fields, Jo Anne Jameson, Robert Johanson, Peter Webster, Herman Tuider, Barbara Selden, Robert Bell, William R. Brown, Lawrence Cappiello, Tom Graff, Richard Haverinen, Nina Jones, Nicholas Kaledin, Cheryl Moore, Robert Nadir, Michael O'Brien, Polly Penn, Kathryn Meisle

PRODUCTIONS

"The Tempest," "The Comedy of Errors," "Androcles and the Lion," "Dark Lady of the Sonnets," "King Lear"

Harry Marshall Photos

Right: Peter Michael Webster, Robert Johanson in "The Tempest"

Lee McClelland, John H. Fields in "King Lear"

"A Comedy of Errors"

STRATFORD FESTIVAL OF CANADA

Stratford, Ontario
June 9–October 11, 975
Twenty-third Season

Artistic Director, Robin Phillips; Director/Festival Stage, William Hutt; Directors; Bill Glassco; David Jones, Jan Rubes, David Toguri, John Wood; General Manager, Bruce Swerdfager; Business Manager, Gerald Corner; Company Manager, Barry MacGregor; Executive Producer, John Hayes; Design, Daphne Dare; Production Manager, Jack Hutt; Technical Director, Robert Scales; Press, Ann Selby, Douglas Allan, Richard Wolfe; Directors of Music, Alan Laing, Raffi Armenian; Fencing Master, Patrick Crean; Stage Managers, Jack Merigold, Vincent Berns, Nora Polley, Colleen Stephenson, R. Lorne McFarland, Catherine McKeehan, Peter Roberts, David Walsh, Thomas Schweitzer, Penelope Ritco, Wardrobe Mistress, Eleanor Nickless; Production Assistant, Heather Kitchen

COMPANY

Mia Anderson, Bob Baker, Keith Batten, Rod Beattie, Brian Bedford, Pat Bentley-Fisher, Mervyn Blake, Geoffrey Bowes, Daniel Buccos, Barbara Budd, Jackie Burroughs, Graeme Campbell, Kenneth Campbell, J. Winston Carroll, Douglas Chamberlain, Marc Connors, Richard Curnock, Eric Donkin, Martin L. Donlevy, Mary Lou Fallis, Denise Fergusson, Michael Fletcher, Pat Galloway, Gale Garnett, John C. Goodin, Lewis Gordon, Diane Grant, Max Helpmann, Martha Henry, Meg Hogarth, Bernard Hopkins, Linda Huffman, Don Junkin, Peter Hutt, John Innes, Terence Kelly, Tom Kneebone, Jan Kudelka, Larry Lamb, Sheena Larkin, Michael Liscinsky, Barry MacGregor, Stephen Macht, Frank Maraden, Marti Maraden, Richard Monette, Robert G. More, William Needles, Robin J. Nunn, Blaine Parker, Richard Partington, Nicholas Pennell, Jack Roberts, Stephen Russell, Melody Ryane, John Sweeney, Robert Vigod, Ian Wallace, Richard Whelan, Kathleen Widdoes, Leslie Yeo

PRODUCTIONS

"Saint Joan," "Twelfth Night," "Measure for Measure," "Trumpet and Drums," "The Comedy of Errors," "Two Gentlemen of Verona," "The Crucible," "Fellowship," "Kennedy's Children," "Oscar Remembered," "The Importance of Being Earnest"

Robert C. Ragsdale Photos

Left: Brian Bedford, Geoffrey Bowes, Richard Monette, Martha Henry in "Measure for Measure" Above: Jackie Burroughs, Nicholas Pennell, Gale Garnett in "A Comedy of Errors" Top: Tom Kneebone, Pat Galloway in "Saint Joan"

William Hutt, Kathleen Widdoes in "Measure for Measure"

Mia Anderson, Nicholas Pennell in "Two Gentlemen of Verona"

Dennis Lipscomb, Betsy Palmer, Alice Elliott
Right: David MacEnulty, Betsy Palmer in "As
You Like It"

THEATRE VENTURE '76

Beverly, Massachusetts
May 3–28, 1976
Managing Director, Stephan Slane; Resident Manager, Theda Taylor; Press, Peter Downs; Stage Manager, Henry Banister; Production Staff, Michael Neelon, Nancy Jean Schertler; Directors, Ada Brown Mather, Russell Treyz; Sets, Eve Lyon; Costumes, Mary Aiello Bruce; Lighting, Theda Taylor; Musical Director, Ken Collins

COMPANY

David Brummel, Deborah Combs, Martin Meredith, Richard Kinter, Jack Honor, David MacEnulty, George Cavey, J. Kenneth Campbell, Michael Kane, David Licht, Alice Elliott, Betsy Palmer, Dennis Lipscomb, Stephen Foster, Christopher Wynkoop, Thomas Barbour, Virgil Roberson, Tom Klunis, Kathleen Forbes, Shanly Heffelfinger, Jason Metaxas, Michael Finnerty, Dan Kirsch

PRODUCTIONS

"As You Like It," "The Fantasticks"

Peter Downs Photos

Martin Meredith, Jack Honor, Deborah Combs
in "The Fantasticks"

PROFESSIONAL RESIDENT COMPANIES

(Failure to meet deadline necessitated several omissions)

ACT: A CONTEMPORARY THEATRE

Seattle, Washington
June 1, 1975–May 31, 1976
Artistic Director, Gregory A. Falls; General Manager, Andrew M. Witt; Press, Edna K. Hanna, Louise Mortenson; Assistant to General Manager, Warren Sklar; Musical Director, Stan Keen; Directors, Greg Falls, James Higgins, Robert B. Loper, Jack Sydow, M. Burke Walker, Eileen MacRae Murphy; Sets, Bill Forrester, Jerry Williams; Costumes, Donna Eskew, Sally Richardson; Lighting, Al Nelson, Phil Schermer; Technical Director, Michael Lowther; Stage Managers, Eileen MacRae Murphy, Sandy Cruse, Michael Weholt

COMPANY

Barbara Bercu, Jay Fernandez, William L. Kux, James W. Monitor, Maryann M. Nagel, Ruth Kidder, A. C. Weary, Richard Watson, Donald Ewer, Henry Hoffman, James Higgins, Rod Pillous, Richard Arnold, Tobias Andersen, Alvin Lee Sanders, Edwin Bordo, Ben Tone, Dean Gardner, John Horn, Kurt Garfield, Richard Blackburn, Jane Bray, Tom Spiller, Joseph Edward Meek, Steven W. Herrmann, Kurt Beattie, Daryl Anderson, Bill Myers, Robert Deitrich, Ann H. Topping, Gregory Elliot, Eric Augusztiny, Ivars Mikelson, Tanny McDonald, C. W. Armstrong, Randy Johnstad, David McMahan, D. H. Panchot, Mada Stockley, John Aylward, Patricia Murray, Clayton Corzatte, Frederick Coffin, Robert Donley, Vern Taylor, William C. Witter, Gail Hebert, Henry Kendrick, Glenn Buttkus, Joe Fields, Brian Avery, Eve Robert, G Wood, Leon Bibb, Gail Nelson, Stan Keen

PRODUCTIONS

"Sleuth," "The Resistible Rise of Arturo Ui," "When You Comin' Back, Red Ryder?," "Of Mice and Men," "Oh Coward!," "Contact: Fred Coffin," "We Three," "The Christmas Show," "Fire," "Absurd Musical Revue for Children," "See the Players," and *World Premiere* of "Quiet Caravans" by Barry Dinerman, with Sylvia Gassell, Ben Tone, Marjorie Nelson, John Renforth, Susan Ludlow

Greg Gilbert Photos

**Right: "When You Comin' Back, Red Ryder?"
Above: "Of Mice and Men"**

**Henry Hoffman, Don Ewer
in "Sleuth"**

**Ben Tone, Sylvia Gassell
in "Quiet Caravans"**

ACTORS THEATRE OF LOUISVILLE

Louisville, Kentucky
October 16, 1975–May 23, 1976

Producing Director, Jon Jory; Administrative Director, Alexander Speer; Associate Director, Trish Pugh; Assistant Administrative Director, Stewart Slater; Directors, Clifford Ammon, Ray Fry, Elizabeth Ives, Jon Jory, Charles Kerr, Christopher Murney, Adale O'Brien, Michael Thompson; Set Designers, Paul Owen, Anne A. Gibson, Grady Larkins, Kurt Wilhelm; Costumes, Kurt Wilhelm; Lighting, Geoffrey T. Cunningham, Vincent Faust, Paul Owen; Property Master, Stephen McDowell; Technical Directors, Joseph Ragey, Jeffrey Hill; Costumiere, Mary Lou Owen; Stage Managers, Elizabeth Ives, Don Johnson, Kimberly Francis Kearsley, Lewis Rosen, David Rosenak

COMPANY

Sarah Atkins, Jim Baker, Eric Booth, Leo Burmester, Bob Burrus, William Cain, Barry Corbin, Jean DeBaer, Randi Douglas, Earle Edgerton, Lee Anne Fahey, John H. Fields, Robert Forster, Ray Fry, Michael Gross, Allan Gruet, John Hancock, James Harris, Katharine Houghton, Ken Jenkins, Don Johnson, Victor Jory, Michael Kevin, Susan Cardwell Kingsley, Marsha Korb, Jack Lanron, Jeremy Lawrence, Lauren Levian, Beverly May, Vaughn McBride, John Meadows, Adale O'Brien, Ardeth Pappas, C. C. H. Pounder, Dennis Predovic, Pamela Reed, Peter Silbert, Michael Thompson

PRODUCTIONS

"Arms and the Man," "The Hot l Baltimore," "Ten Little Indians," "Oedipus the King," "Scapino!," "The Last Meeting of the White Magnolia," "The Sunshine Boys," "Dear Liar," "Sea Horse" *World Premiere* of "Scott and Zelda," and *American Premiere* of Marowitz' "Measure for Measure"

David S. Talbott Photos

**Top Right: Robert Forster, Adale O'Brien
in "The Sea Horse"**

**"The Hot l Baltimore"
Above: "Measure for Measure"**

**Victor Jory, Peter Silbert in "The Last Meeting
of the Knights of the White Magnolia"**

187

ALLEY THEATRE

Houston, Texas
October 18, 1975–May 30, 1976
Producing Director, Nina Vance; Director, Beth Sanford; Sets
William Trotman; Costumes, Barbara A. Cox; Lighting, Jonathan
Duff; Sound, Paul Dupree; Technical Director, William C. Lind
strom; President, McClelland Wallace; Press, Bob Feingold, Marga
ret Genovese; Managing Director, Iris Siff; Business Manager, Bill
Halbert; Production Associate, H. Wilkenfeld; Staff Directors, Bob
Leonard, Beth Sanford, William Trotman; Company Manager, Bob
Leonard; Stage Managers, Bettye Fitzpatrick, George Anderson
Rutherford Cravens, Trent Jenkins

COMPANY

John Adams, Cal Bedford, Mimi Carr, Roderick Cook, Rutherford
Cravens, Philip Davidson, Carl Davis, James Edmonson, Haskell
Fitz-Simons, Brenda Forbes, Larry Ford, Wayne Gagne, Craig R
Gardner, Russell Gold, Dale Helward, John Houser, Stephen Isbell
George Jackson, Rodger McDonald, Margo McElroy, Mark Mur
phy, Jim Nolan, Rand Porter, Rex Rabold, Richard Reed, Richard
Rorke, Tony Russel, Greg Ryan, Dwight Schultz, Daniel Therriault
Concetta Tomei, Ben Wolf, David Wurst, Leslie Yeo, Bettye Fitzpa
trick, Robert Symonds, Bella Jarret, Lyle Talbot

PRODUCTIONS

"Indians," "The Cocktail Party," "The Front Page," "The Last
Meeting of the Knights of the White Magnolia," "Old Times,"
"Juno and the Paycock," "The Show-Off," "Scenes from American
Life," "Tiny Alice," "Purgatory," "The Harmful Effects of To
bacco," "A Christmas Carol"

Dome City Photos

**Top Left: Bettye Fitzpatrick, Mark Murphey,
Leslie Yeo, Cristine Rose in "Juno and the
Paycock" Below: William Troutman, Brenda Forbes
Roderick Cook in "The Cocktail Party"
Center: Dwight Schultz, Bella Jarret in "Tiny Alice"**

**Lyle Talbot, Tony Russel
in "The Front Page"**

Dale Helward in "Indians"

AMERICAN CONSERVATORY
THEATRE

San Francisco, California
October 4, 1975–May 22, 1976
Tenth Season

General Director, William Ball; Executive Producer, James B. McKenzie; Executive Director, Edward Hastings; Development Director, Edith Markson; Conservatory Director, Allen Fletcher; Production Director, Benjamin Moore; General Manager, Charles Dillingham; Press, Cheryle Elliott; Stage Directors, William Ball, Allen Fletcher, Edward Hastings, Jon Jory, Laird Williamson; Sets and Costumes, Robert Blackman, Greg Bolton; Lighting, F. Mitchell Dana; Sound, Bartholomeo Rago; Wardrobe Supervisor, Cathy Edwards; Stage Managers, James Haire, James L. Burke, Julia Fletcher, Raymond Gin, Christian Leigh

COMPANY

Hope Alexander-Willis, Candace Barrett, Joseph Bird, Ray Birk, Carl Boen, Ronald Boussom, Joy Carlin, Megan Cole, Nicholas Cortland, Daniel Davis, Peter Donat, Franchelle Stewart Dorn, Barbara Dirickson, Sabin Epstein, Janice Garcia, Lou Ann Graham, Ross Graham, Nathan Haas, Charles Hallahan, Rick Hamilton, Harry Hamlin, Lawrence Hecht, Elizabeth Huddle, Charles H. Hyman, Daniel Kern, Michael Keys-Hall, Anne Lawder, Deborah May, Fredi Olster, William Paterson, Ray Reinhardt, Stephen Schnetzer, Sandra Shotwell, Anna Deavere Smith, Francine Tacker, Anthony S. Teague, Sydney Walker, Marrian Walters, Al White, J. Steven White, Laird Williamson, James R. Winkler, Daniel Zippi

Frank Abe, Wayne Alexander, Jane Bolton, Cynthia Burch, Traber Burns, Kraig Cassity, Charles Coffey, Linda Connor, William Ferriter, Gina Franz, Bruce Gerhard, Bennet Guillory, Barta Heiner, Gregory Itzin, Delores Mitchell, William Peck, Susan Pellegrino, Peter Schuck, Caroline Smith, Katharine Stapleton, Mary Lou Stewart

PRODUCTIONS

"Tiny Alice," "The Matchmaker," "Desire under the Elms," "The Merry Wives of Windsor," "Equus," "Peer Gynt," "The Taming of the Shrew" and World Premieres of "General Gorgeous" by Michael McClure, and "This Is (An Entertainment)" by Tennessee Williams

William Ganslen, Hank Kranzler Photos

**Top: Nicholas Cortland in "General Gorgeous"
Right: Peter Donat, Janice Garcia, Daniel
Zippi in "Equus" Below: Hope Alexander-Willis,
Nicholas Cortland in "Tiny Alice"**

**Earl Boen, Ray Reinhardt, James R. Winker in
"This Is (An Entertainment)" Above: "The
Merry Wives of Windsor"**

ARENA STAGE

Washington, D.C.

Producing Director, Zelda Fichandler; Executive Director, Thomas C. Fichandler; Associate Producer, George Touliatos; Assistant Executive Director, Alton Miller; Directors, Edward Payson Call, David Chambers, John Dillon, Zelda Fichandler, Martin Fried, Norman Gevanthor, Gene Lesser, Tom Moore, John Pasquin, Alan Schneider, Douglas C. Wager; Set Designers, John Lee Beatty, Karl Eigsti, Grady Larkins, Ming Cho Lee, Santo Loquasto; Costumes, Gwynne Clark, Carol Luiken, Marjorie Slaiman; Lighting, Robert Crawley, Allen Hughes, Hugh Lester, William Mintzer; Composer, Robert Dennis; Music Adapter, Vance Sorrells; Stage Managers, Jay Allison, John D. Charlesworth, Robert Crawley, Michael S. Mantel, Gully Stanford, Douglas C. Wager; Technical Director, Henry R. Gorfein; Staff for Living Stage: Director, Robert Alexander; Assistant Director, Rebecca Rice; Musical Director, Joan Berliner; Stage Manager, Bob Alexander; Production Assistant, Roberta Gasbarre; Director's Assistant, Pamela Horner

COMPANY

Tony Abatemarco, Barry Alexander, Jason Alexander, Jay Allison, Stanley Anderson, John Barrett, Richard Bauer, Gary Bayer, Ned Beatty, Sudie Bond, Nancy Boykin, Peggy Lee Brennan, James Broderick, Russell Carr, Barbara Caruso, Leslie Cass, Howland Chamberlain, Neil Churgin, Liam Clark, William Clark, Carolyn Coates, Hal Corley, Christopher Councill, Jan Cremeans, Terrence Currier, Leora Dana, Regina David, MacIntyre Dixon, le Clanche du Rand, Conchata Ferrell, David Garrison, Grayce Grant, Valorie Gear, Mark Hammer, Dorothea Hammond, Bob Harper, Edward Herrmann, John Hollis, Bella Jarrett, Chris Johnstone, Jeffrey Jones, Pat Karpen, Danny Kelly, Linn Klitzkie, David Leary, Bob Leslie, Kathleen Lindsey, Marilyn McIntyre, Howard Marsden, Norman Martin, Steve Mellor, Michael Mertz, Alexander Metcalf, Mark Metcalf, Michael Miller, Michael Joyce Miller, Gene S. Minkow, Bill Moor, Achim Nowak, Gilbert Oakley, Theresa O'Rourke, Joan Pape, Ron Parker, Tony Pasqualini, Robert Pastene, Daniel Pollack, Ray Procter, Robert Prosky, Richard Ramos, Jack Ryland, David Schaeffer, Scott Schofield, Lane Smith, Phyllis Somerville, Vance B. Sorrells, Robert Stattel, Deborah Ann Stern, Barbara Tarbuck, Joy Tauber, Glenn Taylor, James Tolkan, Lily Tomlin, Eric Vickland, Douglas C. Wager, Mary Lou Walton, Lloyd Webber, Jon Weinberg, Bruce Weitz, Eric Weitz, Dianne Wiest, Eleanor D. Wilson, Halo Wines, Howard Witt, Victoria Wood, Max Wright, Wendell W. Wright

PRODUCTIONS

"Long Day's Journey into Night," "An Enemy of the People," "Once in a Lifetime," "Heartbreak House," "What the Babe Said," "Total Recall," "Madmen," "Waiting for Godot," "Busy Dyin'," "Death of a Salesman," "The Front Page," "Our Town," and *PREMIERES* of Istvan Orkeny's "The Tot Family" and a new version of Ray Bradbury's "Dandelion Wine."

Alton Miller Photos

Right: "The Tot Family" Above: "Cabrona"
Top: Leora Dana, Mark Metcalf, Stanley
Anderson, James Broderick in
"Long Day's Journey into Night"

Dianne Wiest, Robert Pastene
in "Heartbreak House"

James Tolkan, Norman Martin
in "Dandelion Wine"

ASOLO STATE THEATER

Sarasota, Florida
June 1, 1975–May 31, 1976

xecutive Director, Richard G. Fallon; Artistic Director, Robert
ane; Managing Director, Howard J. Millman; Sets, Rick Pike;
hting, Martin Petlock; Costumes, Catherine King, Flozanne
n; Technical Director, Victor Meyrich; Press, Edith N. Anson;
ge Managers, Marian Wallace, Stephanie Moss

COMPANY

rtha J. Brown, Burton Clarke, Bernerd Engel, Max Gulack, Ste-
n Johnson, Henson Keys, William Leach, Philip LeStrange, Bar-
a Reid, Robert Murch, Bette Oliver, Joan Rue, Robert Strane, Isa
omas, Bradford Wallace, Ken Costigan, Kelly Fitzpatrick, James
gartner, David S. Howard, Pamela Lewis, Dennis Michaels,
queline Hammond, Steven Ryan, Stephen Van Benschoten, Ritch
nkley, Katherine Rao, Ralph Clanton, Bob Horen, Gerald
mby, William Jay

vis Agrell, Dottie Dee, Pat Hurley, Barry Klassel, Thomas
mby, Anne Sandoe, Alan Smith, Cathy S. Chappell, Nora Ches-
, Janice Clark, Jim Crisp, Jr., John Gray, Stephen Joseph, David
iat, Clark Niederjohn, Patricia Oetken, Frederic-Winslow Oram,
nna Pelc, Robert Stallworth, Romulus E. Zamora, Linda Burn-
n, Fred Davis, Molly DePree, Bill Herman, Peter Ivanov, Beth
cks, Paul Murray, Steven J. Rankin, Deborah Unger, John C.
ll

UEST ARTISTS: S. C. Hastie, John Dillon, Paxton Whitehead,
Hoskins, Salli Parker, William Woodman, Erskine Caldwell,
n Ulmer, Holmes Easley, Joseph Nieminski, Nick Hall, Bennet
eryt, Jim Chestnutt, Neal Kenyon, Peter Harvey, Eberle Thomas,
n Scheffler, Bella Spewack

PRODUCTIONS

obacco Road," "The Sea," "Heartbreak House," "Guys and
lls," "Tartuffe," "There's One in Every Marriage," "King Lear,"
he Patriots," "The New York Idea," "Hogan's Goat," "Boy
ets Girl," "A Streetcar Named Desire," "Look Homeward, An-
," and *World Premieres* of "Trolls and Bridges" by Jon Caulkins
d Sandie Hastie, "Going Ape" by Nick Hall, "The Quibbletown
cruits" by Eberle Thomas, "Win with Wheeler," by Lee Kal-
eim, "1776 . . . And All That Jazz" by Neal Kenyon

Gary Sweetman Photos

**Right: Robert Murch, Ralph Clanton in
"The Patriots" Above: Steven Ryan, Martha J.
own, Barbara Reid in "A Streetcar Named Desire"
Top Right: "Boy Meets Girl"**

**Dennis Michaels, Bradford Wallace
in "Going Ape"**

**William Leach, Barbara Reid
in "Tobacco Road"**

BARTER THEATRE

Abingdon, Virginia
April 1–October 31, 1975
Artistic Director-Manager, Rex Partington; Director, Owen Phillips; Business Manager, Pearl Hayter; Administrative Director Ruth Carr; Press, Lucy Bushore, Patricia Bailey; Designer, Bennet Averyt; Costumes, Cynthia Doty, George Carr Garnett; Lights Michael Dalzell, Richard Marsters; Technical Director, Clayton Austin; Sound, Tony C. Partington; Stage Managers, Peter Dowling, Michael Mantel

COMPANY

Eric Conger, Tiina Cartmell, Mary Carney, Joseph P. Edens, Gwyllum Evans, Holly Cameron, George Hosmer, Margaret Lunsford Katharine Manning, Gale McNeeley, Peggity Price, Robert E. Rutland, Jr.

GUEST ARTISTS: David Darlow, Joe Costa, George Black, Herbert DuVal, Kenneth Frankel, John E. Going, Yolande Bryant, Rail Helsing, Gloria Hayen Herman, Cleo Holladay, Gloria Maddox Charles Maryan, John W. Morrow, Jr., Amy Nathan, Steve Novelli John Spencer

PRODUCTIONS

"The Devil's Disciple," "The Diary of Anne Frank," "The Beaux Stratagem," "The Male Animal," "Broadway," "Light Up the Sky," "Biography," "Sleuth," "Two on an Island," "The America Experiment," "La Ronde," "Subreal"

Eric Conger Photos

Left: John W. Morrow, Jr., Mary Carney in "Diary of Anne Frank," Below: "Broadway" Top Left: "The Devil's Discipline"

"The Beaux' Strategem"

Cleo Holladay, Gale McNeeley in "Biography"

CALIFORNIA ACTORS THEATRE

Los Gatos, California
October 17, 1975–May 29, 1976
Second Season
Artistic Director, Peter Nyberg; Executive Director, Sheldon Kleinman; Producing Director, James Dunn; Directors, Peter Nyberg, James Dunn, John Reich, Milton Lyon, Jack Bender; Sets, Ronald E. Krempetz, Ralph Fetterly, Russell Pyle, Steven T. Howell, Peter Nyberg; Costumes, Marcia Frederick, Gini Vogel; Lighting, Ray Garrett; Press, Barbara Carpenter; Technical Director, Stephen F. Cherry; Stage Managers, Frank Silvey, Earl Frounfelter, Robert Steiger

COMPANY

Martin Ferrero, Bonnie Gallup, Wesley Goddard, David Goldmund, Kit Gross, Michael Hill, Karen Hensel, Dan Johnson, Sarita Johnson, Lee Kopp, Dakin Matthews, Brian McGreen, Thomas Menz, Gregory Meecham, Sandy McCallum, John Napierala, Peter Nyberg, Victor Pappas, Joan Pirkle, Roxann Pyle, Tom Ramirez, Carolyn Reed, Carl Reggiardo, Alice Rorvik, Peggy Schoditsch, Kurtwood Smith, Robert Steiger, Paul Ventura, Gary Voss, Vernon Weddle

PRODUCTIONS

"Our Town," "Earnest in Love," "The Imaginary Invalid," "Three Sisters," "Enrico IV," "What Price Glory?," "A Midsummer Night's Dream," and *World Premiere* of "A Very Gentle Person" by Hans Steinkellner

H. J. Susser Photos

Top: "Earnest in Love"
Below: "The Imaginary Invalid"
Right: "What Price Glory?" Top:
"The Three Sisters"

"A Very Gentle Person"
Above: "Our Town"

193

CENTER STAGE

Baltimore, Maryland
December 3, 1975–June 27, 1976
Artistic Coordinator, Stan Wojewodski, Jr.; Managing Director,
Peter W. Culman; Press, Jonathan D. Rogers, Hillary Aidus; Stage
Managers, Michael McMahon, Julia Gillett

PRODUCTIONS AND CASTS

TARTUFFE by Moliere; Director, Jacques Cartier; Sets, David
Jenkins; Costumes, Nancy Potts; Lighting, Roger Morgan. CAST:
Peter Vogt, Vivienne Shub, Hillary Aidus, Jane House, Trish Haw-
kins, Davis Hall, Christine Baranski, George Ede, Terrance O'-
Quinn, Henry Thomas, John Eames, Stan Wojewodski, Jr., Michael
A. Cook, Joseph Snair

BUSY BEE GOOD FOOD ALL NIGHT DELICIOUS and BOR-
DERS *(World Premiere)* by Charles Eastman; Sets and Costumes,
Kurt Lundell; Lighting, Roger Morgan. CAST: "Busy Bee . . .":
George Ede, Ruth Gilbert, Davis Hall, "Borders": Helen Hanft,
Trinity Thompson, Peter Vogt

DREAM ON MONKEY MOUNTAIN by Derek Walcott; Direc-
tor, Albert Laveau; Choreography, Carol LaChapelle; Musical Di-
rector, Andrew Beddeau; Set, Eugene Lee; Costumes, Robert
Wojewodski; Lighting, Roger Morgan. CAST: Obba Babatunde,
Anthony Chisholm, Charles Grant-Green, Sam Singleton, David
Pendleton, Clayton Corbin, Marilyn Donnenberg, Sullivan Walker,
Malonga Auguste Casquelourd, Luther Fontaine, Randy Grant, Ha-
zel Bryant, Lynette Laveau, Paula Moss, Aramide Pamela Rice,
Michelle Summers

OLD TIMES by Harold Pinter; Director, Stan Wojewodski, Jr.; Set,
Peter Harvey; Costumes, Elizabeth Palmer; Lighting, Ian Calderon.
CAST: Patricia Gage, George Taylor, Lois Markle

THE CHERRY ORCHARD by Anton Chekhov; Director, Jacques
Cartier; Set and Costumes, John Jensen; Lighting, Gilbert V. Hems-
ley, Jr. CAST: Patricia Gage, Patricia Pearcy, Tana Hicken, Henry
Thomas, George Morfogen, Stan Wojewodski, Jr., Paul C. Thomas,
Anita Keal, Yusef Bulos, Christine Baranski, John Eames, Ronald
Frazier, Joseph Snair, Jay Stone, Justin White, Timothy Wolfe

THE REAL INSPECTOR HOUND by Tom Stoppard; Director,
Stan Wojewodski, Jr.; Sets, Peter Harvey; Costumes, Liz Covey;
Lighting, Ian Calderon. CAST: Henry Thomas, Paul C. Thomas,
Paddy Croft, Lee Corbet, Christine Baranski, Patricia Gage, John
Wylie, Dan Szelag

BLACK COMEDY by Peter Shaffer; Director, Stan Wojewodski,
Jr.; Sets, Peter Harvey; Costumes, Liz Covey; Lighting, Ian Cald-
eron. CAST: Andrew Rohrer, Christine Baranski, Paddy Croft,
John Wylie, Charles O. Lynch, Paul C. Thomas. Patricia Gage, Dan
Szelag

Richard Anderson, Anston-Worthington Photos

Top Right: "The Cherry Orchard"
Below: "Dream on Monkey Mountain"

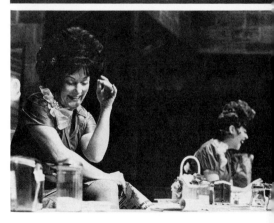

Trinity Thompson, Helen Hanft in
"Busy Bee Good Food All Night Delicious"

CENTER STAGE THEATRE

Austin, Texas
September 1975–May 1976
Artistic Director-Manager, Ken Johnson; Assistant Manager, Laine Leibick; Press, Diane Bertram; Technical Directors, Bob Sertner, Michel Jaroschy; Costumes, Maggie Cox, Mary Lou Stephens

COMPANY

Barbara Amaral, Sandy Leibick, Kim Quillin, Jon Rice, Patti Davis, Melanie Guilbeault, Benjamin Wear, Diane Bertram, Jeff Broyles, Susie Higley, Scott Maynig, Susan Bruton, John Huddleston, Rob Wilds, Brent Thomas, John Bernardoni, Oliver Handley, Ann Armstrong, Adrienne Blalock, Jim Carpetas, Ben Carssons, Bill Chamberlain, Tom Cloutier, Michael Cosentino, Bill Dick, Larry Fitzgerald, Diana Goodman, Patricia Harris, Bruce Kalman, Dorothea Kiker, Glenn Long, Richard McDowell, David Pearson, Karol Phelan, Wanda Pierce, Arthur Rankin, Alison Smith, Allan Stephens, Rex Voland, Jim Baggett, Charles Baumhauer, Dale Bearden, Christine Beato, Jeffrey Benkoe, Sally Bull, James Childs, Maggie Cox, Therese Dean East, Barton Faulks, Bill Johnson, Royce Gehrels, Laura Grayson, Rod Grayson, Sherie Hartle, Karen Sue Hastings, Donald Janda, Peter Lawson, Peter Malof, Duncan McGann, Randy Reece, John Ross, Mack Waldrip, Chris Weismann

PRODUCTIONS

"Macbeth," "West Side Story," "Godspell," "That Championship Season," "Man of La Mancha"

Ken Johnson Photos

Top Right: Bill Dick, Karol Phelan in "Man of La Mancha"
Below: Sandy Leibick, Barbara Amaral in "West Side Story"

Kim Quillin, Jon Rice in "Godspell"

Oliver Handley in "That Championship Season"

CENTER THEATRE GROUP

MARK TAPER FORUM
Los Angeles, California
July 1, 1975–June 30, 1976
Artistic Director, Gordon Davidson; General Manager, William P. Wingate; Associate Director, Edward Parone; Director Forum/-Laboratory, Robert Greenwald; Director Improvisational Theatre Project, John Dennis; Press, Richard Kitzrow, Leigh Charlton, Anthony Sherwood, Thomas Brocato; Lighting, Tharon Musser; Production Manager, John DeSantis; Technical Director, Robert Calhoun; Stage Managers, Don Winton, Madeline Puzo, Richard Serpe, Chuck Linker

PRODUCTIONS AND CASTS

ONCE IN A LIFETIME by Moss Hart, George S. Kaufman; Director, Edward Parone; Designers, Jim Newton, Pete Menefee, Tharon Musser. CAST: Jayne Meadows Allen, Janell Buff, Helen Page Camp, Judy Cassmore, Gordon Connell, Nathan Cook, Lisa Cutler, Dennis Dugan, Wayne C. Dvorak, Antonia Ellis, Stefan Fischer, Aileen Fitzpatrick, Lorry Goldman, Dody Goodman, Harold Gould, John D. Gowans, David Himes, Jerry Hoffman, Richard Lenz, Terry Lumley, Joseph G. Medalis, Louisa Moritz, Charles Thomas Murphy, Julie Payne, Marcia Rodd, Arnold Soboloff, Garn Stephens, Patricia Sturges, Britt Swanson, Donald Torres, Sharon Ullrick, Rick Vartorella

TOO MUCH JOHNSON by William Gillette; Adapted by Burt Shevelove; Director, Gordon Davidson; Designers, Robert Zentis, Tom Rasmussen, H. R. Poindexter. CAST: Mary Carver, Al Checco, Frank Geraci, Rose Gregorio, Cynthia Harris, David Huffman, William Katt, Zale Kessler, Laurence Luckinbill, Simon Oakland, Brad Rearden, Marge Redmond, Tom Rosqui, Joe Zaloom

in repertory with

THE SHADOW BOX (World Premiere) by Michael Cristofer; Director, Gordon Davidson; Designers, Robert Zentis, Tom Rasmussen, H. R. Poindexter. CAST: Mary Carver, Rose Gregorio, Cynthia Harris, David Huffman, Laurence Luckinbill, Simon Oakland, Brad Rearden, Marge Redmond, Tom Rosqui

THE DUCHESS OF MALFI by John Webster; Director, Howard Sackler; Designers, Paul Sylbert, Dorothy Jeakins, John Gleason. CAST: Eileen Atkins, G. W. Bailey, Jeff Bergqvist, Olivia Cole, Marlin Charles, Kermit Christman, Edgar Daniels, Tony De Fonte, Robin Gammell, Rick Garr, Henry Hoffman, Byron Jennings, Sally Kemp, Zale Kessler, Philip Larson, Charles O. Lynch, Herta Ware, Byron Webster, G Wood, Ken Zimmerman

ASHES (American Premiere) by David Rudkin; Director, Edward Parone; Designers, Sally Jacobs, Julie Weiss, F. Mitchell Dana. CAST: Andra Akers, Michael Cristofer, Tyne Daly, Janet Johnson, James Ray

CROSS COUNTRY (World Premiere) by Susan Miller; Director, Vickie Rue; Designers, Sally Jacobs, Julie Weiss, F. Mitchell Dana CAST: Frances Lee McCain, Ron Rifkin, Robin Strasser, Sharon Ullrick

AND WHERE SHE STOPS NOBODY KNOWS (World Premiere) by Oliver Hailey; Director, Gordon Davidson; Designers, Marge Champion, Sally Jacobs, Julie Weiss, F. Mitchell Dana. CAST: Eileen Brennan, Lou Gossett
in repertory with

THREE SISTERS by Anton Chekhov; Translated by Michael Heim; Director, Edward Parone; Designers, Sally Jacobs, F. Mitchell Dana. CAST: Marc Alaimo, Michael Cristofer, Tyne Daly, Lou Gossett, Barra Grant, Warren Hammack, David Himes, Janet Johnson, Laurie Kennedy, Berry Kroeger, Frances Lee McCain, James Ray, Ron Rifkin, Pearl Shear, Delos V. Smith, Jr., David Ogden Stiers, Richard Warrick

Steven Keull Photos

Left Center: "Three Sisters"
Above: Ron Rifkin, Sharon Ullrick,
Frances Lee McCain, Robin
Strasser in "Cross Country"
Top: Marcia Rodd, Dennis Dugan,
Jayne Meadows, Harold
Gould, Charles Thomas Murphy in
"Once in a Lifetime"

Marge Redmond, Simon Oakland
in "The Shadow Box"

IMPROVISATIONAL THEATRE PROJECT

Director, John Dennis; Manager, Michael Lonergan; Stage Manager, Ron Rudolph; Writer, Doris Baizley; Designers, Charles Berner, Dawn Chiang, Joe Tompkins; Music, Harry Aguado; Lyrics, Doris Baizley, Harry Aguado. CAST: Nathan Cook, Brenda Davis, Noreen Hennessy, Hal Landon, Jr., Michael McNeilly, Eric Neuld, Rick Vartorella, Bruce French

FORUM/LABORATORY

Director, Robert Greenwald; Managers, Michael Lonergan, Douglas G. Burns; Production Managers, Erik Brenmark, Ron Rudolph; Stage Managers, Michael Castle, Arni Fishbaugh, Richard Lewis, Stephen Rich, Ron Rudolph, Estela Scarlata, Cathy Zheutlin

THE GREAT POTATO FAMINE by Daniel Wray, Brendan Noel Ward; Director, Richard M. Johnson; Designers, Ron Rudolph, Louise Hayter; Music, Steven Wells, Ray Doyle. CAST: Blanche Bronte, Judy Chaikin, Maryellen Clemons, Duncan Gamble, Sindy Hawke, Kay Howell, Drew Lobenstein, John Megna, Tony Papenfuss, E. A. Sirianni, David Stifel, Steven Wells, Terry Wolf

DIAMONDS IN THE ROUGH by Jeremy Blahnik, David Copelon, Vickie Rue. CAST: Herb Foster, Barra Grant, Henry Hoffman, Mark Jenkins, Julie Payne, Carolyn Reed, Robin Strasser, Sharon Ullrick, Rick Vartorella

OEDIPUS AT COLONUS by Sophocles; Director, Sally Jacobs; Designers, Julie Weiss, Ron Rudolph, Steven Wells. CAST: Andrew Cole, Joe Hudgins, Philip Larson, Ralph Lev Mailer, Julie Payne, John Roddick, Gene Rosen, Benjamin Stewart, Kate Woodville

TO SEE THE ELEPHANT by Elizabeth Clark; Director, Liebe Gray; Designers, Ellyn Gersh, Durinda Wood, Susie Helfond; Music, Cris Williamson. CAST: Terri Carson, E. Marcy Dicterow, Carol-Lynn Fillet, Janet Johnson, Frances Lee McCain, Belita Moreno, Shirley Slater, Sharon Ullrick, Cris Williamson, Carrie Zivetz

ELECTRA by Robert Montgomery; Director, Joseph Chaikin; Dramaturg, Mira Rafalowicz; Designers, Gwen Fabricant, Arden Fingerhut. CAST: Shami Chaikin, Tina Shepard, Paul Zimet

THE COMMON GARDEN VARIETY by Jane Chambers; Director, Gwen Arner; Designers, Robert Zentis, Durinda Wood. CAST: Anne Gee Byrd, Mary Jackson, Marc McClure, Ann O'Donnell, Betsy Slade

JACK STREET by Joan Tewkesbury; Directed by author; Designers, Erik Brenmark, Louise Hayter, Pamela Cooper; Musical Director, Tony Berg; Music, Tony Berg, Albert Greenberg, Melissa Murphy, Ted Neeley, Allan Nichols. CAST: Paul Ainsley, Tony Berg, Ed Buck, Hannah Dean, Bob DoQui, Tom Eden, Scott Glenn, Mariette Hartley, Joan Hotchkis, Lee Jones-DeBroux, Johnn Ray McGhee, John Megna, Melissa Murphy, Ted Neeley, Craig Richard Nelson, Julie Newmar, Paul Potash, Cristina Raines, Rod Rimmer, Susan Tyrrell, Herve Villechaize, Joe Zaloom

UPROOTED by Humberto Robles-Arena; English Adaptation, Severo Perez; Director, Margarita Galban; Designers, Estela Scarlata, Jason Shubb. CAST: Linda Dangcil, Ronald Joseph Godines, Rafael Lopez, Julio Medina, Drew Michaels, Karmin Murcelo, Carmen Zapata

Steven Keull Photos

Top: Michael Cristofer, Tyne Daly in "Ashes"
Right: Lou Gossett, Eileen Brennan in "And Where She Stops Nobody Knows"
Below: "Colonel Montana"
(Improvisational Theatre)

Mariette Hartley, Susan Tyrrell in "Jack Street"
Above: "The Common Garden Variety"

CINCINNATI PLAYHOUSE IN THE PARK

Cincinnati, Ohio
October 21, 1975–May 30, 1976
Producing Director, Michael Murray; General Manager, Robert W. Tolan; Guest Directors, Israel Hicks, John Going, Michael Bawtree; Stage Manager, J. P. Valente; Sets, Neil Peter Jampolis, Eric Head; Costumes, Annie Peacock Warner; Press, Lanni Johnston; Assistant to Producing Director, Jerri Roberts; Production Manager, Richard Lukaszewicz

PRODUCTIONS AND CASTS

DEATH OF A SALESMAN with Sam Gray, Paul Vincent, Richard Kline, Dorothy Stinnette, Robert Beatey, David Stanley Luman, William Myers, Joseph Regalbuto, Diane Danzi, Paul Forste, Georgia Neu, Pat VanOver, David Dreyfoos

RELATIVELY SPEAKING with Leah Chandler, Jo Henderson, Robert Nichols, Douglas Jones

THE LITTLE FOXES with Robert Baines, George Brengel, Louis Edmonds, Jan Farrand, Jo Henderson, Bryan Hull, Robert Johnson, Julia McKenzie, Randall Merrifield, Beatrice Winde

WHAT THE BUTLER SAW with I. M. Hobson, Linda Alper, Philip Anglim, Eric House, Jeanette Landis, Ronald Steelman

THE CONTRAST with Lynn Milgrim, I. M. Hobson, Philip Anglim, Jim Broaddus, Lisa Hemphill, Tom Mardirosian, Fred McCarren, Monica Merryman, Pamela Rohs, Claudia Zahn

WHERE'S CHARLEY? with Adrienne Angel, Dennis Bailey, George Brengel, Dan Diggles, Lee Roy Reams, I. M. Hobson, Sally Mitchell, Marti Rolph, Paul Forste, Keith Mackey, Linda Poser, Linda Lauter, James Braet, Neal Thompson, Bernardo Hiller, Peggy Neeson, Kathryn Cordes, Laura Liebman

Sandy Underwood Photos

Right: "What the Butler Saw" Top: Beatrice Winde, Robert Baines in "The Little Foxes"

Jo Henderson, Robert Nichols in "Relatively Speaking"

Marti Rolph, Dan Diggles in "Where's Charley?"

198

CLEVELAND PLAY HOUSE

Cleveland, Ohio
October 17, 1975–May 2, 1976
Director, Richard Oberlin; Associate Director, Larry Tarrant; Press, Ric Wanetik, Paula Bond; Administrative Coordinator, Nelson Isekeit; Scenic Director, Richard Gould; Assistant Director, Robert Snook; Directors, Jonathan Farwell, Richard Halverson, Paul Lee, Evie McElroy, Richard Oberlin, Robert Snook, Larry Tarrant; Production Coordinator, Larry Tarrant; Designers, Richard Gould, Eugene Hare, Barbara Leatherman, Tim Zupancic; Technical Director, Barbara Leatherman; Costumes, Diane Dalton

COMPANY

Robert Allman, Norm Berman, Sharon Bicknell, John Buck, Jr., Daniel Desmond, Jo Farwell, Jonathan Farwell, June Gibbons, Richard Halverson, Dana Hart, Dee Hoty, Allen Leatherman, Paul Lee, Andrew Lichtenberg, Lizbeth Mackay, Evie McElroy, Spencer McIntyre, David Meyer, Ralph Neeley, Richard Oberlin, Dale Place, Leslie Rapp, Howard Renensland, Jr., James Richards, Dennis Romer, Tedd Rubinstein, Frederic Serino, George Cecil Simms, Robert Snook, Bonnie Sosnowsky, J. D. Sutton

GUEST ARTISTS: Ken Albers, Jean Arthur, Yolande Bavan, David Berman, Jonathan Bolt, George Brengel, Joel Brooks, Victor Caroli, Clayton Corzatte, Mike Dantuono, Carolelinda Dickey, Marji Dodrill, Kenneth Dolin, Melvin Douglas, Ben Evett, Mark Gardner, George Gould, Margaret Hilton, Lee Karnes, Earl Keyes, Greg Krizman, Jerome Lawrence, Robert E. Lee, Vaughn McBride, Christina Moore, Edith Owen, Tony Phelan, J. Ranelli, Ellen Renensland, Ray Walston, William Paterson, William Rhys

PRODUCTIONS

"First Monday in October" *(World Premiere)* by Robert E. Lee and Jerome Lawrence, "The Prague Spring" by Lee Kalcheim, "Bingo" *(American Premiere)* by Edward Bond, "Caesar and Cleopatra," "Abigail Adams: The Second First Lady" by Edith Owen, "Relatively Speaking" by Alan Ayckbourn, "Dr. Jekyll and Mr. Hyde" *(World Premiere)* by Paul Lee, "The Dark at the Top of the Stairs" by William Inge, "A Profile of Benjamin Franklin" by William Patterson, "Get-Rich-Quick Wallingford" by George M. Cohan, "The Last Meeting of the Knights of the White Magnolia" by Preston Jones, "Of Mice and Men" by John Steinbeck, "Scapino" by Frank Dunlop and Jim Dale, "The World of Carl Sandburg" by Norman Corwin

James Fry Photos

Right: "Dr. Jekyll and Mr. Hyde"
Above: "Get-Rich-Quick Wallingford"
Top: "First Monday in October" (Melvyn Douglas
and Jean Arthur guest stars)

Ray Walston, David Meyer in "The Last Meeting
of the Knights of the White Magnolia"

Yolande Bavan, Clayton Corzatte
in "Caesar and Cleopatra"

COMPANY THEATRE

Los Angeles, California
September 1975–June 1976

COMPANY

Alan Abelew, Arthur Allen, David Alperin, Polita Barnes, Pete
Bergren, Dierdre Berthrong, Laurel Bogen, Gar Campbell, War
Carlisle, Larry Cohen, Jim Cypherd, William Dannevik, Jame
DiAngelo, Stephen Downs, Andy Dworkin, Milton Earl Forres
Myrna Gawryn, Susan Gelb, Harvey Gold, Barbara Grover, Da
Grace, Donald Harris, Nora Heflin, Nancy Hickey, Debbie Jame
Lisa James, Lori Landrin, Gil Laurence, Paul Linke, Lance Larse
Sandra Morgan, Bebe Marks, Constance Mellors, Kathi McGinni
Marcina Motter, Liz Palmer, Andrew Parks, Louie Piday, Marsh
Polekoff, Jerry Pojawa, Michael Prichard, Roxann Pyle, Russe
Pyle, Dennis Redfield, Jack Rowe, Carol Rusoff, Billy Schaffne
Sally Schulte, Trish Soodik, Michael Stefani, Diane Uchima, Bo
Walter, Lisette Williams, Dan Wyman

PRODUCTIONS

"Mirror Mirror" *(World Premiere)* adaptation of Pierre Marivaux
"La Dispute" by Louie Piday, "Salt" by Mort Goldberg, "Tw
McClures Sunnyside Up: 'The Pink Helmet,' 'The Masked Choir'
(World Premiere) by Michael McClure

Roger Marshutz Photos

**Left: Milton Earl Forrest, Andrew Parks,
Paul Linke in "The Pink Helmet" Above:
Constance Mellors, Louie Piday in
"The Masked Choir"**

CLARENCE BROWN THEATRE

Knoxville, Tennessee
Director, Ralph G. Allen; Director of Productions, Anthony
Quayle; General Manager, Julian Forrester; Associate Directors,
Thomas Cooke, Fred Fields, Albert Harris, Wandalie Henshaw,
Robert Washburn; Design, Robert Cothran; Technical Director,
Robert Field; Company Manager, Janice Stanton; Wardrobe Mis-
tress, Malou Flato; Assistant to General Manager, Elise Adams;
Stage Managers, Kenneth Leavee, Waller Barret Smith, Maria Alex-
andra Wozniak; Costumes, Marianne Custer

COMPANY

Catherine Byers, Barbara Caruso, Jay Doyle, Bernard Engel, Paul
A. Foley, Richard Galuppi, Jack Gwillim, Wandalie Henshaw,
Earle Hyman, Frederic Major, Harriet Nichols, Anthony Quayle,
Susan Ringwood, Douglas Stender, Eric Schneider, Barry Smith,
Cynthia Woll, Maria Alexandra Wozniak, Richard Bowden, David
Fox-Brenton, Kenneth Gray, Walter Barrett Smith

Elise Adams, Linda Benemann, Bill Duncan, Doug Eckert, John
Ferguson, Warren Gaffney, John Gann, Stephen Martin, Laurie
Metter, Jeff Moore, Terry Morris, Sam O'Donnell, Dwight Percy,
Judy Rye, Chris Smith, Lemmie Smith, Lee Toombs, Ronny Vena-
ble

PRODUCTIONS

"Everyman," "Macbeth," "Rip Van Winkle"

**Andrew McHenry, Anthony Quayle
in "Rip Van Winkle"**

DALLAS THEATER CENTER

Dallas, Texas
October 7, 1975–August 14, 1976

Managing Director, Paul Baker; Assistant Director, Mary Sue Jones; Administrative Assistant, Judith Davis; Press, Lynn Trammell; Guest Directors, Robin Lovejoy, David Healy, Dolores Ferraro; Stage Directors, Ken Latimer, Judith Davis, Paul Baker; Sets, Yoichi Aoki, John Henson, Mary Sue Jones, Sam Nance, Virgil Beavers; Costumes, Diana Devereaux, Kathleen Latimer, Randolf Pearson, Gina Taulane, Susan A. Haynie; Lighting, Robert Duffy, Robyn Flatt, Allen Hibbard, Sam Nance, Randy Moore; Stage Managers, Bryant J. Reynolds, Randy Bonifay, Gina Taulane, Steve Lovett, Nick Dalley, Carolyn Pines, Steve Wallace

COMPANY

Yoichi Aoki, Linda Blase, Judith Davis, John Figlmiller, Robyn Flatt, Martha Robinson Goodman, John Henson, Allen Hibbard, Preston Jones, Mary Sue Jones, Kathleen Latimer, Ken Latimer, Fritz Lennon, John Logan, Rebecca Logan, Steven Robert Mackenroth, Ryland Merkey, Norma Moore, Randy Moore, Louise Mosley, Sam Nance, Sally Netzel, Patti O'Donnell, Mona Pursley, Bryant J. Reynolds, Synthia Rogers, Glenn Allen Smith, John R. Stevens, Randolph Tallman, Jacque Thomas, Matt Tracy, Lynn Trammell

PRODUCTIONS

"The Amorous Flea" by Jerry Devine and Bruce Montgomery, "Promenade, All!" by David V. Robison, "Saturday, Sunday, Monday" by Eduardo de Filippo, "Manny" *(World Premiere)* by Randolph Tallman, Steven Mackenroth, Glenn Allen Smith, "A Place on the Magdalena Flats" *(World Premiere)* by Preston Jones, "Much Ado about Nothing" by William Shakespeare, "Stillsong" *(World Premiere)* by Sallie Laurie

Linda Blase Photos

Top: "A Place on the Magdalena Flats"
elow: "Saturday Sunday Monday" Right: "Manny"

Quinn Mathews, Judith Davis, Ted Bowlin,
William George in "Stillsong"

**Renate Walker in
"The Song of the Whip-Poor-Will"
Left: "The Adding Machine" Top: "In
Abraham's Bosom"**

DETROIT REPERTORY THEATRE

Detroit, Michigan
November 1975–June 1976
Artistic Director, Bruce E. Millan; Executive Director, Dorothy
J. Brown; Press, Betty DuPuis; Sets, Bruce E. Millan, John Knox
Zubek Kachadoorian; Lighting, Dick Smith; Costumes, Marianna
Hoad; Sound, Jack Slater; Assistant Director, Jesse Newton

COMPANY

Willie Hodge, Kwabena Caworrie, Charles Haynie, John W. Hardy
William Boswell, Mark Murri, Joyce Williams, Myrenna Haw
thorne, Robert Williams, Barbara Busby, Yolanda Williams, Chery
Lemans, Michael Joseph, Colleen Davis, Jack Slater, Darlene Black
burn, Jobai Burke, Charles R. Roseborough, Betty Dupuis, Terr
Wilks, Jesse Newton, Myrenna Hawthorne, Ruthe Palmer, Mac
Palmer, Frenchy Hodges, Dee Andrus, John Hardy, Renate Walker
Fred Bennett

PRODUCTIONS

"In Abraham's Bosom" by Paul Green, "The Song of the Whip
Poor-Will" *(World Premiere),* "The Adding Machine" by Elmer
Rice, "Morning's at Seven" by Paul Osborn

**Barbara Busby, Jesse Newton
in "Morning's at Seven"**

DRURY LANE NORTH THEATRE

Lincolnshire, Illinois
May 27, 1975–June 20, 1976
Producer, Richard S. Kordos; Press, Bill Wilson, Aaron D. Cushman Associates; Stage Managers, Ernie Lane, Paul Ferris; Technical Directors, Bill Biltgen, Pat Nesladek; Costumes, Susan Gayford, Susan Clare; Props, Michael Zemenick, Paul Ferris, Jeffrey Harris, William Derl-Davis

PRODUCTIONS AND CASTS

THE FOURPOSTER by Jan de Hartog; Director, Tony Mockus; Set, William B. Fosser. CAST: Leonard Nimoy, Ann Eggert.

BORN YESTERDAY by Garson Kanin; Director, Leland Ball; Set William B. Fosser. CAST: Elke Sommer, Art Kassul, Frank Miller, Don Marston, David Morrison, Fern Persons, Joe Shea, Paul A. Ferris, Dianne Hosken, Michael Zemenick, John Kettermaster, Jon Robb, Fred Michaels

THE CONFIDENCE GAME by Tom Sharkey; Director, Vernon R. Schwartz; Set, William Fosser. CAST: Brooke Tucker, John Burns, Douglas Weiss, Forrest Tucker, Jeannette Leahy, David Carl Starwalt, Sandra Weygandt, Denise Latella, Joe Bell

MY THREE ANGELS by Sam and Bella Spewack; Director, Dick Sasso; Set, William B. Fosser. CAST: Jack Goring, Vera Ward, Wesley Pfenning, Geraldine Power, Chuck Connors, Dick Sasso, David Whitaker, Tom Elrod, Al Nuti, Mark Ullius, B. J. Jones.

SUNDAY IN NEW YORK by Norman Krasna; Director, Dick Sasso; Set, Vernon R. Schwartz. CAST: Brad Bisk, Sandra Dee, Owen Sullivan, B. J. Jones, Fred Michaels, Dianne Hosken

LAST OF THE RED HOT LOVERS by Neil Simon; Director, Alba Oms. CAST: Sheila MacRae, Jack Heller

UNDER PAPA'S PICTURE by Joe Connelly and George Tibbles; Director, Brooks West; Set, Jeffrey Harris. CAST: Clay Taylor, David Rupprecht, Gloria Lynn, Esther Sutherland, Eve Arden, J. J. Butler, Brooks West, Barbara A. Harris, Nikki Zelaya

David H. Fishman Photos

Right: Eve Arden, David Rupprecht, Gloria Lynn in "Under Papa's Picture" Above: Owen Sullivan, Brad Bisk, B. J. Jones, Sandra Dee in "Sunday in New York" Top: Dick Sasso, Chuck Connors, David Whitaker in "My Three Angels"

**Ann Eggert, Leonard Nimoy
in "The Fourposter"**

**Jack Heller, Sheila MacRae
in "Last of the Red Hot Lovers"**

Howard E. Rollins, Jr.
in "Medal of Honor Rag"

FOLGER THEATRE GROUP

Washington, D.C.
October 7, 1975–June 27, 1976

Producer, Louis W. Scheeder; General Manager, Larry Verbit, Company Manager, Mary Ann de Barbieri; Press, Pat Bailey; Technical Director, Thom Shovestull; Stage Managers, David M. Levine, Dorothy Maffei, Pamela Horner; Lighting, Betsy Toth; Assistant to producer, Jonathan Alper

PRODUCTIONS AND CASTS

THE COLLECTED WORKS OF BILLY THE KID (American Premiere) by Michael Ondaatje; Music, Desmond McAnuff; Director, Louis W. Scheeder; Set, David Chapman; Costumes, Randy Barcelo; Lighting, Hugh Lester. CAST: Allan Carlsen, Guy Boyd, Mark Robinson, Sandy Faison, Albert Malafronte, Anne Stone, Brad Sullivan, Richard Greene

THE COMEDY OF ERRORS by William Shakespeare; Director, Jonathan Alper; Music, William Penn; Set, Stuart Wurtzel; Costumes, Bob Wojewodski; Lighting, Arden Fingerhut. CAST: Albert Malafronte, Paul Milikin, Edward Young, Donald Warfield, Mike Champagne, Peter Riegert, Deborah Darr, Kathleen Doyle, Marshall Lee Shnider, Sherry Nehmer, Richard Vernon, Timothy Jenkins, Edward Henry, Joanne Hrkach, Charles Montgomery, June Hansen, Dianne Bye, Tracy Davis, Kurt K. Feuer, Rea Rosno, Sunny Schnitzer

MEDAL OF HONOR RAG (World Premiere) by Tom Cole; Director, David Chambers; Set, Raymond C. Recht; Costumes, Carol Oditz, Deborah Walther; Lighting, Betsy Toth. CAST: David Clennon, Howard E. Rollins, Jr., David M. Levine

HENRY V by William Shakespeare; Director, Lous W. Scheeder; Music, William Penn; Set, Raymond C. Recht; Costumes, Bob Wojewodski; Lighting, Arden Fingerhut. CAST: Tony M. Abatemarco, Patrick Beatey, Mike Champagne, David Cromwell, Clement Fowler, Jeremy Gage, Joanne Hrkach, Kathleen Ireton, Richard Kline, Charles Montgomery, Charles Morey, Antonino Pandolfo, Terrance O'Quinn, Rea Rosno

ALL'S WELL THAT ENDS WELL by William Shakespeare; Director, Jonathan Alper; Music, William Penn; Set, Raymond C. Recht; Costumes, Bob Wojewodski; Lighting, Arden Fingerhut. CAST: Carla Meyer, Mark Winkworth, Etain O'Malley, Clement Fowler, Jo Spiller, Michael Houlihan, Albert Corbin, Robert Hage, Kurt K. Feuer, Jim Brady, Tri Garraty, Barry MacMillan, David Cromwell, Licia Colombi, Mary Carney

Joe B. Mann Photos

**Left: Joanne Hrkach, Richard Kline in
"Henry V" Above: Etain O'Malley,
Albert Corbin in "All's Well That Ends Well"
Top: Marshall Lee Shnider,
Mike Champagne, Peter Riegert in
"Comedy of Errors"**

David Clennon
in "Medal of Honor Rag"

FORD'S THEATRE

Washington, D.C.
September 19, 1975–June 27, 1976
Executive Producer, Frankie Hewitt; General Manager, Maury Sutter; Press, Alma Viator, Wayne Knickel; Assistant to producer, Nora Lee

PRODUCTIONS AND CASTS

ARE YOU NOW OR HAVE YOU EVER BEEN by Eric Bentley; Director, William Devane; Set, Barry Robinson; Lighting, Robert Bye; Stage Manager, Haig Shepherd. CAST: Tom Bower, Beeson Carroll, Jeff David, Wynn Irwin, John Lehne, Heidi Mefford, Allan Miller, Byron Morrow, Stephen Roberts, Ed Rombola, Martin Shakar, David Spielberg, Charles Weldon, M. Emmet Walsh

YOUR ARMS TOO SHORT TO BOX WITH GOD by Vinnette Carroll adapted from the Book of Matthew; Music and Lyrics, Alex Bradford; Orchestrations, Billy Taylor; Sets and Costumes, William Schroder; Lighting, Gilbert Hemsley, Jr; Choreographer, Talley Beatty; Director, Vinnette Carroll. CAST: Lamar Alford, Salome Bey, Alex Bradford, Sharon Brooks, Maryce Carter, Billy Dorsey, Thomas Jefferson Fouse, Jr., Cardell Hall, Delores Hall, William Hardy, Jr., Jan Hazell, Aisha Khabeera, Michele Murray, Stanley Perryman, Zola Shaw, Alwin Taylor

I HAVE A DREAM adapted by Josh Greenfeld; Conceived and Directed by Robert Greenwald; Setting, Donald Harris; Costumes, Terence Tam Soon; Lighting, Martin Aronstein; Associate Producer, Pat Lang; Stage Managers, David Clive, Janyce Ann Wagner. CAST: Billy Dee Williams, Judyann Elder, Marion Ramsey

ELEANOR by Arlene Stadd; Director, Michael Kahn; Set, Ed Wittstein; Costumes, Jane Greenwood; Lighting, John McLain; Stage Manager, Lo Hardin. CAST: Eileen Heckart as Eleanor Roosevelt

**Top: Alwin Taylor, Michelle Murray in
"Your Arms Too Short to Box with God"
Right: "Are You Now or Have You Ever Been"
Below: Billy Dee Williams in "I Have a Dream"**

Eileen Heckart in "Eleanor"

GOODMAN THEATRE CENTER

Chicago, Illinois
October 9, 1975–June 13, 1976
Fiftieth Season
Artistic Director, William Woodman; Managing Director, John Economos; Technical Director, Joseph E. Bates; Press, Rhona Schultz, Ron Christopher; Stage Managers, Peter Dowling, Joseph Drummond, James Greek, James T. McDermott; Stage 2 Coordinator, Gregory Mosher; Sets, Richard Oates; Wardrobe Mistress, Ruth Rinklin; Business Manager, Janet Wade

PRODUCTIONS AND CASTS

MAINSTAGE
OUR TOWN by Thornton Wilder; Director, George Keathley. CAST: Tony Mockus, George Womack, Bruce Powell, Nesbitt Blaisdell, Avril Gentles, Jane Groves, David-James Carroll, Janet Locker, Dennis MacNeille, Harriet Hall, Wiley Harker, Robert Blackburn, Jane MacIver, Glenn Kovacevich, Jane Almquist, Don Marston, William Munchow, Scott Larsson, John Bryson LeGrande, James H. Eckhouse, Timothy J. Murray, Edgar Meyer

BENITO CERENO by Robert Lowell; Director, Michael Montel. CAST: Tony Mockus, Thomas A. Stewart, Gus Kaikkonen, Robert Guillaume, Paul Butler, Lenard Norris, Frank Barrett, Tricia Borha, Geoffrey Clark, Isaac Clay, Karen Ghoston, Frank Rice, Avis LaVelle Sampson, Lionel Smith, William Vines, Steven Williams, Fred Eberle, Mark Hutter, Thomas McKeon, Adrian Smith, Timothy Smith, Mike Genovese, Tony Gillotte, John Heitmanek

MOURNING BECOMES ELECTRA by Eugene O'Neill; Director, William Woodman. CAST: Nesbitt Blaisdell, Murray Nash, Jane MacIver, Brina Rodin, Rosemary Murphy, Laura Esterman, Judith Ivey, Thomas A. Stewart, Robert Murch, Tony Mockus, Tony Lincoln, Brina Rodin, Mike Genovese, Ben Masters, Dennis Kennedy

THE LAST MEETING OF THE KNIGHTS OF THE WHITE MAGNOLIA by Preston Jones; Director, Harold Stone. CAST: Earl Sydnor, Frank Hamilton, Douglas Fisher, Jack Wallace, Gordon Oas-Heim, Chet Carlin, John Wardwell, W. H. Macy, Brad O'Hare

OUR FATHER'S FAILING (World Premiere) by Israel Horovitz; Director, John Dillon. CAST: Dominic Chianese, Joseph Leon, Lawrence Pressman, Lanna Saunders

THE DEVIL'S DISCIPLE by George Bernard Shaw; Director, William Woodman. CAST: Pat Fraser, Wesley Ann Pfenning, Eugene J. Anthony, Robert Murch, Allison Giglio, Michael Tezla, Tony Lincoln, Judy Herbst, Leonard Kraft, Diane Jean Ciesla, Kenneth Welsh, J. J. Johnston, Don Marston, Brian Murray, Tom Birk, Robert Garcia, Tony Gillotte, Ira Goldstein, Tom McKeon, Larry Palmissano, Chris Reynolds, Tim Samuelson, Dan Shapiro, David Wirth

STAGE 2
AMERICAN BUFFALO (World Premiere) by David Mamet; Director, Gregory Mosher. CAST: J. J. Johnston, Bernard Erhard, William H. Macy

THREE PLAYS OF THE YUAN DYNASTY by June Pyskacek; Translated by Liu Jung-en. CAST: Dan Ziskie, Keith Szarabajka, Felicity LaFortune, Michael Tezla, Glenn Kovacevich, Marge Kotlisky

CHICAGO by Sam Shepard; Director, Dennis Zacek. CAST: Jim Jacobs, Mark Nutter, Arlene Schulfer, Sara Asher, Warren Leming, Jeanette Goldberg, Dan Ziskie

THE LOCAL STIGMATIC by Heathcote Williams; Director, Gary Houston. CAST: Jim Jacobs, Warren Leming, Leonard Kraft, Dan Ziskie

DANDELION WINE by Ray Bradbury; Arranged and Adapted by Peter John Bailey; Director, William Woodman. CAST: Scott Stevens, Scott Larsson, Tom McDonald, Danny Goldring, Don Marston, Cordis Fejer, Jane MacIver, Nesbitt Blaisdell, Fern Persons

STATUES and THE BRIDGE AT BELHARBOUR (World Premiere) by Janet L. Neipris; Director, Gregory Mosher. CAST: Mike Genovese, Judith Ivey

Terry Shapiro Photos

Top Right: Lawrence Pressman, Joseph Leon in "Our Father's Failing" Below: Mike Genovese, Judith Ivey in "The Bridge at Belharbour"

"American Buffalo" Above: "Chicago"

HARTFORD STAGE COMPANY

Hartford, Connecticut
September 19, 1975–June 20, 1976
Producing Director, Paul Weidner; Managing Director, Jessica L. Andrews; Press, Dave Skal; Business Manager, Alan Toman; Technical Director, Paul Daniels; Directors, Roderick Cook, Irene Lewis, Charles Turner, Paul Weidner; Sets, Marjorie Kellogg, Hugh Lanwehr, Santo Loquasto; Costumes, Claire Ferraris, Linda Fisher, Caley Summers; Lighting, Ian Calderon, David Chapman, Arden Fingerhut, Peter Hunt; Stage Managers, Fred Hoskins, Gary Lamagna, Fred Mills, Craig Watson

COMPANY

Leon Alexander, Ray Aranha, Joan Astley, Samuel Barton, Gertrude Blanks, Elaine Bromka, Bette Carole, Myra Carter, Rosanna Carter, Dalton Cathey, Frances Chaney, Bill Clemons, Roderick Cook, Cynthia Crumlish, Humphrey Davis, David Downing, Femi Euba, Gary Evans, Al Freeman, Jr., Kimberly Gaisford, Edmond Genest, Alan Gifford, Ted Graeber, Elaine Graham, Charles Grant-Greene, Lois Holmes, Jeffrey Horowitz, Chequita Jackson, Jerry Jarrett, William Jay, Jennifer Jestin, Mel Johnson, Jr., Charles Kaufman, Gary Lamagna, Will Lee, Leroy Lessane, Richard Lieberman, Anne Lynn, Pirie MacDonald, Maura McGeary, Jeffrey B. McLaughlin, Clarkston McPhee, James Maloney, Paul Marin, Joseph Mascolo, Macon McCalman, Candy Minor, Anita Morris, Neil Napolitan, David O. Petersen, David Peterson, Larry Ross, Marco St. John, Seret Scott, Anne Shroshire, Geddeth Smith, Josef Sommer, Regina Stivender, Count Stovall, Margaret Thomson, Edgar Wilcock, Paul Woodard

PRODUCTIONS

"Awake and Sing!" by Clifford Odets, "All Over" by Edward Albee, "Oh Coward!" by Noel Coward and Roderick Cook, "The Estate" by Ray Aranh *(World Premiere)*, "Dream on Monkey Mountain" by Derek Walcott, "Born Yesterday" by Garson Kanin, "Way Back When ..." *(World Premiere)* by Ray Aranha, "Striptease" by Slawomir Mrozek, "Workman! Whoever You Are...." *(World Premiere)*

David Robbins Photos

**Right: "The Estate" Above: "Awake and Sing!"
Top: "Born Yesterday"**

**Myra Carter
in "All Over"**

**Dalton Cathey, Kimberly Gaisford,
Roderick Cook in "Oh Coward!"**

HARTMAN THEATRE COMPANY

Stamford, Connecticut
November 5, 1975–May 16, 1976
First Season
Producing Directors, Del and Margot Tenney; Managing Director, Daniel B. Miller; Press, Steve Rothman; Business Manager, Stanley D. Silver; Production Manager, Roger Meeker; Sets, Robert VerBerkmoes, John Wright Stevens; Costumes, Rachel Kurland; Lighting, John McLain; Music Director, Barbara Damashek; Guest Director, John Beary.

PRODUCTIONS AND CASTS

THE GOVERNMENT INSPECTOR by Nikolai Gogol; Director, Byron Ringland. CAST: Bob Balaban, William Bogert, J. Robert Dietz, Bernard Frawley, Haskell Gordon, George S. Irving, Eren Ozker, Austin Pendleton, Sloane Shelton, Joseph Sommer, David Tabor, Byron Ringland, Patrick Collins, Mark Segal, Rosalyn R. Farinella, Stephen Stabler, Jim Dirlam, Florence Fox, Florence Phillips, George W. Vollano, Bob Callahan, Bill O'Brien, Skip Wolfe, Scott Thomas, Ed Rice, Christian Ericson, Scott Silver, Larry Silbert, Jasper Wellington, John Vichiola, Jack Mason, Mike Lehrman, Nadya Grushetzka Sheehan, Elsa Bastone, Wendell McCombas, Jeanne Harker, Jan Mason, Madlyn O'Neil, Charlotte Smith, Anne Wilcox

THE HOSTAGE by Brendan Behan; Director, John Beary. CAST: Jane Clarke, Greg Kolb, Mark Segal, Bernard Frawley, Sasha von Scherler, Carmel O'Brien, Lark Lee Tyrrell, Leann Enos, Marilynn May, Carole Cortese, Robert Armistead, Patrick Collins, Robert Donley, Gary F. Martin, Eren Ozker, William Bogert, Morgan Redmond, J. Robert Dietz, Susan Stevens, Peter Rogan, David MacNeill, Ed Rice, Gina Dunlap, Kathleen Collins, Ken Perlman

THE RUNNER STUMBLES (*World Premiere*) by Milan Stitt; Director, Austin Pendleton. CAST: Morrie Piersol, Stephen Joyce, Katina Commings, James Noble, Nancy Donohue, Sloane Shelton, William Bogert, Bernard Frawley, Eren Ozker

TOM JONES by Henry Fielding; Adapted and Directed by Larry Arrick. CAST: Stephen Berenson, George Bliss, Roy Brocksmith, Eric Christiansen, J. Robert Dietz, Jill Eikenberry, Kathy Falk, Rosalyn Farinella, Bernard Frawley, Joan Friedman, Haskell Gordon, Victoria Hawken, Shami Jones, Ruth Landowne, Libby Moyer, James Naughton, James Noble, Rico Peterson, Charles Pistone, Teri Ralston, Shellie Sclan, Anne Scurria, Barbara Sieck, Joy Smith, Susan Strickler, Mark Taylor, Margot Tenney, Molly Thompson, Courtney Tucker, Tim Warren

JOAN OF LORRAINE by Maxwell Anderson; Director, Alan Arkin. CAST: Adam Arkin, Matthew Arkin, Deborah Arnold, Roy Brocksmith, Eric R. Christiansen, Patrick Collins, Barbara Dana, Kurt Garfield, Michael Granger, John Horn, Robert Lesser, Ed Rice, Alex Rocco, Anne Scurria, Nikos Valance, Irving Harrison Vincent, Tony Arkin, Sam Luneeta, Tom Gould

AN EVENING OF TENNESSEE WILLIAMS directed by Del Tenney. CAST: Margot Tenney, Louis Turenne, Peter Gatto, Greg Kolb, Sandy Martin, Dennis Cooney

CATCH-22 by Joseph Heller; Director, Larry Arrick. CAST: Robert Balaban, George Martin, T. Richard Mason, Ed Rice, Louis Turenne, David Ackroyd, Betty Gordon, James Brick, Michael Tucker, Ed Hall, Molly Thompson, Barbara Sieck, John Olesen, Courtney Tucker

STAG AT BAY by Charles MacArthur and Nunnally Johnson; Director, Stephen Rothman. CAST: Alan Brooks, William Leach, Judith Light, Henson Keys, John Ulmer, Alfred Drake, Dick Shawn, Heidi Mefford, Joy Smith, Anne Scurria, Marilyn Hase, Joan Friedman, Rosalyn Farinella, Jillian Lindig, Barbara Dana

David Robbins Photos

**Right Center: Stephen Joyce, Nancy Donohue
in "The Runner Stumbles" Above: T. Richard
Mason, George Martin,
Louis Turenne in "Catch-22"
Top: Sloane Shelton, Austin Pendleton,
Erin Ozker in "The Government Inspector"**

Barbara Dana in "Joan of Lorraine"

HIPPODROME THEATRE

San Francisco, California
June 1, 1975–May 31, 1976
BULLSHOT CRUMMOND by Ron House, Diz White, Alan
Shearman, John Neville-Andrews, Derek Cunningham; Producers,
Ron House, Jonathan Gardner, Alan Shearman, Diane White in
association with Gil Adler and Jack Temchin; General Manager,
Jonathan Gardner; Stage Manager, Russell Haney. CAST: Alan
Shearman, Ron House, Louisa Hart, Diz White, Mark Blankfield,
John Achorn, Brandis Kemp, Joyce Harris, Mitch Kreindel

EL GRANDE DE COCA COLA by Ron House, Diz White, Alan
Shearman, John Neville-Andrews; Produced by Low Moan Spec-
tacular and American Conservatory Theatre; Designed by Michael
Garrett; Stage Managers, Russell Haney, Michael Wolf. CAST: Ron
House, James Howard Laurence, Jonathan Gardner, Janet
McGrath, Diz White

**Top Right: Diz White, Alan Shearman in
"Bullshot Crummond"
Below: "That Championship
Season"**

INDIANA REPERTORY THEATRE

Indianapolis, Indiana
October 16, 1975–May 7, 1976
Producing Director, Benjamin Mordecai; Artistic Director, Ed-
ward Stern; Administrative Director, James A. Clark; Press, Gayle
Gordon; Directors, John Abajian, Jack L. Davis, Bernard Kates,
Edward Stern; Sets, Keith Brumley; Costumes, Sherry Lynn Mor-
decai, Florence L. Rutherford; Lighting, Jody Boese, Allen Cornell,
Timothy K. Joyce, Carl Roetter; Technical Directors, Richard
Archer, Ed Collins; Stage Managers, Jody Boese, Leslie Robinson,
Walter Schoen, Robert Stevenson

PRODUCTIONS AND CASTS

THAT CHAMPIONSHIP SEASON with John C. Capodice, Robert Elliott, John Grassilli, Alfred Hinckley, Robert Scogin

THE CARETAKER with John Grassilli, Bernard Kates, Robert
Scogin

ARMS AND THE MAN with Linda Atkinson, Jack L. Davis, Jack
Donner, Robert Elliott, Donald Ewer, Priscilla Lindsay, Steven
Ryan, Dee Victor

LONG DAY'S JOURNEY INTO NIGHT with Edward Binns,
Elizabeth Franz, Priscilla Lindsay, T. Richard Mason, Steven Ryan

THE SEA HORSE with Susan Riskin, Steven Ryan

THE ENVOI MESSAGES (World Premiere) by Louis Phillips,
with Henry Kaimu Bal, Rosanna Carter, Barry Cullison, Brenda
Currin, Jack L. Davis, Maxwell Glanville, Delia Hattendorf, Ber-
nard Kates, Duncan Larson, Chenault Lillard, Robert Machray,
Lou Malandra, Robert Scogin, Linda Selman, Jeffrey V. Thompson,
Loretta Yder

THE REAL INSPECTOR HOUND with John Abajian, John
Guerrasio, Carol Gustafson, Delia Hattendorf, Bernard Kates, Robert Machray, Gun-Marie Nilsson, Robert Scogin

BLACK COMEDY with John Abajian, Carol Gustafson, Delia
Hattendorf, Bernard Kates, Robert Machray, Gun-Marie Nilsson,
Robert Scogin, Edward Stevlingson

THE TAVERN with John Abajian, Jody Boese, Jack L. Davis, John
Guerrasion, Carol Gustafson, Paul Ilg, Carol Mayo Jenkins, Ber-
nard Kates, Robert Machray, Gun-Marie Nilsson, Robin Pearson
Rose, Robert Scogin, Edward Stevlingson, Jeremiah Sullivan, Jeffery
V. Thompson

THE MAN WITH THE FLOWER IN HIS MOUTH with Shelley
Joyce, Bernard Kates, Robert Scogin

Joe McGuire Photos

Right Center: "Long Day's Journey into Night"

**Jeremiah Sullivan, Carol Mayo Jenkins,
Bernard Kates in "The Tavern"**

INNER CITY REPERTORY THEATRE

Los Angeles, California
October 1, 1975–June 30, 1976
Executive Director, C. Bernard Jackson; Press, John C. Thorpe;
Sets and Costumes, Terence Tam Soon; Sets and Lighting, William
Grant III; Assistant Directors, Fred Beauford, Jeanne Joe, Betty
Muramoto; Producers, Virginia Bernache, Nikki Sanz, Virginia
Wing

COMPANY

Ray Adams, Lonnie Bradford, Roger Brown, Gloria Calomee,
Danny de la Paz, Paris Earl, Edloe, Talya Ferro, Jessye Hageman,
Jeanne Joe, Michael Johnson, Barbara O. Jones, Kutee, Lynn
Kuratomi, Frank Michael Liu, Yolanda Marquez, Rosemary Marti-
nez, Michael McKnight, Reginald Montgomery, Steve Reed, Nikki
Sanz, Gloria Scott, Marilyn Tokuda, Les Tuckcho, Dan Turner, A.
J. Walker, Violette Winge, and *Guest Artists* Beah Richards, Carmen
Zapata

PRODUCTIONS

"Maggie D. Mouse Meets De Dirdy Rat Fink," "Piano Bar," "Free
Southern Theatre," "El Teatro Campesino," "Voices Inc.," "Lang-
ston Hughes Said," "A Black Woman Speaks," and *World Premiere*
of "B/C" written by C. Bernard Jackson

**Below: Reggie Montgomery, Jeanne Joe,
Steve Reed in "Piano Bar" Right: A. J. Walker,
Michael Harris in "Maggie D. Mouse Meets
de Dirty Rat Fink"**

IOWA THEATER LAB

Baltimore, Maryland
September 15, 1975–June 30, 1976
Director, Ric Zank; Associate Director, Christopher Amato; Ad-
ministrative Director, Gillian Richards

COMPANY

Christopher Amato	Jamie Le
Scott Duncan	Barry Meine
Rocky Greenberg	Susan Ric
George Kon	Steffen Saif
Helen Szablya	

PRODUCTIONS

"The Naming," "Dancer without Arms," "Moby Dick," and *Wor*
Premieres of "Sweetbird," and "Judas-Pax"

Ric Zank Photos

Top: Carmen Zapata in "B/C"

**Susan Rich, Scott Duncan, Jamie Leo,
Christopher Amato in "Sweetbird"**

JOHN F. KENNEDY CENTER FOR THE PERFORMING ARTS

Washington, D.C.
July 9, 1975–May 31, 1976

Chairman, Roger L. Stevens; Executive Director, Martin Feinstein; Press, Frank Cassidy, Lawrence Weiner Associates; American Bicentennial Theatre Productions presented by The Kennedy Center and Xerox Corporation; Produced by Roger L. Stevens and Richmond Crinkley

PRODUCTIONS AND CASTS

THE SKIN OF OUR TEETH by Thornton Wilder; Director, Jose Quintero. See Broadway Calendar page 11.

THE SCARECROW by Percy MacKaye; Director, Austin Pendleton; Sets, John Conklin; Costumes, Carrie Robbins; Lighting, John Gleason; Incidental Music, Arthur B. Rubinstein; General Manager, Edmonstone Thompson, Jr.; Stage Managers, Franklin Keysar, Pat De Rousie, Kimothy Cruse; Wardrobe Supervisor, Louise Allen; Production Assistant, Frances K. Quigley. CAST: Barbara Baxley (Goody), Leonard Frey (Dickon), Susan Sharkey (Rachel), Kimothy Cruse (Ebenezer), Ralph Byers (Richard), King Donovan (Merton), William Atherton (Lord Ravensbane), Sloane Shelton (Cynthia), Peter Bosche (Micah), Frank Hamilton (Bugby), Patricia Fay (Mistress Dodge), John Wardwell (Dodge), Jon Richards (Rev. Todd), Joseph Mathewson (Rev. Rand)

SUMMER BRAVE by William Inge; Director, Michael Montel. See Broadway Calendar page 20.

SWEET BIRD OF YOUTH by Tennessee Williams; Director, Edwin Sherin. See Broadway Calendar, page 31.

THE ROYAL FAMILY by George S. Kaufman and Edna Ferber; Director, Ellis Rabb. See Broadway Calendar page 32.

LONG DAY'S JOURNEY INTO NIGHT by Eugene O'Neill; Director, Jason Robards; Set, Ben Edwards; Costumes, Jane Greenwood; Lighting, Ken Billington; General Manager, Edmonstone Thompson, Jr.; Stage Managers, Murray Gitlin, Dyanne Hochman, W. T. Martin; Assistant Director, Lois O'Connor. CAST: Jason Robards (James Tyrone), Zoe Caldwell (Mary Tyrone), Walter McGinn (James, Jr.) was succeeded by Kevin Conway, Michael Moriarty (Edmund), Lindsay Crouse (Cathleen)

RIP VAN WINKLE adapted by Joshua Logan and Ralph Allen from Washington Irving's story and from plays attributed to John Kerr, Charles Burke and Dion Boucicault; Director, Joshua Logan; Sets, Robert Cothran; Costumes, Marianne Custer; Lighting, David F. Segal; Traditional Airs adapted by Trude Rittmann; Musical Supervision, Susan Romann; Technical Director, David Nash; Production Supervisor, Jack Hofsiss; Company Manager, Janice Stanton. CAST: Anthony Quayle (Rip Van Winkle), Annie McGreevey (Dame Van Winkle), Bernerd Engel (Diedrich), Richard Galuppi (Nicholas), Jay Doyle (Von Brummel), Andrea McHenry (Tina), Fred Van Winkle (Brom), Ronald Venable (Casper), Michael Petro (Vedder), Deborah Fezelle (Tina), Maria Wozniak (Martha), David Fox-Brenton (Cyrus), Mary Armour, Susan Glaze, Shaun Helton, Billy Jayne Jacoby, Susan Jayne Jacoby, Rex James, Nancy Johnston Smith, Richard Spivey, Patrick Woliver

THE HEIRESS by Ruth and Augustus Goetz; Director, George Keathley. See Broadway Calendar page 47.

A TEXAS TRILOGY: three full-length plays in repertory by Preston Jones; Director, Alan Schneider; Assistant Director, Joan Thorne; Costumes, Jane Greenwood; Produced by Robert Whitehead and Roger L. Stevens; General Manager, Oscar E. Olesen; Stage Managers, Mitchell Erickson, Charles Kindl, Stephen Nasuta; Hairstylist, Steve Atha; Production Assistant, Lee Mastrodonato.

CASTS:

LU ANN HAMPTON LAVERTY OBERLANDER with Kate Wilkinson (Claudine), Diane Ladd (Lu Ann), James Staley (Billy Bob), Graham Beckel (Skip), Everett McGill (Dale), Patrick Hines (Red), Walter Flanagan (Rufe), Thomas Toner (Olin), Baxter Harris (Corky), Josh Mostel (Milo), Kristin Griffin (Charmaine)

THE LAST MEETING OF THE KNIGHTS OF THE WHITE MAGNOLIA with John Marriott (Ramsey), Walter Flanagan (Rufe), Thomas Toner (Olin), Patrick Hines (Red), Henderson Forsythe (L. D.), Fred Gwynne (Colonel), Graham Beckel (Skip), Paul O'Keefe (Lonnie), Josh Mostel (Milo)

THE OLDEST LIVING GRADUATE with Kristin Griffith (Martha Ann), Patricia Roe (Maureen), Fred Gwynne (Colonel), Ralph Roberts (Mike), Lee Richardson (Floyd), Henderson Forsythe (Clarence), William Le Massena (Maj. Ketchum), Paul O'Keefe (Whopper), Kate Wilkinson (Claudine)

Richard Braaten Photos

Fred Gwynne in "The Last Meeting of the Knights of the White Magnolia" Above: Patrick Hines, Diane Ladd in "Lu Ann Hampton Laverty Oberlander" Top: "The Scarecrow"

LONG WHARF THEATRE

New Haven, Connecticut
October 17, 1975–June 11, 1976
Artistic Director, Arvin Brown; Executive Director, M. Edgar Rosenblum; Administrative Associate, Alison Harris; Press, Rosalind Heinz; Stage Directors, Arvin Brown, Kenneth Frankel, Waris Hussein, Peter Levin, Mike Nichols; Sets, Kenneth Foy, David Jenkins, Marjorie Kellogg, Steven Rubin, Tony Walton; Costumes, Linda Fisher, Jania Szatanski, Bill Walker; Lighting, Jamie Gallagher, Judy Rasmuson, Ronald Wallace; Stage Managers, Anne Keefe, Nina Seely, Clint Spencer

PRODUCTIONS AND CASTS

ARTICHOKE *(World Premiere)* by Joanna Glass. CAST: Emery Battis, Louis Beachner, Colleen Dewhurst, James Greene, Brian Murray, Rex Robbins, Ellin Ruskin

THE SHOW-OFF by George Kelly. CAST: William Atherton, Emery Battis, Joyce Ebert, Clarence Felder, Tom Martin, Jan Miner, James Noble, Leon Russom, Susan Sharkey

WHAT EVERY WOMAN KNOWS by J. M. Barrie. CAST: Emery Battis, Blair Brown, Mildred Dunnock, Joyce Ebert, Sean Griffin, Christopher Lloyd, Stephen Mendillo, William Swetland

STREAMERS *(World Premiere)* by David Rabe. CAST: Peter Evans, Joe Fields, John Heard, Herbert Jefferson, Jr., Michael Kell, Kenneth McMillan, Stephen Mendillo, Michael-Raymond O'Keefe, Ron Siebert, Dolph Sweet

ON THE OUTSIDE by Thomas Murphy and Noel O'Donoghue, and ON THE INSIDE by Thomas Murphy *(American Premieres)* CAST: "On the Outside": Jarlath Conroy, Lance Davis, James Greene, Michael Houlihan, Swoosie Kurtz, Suzanne Lederer, Stephen McHattie, "On the Inside": Frank Converse, Don Gantry, Sean Griffin, Bara-Cristin Hansen, James Hummert, Dorothy Lyman, Linda McGuire, Elizabeth Parrish, Ellin Ruskin

THE HOUSE OF MIRTH by Edith Wharton, adapted by John Tillinger. CAST: Emery Battis, Fran Brill, Joyce Ebert, Mary Fogarty, Victor Garber, James Greene, Bara-Cristin Hansen, George Hearn, James Hummert, Ben Kapen, Dorothy Lyman, Linda McGuire, Elizabeth Parrish, Paul Rosson, Susan Sharkey, Douglas Stender, William Swetland, Fiddle Viracola

DAARLIN' JUNO a new musical adaptation of Sean O'Casey's "Juno and the Paycock" by Richard Maltby, Jr. and Geraldine Fitzgerald, with music by Marc Blitzstein. CAST: Emery Battis, Joel Colodner, Jarlath Conroy, Joyce Ebert, James Ferrier, Geraldine Fitzgerald, Victor Garber, James Greene, Sean Griffin, Ruby Holbrook, Suzanne Lederer, Milo O'Shea, Elizabeth Parrish, Fiddle Viracola

William L. Smith Photos

Right: Emery Battis, Milo O'Shea in "Darlin' Juno" Above: Stephen McHattie, James Greene in "On the Outside"

Colleen Dewhurst, Brian Murray in "Artichoke" Top Right: "Streamers"

Fran Brill, Joyce Ebert in "The House of Mirth"

MANITOBA THEATRE CENTRE

Winnipeg, Manitoba, Canada
October 17, 1975–May 15, 1976
Artistic Director, Len Cariou; General Manager, Gregory Poggi; Press, Max Tapper; Production Manager, Dwight Griffin; Technical Director, Kent McKay; Sets and Costumes, Mark Negin, Raymond C. Recht, Taras Korol, Doug McLean, Peter Wingate, Lawrence Schafer, James R. Bakkon; Lighting, Robert R. Scales, Raymond C. Recht, Bill Williams, Gil Wechsler.

PRODUCTIONS AND CASTS

CYRANO DE BERGERAC by Edmond Rostand; Director, Jean Gascon. CAST: Len Cariou, Frank Adamson, Joseph Bahr, Robert Benson, Jay Brazeau, Doreen Brownstone, Claude Dorge, Alexe Duncan, Erik Fredricksen, Marilyn Gardner, Fran Gebhard, David Gillies, Ralph Glass, Harvey Harding, Catherine Harris, Roland Hewgill, David Hurband, Susan Kapilow, Daniel V. Koren, Jack Medley, Louis Negin, Harry Nelken, Sharon Noble, Gilles Paquin, Dixie Seatle, Alf Silver, Howard Storey, Max Tapper, Robin Ward

THE PRICE by Arthur Miller; Director, Robert Bilheimer. CAST: Robert Benson, Roland Hewgill, Milton Selzer, Angela Wood

THE COLLECTED WORKS OF BILLY THE KID by Michael Ondaatje; Director, Arif Hasnain. CAST: Guy Bannerman, Claude Bede, Trudy Cameron, Larry Davis, Patricia Hamilton, Peter Jobin, Des McAnuff, Douglas Millar

A CHRISTMAS CAROL by Charles Dickens; Adapted by David Ball and David Feldshuh; Director, Robert Bilheimer. CAST: Jay Brazeau, Christopher Britton, Doreen Brownstone, David Calderisi, Alexe Duncan, David Gillies, Ralph Glass, Susan Kapilow

EQUUS by Peter Shaffer; Director, Edward Gilbert. CAST: Zoe Alexander, Len Cariou, Ian Deakin, Cliff Gardner, Fran Gebhard, Patricia Hamilton, Jack Mather, Gwen Thomas, Robin Ward

BEYOND WORDS by the Canadian Mime Theatre. CAST: Adrian Pecknold, Harro Maskow, Robin Patterson, Paulette Hallich, Larry Lefevbre

COMPANY by Stephen Sondheim and George Furth; Director, Dean Regan; Musical Director, Victor Davies. CAST: Evelyne Adnerson, Marilyn Boyle, Scot Denton, Roger Dressler, Janis Dunning, Cliff Gardner, Particia Hamilton, Tabby Johnson, Barbara Lawlor, Lynn Marsh, Brian McKay, Nora McLellan, Scott Walker, Steve Weston

ENDGAME by Samuel Beckett; Director, Robert Bilheimer. CAST: Roland Hewgill, David Calderisi, Christopher Britton, Doreen Brownstone

OF MICE AND MEN by John Steinbeck; Director, Len Cariou. CAST: Bob Aaron, Frank Adamson, Martin Doyle, Erik Fredricksen, Cliff Gardner, David Gillies, Delroy Lindo, John-Peter Linton, Janis Nickleson, Scott Walker

CREEPS by David Freeman; Director, Robert Bilheimer. CAST: Aaron Schwartz, Jay Brazeau, Joe Horvath, Christopher Britton, Guy Bannerman, Fran Gebhard, Brian Richardson

PRIVATE LIVES by Noel Coward; Director, Frances Hyland. CAST: Zoe Alexander, Doreen Brownstone, David Calderisi, Clare Coulter, Robin Ward

Gerry Kopelow Photos

**Right Center: Len Cariou as Cyrano de Bergerac
Above: "Company" Top: Doreen
Brownstone, Christopher Britton in "Endgame"**

Ian Deakin, Len Cariou in "Equus"

McCARTER THEATRE COMPANY

Princeton, N. J.
October 9, 1975–April 4, 1976
Producing Director, Michael Kahn; General Manager, Edward
A. Martenson; Producing Manager, Mark S. Krause; Press, Norman
Lombino, David Wynne; Business Managers, Louise Bayer, Marsha
Senack; Technical Director, Mitchell Kurtz; Guest Directors,
Kenneth Frankel, Ellis Rabb; Sets, John Conklin, David Jenkins,
Marjorie Kellogg, Kert Lundell, Oliver Smith; Costumes, Jeanne Button, Lawrence Casey, Jane Greenwood, Ann
Roth; Lighting, L. B. Achziger, John Gleason, John McLain; Stage
Managers, Suzanne Egan, Helaine Head, Arthur Karp

COMPANY

John Arnone, George Axler, Richard Backus, Sally Backus, Donald
Barton, Powers Boothe, Frank Borgman, John Christian Browning,
Forrest Buckman, James C. Burge, Morris Carnovsky, David Chandler, Curt Dawson, Richard Dix, Conrad Fowkes, Richard Gere,
Steven Gilborn, George Grizzard, Jack Gwillim, Sarah-Jane Gwillim, Rosemary Harris, David Haskell, Bette Henritze, Barton Heyman, Pat Hingle, Michael Houlihan, Joseph Jamrog, Elaine Kerr,
Philip Kerr, Jerry Lanning, William Larsen, Paul Larson, Mary
Layne, Eva LeGallienne, Rosetta LeNoire, Richard Lenz, Barbara
Lester, Sam Levene, Miller Lide, Karl Light, Sherman Lloyd, Joan
Lorring, Larry C. Lott, Joseph Maher, Carol Morley, Gabor Morea,
Mary Joan Negro, Deborah Offner, Kristin Paulus, Wyman Pendleton, Sarah Peterson, Eleanor Phelps, John Remme, David Rounds,
Martin Rudy, Chris Sarandon, Anne Sheldon, Marshall Shnider,
Drew Snyder, Josef Sommer, Theodore Sorel, Ian Trigger, Maria
Tucci, Steve Vinovich, Kate Wilkinson, Mary Louise Wilson

PRODUCTIONS

"A Grave Undertaking" *(World Premiere)* by Lloyd Gold, directed
by Michael Kahn, "The Royal Family" by George S. Kaufman and
Edna Ferber, "Section Nine" *(American Premier)* by Philip Magdalany, directed by Michael Kahn, "The Heiress" by Ruth and
Augustus Goetz, "Awake and Sing" by Clifford Odets, "The Winter's Tale" by William Shakespeare

Cliff Moore Photos

**Right: Maria Tucci,
David Haskell in "The Winter's Tale"
Above: Morris Carnovsky (1) in
"Awake and Sing!" Top: Jerry Lanning,
Richard Lenz, Drew Snyder in "Section Nine"**

**Maria Tucci, Richard Backus
in "The Heiress"**

**Chris Sarandon, Deborah Offner
in "A Grave Undertaking"**

MEADOW BROOK THEATRE

Rochester, Michigan
October 9, 1975–May 16, 1976
Artistic Director, Terence Kilburn; Managing Director, David
Robert Kanter; Sets, Peter Hicks; Costumes, Mary Lynn Bonnell;
Stage Managers, R. Joseph Mooney, Robert Neu, James Corrigan;
Business Manager, Vincent L. Ammann; Guest Directors, Anthony
Mockus, Michael Montel, Charles Nolte; Guest Designers, Tom
Aston, Lance Brockman, Larry A. Reed, Nancy Thompson

COMPANY

Mark Addy, Dan C. Bar, Mary Benson, Rolfe Bergsman, James
Corrigan, J. L. Dahlmann, Fred Fonner, Cheryl Giannini, Robert
Grossman, William Halliday, John Hammond, Elizabeth King,
Dennis MacMath, Mark McKinney, Marianne Muellerleile, Patricia
Oliveri, James D. O'Reilly, Elisabeth Orion, John L. Peakes, Su-
sanne Peters, F. Jackson Reilly, Melanie Resnick, Richard Riehle,
Ramona Santiago, Laurie Schirner, Thomas C. Spackman, Eric
Tavaris, Fred Thompson, James Winfield

GUEST ARTISTS: Curtis J. Armstrong, Burneice Avery, Terence
Baker, Evalyn Baron, Stephen Berger, Peter Brandon, Nancy Cole-
man, Donald Ewer, Patricia Gage, Demene Hall, John Hallow,
Polly Holliday, William LeMassena, Mae Marmy, Kent Martin,
Terri McRay, Edgar Meyer, Donald C. Moore, Michele Mullen,
Phillip Piro, David Schurmann, Max Showalter, Guy Stockwell,
Steven Sutherland, Marie Wallace, Joseph Warren

PRODUCTIONS

"A Midsummer Night's Dream," "Witness for the Prosecution,"
"Arms and the Man," "The Little Foxes," "Relatively Speaking,"
"Under Milk Wood," "Born Yesterday," and *World Premiere* of
"Yankee Ingenuity"

Walt Bromley Photos

Right: "The Little Foxes"
Above: "Under Milk Wood"
Top: "Yankee Ingenuity"

Susanne Peters, Mae Marmy, Donald C. Moore,
Eric Tavaris in "Arms and the Man"

Marie Wallace, Guy Stockwell
in "Born Yesterday"

MILWAUKEE REPERTORY THEATER

Milwaukee, Wisconsin
September 12, 1975–May 30, 1976
Artistic Director, Nagle Jackson; Managing Director, Sara O'
Connor; Press, Michael Krawczyk, Denise Masnica; Directors,
Barry Boys, Montgomery Davis, John Dillon, Nagle Jackson, Rob'
ert Lanchester, William McKereghan, John Olon-Scrymgeour, Pa'
Weidner; Sets and Lighting, Christopher M. Idoine, R. H. Graham;
Costumes, Elizabeth Covey, Ellen M. Kozak; Stage Manager, Fre
dric H. Orner

COMPANY

Tom Blair, Robert Dawson, Leslie Geraci, Rose Herron, Rober
Ingham, Robert Lanchester, John Mansfield, Durward McDonal
William McKereghan, Daniel Mooney, James Pickering, Penelop
Reed, Stephen Stout, Jeffrey Tambor

GUEST ARTISTS: Ray Aranha, Glenn Close, Peggy Cowle
Elaine Dale, Daniel Davis, Jill Heavenrich, Josephine Nichols, Rich
ard Risso, Jessie Saunders, Ruth Schudson, Seret Scott, Sirin De
rim Trainer, Beatrice Winde, Mary Wright

PRODUCTIONS

"King Lear," "Democracy," "School for Wives," "My Sister, M
Sister," "Happy Days," "Out at Sea," *American Premieres* of "Th
Visions of Simone Machard" by Bertolt Brecht, "Fanshen" by D
vid Hare, *World Premieres* of "Never a Snug Harbor" by Dav
Ulysses Clarke, "Out" by Robert Ingham and Penelope Reed

Sorgel-Lee-Riordan Photos

Left: "Democracy" Top: "King Lear"

"Never a Snug Harbor"
Above: "My Sister, My Sister"

"The Visions of Simone Machard"
Above: "School for Wives"

**"The Last Meeting of the Knights
of the White Magnolia"
Above: Susan Borneman, Steve
Ryan in "Born Yesterday"
Right: "Much Ado about Nothing"
Below: Meg Myles, Steve Ryan
in "A Streetcar Named Desire"**

MISSOURI REPERTORY THEATRE

Kansas City, Missouri
Producing Director, Patricia McIlrath; Staff Directors, James Asad, Francis J. Cullinan; Production Manager, David Dannenbaum; Technical Director, Alan Kibbe; Costumes, Vincent Scassellati; Sets, Max A. Beatty, G. Philippe de Rosier; Lighting, Joseph Appelt, Curt Osterman; Sound, James Coleman; Stage Managers, John Maddison, Ron Durbian, Joyce McBroom, Joseph dePauw

COMPANY

Bramwell Fletcher, Meg Myles, Susan Borneman, Richard C. Brown, John Q. Bruce, Jr., Al Christy, Lynn Cohen, Liza Cole, John Cothran, Jr., Robert Elliott, Marla Frumkin, Michael LaGue, Harriet Levitt, John Maddison, Walter Rhodes, Leslie Robinson, Steve Ryan, Steve Scearcy, Henry Strozier, Gloria P. Terrell, Eberle Thomas, Ronetta Wallman, Von H. Washington, Ron Durbian, Art Ellison, Jeannine Hutchings

PRODUCTIONS

"Born Yesterday," "The Cherry Orchard," "Much Ado about Nothing," "The Last Meeting of the Knights of the White Magnolia," "A Streetcar Named Desire," "In the Well of the House," "The Rainmaker," "The Morgan Yard"

**"The Morgan Yard" Above: Bramwell Fletcher,
Von H. Washington in "In the Well of the
House"**

OKLAHOMA THEATER CENTER

Oklahoma City, Oklahoma
October 1, 1975 - April 18, 1976
Artistic Director, Lyle Dye, Jr.; Business Director, Russ Walton;
Pat Cacy; Techncical Director, Roger Drummond; Wardrobe Master, Jim Hampton; Directors, Jeanie Miller, Lyle Dye, Paul Nutt, JoAnn Muchmore, Lee Hicks, Eugene Jacobson, Roberta Sloan, Jeanne Adams Wray, Garry Charter, David McElroy, Judith McElroy; Sets, Dale Hall, Steve Estes, David Pape, Sheldon Wilhelm, Chris VanZandt, Roger Drummond; Lighting, Dell Unruh, Steve Estes, David Pape, Sheldon Wilhelm, Chris VanZandt, Roger Drummond, Keith Jones, Dan Diamond; Costumes, Vicki Holden, Charlotte Stratton, Jim Hampton, Judi McElroy; Musical Director, John Robinson; Choreographer, Cheri Ingram

PRODUCTIONS AND CASTS

THE STAR SPANGLED GIRL with Kerry Robertson, Steven Schmidt, David DeBatto

INHERIT THE WIND with Dean Eikleberry, Tammy Wheat, Melissa J. Clifton, Vernon Wall, Mark Goodwin, Jeffery Spelman, Rusty Plumbtree, John Chandler, Mary S. Patterson, Shana Ledet, Pepper Twyford, Christopher VanZandt, Lance Reese, Mike Blakely, Steven B. Tesney, Susan Arleen Winters, Timmy Hoch, Michael Blackmore, T. J. Sommers, John C. Pickard, Jr., John B. Doolin, Florene Merrit Garner, Scotty Dallas, Eric Schoaff, Clyde Martin, Kent Rulon, Dale Bassler, Paul Toles, Helen Overpeck, Steve Higgins, Bruce Meyers, Kenneth Hamilton, Ira McLaughlin, John Amick, Rick DeSpain, Roy Dunlap, James F. Robbinson, David Taylor, Bill Snyder, Dan Murphy, Jack Sterling Pratt, Timothy Aschmann, Richard Sinclair, Hugh A. Baysinger, Curtis Michener, Dana Rojas

YOU'RE A GOOD MAN, CHARLIE BROWN with Curtiss Clayton, Dana Carnett, David M. Scott, Judith McElroy, Brian Tidwell, Lara Teeter

U. S. A. with Richard Darby, Terry Schenk, Harry Parker, Dusty Presler, Linda Magbee, Sue Long

MARY, MARY with Jim Smith, Cheri Ingram, Thomas Sheehan, Richard Sinclair, Patricia Cacy

THE DIARY OF ANN FRANK with Eric Schoaff, Cecilia Bristow, Joan Pickard, Vernon Wall, Tom Brown, Mary Gordon Taft, Marilyn Morris, Dawn Kutz, Robert Wootten, Charles Unger

CATCH ME IF YOU CAN with T. A. Minton, John Thompson, Richard B. Darby, Joyce Bishop, Clyde Martin, Phoebee Revelle, Harry Revelle, Jr.

WHEN YOU COMIN' BACK, RED RYDER? with J. Shane McClure, Suzan Ott, David Earl Hodges, John Webb, Joan Pickard, Rodger W. Smith, Daniel J. Christiaens, Melody Brook

THE LAST MEETING OF THE KNIGHTS OF THE WHITE MAGNOLIA with Steve Higgins, John Patterson, Les Chick, Roy E. Dunlap, David Earl Hodges, James F.   inson, John B. Doolin, Richard B. Doolin, Richard C. White, Marvin G. Shawn

THE HOT L BALTIMORE with David Taylor, Melody Brook, Eleanora Woodruff, Vicki S. Holden, John C. Pickard, Jr., Gloria Barton, John Chandler, Clayton Barnes, Pepper Twyford, Steve Huntress, Larry Bailey, Sally Unger, Les Chick, Rusty Plumbtree

Pat Cacy, Dave Stanton Photos

Top: "Inherit the Wind" Right: "Diary of Anne Frank"
Below: "When You Comin' Back, Red Ryder?"

"The Hot l Baltimore" Above: "The Last Meet
of the Knights of the White Magnolia"

PHILADELPHIA DRAMA GUILD

Philadelphia, Pennsylvania
November 4, 1975 - March 18, 1976

Artistic Director, Douglas Seale; Managing Director, James B.
eydberg; Chairman of the Board, Elkins Wetherill; President,
ney S. Bloom; Artistic-Administrative Coordinator, Lillian Stein-
g; Sets, John Kasarda; Costumes, Jane Greenwood, David
arles; Lighting, Spencer Mosse; Press, James E. McCormick;
ge Directors, Douglas Seale, Richard Maltby, Jr., Brian Murray;
ge Managers, Gerald Nobles, Rusty Swope; Technical Director,
an Trumpler

PRODUCTIONS AND CASTS

IE ROYAL FAMILY by George S. Kaufman and Edna Feber.
AST: Lois De Banzie, Russell Leib, Terrence Markovich, Eric
ler, Rogert Gerringer, Catherine Wolf, Carolyn Younger, Wil-
m Buell, Betty Leighton, Joseph Leon, Louise Troy, John Glover,
k Viola, William LeMassena, Maureen Garrett

IE GLASS MENAGERIE by Tennessee Williams. CAST: Ger-
line Fitzgerald, James Valentine, Margaret Ladd, Edward Albert

IE BIRTHDAY PARTY by Harold Pinter. CAST: William Pres-
n, Betty Leighton, John Glover, Ann Crumb, Leonard Frey, Rob-
Gerringer

EDDA GABLER by Henrik Ibsen. CAST: Betty Leighton, Barra Lester, James Valentine, Roberta Maxwell, Swoosie Kurtz,
bert Gerringer, John Glover

HE MISER by Moliere. CAST: Thom Christopher, Lu Ann Post,
lan Carlsen, Robert Gerringer, Russell Leib, William Buell,
uise Troy, John Glover, Ann Crumb, Peter Sauer, Susan Keller,
illiam Preston, Eric Uhler, Douglas Seale

James McCormick Photos

**Right: Roberta Maxwell,
James Valentine in "Hedda Gabler"
Above: Robert Gerringer,
Leonard Frey in "The Birthday Party"
Top: James Valentine, Geraldine Fitzgerald
in "The Glass Menagerie"**

**William LeMassena, Louise Troy
in "The Royal Family"**

**Robert Gerringer, John Glover
in "The Miser"**

PITTSBURGH PLAYHOUSE

Pittsburgh, Pennsylvania
February 3 - 21, 1976
Producer, Mark Lewis; Assistant to producer, Carole Berger; Director, Jose Ferrer; Set, Oren Parker; Lighting, Hank Graff; Sound, Jack Givens; Costumes, Mary M. Turner; Press, Leo Carlin; Production Coordinator, Janus Purins; Stage Manager, Jean Kahl

PRODUCTION AND CAST

THE INTERVIEW *(World Premiere)* by Tom Thomas. CAST: Jose Ferrer, Michael Wager, Dennis Sakamoto, James Prescott

Season was curtailed because of financial problems.

Guild Photographers Photos

**Michael Wager, Dennis Sakamoto, Jose Ferrer
in "The Interview"**

PITTSBURGH PUBLIC THEATER

Pittsburgh, Pennsylvania
September 17 - December 21, 1975
First Season
General Director, Ben Shaktman; Business Manager, Dolor
Logue; Press, Joel Warren; Administrative Coordinator, Marie N
gent-Head; Stage Directors, Ben Shaktman, John Going; Sets, Pet
Wexler, David Chapman; Costumes, Whitney Blausen, David Cha
man; Lighting, Peter Wexler, Bernard J. Brannigan; Stage Mana
ers, Margaret Peckham, Michael V. Murphy; Production Manage
Bernard J. Brannigan; Wardrobe Mistress, Renee Banks; Scen
Artist, Joseph Bock; Costume Coordinator, Ann Watson

PRODUCTIONS AND CASTS

THE GLASS MENAGERIE by Tennessee Williams. CAST: Dav
Snell, Carol Teitel, Amy Wright, Steve Simpson

ONE FLEW OVER THE CUCKOO'S NEST by Dale Wasserma
CAST: Ralph Roberts, Edward Lee Talmadge, Jake Turner, Car
Mayo Jenkins, Amy Wright, Michael Thompson, Steve Simpso
Albert Corbin, Thomas Carson, John Long, Vic Kleman, Tom A
kins, Tony Aylward, Wayne Darby Cook, Christine Hulter, Micha
V. Murphy, Katherine Clarke, Leonard R. Tolbert, Renee Y. Bar

TWELFTH NIGHT by William Shakespeare. CAST: Dvida Bloo
Fred Bright, Jake Turner, Steve Simpson, Daniel Booth, Mark
Connolly, Pamela Brook, Albert Corbin, Thomas Carson, Jeane
Landis, Michael Flanagan, John Long, Christine Hulter, Leona
Nimoy, Don Wadsworth, Michael V. Murphy, Daniel Booth, Fr
Bright, Fritz Kupfer

Jack Weinhold Photos

**Left Center: Ralph Roberts, Tom Atkins in "On
Flew over the Cuckoo's Nest"**

**Carol Teitel, David Snell, Amy Wright
in "The Glass Menagerie"**

PROFESSIONAL PERFORMING COMPANY

Chicago, Illinois
March - May 1976
Producer, H. Adrian Rehner; Artistic Coordinators, Jack Montgomery, Lenard Norris; Set Designer and Director, Jack Montgomery; Costumes, Leon Natker; Lighting, James Highland; Stage Managers, Michael Smith, Denise Gilchrist; Press, Jimmie Barboquillo

PRODUCTION AND CAST

ANDROCLES AND THE LION by George Bernard Shaw. CAST: . C. Coleman, Robert Cunningham, Madelyn Dowell, Theodore Greene, Anna Grose, Charles Lee, Randy Lindsay, Jonathon Lindsey, James Lloyd, Mary Mabry, Eva McCann, Dennis McCoy, Albert McGhee, Michael Perkins, Ann Ricks, Valerie Rodgers, Dorothy Singleton, Gayle Tolbert, Glen Washington, Paulette Williams

Ray Hasch Photos

"Androcles and the Lion"

STAGE I THEATRE LAB

Boston, Massachusetts
October 10, 1975 - May 24, 1976
Artistic Director, Kaleel Sakakeeny; Managing Director, David L. Archer; Lighting, Debra Margolis

COMPANY

Wendie Flagg, Deirdre O'Connell, Joseph Pilato, Paul Knill, Deborah Desnoo, Michael Fulginetti, Steven Snow

PRODUCTIONS

"The Hamlet Syndrome," and *Premieres* of "The Arrangers," "Gertrude og Ophelia," "Masques," "Icarus"

Warren Goldberg Photos

Michael Fulginitti in "Icarus" Right Center: Wendie Flagg, Dierdre O'Connell in "Gertrude og Ophelia"

Robert Donley, John Wylie in "The Last Meeting of the Knights of the White Magnolia"
Right: Farley Granger, Margaret Hall in "Private Lives" Above: Harry Groener, James Cahill in "Cyrano de Bergerac"

SEATTLE REPERTORY THEATRE

Seattle, Washington
October 22, 1975 - April 1, 1976
Thirteenth Season
Artistic Director, Duncan Ross; Producing Director, Peter Donnelly; Assistant Artistic Director, Arne Zaslove; Costumes, Lewis D. Rampino, Donna Eskew; Sets, Eldon Elder, John Lee Beatty, Jerry Williams, Robert Dahlstrom; Technical Director, Floyd Hart; Lighting, Steven A. Maze, Phil Shermer, Richard Devin, Cynthia Hawkins, Jim McKie; Guest Directors, Harold Scott, Clayton Corzatte, Robert Patrick; Production Manager, Marc Rush; Stage Managers, Jay Moran, Rod Pilloud; Press, Shirley Dennis, Marnie Andrews; Assistant to Producing Director, Jeff Bentley; Company Manager, Charles Younger.

COMPANY

Richard E. Arnold, John Aylward, Andy Backer, Kurt Beattie, Jon Peter Benson, Rafic Bey, Alan Brandon, Henry Butler, David Boushey, Katherine Bruce, Marck Buchan, Gerald Burgess, Genn Buttkus, James Cahill, James Carruthers, Dorothy Chace, Michael Christensen, Jerome Collamore, David Connell, Bill Cobbs, Edwin Cooper, Lee Corbet, Ted D'Arms, Roger DeKoven, Robert Donley, Katherine Ferrand, Loren Foss, John Gilbert, Wesley Grant, Margaret Hall, Maureen Hawkins, Gardner Hayes, Eric Helland, Margaret Hilton, Michael Keenan, Jean Marie Kinney, Zoaunne LeRoy, Madeleine LeRoux, Nick Lewis-Jones, Susan Ludlow, Michael Medeiros, Dean Melang, Marilyn Meyers, Marjorie Nelson, John Newton, Douglas Nigh, Frances Peter, Demetra Pittman, Robin Reeds, Joseph Regalbuto, Gary Reineke, John Renforth, Gil Rogers, William Rongstad, Kimberly Ross, Lucy Rush, Alvin Lee Sanders, Phil Shallat, Robert Sevra, Eric Sinclair, Sharon Spelman, James Staley, Paul C. Thomas, Deems Urquhart, Earl Christopher Williams, Dan Winston, Max Wright, John Wylie, Alan Zampese.

GUEST ARTISTS: Jeannie Carson, Farley Granger

PRODUCTIONS

"Cyrano de Bergerac," "Jumpers," "Seven Keys to Baldpate," "The Last Meeting of the Knights of the White Magnolia," "The Madwoman of Chaillot," "Private Lives," "Benito Cereno," "Entertaining Mr. Sloane," "Kennedy's Children," "The Collected Works of Billy the Kid," and *World Premiere* of "Made for TV"

Greg Gilbert Photos

Marjorie Nelson in "Made for TV"
Above: "Benito Cereno"

222

atricia Cray, David Gale in "Serenading Louie"
Above: "The Balcony" Right: Robert
Pastene, Gwyllum Evans in "Ah, Wilderness!"

STAGE/WEST

West Springfield, Massachusetts
November 15, 1975 - April 25, 1976
Artistic Director, Rae Allen; Managing Director, Stephen E.
ys; General Manager, Susan B. Hutton; Press, Sally Fuller; Stage
nagers, James Riggs, Barbara Dilker; Designers, Laurence King,
arles Stockton, Eugene Warner, Marc B. Weiss, Fredda Slavin;
stumes, Sigrid Insull; Lighting, Ron Wallace, Jamie Gallagher,
dy Rasmuson; Directors, Rae Allen, Martin Fried, Edward Berke-
, John Milligan, Tom Crawley, Marjorie Sigley

COMPANY

aham Beckel, Yusef Bulos, Thomas Carson, Tom Crawley, Pa-
cia Cray, Gwyllum Evans, David Gale, Phillip Littell, Jane
wry, Jerry Mayer, Lillah McCarthy, Michael Miller, John Milli-
, John O'Creagh, Elizabeth Parrish, Robert Pastene, Chris
milly, John Ryan, Franklyn Seales, James Secrest, Nancy Sellin,
ncy Snyder, Barbara Tarbuck, Janis Young

nes Cass, Dan Eaton, David Gosselin, Lisa Grayton, Madonna T.
agher, A. J. Morin, Leigh Plakias, Betsy Tucker, Tommy N.
cker, Jr.

PRODUCTIONS

h, Wilderness!," "The Tempest," "The Balcony," "The Country
rl," "Design for Living," "Serenading Louie," "Christopher Co-
bus," "Hugo"

Paramount Commercial Studios Photos

**Right Center: Michael Miller, John Ryan
in "The Country Girl"**

**Nancy Snyder, Graham Beckel
in "Ah, Wilderness!"**

223

"Replika" Above: "Scapino!"

STUDIO ARENA THEATRE

Buffalo, N. Y.
October 10, 1975 - May 23, 1976
Eleventh Season

Executive Producer, Neal DuBrock; Associate Producer, Ginta
Sileika; Press, Blossom Cohan, Brian T. Whitehill; Production Co
dinator, Tom Pechar; Producers' Assistant, Jane Abbott; Sta
Managers, John Philip Luckacovic, Brennan Roberts, Donald W.
ters, Jean E. Russ; Production Assistant, Jean Bernecky; Technic
Directors, Jim Crossley, Daniel Dour; Wardrobe, Diane R. Schall
Claudia Lynch; Props, Ronald Schroeder, Carl John; Sound, Ric
ard Menke; Sets, Frank J. Boros; David F. Segal

PRODUCTIONS AND CASTS

BUTLEY by Simon Gray; Director, Richard Barr. CAST: To
Tanner, Katherine Bruce, Peter Burnell, Nancy Cushman, I
Herndon, Andrea Stonorov, Bill VandeSande·

SCAPINO! by Frank Dunlop and Jim Dale; Director, Grover Da
CAST: John Christopher Jones, John Abajian, Julia Barr, Al
Benjamin, Nicholas Cosco, Denny Dillon, David Johns, Neal Kle
Mordecai Lawner, Tom Mardirosian, Albert Sanders, James S
mour, Rick Wessler, Shelley Wyant

A DOLL'S HOUSE by Henrik Ibsen; Director, Stephen Port
CAST: Betsy Palmer, James Cahill, Don Gantry, Betty Lutes, B
nie McInerney, Patricia O'Connell, Patricia Weber, Bishop V
Justin DeBlase, Chelsey DiStefano, Adam Martin

EQUUS by Peter Shaffer; Director, Paul Giovanni. CAST: Jerem
Sullivan, Laurinda Barrett, Elizabeth Brown, Kermit Brown, Ca
Mayo Jenkins, Jonathan Howard Jones, Jim Oyster, Peggy Whitt
Ben Fuhrman, Roger Sewall, Lawrence Smith, Richard Tabor, Da
Tucker, Norman Weiler

THE MAGIC SHOW by Stephen Schwartz, Bob Randall, Dc
Henning; Director, Jay Fox. CAST: Joseph Abaldo, Richard Bar
trino, Serhij Bohdan, Gwendolyn Coleman, Connie Day, W. P. D
mak, Anthony Inneo, Rose Anna Mineo, John-Ann Washingt
Rick Wessler

A LITTLE NIGHT MUSIC by Stephen Sondheim and H
Wheeler; Director, Tony Tanner. CAST: Rosemary Prinz, Willi
Chapman, Paula Laurence, David Holliday, Alan Brasingt
Karen Good, Gail Johnston, Jay Lowman, Leila Martin, Sarah R
Howard Shalwitz

REPLIKA conceived and directed by Jozef Szajna. CAST: E
Kozlowska, Irena Jun, Stanislaw Brudny, Antoni Pszoniak, Jc
Wieczorek

Greenberg, Wrazen and May Photos

Top: Jeremiah Sullivan, Jonathan Howard Jones
"Equus" Left: Tony Tanner, Peter Burnell
in "Butley" Below: Betsy Palmer,
Don Gantry in "A Doll's House"

TRINITY SQUARE REPERTORY COMPANY

Providence, Rhode Island
October 14, 1975 - May 2, 1976

irector, Adrian Hall; Administrator, G. David Black; Press,
on Simon, Patricia Schwadron; Musical Director, Richard
ming; Sets, Eugene Lee, Robert D. Soule; Lights, Mark Rippe,
Custer; Costumes, James Berton Harris, Betsey Potter; Techni-
irector, Douglas Smith; Production Coordinator, David Ward;
Managers, William Radka, Beverly Andreozzi; Stage Direc-
Adrian Hall, Word Baker,Vincent Dowling

COMPANY

rt Black, William Cain, Robert J. Colonna, Timothy Crowe,
am Damkoehler, Lane Davies, Timothy Donahue, John Gar-
Peter Gerety, Brad Gott-Lin, Tom Griffin, Ed Hall, Zina Jas-
Richard Jenkins, David C. Jones, Melanie Jones, Richard
anaugh, Richard Kneeland, Marguerite Lenert, Howard Lon-
Mina Manente, George Martin, Derek Meader, Barbara Meek,
Miterko, Nancy Nichols, Barbara Orson, Bonnie Sacks, Wil-
Sadler, Margo Skinner, Cynthia Strickland, Danie Von Bargen,
Weaver, Ricardo Wiley

PRODUCTIONS

Gentlemen of Verona," "Another Part of the Forest," "The
Foxes," and *Premieres* of "Cathedral of Ice" by James Sche-
"Bastard Son" by Richard Lee Marks, "Eustace Chisholm and
Works" by Adrian Hall and Richard Cumming from a novel by
s Purdy

Dana Duke, William L. Smith, Roger Birn Photos

Right: "Two Gentlemen of Verona"
Top: "Another Part of the Forest"

"Eustace Chisholm and the Works"
Above: "The Little Foxes"

"Bastard Son"

VIRGINIA MUSEUM THEATRE REPERTORY COMPANY

Richmond, Virginia
October 22, 1975 - March 27, 1976
Artistic Director, Keith Fowler; General Manager, Loraine Sl
Stage Directors, Keith Fowler, James Kirkland, Ken Letner, T
Markus; Music Director, William Stancil; Choreographer,
Horne; Designers, Robert Franklin, Richard Norgard, T
Straiges, Frederick Norman Brown, Don Pasco; Lighting, James
Block, Michael Watson; Stage Managers, Rachael Lindhart, D
Flinchum; Press, Fred Haseltine, Michael P. Hickey

COMPANY

David Addis, Nico Boccio, Sarah Brooke, Alan Brooks, Mel C
Jim Cyrus, Dottie Dee, Ron Duncan Maury Erickson, Doug F
chum, Spence Ford, Alan Gilbert, Prudence Wright Holmes, De
Howard, Marie Goodman Hunter, Earle Hyman, James Kirkl
Marjorie Lerstrom, Carl Blackwell Lester, Ken Letner, Rac
Lindhart, Heather MacRae, Carmen Mathews, Milledge Mos
Lynda Myles, Kathy O'Callaghan, Lype O'Dell, Maureen O'Kel
David Pichette, Stan Picus, William Pitts, Roger Rathburn, Bar
Redmond, Walter Rhodes, Dino Shorte, William Stancil, St
Streater, John Wylie, Eloise Zeigler

PRODUCTIONS

"Guys and Dolls," "Sherlock Holmes in Scandal in Bohemia," "
Member of the Wedding," "The Crucible," "The Emperor Jon
"The Contrast," and *Premiere* of "Children" by A. R. Gurney

Virginia Museum Theatre Photos

**Left: Carmen Mathews, Lynda Myles
in "Children"**

**Earle Hyman
in "The Emperor Jones"**

**Nico Boccio, Carl Blackwell Lester, also
above in "Guys and Dolls"**

lma Cuervo, Dan Hamilton, Carmen de Lavallade in
"General Gorgeous" Right: Eugene
Troobnick, Norma Brustein, Tom Hill,
hristine Estabrook in "Walk the Dog, Willie" Right:
Eugene Troobnick, Paul Schierhorn, Linda Lavin,
Alvin Epstein in "Dynamite Tonite!"
Below: Philip Kerr, Victor Garber,
Stephen Rowe in "Don Juan"

YALE REPERTORY THEATRE

New Haven, Connecticut
October 4, 1975–May 15, 1976
Director, Robert Brustein; Associate Director, Alvin Epstein;
Managing Director, Robert J. Orchard; Business Manager, Abigail
earon; Press, Jan Geidt; Designers, Michael H. Yeargan, Tony
traiges; Lighting, William B. Warfel; Production Supervisor, John
obert Hood; Technical Directors, Bronislaw Sammler, George
indsay; Stage Managers, Frank S. Torok, James F. Ingalls; Assis-
nt Managing Directors, Mark Rosenthal, Michael Sheehan; Stage
irectors, Alvin Epstein, Robert Brustein, Walt Jones, Ron Daniels,
awrence Kornfeld; Designers, Tony Straiges, Michael Yeargan,
eidi Ettinger, David Lloyd Gropman, Ursula Belden; Costumes,
ack Brown, Tony Straiges, Suzanne Palmer, Michael Yeargan,
eanne Button, Annette Beck; Lighting, William Warfel, Stephen
oody, Lewis Folden, Donald Bondy Lowy, Steve Pollock, Lloyd
Riford, III, Paul Gallo; Choreographer, Carmen de Lavallade;
onductors, Gary Fagin, Paul Schierhorn

COMPANY

inda Atkinson, Richard Bey, James Brick, Norma Brustein, Rob-
t Brustein, Joseph Capone, Alma Cuervo, Andrew Davis, Carmen
e Lavallade, Randall Duk Kim, Alvin Epstein, Christine Esta-
rook, Victor Garber, Jeremy Geidt, Anne Gerety, Joseph Grifasi,
an Hamilton, Laurie Heineman, Tom Hill, Philip Kerr, Linda
avin, Charles Levin, Jonathan Marks, John Neville-Andrews, Ste-
en D. Nowicki, Lynn Oliver, Peter Phillips, Barry Primus, Marcell
osenblatt, Stephen Rowe, Kenneth Ryan, Paul Schierhorn, Jeremy
mith, Eugene Troobnick, Paula Wagner, Frederick Warriner

PRODUCTIONS

A Midsummer Night's Dream" by William Shakespeare, "Don
uan" a version of Moliere's play by Kenneth Cavander, "Dynamite
onite!" by Arnold Weinstein, William Bolcom, "Bingo: Scenes of
loney and Death" by Edward Bond, "General Gorgeous" by Mi-
nael McClure and Paul Schierhorn, "Troilus and Cressida" by
'illiam Shakespeare, and *World Premiere* of "Walk the Dog, Wil-
" by Robert Auletta, with music and sound by Carol Lees

Eugene Cook, Bruce Siddons, Julie Haber Photos

Anne Gerety, Jeremy Geidt, Alvin Epstein
in "Bingo: Scenes of Money and Death"

227

PULITZER PRIZE PRODUCTIONS

1918–Why Marry?, 1919– No award, 1920–Beyond the Horizon, 1921–Miss Lulu Bett, 1922–Anna Christie, 1923–Icebound, 1924–Hell-Bent fer Heaven, 1925–They Knew What They Wanted, 1926–Craig's Wife, 1927–In Abraham's Bosom, 1928–Strange Interlude, 1929–Street Scene, 1930–The Green Pastures, 1931–Alison's House, 1932–Of Thee I Sing, 1933–Both Your Houses, 1934–Men in White, 1935–The Old Maid, 1936–Idiot's Delight, 1937–You Can't Take It with You, 1938–Our Town, 1939–Abe Lincoln in Illinois, 1940–The Time of Your Life, 1941–There Shall Be No Night, 1942–No award, 1943–The Skin of Our Teeth, 1944–No award, 1945–Harvey, 1946–State of the Union, 1947–No award, 1948–A Streetcar Named Desire, 1949–Death of a Salesman, 1950–South Pacific, 1951–No award, 1952–The Shrike, 1953–Picnic, 1954–The Teahouse of the August Moon, 1955–Cat on a Hot Tin Roof, 1956–The Diary of Anne Frank, 1957–Long Day's Journey into Night, 1958–Look Homeward, Angel, 1959–J. B., 1960–Fiorello!, 1961–All the Way Home, 1962–How to Succeed in Business without Really Trying, 1963–No award, 1964–No award, 1965–The Subject Was Roses, 1966–No award, 1967–A Delicate Balance, 1968–No award, 1969–The Great White Hope, 1970–No Place to Be Somebody, 1971–The Effect of Gamma Rays on Man-in-the-Moon Marigolds, 1972–No award, 1973–That Championship Season, 1974–No award, 1975–Seascape, 1976–A Chorus Line

NEW YORK DRAMA CRITICS CIRCLE AWARDS

1936–Winterset, 1937–High Tor, 1938–Of Mice and Men, Shadow and Substance, 1939–The White Steed, 1940–The Time of Your Life, 1941–Watch on the Rhine, The Corn is Green, 1942–Blithe Spirit, 1943–The Patriots, 1944–Jacobowsky and the Colonel, 1945–The Glass Menagerie, 1946–Carousel, 1947–All My Sons, No Exit, Brigadoon, 1948–A Streetcar Named Desire, The Winslow Boy, 1949–Death of a Salesman, The Madwoman of Chaillot, South Pacific, 1950–The Member of the Wedding, The Cocktail Party, The Consul, 1951–Darkness at Noon, The Lady's Not for Burning, Guys and Dolls, 1952–I Am a Camera, Venus Observed, Pal Joey, 1953–Picnic, The Love of Four Colonels, Wonderful Town, 1954–Teahouse of the August Moon, Ondine, The Golden Apple, 1955–Cat on a Hot Tin Roof, Witness for the Prosecution, The Saint of Bleecker Street, 1956–The Diary of Anne Frank, Tiger at the Gates, My Fair Lady, 1957–Long Day's Journey into Night, The Waltz of the Toreadors, The Most Happy Fella, 1958–Look Homeward Angel, Look Back in Anger, The Music Man, 1959–A Raisin in the Sun, The Visit, La Plume de Ma Tante, 1960–Toys in the Attic, Five Finger Exercise, Fiorello!, 1961–All the Way Home, A Taste of Honey, Carnival, 1962–Night of the Iguana, A Man for All Seasons, How to Succeed in Business without Really Trying, 1963–Who's Afraid of Virginia Woolf?, 1964–Luther, Hello, Dolly!, 1965–The Subject Was Roses, Fiddler on the Roof, 1966–The Persecution and Assassination of Marat as Performed by the Inmates of the Asylum of Charenton under the Direction of the Marquis de Sade, Man of La Mancha, 1967–The Homecoming, Cabaret, 1968–Rosencrantz and Guildenstern Are Dead, Your Own Thing, 1969–The Great White Hope, 1776, 1970–The Effect of Gamma Rays on Man-in-the-Moon Marigolds, Borstal Boy, Company, 1971–Home, Follies, The House of Blue Leaves, 1972–That Championship Season, Two Gentlemen of Verona, 1973–The Hot l Baltimore, The Changing Room, A Little Night Music, 1974–The Contractor, Short Eyes, Candide, 1975–Equus, The Taking of Miss Janie, A Chorus Line, 1976–Travesties, Streamers, Pacific Overtures

AMERICAN THEATRE WING
ANTOINETTE PERRY (TONY) AWARD PRODUCTIONS

1948–Mister Roberts, 1949–Death of a Salesman, Kiss Me, Kate, 1950–The Cocktail Party, South Pacific, 1951–The Rose Tattoo, Guys and Dolls, 1952–The Fourposter, The King and I, 1953–The Crucible, Wonderful Town, 1954–The Teahouse of the August Moon, Kismet, 1955–The Desperate Hours, The Pajama Game, 1956–The Diary of Anne Frank, Damn Yankees, 1957–Long Day's Journey into Night, My Fair Lady, 1958–Sunrise at Campobello, The Music Man, 1959–J. B., Redhead, 1960–The Miracle Worker, Fiorello! tied with Sound of Music, 1961–Becket, Bye Bye Birdie, 1962–A Man for All Seasons, How to Succeed in Business without Really Trying, 1963–Who's Afraid of Virginia Woolf?, A Funny Thing Happened on the Way to the Forum, 1964–Luther, Hello, Dolly!, 1965–The Subject Was Roses, Fiddler on the Roof, 1966–The Persecution and Assassination of Marat as Performed by the Inmates of the Asylum of Charenton under the Direction of the Marquis de Sade, Man of La Mancha, 1967–The Homecoming, Cabaret, 1968–Rosencrantz and Guildenstern Are Dead, Hallelujah, Baby!, 1969–The Great White Hope, 1776, 1970–Borstal Boy, Applause, 1971–Sleuth, Company, 1972–Sticks and Bones, Two Gentlemen of Verona, 1973–That Championship Season, A Little Night Music, 1974–The River Niger, Raisin, 1975–Equus, The Wiz, 1976–Travesties, A Chorus Line

1976 THEATRE WORLD AWARD WINNERS

DANNY AIELLO
of "Lamppost Reunion"

CHRISTINE ANDREAS
of "My Fair Lady"

DIXIE CARTER
of "Jesse and the Bandit Queen"

CHIP GARNETT
of "Bubbling Brown Sugar"

TOVAH FELDSHUH
of "Yentl"

RICHARD KELTON
of "Who's Afraid of Virginia Woolf?"

CHARLES REPOLE
of "Very Good Eddie"

VIVIAN REED
of "Bubbling Brown Sugar"

VIRGINIA SEIDEL
of "Very Good Eddie"

DANIEL SELTZER
of "Knock Knock"

JOHN V. SHEA
of "Yentl"

MERYL STREEP
of "27 Wagons Full of Cotton"

231

1976 THEATRE WORLD AWARDS PARTY, Thursday, May 27, 1976: Top: Jerry Lanning, Maureen Anderman, Colleen Dewhurst, Ben Gazzara, Anthony Perkins, Julie Harris; Ian Richardson; John Cullum, Estelle Parsons, Christopher Walken, Catherine Burns, Gilbert Price Below: Dixie Carter, John Cullum; John, Jennifer and Rosemary Harris Ehle; Ben Gazzara; Richard Kelton, Colleen Dewhurst, Second row from bottom: Vivian Reed, Gilbert Price; Angela Lansbury (L); Anthony Perkins; Carole Schweid, Chuck Cissel, Donna Drake, Marvin Hamlisch, Kelly Bishop, Edward Kleban, Tharon Musser (front), Bottom Row: John V. Shea; Russ Thacker, Joel Grey, Charles Repole; Virginia Seidel; Chip Garnett, Estelle Parsons

Top: Danny Aiello, Rosemary Harris; Angela Lansbury; Julie Harris, Below: Meryl Streep; Daniel Seltzer; Maureen Anderman; Tovah Feldshuh, Anthony Perkins, Second row from bottom: D'Jamin Bartlett (L), Paul Rudd (C); Tovah Feldshuh; Meryl Streep (L), William Atherton (R); Bottom: Stewart Klein, Vivian Reed; Jerry Lanning; Christine Andreas; Christopher Walken, Catherine Burns

Howard Gray, Ron Reagan, Van Williams Photos

Marlon Brando   **Julie Andrews**   **Robert Redford**   **Julie Harris**   **George C. Scott**

PREVIOUS THEATRE WORLD AWARD WINNERS

1944–45: Betty Comden, Richard Davis, Richard Hart, Judy Holliday, Charles Lang, Bambi Linn, John Lund, Donald Murphy, Nancy Noland, Margaret Phillips, John Raitt

1945–46: Barbara Bel Geddes, Marlon Brando, Bill Callahan, Wendell Corey, Paul Douglas, Mary James, Burt Lancaster, Patricia Marshall, Beatrice Pearson

1946–47: Keith Andes, Marion Bell, Peter Cookson, Ann Crowley, Ellen Hanley, John Jordan, George Keane, Dorothea MacFarland, James Mitchell, Patricia Neal, David Wayne

1947–48: Valerie Bettis, Edward Bryce, Whitfield Connor, Mark Dawson, June Lockhart, Estelle Loring, Peggy Maley, Ralph Meeker, Meg Mundy, Douglass Watson, James Whitmore, Patrice Wymore

1948–49: Tod Andrews, Doe Avedon, Jean Carson, Carol Channing, Richard Derr, Julie Harris, Mary McCarty, Allyn Ann McLerie, Cameron Mitchell, Gene Nelson, Byron Palmer, Bob Scheerer

1949–50: Nancy Andrews, Phil Arthur, Barbara Brady, Lydia Clarke, Priscilla Gillette, Don Hanmer, Marcia Henderson, Charlton Heston, Rick Jason, Grace Kelly, Charles Nolte, Roger Price

1950–51: Barbara Ashley, Isabel Bigley, Martin Brooks, Richard Burton, James Daly, Cloris Leachman, Russell Nype, Jack Palance, William Smothers, Maureen Stapleton, Marcia Van Dyke, Eli Wallach

1951–52: Tony Bavaar, Patricia Benoit, Peter Conlow, Virginia de Luce, Ronny Graham, Audrey Hepburn, Diana Herbert, Conrad Janis, Dick Kallman, Charles Proctor, Eric Sinclair, Kim Stanley, Marian Winters, Helen Wood

1952–53: Edie Adams, Rosemary Harris, Eileen Heckart, Peter Kelley, John Kerr, Richard Kiley, Gloria Marlowe, Penelope Munday, Paul Newman, Sheree North, Geraldine Page, John Stewart, Ray Stricklyn, Gwen Verdon

1953–54: Orson Bean, Harry Belafonte, James Dean, Joan Diener, Ben Gazzara, Carol Haney, Jonathan Lucas, Kay Medford, Scott Merrill, Elizabeth Montgomery, Leo Penn, Eva Marie Saint

1954–55: Julie Andrews, Jacqueline Brookes, Shirl Conway, Barbara Cook, David Daniels, Mary Fickett, Page Johnson, Loretta Leversee, Jack Lord, Dennis Patrick, Anthony Perkins, Christopher Plummer

1955–56: Diane Cilento, Dick Davalos, Anthony Franciosa, Andy Griffith, Laurence Harvey, David Hedison, Earle Hyman, Susan Johnson, John Michael King, Jayne Mansfield, Sarah Marshall, Gaby Rodgers, Susan Strasberg, Fritz Weaver

1956–57: Peggy Cass, Sydney Chaplin, Sylvia Daneel, Bradford Dillman, Peter Donat, George Grizzard, Carol Lynley, Peter Palmer, Jason Robards, Cliff Robertson, Pippa Scott, Inga Swenson

1957–58: Anne Bancroft, Warren Berlinger, Colleen Dewhurst, Richard Easton, Tim Everett, Eddie Hodges, Joan Hovis, Carol Lawrence, Jacqueline McKeever, Wynne Miller, Robert Morse, George C. Scott

1958–59: Lou Antonio, Ina Balin, Richard Cross, Tammy Grimes, Larry Hagman, Dolores Hart, Roger Mollien, France Nuyen, Susan Oliver, Ben Piazza, Paul Roebling, William Shatner, Pat Suzuki, Rip Torn

1959–60: Warren Beatty, Eileen Brennan, Carol Burnett, Patty Duke, Jane Fonda, Anita Gillette, Elisa Loti, Donald Madden, George Maharis, John McMartin, Lauri Peters, Dick Van Dyke

1960–61: Joyce Bulifant, Dennis Cooney, Nancy Dussault, Robert Goulet, Joan Hackett, June Harding, Ron Husmann, James MacArthur, Bruce Yarnell

1961–62: Elizabeth Ashley, Keith Baxter, Peter Fonda, Don Galloway, Sean Garrison, Barbara Harris, James Earl Jones, Janet Margolin, Karen Morrow, Robert Redford, John Stride, Brenda Vaccaro

1962–63: Alan Arkin, Stuart Damon, Melinda Dillon, Robert Drivas, Bob Gentry, Dorothy Loudon, Brandon Maggart, Julienne Marie, Liza Minnelli, Estelle Parsons, Diana Sands, Swen Swenson

1963–64: Alan Alda, Gloria Bleezarde, Imelda De Martin, Claude Giraud, Ketty Lester, Barbara Loden, Lawrence Pressman, Gilbert Price, Philip Proctor, John Tracy, Jennifer West

1964–65: Carolyn Coates, Joyce Jillson, Linda Lavin, Luba Lisa, Michael O'Sullivan, Joanna Pettet, Beah Richards, Jaime Sanchez, Victor Spinetti, Nicolas Surovy, Robert Walker, Clarence Williams III

1965–66: Zoe Caldwell, David Carradine, John Cullum, John Davidson, Faye Dunaway, Gloria Foster, Robert Hooks, Jerry Lanning, Richard Mulligan, April Shawhan, Sandra Smith, Lesley Ann Warren

1966–67: Bonnie Bedelia, Richard Benjamin, Dustin Hoffman, Terry Kiser, Reva Rose, Robert Salvio, Sheila Smith, Connie Stevens, Pamela Tiffin, Leslie Uggams, Jon Voight, Christopher Walken

1967–68: Pamela Burrell, Sandy Duncan, Julie Gregg, Bernadette Peters, Alice Playten, Brenda Smiley, David Birney, Jordan Christopher, Jack Crowder, Stephen Joyce, Michael Rupert, Russ Thacker

1968–69: Jane Alexander, David Cryer, Ed Evanko, Blythe Danner, Ken Howard, Lauren Jones, Ron Leibman, Marian Mercer, Jill O'Hara, Ron O'Neal, Al Pacino, Marlene Warfield

1969–70: Susan Browning, Donny Burks, Catherine Burns, Len Cariou, Bonnie Franklin, David Holliday, Katharine Houghton, Melba Moore, David Rounds, Lewis J. Stadlen, Kristoffer Tabori, Fredricka Weber

1970–71: Clifton Davis, Michael Douglas, Julie Garfield, Martha Henry, James Naughton, Tricia O'Neil, Kipp Osborne, Roger Rathburn, Ayn Ruymen, Jennifer Salt, Joan Van Ark, Walter Willison

1971–72: Jonelle Allen, Maureen Anderman, William Atherton, Richard Backus, Adrienne Barbeau, Cara Duff-MacCormick, Robert Foxworth, Elaine Joyce, Jess Richards, Ben Vereen, Beatrice Winde, James Woods

1972–73: D'Jamin Bartlett, Patricia Elliott, James Farentino, Brian Farrell, Victor Garber, Kelly Garrett, Mari Gorman, Laurence Guittard, Trish Hawkins, Monte Markham, John Rubinstein, Jennifer Warren, Alexander H. Cohen (Special Award)

1973–74: Mark Baker, Maureen Brennan, Ralph Carter, Thom Christopher, John Driver, Conchata Ferrell, Ernestine Jackson, Michael Moriarty, Joe Morton, Ann Reinking, Janie Sell, Mary Woronov, Sammy Cahn (Special Award)

1974–75: Peter Burnell, Zan Charisse, Lola Falana, Peter Firth, Dorian Harewood, Joel Higgins, Marcia McClain, Linda Miller, Marti Rolph, John Sheridan, Scott Stevensen, Donna Theodore, Equity Library Theatre (Special Award)

Richard Aaron

Naola Adair

Lloyd Alann

Dru Alexandrine

Arthur Anderson

BIOGRAPHIES OF THIS SEASON'S CAST

AARON, JACK. Born May 1, 1933 in NYC. Attended Hunter Col., Actors Workshop. OB in "Swim Low Little Goldfish," "Journey of the Fifth Horse," "The Nest," "One Flew Over the Cuckoo's Nest," "The Birds," "The Pornographer's Daughter," "Love Death Plays."

AARON, RICHARD. Born Apr. 27, 1946 in Brookline, MA. Graduate Suffolk U., Brandeis U. Debut OB 1972 in "The Lady's Not for Burning," followed by "One Cent Plain," Bdwy 1975 in "Candide."

ABEL, WALTER. Born June 6, 1898 in St. Paul, MN. Attended AADA. Made Bdwy debut in 1918 in "A Woman's Way," subsequently appearing in, among others, "Forbidden," "Back to Methuselah," "Square Peg," "As You Like It," "The Enemy," "Taming of the Shrew," "Hangman's House," "Beyond the Horizon," "Skidding," "The Seagull," "Mourning Becomes Electra," "When Ladies Meet," "Invitation to a Murder," "Merrily We Roll Along," "Wingless Victory," "Mermaids Singing," "Parlor Story," "Biggest Thief in Town," "Wisteria Trees," "The Long Watch," "Pleasure of His Company," "Night Life," "90 Day Mistress," "Saturday Sunday Monday." "Trelawny of the Wells."

ABELS, GREGORY. Born Nov. 6, 1941 in Jersey City, NJ. Studied with Stella Adler. Debut 1970 OB in "War of the Roses," followed by "Macbeth," "Phoebus," "Oedipus at Colonus," "I Love Thee Freely," "Veil of Infamy," "The Boss."

ABRAHAM, F. MURRAY. Born Oct. 24, 1939 in Pittsburgh, Pa. Attended UTex. OB bow 1967 in "The Fantasticks," followed by "An Opening in the Trees," "Fourteenth Dictator," "Young Abe Lincoln," "Tonight in Living Color," "Adaptation," "Survival of St. Joan," "The Dog Ran Away," "Fables," "Richard III," "Little Murders," "Scuba Duba," "Where Has Tommy Flowers Gone?," "Miracle Play," "Blessing," Bdwy debut "The Man In The Glass Booth" (1968), followed by "6 Rms Riv Vu.," "Bad Habits," "The Ritz," "Legend."

ABRAMS, ALAN. Born Mar. 16, 1950 in Boston, MA. Graduate Boston U. Debut OB 1975 in ELT's "Tenderloin."

ABUBA, ERNEST. Born Aug. 25, 1947 in Honolulu, HI. Attended Southwestern Col. Bdwy debut 1976 in "Pacific Overtures."

ACKERMAN, LONI. Born Apr. 10, 1949 in NYC. Attended New School. Bdwy debut 1968 in "George M!," followed by "Dames at Sea" (OB), "No, No, Nanette," "So Long 174th Street," "Magic Show."

ACKROYD, DAVID. Born May 30, 1940 in Orange, NJ. Graduate Bucknell, Yale. Bdwy debut 1971 in "Unlikely Heroes" followed by "Full Circle," "Hamlet" (LC).

ADAIR, NAOLA. Born in Chicago, IL. Graduate Whittier Col. and Portland State U. Debut 1975 OB in "Liberty Call," followed by "Flux."

ADAMS, MASON. Born Feb. 26, 1919 in NYC. Graduate UWisc. Has appeared in "Get Away, Old Man," "Public Relations," "Career Angel," "Violet," "Shadow of My Enemy," "Tall Story," "Inquest," "Trial of the Catonsville 9," "Sign in Sidney Brustein's Window," "Meegan's Game" (OB), "Shortchanged Review" (LC).

ADAMS, MOLLY. Born in Portchester, NY. Graduate Smith College. Debut 1973 OB in "Older People," followed by "Hot l Baltimore."

ADAMS, POLLY. Born in Nashville, TN. Graduate Stanford U., Columbia U. Bdwy debut 1976 in "Zalmen, or the Madness of God."

ADAMS, SHEILA K. Born Mar. 24, 1950 in Omaha, NE. Attended AADA. Bdwy debut 1973 in "A Little Night Music," followed by "Summer Brave."

AGRESS, TED. Born Apr. 20, 1945 in Brooklyn, NY. Attended Adelphi U. Bdwy debut 1965 in "Hello, Dolly!" followed by "Dear World," "Look Me Up" (OB), "Shenandoah."

AIELLO, DANNY. Born June 20, 1935 in NYC. Debut OB 1975 in "Wheelbarrow Closers," followed by "Lamppost Reunion" for which he received a Theatre World Award.

ALANN, LLOYD. Born Aug. 15, 1952 in The Bronx, NY. Attended Lehman Col. Bdwy debut 1975 in "Grease."

ALDREDGE, TOM. Born Feb. 28, 1928 in Dayton, O. Attended Dayton U., Goodman Theatre. Bdwy bow 1959 in "The Nervous Set," followed by "UTBU," "Slapstick Tragedy," "Everything in the Garden," "Indians," "Engagement Baby," "How the Other Half Loves," "Sticks and Bones," "Where's Charley?," "Leaf People," "Rex," OB in "The Tempest," "Between Two Thieves," "Henry V," "The Premise," "Love's Labour's Lost," "Troilus and Cressida," "Butter and Egg Man," "Ergo," "Boys In the Band," "Twelfth Night," "Colette," "Hamlet," "The Orphan," "King Lear," "Iceman Cometh."

ALEXANDER, C. K. Born May 4, 1920 in Cairo, Egypt. American U. graduate. Bdwy debut 1946 in "Hidden Horizon," followed by "The Happy Time," "Flight into Egypt," "Mr. Pickwick," "Can-Can," "Fanny," "The Matchmaker," "La Plume de Ma Tante," "Rhinoceros," "Carnival," "Tovarich," "Poor Bitos," "Ari," OB in "The Dragon," "Corruption in the Palace of Justice," "Justice Box," "Threepenny Opera."

ALEXANDER, JANE. Born Oct. 28, 1939 in Boston, MA. Attended Sarah Lawrence, UEdinburgh. Bdwy debut 1968 in "The Great White Hope" for which she received a Theatre World Award, followed by "6 Rms Riv Vu," "Find Your Way Home," "Hamlet" (LC), "The Heiress."

ALEXANDER, TERRY. Born Mar. 23, 1947 in Detroit, MI. Wayne State U. graduate. Bdwy debut 1971 in "No Place to Be Somebody" OB in "Rashomon," "Glass Menagerie," "Breakout," "Naomi Court," "Streamers."

ALEXANDRINE, DRU. Born Apr. 23, 1950 in Cheshire, Eng. Studied at Royal Ballet School. Bdwy debut 1973 in "Pajama Game," followed by "My Fair Lady" (1976).

ALLEN, DEBORAH. Born Jan. 16, 1950 in Houston, TX. Graduate Howard U. Debut OB 1972 in "Ti-Jean and His Brothers," Bdwy 1973 in "Raisin."

ALLEN, GARY. Born Sept. 4, 1942 in Camden, TN. Attended Memphis State U., Goodman Theatre. Debut 1975 OB in "Ice Age."

ALLEN, SCOTT. Born Aug. 29, 1948 in Morristown, NJ. Attended Union Col., Upsala Col., AMDA. Bdwy debut 1975 in "A Chorus Line."

ALLINSON, MICHAEL. Born in London; attended Lausanne U., RADA. Bdwy bow 1960 in "My Fair Lady," followed by "Hostile Witness," "Come Live with Me," "Coco," "Angel Street," OB in "Importance of Being Earnest," "Staircase."

ALTMAN, JANE. Born Sept. 7 in Philadelphia, Pa. Temple U. graduate. Debut OB in "Importance of Being Earnest," followed by "Taming of the Shrew," "Candida," "A Doll's House," "Magda," "The Three Musketeers," "And So to Bed."

ANDERMAN, MAUREEN. Born Oct. 26, 1946 in Detroit, MI. Graduate U. Mich. Bdwy debut 1970 in ASF's "Othello," followed by "Moonchildren" for which she received a Theatre World Award, "An Evening with Richard Nixon and . . . . ," "The Last of Mrs. Lincoln," "Seascape," "Hamlet" (LC), "Who's Afraid of Virginia Woolf?"

ANDERSON, ARTHUR. Born Aug. 29, 1922 in Staten Island, NY. Attended AmThWing. Made Bdwy debut 1937 in "Julius Caesar," followed by "Shoemakers' Holiday," "1776," OB in "Winkelberg," "The Doctor's Dilemma," "Zoo Story," "American Dream," "Gallows Humor," "The Rivals," "Fantasticks."

ANDREAS, CHRISTINE. Born Oct. 1, 1951 in Camden, NJ. Bdwy debut 1975 in "Angel Street," followed by "My Fair Lady" for which she received a Theatre World Award.

ANDRES, BARBARA. Born Feb. 11, 1939 in NYC. Graduate of Catholic U. Bdwy debut 1969 in "Jimmy," followed by "The Boy Friend," "Rodgers and Hart," "Rex."

ANTHONY, ROBERT. Born May 10, 1941 in Newark, NJ. Attended Boston U., AADA. Off Bdwy in "Jerico-Jim Crow," "Bugs and Veronica," "Dirty Old Man," "Hamlet," "Othello," "Scuba Duba," "Salome," on Bdwy in "Man in the Glass Booth," "Butterflies Are Free," "Legend."

ARBEIT, HERMAN. Born Apr. 19, 1925 in Brooklyn, NY. Attended CCNY, HB Studio, Neighborhood Playhouse. Debut 1959 OB in "The Golem," followed by "Awake and Sing," "A Delicate Balance," "Yentl the Yeshiva Boy," Bdwy 1975 in "Yentl."

ARGO, ALLISON. Born Dec. 23, 1953 in Richmond, VA. Debut OB 1974 in "Neighbors," followed by Bdwy 1976 in "Lady from the Sea."

ARLT, LEWIS. Born Dec. 5, 1949 in Kingston, NY. Graduate Carnegie Tech. Bdwy debut 1975 in "Murder among Friends."

ASHLEY, ELIZABETH. Born Aug. 30, 1939 in Ocala, FL. Attended Neighborhood Playhouse. Bdwy debut 1959 in "The Highest Tree," followed by "Take Her, She's Mine" for which she received a Theatre World Award, "Barefoot in the Park," "Ring Round the Bathtub," "Cat on a Hot Tin Roof," "The Skin of Our Teeth," "Legend."

Armand Assante **Regina Baff** **Roger Baron** **K. T. Baumann** **Michael Beirne**

ASHLEY, MARY ELLEN. Born June 11, 1938 in Long Island City, NY. Queens College graduate. Bdwy debut 1943 in "The Innocent Voyage," followed by "Bobino," "By Appointment Only," "Annie Get Your Gun," "Yentl," OB in "Carousel," "Yentl the Yeshiva Boy," "Polly," "Panama Hattie" (ELT).

ASSANTE, ARMAND. Born Oct. 4, 1949 in NYC. Attended AADA. Debut OB 1971 in "Lake of the Woods," followed by "Yankees 3, Detroit O," "Rubbers," "Boccacio."

ATHERTON, WILLIAM. Born July 30, 1947 in New Haven, CT. Carnegie Tech graduate. Debut 1971 OB in "House of Blue Leaves," followed by "Basic Training of Pavlo Hummel," "Suggs" for which he received a Theatre World Award, "Rich and Famous," Bdwy 1972 in "The Sign in Sidney Brustein's Window."

ATTLES, JOSEPH. Born Apr. 7, 1903 in Charleston, SC. Attended Harlem Musical Conservatory. Bdwy bow in "Blackbirds of 1928," followed by "John Henry," "Porgy and Bess," "Kwamina," "Tambourines to Glory," "The Last of Mrs. Lincoln," "Bubbling Brown Sugar," OB in "Jerico-Jim Crow," "Cabin in the Sky," "Prodigal Son," "Day of Absence," "Cry of Players," "King Lear," "Duplex."

AUMONT, JEAN-PIERRE. Born Jan. 5, 1913 in Paris. Attended Ntl. Sch. of Dramatic Art. Bdwy debut 1942 in "Rose Burke," followed by "My Name Is Aquilon," "Heavenly Twins," "Second String," "Tovarich," "Camino Real" (LC), "Murderous Angels" (OB), "Days in the Trees."

AZITO, ANTONIO. Born July 18, 1948 in NYC. Attended Juilliard. Debut OB 1971 in "Red, White and Black," followed by "Players Project," "Secrets of the Citizens' Correction Committee," "Threepenny Opera."

BACIGALUPI, ROBERT. Born Oct. 21, 1949 in San Francisco, CA. Juilliard graduate. Debut 1975 in "The Robber Bridegroom," followed by "Edwared II," "The Time of Your Life."

BACKUS, RICHARD. Born Mar. 28, 1945 in Goffstown, NH. Harvard graduate. Bdwy debut 1971 in "Butterflies Are Free," followed by "Promenade, All!" for which he received a Theatre Award, "Studs Edsel," "Ah Wilderness."

BAFF, REGINA. Born Mar. 31, 1949 in The Bronx, NY. Attended Western Reserve, Hunter Col. Debut 1969 OB in "The Brownstone Urge," followed by "Patrick Henry Lake Liquors," "The Cherry Orchard," Bdwy in "Story Theatre," "Metamorphosis," "Veronica's Room."

BAILEY, PEARL. Born Mar. 28, 1918 in Newport News, VA. Bdwy debut 1946 in "St. Louis Woman," followed by "Arms and the Girl," "House of Flowers," "Hello, Dolly!"

BAKER, LENNY. Born Jan. 17, 1945 in Boston, MA. Graduate Boston U. Debut OB 1969 in "Frank Gagliano's City Scene," followed by "The Year Boston Won the Pennant," "The Time of Your Life," "Summertree," "Early Morning," "Survival of Joan," "Gallery," "Barbary Shore," "Merry Wives of Windsor," "Pericles," "Secret Service," "Boy Meets Girl," Bdwy 1974 in "Freedom of the City."

BAKER, MARK. Born Oct. 2, 1946 in Cumberland, Md. Attended Wittenberg U., Carnegie-Mellon U., Neighborhood Playhouse, AADA. Debut 1971 OB in "Love Me, Love My Children," Bdwy bow 1972 in "Via Galactica," followed by "Candide" for which he received a Theatre World Award, "Habeas Corpus."

BAMFORD, GEORGE. Born Nov. 6, 1944 in Dundalk, MD. Attended Frostberg State Col., Peabody Cons. Debut OB 1973 in "Anna K," followed by "The Kid," "Killer's Head," "Yanks 3, Detroit O," "Sweet Bird of Youth."

BARBOUR, ELEANOR. Born Jan. 23, 1945 in NYC. Graduate Hofstra U. Debut OB 1976 in "Follies."

BARON, JOANNE. Born Feb. 3, 1953 in New Haven, CT. Attended UConn, Neighborhood Playhouse. Appeared OB in "pops!," "Bah Humbug."

BARON ROGER. Born Nov. 22, 1946 in Chicago, IL. Graduate Northwestern U. Bdwy debut 1976 in "The Heiress."

BARRETT, BILL. Born Oct. 25, 1950 in Jersey City, NJ. Graduate Commonwealth U. Bdwy debut 1975 in "Summer Brave." OB in "The Fifth," "Brick and the Rose," "Absence of Heroes," "Touch," "Fool's Delight," "Leander Stillwell."

BARRETT, JOE. Born Nov. 30, 1950 in Webster, NY. Graduate URochester. Debut 1975 OB in "Boy Meets Boy."

BARROWS, DIANA. Born Jan. 23, 1967 in NYC. Bdwy debut 1975 in "Cat on a Hot Tin Roof," followed by "Panama Hattie" (ELT).

BARRY, ROBERT. Born Mar. 17, 1943 in Spring Valley, NY. Graduate Rockland Com. Col. Debut OB 1971 in "Stag Movie," followed by "The Drunkard," "Alligator Man," "Brass Butterfly," "So Long 174th Street."

BARTLETT, D'JAMIN. Born May 21 in NYC. Attended AADA. Bdwy debut 1973 in "A Little Night Music" for which she received a Theatre World Award, OB in "The Glorious Age," "Boccacio."

BARTON, DANIEL. Born Jan. 23, 1949 in Buffalo, NY. Attended Buffalo State, Albany State. Bdwy debut 1976 in "The Poison Tree."

BARTON, DONALD. Born May 2, 1928 in Eastland, TX. Attended UTex. Credits include "Design for a Stained Glass Window," "Paint Your Wagon," "Wonderful Town," "Goldilocks," "Much Ado about Nothing," "The Royal Family."

BATES, KATHY. Born June 28, 1948 in Memphis, TN. Graduate Southern Methodist U. Debut OB 1976 in "Vanities."

BATTISTA, LLOYD. Born May 14, 1937 in Cleveland, OH. Graduate Carnegie Tech. Bdwy debut 1966 in "Those That Play the Clowns," followed by "The Homecoming," OB in "The Flame and the Rose," "Murder in the Cathedral," "The Miser," "Gorky."

BAUER, BRUCE. Born July 5, 1944 in Santa Monica, CA. Attended Santa Monica Col. Bdwy bow 1975 in "The Ritz."

BAUMANN, K. T. (formerly Kathryn) Born Aug. 13, 1946 in The Bronx, NY. Attended Neighborhood Playhouse. Bdwy debut 1967 in "The Prime of Miss Jean Brodie," followed by "The Penny Wars," OB in "Lemon Sky," "Effect of Gamma Rays . . . ," "Trelawny of the Wells."

BAXLEY, BARBARA. Born Jan. 1, 1925 in Porterville, CA. Attended Pacific Col., Neighborhood Playhouse. Bdwy debut 1948 in "Private Lives," followed by "Out West of Eighth," "Peter Pan," "I Am a Camera," "Bus Stop," "Camino Real," "Frogs of Spring," "Oh, Men! Oh, Women!," "Flowering Peach," "Period of Adjustment," "She Loves Me," "Three Sisters," "Plaza Suite," "Me Jack, You Jill," OB in "Brecht on Brecht," "Measure for Measure," "To Be Young, Gifted and Black," "Oh, Pioneers."

BAYNE, RICHARD COOPER. Born Feb. 25, 1949 in Brooklyn, NY. Graduate NYU. Bdwy debut 1971 in "Hair," followed by "Seesaw," "Rachael Lily Rosenbloom," OB in "The Boy Friend," "Follies."

BEACH, GARY. Born Oct. 10, 1947 in Alexandria, VA. Graduate NC Sch. of Arts. Bdwy bow 1971 in "1776," followed by "Something's Afoot," OB in "Smile, Smile, Smile," "What's a Nice Country. . . . ," "Ionescopade."

BEARD, CHARLES. Born July 24, 1945 in Lake Charles, LA. Attended Butler U. NY debut 1968 in "West Side Story" (LC), followed by "Carnival" (CC), "Gantry," "So Long 174th Street," OB in "Dark of the Moon."

BECKHAM, WILLARD. Born Nov. 6, 1948 in Hominy, OK. Graduate Cleveland Inst. of Music. Debut OB 1972 in "Crazy Now," Bdwy 1974 in "Lorelei," followed by "Something's Afoot."

BEDFORD, BRIAN. Born Feb. 16, 1935 in Morley, Eng. Attended RADA. Bdwy bow 1960 in "Five Finger Exercise," followed by "Lord Pengo," "The Private Ear," "The Knack" (OB), "The Astrakhan Coat," "The Unknown Soldier and His Wife," "Seven Descents of Myrtle," "Jumpers," with APA in "Misanthrope," "Cocktail Party," and "Hamlet," "Private Lives," "School for Wives."

BEIRNE, MICHAEL. Born Apr. 23, 1943 in Endicott, NY. Graduate NYU, Harvard, Neighborhood Playhouse. Bdwy bow 1968 in "Hallelujah Baby," followed by "Cactus Flower," "The Ritz."

BELL, GLYNIS. Born July 30, 1947 in London. Attended Oakland U., AADA. Debut 1975 OB in "The Devils," followed by "The Time of Your Life," "The Robber Bridegroom," "Three Sisters."

BELL, JOAN. Born Feb. 1, 1935 in Bombay, Ind. Studied at Sylvia Bryant Stage Sch. Bdwy debut 1963 in "Something More," followed by "Applause," "Chicago."

BELLOMO, JOE. Born Apr. 12, 1938 in NYC. Attended Manhattan Sch. of Music. Bdwy bow 1960 in "New Girl in Town," followed by CC's "South Pacific" and "Guys and Dolls," OB in "Cindy," "Fantasticks."

BENJAMIN, RICHARD. Born May 22, 1938 in NYC. Graduate Northwestern U. Bdwy bow 1966 in "Star Spangled Girl" for which he received a Theatre World Award, followed by "Little Black Book," "Norman Conquests."

BENNETT, MEG. Born Oct. 4, 1948 in Los Angeles, CA. Graduate Northwestern U. Debut OB 1971 in "Godspell," on Bdwy 1972 in "Grease."

BEREZIN, TANYA. Born Mar. 25, 1941 in Philadelphia, Pa. Attended Boston U. Debut OB 1967 in "The Sandcastle." Member of Circle Rep. Theatre Co. from 1969, and has appeared in "Three Sisters," "Great Nubula in Orion," "him," "Amazing Activity of Charlie Contrare," "Battle of Angels," "Mound Builders," "Serenading Louie."

orothy Blackburn   **Mark Blum**   **Verna Bloom**   **Edwin Bordo**   **Maureen Brennan**

BERK, DAVID. Born July 20, 1932 in NYC. Graduate Manhattan Sch. of Music. Debut OB 1958 in "Eloise," followed by "Carnival" (CC), "So Long 174th Street."

BERRY, ERIC. Born Jan. 9, 1913 in London. Graduate RADA. NY debut 1954 in "The Boy Friend," followed by "Family Reunion," "The Power and the Glory," "Beaux Stratagem," "Pictures in the Hallway," "Peer Gynt," "Great God Brown," "Henry IV," "The White House," "White Devil," "Charley's Aunt," "The Homecoming" (OB), "Capt. Brassbound's Conversion," "Pippin."

BERTRAND, JACQUELINE. Born June 1, 1937 in Quebec City, Can. Attended Neighborhood Playhouse, LAMDA. Debut OB 1957 in "Madwoman of Chaillot," followed by "Geranium Hat," "Rhuy Blas," "Command Performance," "The Elizabethans," "Tovarich," "Dancing for the Kaiser."

BILLINGTON, LEE. Born July 15, 1932 in Madison, WI. Attended UWisc. Bdwy debut 1969 in "But Seriously," OB in "Dance of Death," "3 by O'Neill," "Our Town," "Capt. Brassbound's Conversion," "Henry VIII," "Boy with a Cart," "Epicoene," "The Homecoming."

BISHOP, KELLY (formerly Carole) Born Feb. 28, 1944 in Colorado Springs, CO. Bdwy debut 1967 in "Golden Rainbow," followed by "Promises, Promises," "On the Town," "Rachel Lily Rosenbloom," "A Chorus Line."

BITTNER, JACK. Born in Omaha, NE. Graduate UNeb. Has appeared OB in "Nathan the Wise," "Land of Fame," "Beggar's Holiday," "Rip Van Winkle," "Dear Oscar," "What Every Woman Knows," "By Bernstein."

BLACKBURN, DOROTHY. Born in Buffalo, NY. Bdwy debut 1924 in "New Brooms," followed by "Sweet Land of Liberty," "Pick-up Girl," "Desk Set," "Auntie Mame," "Desert Incident," "Passage to India," "Loves of Cass McGuire," "Harvey," "The Heiress," OB in "Nigh Named Today," "The Father."

BLAIR, PAMELA. Born Dec. 5, 1949 in Arlington, VT. Attended Ntl. Acad. of Ballet. Made Bdwy debut in 1972 in "Promises, Promises," followed by "Sugar," "Seesaw," "Of Mice and Men," "Wild and Wonderful," "A Chorus Line," OB in "Ballad of Boris K."

BLAISDELL, BRAD. Born Mar. 15, 1949 in Baltimore, MD. NY debut OB 1975 in ELT's "Tenderloin."

BLAKE, SYDNEY. Born Feb. 4, 1951 in Rome, Italy. Graduate Smith Col. Debut OB 1971 in "One Flew over the Cuckoo's Nest," followed by "El Grande de Coca Cola," "Fashion," "So Long 174th Street."

BLOCK, LARRY. Born Oct. 30, 1942 in NYC. Graduate URI. Bdwy bow 1966 in "Hail Scrawdyke," followed by "La Turista," OB in "Eh?," "Fingernails Blue as Flowers," "Comedy of Errors" (CP).

BLOOM, VERNA. Born Aug. 7 in Lynn, MA. Graduate Boston U. Bdwy debut 1967 in "Marat/Sade," followed by OB "Kool Aid," "The Cherry Orchard."

BLUM, MARK. Born May 14, 1950 in Newark, NJ. Graduate UPa., UMinn. Debut 1976 OB in "The Cherry Orchard."

BOBBIE, WALTER. Born Nov. 18, 1945 in Scranton, Pa. Graduate UScranton, Catholic U. Bdwy bow 1971 in "Frank Merriwell," followed by "Grass Harp," "Grease," "Drat!" (OB), "Tricks."

BOGERT, WILLIAM. Born Jan. 25, 1936 in NYC. Yale graduate. Bdwy in "Man for All Seasons," "Hamlet," "Star Spangled Girl," "Cactus Flower," "Sudden and Accidental Re-education of Horse Johnson," OB in "Country Wife," "Taming of the Shrew," "Henry V," "Love's Labour's Lost," "A Gun Play," "The Real Inspector Hound," "Conflict of Interest," "Killdeer," "Rubbers," "Yankees 3 . . ."

BOND, SUDIE. Born July 13, 1928 in Louisville, KY. Attended Rollins Col. OB in "Summer and Smoke," "Tovarich," "American Dream," "Sandbox," "Endgame," "Theatre of the Absurd," "Home Movies," "Softly and Consider the Nearness," "Memorandum," "Local Stigmatic," "Billy," "New York! New York!," "The Cherry Orchard," Bdwy in "Waltz of the Toreadors," "Auntie Mame," "The Egg," "Harold," "My Mother, My Father and Me," "The Impossible Years," "Keep It in the Family," "Quotations from Chrmn. Mao Tse-Tung," "American Dream," "Forty Carats," "Hay Fever," "Grease."

BONDS, ROBERT. Born Feb. 27, 1933 in Pasadena, CA. Attended LACC. Debut 1975 OB in ELT's "Another Language."

BOOCKVOR, STEVE. Born Nov. 18, 1942 in NYC. Attended Queens Col., Juilliard. Bdwy debut 1966 in "Anya," followed by "A Time for Singing," "Cabaret," "Mardi Gras," "Jimmy," "Billy," "The Rothschilds," "Follies," "Over Here," "The Lieutenant," "Musical Jubilee."

BORDO, ED. Born Mar. 3, 1931 in Cleveland, OH. Graduate Allegheny Col., LAMDA. Bdwy bow 1964 in "The Last Analysis," followed by "Inquest," "Zalmen or the Madness of God," OB in "The Dragon," "Waiting for Godot," "Saved."

BORRELLI, JIM. Born Apr. 10, 1948 in Lawrence, MA. Graduate Boston Col. NY Debut OB 1971 in "Subject to Fits," followed by "Grease."

BOSCO, PHILIP. Born Sept. 26, 1930 in Jersey City, NJ. Graduate Catholic U. Credits: "Auntie Mame," "Rape of the Belt," "Ticket of Leave Man" (OB), "Donnybrook," "Man for All Seasons," "Mrs. Warren's Profession," with LCRep in "The Alchemist," "East Wind," "Galileo," "St. Joan," "Tiger at the Gate," "Cyrano," "King Lear," "A Great Career," "In the Matter of J. Robert Oppenheimer," "The Miser," "The Time of Your Life," "Camino Real," "Operation Sidewinder," "Amphitryon," "Enemy of the People," "Playboy of the Western World," "Good Woman of Setzuan," "Antigone," "Mary Stuart," "Narrow Road to the Deep North," "The Crucible," "Twelfth Night," "Enemies," "Plough and the Stars," "Merchant of Venice," and "A Streetcar Named Desire."

BOSTWICK, BARRY. Born Feb. 24, 1945 in San Mateo, CA. Graduate Cal-Western, NYU. Bdwy debut with APA in "War and Peace," followed by "Pantagleize," "Misanthrope," "Cock-a-Doodle Dandy," "Hamlet," "Grease," OB in "Salvation," "Colette," "Soon," "Screens," "They Knew What They Wanted."

BOTT, JOHN. Born Mar. 28, 1923 in Douglas, Isle of Man. Bdwy debut 1974 in "Sherlock Holmes," followed by "Travesties."

BOUTSIKARIS, DENNIS. Born Dec. 21, 1952 in Newark, NJ. Graduate Hampshire Col. Debut 1975 OB in ELT's "Another Language."

BOWEN, BOBBY. Born Apr. 8, 1949 in New Haven, CT. Graduate R.I. Sch. of Design. Debut in 1975 OB in "Boy Meets Boy."

BOYER, TRICIA. Born Apr. 14, 1953 in Hagerstown, MD. Attended Mary Baldwin Col., AADA. Debut 1976 OB in "The Shortchanged Review."

BRAHA, HERBERT. (formerly Herb Simon) Born Sept. 18, 1946 in Hyannis, MA. Attended Carnegie Tech. Debut 1971 OB in "Godspell," followed by "The Shortchanged Review."

BREMSETH, LLOYD. Born July 27, 1948 in Minneapolis, MN. Attended UMinn. Debut 1968 in "Kiss Rock," followed by "Klara," "Sweet Shoppe Myriam," "Kiss Now," "Godspell."

BRENNAN, MAUREEN. Born Oct. 11, 1952 in Washington, DC. Attended UCincinnati. Bdwy debut 1974 in "Candide" for which she received a Theatre World Award.

BROCHU, JAMES. Born Aug. 16, 1946 in NYC. Graduate St. Francis Col, AADA. Debut OB 1968 in "Endecott and the Red Cross," followed by "Taming of the Shrew," "Unfair to Goliath," "Skye," "To Be or Not To Be," "Greenwillow," "Berkeley Square."

BROCKSMITH, ROY. Born Sept. 15, 1945 in Quincy, IL. Debut OB 1971 in "Whip Lady," followed by "The Workout," "Beggar's Opera," "Polly," "Threepenny Opera," Bdwy 1975 in "The Leaf People."

BROOKES, JACQUELINE. Born July 24, 1930 in Montclair, NJ. Graduate UIowa, RADA. Bdwy debut in 1955 in "Tiger at the Gates," followed by "Watercolor," "Abelard and Heloise," OB in "The Cretan Woman" for which she received a Theatre World Award, "The Clandestine Marriage," "Measure for Measure," "Duchess of Malfi," "Ivanov," "Six Characters in Search of an Author," "An Evening's Frost," "Come Slowly, Eden," "The Increased Difficulty of Concentration" (LC), "The Persians," "Sunday Dinner," "House of Blue Leaves," "A Meeting by the River," "Owners," "Hallelujah," "Dream of a Blacklisted Actor," "Knuckle."

BROTHERSON, ERIC. Born May 10, 1911 in Chicago, IL. Attended UWisc. Bdwy debut 1937 in "Between the Devil," followed by "Set to Music," "Lady in the Dark," "My Dear Public," "Gentlemen Prefer Blondes," "Room Service," "The Hot Corner," "Musical Jubilee," "My Fair Lady."

BROWN, CANDY A. Born Aug. 19 in San Rafael, CA. Attended MacAlester Col. Bdwy debut 1969 in "Hello, Dolly," followed by "Purlie," "Pippin," "Chicago."

BROWN, CHRISTOPHER J. Born in Port Chester, NY. Emerson Col. and Yale graduate. Bdwy debut 1975 in "The Ritz."

BROWN, DANIEL. Born June 9, 1947 in Little Rock, AR. Graduate LSU. Debut 1972 OB in "Absolutely Time!," followed by "Secret Life of Walter Mitty," "Be Kind to People Week," Bdwy 1976 in "Home Sweet Homer."

Shirley Brown **Terence Burk** **Pamela Burrell** **Miles Chapin** **Mary Carter**

BROWN, GRAHAM. Born Oct. 24, 1924 in NYC. Graduate Howard U. OB in "Widower's Houses," "The Emperor's Clothes," "Time of Storm," "Major Barbara," "Land Beyond the River," "The Blacks," "Firebugs," "God Is a (Guess What?)," "An Evening of One Acts," "Man Better Man," "Behold! Cometh the Vanderkellans," "Ride a Black Horse," "Great MacDaddy," "Eden," on Bdwy in "Weekend," "Man in the Glass Booth," "The River Niger," "Pericles," "Black Picture Show" (LC).

BROWN, GWENDOLYN. (formerly Gwen Saska) Born Sept. 9, 1939 in Mishawaka, IN. Northwestern and Columbia graduate. Debut 1969 OB in "Geese," followed by "Macbeth," "In the Boom Boom Room," "Secret Service," "Boy Meets Girl."

BROWN, SHIRLEY. Born Oct. 5, 1953 in Cincinnati, OH. Attended UCinn. Debut 1976 OB in "Eden."

BROWN, WALTER P. Born Apr. 18, 1926 in Newark, NJ. Attended Bklyn Cons of Music. Bdwy bow in "Porgy and Bess," followed by "Fiorello!," "The Advocate," CC's "Guys and Dolls" and "South Pacific," "Kelly," "Hello, Dolly," "Raisin."

BROWNE, HARRY. Born Aug. 21, 1952 in Flemington, NJ. Graduate Boston U. Debut 1975 OB in "Down by the River Where the Waterlilies are Disfigured," followed by "The Hot 1 Baltimore."

BROWNING, ROBERT. Born Apr. 30, 1942 in Syracuse, NY. Graduate Carnegie Tech, Purdue. Bdwy debut 1970 in "Candida," followed by OB's "Speed Gets the Poppys," "Panama Hattie" (ELT).

BROWNING, SUSAN. Born Feb. 25, 1941 in Baldwin, NY. Graduate Penn. State. Bdwy bow 1963 in "Love and Kisses," followed by "Company" for which she received a Theatre World Award, "Shelter," "Goodtime Charley," OB in "Jo," "Dime A Dozen," "Seventeen," "Boys from Syracuse," "Collision Course," "Whiskey," "As You Like It," "Removalists."

BRUMMEL, DAVID. Born Nov. 1, 1942 in Brooklyn. Bdwy debut 1973 in "The Pajama Game," followed OB by "Cole Porter," "Fantasticks."

BRUNEAU, RALPH. Born Sept. 22, 1952 in Phoenix, AZ. Graduate UNotre Dame. Debut 1974 OB in "The Fantasticks."

BRUNO, JEAN. Born Dec. 7, 1926 in Bklyn. Attended Hofstra Col., Feagin School. Bdwy debut 1960 in "Beg, Borrow or Steal," followed by "Midgie Purvis," "Music Man," "Family Affair," "Minnie's Boys," "The Lincoln Mask," "Lorelei," OB in "All That Fall," "Hector," "Hotel Paradiso," "Pidgeons in the Park," "Ergo," "Trelawny of the Wells," "Song for the First of May."

BRYAN, WAYNE. Born Aug. 13, 1947 in Compton, CA. Graduate UCal. Bdwy debut 1974 in "Good News," followed by "Rodgers and Hart."

BRYDON, W. B. Born Sept. 20, 1933 in Newcastle, Eng. NY debut 1962 in "The Long, the Short and the Tall," followed by "Live Like Pigs," "Sgt. Musgrave's Dance," "The Kitchen," "Come Slowly Eden," "The Unknown Soldier and His Wife," "Moon for the Misbegotten," "The Orphan," "Possession," Bdwy in "The Lincoln Mask," "Ulysses in Nighttown."

BRYNNER, YUL. Born June 15, 1915 in Sakhalin Island, Japan. Bdwy debut 1946 in "Lute Song," followed by "The King and I," "Home Sweet Homer."

BUCKLEY, BETTY. Born July 3, 1947 in Big Spring, TX. Graduate TCU. Bdwy debut 1969 in "1776," followed by "Pippin," OB in "Ballad of Johnny Pot," "What's a Nice Country Like You Doing in a State Like This?," "Circle of Sound."

BURGE, JAMES. Born Dec. 3, 1943 in Miami, FL. Graduate U Okla., Wayne State U. Bdwy bow 1970 in "Grin and Bare It," followed by "The Royal Family."

BURK, TERENCE. Born Aug. 11, 1947 in Lebanon, IL. Graduate S.IL.U. OB in "Religion," "The Future," "Sacred and Profane Love," Bdwy debut 1976 in "Equus."

BURNELL, PETER. Born Apr. 29, 1950 in Johnstown, NY. OB in "Henry IV," "Antony and Cleopatra," "The Tempest," "Macbeth," "Olathe Response," "Ubu Roi/Ubu Bound," "Dancing for the Kaiser," Bdwy debut 1974 in "In Praise of Love" for which he received a Theatre World Award.

BURR, ROBERT. Born in Jersey City, NJ. Attended Colgate U. Has appeared in "Cradle Will Rock," "Mr. Roberts," "Romeo and Juliet," "Picnic," "The Lovers," "Anniversary Waltz," "Top Man," "Remains to Be Seen," "The Wall," "Andersonville Trial," "A Shot in the Dark," "A Man for All Seasons," "Luther," "Hamlet," "Bajour," "White Devil," "Royal Hunt of the Sun," "Dinner at 8," "King John," "Henry VI," "Love Suicide at Schofield Barracks," "Wild and Wonderful."

BURRELL, PAMELA. Born Aug. 4, 1945 in Tacoma, WA. Bdwy debut 1966 in "Funny Girl," followed by "Arms and the Man" (OB) for which she received a Theatre World Award, "Where's Charley?," "Berkeley Square" (OB), "The Boss" (BAM)

BURSTYN, ELLEN. Born Dec. 7, 1932 in Detroit, MI. Attended Actors Studio. Bdwy debut 1957 (then known as Ellen McRae) in "Fair Game," followed by "Same Time, Next Year."

BURTON, RICHARD. Born Nov. 10, 1925 in Pontrhydyfen, S. Wales. Attended Exeter Col., Oxford. Bdwy debut 1950 in "The Lady's Not for Burning" for which he received a Theatre World Award, followed by "Legend of Lovers," "Time Remembered," "Camelot," "Hamlet," "Equus."

BUTLER, RHODA. Born July 25, 1949 in Sanford, ME. Attended Centenary Col. Debut OB 1974 in "Fashion," Bdwy 1974 in "Candide," followed by "Goodtime Charley."

BYERS, CATHERINE. Born Oct. 7 in Sioux City, IA. Graduate UIowa, LAMDA. Bdwy debut 1971 in "The Philanthropist," followed by "Don't Call Back," "Equus," OB in "Petrified Forest," "All My Sons."

BYRDE, EDYE. Born Jan. 19, 1929 in NYC. Bdwy debut 1975 in "The Wiz."

CAHILL, JAMES. Born May 31, 1940 in Brooklyn. Bdwy debut 1967 in "Marat/deSade," OB in "The Hostage," "The Alchemist," "Johnny Johnson," "Peer Gynt," "Timon of Athens," "An Evening for Merlin Finch," "The Disintegration of James Cherry," "Crimes of Passion," "Rain," "Screens," "Total Eclipse," "Entertaining Mr. Sloane," "Hamlet."

CALDWELL, ZOE. Born Sept. 14, 1933 in Melbourne, Aust. Attended Methodist Ladies Col. Bdwy debut 1965 in "The Devils," followed by "Slapstick Tragedy" for which she received a Theatre World Award, "The Prime of Miss Jean Brodie," "The Creation of the World and Other Business," OB in "Colette," "Dance of Death," "Long Day's Journey into Night."

CANNING, JAMES J. Born July 2, 1946 in Chicago, IL. Graduate DePaul U. Debut 1972 in "Grease."

CAPERS, VIRGINIA. Born Sept. 22, 1925 in Sumter, SC. Attended Juilliard. Bdwy debut 1973 in "Raisin."

CAPOZZOLI, GEANINE MICHELE. Born Nov. 8, 1966 in Pittsburg, PA. Bdwy debut 1975 in "The Leaf People."

CAPOZZOLI, RON. Born Feb. 8, 1947 in Pittsburgh, PA. Studied at Pittsburgh Playhouse, HB Studio. Debut 1974 OB in "Sgt. Pepper's Lonely Hearts Club Band," Bdwy 1975 in "The Leaf People."

CARLSON, HARRY. Born Oct. 20, 1926 in Ashland, PA. Graduate Penn State U. Debut 1960 OB in "Here Come the Clowns," followed by "Missouri Legend" (ELT), Bdwy 1963 in "Luther."

CARPENTER, CARLETON. Born July 10, 1926 in Bennington, VT. Attended Northwestern U. Bdwy bow 1944 in "Bright Boy," followed by "Career Angel," "Three to Make Ready," "Magic Touch," "John Murray Anderson's Almanac," "Hotel Paradiso," "A Box of Watercolors," "Hello, Dolly!," OB in "A Stage Affair," "Boys in the Band," "Lyle," "Dylan," "Greatest Fairy Story Ever Told," "Good Old Fashioned Revue."

CARTER, DIXIE. Born May 25, 1939 in McLemoresville, TN. Graduate Memphis State U. Debut 1963 OB in "The Winter's Tale," followed by LC's "Carousel," "Merry Widow," "The King and I," "Sextet," "Jesse and the Bandit Queen" for which she received a Theatre World Award.

CARTER, MARY. Born Oct. 3, 1938 in Washington, DC. Attended Peabody Cons. Debut 1969 OB in "The Glorious Ruler," followed by "Why Hanna's Skirt Won't Stay Down," "Two by John Ford Noonan."

CASSIDY, JACK. Born Mar. 5, 1927 in Richmond Hills, NY. Bdwy debut 1943 in "Something for the Boys," followed by "Sadie Thompson," "Around the World," "Inside U.S.A.," "Small Wonder," "Music in My Heart," "Alive and Kicking," "Wish You Were Here," "Sandhog" (OB), "Shangri-La," "Beggar's Opera" (CC), "She Loves Me," "Fade Out-Fade In," "It's Superman!," "Maggie Flynn," "The Mundy Scheme," "Murder among Friends."

CELLARIO, MARIA. Born June 19, 1948 in Buenos Aires, Arg. Graduate Ithaca Col. Bdwy debut 1975 in "The Royal Family."

CHANNING, CAROL. Born Jan. 31, 1921 in Seattle, Wash. Attended Bennington Col. Bdwy debut 1941 in "No for an Answer," followed by "Let's Face It," "Proof through the Night," "Lend an Ear" for which she received a Theatre World Award, "Gentlemen Prefer Blondes," "Wonderful Town," "The Vamp," "Show Girl," "Hello Dolly!," "Four on a Garden," "Lorelei."

CHAPIN, MILES. Born Dec. 6, 1954 in NYC. Studied at HB Studio. Debut 1974 OB in "Joan of Lorraine," Bdwy 1975 in "Summer Brave."

Roger Chapman

Zan Charisse

Rik Colitti

Deborah Combs

Jeff Conaway

CHAPMAN, ROGER. Born Jan. 1, 1947 in Cheverly, MD. Graduate Rollins Col. Debut 1976 OB in "Who Killed Richard Cory?"

CHARIN, ROBIN. Born July 18 in New Jersey. Attended Boston U. Debut 1974 OB in "Let My People Come."

CHARISSE, ZAN. Born Nov. 14, 1951 in NYC. Debut 1971 OB in "Look Me Up," Bdwy bow 1974 in "Gypsy" for which she received a Theatre World Award.

CHARLES, WALTER. Born Apr. 4, 1945 in East Stroudsburg, PA. Graduate Boston U. Bdwy debut 1973 in "Grease," followed by "1600 Pennsylvania Avenue."

CHINN, LORI. Born in Seattle, WA. Bdwy debut 1970 in "Lovely Ladies, Kind Gentlemen," OB in "Coffins for Butterflies," "Hough in Blazes," "Peer Gynt," "King and I," "Children," "Secret Life of Walter Mitty," "Bayou Legend," "The Primary English Class."

CHODER, JILL. Born Dec. 14, 1948 in Pittsburg, PA. Attended NYU. Bdwy debut 1962 in "Bye Bye Birdie," followed by "Stop the World. . . . ," "The Roar of the Greasepaint," OB in "Best Foot Forward," "Your Own Thing," "Boccaccio."

CHRISTIAN, ROBERT. Born Dec. 27, 1939 in Los Angeles. Attended UCLA. OB in "The Happening," "Hornblend," "Fortune and Men's Eyes," "Boys in the Band," "Behold! Cometh the Vanderkellans," "Mary Stuart," "Narrow Road to the Deep North," "Twelfth Night," "The Past Is the Past," "Going through Changes," "Black Sunlight," "Terraces," "Blood Knot," Bdwy in "We Bombed in New Haven," "Does a Tiger Wear a Necktie?," "An Evening with Richard Nixon," "All God's Chillun."

CHRISTMAS, DAVID. Born May 2, 1942 in Pasadena, Ca. Attended Pasadena City Col., HB Studio. Bdwy debut 1970 in "Grin and Bare It," followed by "Very Good Eddie," OB in "Butter and Egg Man," "Dames at Sea," "Give My Regards to Broadway."

CILENTO, WAYNE. Born Aug. 25, 1949 in The Bronx, NY. Graduate State U. Brockport. Bdwy in "Irene," "Rachel Lily Rosenbloom," "Seesaw," "A Chorus Line."

CINKO, PAULA. Born Dec. 14, 1950. Debut 1972 OB in "A Quarter for the Ladies Room." Bdwy debut 1974 in "Good News," followed by "Candide."

CIOFFI, CHARLES. Born Oct. 31, 1935 in NYC. Graduate UMinn. OB in "A Cry of Players," "King Lear," "In the Matter of J. Robert Oppenheimer," "Antigone," "Whistle in the Dark," "Hamlet" (LC).

CISSEL, CHUCK. Born Oct. 3, 1948 in Tulsa, OK. Graduate UOkla. Bdwy debut 1971 in "Purlie," followed by "Lost in the Stars," "Via Galactica," "Don't Bother Me, I Can't Cope," "A Chorus Line."

CLARK, JOSH. Born Aug. 16, 1955 in Bethesda, MD. Attended NC Sch. of Arts. Debut 1976 in "The Old Glory."

CLARKE, RICHARD. Born Jan. 31, 1933 in Eng. Graduate UReading. With LCRep in "St. Joan," "Tiger at the Gates," "Cyrano de Bergerac," Bdwy debut 1970 in "Conduct Unbecoming," OB in "Old Glory."

CLARKSON, JOHN. Born Jan. 19, 1932 in London. Graduate Oxford U. NY debut OB 1971 in "Murderous Angels," followed by "An Evening with Ma Bell," "Staircase," Bdwy (1973) in "No Sex Please, We're British," "My Fair Lady."

CLAY, LOUISE. Born Mar. 3, 1938 in Lafayette, La. LSU graduate. Bdwy debut 1966 in "Marat/deSade," followed by "Mike Downstairs," OB in "Rondelay," "The Hot l Baltimore."

CLOSE, GLENN. Born Mar. 19, 1947 in Greenwich, CT. Graduate William & Mary Col. Bdwy debut 1974 with Phoenix Co. in "Love for Love," "Member of the Wedding," and "Rules of the Game," followed by "Rex."

COATES, CAROLYN. Born Apr. 29, 1930 in Oklahoma City, OK. Attended UCLA. OB in "The Innocents," "The Balcony," "Electra," "The Trojan Women" for which she received a Theatre World Award, "A Whitman Portrait," "Party on Greenwich Avenue," "Club Bedroom," "A Scent of Flowers," "Effect of Gamma Rays on Man-in-the-Moon Marigolds," LCRep's "Country Wife," "Condemned of Altona," "Caucasian Chalk Circle," and "Disintegration of James Cherry," Bdwy in "Death of Bessie Smith," "American Dream," "Fire!," "All Over."

COFFIN, FREDERICK. Born Jan. 16, 1943 in Detroit, MI. Graduate UMich. Debut 1971 OB in "Basic Training of Pavlo Hummel," followed by "Much Ado about Nothing," "King Lear," "As You Like It," "Boom Boom Room," "Merry Wives of Windsor," "Secret Service," "Boy Meets Girl," Bdwy bow 1975 in "We Interrupt This Program."

COHEN, MARGERY. Born June 24, 1947 in Chicago, IL. Attended UWisc, UChicago. Bdwy debut 1968 in "Fiddler on the Roof," followed by "Jacques Brel Is Alive. . . . ," OB in "Berlin to Broadway," "By Bernstein."

COLE, KAY. Born Jan. 13, 1948 in Miami, Fl. Bdwy debut 1961 in "Bye Bye Birdie," followed by "Stop the World I Want to Get Off," "Roar of the Greasepaint . . . ," "Hair," "Jesus Christ Superstar," "Words and Music," "Chorus Line," OB in "The Cradle Will Rock," "Two if by Sea," "Rainbow," "White Nights," "Sgt. Pepper's Lonely Hearts Club Band."

COLITTI, RIK. Born Feb. 1, 1934 in NYC. Graduate USCal. Deput OB 1961 in "Montserrat," followed by "One Flew over the Cuckoo's Nest," "Gandhi," "The Queen and the Rebels," "Threepenny Opera," Bdwy bow 1975 in "The Ritz."

COLKER, JERRY. Born Mar. 16, 1955 in Los Angeles, CA. Attended Harvard. Deput 1975 OB in "Tenderloin."

COLLENS, GINA. Born in Hollywood, CA. Attended UCLA, USCal. Bdwy deput 1966 in "The Rose Tattoo," followed by "Naomi" (OB).

COLLINS, PAUL. Born July 25, 1937 in London. Attended City and State Col. in Los Angeles. OB in "Say Nothing," "Cambridge Circus," "The Devils," Bdwy in "Royal Hunt of the Sun," "A Minor Adjustment."

COLLINS, STEPHEN. Born Oct. 1, 1947 in Des Moines, IO. Graduate Amherst Col. Bdwy debut 1972 in "Moonchildren," followed by "No Sex Please, We're British" "The Ritz," OB in "Twelfth Night," "More Than You Deserve," "Macbeth" (LC), " Last Days of British Honduras."

COLLINS, SUZANNE. Born in San Francisco, CA. Graduate USan Francisco. Deput 1975 OB in "Trelawny of the Wells."

COLODNER, JOEL. Born May 1, 1946 in Brooklyn, NY. Graduate Cornell U, SMU. Bdwy debut 1973 with CC Acting Co. in "Three Sisters," "Beggar's Opera," "Measure for Measure," OB in "Do I Hear a Waltz?," "A Memory of Two Mondays," "They Knew What They Wanted."

COLTON, CHEVI. Born in NYC. Attended Hunter Col. OB in "Time of Storm," "Insect Comedy" (CC). "The Adding Machine," "O Marry Me," "Penny Change," "The Mad Show," "Jacques Brel Is Alive. . . . ," "Bits and Pieces," "Spelling Bee," Bdwy in "Cabaret."

COLUMBUS, TOBIE. Born May 14, 1951 in Detroit, MI. Graduate Wayne State U. Debut OB 1974 in "Let My People Come."

COLYER, AUSTIN. Born Oct. 29, 1935 in Brooklyn, NY. Attended SMU. Has appeared in "Darwin's Theories," "Let It Ride," "Maggie Flynn," CC revivals of "Brigadoon," "Music Man," and "How to Succeed. . . . ," "Jimmy," "Desert Song," OB in "Show Me Where the Good Times Are," "Maggie Flynn."

COMBS, DAVID. Born June 10, 1949 in Reno, NV. Graduate UNev., Wayne State U. Bdwy debut 1975 in "Equus."

COMBS, DEBORAH. Born July 2, 1951 in Tucson, AZ. Attended UOkla., AMDA. Deput 1974 OB in "The Boy Friend," followed by "Maggie Flynn" (ELT).

CONAWAY, JEFF. Born Oct. 5, 1950 in NYC. Attended NYU. Bdwy debut 1960 in "All the Way Home," followed by "Grease."

CONNELLY, R. BRUCE. Born Aug. 22, 1949 in Meriden, CT. Graduate S. Conn. State Col. Deput 1975 OB in "Godspell."

CONNOLLEY, DENISE. Born Nov. 19, 1951 in Brooklyn, NY. Attended HB Studio. Debut 1974 OB in "Let My People Come."

CONWAY, KEVIN. Born May 29, 1942 in NYC. Debut 1968 OB in "Muzeeka," followed by "Saved," "Plough and the Stars," "One Flew over the Cuckoo's Nest," "When You Comin' Back, Red Ryder?," "Long Day's Journey into Night," on Bdwy in "Indians," "Moonchildren," "Of Mice and Men."

CONWELL, PATRICIA. Born Aug. 17, 1951 in Mexico City, Mex. Graduate Incarnate Word Col. Deput 1974 OB in "Pericles" (NYSF), followed by Bdwy bow in "Love for Love" (1974), "The Cherry Orchard"(OB).

COOLEY, DENNIS. Born May 11, 1948 in Huntington Park, Ca. Attended Northwestern U Bdwy debut 1970 in "Hair," followed by "Jesus Christ Superstar," "Creation of the World and Other Business," "Where's Charley?," "Shenandoah"

COONEY, DENNIS. Born Sept. 19, 1938 in NYC. Attended Fordham U. OB in "Whisper to Me," "Every Other Evening" for which he received a Theatre World Award, "In a Summer House," LCR's "Tiger at the Gates," and "Cyrano de Bergerac," on Bdwy in "Ross," "Love and Kisses," "Lion in Winter," "The Last of Mrs. Lincoln," "Sherlock Holmes."

COOTE, ROBERT. Born Feb. 4, 1909 in London. Bdwy debut 1953 in "The Love of Four Colonels," followed by "Dear Charles," "My Fair Lady" (1956, 1976), "Jockey Club Stakes."

Richard Council   **Lindsay Crouse**   **Jack Davidson**   **Toni Darnay**   **Richard DeFabees**

COPELAND, JOAN. Born June 1, 1922 in NYC. Attended Bklyn Col., AADA. Debut 1945. OB in "Romeo and Juliet," followed by "Othello," "Conversation Piece," "Delightful Season," "End of Summer," Bdwy in "Sundown Beach," "Detective Story," "Not for Children," "Handful of Fire," "Something More," "The Price," "Two by Two," "Pal Joey."

CORMAN, PAUL A. Born Apr. 22, 1946 in Dallas, TX. Graduate Antioch Col., NYU. Debut 1976 in "Maggie Flynn."

COSTER, NICOLAS. Born Dec. 3, 1934 in London. Attended Neighborhood Playhouse. Bdwy bow 1960 in "Becket," followed by "90 Day Mistress," "But Seriously," "Twigs," OB in "Epitaph for George Dillon," "Shadow and Substance," "Thracian Horses," "O, Say Can You See," "Happy Birthday, Wanda June," "Naomi Court.," "Old Glory."

COUNCIL, RICHARD. Born Oct. 1, 1947 in Tampa, Fl Graduate UFla. Debut 1974 in "Merchant of Venice," followed by "Ghost Dance," "Look We've Come Through," "Arms and the Man.", Bdwy 1975 in "The Royal Family."

COURT, GERALDINE. Born July 28, 1942 in Binghamton, NY. Attended AADA. Debut 1968 OB in "Possibilities," followed by "Medea," "Lower Depths," "Midsummer."

COWLES, MATTHEW. Born Sept. 28, 1944 in NYC. Attended Neighborhood Playhouse. Bdwy bow 1966 in "Malcolm," "Sweet Bird of Youth," OB in "King John," "The Indian Wants the Bronx," "Triple Play," "Stop, You're Killing Me!," "The Time of Your Life," "Foursome," "Kid Champion."

CRAIG, JOEL. Born Apr. 26 in NYC. Attended Brandeis U. Bdwy debut 1961 in "Subways Are for Sleeping," followed by "Nowhere to Go but Up," "Hello, Dolly!," "Follies," "Out of This World" (OB), "Cyrano," "Very Good Eddie."

CROMWELL, J. T. Born Mar. 4, 1935 in Ann Arbor, MI. Graduate UCinn. Bdwy bow 1965 in "Half a Sixpence," followed by "Jacques Brel Is Alive . . . " (OB), "1600 Pennsylvania Avenue."

CRONIN, JANE. Born Apr. 4, 1936 in Boston, MA. Attended Boston U. Bdwy debut 1965 in "Postmark Zero," OB in "Bald Soprano," "One Flew over the Cuckoo's Nest," "Hot 1 Baltimore."

CROSSLEY, KAREN. Born May 20 in Cleveland, OH. Attended Case Western Reserve. Bdwy debut 1975 in "Very Good Eddie."

CROUSE, LINDSAY ANN. Born May 12, 1948 in NYC. Graduate Radcliffe. Bdwy debut 1972 in "Much Ado about Nothing," followed OB by "The Foursome," "Fishing," "Long Day's Journey into Night."

CROXTON, DARRYL. Born Apr. 5, 1946 in Baltimore, MD. Attended AADA. Appeared OB in "Volpone," "Murder in the Cathedral," "The Taking of Miss Janie," "Volpone," "Old Glory," Bdwy debut 1969 in "Indians."

CULLUM, JOHN. Born Mar. 2, 1930 in Knoxville, TN. Graduate U. Tenn. Bdwy bow 1960 in "Camelot," followed by "Infidel Caesar," "The Rehearsal," "Hamlet," "On A Clear Day You Can See Forever" for which he received a Theatre World Award, "Man of LaMancha," "1776," "Vivat! Vivat Regina!," "Shenandoah," OB in "Three Hand Reel," "The Elizabethans," "Carousel," "In the Voodoo Parlor of Marie Leveau," "The King and I" (JB).

CURRY, CHRISTOPHER. Born Oct. 22, 1948, in Grand Rapids, MI. Graduate UMich. Debut 1974 OB in "When You Comin' Back, Red Ryder?" followed by "The Cherry Orchard," "Spelling Bee."

CURTIS, ROBBI. Born Sept. 4, 1943 in Boston, MA. Graduate Emmanuel Col. Debut 1976 in ELT's "Follies."

CWIKOWSKI, BILL. Born Aug. 4, 1945 in Newark, NJ. Graduate Monmouth and Smith Cols. Debut 1972 OB in "Charlie the Chicken," followed by "Summer Brave," "Desperate Hours," "Mandragola," "Two by John Ford Noonan."

DAMON, CATHRYN. Born Sept. 11 in Seattle, WA. Bdwy debut 1954 in "By the Beautiful Sea," followed by "The Vamp," "Shinbone Alley," "A Family Affair," "Foxy," "Flora, The Red Menace," "UTBU," "Come Summer," "Criss-Crossing," "A Place for Polly," "Last of the Red Hot Lovers," OB in "Boys from Syracuse," "Secret Life of Walter Mitty," "Show Me Where The Good Times Are," "Effect of Gamma Rays on Man-in-the-Moon Marigolds," "Siamese Connections," "Prodigal," "Down by the River . . .," "Sweet Bird of Youth."

DANA, LEORA. Born Apr. 1, 1923 in NYC. Attended Barnard Col., RADA. Bdwy debut 1947 in "Madwoman of Chaillot," followed by "Happy Time," "Point of No Return," "Sabrina Fair," "Best Man," "Beekman Place," "The Last of Mrs. Lincoln," "The Women," "Mourning Pictures," OB in "In the Summer House," "Wilder's Triple Bill," "Collision Course,""Bird of Dawning Singeth All Night Long," "Increased Difficulty of Concentration,' "Place without Mornings," "Rebel Women."

DANA, MILDRED. Born Apr. 3 in Milford, MA. Attended AADA, NYU. Debut 1975 OB in "Another Language."

DANGLER, ANITA. Born Sept. 26 in NYC. Attended NYU. Bdwy debut 1956 in "Affair of Honor," followed by "The Hostage," APA's "Right You Are," "You Can't Take It with You" and "War and Peace," "Hamlet" (CP), "Cyrano," "Comedy of Errors" (CP), "Trelawny of the Wells."

DANIELE, GRACIELA. Born Dec. 8, 1939 in Buenos Aires. Bdwy debut 1964 in "What Makes Sammy Run?" followed by "Here's Where I Belong," "Promises, Promises," "Follies," "Chicago."

DARNAY, TONI. Born Aug. 11 in Chicago, IL. Attended Northwestern U. Debut 1942 OB in "Name Your Poison," followed by "When the Bough Breaks," "Nocturne in Daylight," "The Gold Watch," "Possibilities," Bdwy 1944 in "Sadie Thompson," followed by "Affair of Honor," "Life with Father" (CC), "The Women," "Molly," "The Heiress."

DARZIN, DAINA. Born Jan. 10, 1953 in Spokane, WA. Attended Carnegie-Mellon U. Debut OB 1974 in "Let My People Come."

DAVIDSON, JACK. Born July 17, 1936 in Worcester, MA. Graduate Boston U. Debut 1968 OB in "Moon for the Misbegotten," followed by "Battle of Angels," "Midsummer Night's Dream," "Hot 1 Baltimore," Bdwy 1972 in "Capt. Brassbound's Conversion."

DAVIDSON, LORRAINE. Born Oct. 11, 1945 in Boston, MA. Attended HB Studio. Debut OB 1974 in "Let My People Come."

DAVIES, JOSEPH C. Born June 29, 1928 in Chariton, IA. Attended Mich. State Col., Wayne U. Debut 1961 OB in "7 at Dawn," followed by "Jo," "Long Voyage Home," "Time of the Key," "Good Soldier Schweik," "Why Hanna's Skirt Won't Stay Down," "Ghandi," Bdwy debut 1975 in "The Skin of Our Teeth."

DAVILA, DIANA. Born Nov. 5, 1947 in NYC. Bdwy debut 1967 in "Song of the Grasshopper," followed by "The Prime of Miss Jean Brodie," "Two Gentlemen of Verona," "Home Sweet Homer," OB in "What the Butler Saw," "The Refrigerators," "People Are Living There," "Last Analysis," "The Seducers."

DAWSON, CURT. Born Dec. 5, 1941 in Kansas. RADA graduate. Debut OB 1968 in "Futz," followed by "Boys in the Band," "Not Now, Darling," "White Nights," "Enter a Free Man," Bdwy 1975 in "Absurd Person Singular."

DEAN, JACQUE. Born Jan. 21 in Washington, DC. Attended UMd., HB Studio. Debut 1961 OB in "Little Mary Sunshine," followed by "Gorky," "Mata Hari," Bdwy in "The Student Gypsy," "Lolita My Love," "Coco," "Dear World," "I'm Solomon," "Drat! The Cat!," "I Had a Ball."

DEARINGER, KEVIN LANE. Born Nov. 23, 1951 in Versailles, KY. Graduate UKy. Bdwy debut 1976 in "My Fair Lady."

DE BEER, GERRIT. Born June 17, 1935 in Amsterdam. Bdwy debut 1965 in "Pickwick," followed by "Illya Darling," "Zorba," "Pajama Game," "All Over Town."

DEE, BLANCHE. Born Jan. 18, 1936 in Wheeling, WV. Graduate Bklyn. Col. Debut 1967 OB in "Rimers of Eldritch," followed by "Tom Paine," "Sunset," "Yentl the Yeshiva Boy," Bdwy in "Grin and Bare It," "Yentl."

DEE, RUBY. Born Oct. 27, 1923 in Cleveland, OH. Graduate Hunter Col. Bdwy debut 1946 in "Jeb," followed by "Anna Lucasta," "Smile of the World," "Long Way Home," "Raisin in the Sun," "Purlie Victorious," OB in "World of Sholom Aleichem," "Boesman and Lena," "Wedding Band," "Hamlet."

DEERING, MARTHA. Born Mar. 6, 1949 in Worcester, MA. Graduate Carnegie-Mellon U. Bdwy debut 1972 in "Jesus Christ Superstar," followed by "Where's Charley?," OB in "Inner City," "Panama Hattie" (ELT).

DeFABEES, RICHARD. Born Apr. 4, 1947 in Englewood, NJ. Georgetown U. graduate. Debut 1973 OB in "Creeps," Bdwy 1975 in "The Skin of Our Teeth."

DeFILIPPS, RICK. Born Apr. 16, 1950 in Binghamton, NY. Attended AMDA. Debut 1976 OB in "Panama Hattie" (ELT).

DEITCH, DAN. Born Oct. 26, 1945 in San Francisco, CA. Graduate Princeton, Harvard, LAMDA. Bdwy debut 1972 in "Grease," OB in "Troilus and Cressida."

DeKOVEN, ROGER. Born Oct. 22, 1907 in Chicago, ILL. Attended UChicago, Northwestern, Columbia. Bdwy bow 1926 in "Juarez and Maximilian," followed by "Mystery Man," "Once in a Lifetime," "Counsellor-at-Law," "Murder in the Cathedral," "Eternal Road," "Brooklyn U.S.A.," "The Assassin," "Joan of Lorraine," "Abie's Irish Rose," "The Lark," "Hidden River," "Compulsion," "Miracle Worker," "Fighting Cock," OB in "Deadly Game," "Steal the Old Man's Bundle," "St. Joan," "Tiger at the Gates," "Walking to Waldheim," "Cyrano de Bergerac," "An Enemy of the People," "Ice Age."

Kaylyn Dillehay

Ed Dixon

Jamie Donnelly

William Duell

Virginia Downing

DELL, GABRIEL. Born Oct. 7, 1930 in Barbadoes, BWI. On Bdwy in "Dead End," "Tickets, Please," "Ankles Aweigh," "Prisoner of Second Ave," CC's "Can-Can," "Wonderful Town," and "Oklahoma!," "Marathon '33," "Anyone Can Whistle," "Sign in Sidney Brustein's Window," "Luv," "Something Different," "Fun City," "Lamppost Renuion." OB in "Chocolates," "Adaptation," "Where Do We Go from Here?"

DeMAIO, PETER. Born in Hartford, Conn. Attended New School, Julliard. Debut OB 1961 in "Threepenny Opera," followed by "Secret Life of Walter Mitty," "Dark of the Moon," "Welcome to Black River," "Last Breeze of Summer," Bdwy in "Billy," "Indians," "The Changing Room."

DEMAS, CAROLE. Born May 16, 1940 in Bklyn. Attended UVt., NYU. OB in "Morning Sun," "The Fantasticsk," "How to Steal an Election," "Rondelay," Bdwy debut 1965 in "Race of Hairy Men," followed by "Grease."

DEMPSEY, JEROME. Born Mar. 1, 1929 in St. Paul, MN. Toledo U-graduate. Bdwy bow 1959 in "West Side Story," followed by "The Deputy," "Spoford," "Room Service," "Love Suicide at Schofield Barracks," OB in "Cry of Players," "Year Boston Won the Pennant," "The Crucible," "Justice Box," "Threlawny of the Wells," "The Old Glory."

DENGEL, JAKE. Born June 19, 1933 in Oshkosh, WI. Graduate Northwestern U. Debut OB in "The Fantasticks," followed by "Red Eye of Love," "Fortuna," "Abe Lincoln in Illinois," "Dr. Faustus," "An Evening with Garcia Lorca," "Shrinking Bride," APA's "Cock-a-Doodle Dandy" and "Hamlet," "Where Do We Go from Here?," "Woyzeck," Bdwy in "Royal Hunt of the Sun," "The Changing Room."

DENNIS, RONALD. Born Oct. 2, 1944 in Dayton. OH. Debut OB 1966 in "Show Boat," followed by "Of Thee I Sing," "Moon Walk," "Please Don't Cry," Bdwy 1975 in "A Chorus Line."

DENNIS, SANDY. Born Apr. 27, 1937 in Hastings, NE. Bdwy debut 1957 in "The Dark at the Top of the Stairs," followed by "Burning Bright" (OB), "Face of a Hero," "Complaisant Lover," "A Thousand Clowns" for which she received a Theatre World Award, "Any Wednesday," "Daphne in Cottage D," "How the Other Half Loves," "Let Me Hear You Smile," "Absurd Person Singular," "Same Time Next Year."

de PIETRI, STEPHEN. Born Apr. 5, 1952 in NYC. Graduate Tufts U. Debut OB 1974 in "Yentl the Yeshiva Boy," Bdwy 1975 in "Yentl."

DeSHIELDS, ANDRE. Born Jan. 12, 1946 in Baltimore, MD. Graduate U Wisc. Bdwy debut 1973 in "Warp," followed by "Rachel Lily Rosenbloom," "The Wiz," OB in $"2008½."

DEWHURST, COLLEEN. Born in Montreal, Can. Attended Downer Col., AADA. Bdwy debut 1952 in "Desire under the Elms," followed by "Tamburlaine the Great," "Country Wife," "Caligula," "All the Way Home," "Great Day in the Morning," "Ballad of the Sad Cafe," "More Stately Mansions," "All Over," "Mourning Becomes Electra," "Moon for the Misbegotten," "Who's Afraid of Virginia Woolf?," OB in "Taming of the Shrew," "The Eagle Has Two Heads," "Camille," "Macbeth," "Children of Darkness" for which she received a Theatre World Award, "Antony and Cleopatra" (CP), "Hello and Goodbye," "Good Woman of Setzuan" (LC), "Hamlet" (NYSF).

DIENER, JOAN. Born Feb. 24, 1934 in Cleveland, O. Attended Sarah Lawrence Col. Bdwy debut 1948 in "Small Wonder," followed by "Season in the Sun," "Kismet" for which she received a Theatre World Award, "Cry for Us All," "Man of La Mancha," "Home Sweet Homer."

DILLEHAY, KAYLYN. Born Dec. 1, 1954 in Oklahoma City, OK. Attended Tex. Christian U., OkCityU. Debut 1976 OB in ELT's "Follies"

DILLON, DENNY. Born May 18, 1951 in Cleveland, O. Graduate Syracuse J. Bdwy debut 1974 in "Gypsy," followed by "The Skin of Our Teeth."

DIXON, DIANNE OYAMA. Born Mar. 24, 1954 in Nashville, TN. Stephens Col. graduate. Debut 1975 OB in "The Taking of Miss Janie."

DIXON, ED. Born Sept. 2, 1948 in Oklahoma. Attended OklaU. Bdwy in "Student Prince," "No, No, Nanette," OB in "By Bernstein."

DIXON, MacINTYRE. Born Dec. 22, 1931 in Everett, MA. Graduate Emeron Col. OB in "Quare Fellow," "Plays for Bleecker St.," "Stewed Prunes," "Cat's Pajamas," "Three Sisters," " 3 X 3," "Second City," "Mad Show," "Meeow!" "Lotta," "Rubbers," Bdwy in "Xmas in Las Vegas," "Cop-Out," "Story Theatre," "Metamorphoses," "Twigs," "Over Here."

DON, CARL. Born Dec. 15, 1916 in Vitebsk, Russia. Attended Western Reserve U. Bdwy debut 1954 in "Anastasia," followed by "Romanoff and Juliet," "Dear Me, the Sky Is Falling," "The Relapse," "The Tenth Man," "Zalmen," OB in "Richard III," "Twelfth Night," "Winterset," "Arms and the Man." "Between Two Thieves," "He Who Gets Slapped," "Jacobosky and the Colo-

DONNELLY, JAMIE. Bdwy debut 1965 in "Flora the Red Menace," followed by "You're a Good Man, Charlie Brown," (OB), "George M!," "Rodgers and Hart," "Rocky Horror Show."

DONOHUE, NANCY. Born Nov. 2, 1938 in Orange, NJ. Graduate Conn. Col. Bdwy debut 1964 in "Never Too Late," followed by OB "Canadian Gothic," "Prometheus Bound," "Little Eyolf," "The Runner Stumbles."

DOUGLASS, PI. Born in Sharon, CT. Attended Boston Conserv. Bdwy debut 1969 in "Fig Leaves Are Falling," followed by "Hello, Dolly!," "Georgy," "Purlie," "Ari," "Jesus Christ Superstar," "Selling of the President," "The Wiz," OB in "Of Thee I Sing."

DOWNING, DAVID. Born July 21, 1943 in NYC. OB in "Days of Absence," "Happy Ending," "Song of the Lusitanian Bogey," "Ceremonies in Dark Old Men," "Man Better Man," "The Harangues," "Brotherhood," "Perry's Mission," "Rosalee Pritchett," "Dream on Monkey Mt.," "Ride a Black Horse," "Ballet behind the Bridge," "Please Don't Cry and Say No," "Richard III," Bdwy in "Raisin."

DOWNING, VIRGINIA. Born Mar. 7, in Washington, DC. Attended Bryn Mawr. OB in "Juno and the Paycock," "Man with the Golden Arm," "Palm Tree in a Rose Garden," "Play with a Tiger," "The Wives," "The Idiot," "Medea," "Mrs. Warren's Profession," "Mercy Street," "Thunder Rock," "Pygmalion," "The First Week in Bogota," "Rimers of Eldritch," Bdwy in "Father Malachy's Miracle," "Forward the Heart," "The Cradle Will Rock," "A Gift of Time," "We Have Always Lived in the Castle."

DRAKE, ALFRED. Born Oct. 7, 1914 in NYC. Graduate Brooklyn Col. Bdwy bow 1935 in "The Mikado," followed by "White Horse Inn," "Babes in Arms," "Two Bouquets," "One for the Money," "Two for the Show," "Straw Hat Revue," "Out of the Frying Pan," "As You Like It," "Yesterday's Magic," "Oklahoma!," "Sing Out, Sweet Land," "Beggar's Holiday," "The Cradle Will Rock," "Joy to the World," "Kiss Me, Kate," "The Liar," "The Gambler," "The King and I," "Kismet," "Kean," "Lorenzo," "Hamlet," "Those That Play the Clowns," "Song of the Grasshopper," "Gigi," "The Skin of Our Teeth."

DRISCHELL, RALPH. Born Nov. 26, 1927 in Baldwin, NY. Attended Carnegie Tech. OB in "Playboy of the Western World," "The Crucible," "The Balcony" "Time of Vengeance," "Barroom Monks," "Portrait of the Artist . . . ," "Abe Lincoln in Illinois," "The Caretaker," "A Slight Ache," "The Room," "Year Boston Won the Pennant," "Time of Your Life," "Camino Real," "Operation Sidewinder," "Beggar on Horseback," "Threepenny Opera," Bdwy in "Rhinoceros," "All in Good Time," "Rosencrantz and Guildenstern Are Dead," "The Visit," "Chemin de Fer," "Ah, Wildnerness."

DRIVAS, ROBERT. Born Nov. 20, in Chicago. Bdwy debut 1958 in "The Firstborn," followed by "One More River," "The Wall," "Lorenzo," "Irregular Verb to Love," "And Things That Go Bump in the Night," "The Ritz," OB in "Mrs. Dally Has a Lover" for which he received a Theatre World Award, "Sweet Eros," "Where Has Tommy Flowers Gone," "Breeze from the Gulf."

DRUMMOND, ALICE. Born May 21, 1929 in Pawtucket, RI. Attended Pembroke Col. OB in "Royal Gambit," "Go Show Me a Dragon," "Sweet of You to Say So," "Gallows Humor," "American Dream," "Giants' Dance," "Carpenters," "Charles Abbott & Son," "God Says There Is No Peter Ott," "Enter a Free Man," "Memory of Two Mondays," "Secret Service," "Boy Meets Girl," Bdwy debut 1963 in "Ballad of the Sad Cafe," followed by "Malcolm," "The Chinese," "Thieves," "Summer Brave."

DUELL, WILLIAM. Born Aug. 30, in Corinth, NY. Attended Ill. Wesleyan, Yale. OB in "Portrait of the Artist . . . ," "Barroom Monks," "Midsummer Night's Dream," "Henry IV," "Taming of the Shrew," "The Memorandum," "Threepenny Opera," Bdwy in "A Cook for Mr. General," "Ballad of the Sad Cafe," "Ilya, Darling," "1776."

DUFF-MacCORMICK, CARA. Born Dec. 12 in Woodstock, Can. Attended AADA. Debut 1969 OB in "Love Your Crooked Neighbor," followed by "The Wager," "Macbeth" (LC), "A Musical Merchant of Venice," Bdwy 1972 in "Moonchildren" for which she received a Theatre World Award, followed by "Out Cry."

DUKES, DAVID. Born June 6, 1945 in San Francisco, CA. Attended Mann College. Bdwy debut 1971 in "School for Wives," followed by "Don Juan," "The Play's the Thing," "The Visit," "Chemin de Fer," "Holiday," "Rules of the Game," "Love for Love," "Travesties," OB in "Rebel Women."

James Dybas

Leslie Easterbrook

Brandt Edwards

Wendy Edmead

Gary Faga

DURNING, CHARLES. Born Feb. 28, 1933 in Highland Falls, NY. Attended Columbia, NYU. Bdwy in "Poor Bitos," "Drat! The Cat!," "Pousse Cafe," "Happy Time," "Indians," "That Championship Season," "Knock Knock," OB in "Two by Saroyan," "Child Buyer," "Album of Gunther Grass," "Huui, Huui," "Invitation to a Beheading," "Lemon Sky," "Henry VI," "Happiness Cage," "Hamlet," "Boom Boom Room," "Au Pair Man."

DURRELL, MICHAEL. Born Oct. 6, 1939 in Brooklyn, NY. Attended Boston U. OB 1961 in "Worm in the Horseradish," "Butterfly Dream," "Phedre," "MacBird," "A Maid's Tragedy," APA's "Cherry Orchard," "Pantagleize," "Misanthrope," "Cock-a-Doodle Dandy," and "Hamlet," "Nuts," Bdwy 1973 in "Emperor Henry IV," "Murder among Friends."

DUTTON, NANCY. Born Aug. 12, 1952 in Long Island, NY. Boston U. graduate. Bdwy debut 1976 in "Zalmen, or the Madness of God."

DVORSKY, PETER. Born Aug. 27, 1948 in Komarno, Czech. Antioch Col. graduate. Debut OB 1972 in "School for Scandal," "Lower Depths," Bdwy in "Three Sisters" (1973), "Beggar's Opera," "Measure for Measure," "Edward II," "The Time of Your Life," "The Robber Bridegroom."

DYBAS, JAMES. Born Feb. 7, 1944 in Chicago, IL. Bdwy debut 1965 in "Do I Hear a Waltz?," followed by "George M!," "Via Galactica," "Pacific Overtures."

EAMES, JOHN. Born Oct. 8, 1924 in Hartford, CT. Graduate Carnegie-Mellon U. Debut 1959 OB in "Leave It to Jane," followed by "The Boss," Bdwy 1972 in "1776."

EARLEY, CANDICE. Born Aug. 18, 1950 in Ft. Hood, TX. Attended Trinity U. Bdwy debut 1971 in "Hair," followed by "Jesus Christ Superstar," "Grease."

EASTERBROOK, LESLIE. Born July 29, 1949 in Los Angeles, CA. Stephens Col. graduate. Bdwy debut 1976 in "California Suite."

EASTON, EDWARD. Born Oct. 21, 1942 in Moline , IL. Graduate Lincoln Col., UIll., Neighborhood Playhouse. Debut 1967 OB in "Party on Greenwich Avenue," followed by "Middle of the Night," "Summer Brave."

EDE, GEORGE. Born Dec. 22, 1931 in San Francisco, CA. Bdwy debut 1969 in "A Flea in Her Ear," followed by "Three Sisters," "The Changing Room," "The Visit," "Chermin de Fer," "Holiday," "Love for Love," "Rules of the Game," "Member of the Wedding," "Lady from the Sea."

EDMEAD, WENDY. Born July 6, 1956 in NYC. Graduate NYCU. Bdwy debut 1974 in "The Wiz."

EDWARDS, BRANDT. Born Mar. 22, 1947 in Holly Springs, MS. Graduate UMiss. NY debut 1975 off and on Bdwy in "A Chorus Line."

EGAN, MICHAEL. Born Aug. 24, 1926 in Washington, PA. Graduate Bucknell U. Bdwy debut 1956 in "The Great Sebastians," followed by "Luther," "A Cry of Players," "The Incomparable Max," "The Ritz," OB in "The Real Inspector Hound," "Drums in the Night," "Duck Variations." "American Buffalo."

EHRLICH, JANICE. Born Sept. 6, 1947 in Elizabeth, NJ. Graduate WVa. U., Neighborhood Playhouse. Debut 1975 OB in "Tenderloin."

EINENKEL, ROBERT. Born Feb. 23, 1944 in NYC. Graduate Queens Col., UMich., Yale. Debut OB 1970 in "AC/DC," followed by "Screens," "Kaspar," "Self-Accusation," "The Importance of Being Earnest," "Rimers of Eldritch," "Ice Age."

ELLIOTT, PATRICIA. Born July 21, 1942 in Gunnison, CO. Graduate U. Colo., London Academy. Debut with LCRep 1968 in "King Lear," and "A Cry of Players," followed by OB in "Henry V," "The Persians," "A Doll's House," "Hedda Gabler," "In Case of Accident," "Water Hen," "Polly," "But Not for Me," "By Bernstein," Bdwy bow 1973 in "A Little Night Music" for which she received a Theatre World Award.

ELLIS, ANTONIA. Born Apr. 30, 1944 in Newport, Isle of Wight. Bdwy debut 1975 in "Pippin."

ENEY, WOODY. Born June 8, 1937 in Canberra, Aust. Attended RADA. Debut OB 1974 in "The Desperate Hours," followed by "Click."

ENGSTROM, JON. Born in Fresno, CA. Bdwy debut 1971 in "No, No, Nanette," followed by "The Pajama Game," "Very Good Eddie."

ENNIS, FLLOYD. Born June 29, 1926 in Philadelphia, PA. Studied with Stella Adler. Debut 1961 OB in "The Octoroon," followed by "Kid Champion," "Sweet Bird of Youth."

ENSERRO, MICHAEL. Born Oct. 5, 1918 in Soldier, PA. Attended Allegheny Col., Pasadena Playhouse. Bdwy in "Me and Molly," "Passion of Josef D," "Song of the Grasshopper," "Mike Downstairs," "Camino Real," "Saturday Sunday Monday," OB in "Penny Change," "Fantasticks," "The Miracle," "The Kitchen," "Rome, Rome," "The Jar."

ENTEN, BONI. Born Feb. 20, 1947 in Baltimore, MD. Attended TCU. Bdwy debut 1965 in "Roar of the Greasepaint," followed by "Rocky Horror Show," "Pal Joey," OB in "You're a Good Man, Charlie Brown," "Oh! Calcutta!," "Salvation," "The Real Inspector Hound."

EPSTEIN, PIERRE. Born July 27, 1930 in Toulouse, France. Graduate UParis, Columbia. Bdwy bow 1962 in "A Shot in the Dark," followed by "Enter Laughing," "Bajour," "Black Comedy," "Fun City," OB in "Incident at Vichy," "Threepenny Opera," "Too Much Johnson," "Second City," "People vs. Ranchman," "Promenade," "Cakes with Wine," "Little Black Sheep," "Comedy of Errors," "A Memory of Two Mondays," "They Knew What They Wanted."

ERIC, DAVID. Born Feb. 28, 1949 in Boston, MA. Graduate Neighborhood Playhouse. Debut OB 1971 in "Ballad of Johnny Pot," followed by "Love Me, Love My Children," Bdwy in "Yentl" (1975), "Shenandoah."

ESPEL, PAUL. Born Aug. 17, 1947 in Clarksburg, WV. Graduate Villanova U., Neighborhood Playhouse. Bdwy debut 1975 in "The Ritz."

ESTERMAN, LAURA. Born Apr. 12, in NYC. Attended Radcliffe, London's AMDA. Debut 1969 OB in "The Time of Your Life" (LCR), followed by "Pig Pen," "The Carpenters," "Ghosts," "Waltz of the Toreadors," "MacBeth (LC)," "The Seagull," "Rubbers," "Yanks 3, Detroit O," "Golden Boy," Bdwy 1974 "God's Favorite."

EVANKO, ED. Born in Winnipeg, Can. Studied at Bristol Old Vic. Bldwy debut 1969 in "Canterbury Tales" for which he received a Theatre World Award, OB in "Love Me, Love My Children," "Leaves of Grass." "Rex,"

EVERHART, REX. Born June 13, 1920 in Watseka, IL. Graduate UMo., NYU. Bdwy bow 1955 in "No Time for Sergeants," followed by "Tall Story," "Moonbirds," "Tenderloin," "Matter of Position," "Rainy Day in Newark," "Skyscraper," "How Now Dow Jones," "1776," "The Iceman Cometh," "Chicago."

EVERSON, JOHN. Born May 21, 1947 in Dawson, MN. Graduate UWisc. Bdwy debut 1974 in "Grease," followed by "The Ritz."

FAGA, GARY. Born Nov. 23, 1953 in Brooklyn, NY. Attended Bklyn Col. Debut OB 1975 in "Hustlers," followed by "Dance with Me," Bdwy 1976 in "Equus."

FAIRBANK, SPRING. Born Mar. 15, 1941 in Chicago, IL. Attended New Eng. Conserv. Debut 1968 in "My Fair Lady" (CC), followed by "Oh, Lady, Lady" (ELT), Bdwy 1975 in "Very Good Eddie."

FANN, ALBERT. Born Feb. 21, 1933 in Cleveland. OH. Attended Cleveland Inst. of Music. Debut 1970 OB in "King Heroin," Bdwy 1975 in "The Wiz."

FARENTINO, JAMES. Born Feb. 24, 1938 in Brooklyn, NY. Attended AADA. Bdwy debut 1961 in "Night of the Iguana," followed by "Death of a Salesman," OB in "Days and Nights of Beebee Fenstermaker," "In the Summer House," LC's "Streetcar Named Desire," for which he received a Theatre World Award.

FARR, KIMBERLY. Born Oct. 16, 1948 in Chicago. UCLA graduate. Bdwy debute 1972 in "Mother Earth," followed by "The Lady from the Sea," OB in "More than You Deserve," "The S.S. Benchley," "At Sea with Benchley."

FASO, LAURIE. Born Apr. 11, 1946 in Buffalo, NY. Graduate Denison U., Carnegie Tech. Debut OB 1974 in "Godspell," followed by "The Glorious Age," "Comedy of Errors" (CP)

FEARL, CLIFFORD. Born in NYC. Graduate Columbia U. Bdwy debut 1950 in "Flahooley," followed by "Three Wishes for Jamie," "Two's Company," "Kismet," "Happy Hunting," "Oh, Captain," "Redhead," "Let It Ride," "110 in the Shade," "Ben Franklin in Paris," "Mame," "La Plume de Ma Tante," "Dear World," "Jimmy," "My Fair Lady."

FELDER, CLARENCE. Born Sept. 2, 1938 in St. Matthews, SC. Debut 1964 in "The Room," followed by "Are You Now or Have You Ever Been," Bdwy 1969 in "Red, White and Maddox," "Love for Love," "Rules of the Game," "Golden Boy," "A Memory of Two Mondays," "They Knew What They Wanted."

FELDSHUH, TOVAH. Born Dec. 27 in NYC. Graduate Sarah Lawrence Col. Bdwy debut 1973 in "Cyrano," followed by "Drefus in Rehearsal," "Rodgers and Hart," "Yentl" for which she received a Theatre World Award, OB in "Yentl the Yeshiva Boy," "Straws in the Wind."

Conchata Ferrell

Jack Finnegan

Niki Flacks

Timm Fujii

Julie Garfield

FERNANDES, YUYE. Born Nov. 9, 1948 in Wareham, MA. Graduate Smith Col. Debut OB 1970 in "Pig," followed by "Silver Queen," "La Gente," "Inner City," "Three Musketeers," Bdwy in "Scapino" (1974), "Skin of Our Teeth."

FERRELL, CONCHATA. Born Mar. 28, 1943 in Charleston, WV. Graduate Marshall U. Debut 1973 OB in "The Hot l Baltimore," "The Sea Horse" for which she received a Theatre World Award, "Battle of Angels," "Elephant in the House," "Wine Untouched."

FIELDS, JUDY. Born in Louisville, KY. Graduate Georgetown Col., Northwestern U. Debut 1973 OB in "Summer Brave," followed by "Love Death Plays."

FINEMAN, VIVIAN. Born June 23, 1951 in Philadelphia, PA. Debut OB 1973 in "Call Me Madam," followed by "Panama Hattie."

FINKEL, FYVUSH. Born Oct. 9, 1922 in Brooklyn, NY. Bdwy debut 1970 in "Fiddler on the Roof," OB in "Gorky."

FINNEGAN, JACK. Born Mar. 21, 1927 in NYC. Attended AADA AmTh-Wing. Debut 1961 OB in "Follies of 1910," followed by "Follies" (ELT).

FIRTH, PETER. Born Oct. 27, 1953 in Bradford, Eng. Bdwy debut 1974 in "Equus" for which he received a Theatre World Award.

FITCH, ROBERT. Born Apr. 29, 1934 in Santa Cruz, CA. Attended U Santa Clara. Bdwy debut 1961 in "Tenderloin," followed by "Do Re Mi," "My Fair Lady" (CC), "Girl Who Came to Supper," "Flora the Red Menace," "Baker Street," "Sherry," "Mack and Mabel," "Henry, Sweet Henry," "Mame," "Promises, Promises," "Coco," "Lorelei," OB in "Lend an Ear," "Half-Past Wednesday," "Anything Goes," "Crystal Heart," "Broadway Dandies," "One Cent Plain."

FITZGERALD, GERALDINE. Born Nov. 24, 1914 in Dublin, Ire. Bdwy debut 1938 in "Heartbreak House," followed by "Sons and Soldiers," "Doctor's Dilemma," "King Lear," "Hide and Seek," "Ah, Wilderness," OB in "Cave Dwellers," "Pigeons," "Long Day's Journey into Night," "Everyman and Roach."

FITZPATRICK, LYNN. Born in Philadelphia, PA. Graduate Ohio Dominican Col. Bdwy debut 1972 in "Ambassador," followed by "You Never Know" (OB), "My Fair Lady."

FLACKS, NIKI. Born Apr. 7, 1943 in Daytona Beach, Fl Attended Northwestern, UMinn. Bdwy debut 1966 in "Dinner at 8," followed by "Private Lives," "Candide."

FLAGG, TOM. Born Mar. 30, 1949 in Canton, OH. Attended Kent State U., AADA. Debut 1975 OB in "The Fantasticks," followed by "Give Me Liberty."

FLANAGAN, NEIL. Born May 3, 1934 in Springfield, IL. Debut 1966 OB in "Fortune and Men's Eyes," followed by "Haunted Host," "Madness of Lady Bright," "Dirtiest Show in Town," "The Play's the Thing," "As You Like It," "Hedda Gabler," "Design for Living," "him," "Partnership," "Down by the River . . . ," "Lisping Judas," "Elephant in the House," Bdwy in "Sheep on the Runway," "Secret Affairs of Mildred Wild," "Knock Knock."

FLEISCHMAN, MARK. Born Nov. 25, 1935 in Detroit, MI. Attended UMich Bdwy debut 1955 in "Tonight in Samarkand," followed by "A Distant Bell," "The Royal Family," OB in "What Every Woman Knows," "Lute Song," "The Beautiful People," "Big Fish, Little Fish."

FLIPPIN, LUCY LEE. Born July 23, 1943 in Philadelphia, PA. Graduate Northwestern U. Debut OB 1970 in "The Playground," followed by "Shoestring Revue," "Rip Van Winkle," "Midsummer Night's Dream," "Rebirth and Celebration of the Human Race."

FLYNN, MARYELLEN. Born Aug. 22, 1940 in Boston, MA. Attended Fordham U., AADA. Debut 1963 OB in "Pullman Car Hiawatha," followed by "Babes Don't Cry Anymore," "Guimpes and Saddles," "Hot l Baltimore," "Battle of Angels," "Dancing for the Kaiser."

FOGARTY, JACK. Born Oct. 23, 1923 in Liverpool, Eng. Attended Fordham and Columbia U. Debut 1952 OB in "No Exit," followed by "Hogan's Goat," "Sweeney Todd," "The Fantasticks."

FOOTE, GENE. Born Oct. 30, 1936 in Johnson City, TN. Attended ETSU. Bdwy debut 1961 in "Unsinkable Molly Brown," followed by "Bajour," "Sweet Charity," "Golden Rainbow," "Applause," "Pippin," "Chicago," "Celebration" (OB).

FORBES, BRENDA. Born Jan. 14, 1909 in London Bdwy debut 1931 in "Barretts of Wimpole Street," followed by "Candida," "Lucrece," "Flowers of the Forest," "Pride and Prejudice," "Storm over Patsy," "Heartbreak House," "One for the Money," "Two for the Show," " Three to Make Ready," "Yester-

day's Magic," "Morning Star," "Suds in Your Eyes," "Quadrille," "The Reluctant Debutante," "Loves of Cass McGuire," "Darling of the Day," "The Constant Wife," "My Fair Lady."

FORD, SUZANNE. Born Sept. 22, 1949 in Auburn, NY. Attended Ithaca Col., Eastman Ach. Debut 1973 OB in "Fashion," followed by "El Grande de Coca Cola," "Tenderloin" (ELT).

FORSLUND, CONNIE. Born June 19, 1950 in San Diego, CA. Graduate NYU. Debut OB 1972 in "The Divorce of Judy and Jane," followed by "The Cretan Bull," "The Kiss-Off," Bdwy in "The Women" (1973), "Habeas Corpus."

FRANK, ALLAN. Born Apr. 5, 1915 in Brooklyn, NY. Bdwy bow 1941 in "Liberty Jones," followed by "I Never Sang for My Father," "Daughter of Silence," "A Shadow of My Enemy," "Skipper Next to God," "A Flag Is Born," "Collector's Item," "Angel Street," OB in "The Boss."

FRAZIER, RONALD C. Born Feb. 18, 1942. Graduate Carnegie Tech. Bdwy debut 1970 in "Wilson in the Promise Land," followed by "Enemy of the People," "What Every Woman Knows," "Death Story," OB in "Another Language" (ELT).

FREED, SAM. Born Aug. 29, 1948 in York, PA. Graduate Pa. State U. Debut OB 1972 in "The Proposition," followed by "What's a Nice Country Like You . . . ," Bdway 1974 in "Candide."

FREEMAN, ANN. Born in Portsmouth, Eng. Bdwy debut 1967 in CC's "Life with Father," followed by OB "Present Laughter," "The Home."

FREY, LEONARD. Born Sept. 4, 1938 in Brooklyn. Attended Cooper Union, Neighborhood Playhouse. OB in "Little Mary Sunshine," "Funny House of a Negro," "Coach with Six Insides," "Boys in the Band," "Time of Your Life," "Beggar on Horseback," "People Are Living There," "Twelfth Night," "Troilus and Cressida," on Bdwy in "Fiddler on the Roof," "The National Health," "Knock Knock."

FUJII, TIMM. Born May 26, 1952 in Detroit, MI. Attended CalStateU. Bdwy debut 1976 in "Pacific Overtures."

FULLER, JANICE. Born June 4 in Oakland, CA. Attended RADA. Debut OB 1975 in "Ice Age."

FULLER, PENNY. Born in 1940 in Durham, NC. Attended Northwestern U. Credits include "Barefoot in the Park," "Cabaret," "Richard III," "As You Like It," "Henry IV," "Applause," "Rex."

GABLE, JUNE. Born June 5, 1945 in NY. Graduate Carnegie Tech. OB in "MacBird," "Jacques Brel Is Alive and Well and Living In Paris," "A Day in the Life of Just about Everyone," "Mod Donna," "Wanted," "Lady Audley's Secret," "Comedy of Errors," Bdwy 1974 in "Candide."

GALE, DAVID. Born Oct. 2, 1936 in England. Debut 1958 OB in "Elizabeth the Queen," followed by "Othello," "White Devil," "Baal," "What Do They Know about Love Uptown," "Joe Egg," "The Trial," "Dumbwaiter," Bdwy 1974 in "Of Mice and Men," "Sweet Bird of Youth."

GALLAGHER, HELEN. Born in 1926 in Brooklyn, NY. Bdwy debut 1947 in "Seven Lively Arts," followed by "Mr. Strauss Goes to Boston," "Billion Dollar Baby," "Brigadoon," "High Button Shoes," "Touch and Go," "Make a Wish," "Pal Joey," "Guys and Dolls," "Finian's Rainbow," "Oklahoma!," "Pajama Game," "Bus Stop," "Portofino," "Sweet Charity," "Mame," "Cry for Us All," "No, No, Nanette," OB in "Hothouse," "Tickles by Tucholsky."

GALLEGLY, DAVID. Born June 2, 1950 in Pampa, TX. Attended WTexState U., NTex State. Debut 1975 OB in "Boy Meets Boy."

GALLERY, JAMES. Born in Auburn, NY. Graduate Lemonye Col. Debut 1967 OB in "Arms and the Man," followed by "Shadow of a Gunman," "Where Do We Go from Here," "A Doll's House," "Hamlet," Bdwy 1970 in "Wilson in the Promise Land."

GANTRY, DONALD. Born June 11, 1936 in Philadelphia, PA. Attended Temple U. Bdwy debut 1961 in "One More River," followed by "Ah, Wilderness," OB in "The Iceman Cometh," "Children of Darkness," "Here Come the Clowns," "Seven at Dawn," "Long Day's Journey into Night," "Enclave."

GARBER, VICTOR. Born Mar. 16, 1949 in London, Can. Debut 1973 OB in "Ghosts" for which he received a Theatre World Award, followed by "Joe's Opera," "Cracks."

GARFIELD, JULIE. Born Jan. 10, 1946 in Los Angeles. Attended UWisc., Neighborhood Playhouse Debut OB 1969 in "Honest-to-God Schnozzola," "East Lynne," "The Sea," followed by "Uncle Vanya" for which she received a Theatre World Award, Bdwy in "The Good Doctor," "Death of a Salesman."

Kelly Garrett　　**Larry Gates**　　**Deborah Geffner**　　**Robert Giber**　　**Eleanor Cody Goul**

GARNETT, CHIP. Born May 8, 1953 in New Kensington, PA. Attended Indiana U. Debut 1973 OB in "Inner City," followed by Bdwy "Candide" (1974), "Bubbling Brown Sugar" for which he received a Theatre World Award.

GARRETT, BOB. Born Mar. 2, 1947 in NYC. Graduate Adelphi U. Debut OB 1971 in "Godspell," Bdwy in "Grease."

GARRETT, KELLY. Born Mar. 25, 1948 in Chester, PA. Attended Cincinnati Cons. Bdwy debut 1972 in "Mother Earth" for which she received a Theatre World Award, followed by "Words and Music," "The Night That Made America Famous,"

GARRICK, BEULAH. Born June 12, 1921 in Nottingham, Eng. Bdwy debut 1959 in "Shadow and Substance," followed by "Auntie Mame," "Juno," "Little Moon of Alban," "High Spirits," "The Hostage," "Funny Girl," "Lovers," "Abelard and Heloise," "Ulysses in Nighttown," OB in "Berkeley Square."

GATES, LARRY. Born Sept. 24, 1915 in St. Paul, MN. Attended UMinn. Bdwy bow 1939 in "Speak of the Devil," followed by "Twelfth Night," "Bell, Book and Candle," "Taming of the Shrew," "Love of Four Colonels," "Teahouse of the August Moon," "Sing Me No Lullaby," "Carefree Tree," OB in "A Case of Libel," "Carving a Statue," "Hamlet."

GAVON, IGORS. Born Nov. 14, 1937 in Latvia. Bdwy bow 1961 in "Carnival," followed by "Hello, Dolly," "Marat/deSade," "Billy," "Sugar," "Mack and Mabel," "Musical Jubilee," OB in "Your Own Thing," "Promenade," "Exchange," "Nevertheless They Laugh," "Polly," "The Boss."

GAZZARA, BEN. Born Aug. 28, 1930 in NYC. Attended CCNY. Bdwy debut 1953 in "End as a Man" for which he received a Theatre World Award, followed by "Cat on a Hot Tin Roof," "Hatful of Rain," "Night Circus," "Strange Interlude," "Traveller without Luggage," "Hughie," "Duet," "Who's Afraid of Virginia Woolf?"

GEFFNER, DEBORAH. Born in August in West Virginia. Attended Juilliard, HB Studio. Debut 1975 OB in "Tenderloin" (ELT).

GENNARO, MICHAEL. Born Sept. 20, 1950 in NYC. Graduate UNotre Dame, Neighborhood Playhouse. Debut 1975 OB in "The Three Musketeers," followed by "Godspell."

GERSHENSON, SUEANNE. Born Feb. 18, 1953 in Chicago, IL. Attended Indiana U. Debut 1976 OB in "Panama Hattie."

GIBER, ROBERT. Born Oct. 13, 1950 in Youngstown, OH. Graduate UMich., Neighborhood Playhouse. Debut 1975 OB in "The Love Death Plays of William Inge."

GIBSON, JUDY. Born Sept. 11, 1947 in Trenton, NJ. Graduate Rider Col. Bdwy debut 1970 in "Purlie," followed by "Seesaw," "Rachel Lily Rosenbloom," "Rockabye Hamlet," OB in "Sensations," "Manhattan Arrangement," "Two if by Sea," "Let My People Come."

GIBSON, KAREN. (formerly Karen Zenker) Born Jan. 9 in Columbus, OH. Attended Ohio State U. Debut 1975 OB in ELT's "Three Musketeers," followed by Bdwy 1976 in "My Fair Lady."

GILBERT, ALAN. Born Mar. 4, 1949 in Seneca, KS. Graduate USyracuse. Debut 1972 OB in "No Strings," followed by "Follies" (ELT).

GILBERT, JOAN G. Born July 4, 1935 in NYC. Graduate Barnard Col., NYU. Debut OB 1976 in "The Rimers of Eldritch."

GILCHRIST, REBECCA. Born June 10, 1948 in Parkersburg, WV. Graduate WVa. U. Debut OB 1972 in "The Proposition," Bdwy debut 1974 in "Grease."

GILLETTE, ANITA. Born Aug. 16, 1938 in Baltimore, MD. Debut 1960 OB in "Russell Patterson's Sketchbook" for which she received a Theatre World Award, followed by Bdwy's "Carnival," "All American," "Mr. President," "Guys and Dolls" (CC), "Don't Drink the Water," "Cabaret," "Jimmy," "Rich and Famous" (OB).

GILMANN, LARRY. Born Apr. 3, 1950 in NYC. Graduate Franklin & Marshall Col. Debut OB 1973 in "Tubstrip," Bdwy bow 1975 in "The Ritz."

GISH, LILLIAN. Born Oct. 14, 1896 in Springfield, OH. Bdwy debut 1930 in "Uncle Vanya," followed by "Camille," "9 Pine Street," "Joyous Season," "Hamlet," "Star Wagon," "Dear Octopus," "Life with Father," "Mr. Sycamore," "Crime and Punishment," "Curious Savage," "Trip to Bountiful," "Family Reunion" (OB), "All the Way Home," "Too True to Be Good," "Anya," "I Never Sang for My Father," "Uncle Vanya" (1973), "Musical Jubilee."

GLASER, DAREL. Born Jan. 12, 1957 in Chicago, IL. Bdwy debut 1966 in "Wozzeck," followed by "Tea Party" (OB), "Cry for Us All," "Home Sweet Homer."

GLENN, BETTE. Born Dec. 13, 1946 in Atlantic City, NJ. Graduate Montepelier Col. Debut 1971 OB in "Ruddigore," followed by "Maggie Flynn," Bdwy in "Irene."

GLOVER, JOHN. Born Aug. 7, 1944 in Kingston, NY. Attended Towson State Col. Debut OB 1969 in "A Scent of Flowers," followed by "Subject to Fits," "House of Blue Leaves," "Government Inspector," "Rebel Women," Bdwy in "The Selling of the President," "Great God Brown," "Don Juan," "The Visit," "Chemin de Fer," "Holiday."

GOLDSMITH, MERWIN. Born Aug. 7, 1937 in Detroit, MI. Graduate UCLA. Studied at Old Vic. Bdwy debut 1970 in "Minnie's Boys," followed by "The Visit," "Chemin de Fer," "Rex," OB in "Hamlet as a Happening," "Chickencoop Chinaman," "Wanted," "Comedy," "Rubbers," "Yankees 3, Detroit 0," "Trelawny of the Wells."

GONZALEZ, ERNESTO. Born Apr. 8, 1940 in San Juan, PR. Attended UPR. Bdwy debut 1953 in "Camino Real," followed by "Saint of Bleecker St.," "The Innkeepers," "Cut of the Axe," "Ride the Winds," "The Strong Are Lonely," "Oh, Dad, Poor Dad. . . .," "The Leaf People," OB in "The Kitchen," "Secret Concubine," "Life Is a Dream."

GOODMAN, ROBYN. Born Aug. 24, 1947 in NYC. Graduate Brandeis U. Debut OB 1973 in "When You Comin' Back, Red Ryder?," followed by "Richard III.," "Spelling Bee."

GORBEA, CARLOS. Born July 3, 1938 in Santurce, PR. Graduate Fordham U. Bdwy debut 1964 in "West Side Story," followed by "Fiddler on the Roof," "Cabaret," "Candide," OB in "Time of Storm," "Theatre in the Street."

GORDON, CARL. Born Jan. 20, 1932 in Richmond, VA. Bdwy bow 1966 in "Great White Hope," followed by "Ain't Supposed to Die a Natural Death," OB in "Day of Absence," "Happy Ending," "Strong Breed," "Trials of Brother Jero," "Kongi's Harvest," "Welcome to Black River," "Shark," "Orrin and Sugar Mouth," "A Love Play."

GORDON, PEGGY. Born Dec. 26, 1949 in NYC. Attended Carnegie Tech. Debut OB 1971 in "Godspell."

GORDON, RITA. Born Sept. 9, 1952 in Philadelphia, PA. Attended HB Studio. Debut 1975 OB in "Boy Meets Boy."

GORDON, RUTH. Born Oct. 30, 1896 in Wollaston, MA. Attended AADA. Bdwy debut 1915 in "Peter Pan," followed by "Seventeen," "Clarence," "Saturday's Children," "Serena Blandish," "Hotel Universe," "Church Mouse," "Three Cornered Moon," "Ethan Frome," "Country Wife," "Doll's House," "Three Sisters," "Over 21," "Leading Lady," "Smile of the World," "Matchmaker," "Good Soup," "My Mother, My Father and Me," "A Very Rich Woman," "Loves of Cass McGuire," "Dreyfus in Rehearsal," "Mrs. Warren's Profession" (OB).

GORWIN, PETER. Born June 26, 1948 in Duluth, MN. Attended Loyola U. Bdwy debut 1971 in "Trial of the Catonsville 9," followed by OB "Feast of Flies."

GOULD, ELEANOR CODY. Born in Bradford, PA. Attended Elkins Col., AADA . . . where she became a teacher for many years. Returned to acting and appeared OB in "Ice Age."

GRAY, BRUCE. Born Sept. 7, 1936 in San Juan, PR. Graduate UToronto. Debut 1976 OB in "Who Killed Richard Cory?"

GREEN, MARY-PAT. Born Sept. 24, 1951 in Kansas City, MO. Attended UKan. Bdwy debut 1974 in "Candide."

GREENE, ELLEN. Born Feb. 22 in NYC. Attended Ryder Col. Debut 1973 in "Rachel Lily Rosenbloom," followed by "In the Boom Boom Room," "Threepenny Opera."

GREENE, GAYLE. Born Jan. 22, 1948 in NYC. Graduate Carnegie Tech, NYU. Debut 1975 OB in "The Love Death Plays of William Inge."

GREENFIELD, EDITH. Born Jan. 19 in Poughkeepsie, NY. Graduate NYU, Central Sch. in London. Debut 1974 OB in "The Poseur," followed by "Rites of Passage," "Rimers of Eldritch."

GREENHOUSE, MARTHA. Born June 14 in Omaha, NE. Attended Hunter Col., Theatre Wing. Bdwy debut 1942 in "Sons and Soldiers," followed by "Dear Me, the Sky Is Falling," "Family Way," "Woman Is My Idea," "Summer Brave," OB in "Clerambard," "Our Town," "3 by Ferlinghetti," "No Strings," "Cackle."

GRIFFIS, WILLIAM. Born July 12, 1917 in Hollywood, CA. Debut 1946 OB in "The Would-Be Gentleman," followed by "The Corn Is Green," "Major Barbara," "Babes in Arms," "Capacity for Wines," "No Trifling with Love," "Oklahoma" (LC), Bdwy in "A Pin to See the Peepshow" (1953), "Look after Lulu," "Here's Love," "The Cradle Will Rock," "Never Too Late," "Philadelphia, Here I Come," "Jimmy," "Cry for Us All," "Over Here," "Rex."

GRIMALDI, DENNIS. Born Sept. 30, 1947 in Oak Park, IL. Graduate Goodman Sch. Debut 1970 OB in "Me and Juliet," followed by "Workers," "Apple Pie."

David Groh   **Elaine Grollman**   **Gordon Halliday**   **Bara-Cristin Hansen**   **Charles T. Harper**

GRIMES, TAMMY. Born Jan. 30, 1934 in Lynn, MA. Attended Stephens Col., Neighborhood Playhouse. Debut 1956 OB in "The Littlest Revue," followed by "Clerambard," Bdwy bow 1959 in "Look after Lulu" for which she received a Theatre World Award, "The Unsinkable Molly Brown," "Rattle of a Simple Man," "High Spirits," "The Only Game in Town," "Private Lives," "Musical Jubilee."

GRIZZARD, GEORGE. Born Apr. 1, 1928 in Roanoke Rapids, VA. Graduate UNC. Bdwy bow 1954 in "All Summer Long," followed by "The Desperate Hours," "Happiest Millionaire" for which he received a Theatre World Award, "Disenchanted," "Big Fish, Little Fish," with APA 1961–61, "Who's Afraid of Virginia Woolf?," "Glass Menagerie," "You Know I Can't Hear You . . .," "Noel Coward's Sweet Potato," "Gingham Dog," "Inquest," "Country Girl," "Creation of the World and Other Business," "Crown Matrimonial," "The Royal Family."

GRODIN, CHARLES. Born Apr. 21, 1935 in Pittsburgh, PA. Attended UMiami, Pittsburgh Playhouse. Bdwy debut 1962 in "Tchin-Tchin," followed by "Absence of a Cello," "Same Time, Next Year," OB in "Hooray! It's a Glorious Day," "Steambath."

GROH, DAVID. Born May 21, 1939 in NYC. Graduate Brown U., LAMDA. Debut OB 1963 in "The Importance of Being Earnest," followed by "Elizabeth the Queen" (CC), "The Hot l Baltimore."

GROLLMAN, ELAINE. Born Oct. 22, 1928 in The Bronx, NY. Debut 1974 OB in "Yentl the Yeshiva Boy," followed by "Kaddish," "The Water Hen," Bdwy 1975 in "Yentl."

GUILLAUME, ROBERT. Born Nov. 30, 1937 in St. Louis, MO. Bdwy debut 1961 in "Kwamina," followed by "Finian's Rainbow," "Tambourines to Glory," "Golden Boy," "Purlie," OB in "Charlie Was Here and Now He's Gone," "Life and Times of J. Walter Smintheus," "Jacques Brel Is Alive . . .," "Music! Music!," "Miracle Play," "Apple Pie."

GUITTARD, LAURENCE. Born July 16, 1939 in San Francisco, CA. Graduate Stanford U. Bdwy debut 1965 in "Baker Street," followed by "Anya," "Man of La Mancha," "A Little Night Music" for which he received a Theatre World Award, "Rodgers and Hart."

GULACK, MAX. Born May 19, 1928 in NYC. Graduate CCNY, Columbia U. Debut OB 1952 in "Bonds of Interest," followed by "Warrior's Husband," "Worm in the Horseradish," "Marcus in the High Grass," "Country Scandal," "Song for the First of May," "Threepenny Opera."

GUNN, MOSES. Born Oct. 2, 1929 in St. Louis, MO. Graduate TN. AIU, UKan. OB in "Measure for Measure," "Bohikee Creek," "Day of Absence," "Happy Ending," "Baal," "Hard Travelin'," "Lonesome Train," "In White America," "The Blacks," "Titus Andronicus," "Song of the Lusitanian Bogey," "Summer of the 17th Doll," "Kongi's Harvest," "Daddy Goodness," "Cities in Bezique," "Perfect Party," "To Be Young, Gifted and Black," "Sty of the Blind Pig," "Twelfth Night," Bdwy in "A Hand Is on the Gate," "Othello," "First Breeze of Summer." "The Poison Tree."

GUTIERREZ, GERALD. Born Feb. 3, 1950 in Brooklyn, NY. Graduate SUNY Stony Brook, Juilliard. Debut 1972 OB in "School for Scandal," followed by "Lower Depths," "U.S.A.," "The Hostage," "The Time of Your Life," Bdwy 1973 in "Measure for Measure," "Beggar's Opera," "Scapin," "Three Sisters."

HALL, GEORGE. Born Nov. 19, 1916 in Toronto, Can. Attended Neighborhood Playhouse. Bdwy bow 1946 in "Call Me Mister," followed by "Lend an Ear," "Touch and Go," "Live Wire," "Boy Friend," "There's a Girl in My Soup," "An Evening with Richard Nixon . . .," "We Interrupt This Program," OB in "The Balcony," "Ernest in Love," "A Round with Ring," "Family Pieces," "Carousel," "Case against Roberta Guardino," "Marry Me! Marry Me!," "Arms and the Man," "The Old Glory," "Dancing for the Kaiser."

HALL, MARGARET. Born in Richmond, VA. Graduate Wm. & Mary Col. Bdwy debut 1960 in "Becket," followed by "High Spirits," "Mame," "The Leaf People," OB in "The Boy Friend," "Fallout," "U.S.A.," "Midsummer Night's Dream," "Little Mary Sunshine."

HALL, PHILIP BAKER. Born Sept. 10, 1934 in Toledo, OH. Graduate UToledo. Debut OB 1961 in "Donogoo," followed by "The Skin of Our Teeth," "In White America," "The World of Gunter Grass," "The Fantasticks," "Gorky."

HALLIDAY, GORDON. Born Apr. 2, 1952 in Providence, RI. Attended RI Col., AADA. Bdwy debut 1975 in "Shenandoah."

HALPERN, RICHARD. Born May 18, 1948 in The Bronx, NY. Graduate Columbia U. Debut 1976 OB in "Maggie Flynn."

HAMILTON, ALMA. Born Nov. 27, 1886 in Crystal Springs, MS. Attended Goodnight Col. Debut OB 1972 in "Life and Times of Joseph Stalin," Bdwy 1975 in "A Letter to Queen Victoria."

HAMILTON, ROGER. Born in San Diego, CA., May 2, 1928. Attended San Diego Col., RADA. OB in "Merchant of Venice," "Hamlet," "Live Like Pigs," "Hotel Passionato," "Sjt. Musgrave's Dance," Bdwy in "Someone Waiting," "Separate Tables," "Little Moon of Alban," "Luther," "The Deputy," "Rosencrantz and Guildenstern Are Dead," "The Rothschilds," "Pippin."

HANEY, MICHAEL. Born Dec. 12, 1949 in Annapolis, MD. Graduate Catholic U. Bdwy debut 1976 in "Zalmen or the Madness of God."

HANLEY, KATIE. Born Jan. 17, 1949 in Evanston, IL. Attended Carnegie-Mellon U. Debut 1971 OB in "Godspell," followed by "Grease."

HANSEN, BARA-CRISTIN. Born Feb. 26, 1955 in NYC. Graduate AADA. Bdwy debut 1975 in "Death of a Salesman."

HARADA, ERNEST. Born Oct. 20, 1946 in Honolulu, HI. Attended Syracuse U., LAMDA. Bdwy debut 1976 in "Pacific Overtures."

HAREWOOD, DORIAN. Born Aug. 6, in Dayton, OH. Attended UCincinnati. Bdwy debut 1972 in "Two Gentlemen of Verona," followed by "Over Here," "Don't Call Back" for which he received a Theatre World Award, "Streamers."

HARGER, GARY. Born Aug. 19, 1951 in New Haven, CT. Ithaca Col. graduate. Bdwy debut 1975 in "Shenandoah."

HARNEY, BEN. Born Aug. 29, 1952 in Brooklyn, NY. Bdwy debut 1971 in "Purlie," followed by "Pajama Game," "Treemonisha," "Pippin," OB in "Don't Bother Me, I Can't Cope."

HARPER, CHARLES THOMAS. Born Mar. 29, 1949 in Carthage, NY. Graduate Webster Col. Debut 1975 OB in "Down by the River Where Waterlilies Are Disfigured Every Day." "Holy Ghosts."

HARPER, J. W. Born Oct. 8, 1948 in Bell, CA. Attended Marin Col., Juilliard. Bdwy debut 1975 in "The Robber Bridegroom," followed by "Edward II," "The Time of Your Life," "Three Sisters."

HARRELSON, HELEN. Born in Missouri; graduate Goodman Theatre Sch. Bdwy debut 1950 in "The Cellar and the Well," followed by "Death of a Salesman," OB in "Our Town," "His and Hers," "House of Atreus."

HARRIS, JULIE. Born Dec. 2, 1925 in Grosse Point, MI. Attended Yale. Bdwy debut 1945 in "It's a Gift," followed by "Henry V," "Oedipus," "The Playboy of the Western World," "Alice in Wonderland," "Macbeth," "Sundown Beach" for which she received a Theatre World Award, "The Young and The Fair," "Magnolia Alley," "Montserrat," "The Member of the Wedding," "I Am a Camera," "Mlle Colombe," "The Lark," "Country Wife," "Warm Peninsula," "Little Moon of Alban," "A Shot in the Dark," "Marathon '33," "Ready When You Are, C. B.," "Hamlet" (CP), "Skyscraper," "40 Carats," "And Miss Reardon Drinks A Little," "Voices," "The Last of Mrs. Lincoln," "The Au Pair Man" (LC), "In Praise of Love." "Belle of Amherst."

HARRIS, ROSEMARY. Born Sept. 19, 1930 in Ashby, Eng. Attended RADA. Bdwy debut 1952 in "Climate of Eden" for which she received a Theatre World Award, followed by "Troilus and Cressida," "Interlock," "The Disenchanted," "The Tumbler," in APA's "The Tavern," "School for Scandal," "Seagull," "Importance of Being Earnest," "War and Peace," "Man and Superman," "Judith" and "You Can't Take It with You," "Lion in Winter," "Old Times," LC's "Merchant of Venice" and "Streetcar Named Desire," "Royal Family."

HARRIS, TOM. Born Feb. 17, 1949 in Kingston, PA. Graduate King's Col. Debut 1971 OB in "The Basic Training of Pavlo Hummel," followed by "Fishing," Bdwy bow 1972 in "Grease."

HARTZ, BEVERLY. Born Feb. 20 in Pittsburgh, PA. Graduate Ohio U. Debut 1975 OB in ELT's "Tenderloin."

HARVEY, KENNETH. Born Dec. 25, 1918 in Montreal, Can. Bdwy debut 1951 in "Top Banana," followed by "John Murray Anderson's Almanac," "Grand Prize," "Pipe Dream," OB in "Phoenix '55," "Augusta," "The Old Glory."

HATTAN, MARK. Born Mar. 21, 1952 in Portland, OR. Graduate UVa. Debut 1975 OB in "Our Father," followed by ELT's "Maggie Flynn."

HAUSMAN, ELAINE. Born June 8, 1949 in Sacramento, CA. Graduate UCal., Juilliard. Bdwy debut 1975 in "The Robber Bridegroom," followed by "Edward II," "The Time of Your Life," "Three Sisters."

HAVOC, JUNE. Born Nov. 8, 1916 in Seattle, WA. Bdwy debut 1936 in "Forbidden Melody," followed by "The Women," "Pal Joey," "Mexican Hay-

245

| **Every Hayes** | **Barbara Heuman** | **Joel Higgins** | **Jane Hoffman** | **John Holly** |

ride," "Sadie Thompson," "The Ryan Girl," "Dunnigan's Daughter," "Dream Girl," "Affairs of State," "The Infernal Machine," "Beaux Stratagem," "Warm Peninsula," "Dinner at 8," "Habeas Corpus."

HAWKINS, TRISH. Born Oct. 30, 1945 in Hartford, CT. Attended Radcliffe, Neighborhood Playhouse. Debut OB 1970 in "Oh! Calcutta!" followed by "Iphigenia," "The Hot l Baltimore" for which she received a Theatre World Award, "him," "Come Back, Little Sheba," "Battle of Angels," "Mound Builders."

HAYES, EVERY. Born Sept. 1, 1949 in Montclair, NJ. OB in "Step Lively, Boys," "Croecus and the Witch," "The Flies," "Ups and Downs of Theophilus Maitland," Bdwy in "Purlie," "Don't Bother Me, I Can't Cope," "All Over Town."

HAYLE, DOUGLAS. Born Jan. 11, 1942 in Trenton, NJ. Graduate AADA. OB in "Henry IV," "Romeo and Juliet," "King Lear," "A Cry of Players," "In the Matter of J. Robert Oppenheimer," "The Miser," "Trelawny of the Wells," "Oh, Lady! Lady!," "Desperate Hours," "Panama Hattie" (ELT).

HAYNES, TIGER. Born Dec. 13, 1907 in St. Croix, VI. Bdwy bow 1956 in "New Faces," followed by "Finian's Rainbow," "Fade Out—Fade In," "The Pajama Game," "The Wiz."

HEARN, GEORGE. Born June 18, 1934 in St. Louis, MO. Southwestern Col. graduate. In NYSF's "Macbeth," "Antony and Cleopatra," "As You Like It," "Richard III," "Merry Wives of Windsor," "Midsummer Night's Dream," "Hamlet," OB in "Horseman, Pass By," Bdwy in "A Time for Singing," "Changing Room."

HECKART, EILEEN. Born Mar. 29, 1919 in Columbus, OH. Graduate Ohio State U. Debut OB in "Tinker's Dam." followed by Bdwy in "Our Town," "They Knew What They Wanted," "The Traitor," "Hilda Crane," "In Any Language," "Picnic" for which she received a Theatre World Award, "Bad Seed," "View from the Bridge," "Dark at the Top of the Stairs," "Invitation to a March," "Pal Joey," "Everybody Loves Opal," "And Things That Go Bump in the Night," "Barefoot in the Park," "You Know I Can't Hear You When the Water's Running," "Mother Lover," "Butterflies Are Free," "Veronica's Room."

HEFFERNAN, JOHN. Born May 30, 1934 in NYC. Attended CCNY, Columbia, Boston U. OB in "The Judge," "Julius Caesar," "Great God Brown," "Lysistrata," "Peer Gynt," "Henry IV," "Taming of the Shrew," "She Stoops to Conquer," "The Plough and the Stars," "Octoroon," "Hamlet," "Androcles and the Lion," "A Man's a Man," "Winter's Tale," "Arms and the Man," "St. Joan" (LCR), "Peer Gynt" (CP), "Memorandum," "Invitation to a Beheading," "Shadow of a Gunman," "The Sea," Bdwy in "Luther," "Tiny Alice," "Postmark Zero," "Woman Is My Idea," "Morning, Noon and Night," "Purlie," "Bad Habits," "Lady from the Sea," "Knock Knock."

HEMSLEY, WINSTON DeWITT. Born May 21, 1947 in Brooklyn, NY. Bdwy debut 1965 in "Golden Boy," followed by "A Joyful Noise," "Hallelujah, Baby," "Hello, Dolly!," "Rockabye Hamlet," "A Chorus Line," OB in "Buy Bonds Buster."

HENNING, DOUG. Born May 3, 1947 in Winnipeg, Can. Graduate McMaster U. Bdwy debut 1974 in "The Magic Show."

HENRITZE, BETTE. Born May 3 in Betsy Layne, KY. Graduate U. Tenn. OB in "Lion in Love," "Abe Lincoln in Illinois," "Othello," "Baal," "Long Christmas Dinner," "Queens of France," "Rimers of Eldritch," "Displaced Person," "Acquisition," "Crime of Passion," "Happiness Cage," NYSF's "Henry VI," "Richard III," "Older People," "Lotta," Bdwy debut 1948 in "Jenny Kissed Me," followed by "Pictures in the Hallway," "Giants, Sons of Giants," "Ballad of the Sad Cafe," "The White House," "Dr. Cook's Garden," "Here's Where I Belong," "Much Ado about Nothing," "Over Here," "Angel Street."

HEPBURN, KATHARINE. Born Nov. 9, 1909 in Hartford, CT. Graduate Bryn Mawr. Bdwy debut 1928 in "Night Hostess," followed by "These Days," "A Month in the Country," "Art and Mrs. Bottle," "Warrior's Husband," "The Lake," "Philadelphia Story," "Without Love," "As You Like It," "The Millionairess," "Coco," "A Matter of Gravity."

HERLIHY, ED. Born in Boston, MA. Bdwy debut 1968 in "Mame," OB in "Born Yesterday," "Rubbers," "Yankees 3, Detroit 0."

HERRMANN, EDWARD. Born July 21, 1943 in Washington, DC. Graduate Bucknell U., LAMDA. Debut 1970 OB in "Basic Training of Pavlo Hummel," followed by NYSF's "Midsummer Night's Dream," Bdwy 1972 in "Moonchildren," "Mrs. Warren's Profession" (LC).

HEUMAN, BARBARA. Born Feb. 24, 1944 in Montrose, PA. Graduate UWash. Debut 1970 OB in "Dames at Sea," followed by Bdwy in "No, No, Nanette," "Something's Afoot."

HEWETT, CHRISTOPHER. Born Apr 5 in England; attended Beaumont Col. Bdwy debut 1956 in "My Fair Lady," followed by "First Impressions," "Un-

sinkable Molly Brown," "Kean," "The Affair," "Hadrian VII," OB in "Tobias and the Angel," "Trelawny of the Wells."

HIGGINS, JOEL. Born Sept. 28, 1943 in Bloomington, IL. Graduate Mich. State U. Bdwy debut 1975 in "Shenandoah" for which he received a Theatre World Award.

HIGGINS, MICHAEL. Born Jan. 20, in Bklyn. Attended Theatre Wing. Bdwy bow 1946 in "Antigone," followed by "Our Lan'," "Romeo and Juliet," "The Crucible," "The Lark," "Equus," OB in "White Devil," "Carefree Tree," "Easter," "The Queen and the Rebels," "Sally, George and Martha," "L'Ete," "Uncle Vanya," "The Iceman Cometh."

HILL, PARKS. Born July 26, 1949 in Albemarle, NC. Graduate UNC. Debut 1976 OB in ELT's "Maggie Flynn."

HILLGARTNER, JAMES. Born Nov. 14, 1938 in Franklin, NJ. Graduate Lafayette Col., San Francisco State U. Debut OB 1975 in "Bus Stop," followed by "Tenderloin."

HINCKLEY, ALFRED. Born Sept. 22, 1920 in Kalamazoo, MI. Graduate NYU. Bdwy bow 1959 in "Legend of Lizzie," followed by "Subways Are for Sleeping," "Man for All Seasons," "Impossible Years," "More Stately Mansions," "That Championship Season," OB in "A Clearing in the Woods," "Long Voyage Home," "Diff'rent," "Rimers of Eldritch," "People vs Ranchman," "Steambath," "Harry Outside."

HINGLE, PAT. Born July 19, 1923 in Denver, CO. Graduate Tex. U. Bdwy bow 1953 in "End as a Man," followed by "Festival," "Cat on a Hot Tin Roof," "Girls of Summer," "Dark at the Top of the Stairs," "J. B.," "Deadly Game," "Strange Interlude," "Blues for Mr. Charlie," "A Girl Could Get Lucky," "Glass Menagerie," "Johnny No Trump," "The Price," "Child's Play," "Selling of the President," "That Championship Season," "Lady from the Sea."

HIRSCH, JUDD. Born Mar. 15, 1935 in NYC. Attended AADA. Bdwy debut 1966 in "Barefoot in the Park," followed OB by "On the Necessity of Being Polygamous," "Scuba Duba," "Mystery Play," "Hot l Baltimore," "Prodigal," "Knock Knock."

HOFFMAN, JANE. Born July 24 in Seattle, WA. Graduate UCal. Bdwy debut 1940 in " 'Tis of Thee," followed by "Crazy with the Heat," "Something for the Boys," "One Touch of Venus," "Calico Wedding," "Mermaids Singing," "Temporary Island," "Story for Strangers," "Two Blind Mice," "The Rose Tattoo," "The Crucible," "Witness for the Prosecution," "Third Best Sport," "Rhinoceros," "Mother Courage and Her Children," "Fair Game for Lovers," "A Murderer among Us," "Murder among Friends," OB in "American Dream," "Sandbox," "Picnic on the Battlefield," "Theatre of the Absurd," "Child Buyer," "A Corner of the Bed," "Someone's Comin' Hungry," "Increased Difficulty of Concentration," "American Hamburger League," "Slow Memories," "Last Analysis," "Dear Oscar," "Hocus-Pocus."

HOGAN, JONATHAN. Born June 13, 1951 in Chicago, IL. Graduate Goodman Theatre. Debut OB 1972 in "The Hot l Baltimore," followed by "Mound Builders," "Harry Outside."

HOLLAND, ANTHONY. Born Oct. 17, 1933 in Brooklyn, NY. Graduate UChicago. OB in "Venice Preserved," "Second City," "Victim of Duty," "New Tenant," "Dynamite Tonight," "Quare Fellow," "White House Murder Case," "Waiting for Godot," on Bdwy in "My Mother, My Father and Me," "We Bombed in New Haven," "Dreyfus in Rehearsal," "Leaf People."

HOLLANDER, DONN. Born June 9, 1946 in Wilkes-Barre, PA. Graduate Hobart Col., Oberlin Col. Debut 1976 OB in ELT's "Panama Hattie."

HOLLANDER, JACK. Born Jan. 29, 1918 in Chicago, IL. Graduate Goodman Theatre. Bdwy debut 1959 in "Miracle Worker," followed by "All the Way Home," "Gideon," "Impossible Years," "Man in the Glass Booth," "Inquest," "Birthday Party," "Zalmen, or the Madness of God," OB in "Girl of the Golden West," "Dybbuk," "Journey to the Day," "Titus Andronicus," "Comedy of Errors," "Ergo," "Phantasmagoria Historia . . . ," "Troilus and Cressida."

HOLLIDAY, POLLY. Born in Jasper, AL. Attended AL. Col., Fla. State U. Debut 1964 OB in "Orpheo," followed by "Dinner on the Ground," "Wedding Band," "Girls Most Likely to Succeed," "Carnival Dreams," Bdwy bow 1974 in "All over Town."

HOLLY, JOHN. Born May 6, 1944 in St. Louis, MO. Graduate Ariz. State U. Bdwy debut 1973 in "Grease," OB in "Call Me Madam."

HOLM, CELESTE. Born Apr. 29, 1919 in NYC. Attended UCLA, UChicago. Bdwy debut 1938 in "Glorianna," followed by "The Time of Your Life," "Another Sun," "Return of the Vagabond," "Eight O'Clock Tuesday," "My Fair Ladies," "Papa Is All," "All the Comforts of Home," "Damask Cheek," "Oklahoma!," "Bloomer Girl," "She Stoops to Conquer," "Affairs of State," "Anna Christie," "The King and I," "His and Hers," "Interlock," "Third Best Sport," "Invitation to a March," "A Month in the Country" (OB), "Mame," "Candida," "Habeas Corpus."

Elaine Hyman   **Randy Hugill**   **Anne Ives**   **Page Johnson**   **Charlotte Jones**

HOPKINS, ANTHONY. Born Dec. 31, 1937 in Port Talbot, South Wales. Attended Cardiff Col. of Music and Drama, RADA. Bdwy debut 1974 in "Equus."

HORMANN, NICHOLAS. Born Dec. 22, 1944 in Honolulu, HI. Graduate Oberlin, Yale. Bdwy debut 1973 in "The Visit," followed by "Chemin de Fer," "Holiday," "Love for Love," "Rules of the Game," "Member of the Wedding," OB in "Ice Age."

HORNE, CHERYL. Born Nov. 15 in Stamford, CT. Graduate SMU. Debut 1975 OB in "The Fantasticks."

HOWARD, DAVID. Born Sept. 10, 1928 in Mt. Kisco, NY. Graduate Cornell U. Debut 1964 OB in "Cindy," followed by "Hamp," "Hamlet."

HOWARD, JOE. Born Nov. 24, 1948 in Yonkers, NY. Graduate Hamilton Col. Bdwy debut 1976 in "So Long, 174th Street."

HOWARD, KEN. Born Mar. 28, 1944 in El Centro, CA. Yale graduate. Bdwy debut 1968 in "Promises, Promises," followed by "1776" for which he received a Theatre World Award, "Child's Play," "Little Black Sheep" (LC), "The Norman Conquests," "1600 Pennsylvania Avenue."

HOXIE, RICHMOND. Born July 21, 1946 in NYC. Graduate Dartmouth Col., LAMDA. Debut 1975 OB in "Shaw for an Evening," followed by "The Family."

HUDGINS, WAYNE. Born June 19, 1950 in Amarillo, TX. Graduate UWash. Bdwy debut 1976 in "Shenandoah."

HUDSON, TRAVIS. Born Feb. 2 in Amarillo, TX. Graduate UTex. Bdwy debut in "New Faces of 1962," followed by "Pousse Cafe," "Very good Eddie," OB in "Triad," "Tattooed Countess," "Young Abe Lincoln," "Get Thee to Canterbury," "Golden Apple."

HUGHES, BARNARD. Born July 16, 1915 in Bedford Hills, N.Y. Attended Manhattan Col. OB in "Rosmersholm," "A Doll's House," "Hogan's Goat," "Line," "Older People," "Hamlet," "Merry Wives of Windsor," "Pericles," Bdwy in "The Ivy Green," "Dinosaur Wharf," "Teahouse of the August Moon" (CC), "A Majority of One," "Advise and Consent," "The Advocate," "Hamlet," "I Was Dancing," "Generation," "How Now, Dow Jones?," "Wrong Way Light Bulb," "Sheep On The Runway," "Abelard and Heloise," "Much Ado about Nothing," "Uncle Vanya," "The Good Doctor," "All Over Town."

HUGILL, RANDY. Born in Olney, IL. Graduate UFla. Bdwy debut 1974 in "Lorelei," followed by OB "Follies."

HUGO, LAURENCE. Born Dec. 22, 1917 in Berkeley, CA. Attended UCal., Neighborhood Playhouse. Bdwy bow 1941 in "Distant City," followed by "The Skin of Our Teeth," "I'll Take the High Road," "Decision," "Born Yesterday," "Stalag 17," "Double in Hearts," "There's a Girl in My Soup," "Hamlet," OB in "U.S.A.," "Enclave."

HULCE, THOMAS. Born Dec. 6, 1953 in Plymouth, MI. Graduate N.C. School of Arts. Bdwy debut 1975 in "Equus," followed by OB in "A Memory of Two Mondays."

HUNT, LINDA. Born Apr. 2, 1945 in Morristown, NJ. Attended Goodman School. Debut 1975 OB in "Down by the River Where the Waterlilies Are Disfigured," followed by Bdwy in "Ah, Wilderness."

HUNTER, KIM. Born Nov. 12, 1922 in Detroit, MI. Attended Actors Studio. Bdwy debut 1947 in "A Streetcar Named Desire," followed by "Darkness at Noon," "The Chase," "Children's Hour," "Tender Trap," "Write Me a Murder," "Weekend," "Penny Wars," "The Women," OB in "Come Slowly, Eden," "All Is Bright," "The Cherry Orchard."

HYMAN, EARLE. Born Oct. 11, 1926 in Rocky Mount, NC. Attended New School, Theatre Wing. Bdwy debut 1943 in "Run, Little Chillun," followed by "Anna Lucasta," "Climate of Eden," "Merchant of Venice," "Othello," "Julius Caesar," "The Tempest," "No Time for Sergeants," "Mr. Johnson" for which he received a Theatre World Award, "St. Joan," "Hamlet," "Waiting for Godot," "Duchess of Malfi," "Les Blancs," OB in "The White Rose and the Red," "Worlds of Shakespeare," "Jonah," "Life and Times of J. Walter Smintheus," "Orrin," "Cherry Orchard," "House Party," "Carnival Dreams."

HYMAN, ELAINE. Born in Detroit, MI. Graduate Columbia U. Bdwy debut 1962 in "General Seeger," followed by "Say Darling," "The Norman Conquests," OB in "Javelin," "Night of the Dunce," "What the Butler Saw," "Children, Children," "Big Fish, Little Fish."

IACANGELO, PETER. Born Aug. 13, 1948 in Brooklyn, NY. Attended Hofstra U. Bdwy debut 1968 in "Jimmy Shine," OB in "One Flew over the Cuckoo's Nest," "Moonchildren," "Comedy of Errors."

ING, ALVIN. Born May 26, 1938 in Honolulu, HI. Graduate Columbia U. Bdwy debut 1959 in "World of Suzie Wong," followed by "Two Gentlemen of Verona," "Pacific Overtures," OB in "Tenth of an Inch," "Cranes and Peonies," "Coffins for Butterflies," "Six."

IRVING, GEORGE S. Born Nov. 1, 1922 in Springfield, MA. Attended Leland Powers Sch. Bdwy bow 1943 in "Oklahoma!," followed by "Call Me Mister," "Along Fifth Avenue," "Two's Company," "Me and Juliet," "Can-Can," "Shinbone Alley," "Bells are Ringing," "The Good Soup," "Tovarich," "A Murderer Among Us," "Alfie," "Anya," "Galileo" (LC), "The Happy Time," "Up Eden" (OB), "4 on a Garden," "An Evening with Richard Nixon and . . .," "Irene," "Who's Who in Hell," "All over Town," "So Long 174th Street."

IVES, ANNE. Born in Providence, RI. Attended Sargent's Sch., AmThWing. Bdwy debut 1906 in "The Chorus Lady," followed by "Point of No Return," "Masquerade," "Uncle Vanya," OB in "The Crucible," "Effect of Gamma Rays . . .," "Good Woman of Setzuan," "The Contractor," "Ice Age."

JACKSON, ERNESTINE. Born Sept. 18 in Corpus Christi, TX. Graduate Del Mar Col., Juilliard. Debut 1966 in LC's "Show Boat," followed by "Finian's Rainbow" (CC), "Hello, Dolly!," "Applause," "Jesus Christ Superstar," "Tricks," "Raisin" for which she received a Theatre World Award.

JAMES, WILLIAM. Born Apr. 29, 1938 in Jersey City, NJ. Graduate NJ State Teachers Col. Bdwy bow 1962 in "Camelot," followed by "Maggie Flynn," "Coco," "My Fair Lady" (CC & 1976), "Where's Charley?" (CC), OB in "Anything Goes," "Smith."

JAMROG, JOE. Born Dec. 21, 1932 in Flushing, NY. Graduate CCNY. Debut OB 1970 in "Nobody Hears a Broken Drum," followed by "Tango," "And Whose Little Boy Are You?," "When You Comin' Back, Red Ryder?," "Drums at Yale," "The Boy Friend," "Love Death Plays."

JANIS, CONRAD. Born Feb. 11, 1928 in NYC. Bdwy debut 1942 in "Junior Miss," followed by "Dark of the Moon," "The Next Half Four," "Brass Ring" for which he received a Theatre World Award, "Time Out for Ginger," "Terrible Swift Sword," "Visit to a Small Planet," "Make a Million," "Sunday in New York," "Marathon '33," "Front Page," "No Hard Feelings," "Same Time Next Year."

JANSEN, JIM. Born July 27, 1945 in Salt Lake City, UT. Graduate UUtah. NYU. Debut OB 1973 in "Moonchildren," Bdwy 1974 in "All over Town."

JAROWSKY, ANDREW. Born in NYC. Graduate CCNY. Debut OB 1974 in "Festival of Short Plays," followed by "Cakes with Wine," "The Boss."

JAROSLOW, RUTH. Born May 22 in Brooklyn, NY. Attended HB Studio. Debut 1964 OB in "That 5 A.M. Jazz," followed by "Jonah," Bdwy in "Mame," "Fiddler on the Roof," "The Ritz."

JARRETT, JERRY. Born Sept. 9, 1918 in Brooklyn, NY. Attended New Theatre School. Bdwy debut 1948 in "At War with the Army," followed by "Gentlemen Prefer Blonds," "Stalag 17," "Fiorello," "Fiddler on the Roof," OB in "Waiting for Lefty," "Nat Turner," "Me Candido," "That 5 A.M. Jazz," "Valentine's Day," "Tickles by Tucholsky."

JEANNETTE, GERTRUDE. Born Nov. 28, 1918 in Little Rock, AR. Attended New School. Has appeared in "Lost in the Stars," "The Long Dream," "Amen Corner," "Nobody Loves an Albatross," "The Skin of Our Teeth," OB in "This Way Forward," "Deep Are the Roots," "417," "Moon on a Rainbow Shawl," "To Be Young, Gifted and Black."

JENN, STEPHEN. Born Mar. 30, 1950 in London, Eng. Graduate RADA. Debut 1976 with Royal Shakespeare Co. in "Henry V."

JOHNSON, DOTTS. Born Feb. 3 in Baltimore, MD. Bdwy debut 1950 in "Freight," followed by "Anna Lucasta," "Death of a Salesman," OB in "Freeman."

JOHNSON, PAGE. Born Aug. 25, 1930 in Welch, WV. Graduate Ithaca Col. Bdwy bow 1951 in "Romeo and Juliet," followed by "Electra," "Oedipus," "Camino Real," "In April Once" for which he received a Theatre World Award, "Red Roses for Me," "The Lovers," "Equus," "The Enchanged," "Guitar," "4 in 1," "Journey of the Fifth Horse," APA's "School for Scandal," "The Tavern" and "The Seagull," "Odd Couple," "Boys In The Band," "Medea."

JONES, CHARLOTTE. Born Jan. 1, in Chicago. Attended Loyola, DePaul U. OB in "False Confessions," "Sign of Jonah," "Girl on the Via Flaminia," "Red Roses for Me," "Night is Black Bottles," "Camino Real," "Plays for Bleecker St.," "Pigeons," "Great Scot!" "Sjt. Musgrave's Dance," "Papers," "Johnny Johnson," "Beggar's Opera," "200 Years of American Furniture," Bdwy in "Camino Real," "Buttrio Square," "Mame," "How Now Dow Jones," "Skin of Our Teeth," "Matter of Gravity."

Kender Jones   **Bunny Kacher**   **Peter Julian**   **Mimi Kennedy**   **Michael Kell**

JONES, JAMES EARL. Born Jan. 17, 1931 in Arkabutla, MI. Graduate Mich U. OB in "The Pretender," "The Blacks," "Clandestine on the Morning Line," "The Apple," "A Midsummer Night's Dream," "Moon on a Rainbow Shawl" for which he received a Theatre World Award. "PS 193," "Last Minstrel," "Love Nest," "Bloodknot," "Othello," "Baal," "Danton's Death" (LC), "Boesman and Lena," "Hamlet" (NYSF) "Cherry Orchard," Bdwy in "The Egghead," "Sunrise at Campobello," "The Cool World," "A Hand is on the Gate," "Great White Hope," "Les Blancs," "King Lear," "The Iceman Cometh," "Of Mice and Men."

JONES, JEFFREY. Born Sept. 28, 1947 in Buffalo, NY. Graduate Lawrence U., LAMDA. Debut OB 1973 in "Lotta," followed by "The Tempest," "Trelawny of the Wells," "Secret Service," "Boy Meets Girl."

JONES, KENDER. Born Sept. 14, 1939 in Equality, AL. Graduate TexChristianU, Cornell U. Debut 1976 OB in ELT's "Rimers of Eldritch."

JOSLYN, BETSY. Born Apr. 19, 1954 in Staten Island, NY. Graduate Wagner Col. Debut 1976 OB in "The Fantasticks."

JOYCE, STEPHEN. Born Mar. 7, 1933 in NYC. Attended Fordham U. Bdwy bow 1966 in "Those That Play the Clowns," followed by "The Exercise," "The Runner Stumbles," OB in "Three Hand Reel," "Galileo," "St. Joan," "Stephen D" for which he received a Theatre World Award, "Fireworks," "School for Wives."

JULIA, RAUL. Born Mar. 9, 1940 in San Juan, PR. Graduate UPR. OB in "Macbeth," "Titus Andronicus" (CP), "Theatre in the Streets," "Life Is a Dream," "Blood Wedding," "Ox Cart," "No Exit," "Memorandum," "Frank Gagliano's City Scene," "Your Own Thing," "Persians," "Castro Complex," "Pinkville," "Hamlet," "King Lear," "As You Like It," "Emperor of Late Night Radio," "Threepenny Opera," Bdwy bow 1968 in "The Cuban Thing," followed by "Indians," "Two Gentlemen of Verona," "Via Galactica," "Where's Charley?"

JULIAN, PETER. Born Oct. 23, 1945 in NYC. Graduate CCNY, C.W. Post, HB Studio. Debut 1975 OB in "Pursuit of Happiness."

JUNG, CALVIN. Born Feb. 17, 1945 in NYC. Graduate Hillsdale Col. Debut 1972 OB in "Chickencoop Chinaman," followed by "Dawn Song," "Year of the Dragon," "A Memory of Two Mondays," "They Knew What They Wanted."

KACHER, BUNNY. Born Mar. 25, 1936 in Chicago, IL. Graduate UWisc. Bdwy debut 1975 in "Sweet Bird of Youth."

KAGAN, DIANE. Born in Maplewood, NJ. Graduate Fla. State U. Debut OB 1963 in "Asylum," followed by "Days and Nights of Beebee Fenstermaker," "Death of the Well-Loved Boy," "Madam de Sade," "Blue Boys," "Alive and Well in Argentina," "Little Black Sheep," "The Family," Bdwy in "Chinese Prime Minister," "Never Too Late," "Any Wednesday," "Venus Is," "Tiger at the Gates" (LC).

KAPEN, BEN. Born July 2, 1928 in NYC. Graduate NYU. Has appeared OB in "No Trifling with Love," "Good News," "A Memory of Two Mondays," "They Knew What They Wanted," Bdwy in "The Happy Time" (1968), "Man in the Glass Booth," "Penny Wars."

KARIN, RITA. Born Oct. 24, 1919 in Warsaw, Poland. Bdwy debut 1960 in "The Wall," followed by "A Call on Kaprin," "Penny Wars," "Yentl," OB in "Pocket Watch," "Scuba Duba," "House of Blue Leaves," "Yentl the Yeshiva Boy."

KARR, PATTI. Born July 10 in St. Paul, MN. Attended TCU. Bdwy debut 1953 in "Maggie," followed by "Carnival in Flanders," "Pipe Dream," "Bells Are Ringing," "New Girl in Town," "Body Beautiful," "Bye Bye Birdie," "New Faces of 1962," "Come on Strong," "Look to the Lilies," "Different Times," "Lysistrata," "Seesaw," "Irene," "Pippin," OB in "A Month of Sundays," "Up Eden."

KASS, ALAN. Born Apr. 23, 1928 in Chicago, IL. Graduate CCNY. Bdwy bow 1968 in "Golden Rainbow," followed by "Sugar," OB in "Guitar," "Be Kind to People Week."

KAVA, CAROLINE. Born in Chicago, IL. Attended Neighborhood Playhouse. Debut 1975 OB in "Gorky," followed by "Threepenny Opera."

KAYE, STUBBY. Born Nov. 11, 1918 in NYC. Bdwy debut 1950 in "Guys and Dolls," followed by "Li'l Abner," "Everybody Loves Opal," "Good News," "The Ritz."

KEEP, STEPHEN. Born Aug. 24, 1947 in Camden, SC. Attended Columbia, Yale. Bdwy debut 1972 in "Paul Sills Story Theatre" and "Metamorphosis," followed OB in "Clarence," "The Cherry Orchard."

KELL, MICHAEL. Born Jan. 18, 1944 in Jersey City, NY. Attended HB Studio. Debut 1972 OB in "One Flew over the Cuckoo's Nest," followed by "Boom Boom Room," "Golden Boy," "Streamers."

KELLER, JEFF. Born Sept. 8, 1947 in Brooklyn. Graduate Monmouth Col. Bdwy debut 1974 in "Candide."

KELLER, MAY. Born Jan. 25 in Bryn Mawr, PA. Graduate U. Miami. Debut 1976 OB in "Panama Hattie."

KELLERY, KATE. Born Aug. 23, 1950 in Washington, DC. Graduate Temple, Catholic U. Bdwy debut 1975 in "The Skin of Our Teeth."

KELLIN, MIKE. Born Apr. 26, 1922 in Hartford, CT. Attended Trinity Col., Yale. Bdwy bow in 1949 in "At War with the Army," followed by "Bird Cage," "Stalag 17," "The Emperor's Clothes," "Time of Your Life," "Pipe Dream," "Who Was That Lady," "God and Kate Murphy," "Ankles Aweigh," "Rhinoceros," "Odd Couple," "Mother Courage," "The Ritz," OB in "Taming of the Shrew," "Diary of a Scoundrel," " Purple Dust," "Tevya and His Daughters," "Winkelberg," "Winterset," "Joan of Lorraine," "Bread," "American Buffalo."

KELTON, RICHARD. Born Apr. 29, 1943 in Lincoln, NE. Graduate UKan. Bdwy debut 1976 in "Who's Afraid of Virginia Woolf?" for which he received a Theatre World Award.

KENAN, DOLORES. Born June 7 in Bellevue, KY. Graduate Xavier U., Goodman Theatre. Debut 1974 OB in "The Killdeer," followed by "Wedding Band," "Summer Brave," "Bus Stop," "Holy Ghosts."

KENNEDY, MIMI. Born Sept 25, 1948 in Rochester, NY. Graduate Smith College. Bdwy debut 1975 in "Grease."

KERT, LARRY. Born Dec. 5, 1934 in Los Angeles, CA. Attended LACC. Bdwy bow 1953 in "John Murray Anderson's Almanac," followed by "Ziegfeld Follies," "Mr. Wonderful," "Walk Tall," "Look, Ma, I'm Dancin'," "Tickets Please," "West Side Story," "A Family Affair," "Breakfast at Tiffany's," "Cabaret," "La Strada," "Company," "Two Gentlemen of Verona," "Music! Music!," "Musical Jubilee."

KEYES, DANIEL. Born Mar. 6, 1914 in Concord, MA. Attended Harvard. Bdwy debut 1954 in "The Remarkable Mr. Pennypacker," followed by "Bus Stop," "Only in America," "Christine," "First Love," "Take Her, She's Mine," "Baker Street," "Dinner at 8," "I Never Sang for My Father," "Wrong Way Light Bulb," "A Place for Polly," "Scratch," "Rainbow Jones," OB in "Our Town," "Epitaph for George Dillon," "Plays for Bleecker Street," "Hooray! It's A Glorious Day!," "Six Characters in Search of an Author," "Sjt. Musgrave's Dance," "Arms and the Man," "Mourning Becomes Electra," "Salty Dog Saga," "Hot l Baltimore."

KEYS, HENSON. Born Oct. 7, 1949 in Lincoln, IL. Graduate UOkla., Fla. State U. Debut 1975 OB in "Hamlet."

KEZER, GLENN. Born Apr. 2, 1923 in Okemah, OK. Graduate UOkla. Bdwy in "My Fair Lady," "Camelot," "Fade Out—Fade In," "Half a Sixpence," "Little Murders," "Trial of Lee Harvey Oswald," "The Other Man," OB in "Walk in Darkness," "Brigadoon" (CC), "Oh, Say Can You See L.A.," "Firebugs," "The David Show," "Promenade," "Threepenny Opera."

KILEY, RICHARD. Born Mar. 31, 1922 in Chicago, IL. Attended Loyola U. Bdwy debut 1953 in "Misalliance" for which he received a Theatre World Award, followed by "Kismet," "Sing Me No Lullaby," "Time Limit!" "Redhead," "Advise and Consent," "No Strings," "Here's Love," "I Had a Ball," "Man of La Mancha" (also LC), "Her First Roman," "The Incomparable Max," "Voices," "Absurd Person Singular," "The Heiress."

KILLMER, NANCY. Born Dec. 16, 1936 in Homewood, IL. Graduate Northwestern U. Bdwy debut 1969 in "Coco," followed by "Goodtime Charley," "So Long, 174th Street."

KIMBROUGH, CHARLES. Born May 23, 1936 in St. Paul, MN. Graduate Ind. U., Yale, Bdwy bow 1969 in "Cop-Out," followed by "Company," "Love for Love," "Rules of the Game," "Candide," OB in "All in Love," "Struts and Frets," "Troilus and Cressida," "Secret Service," "Boy Meets Girl."

KIMMINS, KENNETH. Born Sept. 4, 1941 in Brooklyn, NY. Graduate Catholic U. Debut 1966 OB in "The Fantasticks," followed by "Adaptation," "All My Sons," Bdwy in "Fig Leaves Are Falling," "Gingerbread Lady," "Company," "Status Quo Vadis," "Magic Show."

KINGSLEY, PETER. Born Aug. 14, 1945 in Mexico City, Mex. Graduate Hamilton Col., LAMDA. Debut 1974 OB in "The Beauty Part," followed by "Purification."

Terry Kiser

Catherine Henry Lamm

Daniel Landon

Nancy Lane

John Lansing

KIRK, LISA. Born Sept. 18, 1925 in Brownsville, PA. Bdwy debut 1945 in "Goodnight Ladies," followed by "Allegro," "Kiss Me, Kate," "Here's Love," "Mack and Mabel," "Me Jack, You Jill."

KIRSCH, CAROLYN. Born May 24, 1942 in Shreveport, LA. Bdwy debut 1963 in "How to Succeed . . .," followed by "Folies Bergere," "La Grosse Valise," "Skyscraper," "Breakfast at Tiffany's," "Sweet Charity," "Hallelujah, Baby!," "Dear World," "Promises, Promises," "Coco," "Ulysses in Nighttown," "A Chorus Line."

KISER, TERRY. Born Aug. 1, 1939 in Omaha, NE. Graduate U. Kan. Debut OB 1966 in "Night of the Dunce," followed by "Fortune and Men's Eyes" for which he received a Theatre World Award, "Horseman, Pass By," "Frank Gagliano's City Scene," "The Ofay Watcher," "Castro Complex," "In Case of Accident," "The Children," "More Than You Deserve," Bdwy in "Paris Is Out," "Shelter," "God's Favorite."

KLINE, KEVIN. Born Oct. 24, 1947 in St. Louis, MO. Graduate Ind. U., Juilliard. Debut 1970 OB in "Wars of Roses," followed by "School for Scandal," "Lower Depths," "The Hostage," "Women Beware Women," "Robber Bridegroom," "Edward II," "The Time of Your Life," Bdwy in "Three Sisters," "Measure for Measure," "Beggar's Opera," "Scapin."

KNIGHT, SHIRLEY. Born July 5 in Goessel, KS. Attended Phillips U., Wichita U. Bdwy debut 1964 in "The Three Sisters," followed by "We Have Always Lived in a Castle," "The Watering Place," "Kennedy's Children," OB in "Journey to the Day," "Rooms."

KNUDSON, KURT. Born Sept. 7, 1936 in Fargo, ND. Attended NDState U., Hamline U, UMiami. Debut 1976 OB in "The Cherry Orchard."

KOLBA, MICHAEL. Born Oct. 1, 1947 in Moorhead, MN. Graduate Moorhead U., UHawaii. Debut 1976 OB in "The Cherry Orchard."

KOLOGI, MARK. Born Mar. 23, 1954 in Jersey City, NJ. AADA graduate. Bdwy debut 1975 in "Don't Call Back," followed by "Summer Brave."

KRAUS, PHILIP. Born May 10, 1949 in Springville, NY. Carnegie Tech graduate. Bdwy debut 1973 in "Shelter," followed by "Equus."

KRAMER, JOEL. Born July 1, 1943 in The Bronx, NY. Graduate Queens Coll., UMich. Debut OB 1963 in "St. Joan of the Stockyards," followed by "Playboy of the Western World," "Measure for Measure," "Man Who Corrupted Hadleyburg," "Call Me Madam," Bdwy 1975 in "Candide."

KREITZBERG, DANNY. Born July 2, 1952 in Newark, NJ. Attended NYU. OB in "The Faggot," "The Hot l Baltimore," Bdwy debut 1971 in "The Last Analysis."

KUBIAK, TOM. Born Dec. 29, 1936 in Lackawanna, NY. Attended Actors Studio. Debut 1969 ON in "End of All Things Natural," followed by "Trial of Denmark Vesey," "Primary English Class."

KUHLMAN, RON. Born Mar. 6, 1948 in Cleveland, OH. Graduate Ohio U. Debut 1972 OB in "A Maid's Tragedy," followed by "A Chorus Line" (Bdwy 1975).

KURTZ, SWOOSIE. Born Sept. 6, 1944 in Omaha, NE. Attended USCal., LAMDA. Debut 1968 OB in "The Firebugs," followed by "The Effect of Gamma Rays. . . .," "Enter a Free Man," Bdwy 1975 in "Ah, Wilderness."

LAM, DIANE. Born Mar. 6, 1945 in Honolulu, HI. Graduate UHi., SMU. Bdwy debut 1976 in "Pacific Overtures."

LAMM, CATHERINE HENRY. Born in Washington, DC. Attended IndU, London Actors Workshop. Debut 1976 OB in "The Boss."

LAMONT, ROBIN. Born June 2, 1950 in Boston, MA. Attended Carnegie-Mellon U. Debut 1971 OB in "Godspell," followed by "Thoughts," Bdwy 1976 in "Godspell."

LANCASTER, LUCIE. Born Oct. 15, 1907 in Chicago, IL. Bdwy debut 1947 in "Heads or Tails," followed by "Mr. Pickwick," "The Girl Who Came to Supper," "Bajour," "How Now, Dow Jones," "Little Boxes" (OB), "70 Girls 70," "Pippin."

LANDERS, MATT. Born Oct. 21, 1952 in Mohawk Valley, NY. Attended Boston Cons. Debut OB 1974 in "Godspell," followed by Bdwy 1975 in "Grease."

LANDON, DANIEL. Born Dec. 29, 1950 in NYC. Bdwy debut 1974 in "Mourning Pictures," followed by "Yanks 3, Detroit 0," "Rimers of Eldritch" (ELT).

LANE, NANCY. Born June 16, 1951 in Passaic, NJ. Attended Va. Commonwealth U., AADA. Debut 1975 OB and Bdwy in "A Chorus Line."

LANNING, JERRY. Born May 17, 1943 in Miami, FL. Graduate USCal. Bdwy debut 1966 in "Mame" for which he received a Theatre World Award, followed by "1776," "Where's Charley?" "My Fair Lady," OB in "Memphis Store Bought Teeth," "Berlin to Broadway," "Sextet."

LANSING, JOHN. Born Oct. 16, 1949 in Baldwin, NY. Attended Hofstra Col. Bdwy debut 1972 in "The Sign in Sidney Brustein's Window," followed by "Grease."

LAPKA, BETSY. Born Nov. 14, 1949 in Chicago, IL. Graduate Ill. Wesleyan U. Debut 1975 OB in ELT's "Tenderloin."

LASKY, ZANE. Born Apr. 23, 1953 in NYC. Attended Manhattan Com. Col., HB Studio. Debut OB 1973 in "The Hot l Baltimore," followed by "Prodigal," Bdwy 1974 in "All over Town."

LATHRAM, ELIZABETH. Born Apr. 23, 1947 in Washington, DC. Graduate UOre. Debut 1971 OB in "Godspell," followed by "Moonchildren," Bdwy 1976 in "Godspell."

LAUGHLIN, SHARON. Graduate UWash. Bdwy debut 1964 in "One by One," followed by "The Heiress," OB in "Henry IV," "Huui, Huui," "Mod Donna," "Subject to Fits," "The Minister's Black Veil," "Esther," "Rag Doll," "Four Friends."

LAVIN, LINDA. Born Oct. 15, 1939 in Portland, ME. Graduate William & Mary Col. Bdwy bow 1962 in "A Family Affair," followed by "Riot Act," "The Game Is Up," "Hotel Passionato," "It's a Bird . . . It's Superman!," "On a Clear Day You Can See Forever," "Something Different," "Cop-Out," "Last of the Red Hot Lovers," "Story Theatre," "The Enemy is Dead," OB in "Wet Paint" for which she received a Theatre World Award, "Comedy of Errors."

LAVREN, CHRISTINE. Born Sept. 7, 1944 in Victoria, TX. Bdwy debut 1971 in "Four on a Garden," followed OB by "An Evening with Ma Bell," "Fame," "Patrick Henry Lake Liquors."

LAWLESS, SUE. Born Sept. 26 in Freeport, IL. Graduate DePaul U. Debut 1961 OB in "The Sudden End of Anne Cinquefoil," followed by "Shoemaker's Holiday," "In the Nick of Time," "Don't Shoot, Mabel, It's Your Husband," "Now," "Love Course," "Good Old Fashioned Revue."

LAWRENCE, ELIZABETH. Born Sept. 6, 1922 in Huntington, WV. Graduate UMich., Yeshiva U. Bdwy debut 1954 in "The Rainmaker," followed by "All the Way Home," "Look Homeward, Angel," "A Matter of Gravity."

LAYNE, MARY. Born June 20, 1950 in Colorado, TX. Attended Houston Baptist Col., UHouston. Bdwy debut 1975 in "The Royal Family."

LEA, BARBARA. Born Apr. 10, 1929 in Detroit, MI. Graduate Wellesley, San Fernando State Col. Debut 1961 OB in "The Painted Days," followed by "Do I Hear a Waltz?," "Follies" (ELT).

LEAGUE, JANET. Born Oct. 13 in Chicago, IL. Attended Goodman Theatre. Debut 1969 OB in "To Be Young, Gifted and Black," followed by "Tiger at the Gates," "The Screens," "Mrs. Snow," "Please Don't Cry and Say No," Bdwy debut 1975 in "First Breeze of Summer."

LEE, IRVING. Born Nov. 21, 1948 in NYC. Graduate Boston U. Debut 1969 OB in "Kiss Now," followed by "Ride the Winds," "A Visit with Death," Bdwy in "Pippin" (1973), "Rockabye Hamlet."

LeGALLIENNE, EVA. Born Jan. 11, 1899 in London, Eng./ Bdwy debut 1915 in "Mrs. Boltay's Daughters," followed by "Bunny," "Melody of Youth," "Mr. Lazarus," "Saturday to Monday," "Lord and Lady Algy," "Off Chance," "Lusmore," "Elsie Janis and Her Gang," "Not So Long Ago," "Liliom," "Sandro Botticelli," "The Rivals," "The Swan," "Assumption of Hannele," "LaVierge Folle," "Call of Life," "Master Builder," "John Gabriel Borkman," "Saturday Night," "Three Sisters," "Mistress of the Inn," "Twelfth Night," "Cradle Song," "Inheritors," "Good Hope," "First Stone," "Improvisations in June," "Hedda Gabler," "Would-Be Gentleman," "Cherry Orchard," "Peter Pan," "Sunny Morning," "Seagull," "Living Corpse," "Romeo and Juliet," "Siegfried," "Alison's House," "Camille," "Dear Jane," "Alice in Wonderland," "L'Aiglon," "Rosmersholm," "Women Have Their Way," "Prelude to Exile," "Madame Capet," "Frank Fay's Music Hall," "Uncle Harry," "Therese," "Henry VIII," "What Every Woman Knows," "Ghosts," "The Corn Is Green" (CC), "Starcross Story," "Southwest Corner," "Mary Stuart," "Exit the King," "The Royal Family."

LEIBMAN, RON. Born Oct. 11, 1937 in NYC. Attended Ohio Wesleyan, Actors Studio. Bdwy debut 1963 in "Dear Me, the Sky Is Falling," followed by "Bicycle Ride to Nevada," "The Deputy," "We Bombed in New Haven" for which he received a Theatre World Award, "Cop-Out," OB in "The Academy," "John Brown's Body," "Scapin," "Legend of Lovers," "Dead End," "Poker Session," "The Premise," "Transfers," "Room Service," "Love Two," "Rich and Famous."

LEIGH, JANET. Born July 6, 1927 in Merced, CA. Attended UPacific. Bdwy debut 1975 in "Murder among Friends."

Robert Lintner   **Sara Louise**   **Alvin Lum**   **Debra Lyman**   **Adeyemi Lythcott**

LeMASSENA, WILLIAM. Born May 23, 1916 in Glen Ridge, NJ. Attended NYU. Bdwy bow 1940 in "Taming of the Shrew," followed by "There Shall Be No Night," "The Pirate," "Hamlet," "Call Me Mister," "Inside U.S.A.," "I Know, My Love," "Dream Girl," "Nina," "Ondine," "Fallen Angels," "Red-head," "Conquering Hero," "Beauty Part," "Come Summer," "Grin and Bare It," "All over Town," OB in "The Coop," "Brigadoon," "Life with Father," "F. Jasmine Addams."

LeNOIRE, ROSETTA. Born Aug. 8, 1911 in NYC. Attended Theatre Wing. Bdwy debut 1936 in "Macbeth," followed by "Bassa Moona," "Hot Mikado," "Marching with Johnny," "Janie," "Decision," "Three's a Family," "Destry Rides Again," "Finian's Rainbow," "South Pacific," "Sophie," "Tambourines to Glory," "Blues for Mr. Charlie," "Great Indoors," "Lost in the Stars," "The Royal Family," OB in "Bible Salesman," "Double Entry," "Clandestine on the Morning Line," "Cabin in the Sky," "Lady Day," LC in "Show Boat," "A Cry of Players," and "Streetcar Named Desire."

LEON, JOSEPH. Born June 8, 1923 in NYC. Attended NYU, UCLA. Bdwy debut 1950 in "Bell, Book and Candle," followed by "Seven Year Itch," "Pipe Dream," "Fair Game," "Gazebo," "Julia, Jake and Uncle Joe," "Beauty Part," "Merry Widow," "Henry, Sweet Henry," "Jimmy Shine," "All over Town," OB in "Come Share My House," "Dark Corners," "Interrogation of Havana," "Are You Now or Have You Ever Been."

LEONARDOS, URYLEE. Born May 14 in Charleston, SC. Attended Manhat-tan Sch. of Music. Bdwy debut 1943 in "Carmen Jones," followed by "Shangri-La," "Bells Are Ringing," "Wildcat," "Sophie," "Milk and Honey," "110 in the Shade," "Bajour," "Ilya, Darling," "Dear World," "Billy Noname"(OB), "Desert Song," "1600 Pennsylvania Avenue."

LEVENE, SAM. Born Aug. 28, 1905 in NYC. Graduate AADA. Bdwy debut 1927 in "Wall Street," followed by "3 Men on a Horse," "Dinner at 8," "Room Service," "Margin for Error," "Sound of Hunting," "Light up the Sky," "Guys and Dolls," "Hot Corner," "Fair Game," "Make a Million," "Heartbreak House," "Good Soup," "Devil's Advocate," "Let It Ride," "Seidman & Son," "Cafe Crown," "Last Analysis," "Nathan Weinstein, Mystic, Conn.," "The Impossible Years," "Paris Is Out," "A Dream out of Time" (OB), "The Sun-shine Boys," "Dreyfus in Rehearsal," "The Royal Family."

LEYDEN, LEO. Born Jan. 28, 1929 in Dublin, Ire. Attended Abbey Theatre Sch. Bdwy debut 1960 in "Love and Libel," followed by "Darling of the Day," "Mundy Scheme," "The Rothschilds," "Capt. Brassbound's Conversion," "The Plough and the Stars" (LC), "Habeas Corpus."

LIDE, MILLER. Born Aug. 10, 1935 in Columbia, SC. Graduate USC, Am ThWing. Debut 1961 OB in "Three Modern Japanese Plays," followed by "Trial at Rouen," "Street Scene," "Joan of Arc at the Stake," Bdwy in "Ivanov" (1966), "Halfway up the Tree," "Who's Who in Hell," "We Interrupt This Program," "The Royal Family."

LINDIG, JILLIAN. Born Mar. 19, 1944 in Johnson City, TX. Debut 1969 OB in "Brownstone Urge," followed by "AC/DC."

LINTNER, ROBERT. Born Oct. 21, 1950 in Norfolf, NE. Graduate Midland Col. Debut 1975 OB in "The Three Musketeers," followed by "Panama Hattie."

LIPSCOMB, DENNIS. Born Mar. 1, 1942 in Brooklyn, NY. Graduate Clark-son Col., UIowa, LAMDA. Debut 1975 OB in "The Rivals," followed by "The Boss."

LIPSON, PAUL. Born Dec. 23, 1913 in Brooklyn. Attended Ohio State, The-atre Wing. Bdwy bow 1942 in "Lily of the Valley," followed by "Heads or Tails," "Detective Story," "Remains to Be Seen," "Carnival in Flanders," "I've Got Sixpence," "The Vamp," "Bells Are Ringing," "Fiorello" (CC), "Sound of Music," "Fiddler on the Roof," OB in "Deep Six the Briefcase," "The Inn at Lydda," "Golden Boy."

LISTMAN, RYAN. Born Dec. 30, 1939 in Newark, NJ. With LCRep in "St. Joan," "Tiger at the Gates," and "Cyrano de Bergerac," OB in "Utopia," "Until the Monkey Comes," "Fortune and Men's Eyes," "Spiro Who?," "Blueberry Mountain," "Midsummer Night's Dream."

LITHGOW, JOHN. Born in Rochester, NY. Graduate Harvard U. Bdwy debut 1973 in "The Changing Room," followed by "My Fat Friend," OB in "Hamlet," "Trelawny of the Wells," "A Memory of Two Mondays," "Secret Service," "Boy Meets Girl."

LITTLE, CLEAVON. Born June 1, 1939 in Chickasha, OK. Attended San Diego State U., AADA. Debut OB 1967 in "MacBird," followed by "Hamlet," "Someone's Coming Hungry," "Ofay Watcher," "Scuba Duba," "Narrow Road to the Deep North," "Great MacDaddy," Bdwy "Jimmy Shine," "Purlie," "All over Town," "The Poison Tree."

LITTLE, DAVID. Born Mar. 21, 1937 in Wadesboro, NC. Graduate William & Mary Col., Catholic U. Debut OB 1967 in "MacBird," followed by "Iphigenia in Aulis," "Antony and Cleopatra," "Antigone," "Enemy of the People," Bdwy bow 1974 in "Thieves," "Zalmen, or the Madness of God."

LITTLE, RON PAUL. Born Apr. 2, 1949 in New Haven, CT. UConn. gradu-ate. Debut OB 1973 in "Thunder Rock," followed by "Summer Brave," "The Hot I Baltimore."

LIVINGSTON, RUTH. Born March 25 in New Haven, CT. Graduate UMich., AmThWing. Debut OB 1976 in "The Rimers of Eldritch."

LoBIANCO, TONY. Born Oct. 19, 1936 in NYC. Bdwy debut 1966 in "The Office," followed by "Royal Hunt of the Sun," "Rose Tattoo," "90 Day Mis-tress," "The Goodbye People," OB in "Three-penny Opera," "Answered the Flute," "Camino Real," "Oh, Dad, Poor Dad. . . . ," "Journey to the Day," "Zoo Story," "Nature of the Crime," "Incident at Vichy," "Tartuffe," "Yan-kees 3, Detroit O."

LONG, AVON. Born June 18, 1910 in Baltimore, MD. Attended New Eng. Cons. Bdwy debut 1942 in "Porgy and Bess," followed by "Memphis Bound," "Carib Song," "Beggar's Holiday," "Don't Play Us Cheap," "Bubbling Brown Sugar," OB in "Ballad of Jazz Street."

LOONEY, PETER. Born Jan. 18, 1937 in Caldwell, ID. Graduate UNev., Neighborhood Playhouse. Debut 1976 OB in ELT's "Missouri Legend."

LOUISE, SARA. Born. Apr. 15 in Brooklyn, NY. Attended Northwestern U., RADA. Debut 1969 OB in "Of Thee I Sing," followed by "Show Me Where the Good Times Are," "Lend an Ear," "I'll Die if I Can't Live Forever," "Follies" (ELT).

LOVETT, MARJORIE. Born Oct. 4, 1932 in Long Branch, NJ. Debut 1975 OB in ELT's "Another Language."

LUM, ALVIN. Born May 28, 1931 in Honolulu, HI. Attended UHawaii. Debut 1969 OB in "In the Bar of a Tokyo Hotel," followed by ELT's "Pursuit of Happiness," Bdwy in "Lovely Ladies, Kind Gentlemen," "Two Gentlemen of Verona."

LUPINO RICHARD. Born Oct. 29, 1929 in Hollywood, CA. Attended LACC, RADA. Bdwy debut 1956 in "Major Barbara," followed by "Conduct Unbe-coming," "Sherlock Holmes."

LuPONE, PATTI. Born Apr. 21, 1949 in Northport, NY. Juilliard graduate. Debut 1972 OB in "School for Scandal," followed by "Women Beware Women," "Next Time I'll Sing to You," "Lower Depths," Bdwy in "Three Sisters," "Measure for Measure," "Next Time I'll Sing to You," "Beggar's Opera," "Scapin," "Robber Bridegroom," "Edward II," "The Time of Your Life."

LYMAN, DEBRA. Born July 17, 1940 in Philadelphia, PA. Graduate Phila. Col. Debut 1967 OB in "By Jupiter," Bdwy in "Sugar" (1972), "My Fair Lady."

LYNCH, RICHARD. Born Feb. 12, 1940 in Brooklyn, NY. Attended Actors Studio. Bdwy debut 1965 in "The Devils," followed by "Lady from the Sea," OB in "Live Like Pigs," "One Night Stands of a Noisy Passenger," "Things That Almost Happen," "12 Angry Men," "The Orphan," "Action."

LYNDECK, EDMUND. Born Oct. 4, 1925 in Baton Rouge, LA. Graduate Montclair State Col., Fordham U. Bdwy debut 1969 in "1776," followed by "The King and I" (JB), OB in "Mandragola," "A Safe Place," "Amoureuse."

LYTHCOTT, ADEYEMI. Born Feb. 19, 1948 in Boston, MA. Graduate Ober-lin Col. Debut 1975 OB in "The Taking of Miss Janie."

MacCAULEY, MARK. Born Dec. 11, 1948 in NYC. Attended UInd. Debut 1969 OB in "Crimes of Passion," followed by "Anna K," "Godspell."

MacDONALD, PIRIE. Born Mar. 24, 1932 in NYC. Graduate Harvard U. Debut OB 1957 in "Under Milk Wood," followed by "Zoo Story," Bdwy in "Shadow and Substance," "Golden Fleecing," "Big Fish, Little Fish," "Death of a Salesman," "But Not for Me."

MacMAHON, ALINE. Born May 3, 1899 in McKeesport, PA. Attended Barnard Col. Bdwy debut 1921 in "Madras House," followed by "Green Ring," "Exciters," "Grand Street Follies," "Beyond the Horizon," "Maya," "Once in a Lifetime," "Heavenly Express," "Eve of St. Mark," "Confidential Clerk," "A Day by the Sea," "I Knock at the Door," "Pictures in the Hallway," "All the Way Home," LC's "The Alchemist," "Yerma," "East Wind," "Galileo," "Walking to Waldheim," "Tiger at the Gates," "Cyrano," "Mary Stuart," "The Crucible," "Trelawny of the Wells."

MADAMA, LINDA. Born July 26, 1947 in Steubenville, OH. Graduate Bosto Conserv. Debut 1976 OB in "Panama Hattie."

MADDEN, SHARON. Born July 8, 1947 in St. Louis, MO. Debut 1975 OB in "The Hot I Baltimore."

Claire Malis   **George Maguire**   **PJ Mann**   **Terrance McKerrs**   **Marcia McClain**

MAGGART, BRANDON. Born Dec. 12, 1933 in Carthage, TN. Graduate U. Tenn. OB in "Sing Muse!," "Like Other People," "Put It In Writing" for which he received a Theatre World Award, "Wedding Band," "But Not for Me," Bdwy in "Kelly," "New Faces of 1968," "Applause," "Lorelei," "We Interrupt This Program."

MAGUIRE, GEORGE. Born Dec. 4, 1946 in Wilmington, DE. Graduate UPa. Debut 1975 OB in "Polly," followed by "Follies."

MALIS, CLAIRE. Born Feb. 17, 1944 in Gary, IN. Graduate UInd., AADA. Debut 1969 OB in "The Man with the Flower in His Mouth," followed by "Berkeley Square."

MANDIS, RENOS. Born in Athens, Greece. Attended Hunter Col., HB Studio. Debut 1972 OB in "Tarot," followed by "Ice Age."

MANN, PJ Born Apr. 9, 1953 in Pasadena, CA. Bdwy debut 1976 in "Home Sweet Homer."

MARCH, ELLEN. Born Aug. 18, 1948 in Brooklyn. Graduate AMDA. Debut OB 1967 in "Pins and Needles," Bdwy 1973 in "Grease."

MARCH, WILLIAM. Born Apr. 3, 1951 in St. Paul, MN. Graduate NYU. Debut 1975 OB in "Gift of the Magi."

MARCUM, KEVIN. Born Nov. 7, 1955 in Danville, IL. Attended UIll. Bdwy debut 1976 in "My Fair Lady."

MARGULIES, DAVID. Born Feb. 19, 1937 in NYC. Graduate CCNY. Debut 1958 OB in "Golden Six," followed by "Six Characters in Search of an Author," "Tragical Historie of Dr. Faustus," "Tango," "Little Murders," "Seven Days of Mourning," "Last Analysis," "An Evening with the Poet Senator," "Kid Champion," Bdwy 1973 in "The Iceman Cometh," "Zalmen, or the Madness of God."

MARR, RICHARD. Born May 12, 1928 in Baltimore, MD. Graduate UPa. Bdwy in "Baker Street," "How to Succeed . . . ," "Here's Where I Belong," "Coco," "The Constant Wife," "So Long, 174th Street," OB in "Sappho," "Pilgrim's Progress," "Pimpernel," "Witness," "Antiques," "Two by Tennessee."

MARSHALL, LARRY. Born Apr. 3, 1944 in Spartanburg, SC. Attended Fordham, Xavier, New Eng. Consv. Bdwy debut in "Hair," followed by "Two Gentlemen from Verona," "Midsummer Night's Dream" (LC), "Rockabye Hamlet."

MARSHALL, NORMAN THOMAS. Born Apr. 28, 1939 in Richmond, VA. Attended UVa., Hunter Col., CCNY. Debut 1966 OB in "Gorilla Queen," followed by "Boy on the Straight-back Chair," "Charlie Was Here and Now He's Gone," "The Rapists," "Home/Work."

MARTIN, LYNN. Born Nov. 13, 1945 in Wilmington, DE. Graduate UDel. Debut 1967 OB in "Shoemaker's Holiday," followed by "Damn Yankees," "The Kid," "Panama Hattie."

MARTIN, NAN. Born in Decatur, IL. Attended UCLA, Actors Studio. Bdwy debut 1950 in "A Story for a Sunday Evening," "The Constant Wife," "J. B.," "Great God Brown," "Under the Yum-Yum Tree," "Summer Brave," OB in "Saturday Night Kid," "Sweet Confession," "Lysistrata," "Much Ado about Nothing," "Phaedra," "Merchant of Venice," "Taming of the Shrew," "Hamlet."

MASIELL, JOE. Born Oct. 27, 1939 in Bklyn. Studied at HB Studio. Debut 1964 OB in "Cindy," followed by "Jacques Brel Is Alive . . . .," "Sensations," "Leaves of Grass," "How to Get Rid of It," "A Matter of Time," "Tickles by Tucholsky," Bdwy in "Dear World," "Different Times," "Jacques Brel is Alive."

MASONER, GENE. Born Jan. 22, in Kansas City, KS. Attended UKan., HB Studio. Debut OB 1969 in "Your Own Thing," followed by "White Devil," "Cherry," "3 Drag Queens from Datona," Bdwy 1975 in "Shenandoah."

MASTERSON, PETER. Born June 1, 1934 in Houston, TX. Graduate Rice U. Debut 1961 OB in "Call Me by My Rightful Name," Bdwy in "Marathon '33," "Blues for Mr. Charlie," "Trial of Lee Harvey Oswald," "Great White Hope," "Poison Tree."

MATHEWS, WALTER. Born Oct. 10, 1926 in NYC. Graduate NYU, Ohio U. Bdwy debut 1951 in "St. Joan," followed by "The Long Dream," "King Lear," "Mr. Roberts," "Equus."

MATHEWSON, JOSEPH. Born Sept. 22, 1938 in Ashland, KY. Yale graduate. Debut 1961 OB in "Tom Jones," followed by "The Sorrows of Frederick," "The Runner Stumbles."

MATSUSAKA, TOM. Born Aug. 8 in Wahiawa, HI. Graduate Mich. State U. Bdwy bow 1968 in "Mame," followed by "Pacific Overtures," OB in "Jungle of Cities," "Ride the Winds," "Santa Anita '42."

MATTHEWS, ANDERSON. Born Oct. 21, 1950 in Springfield, OH. Graduate Carnegie-Mellon U. Bdwy debut 1975 in "The Robber Bridegroom," followed by "Edward II," "The Time of Your Life."

MAXWELL, WAYNE. Born Dec. 22, 1939 in Needesha, KS. OB in "Titus Andronicus," "Boy With a Cart," "Kataki," "Long Voyage Home," "Pictures in a Hallway," "A Whitman Portrait," "Too Close for Comfort," "The Gay Apprentice," "Dog in the Manger," "The Beheading," Bdwy debut 1976 in "Legend."

MAYER, CHARLES. Born Apr. 4, 1904 in Germany. Attended State Th. Sch. Debut OB 1944 in "Korbin," followed by "Beavercoat," "Marriage Proposal," "Jacknife," "Boubouroche," "Golden Boy," "The Lawyer," "Flight into Egypt," "Ice Age," Bdwy in "A Bell for Adano," "Red Mill," "Now I Lay Me Down to Sleep," "Springtime Folly," "Thieves."

MAYER, JERRY. Born May 12, 1941 in NYC. Graduate NYU. Debut OB 1968 in "Alice in Wonderland," followed by NYSF productions, "L'Ete," "Marouf," "Trelawny of the Wells," Bdwy in "Much Ado about Nothing" (1972).

McCALL, NANCY. Born Jan. 12, 1948 in Atlanta, GA. Graduate Northwestern U. Debut 1975 OB in "Godspell."

McCARTY, MARY. Born in 1923 in Kansas. Bdwy debut 1948 in "Sleepy Hollow" for which she received a Theatre World Award, followed by "Small Wonder," "Miss Liberty," "Bless You All," "A Rainy Day in Newark," "Follies," "Chicago."

McCLAIN, MARCIA. Born Sept. 30, 1949 in San Antonio, TX. Graduate Trinity U. Debut 1972 OB in "Rainbow," followed by Bdwy bow 1974 in "Where's Charley?" for which she received a Theatre World Award.

McDERMOTT, KEITH. Born in Houston, TX. Attended LAMDA. Bdwy debut 1976 in "Equus."

McDONALD, TANNY. Born Feb. 13, 1939 in Princeton, IN. Graduate Vassar Col. Debut OB with Am. Savoyards, followed by "All in Love," "To Broadway with Love," "Carricknabauna," "Beggar's Opera," "Brand," "Goodbye, Dan Bailey," "Total Eclipse," "Gorky," Bdwy in "Fiddler on the Roof," "Come Summer," "The Lincoln Mask."

McGANN, MICHAELJOHN. Born Feb. 2, 1952 in Cleveland, OH. Graduate Ohio U. Debut 1975 OB in "The Three Musketeers," followed by "Panama Hattie."

McGILL, EVERETT. Born Oct. 21, 1945 in Miami Beach, FL. Graduate UMo., RADA. Debut OB 1971 in "Brothers," followed by "The Father," "Enemies," Bdwy 1974 in "Equus."

McGREEVEY, ANNIE. Born in Brooklyn, NY. Graduate AADA. Bdwy debut 1971 in "Company," followed by "The Magic Show," OB in "Booth Is Back in Town."

McINTYRE, BILL. Born Sept. 2, 1935 in Rochester, NY. Debut 1970 OB in "The Fantasticks," Bdwy 1972 in "Secret Affairs of Mildred Wild," followed by "Legend."

McKECHNIE, DONNA. Born in Nov. 1944 in Detroit, MI. Bdwy debut 1961 in "How to Succeed. . . ." followed by "Promises, Promises," "Company," "On the Town," "Music! Music!" (CC), "A Chorus Line."

McKERRS, TERRANCE. Born Oct. 11, 1944 in Oakes, ND. Attended St. Cloud Col. Debut 1969 in "Rondalay," followed by "Say When," "Panama Hattie."

McLERNON, PAMELA. Born March 1 in Lynn, MA. Graduate Lowell State Col. Debut 1975 OB in "Tenderloin."

McMILLAN, KENNETH. Born July 2, 1934 in Brooklyn. Bdwy debut 1970 in "Borstal Boy," OB in "Red Eye of Love," "King of the Whole Damn World," "Little Mary Sunshine," "Babes in the Wood," "Moonchildren," "Merry Wives of Windsor," "Where Do We Go from Here?," "Kid Champion," "Streamers."

McMILLIAN LARRY. Born Jan. 15, 1949 in Birmingham, AL. Graduate UAla. Bdwy debut 1975 in "Very Good Eddie."

McMURRAY, SAM. Born Apr. 15, 1952 in NYC. Graduate Washington U. Debut OB 1975 in "The Taking of Miss Janie," followed by "Merry Wives of Windsor," "Clarence."

McWILLIAMS, CAROLINE. Born Apr.4, in Seattle, WA. Attended Carnegie Tech, Pasadena Playhouse. Bdwy debut 1971 in "The Rothschilds," followed by "Cat on a Hot Tin Roof," OB in "An Ordinary Man," "Boccacio."

MEEHAN, DANNY. Born Feb. 17, 1933 in White Plains, NY. Attended AADA. Bdwy bow 1958 in "Whoop-Up," followed by "Do Re Mi," "Funny Girl," "Ulysses in Nighttown," "Poison Tree," OB in "Smiling the Boy Fell Dead," "Thracian Horses," "O, Oysters," "New Cole Porter Revue."

Dione Messina   **Jacob Milligan**   **Linda Miller**   **Craig R. Nelson**   **Chi Chi Navarro**

MENDILLO, STEPHEN. Born Oct. 9, 1942 in New Haven, CT. Graduate Colo. Col., Yale. Debut OB 1973 in "Nourish the Beast," followed by "Loot," "Subject to Fits," "Wedding Band," "As You Like It," Bdwy in "National Health," "Ah, Wilderness."

MERENSKY, JOHN. Born Nov. 4, 1943 in NYC. Attended Neighborhood Playhouse. With APA in "Man and Superman," "Judith," "War and Peace," OB in "Something for Kitty Genovese," "The Nun," "Two Gentlemen of Verona," "As You Like It," "Are You Prepared to Be a Marine?," "Disintegration of James Cherry," "Twentieth Century Tar," "The Home."

MERRILL, DINA. Born Dec. 29, 1925 in NYC. Attended AADA. Bdwy debut 1975 in "Angel Street."

MERSON, SUSAN. Born Apr. 25, 1950 in Detroit, MI. Graduate Boston U. Bdwy debut 1974 in "Saturday Sunday Monday," followed by OB "Vanities."

MESSINA, DIONE. Born Jan. 21 in New Orleans, LA. Graduate La.State U. Debut 1976 OB in "Panama Hattie."

METCALF, MARK. Born Mar. 11 in Findlay, OH. Attended UMich. Debut OB 1973 in "Creeps," followed by "The Tempest" (LC), "Beach Children," "Hamlet," "Patrick Henry Lake Liquors," "Streamers."

MILES, JOANNA. Born Mar. 6, 1940 in Nice, France. Attended Actors Studio. Bdwy debut 1963 in "Marathon '33," followed by "Lorenzo," OB in "Walk-Up," "Cave Dwellers," "Once in a Lifetime," "Home Free," "Drums in the Night," "Dylan," "Dancing for the Kaiser."

MILES, ROSS. Born in Poughkeepsie, NY. Bdwy debut 1962 in "Little Me," followed by "Baker Street," "Pickwick," "Darling of the Day," "Mame," "Jumpers," "Goodtime Charley," "Chicago."

MILLER, LINDA. Born Sept. 16, 1942 in NYC. Graduate Catholic U. Debut 1975 OB in "Black Picture Show" for which she received a Theatre World Award.

MILLER, MARTHA. Born Aug. 30, 1929 in New Bedford, MA. Graduate Carnegie-Mellon U. Debut OB 1956 in "House of Connolly," followed by "A Place without Morning," "Julius Caesar," "Major Barbara," "In the Summer House," "Merry Wives of Windsor," "Rimers of Eldritch."

MILLIGAN, JACOB. Born Mar. 25, 1949 in Kansas City, MO. Graduate UKC. Bdwy debut 1976 in "Equus."

MILLS, STEPHANIE. Born in 1959 in Brooklyn, NY. Bdwy debut 1975 in "The Wiz."

MINER, JAN. Born Oct. 15, 1917 in Boston, MA. Debut 1958 OB in "Obligato," followed by "Decameron," "Dumbbell People," "Autograph Hound," Bdwy in "Viva Madison Avenue," "Lady of the Camelias," "Freaking Out of Stephanie Blake," "Othello," "Milk Train Doesn't Stop Here Anymore," "Butterflies Are Free," "The Women," "Pajama Game," "Saturday Sunday Monday," "The Heiress."

MINTUN, JOHN. Born Jan. 16, 1941 in Decatur IL. Princeton graduate. Debut OB 1969 in "Get Thee to Canterbury," followed by "Boys in the Band," "The Rabinowitz Gambit," "Happy Halloween," "Esther," "The Inn at Lydda," "Carnival Dreams," Bdwy 1975 in "The Ritz."

MIRATTI, T. Born Dec. 6 in Santa Barbara, CA. Attended SBCC, Pasadena Playhouse. Debut 1976 OB in "The Shortchanged Review."

MIXON, ALAN. Born Mar. 15, 1933 in Miami, FL. Attended UMiami. Bdwy bow 1962 in "Something about a Soldier," followed by "Sign in Sidney Brustein's Window," "The Devils," "The Unknown Soldier and His Wife," "Love Suicide at Schofield Barracks," "Equus," OB in "Suddenly Last Summer," "Desire under the Elms," "Trojan Women," "Alchemist," "Child Buyer," "Mr. and Mrs. Lyman," "A Whitman Portrait," "Iphigenia in Aulis," "Small Craft Warnings," "Mourning Becomes Electra," "The Runner Stumbles," "Old Glory."

MIZELLE, VANCE. Born Aug. 6, 1934 in Atlanta, GA. Graduate Davidson Col., UGa. Debut 1975 in "Hamlet" (CP & LC).

MOBERLY, ROBERT. Born Apr. 15, 1939 in Excelsior Springs, MO. Graduate UKan. Debut 1967 OB in "Arms and the Man," followed by "The Millionairess," "A Gun Play," "Shadow of a Gunman," Bdwy "A Place for Polly," "A Matter of Gravity."

MOLDOW, DEBORAH. Born Dec. 18, 1948 in NYC. Graduate Sarah Lawrence Col. Debut OB 1958 in "The Enchanted," followed by "The Power and the Glory," "Pursuit of Happiness."

MOORE, JONATHAN. Born Mar. 24, 1923 in New Orleans, LA. Attended Piscator's Sch. Debut OB 1961 in "After the Angels," followed by "Berkeley Square," Bdwy in "Dylan," "1776."

MORENO, RITA, Born Dec. 11, 1931 in Humacao, PR. Bdwy debut 1945 in "Skydrift," followed by "West Side Story," "Sign in Sidney Brustein's Win-

dow," "Last of the Red Hot Lovers," "The National Health," "The Ritz."

MORENZIE, LEON. Born in Trinidad, WI. Graduate Sir George William U. Debut 1972 OB in "Ti-Jean and His Brothers," followed by "The Cherry Orchard," Bdwy in "The Leaf People."

MORFOGEN, GEORGE. Born Mar. 30, 1933 in NYC. Graduate Brown U., Yale. Debut 1957 OB in "Trial of D. Karamazov," followed by "Christmas Oratorio," "Othello," "Good Soldier Schweik," "Cave Dwellers," "Once in a Lifetime," "Total Eclipse," "Ice Age," Bdwy in "The Fun Couple."

MORIARTY, MICHAEL. Born Apr. 5, 1941 in Detroit, MI. Graduate Dartmouth, LAMDA. Debut OB 1963 in "Antony and Cleopatra," followed by "Peanut Butter and Jelly," "Long Day's Journey into Night," Bdwy in "Trial of the Catonsville 9," "Find Your Way Home" for which he received a Theater World Award, "Richard III" (LC).

MORRIS, MARTI. Born June 8, 1949 in Clarksburg, WV. Graduate UWVa. Debut in 1972 OB in "The Fantasticks," followed by "Riverwind" (ELT), Bdwy 1974 in "Candide."

MORSE, ROBERT. Born May 18, 1931 in Newton, MA. Bdwy debut 1955 in "The Matchmaker," followed by "Say, Darling" for which he received a Theatre World Award, "Take Me Along," "How to Succeed in Business . . .," "Sugar," "So Long, 174th Street."

MORSELL, FRED. Born Aug. 3, 1940 in NYC. Graduate Dickinson Col. Debut 1971 OB in "Any Resemblance to Persons Living or Dead," followed by "Enemies," "Merchant of Venice," "Enclave," "Rubbers," "Yankees 3, Detroit 0."

MORTON, JOE. Born Oct. 18, 1947 in NYC. Attended Hofstra U. Debut OB 1968 in "Month of Sundays," followed by "Salvation," "Charlie Was Here and Now He's Gone," Bdwy in "Hair," "Two Gentlemen of Verona," "Tricks," "Raisin" for which he received a Theatre World Award.

MOSS, LELAND. Born Mar. 30, 1948 in NYC. Graduate Harvard, LAMBDA. Bdwy debut 1975 in "Yentl."

MUNSEL, PATRICE. Born May 14, 1925 in Spokane, WA. Made operatic debut 1943 at Met in "Mignon." Bdwy debut in 1964 in "The Merry Widow," followed by "Musical Jubilee."

MUNSON, ESTELLA. Born in Fairfield, CT. Graduate New Eng. Consv. Debut OB 1965 with Am. Savoyards, followed by "Show Boat" (LC), CC's "Carousel" and "Sound of Music," "Open Season on Butterflies," Bdwy "No, No, Nanette," "Musical Jubilee."

MURPHY, PETER. Born Sept. 13, 1925 in Glenarm, Ireland. Attended ULondon, RADA. Debut 1956 OB in "The Comedian," followed by "Macbeth," "Ghosts," "The Fantasticks," "When We Dead Awaken," "Dancing for the Kaiser."

MURRAY, DON. Born July 31, 1929 in Hollywood, CA. Attended AADA. Debut 1948 in "The Insect Comedy" (CC), followed by "The Rose Tattoo," "The Skin of Our Teeth" (1955), "The Hot Corner," "The Norman Conquests."

MUSANTE, TONY. Born June 30, 1936 in Bridgeport, CT. Oberlin Col. graduate. Debut OB 1960 in "Borak," followed by "The Balcony," "Theatre of the Absurd," "Half-Past Wednesday," "The Collection," "Tender Heel," "Kiss Mama," Mme. Mousse," "Zoo Story," "Match-Play," "Night of the Dunce," "A Gun Play," "A Memory of Two Mondays," "27 Wagons Full of Cotton," Bdwy bow 1975 in "P.S. Your Cat is Dead."

NAVARRO, CHICHI. Born June 22, in Puerto Rico. Attended HB Studio. Bdwy debut in 1975 in "The Ritz."

NEILSON, RICHARD. Born Nov. 30, 1924 in London, Eng. Debut 1959 OB in "Heloise," followed by "O Say Can You See," "Tea Party," Bdwy 1964 in "Pickwick," then "Wise Child," "My Fair Lady," "Equus."

NELSON, BARRY. Born in 1925 in Oakland, CA. Bdwy debut 1943 in "Winged Victory," followed by "Light Up the Sky," "The Moon is Blue," "Wake Up, Darling," "Rat Race," "Mary, Mary," "Nobody Loves an Albatross," "Cactus Flower," "Everything in the Garden," "Only Game in Town," "Fig Leaves Are Falling," "Engagement Baby," "Seascape," "Norman Conquests."

NELSON, CRAIG RICHARD. Born Sept. 17, 1947 in Salt Lake City, UT. Attended NYU. Bdwy debut 1972 in "Two Gentlemen of Verona," followed by "The Runner Stumbles."

NETTLETON, DENISE. Born June 9, 1948 in Branford, Can. Bdwy debut 1974 in "Grease."

NETTLETON, LOIS. Born in Oak Park, IL. Attended Goodman Theatre, Actors Studio. Bdwy debut 1949 in "The Biggest Thief in Town," followed by "Darkness at Noon," "Cat on a Hot Tin Roof," "God and Kate Murphy," "Silent Night, Lonely Night," "A Streetcar Named Desire" (LC), "They Knew What They Wanted" (OB).

| Don Nute | Mary Ann Niles | Ian O'Connell | Sylvia O'Brien | Thomas O'Rourke |

NEWMAN, STEPHEN D. Born Jan. 20, 1943 in Seattle, WA. Stanford graduate. Debut 1971 OB in Judith Anderson's "Hamlet," followed by "School for Wives," "Beggar's Opera," "Pygmalion," "In the Voodoo Parlour of Marie Leveau," "Richard III," "Santa Anita '42," "Polly," Bdwy in "An Evening with Richard Nixon and . . . ," "Emperor Henry IV," "Habeas Corpus," "Rex."

NICKERSON, SHANE. Born Jan. 29, 1964 in Miami, FL. Bdwy debut 1972 in "Pippin."

NICOL, LESSLIE. Born May 27 in Dundee, Scot. NY debut OB in "Man with a Load of Mischief,' Bdwy 1973 in "Grease."

NILES, MARY ANN. Born May 2, 1933 in NYC. Attended Miss Finchley's Ballet Acad. Bdwy debut in "Girl from Nantucket," followed by "Dance Me a Song," "Call Me Mister," "Make Mine Manhattan," "La Plume de Ma Tante," "Carnival," "Flora the Red Menace," "Sweet Charity," "George M!," "No, No, Nanette," "Irene," OB in "The Boys from Syracuse." CC's "Wonderful Town" and "Carnival."

NOBLE, JAMES. Born Mar. 5, 1922 in Dallas, TX. Attended SMU. Bdwy bow 1949 in "The Velvet Glove," followed by "Come of Age," "A Far Country," "Strange Interlude," "1776," "The Runner Stumbles," OB in "Wilder's Triple Bill," "Night of the Dunce," "Rimers of Eldritch," "The Acquisition," "A Scent of Flowers," "A Touch of the Poet."

NOVY, NITA. Born June 13, 1950 in Wilkes-Barre, PA. Graduate Duke U. Bdwy debut 1960 in "Gypsy," followed by "Sound of Music," OB in "How to Succeed . . . ," "Maggie Flynn!"

NUTE, DON. Born Mar. 13, in Connellsville, Pa. Attended Denver U. Debut OB 1965 in "The Trojan Women," followed by "Boys in the Band," "Mad Theatre for Madmen," "The Eleventh Dynasty," "About Time," "The Urban Crisis," "Christmas Rappings," "The Life of a Man," "A Look at the Fifties."

O'BRIEN, SYLVIA. Born May 4, 1924 in Dublin, Ire. Debut OB 1961 in "O Marry Me," followed by "Red Roses for Me," "Every Other Evil," "3 by O'Casey," "Essence of Woman," "Dear Oscar," Bdwy in "Passion of Josef D," "Right Honourable Geltleman," "Loves of Cass McGuire," "Hadrian VII," "Conduct Unbecoming," "My Fair Lady."

O'CONNELL, IAN. Born Nov. 10, 1945 in Sligo, Ire. Graduate UNC. Debut 1976 OB in 'Maggie Flynn."

O'CONNELL, PATRICIA. Born May 17 in NYC. Attended AmThWing. Debut 1958 OB in "The Saintliness of Margery Kemp," followed by "Time Limit," "An Evening's Frost," "Mrs. Snow," "Electric Ice," "Survival of St. Joan," "Rain," "The Rapists," "Who Killed Richard Cory?," Bdwy in "Criss-Crossing," "Summer Brave."

O'DELL, K. LYPE. Born Feb. 2, 1939 in Claremore, OK. Graduate Los Angeles State Col. Debut 1972 OB in "Sunset," followed by "Our Father," "Ice Age."

OH, SOON-TECK. Born June 29, 1943 in Korea. Attended UCLA, Neighborhood Playhouse. Bdwy debut 1976 in "Pacific Overtures."

O'HARA, PAIGE. Born May 10, 1956 in Ft. Lauderdale, FL. Debut 1975 OB in "The Gift of the Magi."

O'NEAL, RON. Born Sept. 1, 1937 in Utica, NY. Attended Ohio State U. Debut 1968 OB in "American Pastoral," followed by "No Place to be Somebody" for which he received a Theatre World Award, "Dream on Monkey Mountain," Bdwy in "All over Town."

ORBACH, JERRY. Born Oct. 20, 1935 in NYC. Attended Northwestern U. Bdwy debut 1961 in "Carnival," followed by "Guys and Dolls," "Carousel," "Annie Get Your Gun," "The Natural Look," "Promises, Promises," "6 Rms Riv Vu," "Chicago," OB in "Threepenny Opera," "The Fantasticks," "The Cradle Will Rock," "Scuba Duba."

ORFALY, ALEXANDER. Born Oct. 10, 1935 in Brooklyn, NY. Appeared in "South Pacific" (LC), "How Now, Dow Jones," "Ari," "Sugar," "Cyrano," OB in "The End of All Things Natural," "Mahogonny," "Johnny Johnson," "Ride the Winds," "Polly," "1600 Pennsylvania Avenue."

O'ROURKE, THOMAS. Born Mar. 28, 1944 in NYC. Attended Goodman Theatre Sch. Debut 1976 OB in "The Old Glory."

ORR, MARY. Born Dec. 21, 1918 in Brooklyn, NY. Attended AADA, Syracuse U. Bdwy debut 1938 in "Bachelor Born," followed by "Jupiter Laughs," "Wallflower," "Dark Hammock," "Sherlock Holmes," "The Desperate Hours," OB in "Grass Widows."

OSBORNE, KIPP. Born Oct. 17, 1944 in Jersey City, NJ. Attended UMich., Neighborhood Playhouse. Bdwy debut 1970 in "Butterflies Are Free" for which he received a Theatre World Award, followed by "Veronica's Room," "Lady from the Sea," OB in "Children's Mass," "Love Gotta Come by Saturday Night."

O'SHEA, MILO. Born June 2, 1926 in Dublin, Ire. Bdwy debut 1968 in "Staircase," followed by "Dear World," "Mrs. Warrens's Profession" (LC).

O'SHEA, TESSIE. Born Mar. 13, 1918 in Caerdydd, GB. Bdwy debut 1963 in "The Girl Who Came to Supper," followed by "A Time for Singing," "Something's Afoot."

OSHEN, GABRIEL. Born Oct. 8, 1950 in NYC. Bdwy debut 1974 in "Equus."

OTTENHEIMER, ALBERT M. Born Sept. 6, 1904 in Tacoma, WA. Graduate UWash. Bdwy debut 1946 in "Affair of Honor," followed by "West Side Story," "Deputy," "Yentl," OB in "Monday's Heroes," "Tiger," "Mother Riba," "A Christmas Carol," "Juno and the Paycock," "Italian Straw Hat," "The Iceman Cometh," "Call It Virtue," "The Immoralist," "The Cat and the Canary," "Exhaustion of Our Son's Love," "Deadly Game," "Brother Gorski," "The Kid," "Holy Ghosts," "Yentl the Yeshiva Boy."

PAGE, GERALDINE. Born Nov. 22, 1924 in Kirksville, MO. Attended Goodman Theatre. OB in "7 Mirrors," "Summer and Smoke" for which she received a Theatre World Award, "Macbeth," "Look Away," Bdwy in "Mid-summer," followed by "The Immoralist," "The Rainmaker," "Innkeepers," "Separate Tables," "Sweet Bird of Youth," "Strange Interlude," "Three Sisters," "P.S. I Love You," "The Great Indoors," "White Lies," "Black Comedy," "The Little Foxes," "Angela," "Absurd Person Singular."

PALMER, LELAND. Born June 16, 1945 in Port Washington, NY. Bdwy debut 1966 in "Joyful Noise," followed by "Applause," "Pippin," OB in "Your Own Thing."

PALMIERI, JOSEPH. Born Aug. 1, 1939 in Bklyn. Attended Catholic U. With NYSF 1965–6, "Cyrano de Bergerac" (LCR), OB in "Butter and Egg Man," "Boys in the Band," "Beggar's Opera," "The Family," Bdwy in "Lysistrata," "Candide."

PAPE, PAUL. Born July 17, 1952 in Rochester, NY. Graduate SUNY Brockport. Debut 1976 OB in "The Cherry Orchard."

PARKER, DON. Born Aug. 29 in NYC. Graduate Bard Col. Bdwy debut 1975 in "Kennedy's Children."

PARS, JULIE M. Born Nov. 29, 1949 in Alton, IL. Graduate Monticello Col. Bdwy debut 1971 in "Follies," followed by "Irene," "Musical Jubilee."

PARSONS, ESTELLE. Born Nov. 20, 1927 in Lynn, MA. Attended Boston U., Actors Studio. OB in "Threepenny Opera," "Automobile Graveyard," "Mrs. Dally Has a Lover" for which she received a Theatre World Award, "In the Summer House." "Monopoly," "Peer Gynt," "Mahagonny," "Silent Partner," "Barbary Shore," "Oh Glorious Tintinnabulation," with LCR in "East Wind," "Galileo," "People Are Living There," and "Mert and Phil," Bdwy in "Happy Hunting," "Whoop-Up!," "Beg, Borrow or Steal," "Ready When You Are, C. B.," "Malcolm," "Seven Descents of Myrtle," "A Way of Life," "and Miss Reardon Drinks a Little," "Norman Conquests."

PASEKOFF, MARILYN. Born Nov. 7, 1949 in Pittsburgh, PA. Graduate Boston U. Debut 1975 OB in "Godspell."

PASSELTINER, BERNE. Born Nov. 21, 1931 in NYC. Graduate Catholic U. OB in "Square in the Eye," "Sourball," "As Virtuously Given," "Now Is the Time for All Good Men," "Rain,' "Kaddish," "Against the Sun," "End of Summer," "Yentl, the Yeshiva Boy," Bdwy in "The Office," "The Jar," "Yentl."

PATIK, VICKIE. Born June 14, 1950 in Los Angeles, CA. Graduate Los Angeles State U. Bdwy debut 1976 in "My Fair Lady."

PATTON, LUCILLE. Born in NYC; attended Neighborhood Playhouse. Bdwy debut 1946 in "A Winter's Tale," followed by "Topaze," "Arms and the Man," "Joy to the World," "All You Need Is One Good Break," "Fifth Season," "Heavenly Twins," "Rhinoceros," "Marathon '33." "The Last Analysis," "Dinner at 8," "La Strada," "Unlikely Heroes," "Love Suicide at Schofield Barracks," OB in "Ulysses in Nighttown," "Failures," "Three Sisters, "Yes, Yes, No,No," "Tango," "Mme. de Sade," "Apple Pie," "Follies."

PAULETTE, LARRY. Born Apr. 10, 1949 in Steubenville, OH. Attended UCinn. Debut OB 1974 in "Let My People Come."

PAYTON-WRIGHT, PAMELA. Born Nov. 1, 1941 in Pittsburgh, PA. Graduate Birmingham Southern Col., RADA. Bdwy debut 1967 with APA in "The Show-Off," followed by "Exit the King," "The Cherry Orchard," "Jimmy Shine," "Mourning Becomes Electra," "Glass Menagerie," OB in "Effect of Marigolds . . . ," "The Crucible."

PEACHENA. Born May 15, 1948 in Salisbury, MD. Graduate Morgan State Col. Debut 1974 OB in "Let My People Come."

PEARL, BARRY. Born Mar. 29, 1950 in Lancaster, PA. Graduate Carnegie Tech. Bdwy debut 1961 in "Bye Bye Birdie," "A Teaspoon Every Four Hours," "Oliver," OB in "The Glorious Age."

Barry Pearl

Penny Peyser

Jeffrey D. Pomerantz

Frances Pole

Howard Porter

PENN, EDWARD. Born In Washington, DC. Studied at HB studio. Debut 1965 OB in "The Queen and the Rebels," followed by "My Wife and I," "Invitation to a March," "Of Thee I Sing," "Fantasticks," "Greenwillow," "One for the Money," "Dear Oscar," "Speed Gets the Poppys," "Man with a Load of Mischief." Bdwy bow 1975 in "Shenandoah."

PERCASSI, DON. Born Jan. 11 in Amsterdam, NY. Bdwy debut 1964 in "High Spirits," followed by "Walking Happy," "Coco," "Sugar," "Molly," "Mack and Mabel," "A Chorus Line."

PERKINS, ANTHONY. Born Apr. 4, 1932 in NYC. Attended Rollins Col., Columbia U. Bdwy debut 1954 in "Tea and Sympathy" for which he received a Theatre World Award, followed by "Look Homeward, Angel," "Greenwillow," "Harold," "Star Spangled Girl," "Steambath" (OB), "Equus."

PERKINS, PATTI. Born July 9 in New Haven, CT. Attended AMDA. Debut 1972 OB in "The Contrast," followed by "Fashion," "Tuscaloosa's Calling Me . . . ," Bdwy in "All Over Town."

PERRIER, MICHAEL. Born Aug. 6, 1942 In Minneapolis, MN. Graduate UMinn. Debut 1972 OB in "Love Me, Love My Children," followed by "Dancing Picture Show," "New Beginnings," "Follies" (ELT).

PETERSON, KURT. Born Feb. 12, 1948 in Stevens Point, WI. Attended AMDA. Bdwy debut 1969 in "Dear World," followed by "Follies," OB in "An Ordinary Miracle," "West Side Story" (LC), "Dames at Sea," "By Bernstein."

PETRICOFF, ELAINE. Born in Cincinnati, OH. Graduate Syracuse U. Bdwy debut 1971 in "The Me Nobody Knows," OB in "Hark!," "Ride the Winds," "Cole Porter," Bdwy debut 1973 in "Grease."

PETTY, ROSS. Born Aug. 29, 1946 in Winnipeg, Can. Graduate UManitoba. Debut OB 1975 in "Happy Time," followed by "Maggie Flynn" (ELT).

PEYSER, PENNY. Born Feb. 9, 1951 in NYC. Emerson Col. graduate. Debut 1975 OB in "Dimaond Studs," followed by "Hot I Baltimore," "Lemon Sky."

PFEIFFER, MARILYN, Born Nov. 7, 1948 in Houston, TX. Graduate Rice U. Bdwy debut 1976 in "The Runner Stumbles."

PHELPS, ELEANOR. Born in Baltimore, MD. Vassar graduate. Bdwy debut 1928 in "Merchant of Venice," followed by "Richard II," "Criminal Code," "Trick for Trick," "Seen But Not Heard," "Flight to the West," "Queen Bee." "We the People," "Six Characters in Search of an Author," "Mr. Big," "Naughty-Naught," "The Disenchanted," "Picnic," "My Fair Lady" (1956 & 76), "40 Carats," "Crown Matrimonial," "Royal Family," OB in "Garden District," "Color of Darkness."

PICKLES, CHRISTINA. Born Feb. 17, 1938 in England. Attended RADA. With APA in "School for Scandal," "War and Peace," "The Wild Duck," "Pantagleize," "You Can't Take It with You," "The Seagull," "The Misanthrope," Bdwy in "Inadmissible Evidence," "Who's Who in Hell," "Sherlock Holmes."

PIERSOL, MORRIE. Born July 6, 1952 in Philadelphia, PA. Graduate Southampton Col. Bdwy debut 1976 in "The Runner Stumbles."

PINCUS, WARREN. Born Apr. 13, 1938 in Brooklyn, NY. Attended CCNY. OB credits: "Miss Nefertiti Regrets," "Circus," "Magician," "Boxcars," "Demented World," "Give My Regards," "Electronic Nigger," "Last Pad," "Waiting for Godot," "In the Time of Harry Harrass," "Yoshe Kolb," Bdwy bow 1976 in "Zalmen, or the Madness of God."

PITCHFORD, DEAN. Born July 29, 1951 in Honolulu, HI. Graduate Yale U. Debut 1971 OB in "Godspell," Bdwy 1973 in "Pippin."

PLUMLEY, DON. Born Feb. 11, 1934 in Los Angeles, CA. Pepperdine Col. graduate. Debut 1961 OB in "The Cage," followed by "A Midsummer Night's Dream," "Richard II," "Cymbeline," "Much Ado about Nothing," "Saving Grace," "A Whistle in the Dark," "Operation Sidewinder," "Enemy of the People," "Back Bog Beast Bait," "The Kid," Bdwy 1974 in "Equus."

POLE, FRANCES. Born June 12, 1907 in St. Paul, MN. Debut 1958 OB in " 'Tis Pity She's a Whore," followed by "Mornings at 7," "Ice Age."

POLLOCK, GEORGE. Born May 26, 1937 in NYC. Juilliard graduate. Bdwy debut 1975 in "Lamppost Reunion."

POMERANTZ, JEFFREY DAVID. Born July 2, 1945 in NYC. Attended Northwestern U., RADA. Bdwy debut (as Jeffrey David-Owen) 1975 in "The Leaf People," followed by "The Ritz," "Equus."

PONAZECKI, JOE. Born Jan. 7, 1934 in Rochester, NY. Attended Rochester U., Columbia. Bdwy bow 1959 in "Much Ado About Nothing," followed by "Send Me No Flowers," "Call on Kuprin,' "Take Her, She's Mine," "Fiddler

on the Roof," "Xmas in Las Vegas," "3 Bags Full," "Love in E-Flat," "90 Day Mistress," "Harvey" "Trial of the Catonsville 9," "Country Girl," "Freedom of the City," "Summer Brave," OB in "The Dragon," "Muzeeka," "Witness," "All Is Bright," "The Dog Ran Away," "Dream of a Blacklisted Actor."

POOLE, ROY. Born Mar. 31, 1924 in San Bernardino, CA. Graduate Stanford U. Bdwy in "Now I Lay Me Down to Sleep," "St. Joan," "Bad Seed," "I Knock at the Door," "Long Day's Journey into Night," "Face of a Hero," "Moby Dick," "Poor Bitos," "1776," "Scratch," Ob in "27 Wagons Full of Cotton," "A Memory of Two Mondays," "Secret Service," "Boy Meets Girl."

PORTER, HOWARD. Born Oct. 31, 1946 in Gary, WV. Attended WVa. U. AMDA. Bdwy debut 1970 in "Hello, Dolly!," followed by "Purlie," "Two Gentlemen of Verona," OB in "Great McDaddy."

PREBLE, ED. Born Nov. 9, 1919 in Chicago, IL. Bdwy bow 1957 in "Inherit the Wind," followed by "Family Way," OB in "Press Cuttings," "Failures," "Krapp's Last Tape," "Marcus in the High Grass," "A Figleaf in Her Bonnet," "Calling in Crazy," "The Family."

PREECE, K. K. Born Nov. 14, 1949 in Anna, IL. Graduate Brenau Col. Debut 1976 OB in "Panama Hattie."

PREMICE, JOSEPHINE. Born July 21, 1926 in Brooklyn, NY. Graduate Columbia, Cornell U. Bdwy debut 1945 in "Blue Holiday," followed by "Caribbean Carnival," "Mr. Johnson," "Jamaica," "A Hand Is on the Gate," "Bubbling Brown Sugar," OB in "House of Flowers," "Cherry Orchard," "American Night Cry."

PRENTISS, PAULA. Born Mar. 4, 1938 in San Tantonio, TX. Graduate Northwestern U. Debut 1969 OB in "Arf" and "The Great Airplane Snatch," Bdwy 1975 in "The Norman Conquests."

PRESTON, BARRY. Born May 31, 1945 in Brooklyn, NY. Attended Utah State Col. Bdwy debut 1964 in "Something More," followed by "A Joyful Noise," "Bubbling Brown Sugar."

PRESTON, WILLIAM, Born Aug. 26, 1921 In Columbia, PA. Graduate Pa. State U. Debut OB 1972 in "We Bombed in New Haven," followed by "Hedda Gabler," "Whisper into My Good Ear," "A Nestless Bird," "Friends of Mine," "Iphigenia in Aulis," "Midsummer."

PRICE, GILBERT. Born Sept. 10, 1942 in NYC. Attended AmThWing. Bdwy bow 1965 in "Roar of the Greasepaint . . . ," followed by "Lost in the Stars," "The Night That Made America Famous," "1600 Pennsylvania Avenue," OB in "Kicks & Co," "Fly Blackbird," "Jerico-Jim Crow" for which he received a Theatre World Award, "Promenade," "Slow Dance on the Killing Ground," "Six," "Melodrama Play."

PRICE, PAUL B. Born Oct. 7, 1933 In Carteret, NJ. Attended Pasadena Playhouse. Debut 1960 OB in "Dead End," followed by "Banquet for the Moon," "O Say Can You See," "Dumbwaiter," "Live Like Pigs," "Medea," "4H Club," "Waiting for Godot," Bdwy in "A Cook for Mr. General," "Let Me Hear You Smile," "The Ritz."

PRIMUS, BARRY. Born Feb. 16, 1938 in NYC. Attended CCNY. Bdwy debut 1960 in "The Nervous Set," followed by "Oh, Dad, Poor Dad . . . ," "Creation of the World and Other Business," OB in "Henry IV," "Huui, Huui," "The Criminals," "Diary of a Scoundrel," "Jesse and the Bandit Queen."

PRITCHARD, TED. Born Sept. 12, 1936 in Lakewood, OH. Graduate Ohio U. Debut 1974 in "Music! Music!" (CC), followed OB 1975 in "Tuscaloosa's Calling Me But I'm Not Going."

PUMA, MARIE. Born in Brooklyn, NY. Graduate CUNY. Debut 1969 OB in "Romeo and Jeannette,' followed by "Purification."

PYSHER, ERNIE. Born in Youngstown, OH. Graduate Youngstown State U. Bdwy debut 1974 in "Good News," followed by "The Night That Made America Famous," OB in "Carousel," "My Fair Lady,"

QUARRY, RICHARD. Born Aug. 9, 1944 in Akron, OH. Graduate UAkron, NYU. Bdwy bow 1970 in "Georgy," followed by "Oh! Calcutta!," "Grease."

RABB, ELLIS. Born June 20, 1930 in Memphis, TN. Attended Carnegie Tech., Yale. Debut OB 1956 in "Midsummer Night's Dream," followed by "Misanthrope," "Mary Stuart," "The Tavern," "Twelfth Night," "The Importance of Being Earnest," "King Lear," "Man and Superman," Bdwy in "Look after Lulu," "Jolly's Progress," "Right You Are . . . ," "Scapin," "Impromtu at Versailles," "Lower Depths," "School for Scandal," "Pantagleize," "Cock-a-Doodle Dandy," "Hamlet," "The Royal Family." Founder and director of APA.

Eugenia Rawls   **John Remme**   **Antonia Rey**   **Jess Richards**   **Elaine Rinehart**

RAITT, JOHN. Born Jan. 29, 1917 in Santa Ana, CA. Graduate Redlands U. Bdwy bow 1945 in "Carousel" for which he received a Theatre World Award, followed by "Magdalena," "Three Wishes for Jamie," "Pajama Game," "A Joyful Noise," "On a Clear Day You Can See Forever," "Musical Jubilee."

RAMOS, RICHARD. Born Aug. 23, 1941 in Seattle, WA. Graduate UMinn. Bdwy debut 1968 in "House of Atreus," followed by "Arturo Ui," OB in "Adaptation," "Screens," "Lotta," "The Tempest," "A Midsummer Night's Dream," "Gorky."

RANDELL, RON. Born Oct. 8, 1920 in Sydney, Aust. Attended St. Mary's Col. Bdwy debut 1949 in "The Browning Version," followed by "A Harlequinade," "Candida," "World of Suzie Wong," "Sherlock Holmes," "Mrs. Warren's Profession" (LC).

RAWLS, EUGENIA. Born Sept. 11. 1916 in Macon, GA. Attended UNC. Bdwy debut 1934 in "The Children's Hour," followed by "To Quito and Back," "Journeyman," "Little Foxes," "Guest in the House," "Man Who Had All the Luck," "Strange Fruit," "The Shrike," "Great Sebastians," "First Love," "Case of Libel," "Poker Session" (OB), "Sweet Bird of Youth."

REAMS, LEE ROY. Born Aug. 23, 1942 in Covington, KY. Graduate U. Cinn. Cons. Bdwy debut 1966 in "Sweet Charity," followed by "Oklahoma!" (LC). "Applause," "Lorelei."

REDGRAVE, LYNN. Born In London Mar. 8, 1943. Attended Central Schl. of Speech. Bdwy debut 1967 in "Black Comedy," follwed by "My Fat Friend," "Mrs. Warren's Profession" (LC), "Knock Knock."

REDGRAVE, VANESSA. Born Jan. 30, 1937 in London, Eng. Attended Central School of Speech and Drama. Bdwy debut 1976 in "The Lady from the Sea."

REED, ALEXANDER. Born June 9, 1916 in Clearfield, PA. Graduate Columbia U. Debut OB 1956 in "Lady from the Sea," followed by "All the King's Men," "Death of Satan," "The Balcony," "Call Me by My Rightful Name," "Studs Edsel," "The Coroner's Plot," on Bdwy in "Witness," "Lost in the Stars," "The Skin of Our Teeth."

REED, BOBBY. Born Sept. 26, 1956 in NYC. Attended AMDA. Debut OB 1975 in "Boy Meets Boy."

REED, VIVIAN. Born June 6, 1947 in Pittsburgh, PA. Attend Pittsburgh Musical Inst., Juilliard. Bdwy debut 1971 "That's Entertainment," followed by "Don't Bother Me, I Can't Cope," "Bubbling Brown Sugar" for which she received a Theatre World Award.

REEHLING, JOYCE. Born Mar. 5, 1949 in Baltimore, MD. Graduate NC School of Arts. Debut 1976 OB in "Hot l Baltimore," followed by "Who Killed Richard Cory?"

REEVE, CHRISTOPHER. Born Sept. 25, 1952 in NYC. Graduate Cornell U., Juilliard. Debut 1975 OB in "Berkeley Square," Bdwy 1976 in "A Matter of Gravity."

REINHARDSEN, DAVID. Born Jan. 13, 1949 in NYC. Graduate Westminster Col. Bdwy debut 1976 in "Zalmen, or the Madness of God."

REINKING, ANN. Born Nov. 10, 1949 in Seattle, WA. Attended Joffrey Sch., HB Studio. Bdwy debut 1969 in "Cabaret," followed by "Coco," "Pippin," "Over Here" for which she received a Theatre World Award, "Goodtime Charley," "A Chorus Line."

REMME, JOHN. Born Nov. 21, 1935 in Fargo, ND. Attended UMinn. Debut 1972 OB in "One for the Money," Bdwy 1975 in "The Ritz," followed by "The Royal Family."

REPOLE, CHARLES. Born May 24 in Brooklyn, NY. Graduate Hofstra U. Bdwy debut 1975 in "Very Good Eddie" for which he received a Theatre World Award.

REXROAD, DAVID. Born Jan. 11, 1950 in Parkersburg, WV. Graduate WVa. U. Debut OB 1973 in "The Fantasticks."

REY, ANTONIA. Born Oct. 12, 1927 in Havana, Cuba. Graduate Havana U. Bdwy debut 1964 in "Bajour," followed by "Mike Downstairs," "Engagement Baby," "The Ritz," OB in "Yerma," "Fiesta in Madrid," "Camino Real" (LC), "Back Bog Beast Bait," "Rain," "42 Seconds from Broadway," "Streetcar Named Desire" (LC).

RICE, SARAH. Born Mar. 5, 1955 in Okinawa. Attended Ariz State U. Debut 1974 OB in "The Fantasticks."

RICHARDS, JESS. Born Jan. 23, 1943 in Seattle, WA. Attended UWash. Bdwy debut 1966 in "Walking Happy," followed by "South Pacific" (LC). "Blood Red Roses," "Two by Two," "On the Town" for which he received a Theatre World Award, "Mack and Mabel," OB in "One for the Money."

RICHARDSON, IAN. Born Apr. 7, 1934 in Edinburgh, Scot. Attended Royal Scottish Acad. Debut 1964 at LC with Royal Shakespeare Co. in "King Lear," "Comedy of Errors," BAM 1975–6 in "Richard II," "Summerfolk," "Love's Labours Lost," "He That Plays the King," Bdwy in "Marat/Sade" (1965), "My Fair Lady" (1976).

RIDGE, JOHN. Born May 13, 1924 in Brooklyn, NY. Attended LIU, NYU, Pratt Inst. Debut OB 1969 in "The Triumph of Robert Emmet," Bdwy 1972 in "Mourning Becomes Electra," followed by "Threepenny Opera" (LC).

RIEGERT, PETER. Born Apr. 11, 1947 in NYC. Graduate UBuffalo. Debut 1975 OB in "Dance with Me."

RIFICI, JOE. Born Nov. 25, 1952 in NYC. Graduate Wagner Col. Bdwy debut 1975 in "Grease."

RINALDI, JOY. Born in Yonkers, NY. Graduate Stephens Col., AADA. Debut OB 1969 in "Satisfaction Guaranteed," Bdwy 1973 in "Grease."

RINEHART, ELAINE. Born Aug. 16, 1952 in San Antonio, TX. Graduate NC School of Arts. Debut 1975 OB in ELT's "Tenderloin."

RITCHARD, CYRIL. Born Dec. 1, 1897 in Sydney, Aus. Attended Sydney U. Bdwy debut 1947 in "Love for Love," followed by "Make Way for Lucia," "The Relapse," "Peter Pan," "Visit to a Small Planet," "The Pleasure of His Company," "Happiest Girl in the World," "Romulus," "Too True to Be Good," "Irregular Verb to Love," "Roar of the Greasepaint . . . ," "Peter and the Wolf," "Sugar," "Musical Jubilee."

RITTER, KATHRYN. Born Aug. 1, 1948 in NYC. Attended NYU. Bdwy debut 1974 in "Candide."

RIVERA, CHITA. Born Jan. 23, 1933 in Washington, DC. Attended AmSch. of Ballet. Bdwy debut 1950 in "Guys and Dolls," followed by "Call Me Madam," "Can-Can," "Shoestring Revue" (OB), "Seventh Heaven," "Mr. Wonderful," "West Side Story," "Bye Bye Birdie," 'Bajour," "Chicago."

ROBARDS, JASON. Born July 26, 1922 in Chicago, IL. Attended AADA. Bdwy debut 1947 with D'Oyly Carte, followed by "Stalag 17," "The Chase," "Long Day's Journey into Night" for which he received a Theatre World Award, "The Disenchanted," "Toys in the Attic," "Big Fish, Little Fish," "A Thousand Clowns," "Hughie," "The Devils," "We Bombed in New Haven," "The Country Girl," "Moon for the Misbegotten," OB in "American Gothic," "The Iceman Cometh," "After the Fall," "But for Whom Charlie," "Long Day's Journey into Night."

ROBBINS, JANA. Born Apr. 18, 1947 in Johnstown, PA. Stephens Col. graduate Bdwy debut 1947 in "Good News," OB in "Tickles by Tucholsky."

ROBBINS, REX. Born in Pierre, SD. Bdwy debut 1964 in "One Flew over the Cuckoo's Nest," followed by "Scratch," "The Changing Room," 'Gypsy," OB in "Servant of Two Masters," "The Alchemist," "Arms and the Man," "Boys in the Band." "A Memory of Two Mondays," "They Knew What They Wanted," "Secret Service," "Boy Meets Girl."

ROBERTS, BILL. Born May 25, 1948 in Sealy, TX. Graduate Sam Houston State U. Debut OB 1976 in "Maggie Flynn."

ROBERTS, RACHEL. Born Sept. 30, 1927 in Llanelly, Wales. Attended RADA. Bdwy debut 1973 in "The Visit," followed by "Chemin de Fer," "Habeas Corpus."

ROBERTS, TONY. Born Oct. 22, 1939 in NYC. Graduate Northwestern U. Bdwy bow 1962 in "Something about a Soldier," followed by "Take Her, She's Mine," "Last Analysis," "The Cradle Will Rock" (OB), "Never Too Late," "Barefoot in the Park," "Don't Drink the Water," "How Now, Dow Jones," "Play It Again, Sam," "Promises, Promises," "Sugar," "Absurd Person Singular."

ROBERTSON, WILLIAM. Born Oct. 9, 1908 in Portsmouth, VA. Graduate Pomona Col. Bdwy debut 1936 in "Tapestry in Grey," followed by "Cup of Trembling," "Liliom," "Our Town," OB in "Uncle Harry," "Shining Hour," "Aspern Papers," "Madame Is Served," "Tragedian in spite of Himself," "Kibosh," "Sun-Up," "The Last Pad," "Hamlet," "Girls Most Likely to Succeed," "The Petrified Forest," "The Minister's Black Veil," "Santa Anita," "Babylon," "Midsummer Night's Dream," "A Touch of the Poet," "The Zykovs," "Rimers of Eldritch."

ROBINSON, HAL. Born in Bedford, IN. Graduate Ind. U. Debut 1971 OB in "Memphis Store-Bought Teeth," followed by "From Berlin to Broadway," "The Fantasticks."

RODGERS, SHEV. Born Apr. 9, 1928 in Holister, CA. Attended SF State Col. Bdwy bow 1959 in "Redhead," followed by "Music Man," "Man of La Mancha" (also LC), "Home Sweet Homer," "Legend." OB in "Get Thee to Canterbury," "War Games," "Moonchildren."

William Roerick   **Judi Rolin**   **David Russell**   **Nancy Salis**   **Craig Schaefer**

ROERICK, WILLIAM. Born Dec. 17, 1912 in NYC. Bdwy bow 1935 in "Romeo and Juliet," followed by "St. Joan," "Hamlet," "Our Town," "Importance of Being Earnest," "The Land is Bright," "Autumn Hill," "This Is the Army," "Magnificent Yankee," "Tonight at 8:30," "The Heiress," "Medea," "Macbeth," "Burning Glass," "Right Honourable Gentlemen," "Marat/-deSade," "Homecoming," "We Bombed in New Haven," "Elizabeth the Queen" (CC), "Waltz of the Toreadors," OB in "Madam, Will You Walk," "Cherry Orchard." "Come Slowly, Eden," "A Passage to E. M. Forster," "Trials of Oz."

ROLFING, TOM. Born Sept. 6, 1949 in Cedar Rapids, IA. Carnegie Tech graduate. Debut 1973 OB in "Godspell," Bdwy in "Godspell," "Equus."

ROLIN, JUDI. Born Nov. 6, 1946 in Chicago, IL. Bdwy debut 1970 in "40 Carats," followed by "Rodgers and Hart."

ROLPH, MARTI. Born March 8 in Los Angeles, CA. Occidental Col. graduate. Bdwy debut 1971 in "Follies," followed by "Good News" for which she received a Theatre World Award.

ROMAN, ANDREW. Born Jan. 25, 1939 in Imlay City, MI. Graduate UMich. Debut 1976 OB in ELT's "Follies."

ROSE, GEORGE. Born Feb. 19, 1920 in Bicester, Eng. Bdwy debut with Old Vic 1946 in "Henry IV," followed by "Much Ado about Nothing," "A Man for All Seasons," "Hamlet," "Royal Hunt of the Sun," "Walking Happy," "Loot," "My Fair Lady" (CC '68). "Canterbury Tales," "Coco," "Wise Child," "Sleuth," "My Fat Friend." "My Fair Lady."

ROSEN, ROBERT. Born Apr. 24, 1954 in NYC. Attended Indiana U., HB Studio. Bdwy debut 1975 in "Shenandoah."

ROSKAM, CATHRYN. Born May 30, 1943 in Hempstead, NY. Middlebury Col. graduate. Debut 1970 OB in "Gandhi," followed by "Autumn Garden.," "Maggie Flynn."

ROSLER, LARRY. Born Apr. 19, 1951 in Newark, NJ. Graduate Seton Hall U. Debut 1976 OB in "Who Killed Richard Cory?"

ROSS, HOWARD. Born Aug. 21, 1934 in NYC. Attended Juilliard, NYU. Bdwy debut 1965 in "Oliver," followed by "1600 Pennsylvania Avenue," OB in "Jacques Brel Is Alive . . . ," "Beggar's Opera," "Philemon."

ROSS, JUSTIN. Born Dec. 15, 1954 in Brooklyn, NY. Debut 1974 OB in "More Than You Deserve, Bdwy 1975 in "Pippin."

ROSSI, GLORIA. Born Nov. 16, 1946 in San Francisco, CA. Attended SF State, Syracuse U. Bdwy debut 1973 in "The Desert Song," followed by "Gypsy," "The Old Glory" (OB).

ROSSOMME, RICHARD. Born Apr. 5, 1936 in Los Angeles, CA. Graduate San Jose State Col., Pasadena Playhouse. Debut OB 1975 in ELT's "Tenderloin."

ROUNDS, DAVID. Born Oct. 9, 1938 in Bronxville, NY. Attended Denison U. Bdwy debut 1965 in "Foxy" followed by "Child's Play" for which he received a Theatre World Award, "The Rothschilds," "The Last of Mrs. Lincoln," "Chicago," OB in "You Never Can Tell," "Money," "The Real Inspector Hound," "Epic of Buster Friend," "Enter A Free Man."

ROUSSEAU, CAROLLE. Born Jan. 21 in Belgium. Studied in Paris. NY debut 1976 with Royal Shakespeare Co. in "Henry V" (BAM).

ROUTLEDGE, PATRICIA. Born Feb. 17, 1929 in Birkenhead, Eng. Attended ULiverpool, Bristol Old Vic. Bdwy debut 1966 in "How's the World Treating You?," followed by "Darling of the Day," "1600 Pennsylvania Avenue."

ROWE, HANSFORD. Born May 12, 1924 in Richmond, VA. Graduate URichmond. Bdwy debut 1968 in "We Bombed in New Haven," OB in "Curley McDimple," "The Fantasticks," "Last Analysis," "God Says There Is No Peter Ott," "Mourning Becomes Electra," "Bus Stop.," "Secret Service," "Boy Meets Girl."

ROWLES, POLLY. Born Jan. 10, 1914 in Philadelphia, PA. Attended Carnegie Tech. Bdwy debut 1938 in "Julius Caesar," followed by "Richard III," "Golden State," "Small Hours, " "Gertie," "Time Out for Ginger," "Wooden Dish," "Goodbye Again," "Auntie Mame," "Look after Lulu," "A Mighty Man Is He," "No Strings," "Best Laid Plans," "Killing of Sister George," "40 Carats," "The Women," OB in "Older People," "Mrs. Warren's Profession."

RUBENSTEIN, BARBARA. Born in Chicago, IL. Graduate Northwestern U. Debut OB 1969 in "Your Own Thing," followed by "Wings," Bdwy in "Much Ado about Nothing" (1972), "Bubbling Brown Sugar."

RUBINSTEIN, JOHN, Born Dec. 8, 1946 in Los Angeles. Attended UCLA. Bdwy debut 1972 in "Pippin" for which he received a Theatre World Award.

RUDD, PAUL. Born May 15, 1940 in Boston, MA. OB in "Henry IV," followed by "King Lear," "A Cry of Players," "Midsummer Night's Dream," "An Evening with Merlin Finch," "In the Matter of J. Robert Oppenheimer," "Elagabalus," "Streamers" (LC), "Henry V" (CP), Bdwy in "The Changing Room," "The National Health," "The Glass Menagerie," "Ah, Wilderness."

RUPERT, MICHAEL. Born Oct. 23, 1951 in Denver, CO. Attended Pasadena Playhouse. Bdwy debut 1968 in "The Happy Time" for which he received Theatre World Award, followed by "Pippin."

RUSKIN, JEANNE. Born Nov. 6 in Saginaw, MI. Graduate NYU. Bdwy debut 1975 in "Equus."

RUSSAK, GERARD. Born Sept. 11, 1927 in Paterson, NJ. Attended NY Col. of Music. Bdwy bow 1967 in "Marat/deSade," followed by "Zorba," OB "The Fantasticks."

RUSSELL, DAVID. Born Aug. 9, 1949 in Allenwood, PA. Ithaca Col. graduate. Bdwy debut 1975 in "Shenandoah."

RYAN, CHARLENE. Born in NYC. Bdwy debut 1964 in "Never Live over a Pretzel Factory," followed by "Sweet Charity," "Fig Leaves Are Falling," "Coco," "A Funny Thing Happened on the Way to the Forum," "Chicago."

SABIN, DAVID. Born Apr. 24, 1937 in Washington, DC. Graduate Cath. U. Debut 1965 OB in "The Fantasticks," followed by "Now Is the Time for All Good Men," "Threepenny Opera" (LC), Bdwy in "The Yearling," "Slapstick Tragedy," "Jimmy Shine," "Gantry," "Ambassador," "Celebration."

SAKAMOTO, DENNIS. Born Jan. 23, 1948 in Chicago, IL. Attended SF State Col. Debut 1975 OB in "The Pursuit of Happiness" (ELT).

SAKATO, ATSUMI. Born in Japan. Graduate Sophia U., UHawaii. Debut 1976 OB in "The Primary English Class."

SALATA, GREGORY. Born July 21, 1949 in NYC. Graduate Queens Col. Bdwy debut 1975 in "Dance with Me," followed by "Equus."

SALIS, NANCY. Born Aug. 14, 1952 in Christopher, IL. Graduate UIll. Debut 1976 OB in ELT's "Follies."

SANDERS, RICHARD. Born Aug. 23, 1940 in Harrisburg, Pa. Graduate Carnegie Tech., LAMDA. Bdwy debut 1973 in "Raisin," followed by "Hamlet" (LC), "The Boss."

SANTELL, MARIE. Born July 8 in Brooklyn, NY. Bdwy debut 1957 "Music Man," followed by "A Funny Thing Happened on the Way . . . "Flora the Red Menace," "Pajama Game," "Mack and Mabel," OB in "Paisano," "Boys from Syracuse," "Peace," "Promenade," "The Drunkard," "Sensations," "The Cast Aways."

SAPPINGTON, FAY. Born May 22, 1906 in Galveston, TX. Attended UT, Pasadena Playhouse. Bdwy debut 1950 in "Southern Exposure," followed by "The Cellar and the Well," "Glad Tidings," "J. B.," "The Yearling," "Gold Rainbow," "Pippin," OB in "Campbells of Boston," "In Case of Accident."

SAUNDERS, LOIS ANN. Born May 14, 1939 in Toledo, OH. Attended Centenary Col., HB Studio. Debut 1964 OB in "Great Scott," followed by "Man with a Load of Mischief," "Follies."

SAUNDERS, MARY. Born Dec. 14, 1945 in Morristown, NJ. Graduate Mt. Holyoke, Middlebury. Debut 1975 OB in "Gift of the Magi."

SAVADGE, DEBORAH. Born Apr. 24 in Detroit, MI. Graduate UWis. Debut 1976 OB in "Rimers of Eldritch."

SCARDINO, DON. Born in Feb. 1949 in NYC. Attended CCNY. On Bdwy in "Loves of Cass McGuire," "Johnny No-Trump," "My Daughter, Your Son," "Godspell," OB in "Shout from the Rooftops," "Rimers of Eldritch," "The Unknown Solider and His Wife," "Godspell," "Moonchildren," "Kid Champion," "Comedy of Errors," "Secret Service," "Boy Meets Girl."

SCHACT, SAM. Born Apr. 19, 1936 in The Bronx, NY. Graduate CCNY. OB in"Fortune and Men's Eyes," "Cannibals," "I Met a Man," "The Increased Difficulty of Concentration" (LCR), "One Night Stands of a Noisy Passenger," "Owners," Bdwy in "The Magic Show."

SCHAEFER, CRAIG. Born Aug. 24, 1953 in San Gabriel, CA. Attended UCLA. Debut 1975 OB in "Tenderloin."

SCHLEE, ROBERT. Born June 13, 1938 in Williamsport, PA. Lycoming Col. graduate. Debut 1972 OB in "Dr. Selavy's Magic Theatre," followed by "Hotel for Criminals," "Threepenny Opera."

SCHMIDT, JACK. Born Sept. 19, 1927 in San Francisco, CA. Attended UCLA, Mex. City Col. Bdwy debut 1976 in "Something's Afoot."

SCHRAMM, DAVID. Born Aug. 14, 1946 in Louisville, KY. Attended Western Ky. U., Juilliard. Debut 1972 OB in "School for Scandal," followed by

r‍ole Schweid **Steve Scott** **Renee Semes** **John Sheridan** **Corie Sims**

‍wer Depths," "Women Beware Women," Bdwy in "Three Sisters," "Next ‍e I'll Sing to You," "Edward II," "Measure for Measure," "Robber Bride-‍m."

‍WEID, CAROLE. Born Oct. 5, 1946 in Newark, NJ. Graduate Boston U., ‍illiard. Bdwy debut 1970 in "Minnie's Boys," followed by "A Chorus Line," ‍B in "Love Me, Love My Children," "How To Succeed in Business . . ."

S‍OTT, GEORGE C. Born Oct. 18, 1927 in Wise, Va. OB in "Richard II" for ‍ich he received a Theatre World Award, followed by "As You Like It," ‍hildren of Darkness," "Desire under the Elms," Bdwy in "Comes a Day," ‍ dersonville Trial," "The Wall," "General Seeger," "Little Foxes," "Plaza Suite," "Uncle Vanya," "Death of a Salesman."

S‍OTT, MARTHA. Born Sept. 22, 1914 in Jamesport, MO. Graduate UMich. ‍dry debut 1938 in "Our Town," followed by "Foreigners," "The Willow and ‍," "Soldier's Wife," "Voice of the Turtle," "It Takes Two," "Design for a ‍ged Glass Window," "Gramercy Ghost," "The Number," "Male Animal," ‍emarkable Mr. Pennypacker," "Cloud 7," "A Distant Bell," "Tumbler," ‍ h Cousin," "Never Too Late," "The Subject Was Roses," "The Skin of Our ‍ ‍."

S‍OTT, STEVE. Born Oct. 11, 1949 in Denver, CO. Graduate UDenver. ‍t 1971 OB in "The Drunkard," followed by "Summer Brave," Bdwy 1975 ‍e Ritz."

S‍EL, VIRGINIA. Born July 26 in Harvey, IL. Attended Roosevelt U. ‍y debut 1975 in "Very Good Eddie" for which she received a Theatre ‍l Award.

S‍LDES, MARIAN. Born Aug. 23, 1928 in NYC. Attended Neighborhood ‍ouse. Bdwy debut 1947 in "Medea," followed by "Crime and Punish-‍nt," "That Lady," "Tower Beyond Tragedy," "Ondine," "On High ‍und," "Come of Age," "Chalk Garden," "The Milk Train Doesn't Stop ‍ Anymore," "The Wall," "A Gift of Time," "A Delicate Balance," "Before ‍ Go," "Father's Day," "Equus," OB in "Different," "Ginger Man," ‍cy Street," "Candle in the Wind."

S‍L, JANIE. Born Oct. 1, 1941 in Detroit, MI. Attended UDetroit. Debut ‍966 in "Mixed Doubles," followed by "Dark Horses," "Dames at Sea," ‍ Bernstein," Bdwy in "George M!," "Irene," "Over Here" for which ‍ eived a Theatre World Award, "Pal Joey."

S‍TZER, DANIEL. Born Feb. 13, 1933 in Passaic, NJ. Graduate Princeton, ‍ford, Harvard. Bdwy debut 1976 in "Knock Knock" for which he received ‍ eatre World Award.

S‍MES, RENEE. Born Feb. 27, 1947 in NYC. Attended NYU. Bdwy debut ‍ 4 in "Candide."

S‍NE, HAL. Born Mar. 17, 1948 in Far Rockaway, NY. Graduate Hofstra ‍ dwy debut 1975 in "Very Good Eddie."

S‍WHAN, APRIL. Born Apr. 10, 1940 in Chicago. Debut OB 1964 in "Jo," ‍ wed by "Hamlet," "Oklahoma!" (LC), "Mod Donna," Bdwy in "Race of ‍ y Men," "3 Bags Full" for which she received a Theatre World Award, ‍ ner at 8," "Cop-Out," "Much Ado about Nothing," "Over Here," "Rex."

S‍WN, DICK. Born Dec. 1 in Buffalo, NY. Attended UMiami. Bdwy debut ‍ 8 in "For Heaven's Sake, Mother," followed by "A Funny Thing Happened ‍ he Way . . . ," "The Egg," "Peterpat," "Fade Out-Fade In," "I'm Solo-‍ ," "Musical Jubilee," OB in "Rebirth Celebration of the Human Race."

S‍A, JOHN V. Born in North Conway, NH. Graduate Bates Col., Yale. ‍ut OB 1974 in "Yentl, the Yeshiva Boy," followed by "Gorky," "Battering ‍ ," Bdwy 1975 in "Yentl" for which he received a Theatre World Award.

S‍EN, MARTIN. Born Aug. 3, 1940 in Dayton, OH. Credits: OB in "The ‍ nnection," "Many Loves," "Jungle of Cities," "Wicked Cooks," "Hamlet," ‍ omeo and Juliet," "Hello and Goodbye," Bdwy in "Never Live over a Pretzel ‍ tory" (1964), "The Subject Was Roses," "Death of a Salesman."

S‍ELLEY, CAROLE. Born Aug. 16, 1939 in London, Eng. Bdwy debut 1965 ‍n "The Odd Couple," followed by "The Astrakhan Coat," "Loot," "Noel Coward's Sweet Potato," "Little Murders" (OB), "Hay Fever," "Absurd Person Singular," "The Norman Conquests."

SHELTON, REID. Born Oct. 7, 1924 in Salem, OR. Graduate UMich. Bdwy bow 1952 in "Wish You Were Here," followed by "Wonderful Town," "By the Beautiful Sea," "Saint of Bleecker Street," "My Fair Lady," "Oh! What a Lovely War!," "Carousel" (CC), "Canterbury Tales," "Rothschilds," "1600 Pennsylvania Avenue," OB in "Phedre," "Butterfly Dream," "Man with a Load of Mischief," "Beggar's Opera," "The Contractor," "Cast Aways."

SHELTON, SLOANE. Born Mar. 17, 1934 in Asheville, NC. Attended Berea Col., RADA. Bdwy debut 1967 in "Imaginary Invalid," followed by "Touch of the Poet," "Tonight at 8:30," "I Never Sang for My Father," OB in "Androcles and the Lion," "The Maids," "Way of the World," "Dark of the Moon," "Basic Training of Pavlo Hummel," "Felix," "Bits and Pieces," "The Runner Stumbles."

SHERIDAN, JOHN. Born May 9, 1947 in Newton, Mass. OB in "Your Own Thing," "Best Foot Forward," "Beggar on Horseback," Bdwy in "No, No, Nanette," "Gypsy" for which he received a Theatre World Award.

SHIMODA, YUKI. Born Aug. 10, 1921 in Sacramento, CA. Graduate Sacramento Jr. Col. Bdwy debut 1952 in "Teahouse of the August Moon," followed by "Auntie Mame," "Pacific Overtures."

SHIMONO, SAB. Born in Sacramento, Cal. Graduate UCal. Bdwy bow 1965 in "South Pacific" (CC), followed by "Mame," "Lovely Ladies, Kind Gentlemen," "Pacific Overtures," OB in "Santa Anita," "Ride the Winds."

SHYRE, PAUL. Born Mar. 8, 1926 in NYC. Attended UFla., AADA. Debut OB 1956 in "Pictures in a Hallway," followed by "Purple Dust," "Cock-a-Doodle Dandy," "U.S.A.," Bdwy in "I Knock at the Door," "Absurd Person Singular."

SIDNEY, SYLVIA. Born Aug. 8, 1910 in NYC. Attended Theatre Guild Sch. Bdwy debut 1926 in "Prunella," followed by "The Squall," "Crime," "Mirrors," "The Breaks," "Gods of the Lightning," "Nice Women," "Cross-Roads," "Many a Slip," "Bad Girl," "To Quito and Back," "Gentle People," "We Will Never Die," "Fourposter," "Very Special Baby," "Enter Laughing," "Barefoot in the Park," "Riverside Drive" (OB), "Me Jack, You Jill."

SIEBERT, CHARLES. Born Mar. 9, 1938 in Kenosha, WI. Graduate Marquette U., LAMDA. Appeared in "Richard III" (CP), "Galileo" (LC), on Bdwy in "Jimmy Shine," "Gingerbread Lady," "Sticks and Bones," "Lysistrata," "The Changing Room," "Cat on a Hot Tin Roof," OB in "Wilde," "Rubbers."

SIGNORELLI, TOM. Born Oct. 19, 1939 in Brooklyn, NY. Attended UCLA. Debut 1960 OB in "Look Back in Anger," followed by "Bury the Dead," "Scapin," "Pretenders," Bdwy debut 1958 in "General Seeger," followed by "Borstal Boy."

SILLIMAN, MAUREEN. Born Dec. 3 in NYC. Attended Hofstra U. Bdwy debut 1975 in "Shenandoah."

SILLS, PAWNEE. Born in Castalia, NC. Attended Bklyn Col. Debut OB 1962 in "Raisin Hell in the Sun," followed by "Mr. Johnson," "Black Happening," "One Last Look" "NY and Who to Blame It On," "Cities in Bezique," "I'd Go to Heaven if I Was Good," "Oakville, U.S.A.," "Hocus-Pocus," "And So to Bed."

SILVER, STUART. Born June 29, 1947 in Hollywood, CA. Attended URochester, AADA. Debut 1969 OB in "Little Murders," followed by "Seven Days of Mourning," "Dance Wi' Me," "Wanted," "The Making of Americans," "Dance with Me."

SIMMONS, KEITH. Born June 2, 1955 in Jamaica, NY. Bdwy debut 1973 in "Seesaw," followed by "Raisin."

SIMS, CORIE. Born Feb. 23, 1948 in NYC. Graduate Hofstra U. Debut OB 1970 in "You're a Good Man, Charlie Brown," followed by "The Hot l Baltimore."

SIMS, MARLEY. Born Feb. 23, 1948 in NYC. Graduate Hofstra U. Debut OB 1971 in "The Me Nobody Knows," followed by "Godspell" OB and Bdwy.

SINDEN, DONALD. Born Oct. 9, 1923 in Plymouth, Eng. Attended Webber-Douglas School. After 33 years in the London theatre, made his Bdwy debut 1974 in "London Assurance," followed by "Habeas Corpus."

SKALA, LILIA. Born in Vienna; graduate UDresden. Bdwy debut 1941 in "Letters to Lucerne," followed by "With a Silk Thread," "Call Me Madam," "Diary of Anne Frank," "Threepenny Opera" (CC), "Zelda," "40 Carats," OB in "Medea and Jason," "Gorky."

SLACK, BEN. Born July 23, 1937 in Baltimore, MD. Graduate Catholic U. Debut 1971 OB in "Oedipus at Colonus," followed by "Interrogation of Havana," "Rain," "Thunder Rock," "Trelawny of the Wells," Bdwy 1976 in "Legend."

SMALL, NEVA. Born Nov. 17, 1952 in NYC. Bdwy debut 1964 in "Something More," followed by "Impossible Years," "Henry, Sweet Henry," "Frank Merriwell," "Something's Afoot," OB in "Ballad for a Firing Squad," "Tell Me Where the Good Times Are," "How Much, How Much?," "F. Jasmine Addams," "Macbeth" (LC), "Yentl, the Yeshiva Boy."

Marcus Smythe

Barbara Spiegel

Scott Stevensen

June Squibb

Mark Syers

SMITH, ALEXANDRA. Born Apr. 25, 1944 in Sydney, Aust. Graduate Poston U. Debut 1974 OB in "The Hot l Baltimore."

SMITH, ALEXIS. Born June 8, 1921 in Penticton, Can. Attended LACC. Bdwy debut 1971 in "Follies," followed by "The Women," "Summer Brave."

SMITH, BARREY. Born in Presque Isle, ME. Graduate Wheaton Col., Princeton. Bdwy debut 1973 in "Grease."

SMYTHE, MARCUS. Born Mar. 26, 1950 in Berea, OH. Graduate Otterbein Col., Ohio U. Debut 1975 OB in "Tenderloin."

SNYDER, ARLEN DEAN. Born Mar. 3, 1933 in Rice, KS. Graduate UTulsa, UIowa. Bdwy bow 1965 in "The Family Way," followed by OB's "Benito Cereno," "Hogan's Goat," "Miss Pete," "Open 24 Hours," "Candyapple," "June Moon," "Big Broadcast," "Thunder Rock," "Streamers."

SNYDER, NANCY E. Born Dec. 2, 1949 in Kankakee, IL. Graduate Webster Col., Neighborhood Playhouse. Bdwy debut 1976 in "Knock Knock."

SOIFFER, FREDA. Born Mar. 10, 1950 in NYC. Attended NYU. Bdwy debut 1974 in "Music! Music!" (CC) followed by "So Long, 174th Street."

SOLEN, PAUL. Born Mar. 27, 1941 in Cincinnati, O. Bdwy debut 1964 in "Hello, Dolly!," followed by "Breakfast at Tiffany's," "Dear World," "Pippin," "Chicago."

SORREL, SCOTT. Born Apr. 9, 1964 in Newport Beach, CA. Attended HB Studio. Debut 1976 OB in "The Old Glory."

SPIEGEL, BARBARA. Born Mar. 12 in NYC. Debut 1969 with LCRep in "Camino Real," "Operation Sidewinder" and "Beggar on Horseback," followed by "Feast for Flies."

SPINELLI, LARRY. Born July 20, 1931 in NYC. Debut 1971 OB in "One Flew over the Cuckoo's Nest," followed by "Soon," "The Hot l Baltimore."

SPONSELLER, HOWARD. Born Dec. 30, 1945 in New London, CT. Attended Carnegie-Mellon U. Debut OB 1971 in "Godspell," followed by "Ionescopade."

SQUIBB, JUNE. Born Nov. 6 in Vandalia, IL. Attended Cleveland Play House, HB Studio. Debut 1956 OB in "Sable Brush," followed by "Boy Friend," "Lend an Ear," "Another Language," Bdwy in "Gypsy" (1960), "The Happy Time."

STADLEN, LEWIS J. Born Mar. 7, 1947 in Brooklyn. Attended Neighborhood Playhouse. Bdwy debut 1970 in "Minnie's Boys" for which he received a Theatre World Award, followed by "Happiness Cage" (OB), "The Sunshine Boys," "Candide."

STANSBURY, HOPE. Born Nov. 23, 1945 in NYC. OB in "Henry and Henrietta," "Just before the War with the Eskimos," "Run to the Sea," "Chocolates," "Couchmates," "Paderefski," "Howies," "Women behind Bars."

STAPLETON, MAUREEN. Born June 21, 1925 in Troy, NY. Attended HB Studio. Bdwy debut 1946 in "Playboy of the Western World," followed by "Antony and Cleopatra," "Detective Story," "Bird Cage," "Rose Tattoo" for which she received a Theatre World Award, "The Emperor's Clothes," "The Crucible," "Richard III," "The Seagull," "27 Wagons Full of Cotton," "Orpheus Descending," "The Cold Wind and the Warm," "Toys in the Attic," "Glass Menagerie," (1965 & 1975), "Plaza Suite," "Norman, Is That You?," "Gingerbread Lady," "Country Girl," "Secret Affairs of Mildred Wild."

STATTEL, ROBERT. Born Nov. 20, 1937 in Floral Park, NY. Graduate Manhattan Col. Debut OB 1958 in "Heloise," followed by "When I Was a Child," "Man and Superman," "The Storm," "Don Carlos," "Taming of the Shrew," NYSFs "Titus Andronicus," "Henry IV," "Peer Gynt," and "Hamlet," LCR's "Danton's Death," "Country Wife," "Caucasian Chalk Circle," and "King Lear," "Iphigenia in Aulis," "Ergo," "The Persians," "Blue Boys," "The Minister's Black Veil," "Four Friends,""Two Character Play," Bdwy in "A Patriot for Me," "Sherlock Holmes."

STENBORG, HELEN. Born Jan. 24, 1925 in Minneapolis, MN. Attended Hunter Col. OB in "A Doll's House," "A Month in the Country," "Say Nothing," "Rosmersholm," "Rimers of Eldrich," "Trial of the Catonsville 9," "Hot l Baltimore," "Pericles," "A Doll's House," "Elephant in the House," Bdwy in "Sheep on the Runway,"

STEPHENS, GARN. Born in Tulsa, OK. Graduate Calif. Western U., Pasadena Playhouse. Debute 1972 OB and Bdwy in "Grease."

STERN, JOSEPH. Born Sept. 3, 1940 in Los Angeles, CA. Graduate UCLA. Debut 1967 OB in "MacBird," followed by "The Homecoming," "Henry IV," "Last Analysis," "Cymbeline," "The Hot l Baltimore."

STERNHAGEN, FRANCES. Born Jan. 13, 1932 in Washington, DC. Vassar Graduate. OB in "Admirable Bashful," "Thieves' Carnival," "Country Wife,"

"Ulysses in Nighttown," "Saintliness of Margery Kemp," "The Room," "A Slight Ache," "Displaced Person," "Playboy of the Western World" (LC), Bdwy in "Great Day in the Morning," "Right Honourable Gentleman," with APA in "Cocktail Party" and "Cock-a-doodle Dandy," "The Sign in Sidney Brustein's Window," "Enemies" (LC), "The Good Doctor," "Equus."

STEVENSEN, SCOTT. Born May 4, 1951 in Salt Lake City, UT. Attended USCal. Bdwy debut 1974 in "Good News" for which he received a Theatre World Award.

STEVENSON, MARGOT. Born Feb. 8, 1918 in NYC. Brearley School graduate. Bdwy debut 1932 in "Firebird," followed by "Evensong," "A Party," "Barretts of Wimpole Street," "Symphony," "Truly Valiant," "Call It a Day," "Stage Door," "You Can't Take It with You," "Golden Wings," "Little Women" (CC), "Rugged Path," "Leading Lady," "The Young and Beautiful," "The Apple Cart," "Triple Play," "Lord Pengo," "Hostile Witness," "The Royal Family," OB in "Autumn Ladies and Their Lovers' Lovers."

STEWART, JEAN-PIERRE. Born May 4, 1946 in NYC Graduate CCNY. Appeared OB in "Henry IV," "King Lear," "Cry of Players," "In the Matter of J. Robert Oppenheimer," "The Miser," "Long Day's Journey into Night," "American Night Cry," "King Lear," "The Old Ones," "Dancing for the Kaiser," "Primary English Class."

STEWART, PATRICIA. Born Aug. 29, 1939 in Bronxville, NY. Graduate St. Lawrence U. Debut OB 1963 in "Best Foot Forward," followed by "The Ginger Man," "Dr. Faustus," "Kid Champion," "Wood Painting," "The Artists," "Elagabalus," "Spelling Bee."

STIERS, DAVID OGDEN. Born Oct. 31, 1942 in Peoria, IL. Attended UOre., Juilliard. Debut OB 1972 in "School for Scandal," followed by "Lower Depths," "The Hostage," "Women Beware Women," Bdwy in "Three Sisters," "Measure for Measure," "Beggar's Opera," "Scapin," "Ulysses in Nighttown," "The Magic Show."

STILLER, JERRY. Born June 8, 1931 in NYC. Graduate Syracuse U., HB Studio, Debut 1953 OB in "Coriolanus," followed by "The Power and the Glory," "Golden Apple," "Measure for Measure," "Taming of the Shrew," "Carefree Tree," "Diary of a Scoundrel," "Romeo and Juliet," "As You Like It," "Two Gentlemen of Verona," Bdwy 1975 in "The Ritz."

STREEP, MERYL. Born Sept. 22 in Summit, NJ. Graduate Vassar, Yale. Debut 1975 OB in "Trelawny of the Wells," followed by "27 Wagons Full of Cotton" for which she received a Theatre World Award, "A Memory of Two Mondays," "Secret Service," "Henry V," "Measure for Measure" (CP).

STUTHMAN, FRED. Born June 27, 1919 in Long Beach, CA. Attended UCal. Debut 1970 OB in "Hamlet," followed by "Uncle Vanya," "Charles Abbot & Son," "She Stoops to Conquer," "Master Builder," "Taming of the Shrew," "Misalliance," "Merchant of Venice," "Conditions of Agreement," "The Play's the Thing," "Ghosts," "The Father," "The Hot l Baltimore," "The Cherry Orchard," Bdwy 1975 in "Sherlock Holmes."

SULLIVAN, IAN. Born Apr. 1, 1933 in NYC. Bdwy debut 1970 in "Man of La Mancha," followed by "Vivat! Vivat! Regina!," "Home Sweet Homer."

SUTORIUS, JAMES. Born Dec. 14, 1944 in Euclid, OH. Graduate Ill. Wesleyan, AMDA. Bdwy debut 1970 in "The Cherry Orchard," followed by "The Changing Room," OB in "Servant of Two Masters," "Hamlet."

SWANSEN, LARRY. Born Nov. 10, 1930 in Roosevelt, OK. Graduate OKU. Bdwy debut 1966 in "Those That Play the Clowns," followed by "Great White Hope," OB in "Dr. Faustus Lights the Lights," "Thistle in My Bed," "A Darker Flower," "Vincent," "MacBird," "Unknown Soldier and His Wife," "Sound of Music," "Conditioning of Charlie One," "Ice Age."

SWEET, DOLPH. Born July 18, 1920 in NYC. Graduate Columbia U. Bdwy debut 1960 in "Rhinoceros," followed by "Romulus," "The Advocate," "Sign in Sidney Brustein's Window," "Great Indoors," "Natural Look," "Billy," "Penny Wars," OB in "The Dragon," "Too Much Johnson," "Sjt. Musgrave's Dance," "Ceremony of Innocence," "Death of J.K.," "Bread," "Streamers."

SYERS, MARK. Born Oct. 25, 1952 in Trenton, NJ. Graduate Emerson Col. Bdwy debut 1976 in "Pacific Overtures."

SYMONDS, ROBERT. Born Dec. 1, 1926 in Bristow, OK. Attended TexU, UMo. With LCRep in "Danton's Death," "Country Wife," "Alchemist," "Galileo," "St. Joan," "Tiger at the Gates," "Cyrano," "Cry of Players," "Inner Journey," "The Miser," "Time of Your Life," "Camino Real," "Disintegration of James Cherry," "Silence," "Scenes from American Life," "Play Strindberg," "Mary Stuart," "Narrow Road to the Deep North," "Enemies," "The Plough and the Stars," "Merchant of Venice," "Streetcar Named Desire," Bdwy 1976 in "The Poison Tree."

Melinda Tanner   **David Thomé**   **Clarice Taylor**   **William Thomas, Jr.**   **Virginia Vestoff**

TABORI, KRISTOFFER. Born Aug. 4, 1952 in Calif. Bdwy debut 1969 in "The Penny Wars," followed by "Henry V," "Habeas Corpus," OB in "Emile and the Detectives," "Guns of Carrar," "A Cry of Players," "Dream of a Blacklisted Actor," "How Much, How Much?" for which he received a Theatre World Award, "The Wager."

TANNER, MELINDA. Born Oct. 5, 1946 in Los Angeles, CA. Attended LACC. Debut 1975 in "The Sea," followed by "Godspell."

TANNER, TONY. Born July 27, 1932 in Hillingdon, Eng. Attended Webber-Douglas School. Bdwy debut 1966 in "Half a Sixpence," followed by "No Sex Please, We're British," "Sherlock Holmes," OB in "Little Boxes," "The Homecoming."

TARLETON, DIANE. Born in Baltimore, MD. Graduate UMd. Bdwy debut 1965 in "Anya," followed by "A Joyful Noise," "Elmer Gantry," "Yentl," OB in "A Time for the Gentle People," "Spoon River Anthology."

TATE, DENNIS. Born Aug. 31, 1938 in Iowa City, IA. Attended Iowa U. OB in "Black Monday," "The Blacks," "The Hostage," "Bohikee Creek," "Happy Bar," "Trials of Brother Jero," "Strong Breed," "Goa," "Electronic Nigger," "Black Quartet," "Life and Times of J. Walter Smintheus," "Jazznite," "Cherry Orchard," "Phantasmagoria Historia . . . ," "Merry Wives of Windsor," Bdwy in "Les Blancs." (1970), "The Poison Tree."

TATUM, BILL. Born May 6, 1947 in Philadelphia, PA. Graduate Catawba Col. Bdwy debut 1971 in "Man of La Mancha," followed by ELT's "Missouri Legend" (OB).

TAYLOR, CLARICE. Born Sept. 20, in Buckingham County, VA. Attended New Theater School. Debut 1943 OB in "Striver's Row," followed by "Major Barbara," "Family Portrait," "Trouble in Mind," "The Egg and I," "A Medal for Willie," "Nat Turner," "Simple Speaks His Mind," "Gold Through the Trees," "The Owl Answers," "Song of the Lusitanian Bogey," "Summer of the 17th Doll," "Kongi's Harvest," "Daddy Goodness," "God Is a (Guess What?)," "An Evening of One Acts," "5 on the Black Hand Side," "Man Better Man," "Day of Absence," "Brotherhood," "Akokawe," "Rosalee Pritchett," "Sty of the Blind Pig," "Duplex" (LC), "Wedding Band," Bdwy 1975 in "The Wiz."

TEITEL, CAROL. Born Aug. 1, 1929 in NYC. Attended AmThWing. On Bdwy in "The Country Wife," "The Entertainer," "Hamlet," "Marat/deSade," "All over Town," OB in "Way of the World," "Plough and the Stars," "The Anatomist," "Country Scandal," "Under Milk Wood," "The Bench," "7 Days of Mourning," "Duet," "Trio," "Figures in the Sand," "The Old Ones."

THACKER, RUSS. Born June 23, 1946 in Washington, DC. Attended Montgomery Col. Debut 1967 in "Life with Father" (CC), followed OB by "Your Own Thing" for which he received a Theatre World Award, "Dear Oscar," "Once I Saw A Boy Laughing," Bdwy in "Grass Harp," "Heathen," "Music! Music!" (CC), "Home Sweet Homer," "Me Jack You Jill."

THEODORE, DONNA. Born July 25, 1945 in Oakland, CA. Debut 1974 OB in "Oh, Lady, Lady." Bdwy 1975 in "Shenandoah" for which she received a Theatre World Award.

THOMAS, WILLIAM, JR. Born in Columbus, O. Graduate Ohio State U. Debut OB 1972 in "Touch," followed by "Natural," "Godspell."

THOMÉ, DAVID. Born July 24, 1951 in Salt Lake City, UT. Bdwy debut 1971 in "No, No, Nanette," followed by "Different Times," "Good News," "Rodgers and Hart," "A Chorus Line."

THOMPSON, ERNEST. Born Nov. 6, 1949 in Bellow Falls, VT. Attended Catholic U., UMd., American U. Bdwy debut 1975 in "Summer Brave."

THOMPSON, ROBERT E. Born Oct. 7, 1916 in Kansas City, MO. Graduate North Central Col., UMich, Goodman Theatre. Debut 1941 OB in "Post Mortum," Bdwy bow 1973 in "Status Quo Vadis," followed by "Angel Street."

TIRELLI, JAIME. Born Mar. 4, 1945 in NYC. Attended UMundial, AADA. Debut 1975 OB in "Rubbers," "Yanks 3, Detroit O."

TOLAYDO, MICHAEL. Born July 23, 1946 in Nairobi, Kenya. Attended Houston Baptist Col., AADA. Bdwy debut 1970 in "The Cherry Orchard," followed by "Robber Bridegroom," "Edward II," "The Time of Your Life," "Three Sisters," OB in "Hamlet."

TORN, RIP. Born Feb. 6, 1931 in Temple, TX. Graduate UTx. Bdwy bow 1956 in "Cat on a Hot Tin Roof," followed by "Sweet Bird of Youth," "Daughter of Silence," "Strange Interlude," "Blues for Mr. Charlie," "Country Girl" (CC), "Glass Menagerie," OB in "Chaparral" (1958) for which he received a Theatre World Award, "The Cuban Thing," "The Kitchen," "Deer Park," "Dream of a Blacklisted Actor," "Dance of Death," "MacBeth," "Barbary Shore."

TORRES, ANDY. Born Aug. 10, 1945 in Ponce, PR. Attended AMDA. Bdwy debut 1969 in "Indians," followed by "Purlie," "Don't Bother Me, I Can't Cope," "The Wiz," OB in "Billy Noname."

TOWB, HARRY. Born July 27, 1925 in Larne, Ire. Attended Belfast Tech. Col. Bdwy debut 1966 in "Under the Weather," followed by "Sherlock Homes," "Travesties."

TRAPANI, LOU. Born Dec. 17, 1947 in Brooklyn, NY. Graduate Hofstra U. Debut OB 1970 in "Journey to Bahia," followed by "Hamlet," "She Stoops to Conquer," "Taming of the Shrew," "Misalliance," "Merchant of Venice," "And They Put Handcuffs on Flowers," "Total Eclipse," "Work."

TRIGGER, IAN J. Born Sept. 30, 1941 in Eng. Graduate RADA. NY debut OB 1973 in "Taming of the Shrew" followed by "Scapino," "True History of Squire Jonathan . . . ," Bdwy in "Scapino" (1974), "Habeas Corpus."

TUCCI, MICHAEL. Born Apr. 15, 1946 in NYC. Graduate C.W. Post Col. Debut 1974 OB in "Godspell," Bdwy 1975 in "Grease."

TUPOU, MANU. Born in 1939 in Fiji Islands. Attended San Francisco State U., ULondon. Bdwy bow 1969 in "Indians," followed by "Othello," "Capt. Brassbound's Conversion," OB in "Madwoman of Chaillot," "Passion of Antigona Perez," "Wedding of Iphigenia," "The Old Glory."

TYRRELL, JOHN. Born Nov. 24, 1948 in Perth Amboy, NJ. Graduate Marquette U., Neighborhood Playhouse. Bdwy debut 1974 in "Equus."

UCHIDA, CHRISTINE. Born Apr. 20, 1952. Bdwy debut 1976 in "Home Sweet Homer."

URMSTON, KENNETH. Born Aug. 6, 1929 in Cincinnati, OH. Attended Xavier U. Bdwy debut 1950 in "Make a Wish," followed by "Top Banana," "Guys and Dolls," "John Murray Anderson's Almanac," "Can-Can," "Silk Stockings," "Oh Captain!," "Bells Are Ringing," "Redhead," "Madison Avenue," "Tenderloin," "We Take the Town," "Lovely Ladies, Kind Gentlemen," "Follies," "Pippin."

VAN BENSCHOTEN, STEPHEN. Born Aug. 27, 1943 in Washington, DC. Graduate LaSalle Col., Yale. Debut 1967 OB in "King John," Bdwy in "Unlikely Heroes," "Grease."

VAN VOOREN, MONIQUE. Born Mar. 25, 1938 in Brussels, Belg. Attended Brussels U., NYU. Bdwy debut 1954 in "John Murray Anderson's Almanac," followed by "Destry Rides Again," "Man on the Moon."

VARRONE, GENE. Born Oct. 30, 1929 in Brooklyn, NY. Graduate LIU. Bdwy in "Damn Yankees," "Take Me Along," "Ziegfeld Follies," "Goldilocks," "Wildcat," "Tovarich," "Subways Are for Sleeping," "Bravo Giovanni," "Drat! The Cat!," "Fade Out—Fade In," "Don't Drink the Water," "Dear World," "Coco," "A Little Night Music," "So Long, 174th Street," OB in "Promenade."

VERDON, GWEN. Born Jan 13, 1926 in Culver City, CA. Bdwy debut 1950 in "Alive and Kicking," followed by "Can-Can" for which she received a Theatre World Award, "Damn Yankees," "New Girl in Town," "Redhead," "Sweet Charity," "Children, Children," "Chicago."

VESTOFF, VIRGINIA. Born Dec. 9, 1940 in NYC. Bdwy bow 1960 in "From A to Z," followed by "Irma La Duce," "Baker Street," "1776," "Via Galactica," "Nash at 9," "Boccaccio," OB in "Boy Friend," "Crystal Heart," "Fall Out," "New Cole Porter Revue," "Man with a Load of Mischief," "Love and Let Love," "Short-changed Review."

VICKERS, LARRY. Born June 8, 1947 in Harrisonburg, VA. Attended Howard U. Bdwy debut in "Purlie," followed by "Shirley McLaine at the Palace."

VITA, MICHAEL. Born in 1941 in NYC. Studied at HB Studio. Bdwy debut 1967 in "Sweet Charity," followed by "Golden Rainbow," "Promises, Promises," "Chicago," OB in "Sensations," "That's Entertainment."

VITELLA, SEL. Born July 7, 1934 in Boston, MA. Graduate San Francisco Inst. of Music. Debut 1975 OB in "Merchant of Venice," Bdwy 1976 in "Something's Afoot."

VON FURSTENBERG, BETSY. Born Aug. 16, 1931 in Westphalia, Ger. Attended Neighborhood Playhouse. Bdwy debut 1951 in "Second Threshold," followed by "Dear Barbarians," "Oh, Men! Oh, Women!," "Chalk Garden," "Child of Fortune," "Nature's Way," "Wonderful Town," "Mary, Mary," "Paisley Convertible," "Gingerbread Lady," "Absurd Person Singular," OB in "The Making of Moo," "Season of Choice," "Measure for Measure."

Chet Walker

Cynthia Wells

Stuart Warmflash

Patricia Wheel

Jim Weston

VON SCHERLER, SASHA. Born Dec. 12. in NYC. Bdwy debut 1959 in "Look after Lulu," followed by "Rape of the Belt," "The Good Soup," "Great God Brown," "First Love," "Alfie," "Harold," "Bad Habits," OB in "Admirable Bashville," "The Comedian," "Conversation Piece," "Good King Charles' Golden Days," "Under Milk Wood," "Plays for Bleecker Street," "Ludlow Fair," "Twelfth Night," "Sondra," "Cyrano de Bergerac," "Crimes of Passion," "Henry VI," "Trelawny of the Wells," "Screens," "Soon Jack November," "Pericles," "Kid Champion," "Henry V."

WAITE, JOHN THOMAS. Born Apr. 19, 1948 in Syracuse, NY. Attended Syracuse U. Debut 1976 OB in "The Fantasticks."

WALKEN, CHRISTOPHER. Born Mar. 31, 1943 in Astoria, NY. Attended Hofstra U. Bdwy debut 1958 in "J. B.," followed by "High Spirits," "Baker Street," "The Lion in Winter," "Measure for Measure" (CP), "Rose Tattoo" (CC'66) for which he received a Theatre World Award, "Unknown Soldier and His Wife," "Rosencrantz and Guildenstern Are Dead," "Scenes from American Life," (LC), "Cymbeline" (NYSF), LC's "Enemies," "The Plough and the Stars," "Merchant of Venice," "The Tempest," "Troilus and Cressida," and "Macbeth," "Sweet Bird of Youth," OB in "Best Foot Forward," "Iphigenia in Aulis," "Lemon Sky," "Kid Champion."

WALKER, CHET. Born June 1, 1954 in Stuttgart, AR. Bdwy debut 1972 in "On the Town," followed by "Ambassador," "Pajama Game," "Lorelei," "Pippin."

WALKER, DOUGLAS W. Born Oct. 18, 1951 in NYC. Attended AMDA. Debut 1976 OB in "Godspell."

WALKER, KATHRYN. Born in Jan. in Philadelphia, PA. Graduate Wells Col., Harvard, LAMDA. Debut 1971 OB in "Alpha Beta," followed by "Kid Champion," "Rebel Women," Bdwy 1973 in "The Good Doctor," "Mourning Pictures."

WALKER, MICHAEL. Born Mar. 11, 1950 in Kenya. Bdwy debut 1974 in "Sherlock Holmes."

WALKER, PETER. Born July 24, 1927 in Mineola, NY. Studied with Stella Adler. Bdwy debut 1955 in "Little Glass Clock," followed by "Dear World," "Follies," "Where's Charley?", OB in "Dancing for the Kaiser."

WALLACE, LEE. Born July 15, 1930 in NYC. Attended NYU. Debut OB 1966 in "Journey of the Fifth Horse," followed by "Saturday Night," "An Evening with Garcia Lorca," "Macbeth," "Booth Is Back in Town," "Awake and Sing," "Shepherd of Avenue B," "Basic Training of Pavlo Hummel," Bdwy in "Secret Affairs of Mildred Wild," "Molly," "Zalmen, or the Madness of God."

WALLACE, TIMOTHY. Born July 24, 1947 in Racine, WI. Graduate UWisc, Penn State U. Debut 1976 OB in "The Rimers of Eldritch" (ELT).

WALSH, THOMAS J. Born Mar. 15, 1950 in Auburn, NY. Attended Boston Consv. Bdwy debut 1973 in "Seesaw," followed by "Rachel Lily Rosenbloom," "Music! Music!," "A Chorus Line."

WARD, DOUGLAS TURNER. Born May 5, 1930 in Burnside, LA. Attended UMich. Bdwy bow 1959 in "A Raisin in the Sun," followed by "One Flew over the Cuckoo's Nest," "Last Breeze of Summer," OB in "The Iceman Cometh," "The Blacks," "Pullman Car Hiawatha," "Bloodknot," "Happy Ending," "Day of Absence," "Kongi's Harvest," "Ceremonies in Dark Old Men," "The Harangues," "The Reckoning," "Frederick Douglass through His Own Words," "River Niger."

WARD, JANET. Born Feb. 19 in NYC. Attended Actors Studio. Bdwy debut 1945 in "Dream Girl," followed by "Anne of a Thousand Days," "Detective Story," "King of Friday's Men," "Middle of the Night," "Miss Lonelyhearts," "J. B.," "Cheri," "The Egg," "Impossible Years," "Of Love Remembered," OB in "Chaparral," "The Typists and The Tiger," "Summertree," "Dream of a Blacklisted Actor," "Cruising Speed 600MPH," "One Flew over the Cuckoo's Nest," "Love Gotta Come by Saturday Night," "Home Is the Hero," "Love Death Plays."

WARFIELD, MARLENE. Born June 19, 1941 in Queens, NY. Attended Actors Studio. Bdwy debut 1968 in "The Great White Hope" for which she received a Theatre World Award, OB in "The Blacks," "All's Well That Ends Well," "Volpone," "Taming of the Shrew," "Who's Got His Own," "Elektra," "2 by Cromwell," "Midsummer Night's Dream," "So Nice They Named It Twice."

WARMFLASH, STUART. Born June 27, 1949 in NYC. Graduate NYU. Debut 1970 OB in "The Lady from Maxim's," followed by "Secret Service," "Boy Meets Girl."

WARREN, JENNIFER. Born Aug. 12, 1941 in NYC. Graduate UWisc. Debut 1967 OB in "Scuba Duba," followed by "Trees in the Wind," Bdwy 1972 in "6 Rms Riv Vu" for which she received a Theatre World Award, followed by "P.S. Your Cat Is Dead."

WASHINGTON, VERNON. Born Aug. 10, 1927 in Hartford CT. Attended Wholter School of Drama. OB in "Cabin in the Sky," "The Strong Breed," "Trials of Brother Jero," "Scuba Duba," "Hocus-Pocus," Bdwy 1976 in "Bubbling Brown Sugar."

WATERSTON, SAM. Born Nov. 15, 1940 in Cambridge, MA. Graduate Yale. Bdwy bow 1963 in "Oh, Dad, Poor Dad . . . ," followed by "First One Asleep, Whistle," "Halfway up the Tree," "Indians," "Hay Fever," "Much Ado about Nothing," OB in "As You Like It," "Thistle in My Bed," "The Knack," "Fitz," "Biscuit," "La Turista," "Posterity For Sale," "Ergo," "Muzeeka," "Red Cross," "Henry IV," "Spitting Image," "I Met a Man," "Brass Butterfly," "Trial of the Catonsville 9," "Cymbeline," "Hamlet," "A Meeting by the River," "The Tempest," "A Doll's House," "Measure for Measure."

WATSON, DOUGLASS. Born Feb. 24, 1921 in Jackson, GA. Graduate UNC. Bdwy bow 1947 in "The Iceman Cometh," followed by "Antony and Cleopatra" for which he received a Theatre World Award, "Leading Lady," "Richard III," "Happiest Years," "That Lady," "Wisteria Trees," "Romeo and Juliet," "Desire under the Elms," "Sunday Breakfast," "Cyrano de Bergerac," "Confidential Clerk," "Portrait of a Lady," "Miser," "Young and Beautiful," "Little Glass Clock," "Country Wife," "Man for All Seasons," "Chinese Prime Minister," "Marat/deSade," "Prime of Miss Jean Brodie," "Pirates of Penzance," NYSF's "Much Ado about Nothing," "King Lear," and "As You Like It," "Over Here," OB in "The Hunter," "Dancing for the Kaiser," "Money."

WEAVER, FRITZ. Born Jan. 19, 1926 in Pittsburgh, PA. Graduate UChicago. Bdwy debut 1955 in "Chalk Garden" for which he received a Theatre World Award, followed by "Protective Custody," "Miss Lonelyhearts," "All American," "Lorenzo," "The White House," "Baker Street," "Child's Play," "Absurd Person Singular," OB in "The Way of the World," "White Devil," "Doctor's Dilemma," "Family Reunion," "The Power and the Glory," "Great God Brown," "Peer Gynt," "Henry IV," "My Fair Lady" (CC).

WEBB, ROBB. Born Jan. 29, 1939 in Whitesburg, KY. Attended Ohio State U. Debut 1976 OB in "Who Killed Richard Cory?"

WEINER, ARN. Born July 19, 1931 in Brooklyn, NY. Attended Pratt, LACC. Bdwy debut 1966 in "Those That Play the Clowns," followed by "Yentl," OB in "Come Walk with Me," "Saving Grace," "Come Out, Carlo," "Evening with Chekhov," "Sunset."

WELCH, CHARLES C. Born Feb. 2, 1921 in New Britain, CT. Attended Randall Sch., AmThWing. Bdwy debut 1958 in "Cloud 7," followed by "Donnybrook," "Golden Boy," "Little Murders," "Holly Go Lightly," "Darling of the Day," "Dear World," "Follies," "Status Quo Vadis," "Shenandoah," OB in "Half-Past Wednesday," "Oh, Lady! Lady!"

WELLER, PETER. Born June 24, 1947 in Stevens Point, WI. Graduate AADA. Bdwy bow 1972 in "Sticks and Bones," followed by "Full Circle," "Summer Brave," OB in "Children," "Merchant of Venice," "Macbeth," "Rebel Women."

WELLS, CYNTHIA. Born Mar. 6, 1942 in Jackson, MN. Graduate Macalester Col, UMinn. Bdwy debut 1975 in "Very Good Eddie."

WENTZ, EARL. Born Mar. 22, 1938 in Charlotte, NC. Attended Charlotte, Wingate, Queens Cols. Debut 1976 OB in ELT's "Missouri Legend."

WESTON, JIM. Born Aug. 2, 1942 in Montclair, NJ. Attended Manchester Col. AADA. Bdwy bow 1969 in "Red, White and Maddox," followed by "Lovely Ladies, Kind Gentlemen," "Grease," "Over Here," OB in "She Loves Me," "Ballad of Johnny Pot," "A Gun Play."

WHEEL, PATRICIA. Born in NYC. Has appeared in "Cyrano," "The Tempest," "Arms and the Man," "Little Brown Jug," "Stars Weep," "Browning Version," "Cry of the Peacock," "Gertie," "Sacred Flame," "Soldiers," "Butterflies Are Free," "Voices," "The Women," "Grass Widows" (OB).

WHITEHEAD, PAXTON. Born in Kent, Eng. Attended Webber-Douglas Drama Sch. Bdwy debut 1962 in "The Affair," followed by "Beyond the Fringe," "Candida," "Habeas Corpus," OB in "Gallows Humour," "One Way Pendulum," "A Doll's House," "Rondelay."

Margaret Whitton   **J. Thomas Wierney**   **Elizabeth Wilson**   **Jerrold Ziman**   **Madonna Young**

WHITMORE, CHRISTINEA. Born Dec. 24, 1952 in Derby, CT. Attended HB Studio. Debut 1972 OB in "Trelawny of the Wells," Bdwy in "The National Health" (1974), "Ah, Wilderness."

WHITTON, MARGARET. (formerly Peggy) Born Nov. 30, 1950 in Philadelphia, PA. Debut 1973 OB in "Baba Goya," followed by "Arthur."

WIERNEY, J. THOMAS. Born Jan. 11, 1953 in Honolulu, HI. Graduate Syracuse U. Debut 1976 OB in ELT's "Panama Hattie."

WILCOX, RALPH. Born Jan. 30, 1951 in Milwaukee, WI. Attended UWisc. Debut 1971 OB in "Dirtiest Show in Town," followed by "Broadway," "Miracle Play," Bdwy in "Ain't Supposed to Die a Natural Death," "The Wiz."

WILKINSON, LISA. Born in NYC. Graduate NYU. Debut 1970 in "Slave Ship," followed by "Don't Fail Your Lovin' Daddy, Lily Plum," Bdwy 1974 in "Candide."

WILLIAMS, CURT. Born Nov. 17, 1935 in Mt. Holly, NJ. Graduate Oberlin Col., UMiami. Debut 1964 OB in "The Fantasticks," followed by "Pinafore," "Mikado," "Night Must Fall," "The Hostage," "Macbeth," "Ice Age," Bdwy 1970 in "Purlie."

WILLIAMS, DICK ANTHONY. Born Aug. 9, 1938 in Chicago, IL. Debut 1968 OB in "Big Time Buck White," followed by "Jamimma," "What the Winesellers Buy," Bdwy in "Ain't Supposed to Die a Natural Death," "We Interrupt This Program," "The Poison Tree."

WILLIAMS, SAMMY. Born Nov. 13, 1948 in Trenton, NJ. Bdwy debut 1969 in "The Happy Time," followed by "Applause," "Seesaw," "A Chorus Line."

WILLISON, WALTER. Born June 24, 1947 in Monterey Park, CA. Bdwy debut 1970 in "Norman, Is That You?," followed by "Two by Two" for which he received a Theatre World Award, "Wild and Wonderful," "Pippin."

WILSON, ELIZABETH. Born Apr. 4, 1925 in Grand Rapids, MI. Attended Neighborhood Playhouse. Bdwy debut 1953 in "Picnic," followed by "Desk Set," "Tunnel of Love," "Big Fish, Little Fish," "Sheep on the Runway," "Sticks and Bones," "Secret Affairs of Mildred Wild," OB in "Plaza 9," "Eh?," "Little Murders," "Good Woman of Setzuan," "Uncle Vanya," "Threepenny Opera."

WILSON, MARY LOUISE. Born Nov. 12, 1936 in New Haven, CT. Graduate Northwestern. OB in "Our Town," "Upstairs at the Downstairs," "Threepenny Opera," "A Great Career," "Whispers on the Wind," "Beggar's Opera," Bdwy in "Hot Spot," "Flora, the Red Menace," "Criss-Crossing," "Promises, Promises," "The Women," "Gypsy," "The Royal Family."

WINDE, BEATRICE. Born Jan. 6 in Chicago, Ill. Debut 1966 OB in "In White America," followed by "June Bug Graduates Tonight," "Strike Heaven on the Face." Bdwy 1971 in "Ain't Supposed to Die a Natural Death" for which she received a Theatre World Award.

WINTERS, NEWTON. Born in Henderson, NV. Bdwy debut 1976 in "Bubbling Brown Sugar."

WINTERS, WARRINGTON. Born July 28, 1909 in Bigstone County, MN. Graduate UMinn. Debut OB 1975 in ELT's "Another Language."

WISE, WILLIAM. Born May 11, 1940 in Chicago, IL. Attended Bradley U. Northern Ill. U. Debut 1970 in "Adaptation/Next," followed by "Hot l Baltimore."

WISEMAN, JOSEPH. Born May 15, 1919 in Montreal, Can. Attended CCNY. Bdwy in "Journey to Jerusalem," "Abe Lincoln in Illinois," "Candle in the Wind," "Three Sisters," "Storm Operation," "Joan of Lorraine," "Antony and Cleopatra," "Detective Story," "That Lady," "King Lear," "Golden Boy," "The Lark," "Zalmen, or the Madness of God," OB in "Marco Millions," "Incident at Vichy," "In the Matter of J. Robert Oppenheimer," "Enemies," "Duchess of Malfi," "Last Analysis."

WITHAM, JOHN. Born Apr. 3, 1947 in Plainfield, NJ. Graduate AMDA. Debut 1972 OB in "Two if by Sea," followed by "Comedy," Bdwy 1976 in "1600 Pennsylvania Avenue."

WOLFE, JOEL. Born Sept. 19, 1936 in NYC. Graduate CCNY. Debut 1968 OB in "Ergo," followed by "Room Service," "The Co-op," Bdwy 1975 in "All over Town."

WOLFSON, ROB. Born Dec. 3, 1953 in NYC. Debut 1974 OB in "The Hot l Baltimore."

WOOD, JOHN. Born in 1931 in Derbyshire, Eng. Attended Jesus Col. Oxford. Bdwy debut 1967 in "Rosencrantz and Guildenstern Are Dead," followed by "Sherlock Holmes," "Travesties."

WOODS, RICHARD. Born May 9, 1921 in Buffalo, NY. Graduate Ithaca Col. Bdwy in "Beg, Borrow or Steal," "Capt. Brassbound's Conversion," "Sail Away," "Coco." Last of Mrs. Lincoln," "Gigi," "Sherlock Homes," "Murder among Friends," OB in "The Crucible," "Summer and Smoke," "American Gothic," "Four-in-One," "My Heart's in the Highlands," "Eastward in Eden," "The Long Gallery," "The Year Boston Won the Pennant" and "In the Matter of J. Robert Oppenheimer" (LC), with APA in "You Can't Take It with You," "War and Peace," "School for Scandal," "Right You Are," "The Wild Duck" "Pantagleize," "Exit the King," "The Cherry Orchard," "Cock-a-Doodle Dandy," and "Hamlet."

WORONOV, MARY. Born Dec. 8, 1946 in Brooklyn, NY. Graduate Cornell U. Debut OB 1968 in "Kitchenette," followed by "Clearing House," "Queen of Greece," "Two Noble Kinsmen," "Boom Boom Room" for which she received a Theatre World Award, "Women behind Bars."

WORTH, IRENE. Born June 23, 1916 in Nebraska. Graduate UCLA. Bdwy debut 1943 in "The Two Mrs. Carrolls," followed by "The Cocktail Party," "Mary Stuart," "Toys in the Attic," "King Lear," "Tiny Alice," "Sweet Bird of Youth."

WRIGHT, TERESA. Born Oct. 27, 1918 in NYC. Bdwy debut 1938 in "Our Town," followed by "Life with Father," "Dark at the Top of the Stairs," "Mary, Mary," "I Never Sang for My Father," "Death of a Salesman," "Ah, Wilderness," OB in "Who's Happy Now," "A Passage to E. M. Forster."

WRIGHT, WILLIAM. Born Jan. 21, 1943 in Los Angeles, CA. Graduate UUtah, Bristol Old Vic. Debut 1973 OB in "Merchant of Venice" (LC), Bdwy 1976 in "Equus."

WYMAN, NICHOLAS. Born May 18, 1950 in Portland, ME. Graduate Harvard. Bdwy debut 1975 in "Very Good Eddie."

WYNKOOP, CHRISTOPHER. Born Dec. 7, 1943 in Long Branch, NJ. Graduate AADA. Debut 1970 OB in "Under the Gaslight," followed by "And So to Bed," "Panama Hattie" (ELT).

WYNNE, JONATHAN. Born Mar. 7, 1947 in Los Angeles, CA. Graduate LACC. Bdwy debut 1975 in "Hello, Dolly!"

YANCY, EMILY. Born in 1947 in NYC. Attended Bklyn Col. Bdwy debut 1967 in "Hello, Dolly!," followed by "Man of La Mancha," "Your Own Thing" (OB), "1600 Pennsylvania Avenue."

YATES, CRAIG. Born Feb. 13, 1948 in Harvey, IL. Attended UCLA, LACC. Bdwy debut 1971 in "On the Town," followed by "Mame," "A Musical Jubilee."

YATES, JOHN ROBERT. Born Sept. 12, 1948 in Chicago, IL. Graduate UIll. Debut OB 1976 in "Medal of Honor Rag."

YOSHIDA, PETER. Born May 28, 1945 in Chicago, IL. Graduate UIll., Princeton U., AADA, AmThWing. Debut 1965 OB in "Coriolanus," followed by "Troilus and Cressida," "Santa Anita '42," "Pursuit of Happiness."

YOUNG, MADONNA. Born July 16 in Lackawanna, NY. Graduate NYU, AADA. Debut 1972 OB in "DuBarry Was a Lady," followed by "Brainwashed."

ZACHAR, GLENN. Born Nov. 30, 1961 in NYC. Bdwy debut 1975 in "Ah, Wilderness."

ZAKS, JERRY. Born Sept. 7, 1946 in Germany. Graduate Dartmouth, Smith Col. Bdwy debut 1973 in "Grease," OB in "Death Story," "Dream of a Blacklisted Actor," "Kid Champion," "Golden Boy."

ZANG, EDWARD. Born Aug. 19, 1934 in NYC. Graduate Boston U. OB in "Good Soldier Schweik," "St. Joan," "Boys in the Band," "The Reliquary of Mr. and Mrs. Potterfield," "Last Analysis," "As You Like It," "More Than You Deserve," "Polly," "Threepenny Opera."

ZIMAN, JERROLD J. Born in Colorado. Graduate UChicago. Debut OB 1969 in "Brass Butterfly," followed by "The Screens," "Kaddish," "Beggars Opera," "Sunset," "Lotta," "Universal Nigger," "Ice Age," Bdwy in "The Beauty Part" (1962)

ZORICH, LOUIS. Born Feb. 12, 1924 in Chicago, IL. Attended Roosevelt U. OB in "Six Characters in Search of an Author," "Crimes and Crimes," "Henry V," "Thracian Horses," "All Women Are One," "Good Soldier Schweik," "Shadow of Heroes," "To Clothe the Naked," "Sunset," "A Memory of Two Mondays," "They Knew What They Wanted," Bdwy in "Becket," "Moby Dick," "The Odd Couple," "Hadrian VII," "Moonchildren," "Fun City," "Goodtime Charley."

ZWICK, JOEL. Born Jan. 11, 1942 in Brooklyn, NY. Graduate Bklyn Col. Debut 1967 OB in "Macbird!," followed by "Dance with Me."

OBITUARIES

John Baragrey (1971)

Larry Blyden (1966)

Pamela Brown (1960)

SIG ARNO, 79, German-born stage and film character actor, died in Los Angeles Aug. 17, 1975 from complications of Parkinson's disease. He came to the U.S. in 1939 and appeared in films before making his Broadway debut in 1940 in "Victoria Regina." Subsequently he appeared in "Song of Norway," "The Play's the Thing," "Time Remembered" (for which he received a Tony nomination), "The Cold Wind and the Warm," and the 1964 revival of "The Merry Widow." Surviving are his widow, and a son by his first wife.

MARGARET BANNERMAN, 83, Canadian-born actress, died Apr. 25, 1976 in Englewood, NJ. After her London stage debut in 1915, she rose to stardom in 1923 in "Our Betters." Her first Bdwy role was in 1942 in "By Jupiter," followed by "Our Betters," "One Touch of Venus," "Rebecca," "The Deep Mrs. Sykes," "John Loves Mary," "Getting Married," "Star-cross Story," "Thor with Angels," "Garden District," and "My Fair Lady." She was twice married and divorced. There are no survivors.

JOHN BARAGREY, 57, Alabama-born actor, died Aug. 4, 1975 in his NYC home. Made his Bdwy debut 1943 in "Sons and Soldiers," followed by "A Flag Is Born," "The Enchanted," "The Royal Family" (CC), "One Eye Closed," "The Crucible," "The Devils," "Elizabeth the Queen" (CC), "The Grass Harp," and "Murderous Angels." He also appeared in several films and many tv productions. Surviving is his widow, actress Louise Larabee.

ALAN BAXTER, 67, Ohio-born actor died of cancer, May 8, 1976 in Woodland Hills, CA. Made Bdwy debut in 1933 in "Lone Valley," followed by "Men in White," "Gold Eagle Guy," "Black Pit," "Winged Victory," "Home of the Brave," "Voice of the Turtle," "The Hallams," "Jenny Kissed Me," and "South Pacific" (CC). He also appeared in over 60 films and on many tv shows. He is survived by his second wife, actress Christy Palmer.

EARL BENHAM, 89, former actor, died Mar. 21, 1976 in his home in Northport, NY. Began his career at 17 traveling with the Primrose Minstrels. He later appeared in many Bdwy musicals, including "The Little Millionaire," "Winsome Widow," "Carnival," "Very Good Eddie," and "Hitchy-Koo." In 1920 he went into business as a custom tailor for entertainers. He was a trustee of the Actors Fund. His son James survives.

LARRY BLYDEN, 49, versatile performer who also produced, and directed for stage, film and tv, died June 6, 1975 while on vacation in Agadir, Morocco, from injuries received in an automobile accident. He had just completed 250 performances in "Absurd Person Singular" and was vacationing before beginning his tv game show "The Showoff." His Bdwy debut was in 1948 in "Mr. Roberts," followed by "The Miser," "Wish You Were Here," "Oh! Men! Oh! Women!," "Italian Straw Hat," "Who Was That Lady I Saw You With?," "Flower Drum Song," "Foxy," "Blues for Mr. Charlie," "Luv," "The Apple Tree," "Mother Lover," "You Know I Can't Hear You When the Water's Running," "A Funny Thing Happened on the Way to the Forum." He was divorced from the late Carol Haney. A son and daughter survive.

CHARLES BROKAW, 77, actor, died in a NYC hospital Oct. 23, 1975. His Bdwy appearances include "The Road to Rome," "The Decoy," "Elizabeth the Queen," "Jenny," "The Squall." He also had roles in several films. A brother and stepson survive.

JOSEPHINE BROWN, 84, Chicago born actress, died Apr. 26, 1976 at her home in Ibiza, Spain, where she had been in retirement for 10 years. Made her debut at 11 with Lillian Russell, and subsequently appeared with William Gillette, John Barrymore, Arnold Day, and George Fawcett. Her most recent appearances were in "Bachelor Born," "I Remember Mama," "Gigi," "Anniversary Waltz," and off-Bdwy in "Diary of a Scoundrel." She was painted by Augustus John, sculpted by Auguste Rodin, and rejected Caruso's proposal of marriage. Her daughter, Wauna Paul, died in 1973.

PAMELA BROWN, 58, a prominent British actress, died Sept. 18, 1975 in London. She made her Bdwy debut in 1947 in "The Importance of Being Earnest," and subsequently returned for roles in "Love for Love," "The Lady's Not For Burning," "The Country Wife," and "Heartbreak House." She was divorced from actor Peter Copley.

ANGUS CAIRNS, 65, actor, died in NYC Oct. 14, 1975. He made his NY debut in "Othello," followed by "Henry VIII," "What Every Woman Knows," "Androcles and the Lion," "Yellow Jack," "Alice in Wonderland," "Mock Turtle," "Brigadoon," "Kiss Me, Kate," "Paint Your Wagon," "Threepenny Opera," "The Engagement Baby," and "Soon." He is survived by his brother and sister.

FRANK CARRINGTON, 73, co-founder, producer and director of the Paper Mill Playhouse, Millburn, NJ, died July 3, 1975 in his Millburn home. In 1938, with Antoinette Scudder, he opened the Playhouse and in 1972 it was proclaimed the State Theater of New Jersey. No reported survivors.

JACQUES CHARON, 55, director and leading actor of the Comedie Francaise, died of a heart attack in his Paris home Oct. 15, 1975. His last NY appearance with the company was in February 1970 at City Center. No reported survivors.

EDWARD CHOATE, 67, producer and manager, died in a NYC hospital July 23, 1975. He was a member of the Shubert staff for 12 years, serving as producer and casting director, and also produced independently. He had been in retirement for 6 months. Surviving are his second wife, a daughter, and 3 sons.

AGATHA CHRISTIE, 85, a tremendously successful writer, died Jan. 12, 1976 at her home in Wallingford, Eng. Among her many works are 14 plays, including "Ten Little Indians," "Appointment with Death," "Hidden Horizons," "Witness for the Prosecution," and "The Mousetrap" which has been running in London since 1952. She was made a Dame of the British Empire in 1956. She is survived by her second husband, Sir Max Mallowan, and a grandson.

LEE J. COBB, 64, actor, died Feb. 11, 1976 in his home in Woodland Hills, CA. He was born Leo Jacob in NY's Lower East Side, and studied to become a violinist. His Bdwy debut was in "Crime and Punishment" (1935), followed by "Till the Day I Die," "Waiting for Lefty," "Mother," "Bitter Stream," "Johnny Johnson," "Golden Boy," "The Gentle People," "The Fifth Column," "Thunder Rock," "Clash by Night," "Jason," "Death of a Salesman," "The Emperor's New Clothes," and "King Lear" (LC). He was well known for his tv series "The Virginian," and had appeared in over 80 films. Surviving are his second wife, a daughter, and two sons.

BARBARA COLBY, 35, actress, was shot and killed July 24, 1975, by unknown gunmen as she left an acting class in Venice, CA. She made her Bdwy debut in 1965 in "The Devils," and appeared Off-Bdwy in "Under Milkwood," "Six Characters in Search of an Author," "Murderous Angels," and Lincoln Center productions of "Richard III" and "A Doll's House." No reported survivors.

CLANCY COOPER, 68, actor, died in Hollywood, June 14, 1975, of a heart attack while driving his car on Mulholland Drive. He made his Bdwy debut in 1938 in "Casey Jones," and subsequently had roles in over 35 plays, including "The Fabulous Invalid" and "Juno and the Paycock." He also appeared in over 60 films. He is survived by his authoress wife, Elizabeth Cooper, and a son.

KEVIN COUGHLIN, 30, stage, film and tv actor, died Jan. 19, 1976 of multiple injuries resulting from a hit-and-run accident in North Hollywood, CA. He was struck while cleaning his car. Before going to Hollywood, he had appeared on Bdwy in "Frogs of Spring," "The King and I," "Life with Mother," and "The Square Root of Wonderful." He was a regular on tv's "Horn and Hardart Children's Hour" and "I Remember Mama." Surviving are his wife and mother.

Lee J. Cobb (1970)

GEORGE CURZON, 77, British actor, died May 10, 1976 in London. He made his Bdwy debut in 1935 in "Parnell," subsequently appearing in "Hitch Your Wagon," "Black Lime-light," "Yes, M'Lord," and "The Little Glass Clock." No reported survivors.

DOLORES, 83, British-born "Ziegfeld girl," died Nov. 7, 1975 in Paris. She was one of the most publicized and beautiful girls from Ziegfeld's "Follies," and appeared in them for several years beginning in 1917. She was "The Empress of Fashion" and "The Peacock Girl." She also appeared in the musical "Sally." She was born Kathleen Mary Rose and became a prominent London model before Ziegfeld offered her a spot in the "Follies." In 1923 she sailed for France to marry Tudor Wilkinson, a millionaire art collector, and from then on lived a quiet life in Paris. During WWII she was arrested by the Germans on a charge of aiding the Resistance and kept in jail until Paris was liberated in 1944. There are no reported survivors.

VINCENT J. DONAHUE, 58, Actors Equity Assistant Executive Secretary, and former actor, was found stabbed to death Feb. 10, 1976 in his NYC hotel room. Before joining Equity's staff he had appeared in numerous Broadway productions, including "20th Century," "Stalag 17," "The Andersonville Trial," City Center productions of "Cyrano de Bergerac," "The Shrike," and "Charley's Aunt," and his last Bdwy play in 1961 "Daughter of Silence." A sister survives.

EDDIE DOWLING, 81, singer, dancer, actor, playwright, songwriter, director, and producer, died Feb. 18, 1976 in Smithfield, RI. He was born Joseph Nelson Goucher in Woonsocket, RI, and made his Bdwy debut in 1919 in "The Velvet Lady" singing two songs he had composed. Subsequently he appeared in "Ziegfeld Follies," "Sally, Irene and Mary" which he co-authored, co-produced, and co-directed, "Honeymoon Lane," "Sidewalks of New York," "Thumbs Up!," "Here Come the Clowns," "The Time of Your Life," "Magic," "Hello Out There," "The Greatest of These," "Manhattan Nocturne," "The Glass Menagerie," "The Home Life of the Buffalo," "Minnie and Mr. Williams," "Angel in the Pawnshop," and "Paint Your Wagon." He retired in the early 1960's. He leaves his widow, dancer-comedienne Rae Dooley whom he married in 1914, and a daughter.

JOE DOWNING, 71, actor, died during February 1976. Among his many Broadway appear-ances were roles in "Garrick Gaieties," "Farewell to Arms," "Shooting Star," "Heat Light-ning," "Page Miss Glory," "Ceiling Zero," "Dead End," and "Ramshackle Inn." No survivors reported.

Robert Downing (1960)

ROBERT DOWNING, 61, drama critic for the Denver Post, and former actor and manager, died June 14, 1976 following abdominal surgery in Denver, CO. After several years in stock and touring companies, he made his Bdwy debut in 1940 with the Lunts in "The Taming of the Shrew," followed by "There Shall Be No Night," "The Naked Genius," "Wake Up, Darling," "Say, Darling," "Butter and Egg Man." He was stage manager for more than 26 Bdwy productions, and a book reviewer for Variety. No survivors reported.

ROBERT ECKLES, 55, singer-actor, died of a heart attack Aug. 9, 1975 in his NYC home. He appeared in numerous Gilbert and Sullivan revivals, and in "The Lady's not for Burning," "Cyrano de Bergerac," and "Becket." No survivors reported.

CHARLES ELLIS, 83, an abstract painter and former actor, died Mar. 11, 1976 in Pittsfield, Mass. In NY he had appeared in "The Rope," "Moon of the Caribbees," "Desire under the Elms," "Show Boat" (1932), "Valley Forge," "Key Largo," "The Eve of St. Mark," "Joan of Lorraine," and "Anne of the Thousand Days." He leaves his wife, former actress Norma Millay.

PAUL FORD, 74, retired actor, died Apr. 12, 1976 in Mineola, NY. Born Paul Ford Weaver in Baltimore, he did not become an actor until his late 30's. He made his Bdwy debut in 1944 in "Decision," and subsequently appeared in "Lower North," "Kiss Them for Me," "Fla-mingo Road," "On Whitman Avenue," "Another Part of the Forest," "As We Forgive Our Debtors," "Command Decision," "Brass Ring," "Teahouse of the August Moon," "Good as Gold," "Whoop-Up," "Music Man," "A Thurber Carnival," "Never Too Late," "3 Bags Full," "What Did We Do Wrong?," "3 Men on a Horse," "Front Page," and "Fun City." For 5 years he was Col. Hall on tv's "Sgt. Bilko" show. Surviving are his widow, two sons and two daughters.

Paul Ford (1966)

Frieda Inescort (1937)

Margaret Leighton (1973)

Tilly Losch (1936)

CHARLES GAYNOR, 66, writer of sketches, music and lyrics, died of a heart attack Dec. 19, 1975 in Washington, D.C. He was the creator of "Lend an Ear" and "Show Girl" starring Carol Channing. He wrote additional numbers for the 1973 revival of "Irene." No reported survivors.

PAUL KIRK GILES, 80, retired actor, died Apr. 23, 1976 in NYC. Among his Broadway appearances were roles in "Born Yesterday," "Ah, Wilderness" and "Pillar to Post." Surviving are his widow and two daughters.

RUTH GILLMORE, former actress and teacher, died Feb. 12, 1976 at her home in Nantucket, Mass. She made her debut in 1918 in "The Betrothal," subsequently appearing in "No More Frontier," and "The Farmer Takes a Wife." Surviving are her husband and son, and a sister, actress Margalo Gillmore.

FERNANDO GRAHAL, 32, Puerto Rican-born dancer and choreographer, was killed Sept. 4, 1975 in San Juan, P.R., when an armed fugitive tried to use him as a shield. On Bdwy he had appeared in "Carnival," "Bajour," "Man of La Mancha," "Guys and Dolls," and "Around the World in 80 Days" at Jones Beach. He is survived by his mother, a brother and sister.

ETHEL GRIFFIES, 97, British actress, died of a stroke Sept. 9, 1975 in London. She was the oldest working actress in the English-speaking theatre, and began her career as a child in 1881. She made her Bdwy debut in 1924 in "Havoc," followed by "Interference," "Pygmalion," "Mariners," "Loose Ends," "Old English," "The Cherry Orchard," "Lady Dedlock," "Criminal Code," "The Druid Circle," "The Hallams," "The Leading Lady," "Shop at Sly Corner," "Miss Liberty," "Legend of Sarah," "The Royal Family" (CC), "Autumn Garden," "Write Me a Murder," "A Very Rich Woman," "Ivanov," "Billy Liar," and "The Natural Look" in 1967. She also appeared in over 100 films. Her first husband, actor Walter Beaumont, died in 1910, and her second, actor Edward Cooper, died in 1956. There were no immediate survivors reported.

WILLIAM HANSEN, 64, character actor, died June 23, 1975 in Woodland Hills, CA. He made his Bdwy debut in 1934 in "My Heart's in the Highlands," subsequently appearing in "Night Music," "Medicine Show," "Twelfth Night," "Macbeth," "The Assassin," "Brigadoon," "Montserrat," "The Member of the Wedding," "Barefoot in Athens," "Golden Boy," "Teahouse of the August Moon," and "Lorenzo." He also appeared in films. No reported survivors.

FRIEDA INESCORT, 75, Scottish-born actress, died of multiple sclerosis Feb. 21, 1976 in Motion Picture Country Hospital where he had been a patient since 1969. She made her Bdwy debut in 1922 in "The Truth about Blayds," followed by "Escape," "Merchant of Venice," "Major Barbara," "Pygmalion," "When Ladies Meet," "False Dreams, Farewell," "Soldier's Wife," "Mermaids Singing," and "You Never Can Tell." She also appeared in many films. A sister survives.

ROBERTA JONAY, 54, singer-actress, died of cancer Apr. 19, 1976 in Tarzana, CA. Her Bdwy credits include "Allegro" and "As You Like It." She is survived by her husband, actor Judson Pratt, and two sons.

ANNETTE KELLERMANN, 87, "Australia's million dollar mermaid," died Nov. 5, 1975 in Southport, Aust. After winning international fame as a swimmer, she became the sensation of Bdwy and vaudeville in an aquatic act. She was arrested in Boston for wearing her original one-piece bathing suit. A sister survives.

MARGOT KELLY, 82, English-born retired actress, died Mar. 10, 1976 in Summit, NJ. She came to NY in 1916 to make her debut in "A Little Bit of Fluff," followed by "Pierrot The Prodigal," "Carnival," "Deburau," "Floradora," "The Second Mrs. Tanqueray," and "The Pearl of Great Price." She was the widow of NY deputy police commissioner James Sinnott. She is survived by her daughter, actress Patricia Sinnott.

JAMES KIERNAN, 35, actor, was shot and killed July 24, 1975 as he was leaving an acting class in Venice, CA. A native of Brooklyn, he had appeared Off-Broadway in "Colette" and "When You Comin' Back, Red Ryder?"

HYMAN KRAFT, 76, playwright, died in NYC July 29, 1975. He wrote "Mr. Papavert," "Ten Percent," "Cafe Crown," "Thank You, Svoboda," "Hot-Cha," "Cue for Passion" with Edward Chodorov, and "Top Banana." His widow survives.

MARGARET LEIGHTON, 53, British-born actress, died of multiple sclerosis Jan. 13, 1976 in Chichester, Eng. Her Bdwy debut in 1946 was with the Old Vic in "Henry IV Parts I & II," and "Uncle Vanya." She subsequently appeared on Bdwy in "Separate Tables," "Much Ado about Nothing," "The Night of the Iguana," "Tchin-Tchin," "The Chinese Prime Minister," "Homage to Shakespeare," "Slapstick Tragedy," and "The Little Foxes." She received "Tony" awards for "Separate Tables" and "Night of the Iguana." Surviving is her third husband, actor Michael Wilding.

DAVID LIGHT, 71, Polish-born director and former Yiddish actor, died of a heart attack in NYC July 31, 1975. He came to the U. S. in 1945 from Buenos Aires, and for 30 years was associated with the Folksbiene. In 1973 he received an "Obie" for his direction of "Hard to Be a Jew." His widow survives.

TILLY LOSCH, an internationally recognized Vienna-born dancer, actress, choreographer and painter, in her 70's, died of cancer Dec. 24, 1975 in a NY hospital. After becoming a prima ballerina in Europe, she made her Bdwy debut in 1927 in Max Reinhardt's "A Midsummer Night's Dream," followed by "Everyman," "Danton's Death," "Servant of Two Masters," "This Year of Grace," "Wake Up and Dream," "The Band Wagon," "The Miracle," and "Topaze." Two marriages to prominent Britons ended in divorce. She had no immediate survivors.

MARTY MAY, 77, comedian, singer and actor, died of a heart ailment Nov. 11, 1975 in Las Vegas. After a career in vaudeville, he appeared in such Bdwy productions as "Roberta," "Walk with Music," "Best Foot Forward," "Artists and Models," "Annie Get Your Gun," "Sons o' Fun," "Funzapoppin," and "Pardon Our French." In 1962 he moved to Las Vegas where he entertained in and helped produce hotel-casino shows. Surviving are his widow, actress June Johnson, and a son.

RUTH McDEVITT, 80, character actress, died May 27, 1976 in her Hollywood home. After the death of her husband Patrick J. McDevitt, she turned to acting, and made her Bdwy debut 1940 in "Young Couple Wanted." She subsequently appeared in "Goodbye in the Night," "Arsenic and Old Lace," "Meet a Body," "Harvey," "Sleepy Hollow," "Picnic," "Solid Gold Cadillac," "Diary of a Scoundrel," "Clerambard," "The Best Man," "Save Me a Place at Forest Lawn," and "Absence of a Cello." She was the mother of Wally Cox in the popular tv series "Mr. Peepers." No survivors reported.

JOHN McGIVER, 62, a Bronx high school teacher who became a noted character actor, died of a heart attack Sept. 9, 1975 at his home in West Fulton, NY. After his Bdwy debut in 1956 in "Little Glass Clock," he had roles in "Cloud 7," "Drink to Me Only," "God and Kate Murphy," "A Thurber Carnival," "A Cook for Mr. General," "Happiness Is Just a Little Thing Called a Rolls Royce," "A Way of Life," "Front Page," and "Our Town." He appeared in films and many tv roles. He is survived by his wife, six sons and four daughters.

DORO MERANDE, Kansas-born character actress in her 70's, died Nov. 1, 1975 in Miami, Fla., where she had gone to act in a Jackie Gleason "Honeymooners" tv special. She first appeared on Bdwy in 1935 in "Loose Moments," followed by "One Good Year," "Fulton of Oak Falls," "Red Harvest," "Angel Island," "Our Town," "Love's Old Sweet Song," "Beverly Hills," "The More the Merrier," "Junior Miss," "Hope for a Harvest," "Three's a Family," "Naked Genius," "Pick-up Girl," "Violet," "Hope for the Best," "Apple of His Eye," "The Silver Whistle," "Rat Race," "4 Twelves Are 48," "Lo and Behold!," "Diary of a Scoundrel," and "Front Page" (1969). No reported survivors.

JO MIELZINER, 74, versatile and imaginative scenic designer, collapsed in a NYC taxicab of a massive stroke and was dead on arrival at the hospital Mar. 15, 1976. He had created the settings, and usually the lighting, for more than 300 plays, musicals, operas and ballets. Born of American parents in Paris, he came to the U. S. in 1909. He began his theatrical career in 1923 as an actor and stage manager, but changed to scenic design a year later, creating the set for the Lunts' production of "The Guardsman." Among his most memorable designs are "South Pacific," "Winterset," "Guys and Dolls," "Death of a Salesman," "Streetcar Named Desire," "Pal Joey," "Carousel," "Annie Get Your Gun," "The King and I," "Can-Can," "Gypsy," "Strange Interlude," "Street Scene," "Glass Menagerie," "Summer and Smoke," "Cat on a Hot Tin Roof," "Barretts of Wimpole Street," "Tea and Sympathy," and "Picnic." His designs received 5 "Tony" Awards, 5 Donaldson Awards, and an Academy Award for the film "Picnic." Surviving are two sons and a daughter, and his wife from whom he had been separated for many years.

SAL MINEO, 37, actor, was stabbed to death by an unknown assailant Feb. 12, 1976 as he was returning to his Hollywood home from a rehearsal. He made his Bdwy debut at 11 in "The Rose Tattoo," followed by "The King and I," "Something about a Soldier." He appeared in many tv roles, and in films. He is survived by his mother, a sister, and two brothers.

KARL NIELSEN, 85, retired stage manager, died Sept. 8, 1975 in West Palm Beach, Fla., where he had been living for several years. Before his retirement in 1970, he had managed over 100 productions, and for 34 years was associated with the Theatre Guild. No reported survivors.

PATRICIA O'CONNELL, 73, Alabama-born singer-actress, died Dec. 24, 1975 in New Haven, Conn. She had appeared in the original companies of "The Student Prince," "The Desert Song," "The Great Waltz," and "Rosalie." She also sang with the Chicago Opera and the New York Opera Comique. The widow of journalist Angus Shaw McCabe, she is survived by two sisters.

DONALD M. OENSLAGER, 73, scenic designer and teacher, died June 21, 1975 in his summer home near Bedford, NY. Among the more than 250 productions he designed are "The Emperor Jones," "The Farmer Takes a Wife," "First Lady," "Stage Door," "You Can't Take It With You," "I'd Rather Be Right," "Of Mice and Men," "The Man Who Came to Dinner," "Pygmalion," "Born Yesterday," "Sabrina Fair," "Major Barbara," "The Pleasure of His Company," "Good News," "A Doll's House," and "A Majority of One." For 46 years he was on the faculty at Yale. His widow survives.

REX O'MALLEY, 75, British-born actor, died May 1, 1976 in the Mary Manning Walsh Home in NYC. He came to the U. S. in 1926 to appear in "The Strange Prince," subsequently he had roles in "The Comic," "The Marquise," "Bachelor Father," "The Apple Cart," "Lost Sheep," "Wonder Bar," "Experience Unnecessary," "The Mad Hopes," "The Best Sellers," "No More Ladies," "The Red Cat," "Revenge with Music," "Simpleton of the Unexpected Isles," "Matrimony Pfd.," "Merely Murder," "You Never Know," "The Man Who Came to Dinner," "Naked Genius," "The Cherry Orchard," "Many Happy Returns," "Devils Galore," "Lute Song," "Lady Windermere's Fan," "Charley's Aunt," "The Sleeping Prince," "The Lady of the Camellias," and "Say Nothing." No known survivors.

SANTOS ORTEGA, 76, stage, tv and radio actor, died Apr. 10, 1976 while visiting Fort Lauderdale, Fla. He began his career at 17 singing at the Hippodrome Theatre. His most important stage role was in "Jeb" in 1946. He was skilled in accents and played in many radio serials, including "Ellery Queen," "Perry Mason," "Charlie Chan," and "Boston Blackie." He was probably best known as Grandpa Hughes on the tv serial "As the World Turns." He leaves a son and daughter.

Ruth McDevitt (1963)

John McGiver (1965)

Doro Merande (1964)

Paul Robeson (1933)

Ethel Shutta (1963)

Arthur Treacher (1949)

B. IDEN PAYNE, 94, British-born actor-director-teacher and Shakespearean authority, died Apr. 6, 1976 in Austin, Tex., where he had been on the faculty of the Univ. of Tex. He made his Bdwy bow in 1915 in "The Critic," followed by "The Great Broxoff," "Candida," and directed numerous other plays with some of the great stars of the theatre. During the latter part of his life, he adopted university theatre as his metier, and was a visiting professor at several universities and colleges. He is survived by his second wife, a son and a daughter.

LOU POLAN, 71, Russian-born character actor, died Mar. 3, 1975 in Freeport, ME. He made his Bdwy debut in 1922 in "R.U.R.," followed by "The Bootleggers," "The Jolly Roger," "Cyrano de Bergerac," "Othello," "Hamlet," "Goat Song," "Immortal Thief," "Electra," "Henry V," "Merchant of Venice," "The Firebird," "Yoshe Kalb," "Sweet Mystery of Life," "Haiti," "Night Music," "Liberty Jones," "Walk into My Parlor," "Cafe Crown," "The Whole World Over," "Gentleman from Athens," "Golden State," "Desire under the Elms," "Bus Stop," and "Hamlet." No reported survivors.

RONALD RADD, 47, British-born actor, died of a brain hemorrhage Apr. 23, 1976 in Toronto, Can., where he was appearing in "Great Expectations." He made his Bdwy debut in 1957 in "Hotel Paradiso," followed by four years in "My Fair Lady" as successor to Stanley Holloway, "Ivanov," and "Abelard and Heloise." His widow and three children survive.

PAUL ROBESON, 77, singer and actor, died of a severe cerebral vascular disorder Jan. 23, 1976 in Philadelphia, Pa. After graduating from Rutgers U. as an All-American football player with a Phi Beta Kappa key, he decided to turn to acting and singing. He made his stage debut in 1921 in "Simon the Cyrenian," and subsequently appeared in "Taboo," "All God's Chillun Got Wings," "Emperor Jones," "Black Boy," "Porgy," "Show Boat" (NY, London, and 1930 NY revival), and "Othello" in 1945. He became an international concert favorite and film star. He had been in retirement since 1963. He leaves a son and a sister

SHIMEN RUSKIN, 69, Polish-born character actor, died of cancer Apr. 23, 1976 in Los Angeles. His Bdwy debut in 1937 in "Having Wonderful Time," was followed by "Saturday Night," "Little Murders," "7 Days of Mourning," "The Corner Bar," and "The Last Analysis." Surviving are his widow and a son.

EVELYN RUSSELL, 49, actress, died Jan. 28, 1976 in her Sherman Oaks, Cal., home. She began her career at 5 in radio serials, and made her Bdwy debut in 1961 in "Sail Away," followed by "Nobody Loves an Albatross," "A Warm Body," "A Place for Polly," and "Lysistrata" with Melina Mercouri. In an off-Bdwy revival of "On the Town" she came to the attention of choreographer Joe Layton who became her husband. He and a son survive.

ETHEL SHUTTA, 79, singer-actress, died Feb. 5, 1976 in NYC. She began her career at 7 in vaudeville as "The Little Girl with the Big Voice" with her family. Her Bdwy debut was in "The Passing Show of 1922," followed by "Louie the 14th," several "Ziegfeld Follies," "Whoopee," "Marjorie," "My Dear Public," "Jennie," and "Follies." She was the singer with the George Olsen Band and became a radio favorite. Two sons survive. She was divorced from George Olsen.

SYBIL THORNDIKE, 93, versatile British-born actress, died June 9, 1976 after a heart attack in her London home. Began her career in 1904 and gave her last performance in 1969, after playing every possible type of role in a list of plays that would be too lengthy to enumerate. After George Bernard Shaw saw her play "Candida," he wrote "St. Joan" for her and she performed it over 2000 times to great acclaim. She toured the U.S. for four years (1904–08) playing Shakespeare with the Ben Greet Co., and subsequently appeared on Bdwy in "Smith," "The Distaff Side," "Time and the Conways," and "The Potting Shed." She met and married actor-producer Lewis Casson in 1908 and until his death in 1969 they formed one of the great partnerships of the theatre. In 1931 George V made her a Dame of the British Empire. Two daughters and two sons survive, all actors: John, Christopher, Mary and Ann Casson.

ARTHUR TREACHER, 81, British-born character actor, died from a heart ailment Dec. 14, 1975 in Manhasset, NY. He made his stage debut in London as a chorus boy in 1919 and performed steadily until he came to the U. S. in 1926 for his Bdwy debut in "Great Temptations." He subsequently appeared in "A Night in Paris," "The Madcap," "The Silent House," "Colonel Satan," "Wonder Bar," "School for Scandal," "The Cat and the Fiddle," "Panama Hattie," "Ziegfeld Follies," "Caesar and Cleopatra," "Getting Married," "Back to Methuselah," "The Fighting Cock," and "Camelot." He appeared in over 40 films, usually as snobbish butler, and was a regular for several years on Merv Griffin's tv show. His widow survives.

FRANCES UPTON, 71, retired comedienne, died Nov. 27, 1975 in Philadelphia. Pa. She had been featured in several musicals, including "Little Jesse James," "Ziegfeld Follies" for three years, "Twinkle, Twinkle," and "You Said It." She gave up her career in 1934 when she married the late Bert Bell, NFL commissioner. Surviving are two sons and a daughter.

HOWARD D. WENDELL, 67, Pennsylvania-born character actor, died Aug. 11, 1975 at his home in Oregon City, Ore. After beginning his career at the Cleveland Play House, and performing in many stock companies, he appeared on Bdwy in "The Curious Savage," "Julius Caesar," "Arms and the Man," and "Make a Wish." He went to Hollywood in 1950 and played many films and tv roles. His widow, three sons and a daughter survive.

LEIGH WHIPPER, 98, character actor, and the first black member of Actors Equity, died July 26, 1975 in NYC. He retired in 1972 after 65 years in the theatre, and 21 Broadway productions. His credits include "Those Who Walked in Darkness," "Stevedore,' "In Abraham's Bosom," "Three Men on a Horse," "Of Mice and Men," "Volpone," "Set My People Free," "Lysistrata," "Porgy," "The Shrike." He was a founder of the Negro Actors Guild. A son and a daughter survive.

THORNTON WILDER, 78, actor, novelist, and Pulitzer-Prize-winning playwright, died Dec. 7, 1975 in his sleep in his home in Hamden, Conn. He received three Pulitzer prizes: for his novel "The Bridge of San Luis Rey," and his plays "Our Town" and "The Skin of Our Teeth." His other plays include "The Trumpet Shall Sound," "The Happy Journey from Trenton to Camden," "The Long Christmas Dinner," "Love and How to Cure It," "Lucrece," "The Merchant of Yonkers" which he re-worked and re-titled "The Matchmaker" and eventually became the musical "Hello, Dolly!" Three sisters and a brother survive.

INDEX

271

273

274

278

281

285